Learn
Office XP
Volume 2

John Preston
Sally Preston
Robert L. Ferrett

Prentice Hall

Upper Saddle River, New Jersey 07458

Acquisitions Editor: Melissa Whitaker-Oliver
VP Publisher: Natalie Anderson
Assistant Editor: Melissa Edwards
Editorial Assistant: Mary Ann Broadnax
Development Editor: Jane Ducham
Media Project Manager: Cathleen Profitko
Marketing Manager: Emily Knight
Marketing Assistant: Scott Patterson
Manager, Production: Gail Steier de Acevedo
Project Manager: Lynne Breitfeller
Associate Director, Manufacturing: Vincent Scelta
Manufacturing Buyer: Lynne Breitfeller
Design Manager: Pat Smythe
Interior & Cover Design: Judy Allen
Full-Service Project Management & Composition: Pre-Press Co., Inc.
Printer/Binder: RR Donnelley & Sons Company
Cover Printer: Phoenix Color Corp.

10 9 8 7 6 5 4 3 2 1
ISBN 0-13-047375-8

Learn Office XP *Volume 2*

SERIES EDITORS **John Preston, Sally Preston, Robert L. Ferrett**

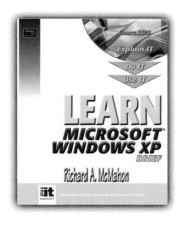

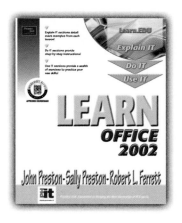

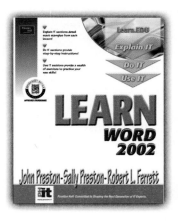

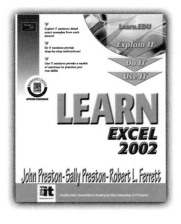

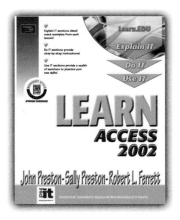

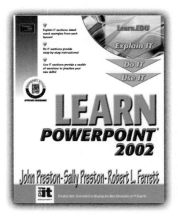

About the Authors

John Preston is an associate professor at Eastern Michigan University in the College of Technology, where he teaches microcomputer application courses at both the undergraduate and graduate levels. He has been teaching, writing, and designing computer training courses since the advent of PCs, and he has authored and co-authored over 40 books on Microsoft Word, Excel, Access, and PowerPoint. He is a series editor for the *Learn 97, Learn 2000,* and *Learn XP* books. Two books on Microsoft Access he co-authored with Robert Ferrett have been translated into Greek and Chinese. He has received grants from the Detroit Edison Institute and the Department of Energy to develop Web sites for energy education and alternative fuels, and has also developed one of the first Internet-based microcomputer applications courses at an accredited university. He has a B.S. in physics, mathematics, and education from the University of Michigan, and an M.S. in physics education from Eastern Michigan University. His doctoral studies are in instructional technology at Wayne State University.

Sally Preston is president of Preston & Associates, which provides software consulting and training. She teaches computing in a variety of settings, which provides her with ample opportunity to observe how people learn, what works best, and what challenges are present when learning a new software program. This diverse experience provides a complimentary set of information, which is blended into the *Learn* series books. Sally has been a co-author on the *Learn* series since its inception. In addition, she has authored books for the *Essentials* and *Microsoft Office User Specialist (MOUS) Essentials* series. Sally has an MBA from Eastern Michigan University and graduated magna cum laude. When Sally is away from her computer, she is often found planting flowers in her garden.

Robert L. Ferrett is the director of the Center for Instructional Computing at Eastern Michigan University, where he provides computer training and support to faculty. He has authored or co-authored more than 40 books on Access, PowerPoint, Excel, Publisher, WordPerfect, and Word, and he was the editor of the *1994 ACM SIGUCCS Conference Proceedings.* He has been designing, developing, and delivering computer workshops for nearly two decades, and is a series editor for the *Learn 97, Learn 2000,* and *Learn XP* books. He has a B.A. in psychology, an M.S. in geography, and an M.S. in interdisciplinary technology from Eastern Michigan University. His doctoral studies are in instructional technology at Wayne State University. As a sidelight, Bob teaches a four-week Computers and Genealogy class and has written books on genealogy and local history.

Contents

Preface

PHILOSOPHY OF THE *LEARN* SERIES

The Preston-Ferrett *Learn* series is designed for students who want to master the core or expert competencies of particular software in an efficient and effective manner. We use the rubric EDU to organize the text into sections labeled "Explain It," "Do It," and "Use It." The books use extensive visual cues to provide immediate feedback to the students. Each step is accompanied by a figure displaying the result of doing that step. Highlights and callouts identify key screen elements. Steps are divided into paragraphs that give specific directions and paragraphs that explain the results of those actions. Special fonts and colors are used to identify the objects of actions and what the student should type. Deeper understanding is provided in asides called "In Depth." Places where students are likely to go astray are identified by asides labeled "Caution." The series uses visual elements, such as buttons and icons, to make it easier for beginners to learn the software. However, it recognizes that students who need to use the software at work are interested in speed. Asides called "Quick Tip" give directions on how to use keyboard shortcuts to accomplish tasks that are likely to be common in the workplace.

The exercises at the end of each lesson promote increasing levels of abstraction similar to those described in Bloom's taxonomy. The "Comprehension" exercises test students' knowledge of the facts and their ability to recognize relationships and visual elements. The "Reinforcement" exercises provide the opportunity to apply these new skills to a different assignment with less-detailed instructions. "Challenge" exercises require students to learn a new skill that is related to the skills covered in the lesson. "On Your Own" provides students with guidelines for applying the newly acquired skills to a unique project of their own. The guidelines specify general requirements to give the student and the instructor a common ground for evaluation but otherwise allow for creativity and innovation. Books in this series give beginners very detailed step-by-step instruction while providing challenging options for more advanced learners.

STRUCTURE OF A *LEARN* SERIES BOOK

Each of the books in the *Learn* series is structured the same and contains elements that explain what is expected, how to do the tasks, and how to transfer this knowledge into daily use. The elements—"Explain It," "Do It," and "Use It" —are described in detail below.

Explain It
Students are provided with a cognitive map of the lesson where they see a list of the tasks, an introduction, and a visual summary.

Introduction
The EDU design relates to the lessons.

Each lesson has an introduction that describes the contents of the lesson to provide an overview of how the tasks are related to a larger concept that is identified by the title of the lesson.

Visual Summary

A visual summary displays the expected results of performing the tasks. Callouts are used to show the student and the instructor where to look in each file to identify the results of following the instructions correctly.

Do It

Once students are oriented to the objective of the lesson and are aware of the expected outcome, they proceed with the task. Tasks begin with an explanation of the relevance of the tasks and are followed by step-by-step, illustrated instructions on how to "Do It."

Why would I do this?

The authors draw upon their experience in education, business, government, and personal growth to explain how this task is relevant to the student's life. Students are motivated to learn when they can relate the task to practical applications in their lives.

Step-by-step instruction

Instructions are provided in a step-by-step format. Explanations follow each instruction and are set off in a new italicized paragraph.

Figures

Each step has an accompanying figure that is placed next to it. Each figure provides a visual reinforcement of the step that has just been completed. Buttons, menu choices, and other screen elements used in the task are highlighted or identified.

Special Notes

Three recurring note boxes are found in the Preston-Ferrett *Learn* series:

An area where trouble may be encountered, along with instructions on how to avoid or recover from these mistakes.

A detailed look at a topic or procedure, or another way of doing it.

A faster or more efficient way of achieving a desired end.

Use It

The end-of-lesson material, "Use It," consists of four elements: "Comprehension"; "Reinforcement"; "Challenge"; and "On Your Own." Students are guided through increasing levels of abstraction until they can apply the skills of the lesson to a completely new situation in the "On Your Own" exercise.

"Comprehension": These exercises are designed to check the student's memory and understanding of the basic concepts in the lesson. Next to each exercise is a notation that references the task number in the lesson where the topic is covered. The student is encouraged to review the task referenced if he or she is uncertain of the correct answer. The "Comprehension" section contains the following three elements:

"True/False": True/false questions test the understanding of the new material in the lesson.

"Matching": Matching questions are included to check the student's familiarity with concepts and procedures introduced in the lesson.

"Visual Identification": A captured screen or screens is used to gauge the student's familiarity with various screen elements introduced in the lesson.

"Reinforcement": These exercises, that provide practice in the skills introduced in the tasks, generally follow the sequence of the tasks in the lesson. Since each exercise is usually built on the previous exercise, it is a good idea to do them in the order in which they are presented.

"Challenge": These exercises test students' abilities to apply skills to new situations with less-detailed instructions. Students are challenged to expand their skills set by using commands similar to those they've already learned.

"On Your Own": This exercise is designed to provide students with an opportunity to apply what they have learned to a situation of their choice. Guidelines are provided to give students and the instructor an idea of what is expected.

Glossary

New words or concepts are printed in italics and emphasized with color the first time they are encountered. Definitions of these words or phrases are provided in the text where they occur and are also included in the glossary at the back of the book.

MOUS Certification

Students may wish to become certified by taking the Microsoft Office User Specialist (MOUS) Core or Expert examinations in Excel. Learn Excel 2002 Comprehensive addresses all the topics required for Core and Expert level certification. Learn books that cover the certification topics in Word 2002, PowerPoint 2002, and Access 2002 are also available. For more information about MOUS certification, visit our website at www.prenhall.com/learn.

Learn Themes

Personal note from the authors to the student: Microsoft Office is a tool that we have used in our professional and personal lives for many years. This experience helps us explain how each lesson in this book relates to practical use. Between the three of us, our interests range across a broad spectrum of activities. We have chosen four themes throughout the *Learn* series that are based on our personal use of Microsoft Office. We hope that one or more of these themes will be of interest to you as well.

Business: Sally's financial experience and Bob's personal experience in pool and spa sales provide the background for the exercises dealing with business. We use a fictional company named Armstrong Pool, Spa, and Sauna Company to illustrate the use of Microsoft Office XP in a business setting. Armstrong is a regional company that was founded in 1957 in Ypsilanti, Michigan. They have expanded to eight locations in Michigan, Indiana, and Ohio, and have sales of around $10 million a year. Armstrong has been trying to improve the communication between their locations and has recently installed Microsoft Office XP. You will see how a company can use Office XP to communicate with customers, manage finances, organize data, and make presentations.

Travel: All three of us love to travel, so we created the fictional Alumni Travel Club, which is an organization that provides travel packages to the alumni of a local college. This theme illustrates how an organization can benefit from the use of Microsoft Office XP. The pictures used for this theme were taken by either Bob or John.

Social Science: Bob's personal interest in genealogy and historical research provides the background for several lessons. Bob's family is from Alcona County, which is a small rural community in northern lower Michigan. Immigrants from Canada, England, Germany, and other pre-dominantly European countries settled there in the late 1800s. Bob Ferrett and his brother Don gathered data from U.S. government census records for that period of time and have published a book on the subject. This information provides interesting clues about the life of people in a rural community before the 20th century and gives us insight into how much the role of women has changed. You will see how Microsoft Office XP applications can be used to explain, tabulate, record, and illustrate research data for a social science project.

John teaches several classes on the Internet and has written papers on how this new form of communication affects the way we learn. These documents are used in the *Learn Word 2002* chapters where you practice formatting long documents.

Science/Environment: John's physics background and interest in energy and the environment are the source of material for several documents and presentations. Every summer he teaches a class on utility power generation to junior high school science teachers.

Bob collaborates on weather-related research and has published articles on the risks associated with tornadoes and lightning. We have included a database of all the tornadoes in the United States from 1950 to 1995 so that users of this book can learn how to use Access and Excel to answer real research questions using a real database with over 38,000 records. We enjoy the excitement of doing this type of research with the tools found in Office and hope to share this excitement with our readers.

SUPPLEMENTS PACKAGE

There are lots of supplements available for both students and teachers. Let's take a look at these now.

Student Supplements

Companion Web site (www.prenhall.com/learn): Includes student data files as well as test questions that allow students to test their knowledge of the material and get instant assessment.

Instructor Supplements

Instructor's Resource CD-ROM: Includes Instructor's Manual, Test Manager, PowerPoint presentations, and the data and solution files for all four applications, which are available for downloading.

TRADEMARK ACKNOWLEDGEMENTS

All terms mentioned in this book that are known to be trademarks or service marks have been appropriately capitalized. Prentice Hall cannot attest to the accuracy of this information. Use of a term in this book should not be regarded as affecting the validity of any trademark or service mark.

ACKNOWLEDGEMENTS

We would like to acknowledge the efforts of the finest team of editing professionals, with whom we have had the pleasure of working. We have worked with editors from four other publishing firms, and none have done as thorough and professional a job as the people who have labored diligently on this series.

Our acquisitions editor, Melissa Whitaker-Oliver, has done an outstanding job of coordinating the efforts of a diverse team, spread across the country, working around the clock in an all-electronic environment.

Other team members include:

Melissa Edwards – Assistant Editor
Mary Ann Broadax – Editorial Assistant
Cathi Profitko – Media Project Manager
Lynne Breitfeller – Project Manager, Pearson
Gail Steier – Manager, Production
Pat Smythe – Design Manager
Jen Carley – Project Manager, Pre-Press

The authors wish to acknowledge the contributions of students at Eastern Michigan University. These students, most of whom are in the Technical Writing Degree Program, worked under the instruction and guidance of Professor Nancy Allen to ensure the accuracy of the final product. The students who participated in this project are:

Tom Barthel
Carrie Bartkowiak
Sandy Becker
Maureen Cousino
Lisa DeLibero
Julie Gibson
Candice Havener
Bill Inman
Jyoti Lal
Jill Money
Ines Perrone
Matt Phillips
Brian Rahn
Darcey Schafer
Jeri Vickerman
Tracy Williams
Christine Zito

Learn.EDU Features

Books in the *Learn 2002* series follow the Learn.EDU philosophy: Explain It, Do It, and then Use It.

*E*xplain It

EXPLAIN IT sections begin each Lesson. Students learn up front what will be covered in a Lesson and what they can expect to learn from it.

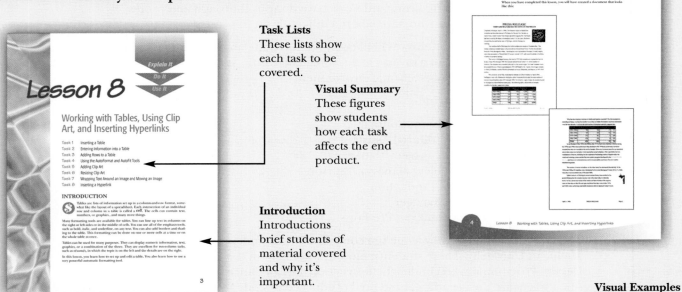

Task Lists
These lists show each task to be covered.

Visual Summary
These figures show students how each task affects the end product.

Introduction
Introductions brief students of material covered and why it's important.

Visual Examples
Numerous screen captures show how the student's own screen should look.

*D*o It

DO IT sections contain numbered steps that walk students through each task, allowing them to do the work themselves along with the instruction.

Why would I do this?
These sections explain the relevance to the student of each concept covered.

Numbered Steps
Students are guided through each task in a step-by-step format with explanations in italics.

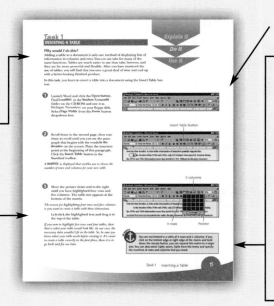

Quick Tip
A faster or more efficient way of doing something.

In Depth
A detailed look at a topic or procedure, or another way of doing something.

Caution
Troubleshooting tips that point out common pitfalls.

*U*se It

USE IT sections give the student opportunities to evaluate and practice skills learned in the Lessons, furthering their knowledge, comprehension, and understanding of the topics.

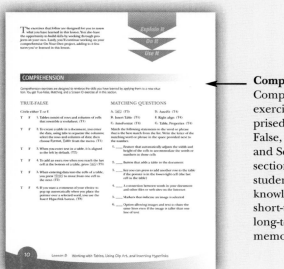

Reinforcement
These exercises provide practice in skills introduced in the tasks.

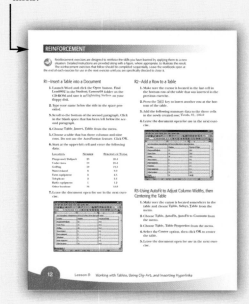

Comprehension
Comprehension exercises, comprised of True-False, Matching, and Screen ID sections help the student transfer knowledge from short-term to long-term memory.

Challenge
The exercises test the student's ability to apply their skills to new situations with less-detailed instructions.

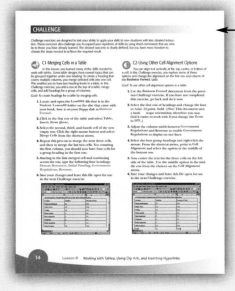

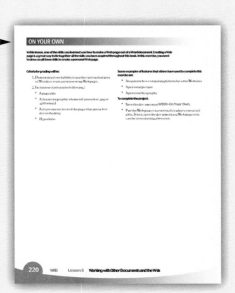

On Your Own
Students are provided with guidelines on how to apply the skills acquired to a project of their choice.

Lesson 9

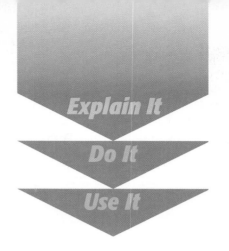

Formatting Paragraphs and Documents

Task 1   Verifying and Clearing Paragraph and Font Formats
Task 2   Creating and Applying Paragraph Styles
Task 3   Creating and Applying Font Styles
Task 4   Updating Paragraph Styles
Task 5   Inserting Line and Page Breaks
Task 6   Formatting Sections

INTRODUCTION

Documents that use many different formats are often time-consuming to set up. There are special techniques and shortcuts that enable you to define a format and store it for quick use. You can also use other techniques to make your document more professional looking.

If you turn on the *task pane*, an area at the right side of the screen that provides relevant information and options, you can quickly see all of the formatting in a paragraph, or the font formatting of selected text.

There are also special *styles* that enable you to select text and apply several formatting options at the same time. You use *font styles* to format selected text, and you use *paragraph styles* to format one or more paragraphs. When you make a change to the style in one place, you can apply the changes to all the other places in the document where that style is used.

Special formatting options can make the document more readable. You can create line breaks that keep the lines of text in the same paragraph, but display them on different lines within the paragraph. You can also insert page breaks to force text to the top of the next page where it may be more appropriate to begin a new topic. When one part of the document needs to have its pages formatted differently from the rest, you can also define a section and use the Page Setup dialog box to apply different page formatting to that section only.

In this lesson, you learn how to use the task pane to verify your formatting, and then to clear formatting. You create and apply both font and paragraph formatting, and you also learn how to add line and page breaks, and how to create and format sections.

VISUAL SUMMARY

When you have completed this lesson, you will have created a document that looks like this:

Task 5: Add a line break to a paragraph

Task 4: Modify existing styles

U.S. Department of Commerce
Economics and Statistics Administration
BUREAU OF THE CENSUS

Introduction

The U.S. population census records contain a wealth of information about people. They are useful in learning about one's family and local social and economic conditions at various times in history. For more recent years especially, they are official documents for persons who need to prove their age (in the absence of a birth certificate), relationship, citizenship, residence, and other facts in order to qualify for pensions; get jobs, naturalization papers, passports, or insurance policies; establish an inheritance; or trace ancestry. There was a population census taken in 1790 and every 10th year after that. (Page 3 lists the items covered in the existing censuses for each year.) The Bureau of the Census publication, 200 Years of U.S. Census Taking: Population and Housing Questions, 1790-1990 (Washington, DC, 1989), shows the specific questions and the way they appear on the records. It also reproduces instructions given to the enumerators for taking each census.

This Factfinder explains what census materials are available and how to obtain them, and also lists the sources for some other useful records about individuals.

Census Schedules Available to the Public

Individual records from the Federal population censuses are confidential for 72 years, by law (Title 44, U.S. Code). Thus, April 2002 is the scheduled date for the National Archives to open the 1930 records to public use.

Microfilm copies of the original population schedules, from 1790 through 1920 (virtually all of the 1890 records were destroyed in a 1921 fire), are available at the National Archives in Washington (http://www.nara.gov) and its 13 regional archives (see p. 4), and many libraries in various parts of the United States. Most have facilities for making paper copies from the microfilm. The National Archives also rents and sells the microfilm rolls (see below). The Textual Reference Branch at National Archives headquarters (see listing on page 4) will accept photocopy orders by mail, given exact page numbers; it will not do research.

There are Soundex (that is, by the sound of the surname rather than its spelling) indexes on microfilm for the 1880, 1900, and 1920 censuses for each State, and for 1910 for 21 States, principally in the South. Ten Southern States, plus a few counties in West Virginia and Kentucky were soundexed for 1930. Alphabetic indexes to the 1790-1860 and most of the 1870 census are available in genealogical libraries. Most States began keeping a more accurate birth registration in the early 1920's.

Researchers may find two Bureau of the Census publications useful; most major libraries have copies: Heads of Families at the First Census of the United States Taken in the Year (12 vols., Washington, DC, 1907-08, reprinted 1965-75), contains specific names. A Century of Population Growth—1790-1900 (Washington, DC, 1909, reprinted 1967-1970), includes the incidence of surnames in 1790, and a variety of summary tables from colonial censuses and 1790 to 1900.

Task 5: Add an artificial page break

Microfilm Rental and Sales

Rental. The National Archives rents microfilm copies of historical records to libraries and individuals. These copies are of Federal population census schedules 1790-1920; Soundex indexes, 1880-1920; Revolutionary War compiled military service records, and pension and bounty-land-warrant application files. For details, contact the National Archives Microfilm Rental Program, P.O. Box 30, Annapolis Junctions, MD 20701-0030, telephone 301-604-3699.

Sales. Microfilmed copies of census schedules, 1790-1920, and Soundex indexes, 1880-1920, can be purchased from National Archives Product Sales, Washington, DC 20408, telephone 202-501-5235 or 800-234-8861. The office has catalogs, prices, and ordering information.

Task 3: Create and apply a font style

Task 2: Create and apply a paragraph style

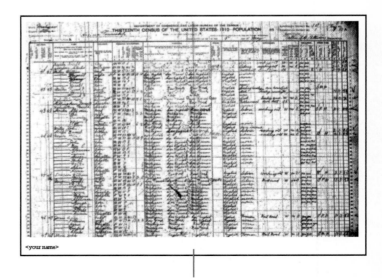

`<your name>`

Task 6: Create a new section with a different page layout

Task 1

VERIFYING AND CLEARING PARAGRAPH AND FONT FORMATS

Explain It

Do It

Use It

Why would I do this?

In many cases, you want to know what type of formatting has been used on a paragraph or selected text. By opening the task pane, you can quickly see all of the formatting. If you want to make changes, you can also do that directly from the task pane.

In this task, you learn how to verify both paragraph and font formatting.

① Start Word and click the **Open** button. Find and open **WD0901** and save it as **WD0901-Federal Census**.

This is an introduction to the Federal Census, from the U.S. Department of Commerce Web site, displayed in Print Layout view without a task pane.

> If your computer opens the file in another view or with the task pane open, click the **Print Layout View** button and close the task pane.

Print Layout View button

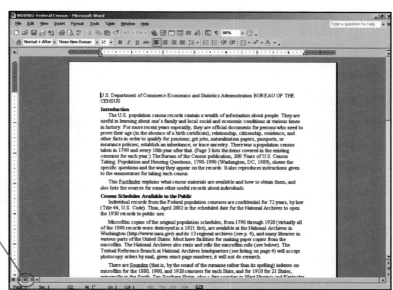

② Click the **Styles and Formatting** button on the left end of the Formatting toolbar.

The task pane is displayed on the right side of the screen showing the formatting and style of the paragraph that contains the insertion point.

> Click the arrow at the top of the task pane and select **Reveal Formatting** from the list. If there are any plus signs next to the Font, Paragraph, or Section areas of the task pane, click them.

The plus signs change to minuses, and all the formatting is displayed. The paragraph formatting shown is for the paragraph containing the insertion point—in this case, the first line.

Styles and Formatting button

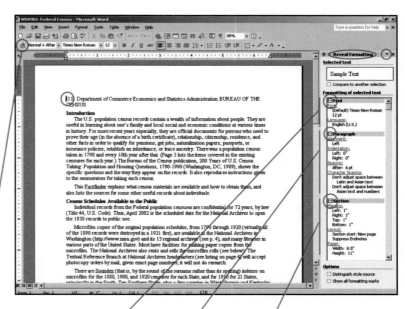

Font formatting   Paragraph formatting   Section formatting

QUICK TIP

You can also open the task pane by selecting **View**, **Task Pane** from the menu.

3 Double-click the word **Introduction** in the third line.

The word is selected, and the Font section shows that the selected text is Bold.

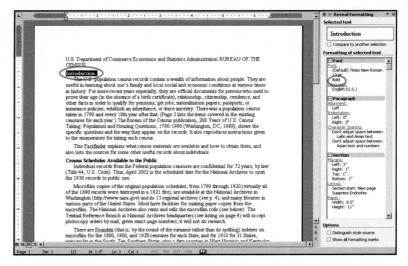

Clear Formatting option

4 Scroll down until you can see all of the text on the second page. Highlight the last two paragraphs.

These are the paragraphs that are in italics.

Click the **Other Task Panes** drop-down arrow and select **Styles and Formatting** from the list.

The Clear Formatting option is displayed at the top of the list. All of the other available paragraph and font styles are displayed.

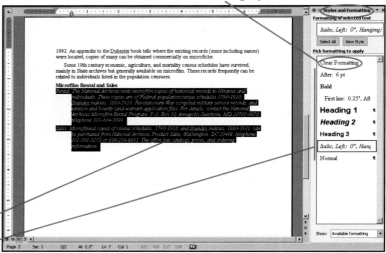

Selected text

Available paragraph and font styles

5 Click the **Clear Formatting** option.

*All of the paragraph and font formatting is removed, and everything is returned to the default **Normal** style. The Normal style is the default paragraph style in the most commonly used template, **Normal.dot**.*

Click anywhere in the selected text to remove the highlight, and then click the Save button. Leave the document open for the next task.

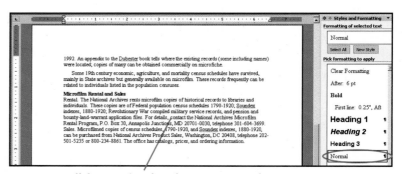

All formatting has been removed

CAUTION

The two paragraphs appear to merge into a single paragraph when you remove the formatting. This is not the case. The first paragraph happens to end at the end of a line.

IN DEPTH

There are additional options at the bottom of each task pane. For example, a drop-down list at the bottom of the Styles and Formatting task pane enables you to see what styles are in use in the rest of the document, or to see all of the styles that are available in addition to the ones used in the current document. Check boxes at the bottom of the Reveal Formatting task pane enable you to quickly reveal all formatting marks, and to show the style for each formatting option.

Task 2

CREATING AND APPLYING PARAGRAPH STYLES

Why would I do this?

You are not limited to the styles shown in the task pane. If none of the styles meet your needs, you can create your own. You can use these new styles in the current document, or add them to a template for use in all documents based on that template. There are several ways to create paragraph styles, but the easiest is to format a paragraph the way you want it, and then type the name into the **Style** box in the Formatting toolbar.

In this task, you learn how to create a new paragraph style, and then apply this new style to other paragraphs in the document.

1 With the **WD0901-Federal Census** document still open, choose the **Styles and Formatting** task pane, if necessary.

Scroll down so that you can see all of the text on the second page. Place the insertion point anywhere in the first paragraph below the Microfilm Rental and Sales heading.

You will now change some of the paragraph formats to create a Hanging Indent style.

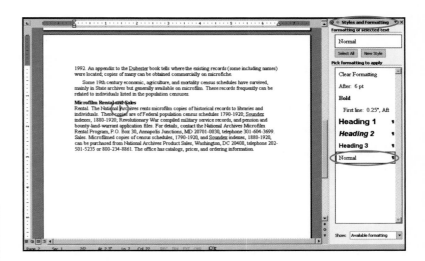

QUICK TIP
You would select the entire paragraph if you were going to change the font or font size, but since all the changes you will make are paragraph formats, all you need to do is place the insertion point anywhere in the paragraph.

2 Choose F**ormat**, **P**aragraph from the menu.

The Paragraph dialog box is displayed.

In the Indentation section, choose **Hanging** from the **Special** list box, and type **.75** in the **By** box. In the Spacing section, choose **6 pt** from the **After** list box, and select 1.5 lines from the Li**n**e spacing box.

QUICK TIP
To see the details of a paragraph style, such as the one you just created, point to a style. A screen tip appears containing the formatting details of that style.

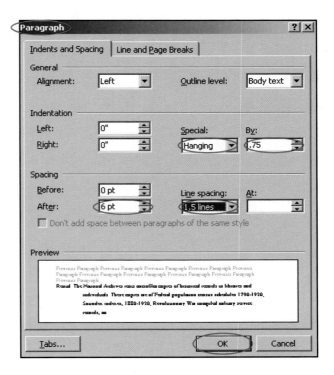

3 Click **OK**.

The paragraph now has 1.5 line spacing, is formatted as a hanging indent, and has an extra 6 points between it and the next paragraph.

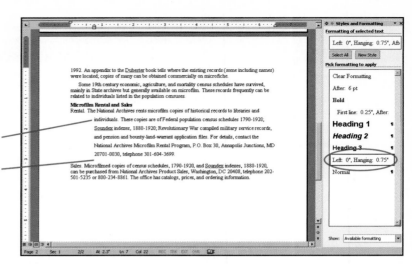

Hanging indent

Extra space between paragraphs

4 Click once in the Style box in the Formatting toolbar.

The text in the Style box is highlighted.

Type **Hanging** and press ⏎Enter.

The Style box displays the new style name; the task pane shows it as well. A paragraph marker to the right of the style name identifies the style as a paragraph style.

⚠ **CAUTION**

To make this procedure work, you must follow all of the steps listed above. If you forget to press ⏎Enter after you type the name in the Style box, your new style will not be created.

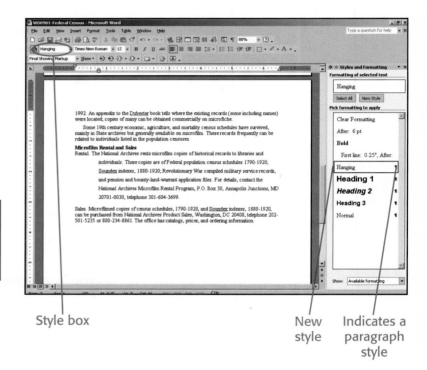

Style box

New style

Indicates a paragraph style

5 Place the insertion point anywhere in the last paragraph, and then click the new Hanging style in the task pane.

The last paragraph now has exactly the same formatting as the paragraph before it.

QUICK TIP

If the task pane is not open, you can get to your new style by clicking the down arrow on the Style list box and selecting the appropriate style.

IN DEPTH

In a hanging indent, if you want the first word following the heading text to line up with the rest of the paragraph, place the insertion point to the left of the word and press Tab.

6 Click the **Save** button to save your work. Leave the document open for the next task.

1992. An appendix to the Dubester book tells where the existing records (some including names) were located; copies of many can be obtained commercially on microfiche.

Some 19th century economic, agriculture, and mortality census schedules have survived, mainly in State archives but generally available on microfilm. These records frequently can be related to individuals listed in the population censuses.

Microfilm Rental and Sales

Rental. The National Archives rents microfilm copies of historical records to libraries and individuals. These copies are of Federal population census schedules 1790-1920; Soundex indexes, 1880-1920; Revolutionary War compiled military service records, and pension and bounty-land-warrant application files. For details, contact the National Archives Microfilm Rental Program, P.O. Box 30, Annapolis Junctions, MD 20701-0030, telephone 301-604-3699.

Sales. Microfilmed copies of census schedules, 1790-1920, and Soundex indexes, 1880-1920, can be purchased from National Archives Product Sales, Washington, DC 20408, telephone 202-501-5235 or 800-234-8861. The office has catalogs, prices, and ordering information.

IN DEPTH

The Show option, at the bottom of the Styles and Formatting task pane, enables you to access a vast library of styles. To see a wider variety, click the arrow in the Show box and choose All styles from the menu.

Task 3
CREATING AND APPLYING FONT STYLES

Why would I do this?

There are times when you might want to create a font format for formatting text without changing the paragraph formatting. In Task 2 you learned a quick way to create paragraph formatting by making all the changes in a paragraph and then naming the new style in the Style box. This technique does not work for creating font styles. Instead, you need to format the text the way you want it, and then click the New Style button in the task pane.

In this task, you learn to create a font style.

1 With the **WD0901-Federal Census** document still open, double-click the word **Rental** in the first line under the Microfilm Rental and Sales heading on the second page.

You want to change the font of the words Rental and Sales at the beginning of the last two paragraphs to make them easy for the reader to distinguish.

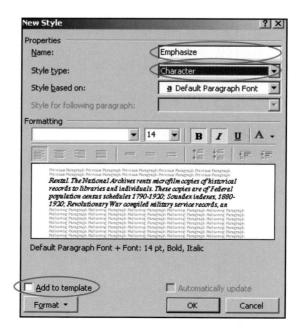

2 Change the font size to 14 points, and then click the **Bold** and **Italic** buttons.

You now want to create a style based on these font formats.

Click the **New Style** button at the top of the task pane.

The New Style dialog box is displayed.

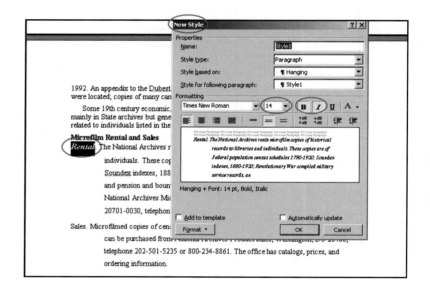

3 In the New Style dialog box, type **Emphasize** in the **Name** box, and then select **Character** from the **Style type** list box.

*Make sure you type **Emphasize**, and not **Emphasis**, which is an existing style. If you don't choose the Character style type, the paragraph formatting will also be transferred to selected text when this new style is used.*

IN DEPTH

The New Style dialog box gives you the option of adding your new style to the template that you are using. If you click the **Add to template** check box, the new style is available in any document based on that template.

4 Click **OK**.

Word adds the new font style to the list of styles in the task pane. The letter to the right of the font style name identifies the new style as a font style.

> Double-click the word **Sales** to select it. Click the Emphasize style from the task pane.

The style of the word is changed.

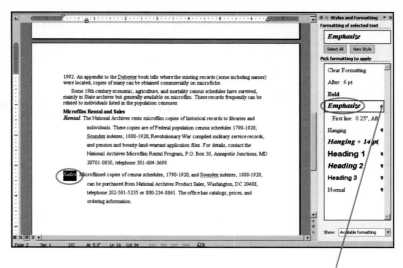

Indicates a font style

5 Click the **Save** button to save your work.
Leave the document open for the next task.

Task 4

UPDATING PARAGRAPH STYLES

Why would I do this?

You create styles with a specific purpose in mind, but often the styles you create don't look just right when you print the document. There is an easy way to modify the style until you get it exactly right. This method works on styles you create, as well as on styles built into the template. In fact, you can change the formatting of styles in the commonly used Normal template (Normal.dot), which will affect all documents based on this template. It is important, therefore, to be very careful when changing Normal template styles.

In this task, you use a heading style on document subtitles, and then modify the existing paragraph style to make the subtitles stand out.

1 With the **WD0901-Federal Census** document still open, click anywhere in the **Introduction** subtitle near the top of the document. Click the **Heading 3** style from the Styles and Formatting task pane.

The paragraph takes on all of the characteristics of the new style. Notice that you do not need to select a whole paragraph to apply a paragraph style.

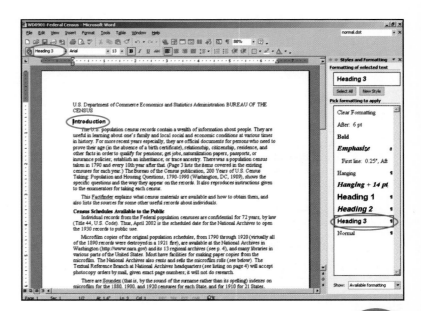

2 Place the insertion point in the **Census Schedules Available to the Public** subtitle and select the **Heading 3** style from the task pane.

Place the insertion point in the **Microfilm Rental and Sales** subtitle and select the **Heading 3** style from the task pane.

*All three of the subtitles now use the **Heading 3** style.*

1969 and 1975) and State Census Records, Ann S. Lainhart, Genealogical Publishing Co., Inc., 1992. An appendix to the Dubester book tells where the existing records (some including names) were located; copies of many can be obtained commercially on microfiche.

Some 19th century economic, agriculture, and mortality census schedules have survived, mainly in State archives but generally available on microfilm. These records frequently can be related to individuals listed in the population censuses.

Microfilm Rental and Sales

Rental. The National Archives rents microfilm copies of historical records to libraries and individuals. These copies are of Federal population census schedules 1790-1920; Soundex indexes, 1880-1920; Revolutionary War compiled military service records, and pension and bounty-land-warrant application files. For details, contact the National Archives Microfilm Rental Program, P.O. Box 30, Annapolis Junctions, MD 20701-0030, telephone 301-604-3699.

Sales. Microfilmed copies of census schedules, 1790-1920, and Soundex indexes, 1880-1920, can be purchased from National Archives Product Sales, Washington, DC 20408, telephone 202-501-5235 or 800-234-8861. The office has catalogs, prices, and ordering information.

3 Scroll to the top of the document and place the insertion point in the **Introduction** subtitle. Right-click on the **Heading 3** style in the Styles and Formatting task pane and select **Modify** from the menu.

*You'll see the Modify Style dialog box displayed. All of the formatting is shown. Notice that the **Heading 3** style is based on the **Normal** style—styles are often variations of other styles. The dialog box has both a Formatting toolbar and a **Format** button, for more control over the formatting.*

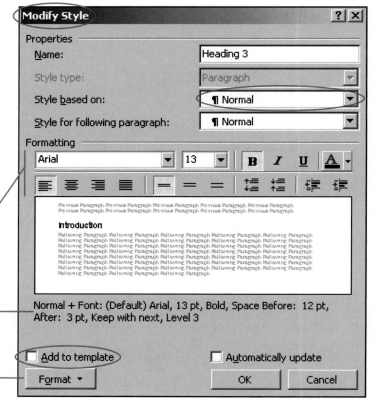

Formatting toolbar

Formatting for this style

Format button

4 Use the **Formatting** toolbar to change the font to **Arial Black**, and the font size to **14** points. Use the drop-down arrow to choose **Red** from the **Font Color** list box.

These changes all help to set off the three subtitles.

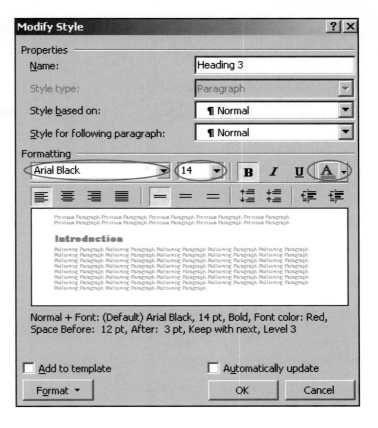

5 Click the F<u>o</u>rmat button, and choose <u>B</u>orders.

The Borders dialog box is displayed.

Click the **Box** option.

This adds a box around all the paragraphs using the **Heading 3** *style.*

The Box option

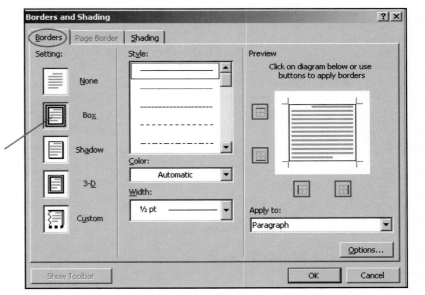

6 Click **OK** to close the Borders dialog box, and then click **OK** again to close the Modify Style dialog box.

*Notice that all of changes have been made to all paragraphs using the **Heading 3** style. Also, the new formats are displayed in Heading 3 style name in the task pane.*

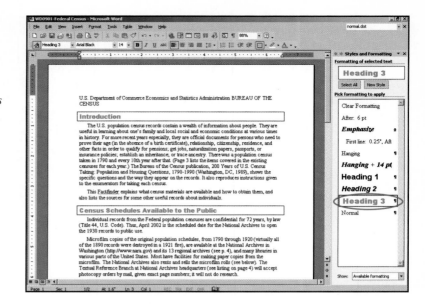

7 Click the **Save** button to save your work. Leave the document open for the next task.

Task 5

INSERTING LINE AND PAGE BREAKS

Why would I do this?

Sometimes you might have a block of text that needs to be broken into two lines, but the paragraph formatting would make the text appear odd. This is particularly true for titles and table entries, where pressing ↵Enter adds too much space before or after the text, or the line spacing leaves too much room between the lines. You can also separate text by adding artificial page breaks. These enable you to keep text or tables together when they would normally be broken over two pages.

In this task, you add line breaks to the title, and a page break at the end of a page.

1 With the **WD0901-Federal Census** document still open, highlight the title of the document.

The title includes the first two lines of the document.

Click the **Bold** button. Use the **Font Color** button to change the color of the title to red to match the subtitles. Change the **Font** to **Arial Rounded MT Bold**, and the **Font Size** to **16** points. Click anywhere in the title to turn off the highlighting.

The title now matches the subtitles.

U.S. Department of Commerce Economics and Statistics Administration BUREAU OF THE CENSUS

Introduction

The U.S. population census records contain a wealth of information about people. They are useful in learning about one's family and local social and economic conditions at various times in history. For more recent years especially, they are official documents for persons who need to prove their age (in the absence of a birth certificate), relationship, citizenship, residence, and other facts in order to qualify for pensions; get jobs, naturalization papers, passports, or insurance policies; establish an inheritance; or trace ancestry. There was a population census taken in 1790 and every 10th year after that. (Page 3 lists the items covered in the existing censuses for each year.) The Bureau of the Census publication, 200 Years of U.S. Census Taking: Population and Housing Questions, 1790-1990 (Washington, DC, 1989), shows the specific questions and the way they appear on the records. It also reproduces instructions given to the enumerators for taking each census.

This Factfinder explains what census materials are available and how to obtain them, and also lists the sources for some other useful records about individuals.

Census Schedules Available to the Public

Individual records from the Federal population censuses are confidential for 72 years, by law (Title 44, U.S. Code). Thus, April 2002 is the scheduled date for the National Archives to open the 1930 records to public use.

Microfilm copies of the original population schedules, from 1790 through 1920 (virtually all of the 1890 records were destroyed in a 1921 fire), are available at the National Archives in Washington (http://www.nara.gov) and its 13 regional archives (see p. 4), and many libraries in various parts of the United States. Most have facilities for making paper copies from the microfilm. The National Archives also rents and sells the microfilm rolls (see below). The Textual Reference Branch at National Archives headquarters (see listing on page 4) will accept photocopy orders by mail, given exact page numbers; it will not do research.

2 Place the insertion point just to the left of the word **Economics** in the title and press ⏎Enter.

Notice the distance between the first and second lines. This is because the formatting places an extra 6 points after the paragraph.

Click the Undo button. Hold down ⇧Shift and press ⏎Enter.

Notice that the distance between the first and second lines no longer includes the extra 6 points.

3 Place the insertion point just to the left of the word **BUREAU** in the title, hold down ⇧Shift and press ⏎Enter.

A second line break is placed in the paragraph.

Click the Center button on the Formatting toolbar, and then click the Show/Hide button in the Standard toolbar.

The title is centered, and the formatting marks show the difference between a paragraph mark and a line break.

4 Click the Show/Hide button.

This removes the formatting marks from the document.

Scroll down so that you can see the document's third subtitle, which is located on the second page.

This shows the rental and sales information, and should be placed on a separate page.

U.S. Department of Commerce
Economics and Statistics Administration BUREAU OF THE CENSUS

Introduction

The U.S. population census records contain a wealth of information about people. They are useful in learning about one's family and local social and economic conditions at various times in history. For more recent years especially, they are official documents for persons who need to prove their age (in the absence of a birth certificate), relationship, citizenship, residence, and other facts in order to qualify for pensions; get jobs, naturalization papers, passports, or insurance policies; establish an inheritance; or trace ancestry. There was a population census taken in 1790 and every 10th year after that. (Page 3 lists the items covered in the existing censuses for each year.) The Bureau of the Census publication, 200 Years of U.S. Census Taking: Population and Housing Questions, 1790-1990 (Washington, DC, 1989), shows the specific questions and the way they appear on the records. It also reproduces instructions given to the enumerators for taking each census.

This Factfinder explains what census materials are available and how to obtain them, and also lists the sources for some other useful records about individuals.

Census Schedules Available to the Public

Individual records from the Federal population censuses are confidential for 72 years, by law (Title 44, U.S. Code). Thus, April 2002 is the scheduled date for the National Archives to open the 1930 records to public use.

Microfilm copies of the original population schedules, from 1790 through 1920 (virtually all of the 1890 records were destroyed in a 1921 fire), are available at the National Archives in Washington (http://www.nara.gov) and its 13 regional archives (see p. 4), and many libraries in various parts of the United States. Most have facilities for making paper copies from the microfilm. The National Archives also rents and sells the microfilm rolls (see below). The

---

Show/hide ¶ button

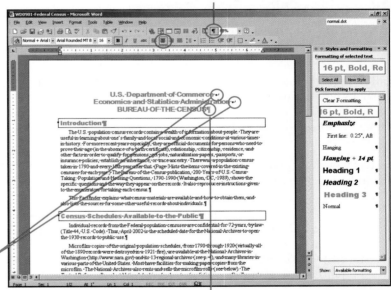

Line break mark

Paragraph mark

A number of State and territorial censuses were taken in the intradecennial years, particularly in the 19th century. See Henry J. Dubester, An Annotated Bibliography of Censuses Taken After the Year 1790, by States and Territories of the United States (Washington, DC, 1948, reprinted 1969 and 1975) and State Census Records, Ann S. Lainhart, Genealogical Publishing Co., Inc., 1992. An appendix to the Dubester book tells where the existing records (some including names) were located; copies of many can be obtained commercially on microfiche.

Some 19th century economic, agriculture, and mortality census schedules have survived, mainly in State archives but generally available on microfilm. These records frequently can be related to individuals listed in the population censuses.

Microfilm Rental and Sales

Rental. The National Archives rents microfilm copies of historical records to libraries and individuals. These copies are of Federal population census schedules 1790-1920; Soundex indexes, 1880-1920; Revolutionary War compiled military service records, and pension and bounty-land-warrant application files. For details, contact the National Archives Microfilm Rental Program, P.O. Box 30, Annapolis Junctions, MD 20701-0030, telephone 301-604-3699.

Sales. Microfilmed copies of census schedules, 1790-1920, and Soundex indexes, 1880-1920, can be purchased from National Archives Product Sales, Washington, DC 20408, telephone 202-501-5235 or 800-234-8861. The office has catalogs, prices, and ordering information.

5 Place the insertion point to the left of the **Microfilm Rental and Sales** subtitle.

This is where you want the new page to begin.

Hold down Ctrl and press ↵Enter.

The rental and sales information moves to a new page. You can also insert a page break by selecting Insert, Break from the menu, and selecting Page break from the Break dialog box.

> **Microfilm Rental and Sales**
>
> *Rental*. The National Archives rents microfilm copies of historical records to libraries and individuals. These copies are of Federal population census schedules 1790-1920; Soundex indexes, 1880-1920; Revolutionary War compiled military service records, and pension and bounty-land-warrant application files. For details, contact the National Archives Microfilm Rental Program, P.O. Box 30, Annapolis Junctions, MD 20701-0030, telephone 301-604-3699.
>
> *Sales*. Microfilmed copies of census schedules, 1790-1920, and Soundex indexes, 1880-1920, can be purchased from National Archives Product Sales, Washington, DC 20408, telephone 202-501-5235 or 800-234-8861. The office has catalogs, prices, and ordering information.

6 Click the Save button to save your work. Leave the document open for the next task.

Task 6
FORMATTING SECTIONS

Why would I do this?

In most cases, the page layout will be consistent throughout each document. You can, however, break your document into two or more sections, each of which has different page or text layouts. You can use sections to separate two-column text from a single-column title. You can also change the page layout so that you can print some pages in *portrait* (vertical) orientation, and some in *landscape* (horizontal) orientation. This is very convenient for displaying images, or wide charts or tables.

In this task, you create a section in which you paste a scanned image that will print in landscape orientation.

1 With the **WD0901-Federal Census** document still open, scroll to the bottom of the document and place the insertion point at the end of the last sentence. Press ↵Enter.

This is where you insert a section break.

> **Microfilm Rental and Sales**
>
> *Rental*. The National Archives rents microfilm copies of historical records to libraries and individuals. These copies are of Federal population census schedules 1790-1920; Soundex indexes, 1880-1920; Revolutionary War compiled military service records, and pension and bounty-land-warrant application files. For details, contact the National Archives Microfilm Rental Program, P.O. Box 30, Annapolis Junctions, MD 20701-0030, telephone 301-604-3699.
>
> *Sales*. Microfilmed copies of census schedules, 1790-1920, and Soundex indexes, 1880-1920, can be purchased from National Archives Product Sales, Washington, DC 20408, telephone 202-501-5235 or 800-234-8861. The office has catalogs, prices, and ordering information.
>
>

2 Choose <u>I</u>nsert, <u>B</u>reak from the menu.

The Break dialog box is displayed. You can add either page breaks or section breaks.

Select the <u>N</u>ext page section break option.

Next page section break option ⎯

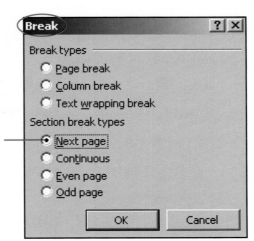

3 Click **OK** to close the Break dialog box.

A new section is created on a new page, but the formatting is still exactly the same as the previous pages. To change the formatting of the section, you need to use page setup options.

Place the insertion point at the beginning of the new section. Choose <u>F</u>ile, **Page Set<u>u</u>p** from the menu.

The Page Setup dialog box is displayed.

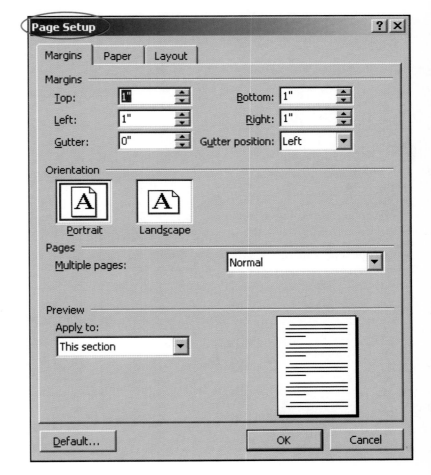

4 Choose **Landscape** from the Orientation area of the Page Setup dialog box. Make sure **This section** is selected from the **Apply to** list box.

You can change as many page setup options as needed. They will apply only to this new section.

Click **OK** to close the Page Setup dialog box. Choose **50%** from the **Zoom** list box.

The smaller size shows clearly that the new section is in landscape orientation.

The new section is in landscape orientation

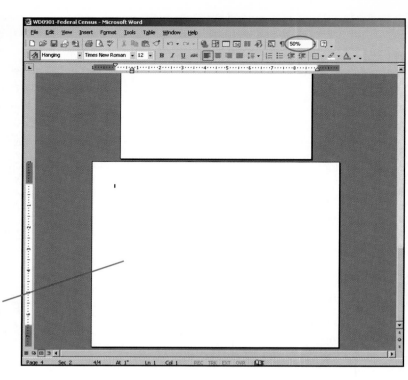

5 Choose **Insert**, **Picture**, **From File** from the menu.

The Insert Picture dialog box is displayed.

Find and select the **WD0902** file in the **Student** folder. Click the **Insert** button.

The picture is inserted into the new section. Because the orientation of the picture is landscape, it fits nicely on the page.

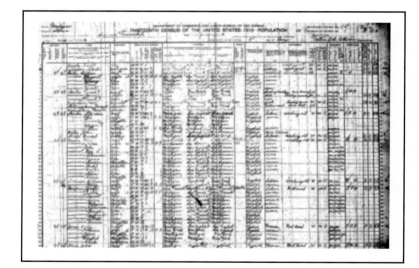

6 Press ↵Enter to start a new text line and type your name. Click the **Print** button to print the whole document.

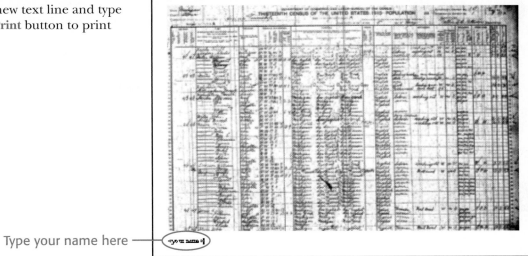

Type your name here ⎯⎯⎯○ <your name>

7 Click the **Save** button to save your work. Close the document.

The exercises that follow are designed for you to review and use what you have learned in this lesson. You also have the opportunity to practice your skills and then expand on them by applying them to new situations.

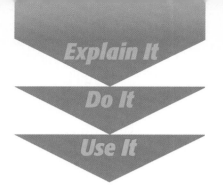

COMPREHENSION

Comprehension exercises are designed to check your memory and understanding of the basic concepts in this lesson. You distinguish between true and false statements, identify new screen elements, and match terms with related statements. If you are uncertain of the correct answer, refer to the task number following each item (for example, T4 refers to Task 4) and review that task until you are confident that you can provide a correct response.

TRUE-FALSE

Circle either T or F.

T   F   **1.** You can change the font of a paragraph using a font style by clicking anywhere in the paragraph and selecting the font style. **(T2)**

T   F   **2.** When you create a style using the Style box in the Formatting toolbar, you must press ↵Enter after you type in the new style name. **(T2)**

T   F   **3.** You cannot create a font style by making the changes and then typing the name in the Style box in the Formatting toolbar. **(T3)**

T   F   **4.** The New Style dialog box enables you to add your new style to an existing template. **(T3)**

T   F   **5.** You cannot make changes to the Normal.dot template. **(T4)**

T   F   **6.** Changes made to a section do not affect other sections. **(T6)**

MATCHING QUESTIONS

A. Line break   **D.** Task pane

B. Font style   **E.** Normal.dot

C. Normal style   **F.** Paragraph style

Match the following statements to the word or phrase that is the best match from the list. Write the letter of the matching word or phrase in the space provided next to the number.

1. _____ Area of the screen that enables style creation and modification **(Intro)**

2. _____ A quick way to format text, but not paragraphs **(Intro)**

3. _____ Method of separating text without creating a new paragraph **(T4)**

4. _____ Controls all aspects of a paragraph's formatting **(Intro)**

5. _____ Default paragraph settings **(T1)**

6. _____ A commonly used template **(T1)**

IDENTIFYING PARTS OF THE WORD SCREEN

Refer to the figure and identify the numbered parts of the screen. Write the letter of the correct label in the space next to the number.

1. _____

2. _____

3. _____

4. _____

5. _____

6. _____

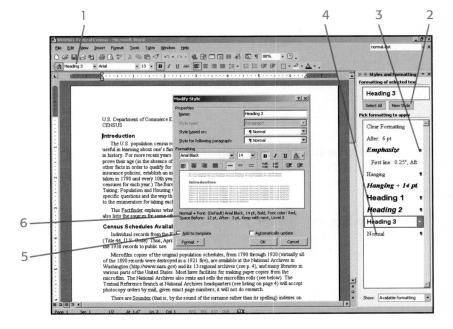

A. All of the formatting in the selected paragraph style (T4)

B. Style box (T4)

C. Way to place a new style into a template (T4)

D. Indicates a font style (T5)

E. Place you go to create a font style (T4)

F. Default paragraph style (T5)

REINFORCEMENT

Reinforcement exercises are designed to reinforce the skills you have learned by applying them to new situations. Detailed instructions are provided along with a figure, where appropriate, to illustrate the result. Complete the following reinforcement exercises sequentially. Leave the document open at the end of each exercise for use in the next exercise until you are specifically directed to close it.

In these exercises, you will work with a press release about research on tornadoes in Michigan during a 40-year time span.

R1—Verifying and Clearing Paragraph Formats

1. Start Word, if necessary. Open the document **WD0903** and save it as **WD0903-Tornado Research**. Switch to Print Layout View, if necessary.

2. Choose **V**iew, Tas**k** Pane from the menu, and select **Reveal Formatting** from the **Other Task Panes** drop-down list, if necessary. Place the insertion point in several of the paragraphs near the top of the document and watch the styles change in the task pane.

3. Select **Styles and Formatting** from the **Other Task Panes** drop-down list. Place the insertion point in the two-line bold title and choose the **Clear Formatting** option from the task pane.

4. Place the insertion point in the first full paragraph and click the **Clear Formatting** option from the task pane. Both the title and the first paragraph have now reverted to the default **Normal** style.

5. Click the **Undo** button once to reverse the style change to the paragraph.

6. Click the **Save** button to save your work. Leave the document open for the next exercise.

R2—Creating and Applying Paragraph Styles

1. Double-click the **Background** heading, located about halfway down the first page.

2. Click the **Bold** button. Use the **Font Size** list to change the font size to 14 points.

3. Select the **Broadway** font from the **Font** list. If this font is not available, choose another heavy-looking font. Click the **Center** button to center the heading.

4. Click once in the Style box in the Formatting toolbar. Type **New Heading** and press **↵Enter**.

5. Place the insertion point in the **Statistics** heading at (or near) the top of the second page. Scroll down and select **New Heading** from the list of styles in the task pane.

6. Use the same procedure you used in step 5 to change the style of the **Conclusion** heading (near the end of the document) to the **New Heading** style.

7. Place the insertion point in the last paragraph. Click once in the Style box in the Formatting toolbar. Type **Regular Paragraph** and press **↵Enter**.

8. Move up through the document, click in each regular paragraph (not the headings or titles), and select the Regular Paragraph style each time. You can also select several paragraphs at the same time and format them all at once. Be careful you don't accidentally include a heading. (Note: You may have to scroll down in the **Pick formatting to apply** box to see the Regular Paragraph style.)

9. Click the **Save** button to save your work. Leave the document open for the next exercise.

R3—Creating and Applying Font Styles

1. In this press release, you want the important information to jump out at the reader. Select the text from the third full paragraph that begins with **the June 8, 1953 Flint tornado** and ends at the end of the paragraph's second sentence.

2. Click the **Bold** and **Italic** buttons from the Formatting toolbar.

3. Click the **New Style** button at the top of the task pane.

4. In the New Style dialog box, type **Important** in the **Name** box, and then select **Character** from the **Style type** list box. Click **OK** to finish creating the font style.

5. In the first paragraph under the **Statistics** heading, highlight from **Michigan is tied with Alabama** to the end of the sentence.

6. Select the **Important** font style from the task pane.

7. Use the same font style on the sentence that begins, **Without doubt** in the **Statistics** paragraph.

8. Use the same font style on the following text in the last paragraph: **about nine-tenths of the deaths and three-fourths of the injuries occurred on four days in the 40-year span**.

9. Click the **Save** button to save your work. Leave the document open for the next exercise.

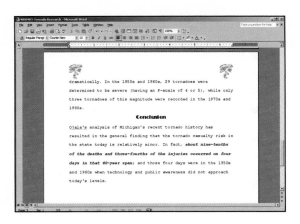

R4—Updating Paragraph Styles

1. Scroll to the point where the **Statistics** heading is at the top of the screen. Right-click on the **Regular Paragraph** style in the task pane and select the <u>M</u>odify option.

2. Click the <u>F</u>ormat button in the **Modify Style** dialog box. Select the <u>P</u>aragraph option.

3. Select **First line** from the <u>S</u>pecial list box, and accept the **0.5"** default in the <u>B</u>y box. Click **OK** twice. Notice that all the paragraphs using the **Regular Paragraph** style have changed.

4. Right-click on the **New Heading** style in the task pane and select the <u>M</u>odify option.

5. Click the drop-down arrow on the **Font Color** button and change the color to a dark blue. Click **OK**. Scroll through the document to make sure all three headings have changed.

6. Leave the document open for the next exercise. Scroll to the top of the document and add Formatted by <your name> just under the title. Click **Save** to save your changes.

R5—Inserting Line Breaks

1. Scroll to the top of the document. Click anywhere in the title of the document (not the PRESS RELEASE line).

2. Select the **New Heading** style from the task pane.

3. Place the insertion point just to the left of **TORNADO** in the title, hold down ⬆Shift), and press ↵Enter).

4. Select the title and choose <u>F</u>ormat, <u>P</u>aragraph from the menu. Select **12 pt** from the Aft<u>e</u>r box, and choose **Single** from the Li<u>n</u>e spacing box. Click **OK**. Notice that when you format text from the menu, it does not change the other paragraphs based on the same style. Instead, it creates another style based on the original paragraph style.

5. Change the **Font Size** to **16** points. Notice that using a formatting button also does not affect other paragraphs based on that style.

6. Click **OK**. Save your changes and leave the document open for the next exercise.

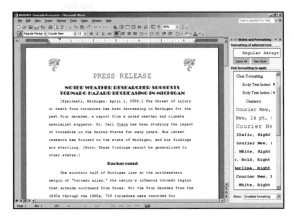

R6—Formatting Sections

1. Scroll to the bottom of the document and place the insertion point at the end of the last sentence. Press ↵Enter).

2. Choose <u>I</u>nsert, <u>B</u>reak from the menu. Select the <u>N</u>ext page section break option and click **OK**.

3. Choose <u>F</u>ile, Page Set<u>u</u>p from the menu.

4. Choose **Landscape** from the Orientation area of the Page Setup dialog box. Make sure **This section** is selected from the **Apply to** list box. Click **OK**.

5. Open the **WD0904** file in the **Student** folder. Choose <u>E</u>dit, Select A<u>l</u>l from the menu.

6. Click the **Copy** button. Close **WD0904**, and click the **Paste** button to paste the table and title into the current document.

7. Click **Save** to save your changes. Print the document, then close both the document and Word, unless you are going to move on to the Challenge exercises.

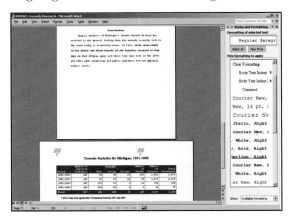

Challenge exercises are designed to test your ability to apply your skills to new situations with less-detailed instructions. These exercises also challenge you to expand your repertoire of skills by using commands that are similar to those you have already learned. The desired outcome is clearly defined, but you have more freedom to choose the steps needed to achieve the required result.

The following exercises use different files to illustrate procedures you should find helpful.

C1—Creating a Paragraph Style Using the New Style Dialog Box

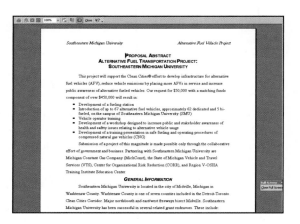

In this lesson, you learned how to create a paragraph style by making the changes in the paragraph and then typing a style name in the Style box. You can also create a style by placing the insertion point in a paragraph and then making all the changes in the New Style dialog box. In addition, you can create styles this way after selecting several paragraphs at the same time. The document you use is a proposal to employ alternative fuel vehicles at a university. There are two types of paragraphs left to format—the subheadings and the standard text paragraphs.

Goal: To create a paragraph style by using the New Style dialog box.

1. Locate and open the **WD0905** document and save it as **WD0905-Alternative Fuel**.

2. Open the Styles and Formatting task pane, if necessary.

3. Click the New Style button to open the New Style dialog box.

4. Name the new style **Subheading**. Make it bold, italic, and centered. Use the F**o**rmat, **P**aragraph option in the dialog box to add 6 points after the paragraph. (Note: Some of these options may be selected already if the insertion point is in the title. Don't worry—creating a new style does not change the formatting of the paragraph that contains the insertion point.)

5. Use the new Subheading style to change the style of the **General Information** and the **Goal and Objectives of the Project** subheadings.

6. Use the same procedure to create a new style called **Regular Text**. It should have a half-inch first line indent, line spacing of 1.5, and it should be aligned left. The font should be 12-point Times New Roman. It should not use bold or italic formatting. (Note: If the insertion point was in the title, you will have to deselect small caps from the F**o**rmat, F**o**nt option.)

7. Type your name at the bottom of the document. Save your changes, and then print and close the document. Leave Word open if you are going to do another exercise.

C2—Creating Your Own Template

If you create a lot of documents, you will probably find yourself creating the same group of styles over and over for each document. You can save yourself time and effort by putting all of your commonly used styles in a template, and then basing future documents on that template. One nice feature of templates is that you can modify them as your needs change.

The document that you will use as a basis for a new template is a short story by Frank Stockton that was one of many stories printed in an anthropological study of cultural behaviors described in late 19th century popular fiction. In this exercise, assume you will scan in other old stories and give them a standard look using the formats created for this short story.

Goal: To create a template based on the styles in a document, and to create a new document based on that template.

1. Locate and open the **WD0906** document. You do not need to save it yet.

2. Open the Reveal Formatting task pane, and then click the **Distinguish style source** option at the bottom of the pane. Click in any paragraph and look at the style name and formatting for the Column Text style. Open the header and look at the three styles created for use in the header.

3. Click the **Show all formatting marks** check box at the bottom of the pane so you can see section breaks, which you want to keep in the template. Highlight all the column text, and type **Use this area to paste the story that you've scanned. Delete this text.** Change the paragraph style to Column Text, if necessary.

4. Open the header (you can double-click anywhere in the header instead of using the menu). Change the title to **TITLE**, the author's name to **Author**, and then replace the biography with **Biography**. Make sure they have the appropriate styles.

5. Choose <u>F</u>ile, Save <u>A</u>s from the menu. Select **Document Template** from the **Save as type** box. Name the new template **WD0906-Story Template** and save it. The template is saved in the **Templates** folder.

6. Close the document. Choose <u>F</u>ile, <u>N</u>ew from the menu. Click the **General Templates** option from the New Document task pane. Choose **WD0906-Story Template** from the list of available templates.

7. Open the Styles and Formatting task pane. Notice that all of the styles you used in previous documents are available in this new document. Also notice that the document is unnamed. This protects you from accidentally saving over the template.

8. Type your name in the header and print this very short document. Close the document, but do not save your work.

C3—Avoiding Unwanted Text Breaks

The way text breaks over pages can affect the look of your document. If text breaks badly, or tables overlap pages, your document will look amateurish, which may affect the reaction of people reading it. In addition to tables and lists that should be kept together, there are also two paragraph breaks that are important enough that they have been given their own names. *Widows* are the last line of a paragraph that appears by itself on the top of a page. *Orphans* are first lines of paragraphs that appear at the bottom of a page. It is considered good form to force a second line to accompany a widow, and to send orphans to the next page to rejoin their paragraphs. Finally, you should keep titles together with at least two lines of text from the following paragraphs.

Goal: To use widow and orphan control, page breaks, and paragraph formatting to avoid awkward text breaks.

1. Locate and open the **WD0907** document and save it as **WD0907-Statistics**. Change to Print Layout View, if necessary.

2. Scroll down so that you can see the page break between the first two pages. Notice that the first line of step 1 is at the bottom of the page.

3. Place the insertion point anywhere in the step 1 text. Choose <u>F</u>ormat, <u>P</u>aragraph from the menu. Select the **Line and <u>P</u>age Breaks** tab. Turn on <u>W</u>idow/Orphan control and click **OK**. Notice that the first line of step 1 has moved to the top of the second page. However, this causes a problem with the **Conventions used in this module** heading and the single line of text below it. These lines should be kept with the following text.

4. Highlight the **Conventions used in this module** heading and the line below it. Choose <u>F</u>ormat, <u>P</u>aragraph from the menu. Select the **Line and <u>P</u>age Breaks** tab, if necessary. Select the **Keep with next** option and click **OK**. This forces these two lines to stay with the following paragraph when they occur at a page break.

5. Scroll to the bottom of the second page. Notice that the table overlaps two pages. Place the insertion point just above the table, hold down Ctrl, and press ↵Enter to add an artificial page break. The table is now together on the third page. (Note: There is another way to handle this problem in the table properties box. See if you can find it.)

6. Type your name at the bottom of the document. Save, print, and close the document.

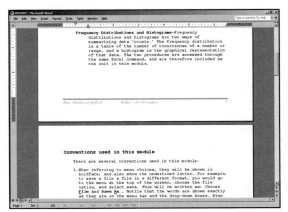

C4—Using the Reveal Formatting task pane to Format Paragraphs

Formatting individual paragraphs using the menu can be quite time-consuming. You can format easily from the Reveal Formatting task pane and save a few steps for each procedure. Using this technique typically requires leaving the task pane open while you are editing, which means that you will probably need a larger monitor (at least 17"). If you are using a small monitor, the task pane will probably make the document too small to read. The document you will use is a brief discussion of copyright and public domain issues—a topic growing more important to everyone with a computer.

Goal: To format paragraphs using the Reveal Formatting task pane.

1. Locate and open the **WD0908** document and save it as **WD0908-Copyright**. Change to Print Layout View, if necessary. Open the Reveal Formatting task pane.

2. Make sure the insertion point is in the first (title) line. Choose the **Alignment** option in the **Paragraph** section. Center the title and add 6 points after the paragraph.

3. Select the title so you can change the font characteristics. Click Font in the Font area. Make the title bold, 18 points, using small caps.

4. Select the second and third lines (the names). Use the same procedure as in steps 2 and 3 to center the text and make the font bold.

5. Open the Section area of the Reveal Formatting task pane. Click Margins and change the left and right margins to 1".

6. Type your name in the third row of the document where indicated. Save, print, and close the document.

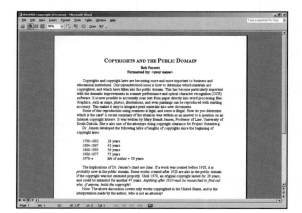

ON YOUR OWN

In this lesson, you saw how styles can save time. You can get templates that contain preformatted styles to perform specific tasks from the Microsoft Web site. These templates are set up to form the basis for everything from Newsletter styles to Fax cover sheet styles. You can download as many as you like, and can even pick and choose styles from several templates to build a template of your own.

This exercise is intended to give you experience finding, downloading, customizing, and using special-purpose templates. Find a newsletter, brochure, or other type of document on the Microsoft site and create a short document based on that template. Save both the template and the document. You only need to add a little information to the document to show that you have made some alterations. Be sure to include your name. Hint: The easiest way to get to the right section of the Microsoft Web site is to use the **Help**, **Office on the Web** menu option.

Criteria for grading will be:

1. Demonstration of ability to use Microsoft Word help and to find and use appropriate templates

2. Demonstration of the ability to create a template

Some examples of features that others have used to complete this exercise are:

- The new template is saved under your name.

- The document created using the new template contains your name, the date, and the name of the template you downloaded.

To complete the project:

- Make sure you identify yourself in the document.

- Print a copy of the document.

Lesson 10

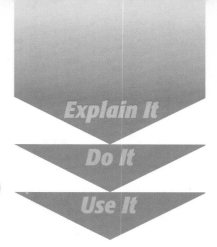

Explain It
Do It
Use It

Integrating Word with Other Office Programs

INTRODUCTION

Microsoft Office makes it easy to move information between applications. You can export Word outlines to PowerPoint to create presentations. You can place Excel charts and data in Word documents, and you can import Excel data into *Microsoft Graph* so you can create charts based on that data. You can use Access tables to create mail merge letters and mailing labels. This easy transfer of information is a nice feature of Office. There are several ways you can add information to a Word document from another program. The simplest way to move text into a document is to use the copy and paste method. This places the text directly into the document, usually in a table. You can also *embed* an object. Embedding a picture, chart, or other object takes the object from the source application and places it in the document, where it takes on the characteristics of a picture. Another way to place information in a document is to create a *link* between the source document and a Word document. The link keeps the relationship between the source and the Word document active—if you make a change in the source document, it is automatically updated in the Word document. Linking is often done when data changes frequently and the text stays the same. For example, if you have to turn in a report every week that consists of the same text with different numbers that come from a worksheet, you can link the worksheet to your Word document and print a new weekly report with little additional effort. You can also use linking when there are a lot of images that would make the document too large. Finally, you can import the data into a subprogram, such as Microsoft Graph, and create charts based on that data, although the Excel data itself might never be displayed.

When you bring Excel or Access text or data into a Word document, it is always entered into a table. There are table features that enable you to work with the data. If the data is numeric, you can use formulas to make calculations by row or column. If you import an Excel table that has had cells merged to create custom titles, Word enables you to split the cells so that you can sort the data.

In this lesson, you learn how to link and embed information from other applications into a Word document. You then use special table functions to make calculations and to split cells.

VISUAL SUMMARY

By the time you complete this lesson, you will have embedded and linked data from other sources. If this was a final document, you could adjust margins, remove spaces, and resize charts to create more logical page breaks. The first three pages of the document will look like this:

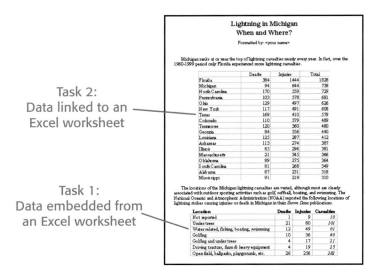

Task 2: Data linked to an Excel worksheet

Task 1: Data embedded from an Excel worksheet

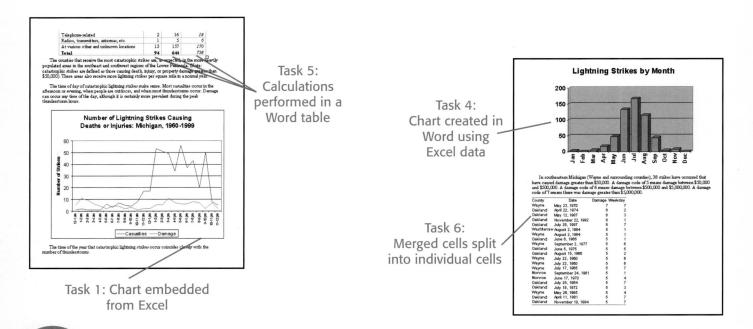

Task 5: Calculations performed in a Word table

Task 4: Chart created in Word using Excel data

Task 1: Chart embedded from Excel

Task 6: Merged cells split into individual cells

Task 1

EMBEDDING EXCEL DATA AND CHARTS

Why would I do this?

Each Office application has its strengths and weaknesses. To create the most effective documents, it is often advisable to take information from several different types of documents and combine them, usually in Word. One way you can do this is to copy information from one application and paste it into another. Excel-to-Word moves are the most common. Excel is a great program for analyzing numerical data, but its report-generating capabilities are limited. It is common to create datasheets and charts in Excel and paste them into Word when they are finished.

In this task, you copy a small Excel data table and a chart and paste them into a Word document.

① Start Word and click the **Open** button. Find and open **WD1001** and save it as **WD1001-Where and When**. Turn off the task pane and click the **Print Layout View** button, if necessary.

This document is a brief synopsis of lightning statistics for the state of Michigan from 1960-1999.

Place the insertion point to the left of the paragraph that begins **The counties that receive**, about one-quarter of the way down the first page.

You will insert a table from an Excel file here.

If you are downloading the sample files from an online source, you will need to get the WD1001 through WD1008 files.

Lightning in Michigan
When and Where?

Formatted by: <your name>

Michigan ranks at or near the top of lightning casualties nearly every year. In fact, over the 1960-1999 period only Florida experienced more lightning casualties.

The locations of the Michigan lightning casualties are varied, although most are clearly associated with outdoor sporting activities such as golf, softball, boating, and swimming. The National Oceanic and Atmospheric Administration (NOAA) reported the following locations of lightning strikes causing injuries or death in Michigan in their *Storm Data* publications.

The counties that receive the most catastrophic strikes are, as expected, in the more heavily populated areas in the southeast and southwest regions of the Lower Peninsula. (Note: catastrophic strikes are defined as those causing death, injury, or property damage greater than $50,000). These areas also receive more lightning strikes per square mile in a normal year.

The time of day of catastrophic lightning strikes make sense. Most casualties occur in the afternoon or evening, when people are outdoors, and when most thunderstorms occur. Damage can occur any time of the day, although it is certainly more prevalent during the peak thunderstorm hours.

The time of the year that catastrophic lightning strikes occur coincides closely with the number of thunderstorms.

2 Start Excel and open **WD1002**. Choose **F**ile, Save **A**s from the menu and rename the file **WD1002-Lightning Data**. Click the **Location** tab at the bottom of the Excel window.

This is an Excel file that has four worksheets. You will use all the worksheets in this lesson.

Scroll to the right until you can see all the location data. Click in the upper-left corner of the location data (in cell **P2**) and drag down and to the right (to cell **S12**) until the entire area is selected.

The cell references refer to the row and column headings. The first cell you selected was in column P, row 2, and is referred to as cell P2. Cell P2 does not look like it is selected, but it is.

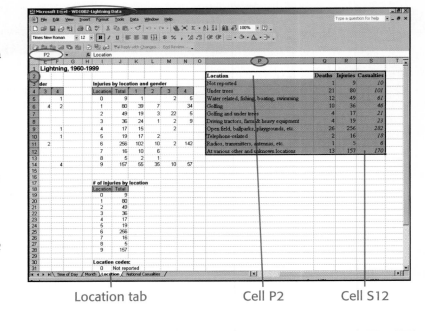

Location tab   Cell P2   Cell S12

3 Click the **Copy** button. Click the **WD1001-Where and When** button on the taskbar.

This returns you to your Word document, but leaves the Excel document open.

With the insertion point still to the left of the third text paragraph, click the **Paste** button.

The Excel data is pasted into the Word document at the insertion point. It is in table format, and you can format it the same way you would format a table created in Word.

Lightning in Michigan
When and Where?

Formatted by: <your name>

Michigan ranks at or near the top of lightning casualties nearly every year. In fact, over the 1960-1999 period only Florida experienced more lightning casualties.

The locations of the Michigan lightning casualties are varied, although most are clearly associated with outdoor sporting activities such as golf, softball, boating, and swimming. The National Oceanic and Atmospheric Administration (NOAA) reported the following locations of lightning strikes causing injuries or death in Michigan in their *Storm Data* publications.

Location	Deaths	Injuries	Casualties
Not reported	1	9	10
Under trees	21	80	101
Water related, fishing, boating, swimming	12	49	61
Golfing	10	36	46
Golfing and under trees	4	17	21
Driving tractors, farm & heavy equipment	4	19	23
Open field, ballparks, playgrounds, etc.	26	256	282
Telephone-related	2	16	18
Radios, transmitters, antennas, etc.	1	5	6
At various other and unknown locations	13	157	170

The counties that receive the most catastrophic strikes are, as expected, in the more heavily populated areas in the southeast and southwest regions of the Lower Peninsula. (Note: catastrophic strikes are defined as those causing death, injury, or property damage greater than $50,000). These areas also receive more lightning strikes per square mile in a normal year.

4 Place the insertion point anywhere in the new table. Choose **Table**, **Table Properties** from the menu.

The Table Properties dialog box is displayed.

Click the **Center** button.

You also have the option of wrapping text around the table if it is a small one.

Center button

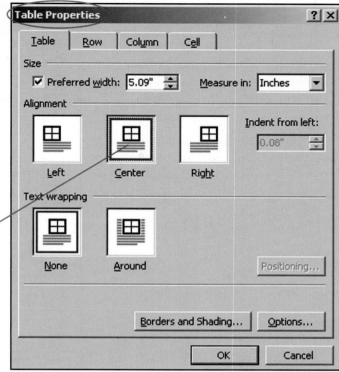

5 Click **OK**.

The table is centered between the left and right margin.

The table is centered

6 Place the insertion point to the left of the paragraph that begins **The time of the year**, near the bottom of the first page. Click the **Microsoft Excel–WD1002-Lightning Data** button in the taskbar.

This takes you back to the Excel document that contains the lightning data.

Click the **Time of Day** tab at the bottom of the Excel window. Click on the chart near the edge.

Handles appear showing that the chart is selected.

Handles indicate that the chart is selected

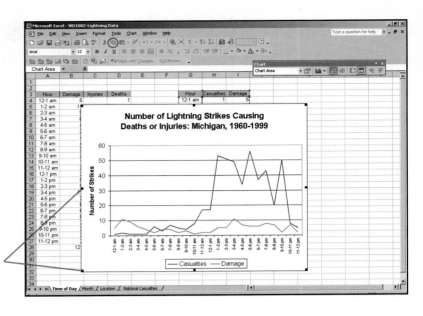

7 Click the **Copy** button. Move back to the **Word** document and click the **Paste** button.

The chart is pasted at the insertion point as a graphic, just the same as a character typed from the keyboard.

Press ⏎Enter.

The chart is now in its own paragraph.

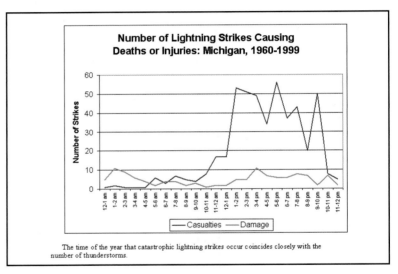

8 Click the **Save** button to save your work. Leave the document open for the next task.

IN DEPTH

When you embed data into Word from another program, the data becomes part of the Word document. All connections to the old document are severed. If you edit the original document, in this case the Excel worksheet, the changes you make will not be reflected in the Word document.

Task 2
LINKING TO EXCEL DATA

Why would I do this?
In the first task, you copied and pasted data from an Excel worksheet into a Word document. If you print the Word document on a regular basis, however, and the data in the table changes over time, it is usually best to link the Word table to the Excel worksheet. That way every change you make to the worksheet will be reflected in the Word document.

In this task, you learn how to link Excel data to a Word document.

1 With the **WD1001-Where and When** document still open, place the insertion point next to the second text paragraph that begins **The locations**.

*Use the taskbar to go to the **WD1002-Lightning Data** Excel document. Click the **National Casualties** tab at the bottom of the Excel window. Highlight all the information on the worksheet except the first row to select the table of data without the title.*

The only data on that datasheet is a list of states with more than 300 lightning casualties over a 40-year time span. The problem with this data is that the most recent two years are tentative. As final numbers come in for each month, small changes are made to the data. This is a perfect use for linking, rather than embedding.

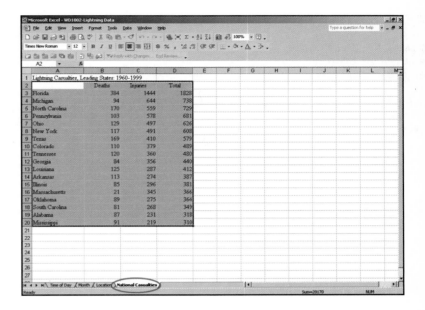

2 Click the Copy button.

The information is copied to the Clipboard.

Use the taskbar to move back to the Word document. Choose **Edit**, **Paste Special** from the menu.

The Paste Special dialog box is displayed.

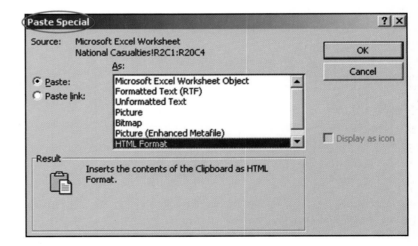

3 Choose **Paste link**, and then select **Microsoft Excel Worksheet Object** as the type of object to link.

Notice that one of the options on the Paste Link dialog box is to insert an Excel icon in the document rather than the data itself.

Inserts an Excel button rather than the data

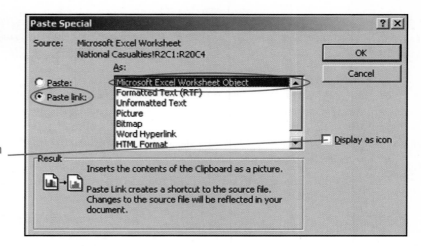

4 Click **OK**.

The data is pasted into a table, just as it was when you used the paste option in Task 1. The data, however, is still linked to the worksheet. Because it was pasted as an object, it is placed in the text the same as any other character.

Press ↵Enter.

The following paragraph is now separated from the table.

When and Where?

Formatted by: <your name>

Michigan ranks at or near the top of lightning casualties nearly every year. In fact, over the 1960-1999 period only Florida experienced more lightning casualties.

	Deaths	Injuries	Total
Florida	384	1444	1828
Michigan	94	644	738
North Carolina	170	559	729
Pennsylvania	103	578	681
Ohio	129	497	626
New York	117	491	608
Texas	169	410	579
Colorado	110	379	489
Tennessee	120	360	480
Georgia	84	356	440
Louisiana	125	287	412
Arkansas	113	274	387
Illinois	85	296	381
Massachusetts	21	345	366
Oklahoma	89	275	364
South Carolina	81	268	349
Alabama	87	231	318
Mississippi	91	219	310

The locations of the Michigan lightning casualties are varied, although most are clearly associated with outdoor sporting activities such as golf, softball, boating, and swimming. The

5 Click anywhere on the new table.

Notice that there are handles in the corners—you cannot directly edit this object. You can treat it as a picture until you need to change something.

Click the **Center** button on the Formatting toolbar.

The table is not centered between the margins. It is being treated like text with a half-inch indent of the first line.

Choose **Format**, **Paragraph** from the menu, select **(none)** from the **Special** box, and click **OK**.

The table is now centered. It is time to change some of the data.

When and Where?

Formatted by: <your name>

Michigan ranks at or near the top of lightning casualties nearly every year. In fact, over the 1960-1999 period only Florida experienced more lightning casualties.

	Deaths	Injuries	Total
Florida	384	1444	1828
Michigan	94	644	738
North Carolina	170	559	729
Pennsylvania	103	578	681
Ohio	129	497	626
New York	117	491	608
Texas	169	410	579
Colorado	110	379	489
Tennessee	120	360	480
Georgia	84	356	440
Louisiana	125	287	412
Arkansas	113	274	387
Illinois	85	296	381
Massachusetts	21	345	366
Oklahoma	89	275	364
South Carolina	81	268	349
Alabama	87	231	318
Mississippi	91	219	310

The locations of the Michigan lightning casualties are varied, although most are clearly associated with outdoor sporting activities such as golf, softball, boating, and swimming. The

6 Double-click on the new table.

An Excel window opens, and the worksheet that is linked to the table is displayed. If Excel is not open, this procedure will start the program, open the file, and go to the correct worksheet.

Change the Florida injuries in cell **C3** to **1444** and the Michigan injuries in cell **C4** to **644**.

Notice that the number in the Totals column changes for the two states.

Change these numbers

WD1002-Lightning Data									
A	B	C	D	E	F	G	H	I	J
1 Lightning Casualties, Leading States: 1960-1999									
2	Deaths	Injuries	Total						
3 Florida	384	1444	1828						
4 Michigan	94	644	738						
5 North Carolina	170	559	729						
6 Pennsylvania	103	578	681						
7 Ohio	129	497	626						
8 New York	117	491	608						
9 Texas	169	410	579						
10 Colorado	110	379	489						
11 Tennessee	120	360	480						
12 Georgia	84	356	440						
13 Louisiana	125	287	412						
14 Arkansas	113	274	387						
15 Illinois	85	296	381						
16 Massachusetts	21	345	366						
17 Oklahoma	89	275	364						
18 South Carolina	81	268	349						
19 Alabama	87	231	318						

Time of Day / Month / Location \ **National Casualties** /

The totals change automatically

7 Close Excel and save your changes. Return to the Word document.

Notice that the Word table reflects the changes you made in the Excel worksheet.

When and Where?

Formatted by: <your name>

Michigan ranks at or near the top of lightning casualties nearly every year. In fact, over the 1960-1999 period only Florida experienced more lightning casualties.

	Deaths	Injuries	Total
Florida	384	1444	1828
Michigan	94	644	738
North Carolina	170	559	729
Pennsylvania	103	578	681
Ohio	129	497	626
New York	117	491	608
Texas	169	410	579
Colorado	110	379	489
Tennessee	120	360	480
Georgia	84	356	440
Louisiana	125	287	412
Arkansas	113	274	387
Illinois	85	296	381
Massachusetts	21	345	366
Oklahoma	89	275	364
South Carolina	81	268	349
Alabama	87	231	318
Mississippi	91	219	310

The locations of the Michigan lightning casualties are varied, although most are clearly associated with outdoor sporting activities such as golf, softball, boating, and swimming. The

8 Click the **Save** button to save your work. Close the Word document and close Word.

Task 3

UPDATING LINKS TO OTHER PROGRAMS

Why would I do this?
On occasion, you will move files to other folders, other disk drives, or even other servers. When this happens, links no longer work. You need to let the document know where the source file is located. You will need a clean floppy disk for the next three tasks.

In this task, you learn to repair a broken link.

1 Go to Windows Explorer, copy the **WD1002-Lightning Data** Excel file, and paste it in drive A. Go back to the **Student** folder (or wherever the **WD1002-Lightning Data** file was originally) and delete it.

This should break the link that you created in the last task.

Run Word and open the **WD1001-Where and When** document.

A message appears telling you that there are links that cannot be found or updated.

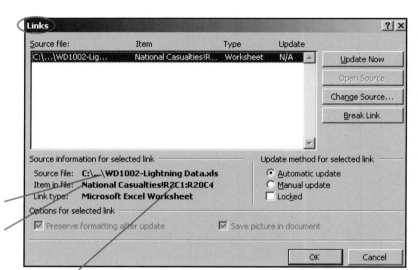

2 Click **OK** to close the message box.

The table appears with the data that existed when you closed the document. If you had made changes to the Excel file, they would not be transferred to the Word document.

Click once on the table to select it, and then choose **Edit**, **Links** from the menu.

The Links dialog box is displayed. It shows the location of the linked file, the name of the worksheet, and even the cell locations.

Source file

Worksheet name

Cell range

3 Click the **Change Source** button on the Links toolbar.

The Change Source dialog box is displayed.

Find the **WD1002-Lightning Data** file in drive A.

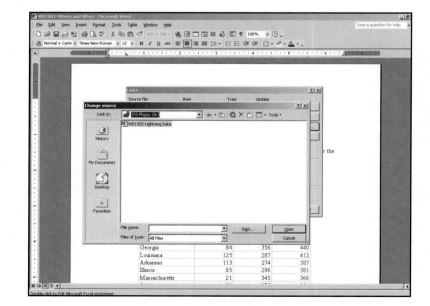

4 Double-click the **WD1002-Lightning Data** file.

The Links dialog box now reflects the new location of the linked file.

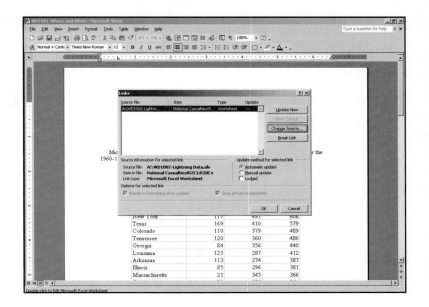

5 Click **OK** to finalize the link change. Double-click the linked table.

The Word document and the Excel worksheet are once again linked.

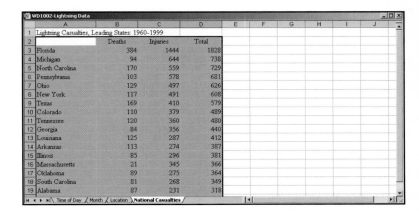

6 Close Excel. Click the Save button to save your work. Leave the document open for the next task.

IN DEPTH

If you know you have to move a file to which you are linked, you can double-click to open the link, and then use the **File, Save As** option to send the file to a new location. Word automatically updates the link to the new folder.

Task 4
USING EXCEL DATA TO CREATE AND REVISE CHARTS

Why would I do this?

There are two ways to get data into Microsoft Chart. You can type the data into the chart datasheet, or, if the data is in an Excel worksheet, there is an easy way to move the data directly from Excel into your chart. Once you complete the chart, you can edit it in Microsoft Chart, but not in Excel—there is no link between the Excel data and the Word chart.

In this task, you create a chart using Excel data.

1 With the **WD1001-Where and When** document still open, find and open **WD1002**—the original Excel file you used at the beginning of this lesson.

This is the Excel file you have been working on.

Click the **Month** tab at the bottom of the Excel window.

This is the data that you will chart in the Word document.

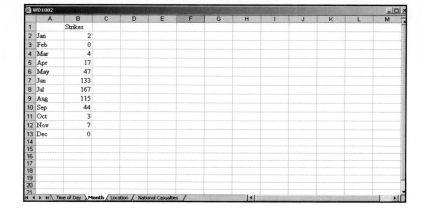

2 Use the taskbar to move back to the Word document and place the insertion point next to the paragraph that begins **In southeastern Michigan**.

The new chart will be placed at this point.

Choose **I**nsert, **P**icture, **Ch**art from the menu.

A new window opens with a sample chart and the chart datasheet. An area is also reserved in the document for the chart.

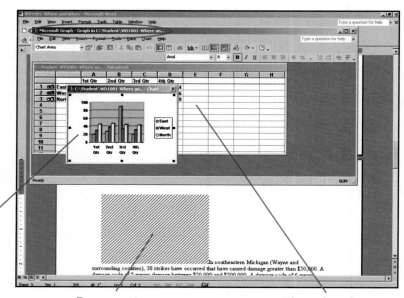

Sample chart

Document area reserved for chart

Chart datasheet

IN DEPTH

The way Microsoft Graph looks depends on the view you are in. If you are in Print Layout view, a separate window opens. If you are in Normal view, the chart and datasheet appear in the same window as the document you are working on.

3 Choose **E**dit, **I**mport File from the Microsoft Graph menu.

The Import File dialog box is displayed.

Find and double-click the **WD1002-Lightning Data** file.

The Import Data Options dialog box is displayed.

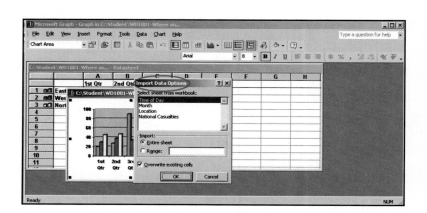

4 Choose Month to select the Month worksheet. Make sure **Entire sheet** is selected, and make sure **Overwrite existing cells** is selected.

If you only want to use a portion of a worksheet, you type the range into the Range box.

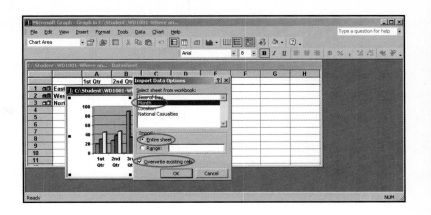

 If you do not select the Overwrite existing cells option, you need to select all of the data in the datasheet and delete it before you begin this procedure.

The data is entered into the datasheet

The chart is updated

5 Click **OK**.

The data is entered into the datasheet, which updates the chart in both the Microsoft Graph window and the document.

Click the **By Column** button on the Formatting toolbar.

This changes the chart from an awkward looking By Row format, putting the data labels on the horizontal axis instead of in the legend.

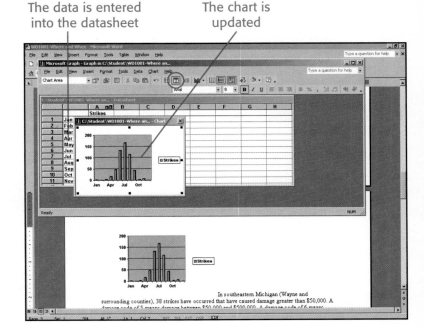

 If all your buttons are on one row, the By Column button may not be displayed. Click the More buttons arrow at the end of the Formatting toolbar to find the button.

6 Click the **Close** button to close Microsoft Graph. Press ⏎Enter to place the chart in a separate paragraph. Click the sizing handle and drag the chart until it is the width of the paragraph and about 4" high.

You might need to zoom out to see enough of the page to perform this action. The chart now fills the page, but needs some formatting.

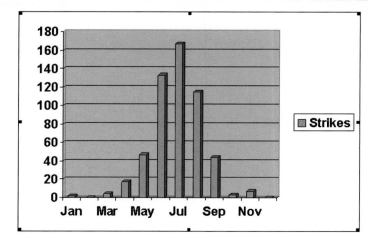

In southeastern Michigan (Wayne and surrounding counties), 38 strikes have occurred that have caused damage greater than $50,000. A damage code of 5 means damage between $50,000 and $500,000. A damage code of 6 means damage between $500,000 and $5,000,000. A damage code of 7 means there was damage greater than $5,000,000.

7 Double-click the chart.

The Microsoft Graph toolbar appears at the top of the screen. Depending on the view you are in, you may also see the datasheet or even the Microsoft Graph window. The following procedure works regardless of how the screen appears.

Choose **Chart**, **Chart Options** from the menu.

The Chart Options dialog box is displayed.

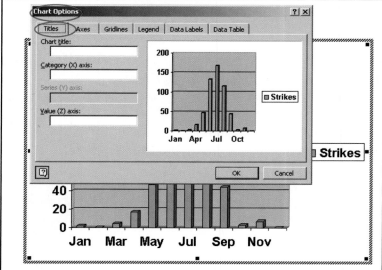

In southeastern Michigan (Wayne and surrounding counties), 38 strikes have occurred that have caused damage greater than $50,000. A damage code of 5 means damage between $50,000 and $500,000. A damage code of 6 means damage between $500,000 and $5,000,000. A damage code of 7 means there was damage greater than $5,000,000.

8 Type **Lightning Strikes by Month** in the **Chart title** box. Click on the Legend tab and deselect **Show legend**. Click **OK**.

The title is added to the chart, and the legend is removed.

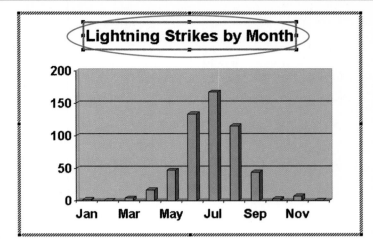

In southeastern Michigan (Wayne and surrounding counties), 38 strikes have occurred that have caused damage greater than $50,000. A damage code of 5 means damage between $50,000 and $500,000. A damage code of 6 means damage between $500,000 and $5,000,000. A damage code of 7 means there was damage greater than $5,000,000.

9 Double-click the months on the horizontal axis. Click the Font tab and change the font size to **14** points.

This reduces the font size slightly.

Click the Alignment tab and change the orientation to **90** degrees.

These changes ensure that all of the months are displayed.

All the month names are displayed

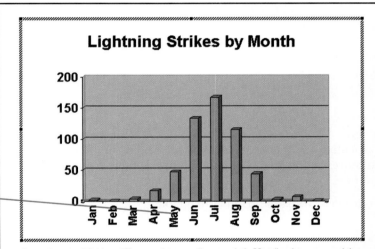

In southeastern Michigan (Wayne and surrounding counties), 38 strikes have occurred that have caused damage greater than $50,000. A damage code of 5 means damage between $50,000 and $500,000. A damage code of 6 means damage between $500,000 and $5,000,000. A damage code of 7 means there was damage greater than $5,000,000.

10 Click **OK**. Double-click one of the columns.

The Format Data Series dialog box is displayed.

Click the Options tab and change the Gap width to **50**. Click **OK**.

This makes the columns wider.

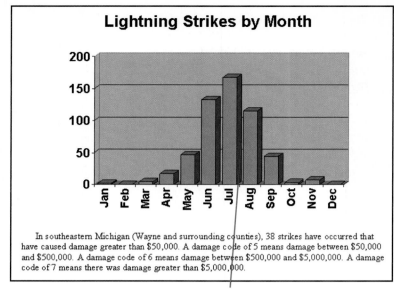

Lightning Strikes by Month

In southeastern Michigan (Wayne and surrounding counties), 38 strikes have occurred that have caused damage greater than $50,000. A damage code of 5 means damage between $50,000 and $500,000. A damage code of 6 means damage between $500,000 and $5,000,000. A damage code of 7 means there was damage greater than $5,000,000.

The gap between columns is reduced

11 Click the **Save** button to save your work. Leave the document open for the next task.

Task 5
USING FORMULAS IN TABLES

Why would I do this?
In most cases, you will probably use Excel to do calculations on numeric data, particularly complicated calculations. For any mathematical operation, Excel is far more flexible than Word. If you have a table that needs a simple calculation, however, you can create formulas quickly in Word.

In this task, you add formulas to a table.

1 With the **WD1001-Where and When** document still open, scroll up until you can see the bottom of the second table.

This is the table with lightning-strike locations.

Click at the end of the last cell and press Tab⇥.

A new row is added to the bottom of the table.

A new row has been added

⚠ **CAUTION**
If the gridlines are not turned on when you press Tab⇥, the new row will not have guidelines, and will look like it increased the height of the last row. To see the guidelines for the new row, choose **Table, Show Gridlines** from the menu.

lightning strikes causing injuries or death in Michigan in their *Storm Data* publications.

Location	Deaths	Injuries	Casualties
Not reported	1	9	10
Under trees	21	80	101
Water related, fishing, boating, swimming	12	49	61
Golfing	10	36	46
Golfing and under trees	4	17	21
Driving tractors, farm & heavy equipment	4	19	23
Open field, ballparks, playgrounds, etc.	26	256	282

Telephone-related	2	16	18
Radios, transmitters, antennas, etc.	1	5	6
At various other and unknown locations	13	157	170

The counties that receive the most catastrophic strikes are, as expected, in the more heavily populated areas in the southeast and southwest regions of the Lower Peninsula. (Note: catastrophic strikes are defined as those causing death, injury, or property damage greater than $50,000). These areas also receive more lightning strikes per square mile in a normal year.

2 Press `Tab⇄` again to move the insertion point to the bottom of the first column of numbers. Select **T**able, **Fo**rmula from the menu.

*The Formula dialog box is displayed. The =SUM(ABOVE) function is displayed in the **Formula** box. This is by far the most commonly used function in Word tables.*

IN DEPTH

If you click the arrow in the **Paste function** box, the other mathematical functions that are available in Word tables are displayed.

Functions available in Word tables

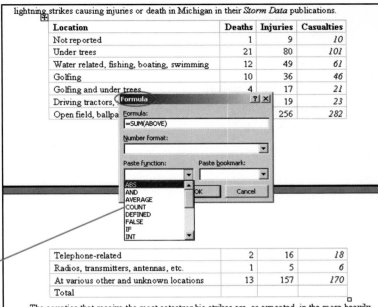

lightning strikes causing injuries or death in Michigan in their *Storm Data* publications.

Location	Deaths	Injuries	Casualties
Not reported	1	9	10
Under trees	21	80	101
Water related, fishing, boating, swimming	12	49	61
Golfing	10	36	46
Golfing and under trees	4	17	21
Driving tractors,		19	23
Open field, ballpa		256	282

Formula

Formula:
=SUM(ABOVE)

Number format:

Paste function: Paste bookmark:

ABS
AND
AVERAGE
COUNT
DEFINED
FALSE
IF
INT

OK   Cancel

Telephone-related	2	16	18
Radios, transmitters, antennas, etc.	1	5	6
At various other and unknown locations	13	157	170
Total			

The counties that receive the most catastrophic strikes are, as expected, in the more heavily populated areas in the southeast and southwest regions of the Lower Peninsula. (Note: catastrophic strikes are defined as those causing death, injury, or property damage greater than $50,000). These areas also receive more lightning strikes per square mile in a normal year.

3 Click **OK**.

The total for the column is displayed.

Change the number just above the new total (13) to **14** and click in any other cell of the table.

The total for the column does not change.

CAUTION

If you are familiar with Excel, you may change a number in a table and expect the total to be recalculated. However in Word, if you change a number, you need to reinsert any formulas that use that number.

lightning strikes causing injuries or death in Michigan in their *Storm Data* publications.

Location	Deaths	Injuries	Casualties
Not reported	1	9	10
Under trees	21	80	101
Water related, fishing, boating, swimming	12	49	61
Golfing	10	36	46
Golfing and under trees	4	17	21
Driving tractors, farm & heavy equipment	4	19	23
Open field, ballparks, playgrounds, etc.	26	256	282

Telephone-related	2	16	18
Radios, transmitters, antennas, etc.	1	5	6
At various other and unknown locations	14	157	170
Total	94		

The counties that receive the most catastrophic strikes are, as expected, in the more heavily populated areas in the southeast and southwest regions of the Lower Peninsula. (Note: catastrophic strikes are defined as those causing death, injury, or property damage greater than $50,000). These areas also receive more lightning strikes per square mile in a normal year.

The change in data is not reflected in the total

4 Change the number back from 14 to **13**. Press Tab. Place the insertion point in the cell at the bottom of the second column of numbers.

You now add up the second column.

Select **Table**, **Formula** from the menu, and then click **OK**.

The second row is added up.

lightning strikes causing injuries or death in Michigan in their *Storm Data* publications.

Location	Deaths	Injuries	Casualties
Not reported	1	9	10
Under trees	21	80	101
Water related, fishing, boating, swimming	12	49	61
Golfing	10	36	46
Golfing and under trees	4	17	21
Driving tractors, farm & heavy equipment	4	19	23
Open field, ballparks, playgrounds, etc.	26	256	282

Telephone-related	2	16	18
Radios, transmitters, antennas, etc.	1	5	6
At various other and unknown locations	13	157	170
Total	94	644	

The counties that receive the most catastrophic strikes are, as expected, in the more heavily populated areas in the southeast and southwest regions of the Lower Peninsula. (Note: catastrophic strikes are defined as those causing death, injury, or property damage greater than $50,000). These areas also receive more lightning strikes per square mile in a normal year.

5 Press Tab. Select **Table**, **Formula** from the menu, and then click **OK**.

The final column is totaled.

Highlight the last row to select it and click the **Bold** button. Click anywhere outside of the row to turn off the highlight.

The Total row is now highlighted.

lightning strikes causing injuries or death in Michigan in their *Storm Data* publications.

Location	Deaths	Injuries	Casualties
Not reported	1	9	10
Under trees	21	80	101
Water related, fishing, boating, swimming	12	49	61
Golfing	10	36	46
Golfing and under trees	4	17	21
Driving tractors, farm & heavy equipment	4	19	23
Open field, ballparks, playgrounds, etc.	26	256	282

Telephone-related	2	16	18
Radios, transmitters, antennas, etc.	1	5	6
At various other and unknown locations	13	157	170
Total	**94**	**644**	**738**

The counties that receive the most catastrophic strikes are, as expected, in the more heavily populated areas in the southeast and southwest regions of the Lower Peninsula. (Note: catastrophic strikes are defined as those causing death, injury, or property damage greater than $50,000). These areas also receive more lightning strikes per square mile in a normal year.

6 Click the **Save** button to save your work. Leave the document open for the next task.

IN DEPTH

As you have seen in this task, there are many reasons why it is better to use Excel for all but the simplest calculations. Among the most striking weaknesses of Word formulas is the inability to recalculate when numbers are changed, and the inability to add a formula to more than one cell at a time.

Task 6

MERGING AND SPLITTING TABLE CELLS

Why would I do this?

Merging cells to eliminate repetitive data can make a table much more attractive. In the table at the bottom of the current document, the first column contained county names in each cell. Merging the cells for each county made the table much easier to read. Usually this is the final step in the creation of a table. However, if you ever need to change a table, there are going to be problems with merged cells. Word has a feature that enables you to split merged cells so that you can manipulate the table again.

In this task, you split cells that have been merged.

1 With the **WD1001-Where and When** document still open, scroll down until you can see the top of the last table.

The table is sorted by county, but you might like to sort the table by damage code or date.

Click in any cell in the table. Choose **Table**, **Select**, **Table** from the menu.

The table is now selected.

Merged cells

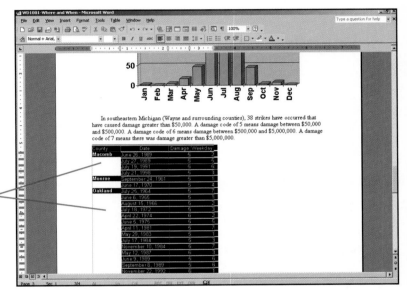

2 Choose **Table**, **Sort** from the menu.

A message box tells you that you cannot sort a table with merged cells.

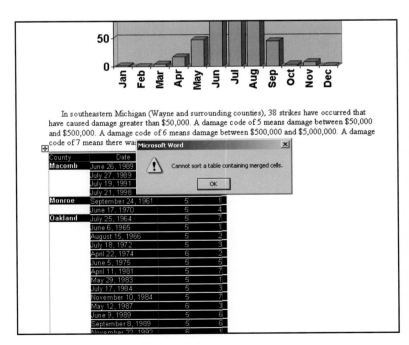

3 Click **OK**. Click on **Macomb** in the first column.

Notice that there are four entries for Macomb County—you need to know this for the following steps.

Choose **T̲able**, **S̲plit Cells** from the menu

The Split Cells dialog box is displayed. The program guesses what you want to do. In this case, it thinks you want split the cell into two columns, which is incorrect.

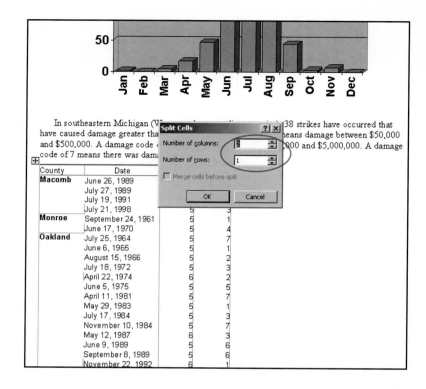

4 Change the **Number of c̲olumns** to **1** and the **Number of r̲ows** to **4**. Click **OK**.

There are now four cells instead of one for Macomb County, although the name is not copied into the other cells—you need to do that yourself in a later step.

One cell has been split into four cells

QUICK TIP

When you change the number of columns to 1, you can click the spinner (up and down arrows) in the **Number of rows** box and the number of merged cells will appear in the box.

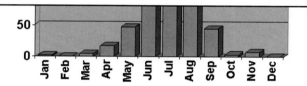

5 Use the same procedure you used in steps 3 and 4 to split the cells for Monroe, Oakland, Washtenaw, and Wayne counties.

Monroe has two cells, Oakland has 17 (don't forget to include the ones that follow the page break), Washtenaw has five, and Wayne has 10.

Copy the county names and paste them in the blank spaces below each.

All the cells in the first column should now contain county names.

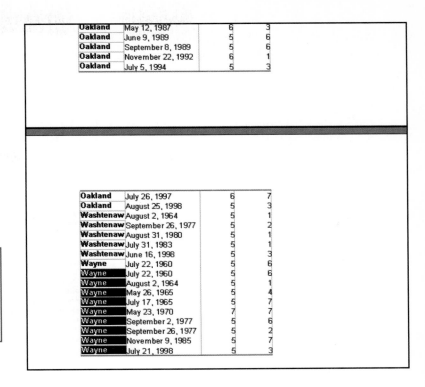

Oakland	May 12, 1987	6	3
Oakland	June 9, 1989	5	6
Oakland	September 8, 1989	5	6
Oakland	November 22, 1992	6	1
Oakland	July 5, 1994	5	3

Oakland	July 26, 1997	6	7
Oakland	August 25, 1998	5	3
Washtenaw	August 2, 1964	5	1
Washtenaw	September 26, 1977	5	2
Washtenaw	August 31, 1980	5	1
Washtenaw	July 31, 1983	5	1
Washtenaw	June 16, 1998	5	3
Wayne	July 22, 1960	5	6
Wayne	July 22, 1960	5	6
Wayne	August 2, 1964	5	1
Wayne	May 26, 1965	5	4
Wayne	July 17, 1965	5	7
Wayne	May 23, 1970	7	7
Wayne	September 2, 1977	5	6
Wayne	September 26, 1977	5	2
Wayne	November 9, 1985	5	7
Wayne	July 21, 1998	5	3

QUICK TIP

There is a quick way to fill in repetitive data in a Word table. Copy the cell contents you want to repeat (in this case a county name), highlight all the empty cells below it, and click the Paste button. This fills in the Clipboard contents in all the selected cells.

6 Choose **Table**, **Select**, **Table** from the menu. Choose **Table**, **Sort** from the menu.

The Sort dialog box is displayed.

Choose **Damage** in the **Sort by** box, and select **Descending** order. Choose **Date** in the **Then by** box and accept the **Ascending** order default.

This sorts the strikes with the highest damage first.

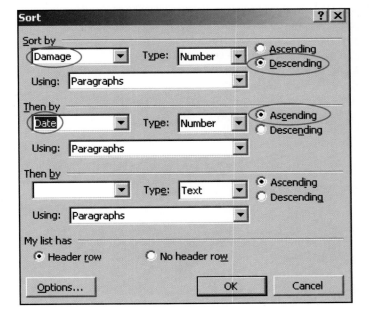

7 Click **OK**. Click anywhere to turn off the highlight, and then scroll up so you can see the top of the table.

Notice that the strikes that caused the most property damage are at the top of the table.

In southeastern Michigan (Wayne and surrounding counties), 38 strikes have occurred that have caused damage greater than $50,000. A damage code of 5 means damage between $50,000 and $500,000. A damage code of 6 means damage between $500,000 and $5,000,000. A damage code of 7 means there was damage greater than $5,000,000.

County	Date	Damage	Weekday
Wayne	May 23, 1970	7	7
Oakland	April 22, 1974	6	2
Oakland	May 12, 1987	6	3
Oakland	November 22, 1992	6	1
Oakland	July 26, 1997	6	7
Washtenaw	August 2, 1964	5	1
Wayne	August 2, 1964	5	1
Oakland	June 6, 1965	5	1
Wayne	September 2, 1977	5	6
Oakland	June 5, 1975	5	5
Oakland	August 15, 1966	5	2
Wayne	July 22, 1960	5	6
Wayne	July 22, 1960	5	6
Wayne	July 17, 1965	5	7
Monroe	September 24, 1961	5	1
Monroe	June 17, 1970	5	4
Oakland	July 25, 1964	5	7
Oakland	July 18, 1972	5	3
Wayne	May 26, 1965	5	4
Oakland	April 11, 1981	5	7
Oakland	November 10, 1984	5	7

8 Type your name at the top of the document where indicated. Click the **Save** button to save your work. Print the document, and then close Word. Close **WD1002-Lightning Data** and close Excel. Make sure you label and turn in the floppy disk you used in Tasks 3 and 4.

The exercises that follow are designed for you to review and use what you have learned in this lesson. You also have the opportunity to practice your skills and then expand on them by applying them to new situations.

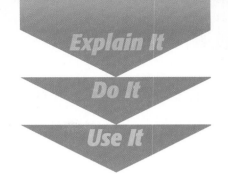

COMPREHENSION

Comprehension exercises are designed to check your memory and understanding of the basic concepts in this lesson. You distinguish between true and false statements, identify new screen elements, and match terms with related statements. If you are uncertain of the correct answer, refer to the task number following each item (for example, T4 refers to Task 4) and review that task until you are confident that you can provide a correct response.

TRUE-FALSE

Circle either T or F.

T F **1.** When you embed a chart from Excel into Word, changes you make in Excel are reflected in the Word document. **(T1)**

T F **2.** If you move a linked document to another folder, the link is broken. **(T3)**

T F **3.** When you place a formula in a Word table, changes you make to the data are automatically recalculated. **(T5)**

T F **4.** You cannot sort a table that contains merged cells. **(T6)**

T F **5.** The chart that you create in Word 2002 is actually created in Excel. **(T4)**

T F **6.** When you paste Excel data into a Word document, it is placed in a Word table. **(Intro)**

MATCHING QUESTIONS

A. Paste Special   **D.** Paste link

B. Embed   **E.** Link

C. Microsoft Graph   **F.** Paste function

Match the following statements to the word or phrase that is the best match from the list. Write the letter of the matching word or phrase in the space provided next to the number.

1. ____ A subprogram that can use Excel data to create a chart **(T4)**

2. ____ Place an object into a document without keeping a link to the original source **(T1)**

3. ____ A way to place a formula in a table **(T5)**

4. ____ A method used to create a connection to a source document **(T2)**

5. ____ Keep a connection to data from another source **(T2)**

6. ____ Use this instead of the Paste function to start the link process **(T2)**

IDENTIFYING PARTS OF THE WORD SCREEN

Refer to the figure and identify the numbered parts of the screen. Write the letter of the correct label in the space next to the number.

1. _____

2. _____

3. _____

4. _____

5. _____

6. _____

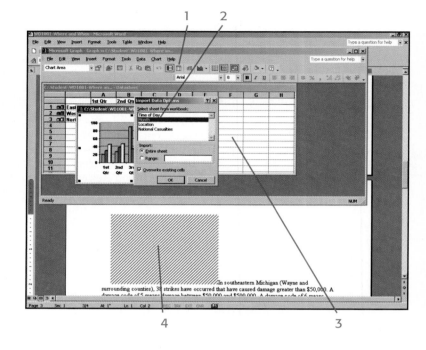

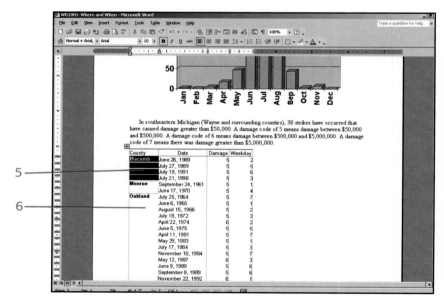

A. Chart datasheet (T4)

B. Split cells (T4)

C. Changes the chart from row to column format (T4)

D. Area reserved for chart (T5)

E. Merged cells (T4)

F. Data source for the chart (T5)

REINFORCEMENT

Reinforcement exercises are designed to reinforce the skills you have learned by applying them to new situations. Detailed instructions are provided along with a figure, where appropriate, to illustrate the result. Complete the following reinforcement exercises sequentially. Leave the document open at the end of each exercise for use in the next exercise until you are specifically directed to close it.

In these exercises, you work with year-end review business data from the Armstrong Pool, Spa, and Sauna Co.

R1—Embedding Excel Data

1. Start Word, if necessary. Open the document **WD1003** and save it as **WD1003-Year End Review**. Switch to Print Layout View, if necessary.

2. Place the insertion point to the left of the paragraph that begins **The following is a list**, about one-third of the way down the first page.

3. Start Excel, open **WD1004**, and save it as **WD1004-Pools**. Click the **Sales by Store** tab at the bottom of the Excel window. Click in cell **A1** and drag down and to the right to cell **E10**. All the data in the worksheet should be selected. Click the **Copy** button.

4. Use the taskbar to move back to the Word document. With the insertion point still to the left of the third text paragraph, click the **Paste** button.

5. Click the **Save** button to save your work. Leave the document open for the next task.

R2—Linking to Excel Data

1. With the **WD1003-Year End Review** document still open, place the insertion point next to the paragraph that begins **Here is a graph**.

2. Use the taskbar to go to the **WD1004-Pools** Excel document. Click the **Year-End Summary** tab at the bottom of the Excel window. Highlight all the information on the worksheet to select it. Click the **Copy** button.

3. Use the taskbar to move back to the Word document. Choose **Edit**, **Paste Special** from the menu. Select **Paste link** as the type of paste, and select **Microsoft Excel Worksheet Object** as the object type. Click **OK**.

4. Press **⏎Enter** to move the paragraph down.

5. Double-click on the new table. Change the 15' pool size for the first quarter to **147** and the 18'×33' pool size for the first quarter to **95**.

6. Switch back to WD1003-Year End Review. Click anywhere else in the document to move out of the worksheet. Notice the changes. Use the same procedure to return the two numbers you just changed back to **127** and **105**, respectively.

7. Click the **Save** button to save your work. Close the document. Close **WD1004-Pools** and close Excel. Save your changes in the Excel file.

R3—Updating Links to Other Programs

1. Put a floppy disk in drive A. Go to Windows Explorer, copy the **WD1004** Excel file, and paste it in drive A. Go back to the **Student** folder (or wherever the **WD1004-Pools** file was originally) and delete it.

2. Open the **WD1003-Year End Review** document. Read the message and close the message box.

3. Click once on the second table to select it, and then choose **Edit**, **Links** from the menu.

4. Click the **Change Source** button on the Links toolbar. Find and double-click the **WD1004-Pools** file in drive A, and click **OK** to close the dialog box.

5. Click the **Save** button to save your work. Leave the document open for the next task.

R4—Using Excel Data to Create a Chart

1. With the **WD1003-Year End Review** document still open, start Excel and open the original **WD1004** file. Click the **Year-End Summary** tab at the bottom of the Excel window, if necessary. Notice that the data you want to chart is in the range from cell **A2** to cell **H6**.

2. Use the taskbar to move back to the Word document. Place the insertion point next to the paragraph that begins **If any of you have ideas**. Choose **Insert**, **Picture**, **Chart** from the menu.

3. Choose **Edit**, **Import File** from the Microsoft Graph menu. Find and double-click the **WD1004** file.

4. Choose **Year-End Summary** to select the Year-End Summary worksheet. In the Import area, type **A2:H6** in the **Range** box. Make sure **Overwrite existing cells** is selected, and then click **OK**. (Note: In Excel, A2:H6 identifies the range from cell A2 through cell H6.)

5. Click the **Close** button to close Microsoft Graph. Press Enter to place the chart in a separate paragraph. Click the sizing handle in the lower right corner and drag the chart until it is the width of the paragraph and about 4" high.

6. Place the insertion point to the left of the paragraph that begins **Here is a graph**. Press Ctrl+Enter to insert a page break at that point.

7. Click **Save** to save your changes. Leave the document open for the next exercise.

R5—Using Formulas in Tables

1. With the **WD1003-Year End Review** document still open, scroll to the first table of the document. Place the insertion point in the last cell in the table and press Tab.

2. Type **Total** in the first cell of the new row, and then press Tab.

3. Select **Table**, **Formula** from the menu. Click **OK** to accept the default **=SUM(ABOVE)** function.

4. Repeat the same procedure to add up the next three columns.

5. Select the new row and click the **Bold** button.

6. Save your changes and leave the document open for the next exercise.

R6—Merging Table Cells

1. With the **WD1003-Year End Review** document still open, select all five cells in the first row of the first table.

2. Choose **Table**, **Merge Cells** from the menu. Click the **Center** button to center the title text.

3. There is also a way to merge cells in the table linked to Excel. Double-click the second table. Click in cell **B1** and drag to cell **H1**.

4. Find and click the **Merge and Center** button on the Formatting toolbar. Close Excel and save your changes when prompted. Notice that the title is not centered.

5. Choose **Edit**, **Update Link** from the menu. Notice that the title is now centered.

6. Type your name where indicated in the **FROM:** area at the top of the document. Save your changes, print the document, and then close Word. Close Excel. Make sure you label and turn in the floppy disk you used in exercises 3 and 4.

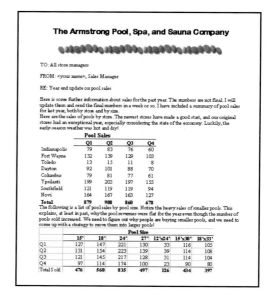

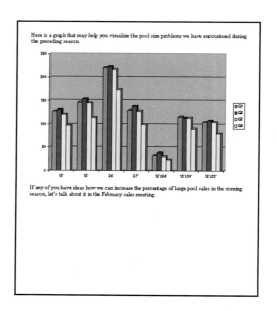

CHALLENGE

Challenge exercises are designed to test your ability to apply your skills to new situations with less-detailed instructions. These exercises also challenge you to expand your repertoire of skills by using commands that are similar to those you have already learned. The desired outcome is clearly defined, but you have more freedom to choose the steps needed to achieve the required result.

The following exercises use different files to illustrate procedures you should find helpful.

C1—Using Mail Merge to Create Mailing Labels from an Access Table

The Mail Merge Wizard that you use to customize a series of letters can also be used to create mailing labels—you can even identify the label's brand name and number and Word sets up the label layout for you. The label mail merge feature is particularly helpful, since it enables you to browse through your labels and decide who should (and who should not) receive the mailing. It also enables you to sort the labels, and to format the address block in several different ways.

For this exercise, you use the customer list of the Armstrong Pool, Spa, and Sauna Co. This list is kept in an Access table. You can also retrieve mail merge data from an Access query, or even an Excel worksheet.

Goal: To create a set of mailing labels based on information stored in an Access table.

1. Click the **New Blank Document** button on the Standard toolbar. Save the document as **WD10-Challenge1**.

2. Choose **Tools**, **Letters and Mailings**, **Mail Merge Wizard** from the menu. The new document automatically switches to Print Layout view if you are in Normal view.

3. Select **Labels** as the document type and move to the next wizard pane.

4. Click **Label options**. Choose **Avery Standard** from the **Label products** list box, and select **5160-Address** as the **Product number**.

5. Move to the next wizard pane, choose to **Use an existing list**, and click **Browse**. Find the **WD1005** Access file and select **tblCustomers** from the list of tables.

6. Click the **LastName** column heading to sort by last name. At this point, you could uncheck anyone for whom you don't want to print a mailing label.

7. Move to the next wizard pane and choose **Address block**. Select the second name option, and deselect the company name. Click the **Update all labels** button.

8. Move to the next wizard pane and check your labels. If you want to change anything, you can move back to a previous wizard pane.

9. Move to the last wizard pane and click **Print**. Print all the records. Close the document and save your changes when prompted.

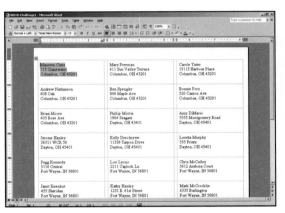

C2—Completing Mail Merge Using Outlook Information as the Source

The interconnectedness of Office applications does not end with Word, Excel, PowerPoint, and Access. You can also use your Outlook Contacts list as the data source for a mail merge. If you are using a computer in a lab, or if you do not have any names or addresses in your Contact list, you will not be able to do this exercise. The document used in this activity is a letter about a travel adventure to Alaska.

Goal: To use a Contact list from Outlook as a source of data for a mail merge.

CAUTION

The way Outlook works with the mail merge feature depends on how your computer is set up. Computers that have multiple users with user profiles will work differently than standalone computers with no administrator. If your options vary from those mentioned in this exercise, use the ones that seem appropriate to continue the merge process.

1. Locate and open the **WD1006** document. Save it as **WD1006-Challenge2**. Make sure the insertion point is at the top of the document because the Mail Merge Wizard will put the address block in the insertion point location.

2. Choose **Tools, Letters and Mailings, Mail Merge Wizard** from the menu.

3. Select **Letters** as the document type and move to the next wizard pane.

4. Choose the **Use the current document** option. Move to the next wizard pane and choose **Select from Outlook contacts**.

5. Click the **Choose Contacts Folder** option and select your profile name. This will probably be **Outlook** if you are the only one who uses the computer.

6. Choose the appropriate **Contacts** name from the **Select Contact List folder** dialog box. Sort on any field by clicking the column heading of the field. Deselect all but a few of the contacts in your list. Click **OK** when you are finished.

7. Move to the next wizard pane and click the **Address block** option. Choose the second option in the list. The address block indicator is inserted at the insertion point.

8. Select **Member** in the greeting. Click **More items** in the task pane, select **First** from the list of available fields, and click **Insert**.

9. Move to the next screen and scroll through a few of the letters. Move to the final wizard pane.

10. Instead of printing all the letters, select **Edit individual letters**, and choose **All**. The letters merge into a word document.

11. Type your name at the bottom of the first page and print just that page. Save your changes and close the document.

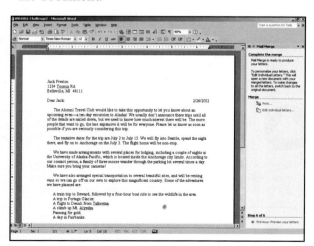

 ## C3— Using the Database Toolbar to Import Access Data

In this lesson, you brought Excel data into a Word document. There is also a way to import Access data directly. In fact, there are two ways you can move information from Access to Word. The first is to open Access, open the table, query, form, or report and choose **Tools, Office Links, Publish It with Microsoft Word** from the menu. This sends the data directly to a table in a new document. If you want to insert data from Access into an existing Word document, you can use the Database toolbar. You can even set criteria to limit the data in any way you want.

In this lesson, you use the Armstrong database that you used in the first Challenge exercise.

Goal: To import data from an Access table into a Word document.

1. Locate and open the **WD1007** document and save it as **WD1007-Challenge3**. Right-click on any toolbar and select the **Database** toolbar from the list.

2. Place the insertion point in the blank line after the first full paragraph. Find and click the **Insert Database** button on the Database toolbar.

3. Choose **Get Data**. Find and open the **WD1005** Access file. Select **tblProducts** from the list of tables and queries.

4. Click **Query Options**. Take a look at how you can restrict the data to be imported, even though you want to copy all the data in this case.

5. Click **Insert Data** and select **All** when asked which records to import.

6. Adjust the column widths on the table until each record is on a single line.

7. Type your name where indicated. Save and print the document, and then close it.

C4—Send a Word Outline to PowerPoint

The most frequently used interactions between Word and the other Office applications are with Excel and Access, with exchanges between Word and Excel being the most common. However, there may be times when you will want to send a Word outline to PowerPoint to provide the basis of a presentation. To do this, you need a document that has been created using the Outline feature, or a document in which you have used the Heading styles from the Normal.dot template. The **Heading 1** style will translate as a slide title, and the **Heading 2** style will become the top-level bulleted points.

In this exercise, you use an outline for a workshop you are giving. The topic is how to make an effective presentation.

Goal: To use a Word outline to create a PowerPoint presentation.

1. Locate and open the **WD1008** document. Change to Normal view, if necessary.

2. Choose **Tools**, **Options** from the menu. Click the **View** tab, if necessary. In the **Outline and Normal options** area, change the **Style area width** to **.6** and close the dialog box. Notice the styles of the outline.

3. Choose **File**, **Send to**, **Microsoft PowerPoint** from the menu. PowerPoint opens, and the outline becomes the titles and bulleted points for the presentation. Notice that the title slide needs some work—you will always need to tweak the presentation.

4. Scroll down to slide 9. Notice that the **Heading 3** styles are subpoints to the **Heading 2** styles.

5. Click at the end of the last point on the page and type your name.

6. Save the presentation as **WD10-Challenge4**. With slide 9 on the screen, choose **File**, **Print** from the menu. Select **Current slide** from the **Print range** area and click **OK**. When you are done, close both PowerPoint and Word.

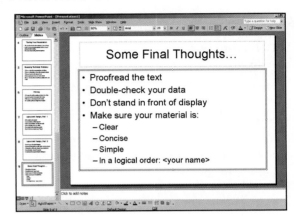

ON YOUR OWN

This lesson dealt with the capability of the various Office applications to relate to each other and exchange information. There are also many things that the programs share, such as a dictionary and several AutoCorrect features. Another feature that most Office applications share is the Clip Gallery, where clip art images are stored.

Office XP has added a number of online features to help you with images, sounds, and animations. In this exercise, you find out how to use the online resources to build your own graphics library. Hint: When you first open the clip gallery, turn on the task pane.

Criteria for grading will be:

1. Demonstration of ability to use Microsoft Word help and to find and use appropriate templates

2. Demonstration of the ability to create a template

To complete the project:

- Write a brief paragraph about how you find and download graphics, including the location of the clip art images.

- Insert two of the new images into the document.

- Write a brief paragraph on how to find animations on the Microsoft Web site.

- Add your name and print a copy of the document.

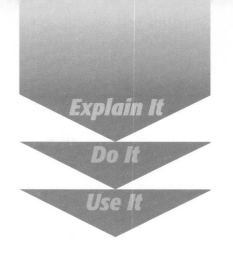

Lesson 11

Collaborating on Documents

Task 1   Setting Document Protection
Task 2   Tracking Changes and Adding Comments
Task 3   Reviewing Changes by Type and Reviewer
Task 4   Responding to Proposed Changes
Task 5   Merging Multiple Revisions of the Same Document
Task 6   Creating Versions of Documents
Task 7   Saving and Editing a Web Page

INTRODUCTION

As Microsoft Office has progressed over the years, the features that enable people to collaborate on documents have increased greatly. You could argue that the ability of a number of people to work on the same document (or set of documents) from any location in the world is one of the most important advancements in computer software

You can collaborate on documents at several levels. The first, and most commonly used collaboration feature is the ability to track changes. Once you activate this tool, any changes you make to an existing document are displayed on the screen— additions are shown in a different color, deleted text has a line through it, and balloons in the margin show deleted text and comments. If you turn the balloons off, the program displays a line through deleted words and shows additions in a different color. You can also add notes to the document, and every change is identified by the name of the person who made the changes and the date and time the changes were made. If more than one person edits a document, the changes each person makes are displayed in a different color. The person doing the final edit can even have the program show only the changes made by a specific person. To keep people from accepting or rejecting changes made by others, you can set up protection to ban changes to other people's edits, and to password protect the entire document.

Documents, as they work their way through various people and departments, are often revised, and then changed again. Sometimes you may find that recent changes are taking the document in the wrong direction, and you'd like to go back to an earlier version. Word has a feature that enables you to save multiple revisions, so that you can view a former version, and revert to that version if necessary.

If you want to put a document out for wide distribution and comment, you can save the document as a Web page, and post it on your company's intranet. This enables a large number of people to read and comment on the document simultaneously.

Finally, you can certify a document by attaching a *digital signature*, which is an assurance to the reader that the document came from you and has not been changed along the way. There are three different levels of certification: a local signature that you can create yourself, a signature that a company network administrator sets, and a registered (for pay) signature that can be used when transferring documents to anyone, anywhere.

In this lesson, you learn how to use some of Word's collaboration features.

VISUAL SUMMARY

By the time you complete this lesson, you will have made and tracked changes to a document. The pages of the document will look like this:

Task 1: Password protect the document

Task 3: Track changes by type

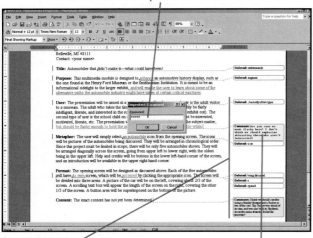

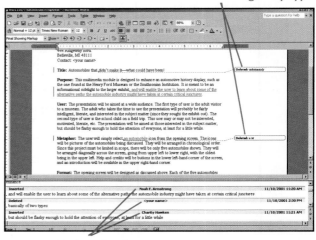

Task 1: Password protect changes made by multiple users

Task 2: Add comments

Task 3: Track changes by person

Task 7: View source code

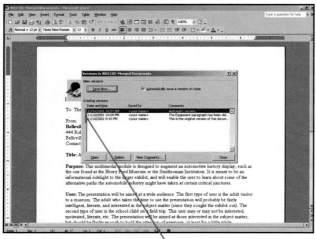

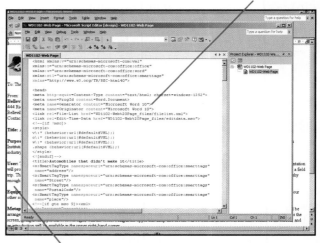

Task 6: Attach previous versions to the current document

Task 7: Create a Web page

Task 1
SETTING DOCUMENT PROTECTION

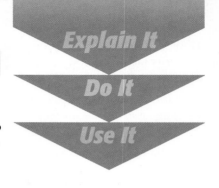

Why would I do this?

Some documents are sensitive—meant to be read by only the author or a select group of people. You can add a password to a document to keep unwanted readers from opening it. When the password protection is no longer necessary, you can remove the password.

When you are collaborating on a document, you often have several people involved in the editing process, each with different motivations for seeing that the document matches their objectives. With the track changes feature active, it is easy for any user to accept or reject changes made by others. Usually, it is a good idea to make sure this doesn't happen. There is a way to protect changes so that only the primary author can decide what should or shouldn't be modified.

In this task, you add password protection to a Word document that has already been edited by others. You also set protection to keep users from editing the changes of others. You begin making and tracking your own changes to the document in Task 2.

1 Start Word and click the **Open** button. Find and open **WD1101** and save it as **WD1101-Multimedia Proposal**. Turn off the Task Pane, click the **Print Layout View** button, and change the **Zoom** to **Page Width**, if necessary.

This document is a proposal by a multimedia company to produce a standalone presentation of automobiles that were not successful. One person wrote it, and two others made changes.

If the changes are not visible on the screen, choose <u>T</u>ools, <u>T</u>rack Changes from the menu to open the Reviewing toolbar, and then click the Track Changes button on the Reviewing toolbar. Select **Final Showing Markup** from the **Display for Review** box.

Clicking the Track Changes button does not change anything on the screen; instead, it turns the feature on to keep track of future changes that you make.

Reviewing toolbar

Display for Review box   Track Changes button   Changes made by others

QUICK TIP

If you are downloading the sample files from an online source, you need to get the WD1101 through WD1110 files.

IN DEPTH

The way Track Changes displays changes depends on the settings the last time this feature was used. If you select Print Layout view and do not see the balloons, choose <u>T</u>ools, <u>O</u>ptions, Track Changes, and then select **Use <u>b</u>alloons in Print and Web Layout** from the Options dialog box.

2 Choose <u>T</u>ools, <u>O</u>ptions from the menu, and click the **Security** tab. Type **learn** in the **Password to <u>o</u>pen** box and click **OK**.

The password is entered, but asterisks take the place of the letters you are typing. A dialog box asks you to reenter the password.

Type **learn** in the **Confirm Password** dialog box.

This checks to make sure you didn't make a mistake typing the password. You have now set the password required to open this document. Read the Caution for further information on passwords.

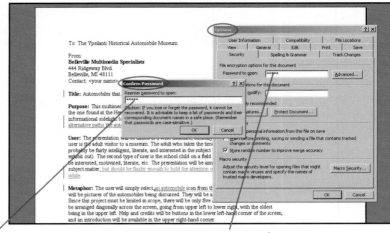

Confirmation of password   New password

3 Click **OK**. Close the document. Click **Yes** to save the changes. Reopen the document.

A Password dialog box asks you to enter the document password.

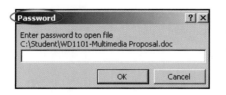

4 Type **learn** in the Password dialog box and click **OK**.

The document opens.

Choose <u>T</u>ools, <u>O</u>ptions from the menu. Highlight and delete the password in the **Password to <u>o</u>pen** box.

This removes the password protection from the document.

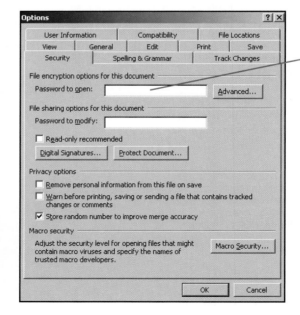

The password has been deleted

IN DEPTH

There is an alternative method for protecting a document that works if you don't mind people reading the document, but need to restrict their ability to make changes to it. If you type the password in the **Password to <u>m</u>odify** box, those who type in the password can make modifications; the document still opens for everyone else in read-only mode.

5 Click **OK**.

The password is removed. Now you will protect the changes made by each of the people editing the document.

Choose **Tools**, **Protect Document** from the menu.

The Protect Document dialog box is displayed.

6 Make sure the **Tracked changes** option is selected, and type **learn** in the **Password** box.

The password makes sure that no one can turn the protection off except you.

The Tracked changes option is selected

A password has been added

7 Click **OK**. Type **learn** again to confirm the password and click **OK**.

The tracked changes are now protected.

Click the **Save** button to save your work. Leave the document open for the next task.

IN DEPTH

Some documents are distributed for comment or review, but are not meant to be changed. When many users can download a document from the Web, a simple way to keep most of them from changing the document is to make it read-only. To do this, find the document using Windows Explorer or My Computer. Right-click on the file name, choose Properties from the shortcut menu, and click the Read-only check box in the Properties dialog box.

Task 2
TRACKING CHANGES AND ADDING COMMENTS

Why would I do this?

In the first task you learned how to protect the changes made to a document. Now you change the name and initials currently registered on your computer, and make some changes of your own. You also learn how to add comments to the document. A comment is not a change to the document. Rather, it is a note you can leave as a reminder, or to raise an issue for consideration.

In this task, you make changes and add comments to the document.

1 With the **WD1101-Multimedia Proposal** document still open, choose **Tools**, **Options** from the menu.

The Options dialog box opens, with the last active sheet.

Click the **User Information** tab to open that sheet. Type your name in the **Name** box and your initials in the **Initials** box.

From this point on (until the name is changed again), your name is properly identified with any changes made.

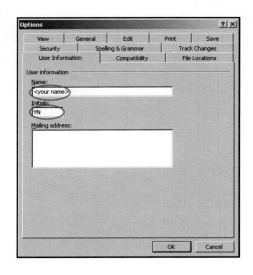

CAUTION

If you are using a computer in a computer lab, or if you are using someone else's machine, jot down the name and initials in the User Information sheet. You will change this information back at the end of Task 4.

2 Click **OK** to register your name. In the **Purpose** paragraph, change **augment** to **enhance**.

Notice that the change is displayed in a different color.

Move the pointer onto the change you just made and hold it there for a second.

A pop-up box is displayed. This box shows your name, the current date and time, and the type of change you made. A change line is also displayed on the left edge of the document, showing that a change was made in that line. A balloon on the right margin also shows any deleted items.

Your name — The date and time of the change — Change balloon

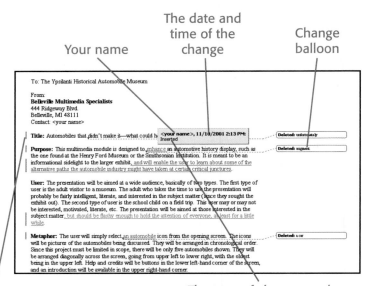

Change line — The type of change made

3 Find the **User** section. In the first line, highlight **basically of two types** (including the leading comma). Press Del.

The text is removed, but another balloon is added in the margin showing what has been removed.

In the second line of the **Format** section, highlight the word **a** from **will have a screen**. Type **its own**.

The new text replaces the old text, and the change is marked.

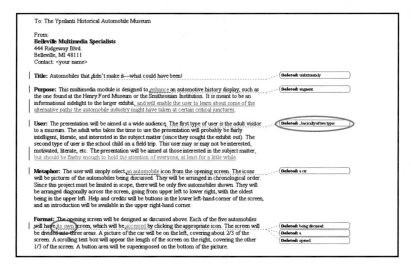

4 Place the insertion point at the end of the **User** paragraph. Choose **V**iew, **T**oolbars, **Reviewing** if the Reviewing toolbar is not visible. Click the **New Comment button**.

A balloon opens up in the margin to the right of the insertion point.

Type **Are you sure we want flashy here? I don't think we should emphasize attracting those who aren't interested!**

Your comment is displayed in the balloon, but is not added to the document.

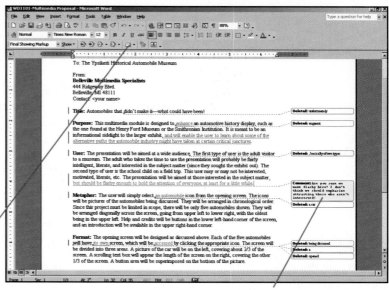

New Comment button

New Comment

5 Choose **V**iew, **M**arkup from the menu.

The Markup option is an on/off switch, and lets you look at what the document would look like with all the revisions accepted and Track Changes turned off.

6 Choose **V**iew, **M**arkup again to display the changes. Click the **Save** button to save your work. Leave the document open for the next task.

Task 3
REVIEWING CHANGES BY TYPE AND REVIEWER

Why would I do this?

It is often helpful to be able to look at only the comments attached to a document. It can also be useful to view tracked changes by the type of change, or look at all the comments by one individual. If the text in the balloons is too small, you can also open a Reviewing Pane at the bottom of the screen to see what changes have been made.

In this task, you look at all deletions and insertions, and all comments attached to a document.

1 With the **WD1101-Multimedia Proposal** document still open, click the <u>S</u>how button on the Reviewing toolbar.

Check marks indicate which features are shown—in this case the comments, insertions and deletions, and formatting.

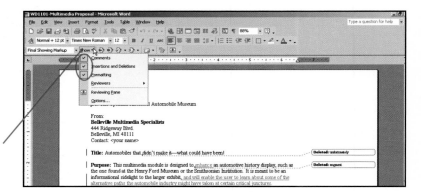

Show button

QUICK TIP

If you want to turn off the balloons, choose <u>T</u>ools, Options, Track Changes, and then deselect **Use <u>b</u>alloons in Print and Web Layout** from the Options dialog box.

2 Click on the <u>C</u>omments option on the <u>S</u>how button drop-down menu to turn the comments display off. Repeat this procedure to turn off the <u>F</u>ormatting display option.

The comments and formatting changes are no longer displayed, leaving just the inserted text and the deleted text.

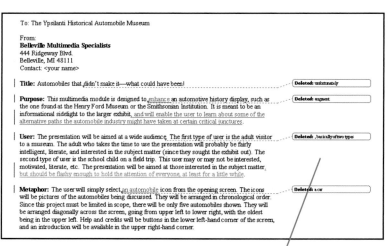

The comments are hidden

3 Click the arrow on the <u>S</u>how button on the Reviewing toolbar. Click on the <u>C</u>omments option.

The comments are displayed once again. You do not need to turn the Formatting option back on, since there are no formatting changes to display.

Click the <u>S</u>how button, move the pointer down until <u>R</u>eviewers is highlighted, and then deselect your name from the list of people who have edited the document. Deselect everyone except **Noah F. Armstrong**. Scroll down so you can see the bottom of the document.

Only the changes and comments made by Mr. Armstrong are shown.

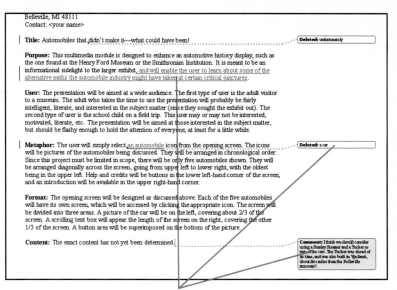

Changes and comments by one reviewer

CAUTION

The number of reviewers shown in the list do not necessarily reflect the number of people who have actually worked on the document. If you have many reviewers showing, choose Show, Reviewers, All Reviewers. This deselects all the reviewers. You can then use the same procedure to select the reviewer you want to see.

4 Click the **Reviewing Pane** button.

The Reviewing Pane is displayed at the bottom of the screen.

Scroll down until you can see the first change made by **Charity Hawken**.

Notice that all the changes and comments are displayed, even if they are turned off in the document. The Reviewing Pane displays the name of the reviewer, the date and time of the changes, what was changed, and what type of change was made.

Reviewing Pane button

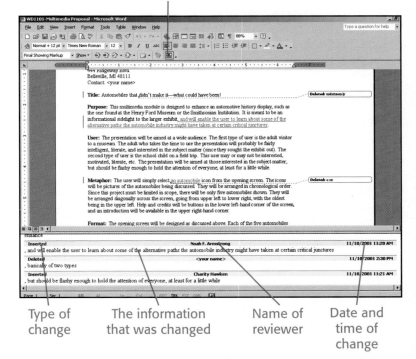

Type of change   The information that was changed   Name of reviewer   Date and time of change

5 Click the <u>S</u>how button, move the pointer down until **Reviewers** is highlighted, and then select the **All Reviewers** option.

All the changes and comments are displayed.

Click the **Reviewing Pane** button.

The Reviewing Pane is removed from the screen.

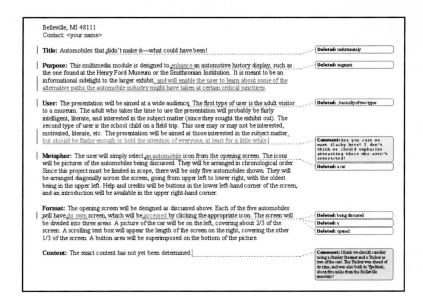

6 Choose <u>F</u>ile, Save <u>A</u>s from the menu. Save the file as **WD1101-Multimedia Proposal-Task 3** to hand in, if required. Close the document.

Task 4
RESPONDING TO PROPOSED CHANGES

Why would I do this?
Once all of the editing suggestions have been made and discussed, it is usually the responsibility of one person to make the final changes. If the changes are protected, the first thing you need to do is unprotect them. At that point, you can move from one suggested change to another and decide whether to accept or reject the suggestion.

In this task, you unprotect the changes and then act on the suggestions.

1 Open the **WD1101-Multimedia Proposal** document. Choose **Tools, Unprotect Document** from the menu.

The Unprotect Document dialog box asks for the password that you typed in when you protected the document.

Type **learn** into the **Password** box.

This releases the change protection.

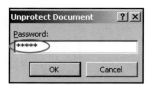

2 Click **OK**. Make sure the insertion point is at the beginning of the document and click the **Next** button on the Reviewing toolbar.

*The deleted word **unfortunately** is highlighted.*

Click the **Accept Change** button on the Reviewing toolbar.

The Deletion balloon disappears, and the change is accepted.

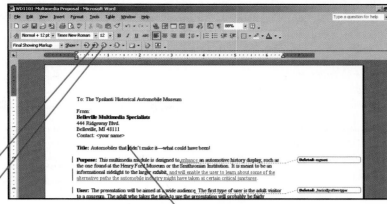

Next button

Accept Change button

The deletion is accepted

3 Click the **Next** button on the Reviewing toolbar.

*The deleted word **augment** is highlighted.*

Click the **Reject Change/Delete Comment** button on the Reviewing toolbar.

*The deleted word **augment** is placed back in the sentence, but the inserted word **enhance** is left in the sentence.*

The inserted word is not removed

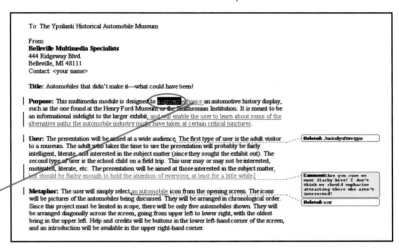

4 Click the **Next** button on the Reviewing toolbar.

*The inserted word **enhance** is now highlighted.*

Click the **Reject Change/Delete Comment** button on the Reviewing toolbar.

Notice that replacing a word actually requires two steps—a deletion and an insertion. First you deal with the deletion, then the insertion.

5 Click the arrow on the **Accept Change** button and select **Accept All Changes Shown** from the menu.

All the changes are accepted. The only things left to work on are the comments. Assume that the comments have been considered and acted upon, where necessary.

Click the arrow on the **Reject Change/ Delete Comment** button on the Reviewing toolbar. Choose the **Delete All Comments in Document** option.

Both comments are removed from the document. There are no balloons in the margin.

To: The Ypsilanti Historical Automobile Museum

From:
Belleville Multimedia Specialists
444 Ridgeway Blvd.
Belleville, MI 48111
Contact: <your name>

Title: Automobiles that didn't make it—what could have been!

Purpose: This multimedia module is designed to augment an automotive history display, such as the one found at the Henry Ford Museum or the Smithsonian Institution. It is meant to be an informational sidelight to the larger exhibit, and will enable the user to learn about some of the alternative paths the automobile industry might have taken at certain critical junctures.

User: The presentation will be aimed at a wide audience. The first type of user is the adult visitor to a museum. The adult who takes the time to use the presentation will probably be fairly intelligent, literate, and interested in the subject matter (since they sought the exhibit out). The second type of user is the school child on a field trip. This user may or may not be interested, motivated, literate, etc. The presentation will be aimed at those interested in the subject matter, but should be flashy enough to hold the attention of everyone, at least for a little while.

Metaphor: The user will simply select an automobile icon from the opening screen. The icons will be pictures of the automobiles being discussed. They will be arranged in chronological order. Since this project must be limited in scope, there will be only five automobiles shown. They will be arranged diagonally across the screen, going from upper left to lower right, with the oldest being in the upper left. Help and credits will be buttons in the lower left-hand corner of the screen, and an introduction will be available in the upper right-hand corner.

All balloons have been removed

6 Click the **Save** button to save your work. Close the document, but leave Word open for the next task.

Task 5

MERGING MULTIPLE REVISIONS OF THE SAME DOCUMENT

Why would I do this?
In the first four tasks of this lesson you have worked with the Track Changes feature. If at all possible, tracking changes in a single document is the preferred method for document collaboration. That method, however, is linear in nature, and does not work well when speed is a factor. If you need to get a number of people to make recommendations at the same time, you will probably need to distribute the same document to all the reviewers, and then merge the documents when they are returned.

In this task, you merge three different revisions of a document.

1 Click the **Open** button. Find and open **WD1102**. Click the **Print Layout View** button, if necessary.

This is the same document you worked on in the first four tasks.

Choose **Tools, Compare and Merge Documents** from the menu.

The Compare and Merge dialog box is displayed.

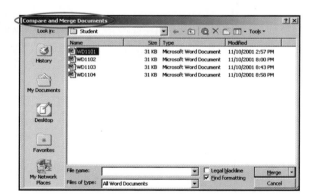

2 Find and select **WD1103**. Click the arrow on the <u>M</u>erge button.

Three options are displayed. You can merge into the new document you are opening (in this case WD1103), you can merge the new document with the open document, or you can merge the two documents into a new document.

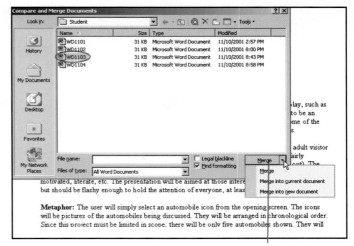

Merge button

If you accidentally click the Merge button instead of the arrow on the button, there is no way to back up. You have to close the document without saving and start over.

3 Choose the **Merge into <u>n</u>ew document** option.

The original document and the document you just selected are merged into a new document. The new document is unnamed, and the title bar shows a generic name, such as Document1.

Scroll down to see the deletion and the new paragraph added from the second document.

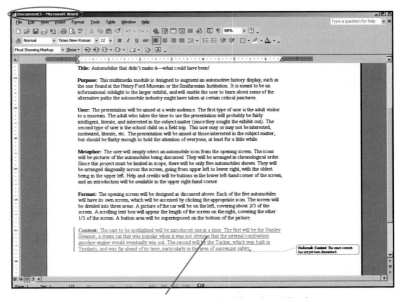

Differences are automatically identified

The people editing the documents to be merged do not need to have Track Changes turned on. When you merge two or more revisions of a document, Word automatically tracks and marks all differences among the documents.

4 Choose Tools, Compare and Merge Documents from the menu again.

There is another revision of the same document.

Find and select **WD1104**. Click the arrow on the Merge button, but this time choose the Merge into current document option.

The changes in WD1104 merge with the new document you created in step 3.

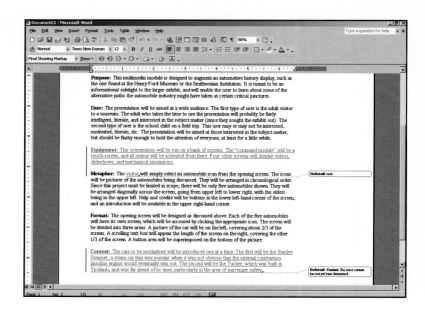

5 Click the arrow on the Accept Change button.

You accept or reject changes the same way you did in Task 4.

Choose the Accept All Changes in Document option.

All the changes from the second and third documents merge with the first document you opened.

User: The presentation will be aimed at a wide audience. The first type of user is the adult visitor to a museum. The adult who takes the time to use the presentation will probably be fairly intelligent, literate, and interested in the subject matter (since they sought the exhibit out). The second type of user is the school child on a field trip. This user may or may not be interested, motivated, literate, etc. The presentation will be aimed at those interested in the subject matter, but should be flashy enough to hold the attention of everyone, at least for a little while.

Equipment: This presentation will be run on a bank of screens. The "command module" will be a touch-screen, and all menus will be activated from there. Four other screens will display videos, slideshows, and mechanical simulations.

Metaphor: The visitor will simply select an automobile icon from the opening screen. The icons will be pictures of the automobiles being discussed. They will be arranged in chronological order. Since this project must be limited in scope, there will be only five automobiles shown. They will be arranged diagonally across the screen, going from upper left to lower right, with the oldest being in the upper left. Help and credits will be buttons in the lower left-hand corner of the screen, and an introduction will be available in the upper right-hand corner.

Format: The opening screen will be designed as discussed above. Each of the five automobiles will have its own screen, which will be accessed by clicking the appropriate icon. The screen will be divided into three areas. A picture of the car will be on the left, covering about 2/3 of the screen. A scrolling text box will appear the length of the screen on the right, covering the other 1/3 of the screen. A button area will be superimposed on the bottom of the picture.

Content: The cars to be spotlighted will be introduced one at a time. The first will be the Stanley Steamer, a steam car that was popular when it was not obvious that the internal combustion gasoline engine would eventually win out. The second will be the Tucker, which was built in Ypsilanti, and was far ahead of its time, particularly in the area of passenger safety.

CAUTION

When you use the **Accept All Changes in Document** option, you do not have the option of viewing changes one at a time—they are all accepted at once. If you decide that you do not want to make all of the changes, click the Undo button.

6 Click the Save button. Save the document as **WD1102-Merged Documents**. Leave the document open for the next task.

Task 6
CREATING VERSIONS OF DOCUMENTS

Why would I do this?

If you are working on a document that will be revised several times, you may want to go back to an earlier revision to retrieve something that has been changed. There are several ways to solve this problem. The first is to save each revision with a new file name that indicates, by way of a version number or date, the chronological order of the documents. The other way to keep track of revisions is to use the Versions feature. A *version* is a revision that you save with the current document. If you save versions, you can open any previous revision along with the current version and cut-and-paste between documents.

In this task, you save different versions of the same document.

1 With the **WD1102-Merged Documents** document still open, right-click on any toolbar and choose Reviewing from the shortcut menu to turn the Reviewing menu off, if necessary. Choose **File**, **Versions** from the menu.

The Versions dialog box is displayed. The title of the dialog box is the word Versions followed by the file name. Notice that there are currently no versions of this document.

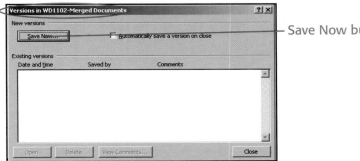

— Save Now button

2 Click the **Save Now** button.

The Save Version dialog box is displayed.

In the **Comments on version** box, type **This is the original version of the document.**

Include the period at the end of the sentence. The text you type into this box will be associated with the version that you save.

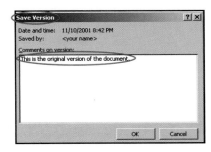

3 Click **OK**. Scroll down, select the **Equipment** paragraph and the following blank line, and press Del.

The paragraph is deleted.

Choose **File**, **Versions** from the menu. Click the **Automatically save a version on close** check box.

This saves a version of the document every time you close the document.

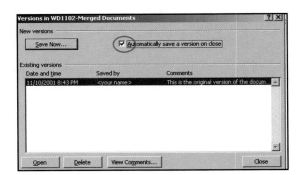

4 Click the <u>S</u>ave Now button.

The Save Version dialog box is displayed.

> In the **Comments on version** box, type **The Equipment paragraph has been deleted.**

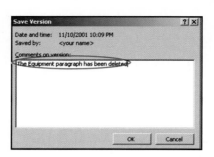

5 Click **OK**. Scroll to the top and place the insertion point at the beginning of the document.

You will add a graphic at this point.

> Choose <u>I</u>nsert, <u>P</u>icture, <u>C</u>lip Art from the menu. Type **car** in the **Search Text** box and click the **Search** button.

The Insert Clip Art pane displays images that are associated with automobiles.

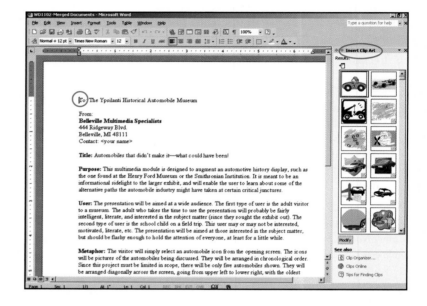

6 Click one of the images. Choose one of the images near the top to insert it at the insertion point location. Press ↵Enter twice.

The first line moves below the image.

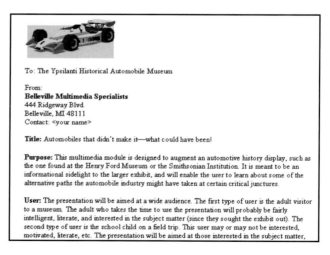

⚠ **CAUTION**

> If you are working in a lab, you might not have very many clip art images installed. If you try to select an image that is not installed, you will see a dialog box that asks you to insert the program disk. Click Cancel and choose an image nearer the top.

7 Close the **Insert Clip Art** pane. Close the document, and save the changes when prompted. Also, close the **WD1102** file that is still open.

A new version is saved because you chose to ***Automatically save a version on close***.

Open the **WD1102-Merged Documents** document again. Choose **File**, **Versions** from the menu.

Notice that there are now three versions saved with the document.

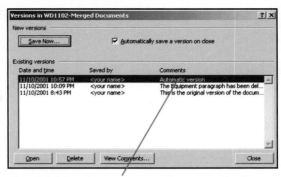

The third version was saved automatically

QUICK TIP

No comment was saved when you closed the document. If you want to add a comment to a version, use the **File**, **Versions**, **Save Now** procedure rather than having it saved automatically.

8 Double-click the first version you saved (the one on the bottom).

The screen is split, and your first version and the current version are in separate windows.

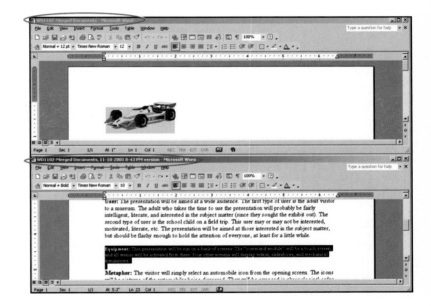

9 With the paragraph you deleted from the first version still selected, click the **Copy** button in that window. Place the insertion point before the paragraph on **Metaphor** in the current document and click the **Paste** button in the current document window.

The deleted text that you wanted to retrieve is now in the current document.

Select the Equipment paragraph and the following blank line. Click the arrow on the **Font Size** button and choose **12** points for the font.

The text now matches the rest of the document.

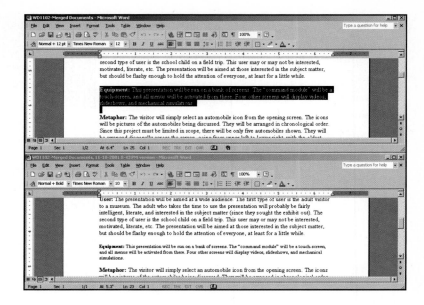

10 Click the **Close** button to close the bottom window. Click the **Maximize** button to maximize the Word window. Click the **Save** button and leave the document open for the next task.

Task 7

SAVING AND EDITING A WEB PAGE

Why would I do this?

There are Web page and Web site development programs that enable you to create and maintain very sophisticated pages and sites. If you just need to make a simple Web page, however, it is much easier to do it in Word. You can create a surprisingly attractive Web page, and you can also edit the Web page, even after it has been converted to HTML.

In this task, you create and then edit a Web page using Word.

1 With the **WD1102-Merged Documents** document still open, choose **File**, **Save as Web Page** from the menu.

Choose a place to save the Web page, and change the **File name** to **WD1102-Web Page**.

The program saves an HTML file called WD1102-Web Page, and also creates a folder containing other Web page elements.

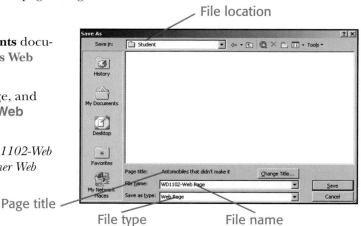

2 Click **S**ave.

A message box tells you that you some of the document features will be lost if the person reading the Web page is using an old version of Internet Explorer or Netscape Navigator.

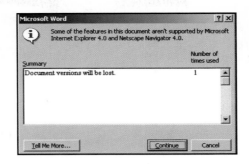

3 Click the **C**ontinue button.

The Web page is created, and the document switches to Web Layout view. The text adjusts to the screen width. The New Blank Document button in the Standard toolbar also changes to a New Web Page button.

New Web Page button
Web Layout View button

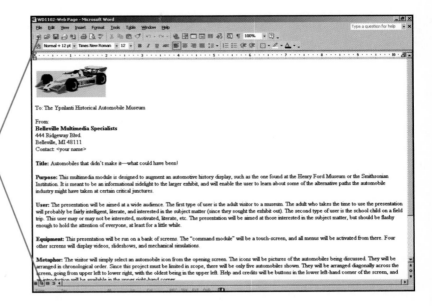

4 Choose **V**iew, HTML **S**ource from the menu.

The Microsoft Script Editor window opens, showing the HTML source for the new Web page. If you know HTML, you can edit this code to change your Web page.

HTML code

5 Close the Microsoft Script Editor window, and then close the WD1102-Web Page document.

At this point, you can upload your Web page HTML document and the associated folder to a Web server.

Click the **Open** button on the Standard toolbar. Find and select the **WD1102-Web Page** file.

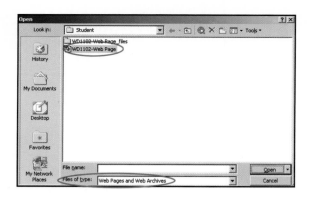

6 Click the **Open** button in the Open dialog box.

The document opens in Web Layout view.

In the seventh line of text, change **what could have been** to **what might have been**. Click the **Save** button. Also, type your name as the Contact person in the sixth line of text

The change is made to the Web page.

Type your name here

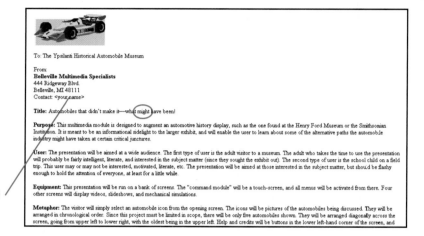

7 Close the document and save your changes. Click the **Open** button on the Standard toolbar. Find and select the **WD1102-Web Page** file. Click the arrow on the **Open** button in the Open dialog box and choose **Open in Browser**.

The Web page opens in your default browser. The change you made is reflected in the document.

Choose **File**, **Print** from the browser menu.

The page prints as a Web page.

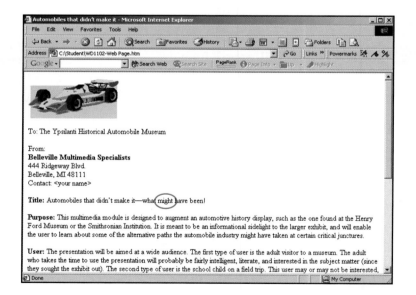

8 Close the browser and close Word.

The exercises that follow are designed for you to review and use what you have learned in this lesson. You also have the opportunity to practice your skills and then expand on them by applying them to new situations.

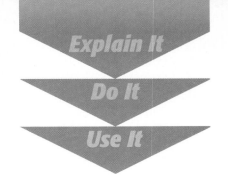

COMPREHENSION

Comprehension exercises are designed to check your memory and understanding of the basic concepts in this lesson. You distinguish between true and false statements, identify new screen elements, and match terms with related statements. If you are uncertain of the correct answer, refer to the task number following each item (for example, T4 refers to Task 4) and review that task until you are confident that you can provide a correct response.

TRUE-FALSE

Circle either T or F.

T   F   1. You can use a password to protect changes made by other users of a document. **(T1)**

T   F   2. If you forget a password to a document, you can always open it in read-only mode and use the **File, Save As** menu option to save it in a format you can edit. **(T1)**

T   F   3. A comment is a change to a document that you can either accept or reject. **(T2)**

T   F   4. Using the Track Changes feature, you can display comments, insertions and deletions, or formatting changes, but not all three together. **(T3)**

T   F   5. You can unprotect a document only if you know the password that was used to protect it. **(T4)**

T   F   6. You can merge the revisions from two or more files into a new file. **(T5)**

MATCHING QUESTIONS

A. Version   D. HTML

B. Password to <u>m</u>odify   E. Read-only

C. Web Layout View button F. Accept All C<u>h</u>anges in Document

Match the following statements to the word or phrase that is the best match from the list. Write the letter of the matching word or phrase in the space provided next to the number.

1. _____ The language used to create Web pages **(T7)**

2. _____ Enables a user to view the document, but not make changes **(T1)**

3. _____ A saved revision of a document **(T6)**

4. _____ Shows what the document will look like when viewed using a Web browser **(T7)**

5. _____ Enables a user to make changes, not just view a document **(T1)**

6. _____ Makes all suggested changes at once **(T5)**

IDENTIFYING PARTS OF THE WORD SCREEN

Refer to the figure and identify the numbered parts of the screen. Write the letter of the correct label in the space next to the number.

1. _____

2. _____

3. _____

4. _____

5. _____

6. _____

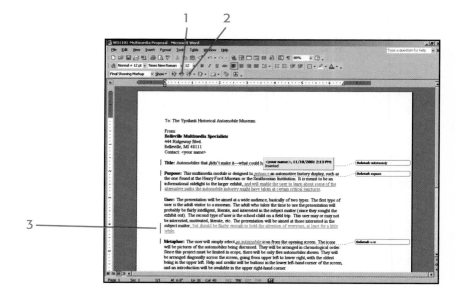

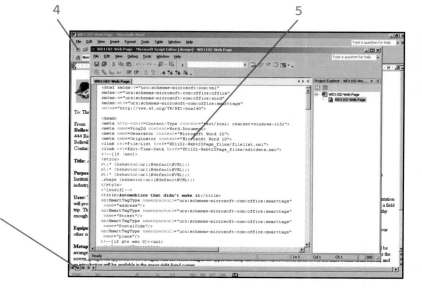

A. HTML code (T7)

B. Accepts the selected change (T4)

C. Shows a Word document in Web format (T7)

D. Moves to the next change (T4)

E. Change bar indicates a change was made (T2)

F. Creates a new Web page (T7)

REINFORCEMENT

Reinforcement exercises are designed to reinforce the skills you have learned by applying them to a new situation. Detailed instructions are provided along with a figure, where appropriate, to illustrate the result. Complete the reinforcement exercises sequentially. Leave the workbook open at the end of each exercise for use in the next exercise until you are specifically directed to close it.

In these exercises, you will work with information about precipitation in Buffalo, New York, and Seattle, Washington.

R1—Setting Document Protection

1. Start Word, if necessary. Open the document **WD1105** and save it as **WD1105-Precipitation**. Switch to Print Layout view, if necessary.

2. If the changes are not visible on the screen, choose **Tools**, **Track Changes** from the menu, and click the **Track Changes** button on the Reviewing toolbar. Select **Final Showing Markup** from the **Display for Review** box.

3. Choose **Tools**, **Options** from the menu, and click the **Security** tab. Type **learn** in the **Password to open** box and click **OK**. (Note: This password is used throughout this book because it is easy to remember. It is used whenever a password is needed.)

4. Type **learn** in the **Confirm Password** dialog box. Click **OK**.

5. Close and reopen the document. Type **learn** in the Password dialog box when prompted, and then click **OK**.

6. To protect changes, choose **Tools**, **Protect Document** from the menu. Type **learn** in the **Password** box and click **OK**. Confirm the password and click **OK**.

7. Click the **Save** button to save your work. Leave the document open for the next exercise.

R2—Tracking Changes and Adding Comments

1. With the **WD1105-Precipitation** document still open, choose **Tools**, **Options** from the menu. Click the **User Information** tab, type your name in the **Name** box, type your initials in the **Initials** box, and click **OK**. (Note: If you are working in a lab, make note of the current name and initials before you change them.)

2. In the first paragraph of the Variance section, highlight **necessary** and type **important**.

3. Scroll down to the last paragraph on the first page. Type **clearly** so that the end of the sentence reads **this is clearly not the case**.

4. Scroll to the top of the document and place the insertion point at the end of the introductory paragraph. Click the **New Comment** button and type **Doesn't this paragraph sound more like an introduction to a statistics text than an introduction to a weather topic?**

5. Click the **Save** button to save your work. Leave the document open for the next exercise. (Note: If you are working in a lab, change the name and initials back to their original settings.)

R3—Reviewing Changes by Type and Reviewer

1. With the **WD1105-Precipitation** document still open, click the **Show** button on the Reviewing toolbar.

2. Click on the **Comments** option to turn the comments display off. Repeat this procedure to turn off the **Formatting** display option. Only insertions and deletions are shown.

3. Click on the **Insertions and Deletions** option to turn it off, and then click on the **Comments** option to see only the comments.

4. Use the same procedure to turn the **Insertions and Deletions** option and the **Formatting** option back on. All three types of changes are now displayed.

5. Use the **Reviewers** option on the **Show** button to deselect all the names but yours. (Note: There will be two extra names of people who did not make any changes. This means that at one time or another, machines with this user information have been used while editing this document.)

6. Click the **Show** button, move the pointer down until **Reviewers** is highlighted, and then select **All Reviewers** to turn all changes back on.

7. Leave the document open for the next exercise.

R4—Responding to Proposed Changes

1. With the **WD1105-Precipitation** document still open, click the **Reviewing Pane** button to review all the changes to the document.

2. Choose **Tools, Unprotect Document** from the menu so you can act on the suggested changes.

3. Type **learn** into the **Password** box and click **OK**.

4. Make sure the insertion point is at the beginning of the document and click the **Next** button on the Reviewing toolbar.

5. Click the **Reject Change/Delete Comment** button on the Reviewing toolbar to reject the deletion. Click the **Next** button. Click the **Reject Change/Delete Comment** button to remove the inserted word.

6. Click the **Next** button. Click the **Reject Change/Delete Comment** button to remove the comment.

7. Click the **Next** button. Click the **Accept Change** button to accept the suggested change.

8. Click the arrow on the **Accept Change** button and select **Accept All Changes in Document** from the menu.

9. Click the **Reviewing Pane** button to close the Reviewing Pane. Click the **Save** button to save your work. Leave the document open for the next exercise.

R5—Merging Multiple Revisions of the Same Document

1. With the **WD1105-Precipitation** document still open, choose **Tools, Compare and Merge Documents** from the menu.

2. Find and select **WD1106**.

3. Click the **Merge** button arrow and choose the **Merge into new document** option.

4. Scroll down to the middle of the second page to see the paragraph deleted from the second document.

5. Choose **Tools, Compare and Merge Documents** from the menu again. Find and select **WD1107**. Click the **Merge** button arrow, but this time choose the **Merge into current document** option. A paragraph has been deleted from the last page of the document.

6. Place the insertion point at the beginning of the document. Click the **Next** button on the Reviewing toolbar. Click the **Accept Change** button to accept the suggested change.

7. Click the arrow on the **Reject Change/Delete Comments** button and select **Reject All Changes in Document** from the menu.

8. Click the **Save** button. Save the document as **WD1105-Merged Documents**.

9. Choose **Window, 2 WD1105-Precipitation** from the menu and close this document. Leave **WD1105-Merged Documents** open for the next exercise.

R6—Creating Versions of Documents

1. With the **WD1105-Merged Documents** document still open, choose **File, Versions** from the menu. Click the **Automatically save a version on close** check box.

2. Click the **Save Now** button. In the **Comments on version** box, type **This version was compiled from several revisions on 12/7/2002 by <your name>**. Substitute your name for <your name>.

3. Click **OK**. Place the insertion point at the end of the second line of the title and press ⏎Enter. Type **edited by <your name>**.

4. Close and save the **WD1105-Merged Documents** document, and then open it again.

5. Choose <u>F</u>ile, Ve<u>r</u>sions from the menu to make sure a new version was automatically saved when you closed the document.

6. Print the first page of the document. Close the document and close Word.

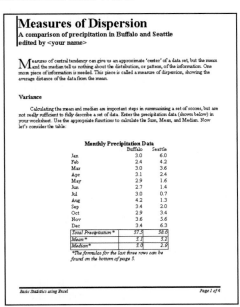

Challenge exercises are designed to test your ability to apply your skills to new situations with less detailed instruction. These exercises also challenge you to expand your repertoire of skills by using commands that are similar to those you have already learned. The desired outcome is clearly defined, but you have more freedom to choose the steps needed to achieve the required result.

The following exercises use different files to illustrate procedures that you should find helpful. Because of the nature of document collaboration features, some of these exercises require network features that may not be available to you. If you are preparing for a certification test, read through the steps for the network exercises and do as many of the steps as possible to get a feel for the dialog boxes that you will need to work with.

C1—Attaching Documents to E-Mail Messages

When several people need to collaborate on or review a document, there are two ways to make the documents available. The first is to place the document in a location available to everyone working on it, such as a shared folder on a server, or as a download from a Web page. The other way to get documents to others is via e-mail. The first two Challenge exercises deal with e-mail attachments and routing documents.

For this exercise, you will use a version of the multimedia proposal that you worked on in this lesson. You will attach this document to an e-mail message, and you will also use the File, Send to menu option.

Goal: To attach a document to an e-mail message using two different techniques.

1. Locate and open the **WD1108** document. Save it as **WD1108-Challenge1**. Close the document.

2. Log in to your e-mail system. In the address box, type your instructor's e-mail address. Add your own e-mail address to send yourself a copy. With most e-mail systems, you can place a comma between e-mail addresses, or you can type the second address in the Copy box.

3. Type **Lesson 11, Challenge 1, Part 1** in the subject box, and then type a short message telling the instructor that you are attaching a document. Make sure you type your name at the bottom of the message.

4. Find the file attachment area for your e-mail system. In AOL, click the Browse button next to the Attach File box. In Hotmail, click the Add/Edit Attachments button, and then click the Browse button next to the Find File box. In Yahoo, click the Add/Delete Attachments button, and then click the Browse button next to the Step 1 box. If you are using a different system, you will find a procedure that is very similar.

5. Find and select the **WD1108-Challenge1** document, attach it by following the instructions on the screen, and then send the e-mail with the document attached.

6. From Word, open the WD1108-Challenge1 document. To send an attachment directly from Word, choose **File, Send to, Mail Recipient (as Attachment)**. You can also send the document as part of the e-mail, or for review only. (Note: For the following procedure to work, you need to use Outlook, Outlook Express, or another MAPI compatible e-mail program. It will probably not work in a lab setting.)

7. Type the instructor's address (or click the **Address Book** button) in the **To** box, and your e-mail address in the **Cc** box. Notice that the attachment is listed in the **Attach** box. Click the **Importance: High** button to flag this as an important message.

8. Type **Lesson 11, Challenge 1, Part 2**. Click the **Send** button.

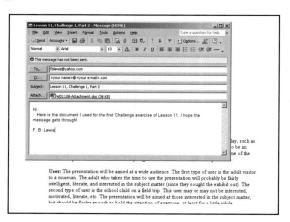

C2—Routing Documents to Colleagues

If you work in an office, you are probably familiar with routing slips, showing the names of all of the people who need to read the document. These are usually attached to the front page of the document. You can use an electronic routing slip to perform the same task. With electronic routing, you can determine a sequential order of people who are to receive the document for review, or you can send the document to everybody at once. If you send it sequentially, after each recipient reads the document, they then send it on to the next person. At the same time, the originator of the document is notified that the document has moved on.

Note: For the following procedure to work, you need to use Outlook, Outlook Express, or another MAPI compatible e-mail program. It will probably not work in a lab setting.

Goal: To use an electronic routing slip to send a document to colleagues.

1. Locate and open the **WD1108** document. Save it as **WD1108-Challenge2**.

2. Choose <u>F</u>ile, Send <u>to</u>, <u>R</u>outing Recipient from the menu. You may see a message box that warns you that a program is trying to access e-mail addresses in Outlook. Since this is a possible virus indicator, the program wants you to confirm that you are initiating this procedure. Security settings on some networks will not allow you to proceed past this point.

3. Click Yes to proceed. Make sure the <u>O</u>ne after another option is selected in the Routing Slip dialog box. Also, make sure the Trac<u>k</u> status check box is selected.

4. Click the <u>A</u>ddress button. Use your address book to choose recipients, or click the New button, choose **In this message only**, click OK, and type the address of the recipient. Make sure you include your instructor.

5. Type a message in the <u>M</u>essage text box, and make sure you add your name to the message.

6. Click the <u>R</u>oute button. The message is sent to the first name on the list. Once the message is read, the recipient needs to choose <u>F</u>ile, Send <u>to</u>, <u>N</u>ext routing Recipient from the menu. Notice the instructions for letting the recipient know how to respond.

7. Close the document.

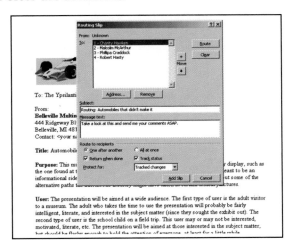

C3—Inserting and Modifying Hyperlinks

Everyone is used to clicking on hyperlinks when using the Web. They are not restricted to the Web, however. You can add hyperlinks to a Word document, so that someone reading the document can click the highlighted word (or words, or image) and the program opens the default browser and goes directly to the Web site. If you place hyperlinks in Word documents and then save the document as a Web page, the links remain active on the Web page. Hyperlinks can help add up-to-the-minute information to documents that have been circulated to employees.

In this lesson, you add hyperlinks to a flyer about an Alaska trip. You use the Web site of your organization (a university or business, for example).

Goal: To add hyperlinks to a Word document.

1. Locate and open the **WD1109** document and save it as **WD1109-Challenge3**.

2. In the opening paragraph, replace <your name> and <your organization> with your name and organization.

3. Select your organization name and click the **Insert Hyperlink** button (the one with a small globe and a chain link) on the Standard toolbar.

4. Make sure **Existing File or Web Page** is selected in the **Link to** area. Type the address of your organization's Web page in the **Addre<u>s</u>s** box. If you do not have a good address to go to, use www.microsoft.com. The program will add **http://** if you type a standard Web address.

5. Click the **Screen Tip** button and type the name of your organization. This appears when you move the pointer on top of the hyperlink. Click OK twice to close the Insert Hyperlink dialog box.

6. Select the word **Alaska** in the first paragraph. Add a hyperlink to **http://www.alaska.com**, with a Screen Tip that says **Welcome to Alaska**.

7. Test your link by holding down Ctrl and click either of your hyperlinks.

8. Close the document and save your changes. Send the file to your instructor as directed.

C4—Setting Up Workgroup Templates

When you create templates, they are stored in the same location as the ones that come with Word. If you want to make templates available to a workgroup, you need to create the template, send it to each person in the group, and then make sure you place it in the right folder. Since the folder location is different for different versions of Windows, this could be a complicated procedure. You would have to repeat this procedure each time the template was changed.

An alternative is to place widely used templates in a location that is available to all workgroup members, such as a shared network folder. Each user would then tell the program where to look for templates just once, and from then on, all changes to templates, or added templates, would be available to each workgroup member immediately.

In this exercise, you create a template, place it in a shared folder, and then point Word to that folder. If you do not have access to a shared folder on a file server, go through the steps to change the template location so you can see how it is done.

Goal: To change the location of templates to a shared folder for use by a workgroup.

1. Locate and open the **WD1110** document. Save the file as **WD1110-Challenge4**.

2. Choose File, Save As from the menu. In the **Save as type** box, select **Document Template**. Keep the default file name. (Note: Check with your network administrator before proceeding with the next step.) Close the template.

3. If you have a shared folder on a network server, choose File, Save As from the menu. (You might want to create a Templates folder in the shared folder, or there may already be one in that location.)

4. Choose Tools, Options from the menu. Click the File Locations tab.

5. Click **Workgroup templates** and click the Modify button. (Note: If you do not have a shared folder, examine the dialog box, and then stop at this point.) Click the Look in arrow, and then find and select the shared folder you want to use for workgroup templates. Click OK.

6. Close the template. Choose File, New from the menu. Find your new template in the **New from template** area of the **New Document** pane. Click the new template to make sure it works.

7. Close Word. Don't save your changes.

ON YOUR OWN

As sending documents electronically has grown more and more common, it has increased the need to confirm the source of the document. With paper documents, a signature and notarization are legal tools to identify the source of the document and the validity of the signature. Signing an electronic document has not been easy, at least not until the advent of *digital signatures*. Digital signatures are your "signature" verified by a digital certificate—an electronic identification card that verifies the source and also verifies that the document has not been changed since the signature was added. The digital certificate contains personal information about the person who signed the document.

You can obtain a digital certificate in one of three ways. The most secure, and the one with the widest acceptance, is to purchase a certificate from one of the commercial verification companies, such as VeriSign or E-Lock. You can also obtain a certificate that is good company-wide from your company's network administrator. Finally, you can create a local certificate using Selfcert.exe, a program that is included with Microsoft Office XP, but which is not automatically installed when you install Office.

In this exercise, you create a digital certificate for yourself, attach a signature to a document, and then describe the process you used to set up your certificate. You need to get the information to complete the exercise from the Help. (Note: If you are working in a lab, you may find that Selfcert.exe has already been installed, or that you cannot create certificates because of security.)

Criteria for grading will be:

1. Demonstration of ability to use Microsoft Word help to discover how to download Selfcert.exe

2. Demonstration of the ability to attach a digital signature to a document

To complete the project:

- Write a description of the process by which you installed Selfcert.exe.

- Save the document as **WD11-On Your Own.**

- Attach a digital signature to the document.

- Describe any differences you see on the screen after you attach the digital signature.

- Describe what the red X means on the certificate, and what differences an authenticated certificate might make.

- Describe what happens when you make changes and save the document and whether the same thing happens if you don't make changes.

- Add your name and print a copy of the document.

- Turn in the file as directed.

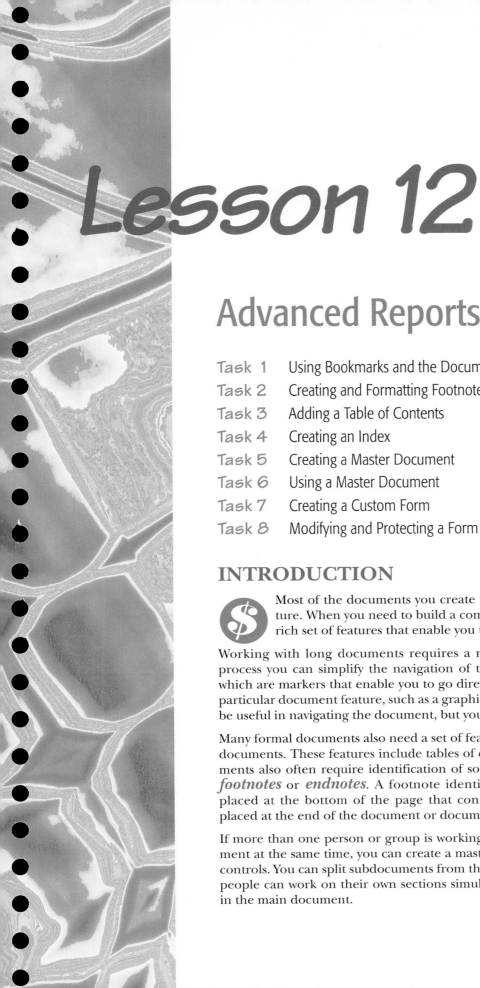

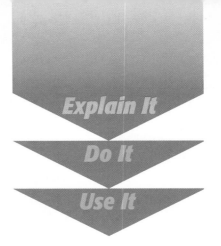

Lesson 12

Explain It
Do It
Use It

Advanced Reports and Forms

Task 1   Using Bookmarks and the Document Map

Task 2   Creating and Formatting Footnotes

Task 3   Adding a Table of Contents

Task 4   Creating an Index

Task 5   Creating a Master Document

Task 6   Using a Master Document

Task 7   Creating a Custom Form

Task 8   Modifying and Protecting a Form

INTRODUCTION

 Most of the documents you create using Word are quite simple in structure. When you need to build a complex document, however, Word has a rich set of features that enable you to do so.

Working with long documents requires a new set of skills. During the editing process you can simplify the navigation of the document by using *bookmarks*, which are markers that enable you to go directly to a section of the document or a particular document feature, such as a graphic or a table. A document map can also be useful in navigating the document, but you must format the document properly.

Many formal documents also need a set of features that are not common in shorter documents. These features include tables of contents and indexes. Scholarly documents also often require identification of sources, such as reference sections and *footnotes* or *endnotes*. A footnote identifies a source of information, and is placed at the bottom of the page that contains the information. Endnotes are placed at the end of the document or document sections.

If more than one person or group is working on different parts of the same document at the same time, you can create a master document that the primary author controls. You can split subdocuments from the main document so that a number of people can work on their own sections simultaneously, with all changes registered in the main document.

311

Finally, you can set up a Word document as a form. Readers can answer questions, click check boxes, or choose responses from drop-down lists. You can even protect the form so that no one can make unauthorized changes.

In this lesson, you learn how to use some of the more advanced report and form features. The first document you use is a review of help-seeking behavior and classroom response systems. This is an analysis and proposed study being put together by a company preparing a bid for a series of technology-assisted classrooms for a university.

VISUAL SUMMARY

By the time you complete this lesson, you will have created a document with indexes, tables of contents, and footnotes. You will also have created a form. The document pages will look like this:

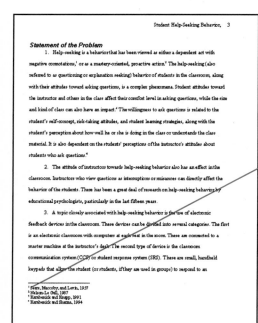

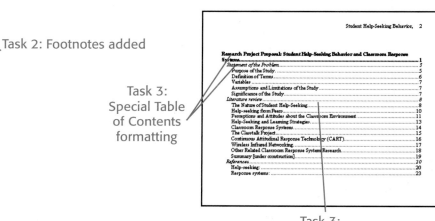

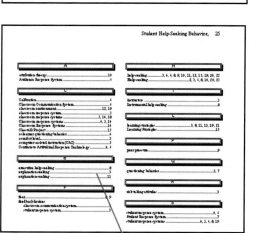

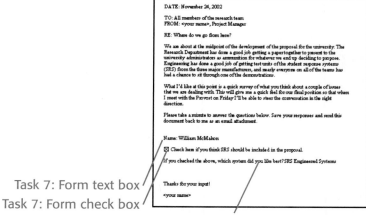

Task 2: Footnotes added

Task 3:
Special Table
of Contents
formatting

Task 3:
Table of contents

Task 4: Words and
phrases marked and
turned into an index

Task 7: Form text box

Task 7: Form check box

Task 7: Form drop-down box

Task 1

USING BOOKMARKS AND THE DOCUMENT MAP

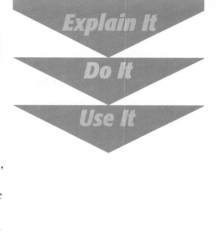

Why would I do this?

Maneuvering through a document, particularly a long one, can be tedious. You can use the Find feature if you can remember a unique word or phrase in the section of the document you want to find. However, Word offers two easy methods to navigate a document.

The first way to move quickly through a document is to add a bookmark, which marks sections of the document so that you can move easily from point to point. The other method of navigating a document is to use the *document map*. A document map is an outline that is based on the Heading styles included with Word. To move around the document, you simply turn the document map on and click on the outline heading of the section you want to see.

In this task, you add bookmarks to a document, and use the document map.

1 Start Word and click the **Open** button. Find and open **WD1201** and save it as **WD1201-Help Seeking Behavior**. Turn off the Task Pane and click the **Print Layout View** button, if necessary.

This document is a proposal that is divided into four sections—a cover page, a statement of the problem, a literature review, and references. A bookmark to each of the sections would be helpful.

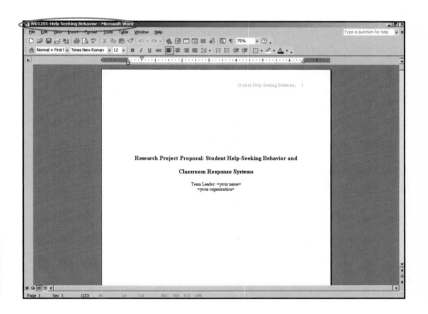

QUICK TIP

If you are downloading the sample files from an online source, you need to get the WD1201 through WD1211 files.

2 Make sure the insertion point is at the beginning of the document. Choose **I**nsert, **Book**mark from the menu.

The bookmark dialog box is displayed.

Type **Title_page** in the **Bookmark name** box.

*The **A**dd button is activated.*

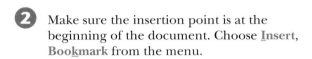
Bookmark name
Add button is activated

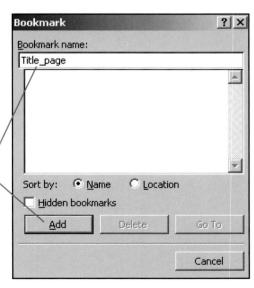

CAUTION

When you create a bookmark that consists of two or more words, you must use the underscore character in place of any spaces.

3 Click **Add**.

The bookmark is created and the Bookmark dialog box closes. There is no indication on the screen that a bookmark exists.

Scroll to the top of page 2 and place the insertion point to the left of **Statement of the Problem.**

This is where you will place the second bookmark.

Statement of the Problem

1. Help-seeking is a behavior that has been viewed as either a dependent act with negative connotations, or as a mastery-oriented, proactive action. The help-seeking (also referred to as questioning or explanation seeking) behavior of students in the classroom, along with their attitudes toward asking questions, is a complex phenomena. Student attitudes toward the instructor and others in the class affect their comfort level in asking questions, while the size and kind of class can also have an impact. The willingness to ask questions is related to the student's self-concept, risk-taking attitudes, and student learning strategies, along with the student's perception about how well he or she is doing in the class or understands the class material. It is also dependent on the students' perceptions of the instructor's attitudes about students who ask questions.

2. The attitude of instructors towards help-seeking behavior also has an effect in the classroom. Instructors who view questions as interruptions or nuisances can directly affect the behavior of the students. There has been a great deal of research on help-seeking behavior by educational psychologists, particularly in the last fifteen years.

3. A topic closely associated with help-seeking behavior is the use of electronic feedback devices in the classroom. These devices can be divided into several categories. The first is an electronic classroom with computers at each seat in the room. These are connected to a master machine at the instructor's desk. The second type of device is the classroom

4 Choose **Insert**, **Bookmark** from the menu.

*The bookmark dialog box is displayed, and the first bookmark is displayed. **Title_page** is also highlighted in the **Bookmark name** box.*

Type **Problem** in the **Bookmark name** box.

New bookmark

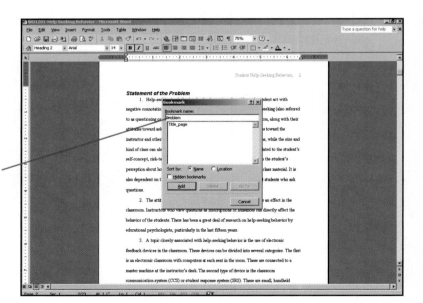

5 Click **Add** to add the second bookmark. Move to page **7** and add a bookmark called **Review** to the **Literature review** title. Click **Add**.

The third bookmark is added.

Move to page 19 and add a bookmark called **References** to the **References** title.

There are three bookmarks, and a bookmark ready to be added.

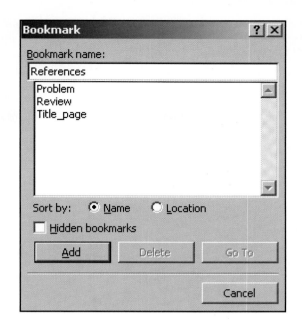

6 Click **Add** to add the final bookmark. Choose **Edit**, **Go To** from the menu.

The Find and Replace dialog box is displayed.

Click the **Bookmark** option in the **Go to what** section. Click the arrow in the **Enter bookmark name** box.

The drop-down menu shows the bookmarks you just created.

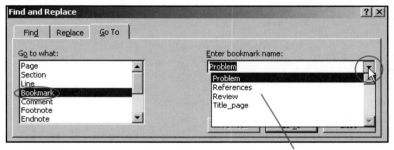

The bookmarks you just created

7 Select **Problem** and click the **Go To** button.

*You immediately move to the title of the **Problem** section of the document. Bookmarks are a good way to move around a document that has been created without using the proper styles. If the document is set up properly with heading styles, the document map will work even better.*

Click **Close** to close the Find and Replace box. Click the **Document Map** button.

An outline appears in the document map pane on the left side of the screen.

IN DEPTH

If you do not use the Heading styles in the document, the document map will not work properly. The Heading 1 style is the top level of the outline, the Heading 2 styles are the next level, and so on. If you want to use a document map on a document that is not formatted properly, you can always change the styles of the titles and subtitles, and then change the fonts and font characteristics of each style to suit your needs.

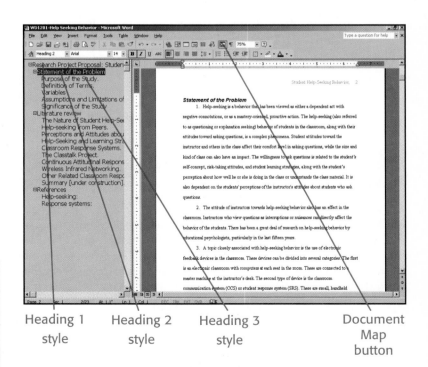

Heading 1 style

Heading 2 style

Heading 3 style

Document Map button

8 Click **Literature review** in the second level of the document map.

The insertion point jumps to the Literature review section of the document.

Click **Wireless Infrared Networking** in the third level of the document map.

The insertion point jumps to the Wireless Infrared Networking section of the document.

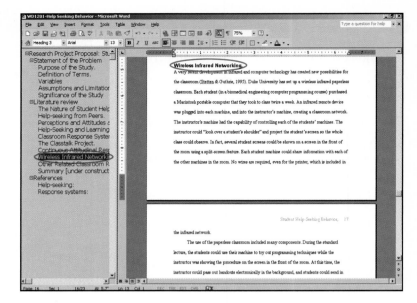

9 Click the **Collapse** button to the left of **Literature review**.

The Collapse button turns into an Expand button. You can collapse or expand any section that you wish. This makes it easier to see the flow of the document.

Click the **Save** button. Leave the document open for the next lesson.

Expand button
Collapse button

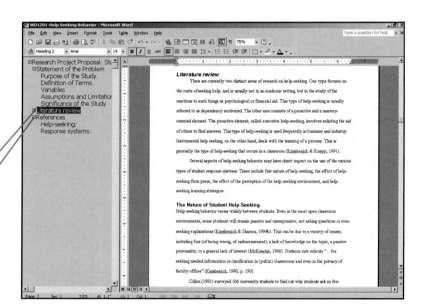

Task 2
CREATING AND FORMATTING FOOTNOTES

Why would I do this?

Footnotes, which appear at the bottom of a page, and endnotes, which appear at the end of a section or the end of the document, are ways of identifying sources of information. They are used most often in scholarly papers or in documents that gather information from many different sources. They also enable the reader to go to the source for further information, if necessary.

The document you are working on originally used sources in a format set up by the American Psychological Association (APA). Your company has decided to change to numbered footnotes of their own design.

In this task, you add footnotes to the help-seeking document.

1 With the **WD1201-Help Seeking Behavior** document still open, click the **Document Map** button.

The document map pane is closed.

Scroll to the top of page 2 and place the insertion point at the end of the first sentence.

Make sure the insertion point follows the period at the end of the sentence. This is where you place your first footnote.

Statement of the Problem

1. Help-seeking is a behavior that has been viewed as either a dependent act with negative connotations, or as a mastery-oriented, proactive action. The help-seeking (also referred to as questioning or explanation seeking) behavior of students in the classroom, along with their attitudes toward asking questions, is a complex phenomena. Student attitudes toward the instructor and others in the class affect their comfort level in asking questions, while the size and kind of class can also have an impact. The willingness to ask questions is related to the student's self-concept, risk-taking attitudes, and student learning strategies, along with the student's perception about how well he or she is doing in the class or understands the class material. It is also dependent on the students' perceptions of the instructor's attitudes about students who ask questions.

2. The attitude of instructors towards help-seeking behavior also has an effect in the classroom. Instructors who view questions as interruptions or nuisances can directly affect the behavior of the students. There has been a great deal of research on help-seeking behavior by educational psychologists, particularly in the last fifteen years.

3. A topic closely associated with help-seeking behavior is the use of electronic

2 Select **I**nsert, **Refere**nce, **Foot**note from the menu.

The Footnote and Endnote dialog box is displayed.

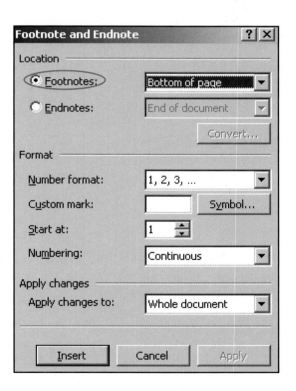

3 Confirm that **Footnotes** is selected and click the **Insert** button.

A footnote area is set aside at the bottom of the page, and the footnote is numbered.

    Type **Nelson-Le Gall, 1987** as the footnote.

Do not type another footnote number.

---

the instructor and others in the class affect their comfort level in asking questions, while the size and kind of class can also have an impact. The willingness to ask questions is related to the student's self-concept, risk-taking attitudes, and student learning strategies, along with the student's perception about how well he or she is doing in the class or understands the class material. It is also dependent on the students' perceptions of the instructor's attitudes about students who ask questions.

    2. The attitude of instructors towards help-seeking behavior also has an effect in the classroom. Instructors who view questions as interruptions or nuisances can directly affect the behavior of the students. There has been a great deal of research on help-seeking behavior by educational psychologists, particularly in the last fifteen years.

    3. A topic closely associated with help-seeking behavior is the use of electronic feedback devices in the classroom. These devices can be divided into several categories. The first is an electronic classroom with computers at each seat in the room. These are connected to a master machine at the instructor's desk. The second type of device is the classroom communication system (CCS) or student response system (SRS). These are small, handheld keypads that allow the student (or students, if they are used in groups) to respond to an instructor's questions. The third type of device uses a keypad that is capable of measuring

[1] Nelson-Le Gall, 1987

---

4 Scroll up so you can see the first paragraph.

The footnote reference number appears at the end of the first sentence. It is a smaller font, and sits slightly above the line (superscripted).

    Place the insertion point at the end of the sentence that ends with the word **impact** in the sixth line.

Make sure the insertion point follows the period at the end of the sentence.

Footnote reference number

Statement of the Problem

    1. Help-seeking is a behavior that has been viewed as either a dependent act with negative connotations, or as a mastery-oriented, proactive action.[1] The help-seeking (also referred to as questioning or explanation seeking) behavior of students in the classroom, along with their attitudes toward asking questions, is a complex phenomena. Student attitudes toward the instructor and others in the class affect their comfort level in asking questions, while the size and kind of class can also have an impact. The willingness to ask questions is related to the student's self-concept, risk-taking attitudes, and student learning strategies, along with the student's perception about how well he or she is doing in the class or understands the class material. It is also dependent on the students' perceptions of the instructor's attitudes about students who ask questions.

    2. The attitude of instructors towards help-seeking behavior also has an effect in the classroom. Instructors who view questions as interruptions or nuisances can directly affect the behavior of the students. There has been a great deal of research on help-seeking behavior by educational psychologists, particularly in the last fifteen years.

    3. A topic closely associated with help-seeking behavior is the use of electronic

---

5 Select Insert, Reference, Footnote from the menu, and then click the Insert button.

A second footnote is placed at the bottom of the page.

> Type **Karabenick and Knapp, 1991** in the new footnote.

You now add a footnote that comes before the two that you just added.

---

the instructor and others in the class affect their comfort level in asking questions, while the size and kind of class can also have an impact.[2] The willingness to ask questions is related to the student's self-concept, risk-taking attitudes, and student learning strategies, along with the student's perception about how well he or she is doing in the class or understands the class material. It is also dependent on the students' perceptions of the instructor's attitudes about students who ask questions.

    2.   The attitude of instructors towards help-seeking behavior also has an effect in the classroom. Instructors who view questions as interruptions or nuisances can directly affect the behavior of the students. There has been a great deal of research on help-seeking behavior by educational psychologists, particularly in the last fifteen years.

    3.   A topic closely associated with help-seeking behavior is the use of electronic feedback devices in the classroom. These devices can be divided into several categories. The first is an electronic classroom with computers at each seat in the room. These are connected to a master machine at the instructor's desk. The second type of device is the classroom communication system (CCS) or student response system (SRS). These are small, handheld keypads that allow the student (or students, if they are used in groups) to respond to an instructor's questions. The third type of device uses a keypad that is capable of measuring

[1] Nelson-Le Gall, 1987
[2] Karabenick and Knapp, 1991

---

6 Scroll up so you can see the first paragraph on page 2, and place the insertion point after **connotations,** in the first sentence. Select Insert, Reference, Footnote from the menu, and then click the Insert button.

> Type **Sears, Maccoby, and Levin, 1957** in the new footnote.

Notice that the existing footnotes are automatically renumbered to make room for this footnote that appears earlier in the document.

The footnotes have been renumbered

CAUTION

When you add the third footnote, the last footnote may move to the bottom of the third page. Word is quirky about footnote placement. The problem often corrects itself when you add another footnote, or if you make slight changes to formatting (such as adding a 6-point space after a document title).

---

the instructor and others in the class affect their comfort level in asking questions, while the size and kind of class can also have an impact.[3] The willingness to ask questions is related to the student's self-concept, risk-taking attitudes, and student learning strategies, along with the student's perception about how well he or she is doing in the class or understands the class material. It is also dependent on the students' perceptions of the instructor's attitudes about students who ask questions.

    2.   The attitude of instructors towards help-seeking behavior also has an effect in the classroom. Instructors who view questions as interruptions or nuisances can directly affect the behavior of the students. There has been a great deal of research on help-seeking behavior by educational psychologists, particularly in the last fifteen years.

    3.   A topic closely associated with help-seeking behavior is the use of electronic feedback devices in the classroom. These devices can be divided into several categories. The first is an electronic classroom with computers at each seat in the room. These are connected to a master machine at the instructor's desk. The second type of device is the classroom communication system (CCS) or student response system (SRS). These are small, handheld keypads that allow the student (or students, if they are used in groups) to respond to an instructor's questions. The third type of device uses a keypad that is capable of measuring

[1] Sears, Maccoby, and Levin, 1957
[2] Nelson-Le Gall, 1987

7 Scroll up so you can see the first paragraph, and place the insertion point at the end of the first paragraph. Select **Insert**, **Reference**, **Footnote** from the menu, and then click the **Insert** button.

Type **Karabenick and Sharma, 1994** in the fourth footnote.

All four footnotes are displayed on the bottom of the page.

Footnote reference numbers

Footnotes for the current page

the instructor and others in the class affect their comfort level in asking questions, while the size and kind of class can also have an impact[3] The willingness to ask questions is related to the student's self-concept, risk-taking attitudes, and student learning strategies, along with the student's perception about how well he or she is doing in the class or understands the class material. It is also dependent on the students' perceptions of the instructor's attitudes about students who ask questions[4]

2. The attitude of instructors towards help-seeking behavior also has an effect in the classroom. Instructors who view questions as interruptions or nuisances can directly affect the behavior of the students. There has been a great deal of research on help-seeking behavior by educational psychologists, particularly in the last fifteen years.

3. A topic closely associated with help-seeking behavior is the use of electronic feedback devices in the classroom. These devices can be divided into several categories. The first is an electronic classroom with computers at each seat in the room. These are connected to a master machine at the instructor's desk. The second type of device is the classroom communication system (CCS) or student response system (SRS). These are small, handheld keypads that allow the student (or students, if they are used in groups) to respond to an

---
[1] Sears, Maccoby, and Levin, 1957
[2] Nelson-Le Gall, 1987
[3] Karabenick and Knapp, 1991
[4] Karabenick and Sharma, 1994

8 Choose **File**, **Print** from the menu. Select the **Current page** option and click **OK**.

The second page prints.

Click the **Save** button and leave the document open for the next lesson.

Task 3
ADDING A TABLE OF CONTENTS

Why would I do this?
A table of contents gives the reader a quick view of the important topics covered in the document. It also lets the reader know the page number of each topic. Word enables you to create an automatic table of contents, and lets you format each level differently.

In this task, you create a table of contents for the proposal.

1 With the **WD1201-Help Seeking Behavior** document still open, scroll to the top of the second page. Place the insertion point to the left of the **Statement of the Problem** heading.

This is where you place the table of contents.

Statement of the Problem

1. Help-seeking is a behavior that has been viewed as either a dependent act with negative connotations,[1] or as a mastery-oriented, proactive action.[2] The help-seeking (also referred to as questioning or explanation seeking) behavior of students in the classroom, along with their attitudes toward asking questions, is a complex phenomena. Student attitudes toward the instructor and others in the class affect their comfort level in asking questions, while the size and kind of class can also have an impact.[3] The willingness to ask questions is related to the student's self-concept, risk-taking attitudes, and student learning strategies, along with the student's perception about how well he or she is doing in the class or understands the class material. It is also dependent on the students' perceptions of the instructor's attitudes about students who ask questions.[4]

2. The attitude of instructors towards help-seeking behavior also has an effect in the classroom. Instructors who view questions as interruptions or nuisances can directly affect the behavior of the students. There has been a great deal of research on help-seeking behavior by educational psychologists, particularly in the last fifteen years.

3. A topic closely associated with help-seeking behavior is the use of electronic

2 Choose **Insert**, **Reference**, **Index and Tables** from the menu.

The Index and Tables dialog box is displayed.

Click the **Table of Contents** tab in the Index and Tables dialog box.

The table of contents sheet shows a print preview and a Web preview of the default table of contents setup. You can also specify the number of levels to show in the table of contents.

Web preview of the table of contents

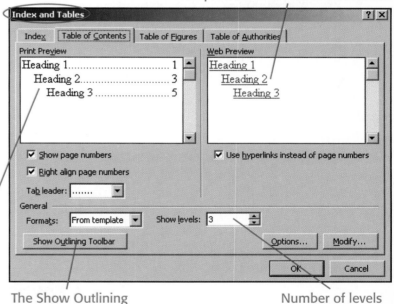

Print preview of the table of contents

The Show Outlining Toolbar button

Number of levels to show

IN DEPTH

If you are creating this document for the Web, the **Use hyperlinks instead of page numbers** option is very valuable. This enables the reader to click on a table of contents entry to move quickly to the desired topic.

3 Make sure **From template** is selected in the **Formats** box.

This style indents the heading levels, adds dots between the headings and the page numbers, and right-aligns the page numbers.

Click the **Show Outlining Toolbar** button in the Index and Tables dialog box and click **OK**.

The Outlining toolbar is displayed somewhere on the screen. The table of contents has been added to the second page of the document. Notice that the Statement of the Problem section remains on the same page, and the page number is shown in the table of contents.

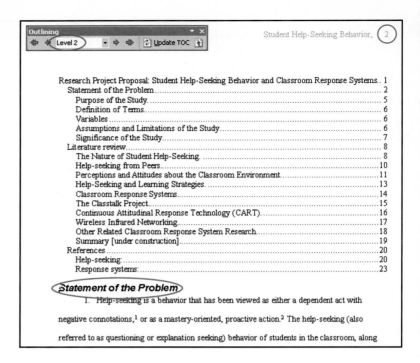

4 With the insertion point still to the left of the **Statement of the Problem** heading, hold down Ctrl and press ↵Enter.

A page break is inserted. The Statement of the Problem section moves to the top of page 3.

Scroll up and look at the table of contents.

The Statement of the Problem heading still shows it on page 2.

Update TOC button

Incorrect page number

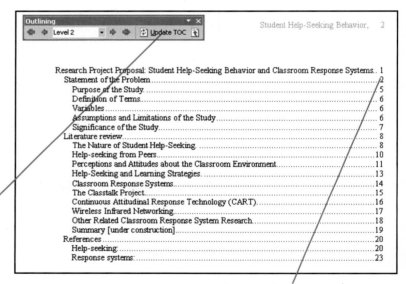

5 Click the **Update TOC** button on the Outlining toolbar.

The Update Table of Contents dialog box is displayed, giving you the option of updating just the page numbers, or if you have made other changes, you can also update the text.

6 Make sure the **Update page numbers only** option is selected and click **OK**.

The page numbers are updated for the entire table of contents. The final task you want to do is format the levels differently to make it easier to read.

Page numbers
have been updated

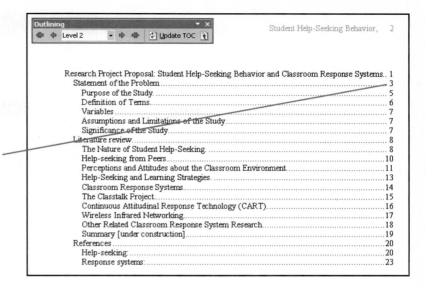

7 Choose **Insert, Reference, Index and Tables** from the menu. Click the **Modify** button on the Index and Tables dialog box.

The Style dialog box is displayed, showing the various table of contents levels.

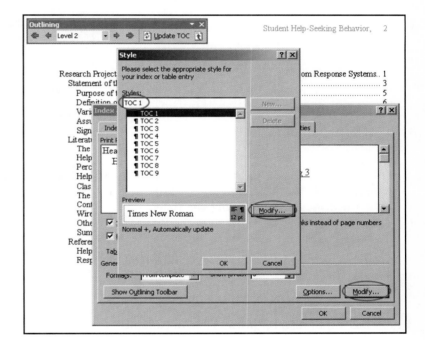

8 Click the **Modify** button on the Style dialog box.

The Modify Style dialog box is displayed.

Click the **Bold** button on the dialog box toolbar.

Any formatting changes you make are made to all entries at the selected level.

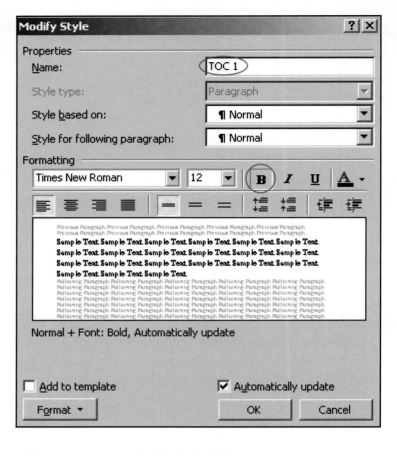

9 Click **OK** to accept the change. Click **TOC 2** in the **Styles** box. Click the **Modify** button on the Style dialog box. Click the **Italic** button and click **OK** on each of the three dialog boxes to close them.

A message box asks if you want to replace the selected table of contents. What you have done is recreated the table.

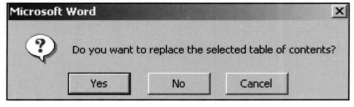

10 Click **Yes** to replace the old table of contents with the new one.

Any formatting changes you make are made to all entries at the selected level.

Click the **Save** button to save your work. Close the document but leave Word open for the next task.

TOC entries have been reformatted

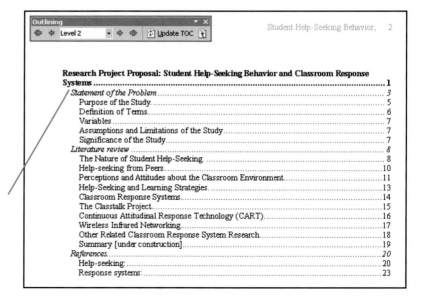

Task 4
CREATING AN INDEX

Why would I do this?

In a long document with a lot of information, it is often difficult to find exactly what you are looking for. An index enables you to look for key words or phrases in the document, and tells you the page number where they can be found. Word has an indexing feature that enables you to quickly create an index and format it in one of several different styles. The first step in the process of creating an index is to mark the words or phrases that you want to include. You can mark them while you are typing the document, or after the document has been created. Once you mark the entries, the rest of the process is automated.

In this task, you create an index for the proposal. (Note: Because of the great amount of time required to mark index entries, a number of entries have already been marked in the new document.)

1 Click the **Open** button. Find and open **WD1202** and save it as **WD1202-Help Seeking Behavior**. Turn off the Task Pane and click the **Print Layout View** button, if necessary.

This is essentially the same document you worked with in the first three tasks.

Scroll down so that you can see the top of page 3. Click the **Show/Hide** button.

*You can now see all paragraph marks, spaces, and other document marks. You can also see the existing index entries. They are shown in brackets with **XE** (for index entry) and then the index term in quotation marks.*

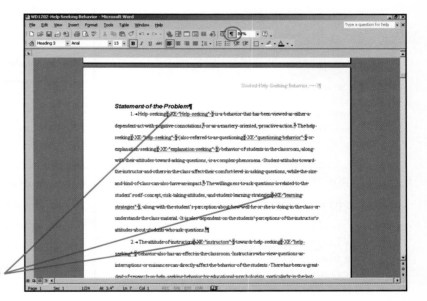

Index entries

② Highlight **comfort level** in the sixth line of the first paragraph.

You add this phrase to the index.

Hold down Alt + ⇧Shift and press **X**.

The Mark Index Entry dialog box is displayed.

Text selected for index

the·instructor·and·others·in·the·class·affect·their·comfort·level·in·asking·questions,·while·the·size· and·kind·of·class·can·also·have·an·impact.·The·willingness·to·ask·questions·is·related·to·the· student's·self-concept,·risk-taking·attitudes,·and·student·learning·strategies{·XE·"learning· strategies"·},·along·with·the·student's·perception·about·how·well·he·or·she·is·doing·in·the·class·or· understands·the·class·material.·It·is·also·dependent·on·the·students'·perceptions·of·the·instructor's· attitudes·about·students·who·ask·questions.¶

2.→ The·attitude·of·instructors{·XE·"instructors"·}·towards·help-seeking{·XE·"help-seeking"·}·behavior·also·has·an·effect·in·the·class interruptions·or·nuisances·can·directly·affect·the·l deal·of·research·on·help-seeking·behavior·by·edu fifteen·years.¶

3.→ A·topic·closely·associated·with·help-s of·electronic·feedback·devices·in·the·classroom.·T categories.·The·first·is·an·electronic·classroom·w are·connected·to·a·master·machine·at·the·instruct

Mark Index Entry [?][X]

Index
Main entry: comfort level

Subentry:

Options
○ Cross-reference: *See*
● Current page
○ Page range
  Bookmark: ▼

Page number format
☐ Bold
☐ Italic

This dialog box stays open so that you can mark multiple index entries.

[Mark] [Mark All] [Cancel]

‖·Sears,·Maccoby,·and·Levin,·1957¶
‖·Nelson-Le·Gall,·1987¶
‖·Karabenick·and·Knapp,·1991¶
‖·Karabenick·and·Sharma,·1994¶

⚓ **IN DEPTH**

There are two ways to enter index entries. You can use the <u>M</u>ark button to mark the highlighted entry, or you can click the Mark All button, which marks all the identical entries in the document. The problem with the second method is that it won't pick up variant forms of a word.

③ Click the <u>M</u>ark button.

An index entry is placed after the phrase in the text.

Click the **Close** button to close the Mark Index Entry dialog box. Highlight **risk-taking attitudes** in the following sentence to select it.

An index entry has been added

the·instructor·and·others·in·the·class·affect·their·comfort·level{·XE·"comfort·level"·}·in·asking· questions,·while·the·size·and·kind·of·class·can·also·have·an·impact.·The·willingness·to·ask· questions·is·related·to·the·student's·self-concept,·risk-taking·attitudes,·and·student·learning· strategies{·XE·"learning·strategies"·},·along·with·the·student's·perception·about·how·well·he·or· she·is·doing·in·the·class·or·understands·the·class·material.·It·is·also·dependent·on·the·students'· perceptions·of·the·instructor's·attitudes·about·students·who·ask·questions.¶

2.→ The·attitude·of·instructors{·XE·"instructors"·}·towards·help-seeking{·XE·"help-seeking"·}·behavior·also·has·an·effect·in·the·classroom.·Instructors·who·view·questions·as· interruptions·or·nuisances·can·directly·affect·the·behavior·of·the·students.·There·has·been·a·great· deal·of·research·on·help-seeking·behavior·by·educational·psychologists,·particularly·in·the·last· fifteen·years.¶

3.→ A·topic·closely·associated·with·help-seeking{·XE·"help-seeking"·}·behavior·is·the·use· of·electronic·feedback·devices·in·the·classroom.·These·devices·can·be·divided·into·several· categories.·The·first·is·an·electronic·classroom·with·computers·at·each·seat·in·the·room.·These· are·connected·to·a·master·machine·at·the·instructor's·desk.·The·second·type·of·device·is·the

‖·Sears,·Maccoby,·and·Levin,·1957¶
‖·Nelson-Le·Gall,·1987¶
‖·Karabenick·and·Knapp,·1991¶
‖·Karabenick·and·Sharma,·1994¶

4 Hold down (Alt)+(Shift) and press **X**. Click the **Mark All** button to mark all instances of this phrase in the document, and then click the **Close** button.

The entry is now marked in the document.

Select **classroom communication system** from the fifth sentence of the third paragraph. Hold down (Alt)+(Shift) and press **X**.

The selected text is listed in the Main entry box, but you want it to be a subentry (a subcategory of another main entry). There is an easy way to do this.

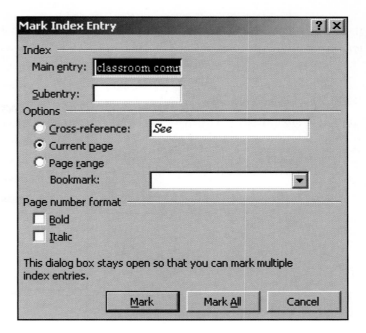

When you use the **Mark All** button, you might notice two of the same words or phrases marked on the same page. It is tempting to remove one, but it is a good idea to leave them both. When Word performs the indexing, it ignores multiple marked entries on the same page. If one of them ends up on another page during the editing process, however, you will be glad you left the index entry mark there.

5 Place the insertion point to the left of **classroom communication system** in the dialog box and type **feedback devices:** .

Make sure you include the colon and the space at the end of the text.

Click **Mark**. Close the dialog box, place the insertion point to the left of **student response system**, open the Mark Index Entry dialog box again, and type **feedback devices:** .

*This is the second subentry for **feedback devices**.*

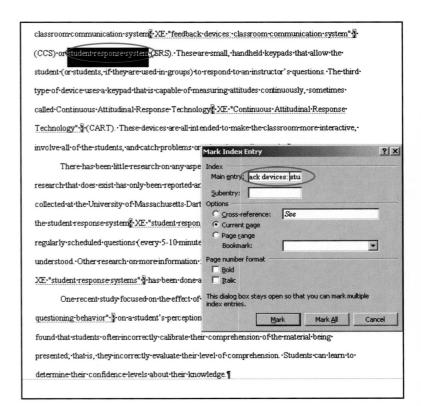

6 Click **Mark**. Click the **Close** button. Scroll to the bottom of the document. Click on the empty line at the bottom of the last page.

You want to place the index at the end of the document, but it should be placed on its own page.

Hold down Ctrl and press ↵Enter.

A page break is inserted, and the insertion point moves to the top of the next page.

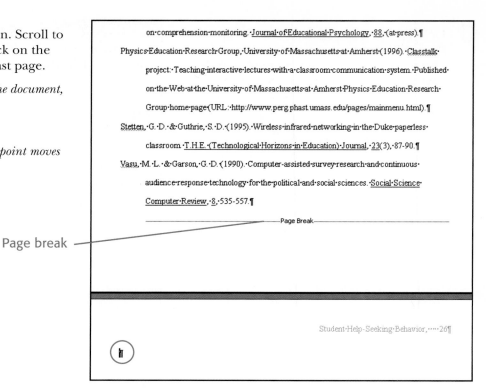

Page break ——

7 Click the **Show/Hide** button.

The paragraph and space marks are turned off.

Choose **Insert, Reference, Index and Tables** from the menu.

The Index and Tables dialog box is displayed.

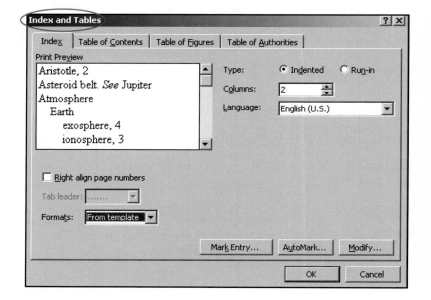

CAUTION

If the Show/Hide button is not turned off, the page numbering will be wrong for the index entries.

8 Click the **Index** tab, if necessary. Make sure the **Right align page numbers** check box is turned on. Choose the dotted line in the **Tab leader** box. Click the arrow in the **Formats** box. Scroll down and select the **Fancy** format.

The Index and Tables dialog box should look like the figure.

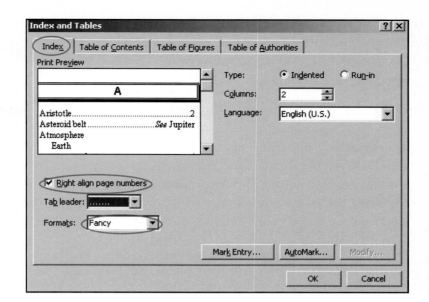

9 Click **OK**.

The index is created.

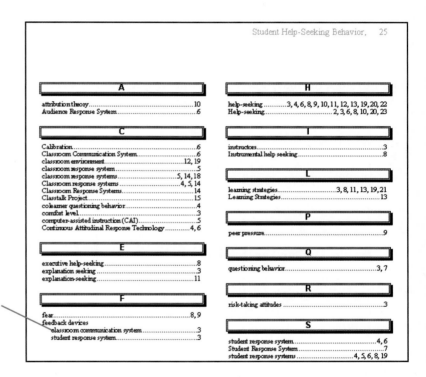

Subentries

10 Click the **Save** button. Print the current (index) page. Close the document, but leave Word open for the next lesson.

CAUTION

You might be tempted to edit the index itself. This is not a good idea unless the document is complete. If you make changes, but then update the index, all your edits will revert to their original form.

IN DEPTH

Indexes require a great deal of work. Notice that the index you just created contains duplicate entries. For example, the index lists help-seeking and Help-seeking separately, although they are clearly the same topic. When you finish creating your index, it is a good idea to print it out and go through the pages, adjusting the text between the quotation marks in the index entries. Once you make the entries consistent, you can right-click on the index and select Update Field from the shortcut menu. (A *field* is an indication to Word that there is information to add or an action to perform in that spot.) If you add more index entries, you can simply recreate the index.

Task 5
CREATING A MASTER DOCUMENT

Why would I do this?

When a group of people collaborate on a document, it is often difficult to know who is working on it, or which is the most recent version. If different people are working on different sections, there is a great solution to this problem—master documents and subdocuments.

A *master document* is the controlling file that coordinates and compiles each individual section, known as *subdocuments*. Each person or group can work on a subdocument, and as the changes are made, they are reflected in the master document, which can be used to update tables of contents, indexes, footnotes, or other reference features that use the whole document.

Using a master document with subdocuments requires that you store all pieces of the final document in the same file folder. In addition, each collaborator must have access to that folder, which will probably require a shared folder on a company intranet.

When you select part of a document and change it to a subdocument, the original document becomes the master document. In this task, you use a file that is similar to the one you have used throughout this lesson. You do not need a shared network folder to do the next two tasks, but it would be a good idea to create a new folder to store the master and subdocuments. You should keep the master document and subdocuments together. A new folder enables you to see the files with which you are working.

① Click the **Open** button. Find and open **WD1203** and save it as **WD1203-Help Seeking Behavior**. Place the document in a new folder, if possible.

This document has four sections, including the index.

Click the **Outline View** button.

The document appears in Outline view, and the Outlining toolbar is displayed. You need to decrease the amount of information in the outline to make the process easier.

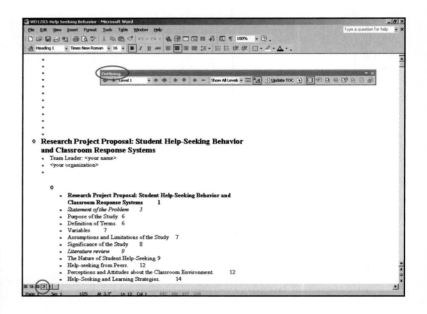

CAUTION

Do not place this document in a folder that others doing this lesson will use, since part of the process involves the creation of subdocuments with the names of the Heading 2 titles. If you are working in a lab situation and only have access to one folder on the hard drive or network drive, use a clean floppy disk and store this document on drive A.

QUICK TIP

If the Outlining toolbar is not displayed on your screen, choose View, Toolbars, Outlining from the menu. You can also right-click on any toolbar and select Outlining from the shortcut menu.

2 Click the arrow in the Show Level box on the Outlining toolbar and select **Show Level 3**.

This is the maximum number of Heading levels in this document, although some nonheading text is also displayed. You need to include all the heading levels in the outline for the master/subdocument process to work correctly. The wavy lines show the location of hidden (non-outline) text.

Indicates hidden text

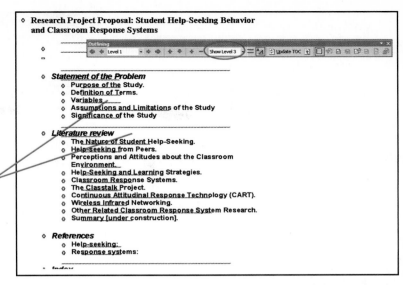

Create Subdocument button

3 Click the plus mark to the left of the **Statement of the Problem** title.

The title, which is a Heading 2 style, and all of the related Heading 3 titles are highlighted.

Click the **Create Subdocument** button on the Outlining toolbar.

A box appears around the selected section, and a Subdocument icon appears in the box. The subdocument has not been saved yet—it will be saved the first time you save the master document.

Subdocument icon
Box around the subdocument

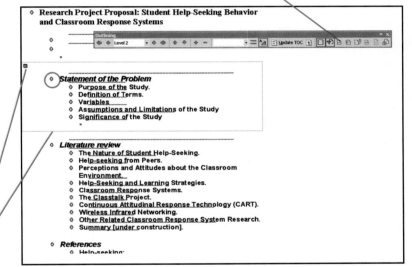

4 Click the plus mark to the left of the **Literature Review** title and click the **Create Subdocument** button.

A second subdocument is marked.

Scroll down, click the plus mark to the left of the **References** title, and click the **Create Subdocument** button.

A third subdocument is marked.

CAUTION

Do not make subdocuments out of automated sections, such as a table of contents or an index. Since these are created for the whole document, you do not want them edited separately.

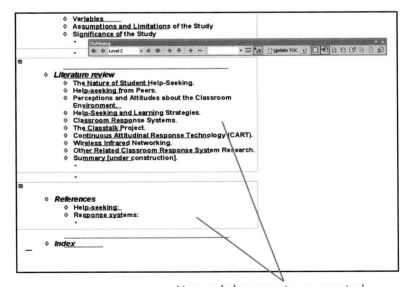

New subdocuments are created

5 Choose <u>F</u>ile, <u>S</u>ave from the menu.

The file is saved, but there is no indication that subdocuments were created.

Open the Windows Explorer or My Computer and look in the folder containing the WD1203-Help Seeking Behavior file.

Notice that there are now files called Literature review, References, and Statement of the Problem. These are the subdocuments for the WD1203-Help Seeking Behavior master document.

Subdocuments

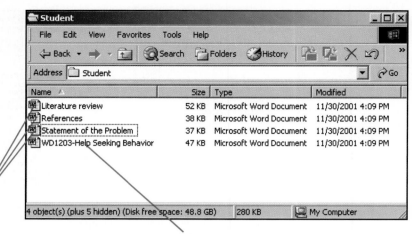

Master document

6 Move back to the WD1203-Help Seeking Behavior document in Word and close it. Leave Word open for the next task.

Task 6
USING A MASTER DOCUMENT

Why would I do this?
Once you have created a master document and made changes to the subdocuments, you need to make sure those changes are reflected in the master document, index, and table of contents, where appropriate.

In this task, you make changes to subdocuments and update the master document.

1 Click the **Open** button. Find and open the new **References** subdocument you created in Task 5. Place the insertion point after the **Help-seeking** heading and type **behavior among students**.

You have to scroll down, because a blank page has been added at the beginning of the document. This change should be reflected in the master document, and since it is a heading, you need to update the table of contents.

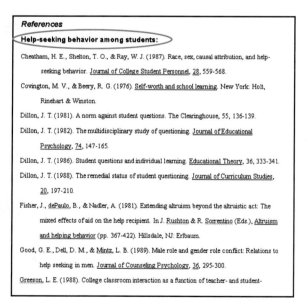

2 Click **Save** button and close the document. Open the WD1203-Help Seeking Behavior master document and scroll down to see the three subdocuments.

The details are no longer displayed. Instead, a hyperlink to the document is shown.

Click the **Expand Subdocuments** button. Scroll down so you can see the **References** subdocument.

Notice that the change you made to the heading is reflected in the master document.

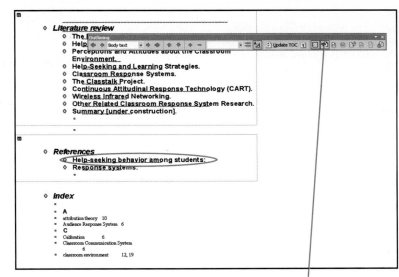

Expand Subdocuments button

QUICK TIP

If you do not want to expand the subdocuments, you can move to them quickly by either clicking the hyperlink, or holding down Ctrl and clicking on the hyperlink, depending on how your computer is set up.

3 Double-click the subdocument button in the upper-left corner of the **Literature review** box.

The Literature review subdocument opens to a blank first page, and the master document remains open.

Replace the first sentence with **Help-seeking research falls into two general categories.**

Literature review

Help-seeking research falls into two general categories. One type focuses on the costs of seeking help, and is usually not in an academic setting, but in the study of the reactions to such things as psychological or financial aid. This type of help-seeking is usually referred to as dependency motivated. The other area consists of a proactive and a mastery-oriented element. The proactive element, called executive help-seeking, involves enlisting the aid of others to find answers. This type of help-seeking is used frequently in business and industry. Instrumental help seeking, on the other hand, deals with the learning of a process. This is generally the type of help-seeking that occurs in a classroom (Karabenick & Knapp, 1991).

Several aspects of help-seeking behavior may have direct impact on the use of the various types of student response systems. These include that nature of help-seeking, the effect of help-seeking from peers, the effect of the perception of the help-seeking environment, and help-seeking learning strategies.

The Nature of Student Help-Seeking.
Help-seeking behavior varies widely between students. Even in the most open classroom environments, some students will remain passive and unresponsive, not asking questions or even

4 Choose <u>W</u>indow, <u>2</u> WD1203-Help Seeking **Behavior** from the menu, but do not close the **Literature review** subdocument. Click the **Print Preview** button and scroll down to the **Literature review** section.

Notice that the change has not been made.

Literature review

There are currently two distinct areas of research on help-seeking. One type focuses on the costs of seeking help, and is usually not in an academic setting, but in the study of the reactions to such things as psychological or financial aid. This type of help-seeking is usually referred to as dependency motivated. The other area consists of a proactive and a mastery-oriented element. The proactive element, called executive help-seeking, involves enlisting the aid of others to find answers. This type of help-seeking is used frequently in business and industry. Instrumental help seeking, on the other hand, deals with the learning of a process. This is generally the type of help-seeking that occurs in a classroom (Karabenick & Knapp, 1991).

Several aspects of help-seeking behavior may have direct impact on the use of the various types of student response systems. These include that nature of help-seeking, the effect of help-seeking from peers, the effect of the perception of the help-seeking environment, and help-seeking learning strategies.

The Nature of Student Help-Seeking.

Help-seeking behavior varies widely between students. Even in the most open classroom environments, some students will remain passive and unresponsive, not asking questions or even seeking explanations (Karabenick & Sharma, 1994b). This can be due to a variety of causes, including fear (of being wrong, of embarrassment), a lack of knowledge on the topic, a passive personality, or a general lack of interest (McKeachie, 1986). Students risk ridicule "...for seeking needed information or clarification in (public) classrooms and even in the privacy of faculty offices" (Karabenick, 1990, p. 190).

Dillon (1981) surveyed 166 university students to find out why students ask so few

5 Choose <u>Window</u>, <u>1</u> **Literature review** from the menu. Click the **Save** button and close the document.

Notice that the change now registers in the Print Preview window of the master document.

Literature review

Help-seeking research falls into two general categories. One type focuses on the costs of seeking help, and is usually not in an academic setting, but in the study of the reactions to such things as psychological or financial aid. This type of help-seeking is usually referred to as dependency motivated. The other area consists of a proactive and a mastery-oriented element. The proactive element, called executive help-seeking, involves enlisting the aid of others to find answers. This type of help-seeking is used frequently in business and industry. Instrumental help seeking, on the other hand, deals with the learning of a process. This is generally the type of help-seeking that occurs in a classroom (Karabenick & Knapp, 1991).

Several aspects of help-seeking behavior may have direct impact on the use of the various types of student response systems. These include that nature of help-seeking, the effect of help-seeking from peers, the effect of the perception of the help-seeking environment, and help-seeking learning strategies.

The Nature of Student Help-Seeking.

Help-seeking behavior varies widely between students. Even in the most open classroom environments, some students will remain passive and unresponsive, not asking questions or even seeking explanations (Karabenick & Sharma, 1994b). This can be due to a variety of causes, including fear (of being wrong, of embarrassment), a lack of knowledge on the topic, a passive personality, or a general lack of interest (McKeachie, 1986). Students risk ridicule "...for seeking needed information or clarification in (public) classrooms and even in the privacy of faculty offices" (Karabenick, 1990, p. 190).

Dillon (1981) surveyed 166 university students to find out why students ask so few

6 Click the <u>Close</u> button on the toolbar. Click the **Print Layout View** button and scroll up so you can see the table of contents.

Notice that the table of contents has been corrupted.

The table of contents is corrupted

CAUTION

In some cases, your screen will not look like the figure. Because of varying Word settings, the corrupted table of contents may not occur on your computer. If page numbers are still displayed on your computer, continue with the following steps to see if the page numbers remain the same.

7 Right-click on the table of contents and select **Update Field** from the shortcut menu. Choose **Update entire table** from the Update Table of Contents dialog box. Click **OK**.

The page references are updated. Notice that the wording of the subheading that you changed in the References section is also been updated.

8 Type your name and organization where indicated on the first page. Print the first two pages of the document. Close the document and save your changes.

Task 7

CREATING A CUSTOM FORM

Why would I do this?

There are form programs that you can use to set up complex surveys online, but they require special server software and some programming. If you just need a form to be filled out and returned by a few people, you can easily create a form using Word that does not require additional setup. You create a form by making a template first. You can either start with a blank template and type the form from scratch, or you can take an existing document and save it as a template. You can use any of the Word features in a form, including the drawing tools, graphics, and tables. When you finish the form, you can post it on a Web page or in a shared folder, or you can send it to the recipients as an e-mail attachment.

In this task, you create a form template from a document and then create a form document from that template.

❶ Click the **Open** button. Find and open **WD1204**. Choose **F**ile, **S**ave **A**s from the menu. If necessary, click the **Show/Hide** button to turn this feature off.

The Save As dialog box is displayed.

Click the arrow in the **Save as type** box and choose **Document Template**. Type **WD1204-Form** in the **File name** box and click the **S**ave button.

The document is saved as a template. You add three different form fields to the template —a text field, a check box, and a drop-down box.

A text field goes here
A check box goes here

⚠ **CAUTION**

If you are working in a lab and cannot save files to the Template folder, you can save it to the new folder you created earlier in this lesson or to the My Documents folder. Check with your instructor about possible file locations.

❷ Place the insertion point after the **Name:** line near the bottom of the document. Choose **V**iew, **T**oolbars, **Forms** from the menu.

The Forms toolbar is displayed.

Click the **Text Form Field** button on the Forms toolbar.

A text box is placed at the insertion point.

DATE: November 24, 2002

TO: All members of the research team
FROM: <your name>, Project Manager

RE: Where do we go from here?

We are about at the midpoint of the development of the proposal for the university. The Research Department has done a good job getting a paper together to present to the university administrators as ammunition for whatever we end up deciding to propose. Engineering has done a good job of getting test units of the student response systems (SRS) from the three major manufacturers, and nearly everyone on all of the teams has had a chance to sit through one of the demonstrations.

What I'd like at this point is a quick survey of what you think about a couple of issues that we are dealing with. This will give me a quick feel for our final position so that when I meet with the Provost on Friday I'll be able to steer the conversation in the right direction.

Please take a minute to answer the questions below. Save your responses and send this document back to me as an email attachment.

Name:

Check here if you think SRS should be included in the proposal.

If you checked the above, which system did you like best?

A drop-down box goes here

Text Form Field button

DATE: November 24, 2002

TO: All members of the research team
FROM: <your name>, Project Manager

RE: Where do we go from here?

We are about at the midpoint of the development of the proposal for the university. The Research Department has done a good job getting a paper together to present to the university administrators as ammunition for whatever we end up deciding to propose. Engineering has done a good job of getting test units of the student response systems (SRS) from the three major manufacturers, and nearly everyone on all of the teams has had a chance to sit through one of the demonstrations.

What I'd like at this point is a quick survey of what you think about a couple of issues that we are dealing with. This will give me a quick feel for our final position so that when I meet with the Provost on Friday I'll be able to steer the conversation in the right direction.

Please take a minute to answer the questions below. Save your responses and send this document back to me as an email attachment.

Text box

Name:

Check here if you think SRS should be included in the proposal.

If you checked the above, which system did you like best?

3 Place the insertion point to the left of the next line of text following the text box you just inserted. Click the **Check Box Form Field** button, and then press [Spacebar].

A check box is placed on the left edge of the sentence followed by a space.

Check Box Form Field button

Check box

DATE: November 24, 2002

TO: All members of the research team
FROM: <your name>, Project Manager

RE: Where do we go from here?

We are about at the midpoint of the development of the proposal for the university. The Research Department has done a good job getting a paper together to present to the university administrators as ammunition for whatever we end up deciding to propose. Engineering has done a good job of getting test units of the student response systems (SRS) from the three major manufacturers, and nearly everyone on all of the teams has had a chance to sit through one of the demonstrations.

What I'd like at this point is a quick survey of what you think about a couple of issues that we are dealing with. This will give me a quick feel for our final position so that when I meet with the Provost on Friday I'll be able to steer the conversation in the right direction.

Please take a minute to answer the questions below. Save your responses and send this document back to me as an email attachment.

Name:

☐ Check here if you think SRS should be included in the proposal.

If you checked the above, which system did you like best?

4 Place the insertion point to the right of the line of text following the check box. Click the **Drop-Down Form Field** button, and then press [Spacebar].

A drop-down box and a space are inserted, although there are no options in it yet. You add options in the next task.

Drop-Down Form Field button

Drop-down box

DATE: November 24, 2002

TO: All members of the research team
FROM: <your name>, Project Manager

RE: Where do we go from here?

We are about at the midpoint of the development of the proposal for the university. The Research Department has done a good job getting a paper together to present to the university administrators as ammunition for whatever we end up deciding to propose. Engineering has done a good job of getting test units of the student response systems (SRS) from the three major manufacturers, and nearly everyone on all of the teams has had a chance to sit through one of the demonstrations.

What I'd like at this point is a quick survey of what you think about a couple of issues that we are dealing with. This will give me a quick feel for our final position so that when I meet with the Provost on Friday I'll be able to steer the conversation in the right direction.

Please take a minute to answer the questions below. Save your responses and send this document back to me as an email attachment.

Name:

☐ Check here if you think SRS should be included in the proposal.

If you checked the above, which system did you like best?

5 Click the **Protect Form** button on the Forms toolbar.

This enables you to see how the form will work when it is used as a document.

Press [Tab⇄] two or three times and watch the insertion point jump from field to field. Click once in the check box.

The check box is selected.

Protect Form button

IN DEPTH

The Protect Form button acts as a toggle switch between the two form modes. When it is selected, you can use the form the way the end user will see it, but you cannot do any editing. When you turn the button off, you can edit the form, but the fields will not work the way they will as a form. You move back and forth between these two views often if you set up complex forms.

DATE: November 24, 2002

TO: All members of the research team
FROM: <your name>, Project Manager

RE: Where do we go from here?

We are about at the midpoint of the development of the proposal for the university. The Research Department has done a good job getting a paper together to present to the university administrators as ammunition for whatever we end up deciding to propose. Engineering has done a good job of getting test units of the student response systems (SRS) from the three major manufacturers, and nearly everyone on all of the teams has had a chance to sit through one of the demonstrations.

What I'd like at this point is a quick survey of what you think about a couple of issues that we are dealing with. This will give me a quick feel for our final position so that when I meet with the Provost on Friday I'll be able to steer the conversation in the right direction.

Please take a minute to answer the questions below. Save your responses and send this document back to me as an email attachment.

Name:

☒ Check here if you think SRS should be included in the proposal.

If you checked the above, which system did you like best?

6 Click the check box once more. Click the **Protect Form** button on the Forms toolbar.

The check box is deselected and the form protection is turned off.

Type your name at the top and bottom of the document where indicated. Click the **Save** button to save the document. Leave it open for the next task.

Task 8
MODIFYING AND PROTECTING A FORM

Why would I do this?
Form fields, when they are first inserted, are seldom exactly the way you want them. For example, fields are shaded by default, text boxes allow unlimited-length responses, and drop-down boxes contain no options. You need to modify one or more of these field *properties* before you create the final form document.

Once the form is complete, you close the template and create a document based on the template. You can then lock the form using the Protect Form button on the Forms toolbar. Any user who knows anything about Word, however, can turn on the toolbar and turn off the form protection. If you want to make sure no one alters the form, the field properties, or the drop-down box options, you need to password-protect the form.

In this task, you modify the form fields, create a new form based on the template, and protect the form with a password.

1 With the **WD1204-Form** document still open, double-click the check box you created in Task 7.

The Check Box Form Field Options dialog box is displayed.

Choose **Checked** from the **Default value** area.

This places an X in the check box as the default value, and the option for the user is to deselect the box.

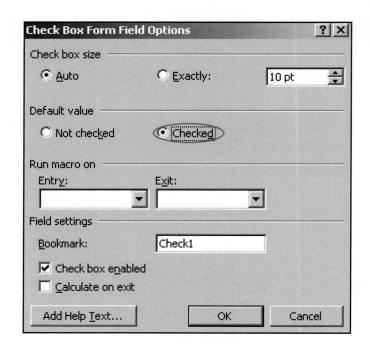

 QUICK TIP

To open the Options dialog box for any field type, you can also right-click the check box and select Properties from the shortcut menu.

2 Click **OK**.

The Drop-Down Form Field Options dialog box is displayed.

Type **SRS Engineered Systems** in the **Drop-down item** box and click the **Add** button.

*The new option is added to the **Items in drop-down** list box.*

Type drop-down list entries here

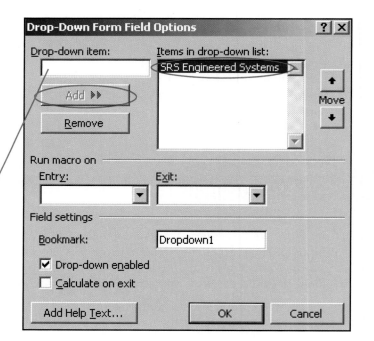

3 Use the same procedure to add **Classroom Response, Inc.** and **Responses Unlimited** to the **Items in drop-down list** box.

These are the three options, but they should be displayed in alphabetical order.

Select the **SRS Engineered Systems** option and click the **Move** down arrow twice.

The options are now in order.

Options are in alphabetical order

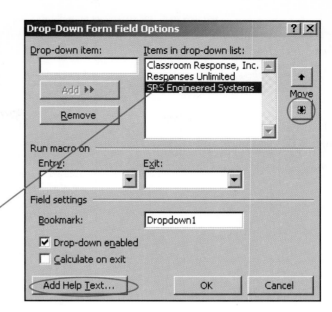

4 Click the Add Help Text button. Make sure the **Status Bar** tab is selected.

The Form Field Help Text dialog box is displayed.

Type **Click the arrow in the box and make your choice from the list**.

Whatever you type here appears in the Status bar.

Type your help message here

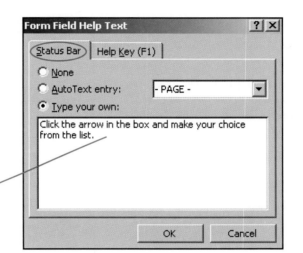

5 Click **OK** on both dialog boxes to close them. Click the **Form Field Shading** button.

The first response is shown in the drop-down box, and the shading is turned off for all fields.

Form Field Shading button
Shading has been turned off

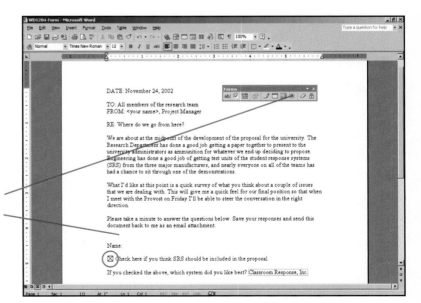

6 Click the **Protect Form** button, click the **Save** button, and close the template.

The template is now ready to be used as the basis for a form document.

Choose **File**, **New** from the menu. Choose **General Templates** from the New Document pane, select **WD1204-Form**, and click **OK**.

The form opens ready to accept data in the first (text) field.

The form is ready to accept data here

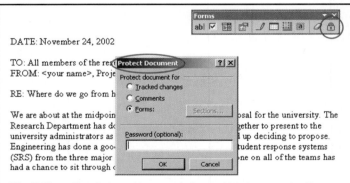

7 Click the **Protect Form** button on the Forms toolbar.

You can still make changes to the form. The only change you want to make is to protect the form so that only those with the password can open it. The form has to be unprotected to do that.

Choose **Tools**, **Protect Document** from the menu.

The Protect Document dialog box is displayed, and the Forms option is selected by default.

8 Type **learn** in the <u>P</u>assword (optional) box. Click **OK**.

The Confirm Password dialog box is displayed.

Type **learn** again.

This makes certain you have typed your password correctly.

Type your password here

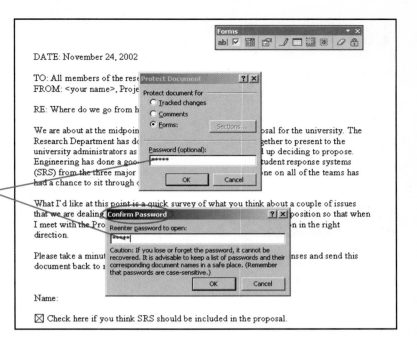

9 Click **OK**. Click the Save button and save the document as **WD1204-Form**.

Both dialog boxes are closed. Notice that the Protect Form button on the Forms toolbar is now selected.

Close the Forms toolbar. Type **William McMahon** in the text box. Press Tab⇆ twice, and click the arrow in the drop-down box.

The default is accepted in the check box, and the list of options in the drop-down box is displayed.

IN DEPTH

Do not worry about saving the file with the same name as the template you saved. The template is saved with a .dot extension, and the document is saved with a .doc extension.

DATE: November 24, 2002

TO: All members of the research team
FROM: <your name>, Project Manager

RE: Where do we go from here?

We are about at the midpoint of the development of the proposal for the university. The Research Department has done a good job getting a paper together to present to the university administrators as ammunition for whatever we end up deciding to propose. Engineering has done a good job of getting test units of the student response systems (SRS) from the three major manufacturers, and nearly everyone on all of the teams has had a chance to sit through one of the demonstrations.

What I'd like at this point is a quick survey of what you think about a couple of issues that we are dealing with. This will give me a quick feel for our final position so that when I meet with the Provost on Friday I'll be able to steer the conversation in the right direction.

Please take a minute to answer the questions below. Save your responses and send this document back to me as an email attachment.

Name William McMahon

☒ Check here if you think SRS should be included in the proposal.

If you checked the above, which system did you like best? Classroom Response, Inc.

> Classroom Response, Inc.
> Responses Unlimited
> SRS Engineered Systems

Thanks for your input!

Drop-down list

10 Select **SRS Engineered Systems** from the list. Choose <u>F</u>ile, Save <u>A</u>s from the menu. Name the file **WD1204-Form Filled In**. Click <u>S</u>ave. Print the form and close the document.

IN DEPTH

You can distribute this form using several methods, but the easiest is to send the document as an attachment, have the recipient fill it out, and then send it back as an e-mail attachment. You can also put the form on a shared folder on the intranet, but you have to make sure everyone saves the document under a different name. Otherwise, each person who uploads the document will write over the previous document.

The exercises that follow are designed for you to review and use what you have learned in this lesson. You also have the opportunity to practice your skills and then expand on them by applying them to new situations.

COMPREHENSION

Comprehension exercises are designed to check your memory and understanding of the basic concepts in this lesson. You distinguish between true and false statements, identify new screen elements, and match terms with related statements. If you are uncertain of the correct answer, refer to the task number following each item (for example, T4 refers to Task 4) and review that task until you are confident that you can provide a correct response.

TRUE-FALSE

Circle either T or F.

T   F   1. A bookmark enables you to move quickly to a marked spot in a document. (T1)

T   F   2. A table of contents is updated automatically every time you make a change. (T3)

T   F   3. Once you create an index entry, you cannot modify it. (T4)

T   F   4. When you make a change to a subdocument, you need to click the **Update** button to make the changes in the master document. (T6)

T   F   5. The first step in creating a form is to create a form template. (T7)

T   F   6. Clicking the Protect Form button eliminates the possibility that anyone else can modify the form. (T8)

MATCHING QUESTIONS

A. Subdocument   **D.** Drop-down box

B. Document map   **E.** Property

C. Footnote   **F.** Endnote

Match the following statements to the word or phrase that is the best match from the list. Write the letter of the matching word or phrase in the space provided next to the number.

1. _____ A characteristic of a form field (T8)

2. _____ Gives the user choices in a form field (T7)

3. _____ Changes to this are reflected in the master document (T5)

4. _____ Reference at the end of a section or document (Intro)

5. _____ Outline navigation tool (T1)

6. _____ Reference shown at the bottom of a page (T2)

IDENTIFYING PARTS OF THE WORD SCREEN

Refer to the figure and identify the numbered parts of the screen. Write the letter of the correct label in the space next to the number.

1. _____

2. _____

3. _____

4. _____

5. _____

6. _____

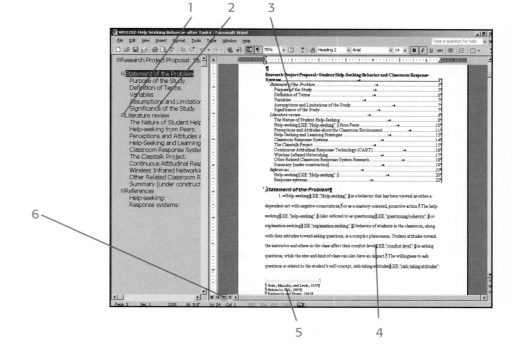

A. Collapse button (T1)

B. Footnotes (T2)

C. Table of contents (T3)

D. Index entry (T4)

E. Outline View button (T5)

F. Document map (T1)

Reinforcement exercises are designed to reinforce the skills you have learned by applying them to a new situation. Detailed instructions are provided along with a figure, where appropriate, to illustrate the result. Complete the reinforcement exercises sequentially. Leave the workbook open at the end of each exercise for use in the next exercise until you are specifically directed to close it.

In these exercises, you work with a detailed statistical analysis of census data from the 1880 Alcona County, Michigan federal census. This document is meant to be used as an introduction to a census transcription.

R1—Using Bookmarks and the Document Map to Navigate a Document

1. Start Word, if necessary. Open the document **WD1205** and save it as **WD1205-1880 Census**. Turn off the Task Pane and click the **Print Layout View** button, if necessary.

2. Choose **I**nsert, **Bookmark** from the menu and type **Profile** in the **Bookmark name** box. Click the **Add** button to add the bookmark.

3. Move to the top of page 2 and place the insertion point to the left of the **About the Census** title.

4. Choose **I**nsert, **Bookmark** from the menu, type **Census_Info** in the **Bookmark name** box, then click the **Add** button. Make sure you use an under-score instead of a space.

5. Move to the top of page 4 and place the insertion point to the left of the **About the People** title. Add a bookmark called **People**.

6. Move to the top of page 19 and place the insertion point to the left of the **About the Community** title. Add a bookmark called **Community**.

7. Choose **E**dit, **G**o To from the menu. Click the **Bookmark** option in the **Go to what** section. Click the arrow in the **Enter bookmark name** box. Select **Community** and click the **Go T**o button. Test this option on each of the bookmarks to make sure they all work.

8. Click the **Document Map** button. Click Agriculture near the bottom of the outline. Try a few of the other headings.

9. Click the **Collapse** button next to the three second-level headings. Click the **Expand** button next to the **About the Census** heading.

10. Click the **Document Map** button to close the document map. Click the **Save** button to save your work. Leave the document open for the next exercise.

R2—Creating and Formatting Endnotes

1. With the **WD1205-1880 Census** document still open, scroll to the top of page 2 and place the insertion point at the end of the first paragraph.

2. Select **I**nsert, **Refere**nce, **Foot**note from the menu. Click the **Endnotes** option in the Location area. Make sure **End of document** is selected. You will add informational footnotes to the end of this document.

3. In the **Number format** box, select A, B, C from the list. Click the **I**nsert button.

4. Type the following endnote: **Although the fire destroyed most of the records, the aggregate statistics and the Union Civil War veterans schedule still exist.**

5. Move to the middle of page 2. Place the insertion point after **Greenbush Township** in the bulleted list. Select **I**nsert, **Refere**nce, **Foot**note from the menu. Click the **I**nsert button.

6. Type the following endnote: **Greenbush Township was called Yewell Place in the 1860 census.**

7. Move back to page 2 and place the insertion point after the **Alcona Township** entry in the bulleted list. Select **I**nsert, **Refere**nce, **Foot**note from the menu. Click the **I**nsert button.

8. Type the following endnote: **The Sturgeon Point lighthouse and Life-Saving Service were also included in Alcona Township.**

9. Click the **Save** button. Leave the document open for the next exercise.

Manufacturing

There were four manufacturing facilities reported in the county in 1870, and that number had only increased to six by 1880 (see Table 27). There is a great deal more information on Alcona County manufacturing and manufacturing production in the Production of Industry schedule, which begins on page 201. The schedule provides business and production statistics for each of the six manufacturing establishments in the county.

Table 27: 1880 Alcona County manufacturing establishments.

	Total
Number of establishments	6
Capital	$146,000
Average number of hands employed—Males above 16	97
Average number of hands employed—Females above 15	0
Average number of hands employed—Children and youth	5
Total amount paid in wages during the year	$31,325
Materials	$3,492,604
Products	$4,489,555

A Although the fire destroyed most of the records, the aggregate statistics and the Union Civil War veterans schedule still exist.
B The Sturgeon Point lighthouse and Life-Saving Service were also included in Alcona Township.
C Greenbush Township was called Yewell Place in the 1870 census.

R3–Adding a Table of Contents

1. With the **WD1205-1880 Census** document still open, scroll to the top of the document. Place the insertion point in the first blank line after the third full paragraph (ending **released in 1992.**). Press ↵Enter to create blank line.

2. Choose **I**nsert, **Referen**c**e**, In**d**ex and Tables from the menu. Click the **Table of **C**ontents** tab in the Index and Tables dialog box.

3. Click the arrow in the **Forma**t**s** box and select **Distinctive**. Click the **Show O**u**tlining Toolbar** button in the Index and Tables dialog box and click **OK**.

4. Choose **I**nsert, **Referen**c**e**, In**d**ex and Tables from the menu. Notice that the **M**odify button is not active; that feature is only available if you use the **From template** format. Click the **Cancel** button to close the dialog box.

5. Click the **Save** button. Leave the document open for the next exercise.

```
Alcona County, Michigan
1880 Statistical Profile

Introduction

    A United States Federal census has been taken every ten years since 1790, and Michigan has been involved
in all but the first, being under British rule in 1790. The 1850 census was the first to include the names of all
people in every household. The earlier census returns listed the names of only the heads of households and
number of males and females in various age brackets.
    The current geographic boundaries of Alcona County, then called Negwegon, were created on April 1,
1840. Three years later the name was changed to Alcona. In 1850, Alcona was not a yet a full-fledged county,
but still part of a vast section of the state referred to as Michilimackinac, and the few people living within the
boundaries of the county were not enumerated separately. The 1860 census was the first Federal census to
directly cover the area currently known as Alcona County. The county was not self-governing until 1869.
    A Federal law requires that 72 years pass before the actual census results are released to the public,
although summary data is made available almost immediately. At the time of publication, the 1920 census is
the most recent complete census available, having been released in 1992.


Alcona County, Michigan _____ 5
1880 Statistical Profile _____ 5
Introduction _____ 5
About the Census _____ 6
    Total Population _____ 6
    Census Dates _____ 6
About the People _____ 7
    Place of Origin _____ 7
    Age Distribution _____ 7
    Literacy _____ 7
    Marital Status _____ 7
    School Attendance _____ 7
    Occupations _____ 7
    Given Names _____ 7
    Surnames _____ 7
About the Community _____ 7
    Valuation of Real and Personal Estates _____ 7
    State, County, and Local Taxation _____ 7
    Public Debt _____ 7
    Agriculture _____ 7
    Manufacturing _____ 7
```

R4–Creating an Index

1. With the **WD1205-1880 Census** document still open, scroll to the top of the document. You will add index entries to this document. None have been marked, so you will be create the start of an index. Because of this, the index itself will be very short.

2. Click the **Show/Hide ¶** button. Highlight **Negwegon** in the first line of the second paragraph. Hold down Alt + ⬆Shift and press **X**. Click the **M**ark button and close the dialog box.

3. Highlight **Alcona County** earlier in the same line. Hold down Alt + ⬆Shift and press **X**. Click the **Mark All** button.

4. Scroll to the second page. Highlight **Alcona Township** in the bulleted list. Hold down Alt + ⬆Shift and press **X**. Click the **Mark **A**ll** button. Repeat the procedure for **Harrisville Township** and **Greenbush Township**.

5. Use the same procedure to mark all the entries for the three villages mentioned in the same bulleted list.

6. Scroll to the bottom of the document. Place the insertion point above the endnote line. Choose **I**nsert, **B**reak, **N**ext page to create a new section in the document. You have to do this if you want the endnotes to appear before the index.

7. Select **I**nsert, **Referen**c**e**, **Foot**n**ote** from the menu. Choose **End of section** from the **E**ndnotes box. Click the **A**pply button. The endnotes move up, and the insertion point is at the top of the next page.

8. Click the **Show/Hide ¶** button. Choose **I**nsert, **Referen**c**e**, In**d**ex and Tables from the menu. Click the **Inde**x tab in the Index and Tables dialog box.

9. Accept the default settings and click **OK**. Move back to the first page of the document. Type your name in parentheses after the **1880 Statistical Profile** heading.

10. Click the **Save** button. Print the first two pages of the document, and then scroll down and print the page with the endnotes and the index. Close the document, but leave Word open for the next exercise.

```
Alcona County 1, 2, 4, 5, 6, 7, 8, 9, 10, 11, 12,    Greenbush Township.................2, 3, 17, 22
    15, 16, 17, 19, 20, 21, 22                        Harrisville Township.................2, 3, 4, 17
Alcona Township ................2, 3, 4, 17, 22        Harrisville Village ...................2, 3, 10, 17
Alcona Village ...........................2, 3, 10, 17  Negwegon ...................................................1
Black River Village ..................2, 3, 10, 17
```

R5–Creating a Master Document and Subdocuments

1. Open the document **WD1206** and save it as **WD1206-1880 Census**. Click the **Outline View** button.

2. Click the arrow in the **Show Level** box on the Outlining toolbar and select **Show Level 2**. There are no Level 3 headings in this document.

3. Click the plus mark to the left of the **About the People** title. Click the **Create Subdocument** button on the Outlining toolbar.

4. Use the same procedure to create a subdocument of the **About the Community** heading. These are the two sections others will work on.

5. Click the Save button. Close the **WD1206-1880 Census** document. Open the **About the People** subdocument.

6. Scroll down and change the first heading from **About the People** to About the People of Alcona County. Save the document and close it.

7. Open the **About the Community** subdocument. Scroll down and change the first heading from **About the Community** to About the Alcona County Community. Save the document and close it.

8. Open the **WD1206-1880 Census** document. Click the Expand Subdocuments button on the Outlining toolbar.

9. Choose **Show Level 2** from the **Show Level** box on the Outlining toolbar. Notice that the main document reflects the changes you made in the subdocuments.

10. Click the Print Layout View button. Scroll down so you can see the table of contents. Notice that the changes are not reflected here.

11. Right-click the table of contents. Choose Update Field from the shortcut menu. Choose the **Update entire table** option and click OK. The changes are now displayed.

12. Click the Save button. Print the first page. Close the document, but leave Word open for the next exercise.

Alcona County, Michigan
1880 Statistical Profile (<your name>)

Introduction

    A United States Federal census has been taken every ten years since 1790, and Michigan has been involved in all but the first, being under British rule in 1790. The 1850 census was the first to include the names of all people in every household. The earlier census returns listed the names of only the heads of households and number of males and females in various age brackets.

    The current geographic boundaries of Alcona County, then called Negwegon, were created on April 1, 1840. Three years later the name was changed to Alcona. In 1850, Alcona was not a yet a full-fledged county, but still part of a vast section of the state referred to as Michilimackinac, and the few people living within the boundaries of the county were not enumerated separately. The 1860 census was the first Federal census to directly cover the area currently known as Alcona County. The county was not self-governing until 1869.

    A Federal law requires that 72 years pass before the actual census results are released to the public, although summary data is made available almost immediately. At the time of publication, the 1920 census is the most recent complete census available, having been released in 1992.

R6—Creating a Custom Form

1. Open the document **WD1207**. Choose File, Save As from the menu. Select **Document Template** from the **Save as type box**, and then save the template as WD1207-Transcription Errors. Click the Print Layout View button, if necessary.

2. Place the insertion point to the left of the **I found no errors** line in the box. Choose View, Toolbars, Forms from the menu. Click the Check Box Form Field button, and then press Spacebar.

3. Place the insertion point to the right of the **I am working on** line (after the space at the end of the line). Click the Drop-Down Form Field button.

4. Place the insertion point to the right of the **The error is on page:** line, but before the word **Line:**, and then click the Text Form Field button. Place another text form field at the end of the same line (after the word **Line:**).

5. Place the insertion point to the right of the **Here is the problem:** line (after the space at the end of the line). Click the Text Form Field button.

6. Click the Protect Form button and press Tab several times to see how the form works. Click the Protect Form button again so you can edit the form.

7. Double-click the combo box field. Type Alcona Township in the Drop-down item box and click the Add button. Use the same procedure to add Greenbush Township and Harrisville Township, and then click OK.

8. Double-click on the **Line** field. In the **Type** box, select **Number**. In the **Maximum length** box, select **2**. This restricts the entry to a double-digit number. Click OK.

9. Type your name where indicated at the top of the document. Click the Protect Form button, click the Save button, and close the template. Choose File, New from the menu. Choose **General Templates** from the New Document pane, select **WD1207-Transcription Errors**, and click OK.

10. Select Harrisville Township from the combo box. Place the error on page **3A**, line **42**. As the problem, type: Change the occupation from "surtman" to "surfman"

11. Click the **Save** button. Save the document as
WD1207-Transcription Errors. Print the document and close Word.

TO: 1880 Alcona County census transcription proofreaders

FROM: <your name>

RE: Final corrections

Hi everyone!

  Here we are in the homestretch! We've done all of the transcribing and proofing. Now we're doing one last check before we send this book to the printers. There should be VERY FEW errors to be found now. In fact, you may find that there are no changes at all on your page. Please check your page, fill out this form, and send it back to me by next Friday. I'll compile everything over the weekend, and we should be read to go to press on Monday.

  It's hard to believe ten years of work will finally be finished. Once again, congratulations and thanks to everyone who has worked on this project. We're planning a big celebration for sometime next month!

Please answer the following:

☐ I found no errors [you can skip the other questions]

I am working on the following township: Harrisville Township

The error is on page: 3A   Line: 42

Here is the problem: Change the occupation from "surtman" to "surfman"

CHALLENGE

Challenge exercises are designed to test your ability to apply your skills to new situations with less detailed instruction. These exercises also challenge you to expand your repertoire of skills by using commands that are similar to those you have already learned. The desired outcome is clearly defined, but you have more freedom to choose the steps needed to achieve the required result.

The following exercises use different files to illustrate advanced report and form features that you should find helpful.

C1—Adding a Table of Figures

In this lesson, you learned how to create a table of contents and an index. You can use a similar procedure to create a table of figures and a table of tables. You need to mark tables and figures before they can be compiled and presented by Word. With a table of contents, you mark the appropriate headings using the Heading styles. With the index, you use a key combination to mark individual words or phrases for inclusion. With tables and figures, you need to add captions that can be compiled.

For this exercise, you use a much-abbreviated version of the Alcona County census file that you used earlier in this lesson.

Goal: To create a table of figures and a table of tables in a document.

1. Locate and open the **WD1208** document. Save it as **WD1208-Tables**.

2. Move to the last table in the document. Select the table. Choose **Insert**, **Reference**, **Caption** from the menu.

3. In the Caption box, type **Table 10: Manufacturing establishments**. The other nine tables and the lone figure have already had captions added.

4. Accept the other defaults, but take a look at the options available in the **Label** box and the **Position** box. When you are through, click **OK**.

5. Scroll to the top of the document. Place the insertion point in the blank line between the Tables and Figures headings. Choose **Insert**, **Reference**, **Index and Tables** from the menu. Click the Table of Figures tab, choose the **Formal** format, and click **OK**.

6. Place the insertion point in the blank line under the Figures heading. Choose **Insert**, **Reference**, **Index and Tables** from the menu, but this time select Figure from the **Caption label** box. Choose the **Formal** format and click **OK**.

7. Type your name where indicated in the heading at the top of the first page. Save your work, print the first page of the document, and close Word.

Alcona County, Michigan
1880 Statistical Profile (<your name>)

Introduction

A United States Federal census has been taken every ten years since 1790, and Michigan has been involved in all but the first, being under British rule in 1790. The 1850 census was the first to include the names of all people in every household. The earlier census returns listed the names of only the heads of households and number of males and females in various age brackets.

The current geographic boundaries of Alcona County, then called Negwegon, were created on April 1, 1840. Three years later the name was changed to Alcona. In 1850, Alcona was not a yet a full-fledged county, but still part of a vast section of the state referred to as Michilimackinac, and the few people living within the boundaries of the county were not enumerated separately. The 1860 census was the first Federal census to directly cover the area currently known as Alcona County. The county was not self-governing until 1869.

A Federal law requires that 72 years pass before the actual census results are released to the public, although summary data is made available almost immediately. At the time of publication, the 1920 census is the most recent complete census available, having been released in 1992.

Tables

Figures

C2—Inserting Cross-References

When you work on a long document, there are times you might want to let the reader move quickly to other locations in the document, such as tables, figures, maps, or document sections. Cross references send you quickly to the appropriate spot. They work like hyperlinks, but are continuously updated as you edit the document. This is because cross references are linked to document elements such as bookmarks, figure or table captions, or footnotes/endnotes. You insert cross references into the document the same way you do index entries—as fields with brackets, but instead of {XE} you see {REF} when you use the reveal codes options.

For this exercise, you use a short, severe weather document. The document contains no captions or bookmarks, so you need to add those before you can create the cross-references.

Goal: To add cross-references to bookmarks and captions.

1. Locate and open the **WD1209** document. Save it as **WD1209-Cross References**.

2. Add a bookmark to the **Tornadoes** heading on the first page, and call it **Tornadoes**. Add a bookmark to the **Lightning** heading on the second page, and call it **Lightning**. (Note: Make sure you don't include the paragraph mark when you highlight the words! If you do, the cross reference to that bookmark will add an extra paragraph mark.)

3. Add a caption to the tornado table on the first page. Call it **Table 1: Michigan tornado casualties**. If you did not do the first Challenge exercise, look at steps 2-4 to see how it is done.

4. Add a caption to the lightning chart on the third page. Call it **Figure 1: National lightning casualties**.

5. Move to the first paragraph. Place the insertion point to the right of the space after (**see** in the third sentence. Choose <u>I</u>nsert, Refere<u>n</u>ce, Cross-<u>r</u>eference from the menu. Choose **Figure** from the **Reference <u>t</u>ype** box. Choose **Only label and number** from the **Insert <u>r</u>eference to** box. Make sure the **Insert as <u>h</u>yperlink** check box is selected, and only the figure in the document is highlighted. Click the <u>I</u>nsert button and close the dialog box.

6. Go to the first paragraph of the **Lightning** section. Type **(see)** after the word tornadoes in the first sentence. Add a cross reference to the table on the first page the same way you added the lightning reference.

7. Add a cross reference to the **Tornadoes** and **Lightning** bookmarks from the words **tornadoes** and **lightning** in the second sentence of the introductory paragraph. You need to reformat the text. (Hint: You can reformat the bold text in the normal way, but you need to right-click on each word, edit the field, and choose lowercase from the dialog box.)

8. To test your cross references, move the pointer to the phrases you highlighted, hold down Ctrl and click. (Note: Your machine may be set up to click the hyperlinks directly.)

9. Save your work. Type your name at the top of the document where indicated. Turn in the WD1209-Cross References file as directed.

Severe Weather in Michigan

Compiled by: <your name>

Michigan is on the receiving end of several types of severe weather, according to statistics compiled by the National Oceanic[lightning] [CTRL + click to follow link] [ministration (NOAA). These weather events include tornadoes, lightning, hail, and snow/ice storms. Surprisingly, Michigan ranks second in lightning casualties (see Figure 1). Hurricanes are never reported in the state. Flooding, when it occurs, tends to be minor; severe flooding is rare and often localized. Casualties as a result of flooding are extremely rare.

Tornadoes

The southern half of Michigan lies at the northeastern margin of "tornado alley," the nation's infamous tornado region which extends northward from Texas. For the four decades from the 1950s through the 1980s, 718 tornadoes were recorded for Michigan. In total, slightly more than one quarter of them killed 237 people, injured 3,157, and caused hundreds of millions of dollars

C3— Rearranging a Document

You might wonder why there is an outline view when the table of contents feature is so powerful. In this exercise, you try to use both the table of contents and the outline view to rearrange large sections of a document. By updating the table of contents, you can see which method worked. You are also be introduced to some of the problems you can create by using some of the advanced features.

The document you use in this exercise is the census introduction you used in the Reinforcement exercises. It has a table of contents and an index. The index starts page numbering at 1, which causes problems.

In this lesson, you find out which method(s) of rearranging sections of a document work.

Goal: To rearrange large sections of a complex document.

1. Locate and open the **WD1210** document and save it as **WD1210-Rearrange**. Type your name where indicated at the top of the document.

2. Click on the table of contents on the first page. Scroll down until you can see the whole table. Click to the left of the **About the Community** section and highlight the whole section. You can tell it is highlighted when it is black and the rest of the table is gray.

3. Click and drag the highlighted section up and drop it just before the **About the Census** section. Scroll down and see if the sections have moved. Scroll back to the top, right-click the table of contents, and update the entire table. Notice what happens to the section you moved. (Note: You can click the **Document Map** button and use the document map to check the new location of the sections.)

4. Switch to outline view and show three levels. Click the plus to the left of the About the Community section, drag it, and drop it above the About the People section.

5. Move back to Print Layout view and notice where the About the Community section is now located. Scroll to the top of the document, right-click the table of contents, and update the entire table. Notice that the page numbers are way off. This is because of the section that is numbered differently than the rest.

6. Scroll down to page 7. Notice that the footnotes are also in the wrong spot. Show the paragraph marks. Highlight the section break and delete it. Update the table of contents again.

7. Save your work, print the first page, and close the document.

Severe Weather in Michigan

Compiled by: <your name>

Michigan is on the receiving end of several types of severe weather, according to statistics compiled by the National Oceanic [Lightning] inistration (NOAA). These weather
[CTRL + click to follow link]
events include tornadoes, lightning, hail, and snow/ice storms. Surprisingly, Michigan ranks second in lightning casualties (see Figure 1). Hurricanes are never reported in the state. Flooding, when it occurs, tends to be minor; severe flooding is rare and often localized. Casualties as a result of flooding are extremely rare.

Tornadoes

The southern half of Michigan lies at the northeastern margin of "tornado alley," the nation's infamous tornado region which extends northward from Texas. For the four decades from the 1950s through the 1980s, 718 tornadoes were recorded for Michigan. In total, slightly more than one quarter of them killed 237 people, injured 3,157, and caused hundreds of millions of dollars

C4–Adding Help to a Form

When many people use Microsoft products and need help, they press F1. When you create forms, you can add help to a message box that is activated by using that key. In this exercise, you use a modified version of the transcription errors form that you worked with in the Reinforcement exercises.

Goal: To add a help message to a dialog box that is activated by pressing F1.

1. Locate and open the **WD1211** document. Save the file as **WD1211-Help**. Type your name where indicated.

2. See if you can figure out how to add help to F1. If not, use the Help menu.

3. Add the following message to the **I am working on the following township** combo box: **If you are working on a village, please indicate the township in which the village is located. The page and line numbers will give us the information we need to find the error.** (Note: If your text does not fit into the text field, you might want to take a closer look at where you are entering it.)

4. Add the following message to the **Here is the problem:** text box: **You can make your response as detailed as necessary. If you would like someone else to try and interpret difficult writing, please state that here!**

5. Test your help messages. Save the document. Turn in the file to your instructor, or attach it as an e-mail, as directed.

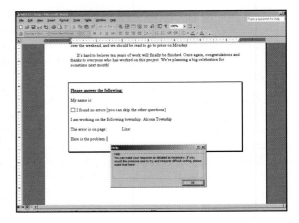

ON YOUR OWN

In this lesson, you created your own template as the basis for a form. If you need more complex forms, particularly of a business nature, Microsoft provides templates at its Web site.

To complete this exercise, you go to the Microsoft site and find a template that contains a form, find a way to edit the form in Word, and save the form for future use. The form should use form fields such as check boxes or text fields. If you cannot find one, use a standard form design and add a couple of form fields, one of which should be a text field for your name. (Hint: To get started, choose **File**, **New** from the menu and look in the New Document Task Pane.)

Criteria for grading will be:

1. Demonstration of ability to go to the Microsoft site and find a form template

2. Demonstration of the ability to save a document based on the template

To complete the project:

- Fill out the new form.

- Include your name somewhere near the top of the form.

- Print the form.

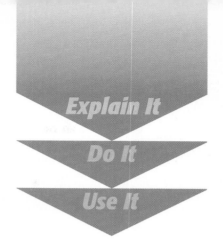

Lesson 13

Customizing Word

Task 1 Creating a Keyboard-Activated Macro

Task 2 Creating a Button-Activated Macro

Task 3 Editing Macros Using the Visual Basic Editor

Task 4 Creating a Custom Menu

Task 5 Adding Buttons to a Toolbar

Task 6 Moving Word Customizations to Another Computer

INTRODUCTION

Repetitive tasks are common in the workplace; tasks that you wish could be done more easily. The solution to that problem is to customize Word to fit your needs. You can customize the entire program, or you can create little programs that perform several functions with a single command.

One way to automate functions in Word is to use *macros*. Macros are predefined commands that you can invoke and apply to selected text, objects in your document, or even the entire document. By using macros you can automate a wide range of tasks. You run macros by using either a keystroke combination, or by clicking a button in a toolbar.

You can create macros without any knowledge of programming languages. Word has a built-in recorder that records each step that you perform. When you create a macro, you turn on the recorder, perform each step in the operation, and close the recorder. The steps are then assigned to either a keystroke combination of your choice, or placed in a button in a toolbar.

Macros are written in a language called *Visual Basic for Applications (VBA)*. VBA is a common programming language used in many Microsoft products. The *Visual Basic Editor (VBE)* enables you to make changes to your macros after they have been created. You can even use VBA to write macros from scratch, although it is almost always easier to record the macro and make minor changes later.

Word enables you to change the toolbars and menus. You can add or remove buttons from a toolbar, or create your own toolbar. You can create a custom menu option. Custom menus also provide a convenient, easy way to access to your macros.

Finally, Word gives you the option of saving all your Microsoft Office customizations and moving them to another computer. This enables you to transfer your templates, dictionaries, toolbars, menus, defaults, and other customizations quickly when you get a new computer or change your workstation.

Note: The topics covered in this lesson involve modifications to Microsoft Word. If you are using a computer in a computer lab, you need to check with your instructor before proceeding. Certain security programs used in labs will not allow you to make some of these changes. If you can make these changes in a lab setting, make sure you return the computers to their original settings. If you are using Windows 2000 or Windows XP operating systems, the changes are limited to the user profile you used when you logged onto the computer.

In this lesson, you create one macro that is activated by a keystroke combination and one that is activated by a toolbar button. You edit a macro using the Visual Basic Editor. You then put the macros you created into a new menu. Finally, you add buttons to a Word toolbar. You will work with several short stories that have been scanned into the computer. They have special formatting problems that need to be cleaned up, such as paragraph marks at the end of each line instead of at the end of each paragraph. The copyright on these stories has expired, so it is legal to make copies of them without obtaining the author's permission.

VISUAL SUMMARY

By the time you complete this lesson, you will have created a custom menu option and added a button to a toolbar. You will have also edited a macro in the Visual Basic editor:

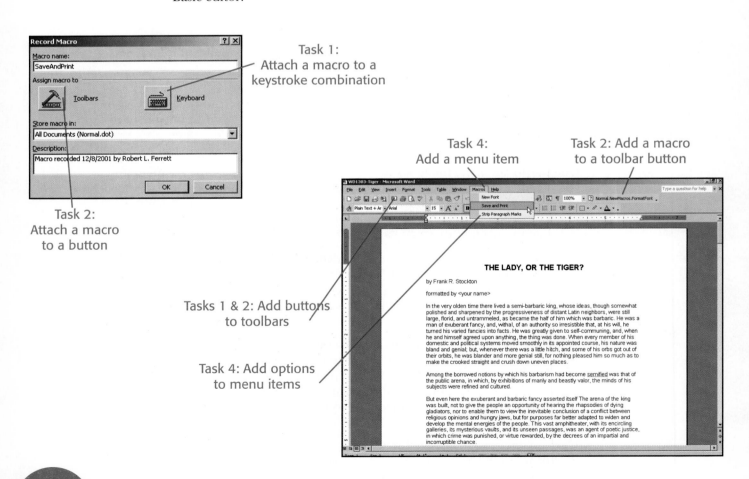

Task 1
CREATING A KEYBOARD-ACTIVATED MACRO

Why would I do this?

If you are going to use a few macros on a regular basis, it is usually a good idea to assign them to keystroke combinations. These are ordinarily quicker than clicking buttons with the mouse, since you don't have to take your hand off the keyboard.

In this task you create two macros. The first will select the whole document, change the font size, and change the font. The second will perform two tasks—saving the document, and then printing it. You will record the macros on one document, and then test them on another, similar document. (Note: In this lesson, all macros are attached to the Normal.dot template unless otherwise directed. This makes it convenient to clear the machine of macros when you are through.)

Type macro name here

1 Start Word and click the **Open** button. Change **Files of type** to **All Files**. Find and open **WD1301**. Choose **File, Save As** from the menu. Change **Save as type** to Word Document and save it as **WD1301-Inheritance**. Click the **Print Layout View** button.

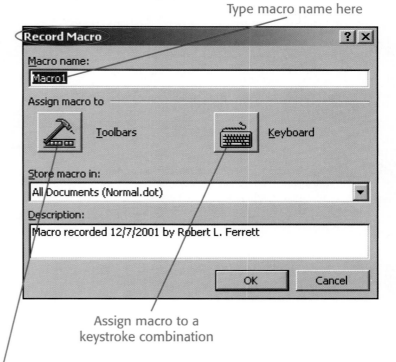

This document is a text file that has been scanned using software that changes paper text to a word processing file. It is a story by Ambrose Bierce (1842-1914) from the 1899 edition of a book called Fantastic Fables. *It is saved in text format, which means it has very little formatting other than paragraph marks. Many documents that are downloaded from the Internet or taken from email messages will be formatted the same way.*

Choose **Tools, Macro, Record New Macro** from the menu.

The Record Macro dialog box is displayed.

Assign macro to a toolbar

Assign macro to a keystroke combination

QUICK TIP

If you are downloading the sample files from an online source, you will need to get the WD1301 through WD1310 files.

2 Type **FormatFontandSize** in the **Macro name** box. Click the <u>K</u>eyboard button.

The Customize Keyboard dialog box is displayed.

Hold down Alt and press **C**.

*If the keystroke combination is unassigned, the new shortcut key is displayed in the **Press new shortcut key** box.*

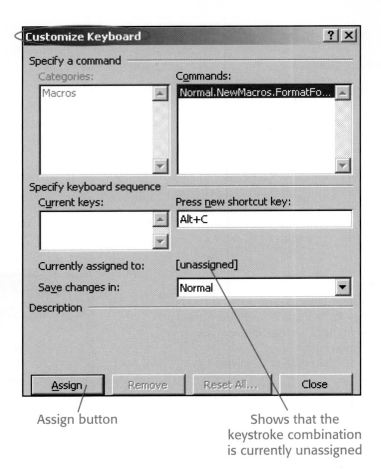

Assign button

Shows that the keystroke combination is currently unassigned

IN DEPTH

You cannot use spaces when you create a macro name. If you want to separate words visually in the macro name, use the underscore character between words. You can also begin each word with a capital letter to indicate where every new word in the macro name begins. Also, if you only have one or two macros, the name you give them is probably not very important. If you are going to use a number of macros, however, or if someone else is going to be working with the same macros, it is very helpful if you create descriptive names.

CAUTION

You may be informed that the keystroke combination you have chosen is already assigned. In that case, simply select other combinations until you find one that is not assigned.

Stop Recording button

Pause Recording button

3 Click the <u>A</u>ssign button.

*The keystroke combination is assigned to the new macro, and is listed in the **Current keys** box.*

Click the **Close** button.

The Stop Recording toolbar indicates that you are now ready to record a macro. Notice that the insertion point has a cassette icon by it, and the status bar shows REC in black letters. The Stop Recording toolbar consists of a Stop Recording button and a Pause Recording button.

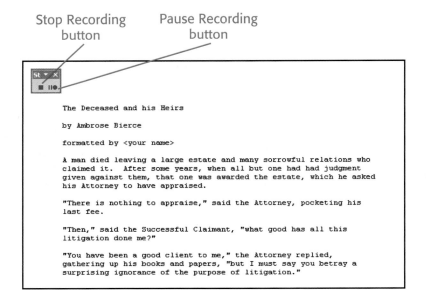

4 Choose **E**dit, **S**elect **All** from the menu.

All of the text in the document is selected.

Choose **F**ormat, **F**ont from the menu. Choose **Times New Roman** from the **Font** box, and **12** from the **Size** box. Click **OK**.

The document is now formatted differently. You now want to stop the macro from recording any further actions.

Stop Recording button

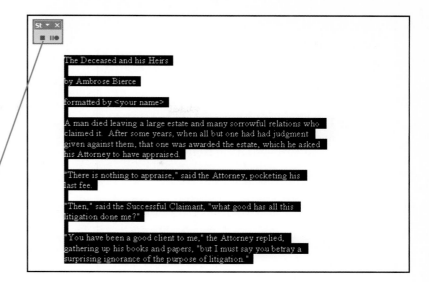

5 Click the **Stop Recording** button on the Stop Recording toolbar.

The macro is created.

Type your name at the top of the document where indicated. Click the **Open** button. Find and open **WD1302**. Choose **F**ile, **Save As** from the menu. Change **Save as type** to Word Document and save it as **WD1302-Three Recruits**.

Another document is displayed. It is formatted the same way the first one was.

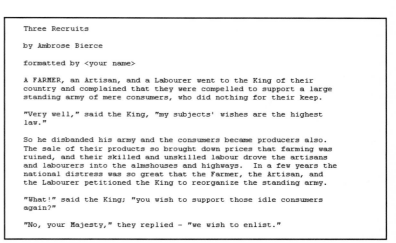

6 Type your name at the top of the new document where indicated. Press Alt+C. Click anywhere in the document to turn off the highlight.

The new document is formatted the same as the first one you opened. Now you create a second macro using this new file.

Choose **T**ools, **M**acro, **R**ecord New Macro from the menu. Type **SaveAndPrint** in the **Macro name** box.

Make sure there are no spaces in the file name.

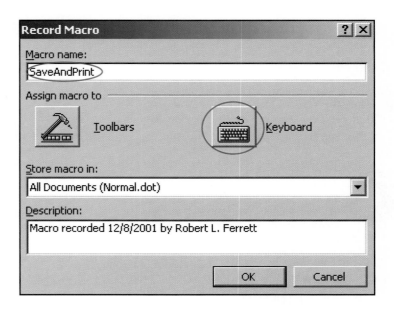

7 Click the **Keyboard** button. Hold down [Alt] and press **P** as the new shortcut key. Click the <u>A</u>ssign button, and then click the Close button.

The macro is ready to be recorded.

Choose <u>F</u>ile, <u>S</u>ave from the menu. Choose <u>F</u>ile, <u>P</u>rint from the menu. Choose the **Curre<u>n</u>t page** option and click OK.

These are the two steps in this short macro.

Three Recruits

by Ambrose Bierce

formatted by <your name>

A FARMER, an Artisan, and a Labourer went to the King of their country and complained that they were compelled to support a large standing army of mere consumers, who did nothing for their keep.

"Very well," said the King, "my subjects' wishes are the highest law."

So he disbanded his army and the consumers became producers also. The sale of their products so brought down prices that farming was ruined, and their skilled and unskilled labour drove the artisans and labourers into the almshouses and highways. In a few years the national distress was so great that the Farmer, the Artisan, and the Labourer petitioned the King to reorganize the standing army.

"What!" said the King; "you wish to support those idle consumers again?"

"No, your Majesty," they replied - "we wish to enlist."

8 Click the Stop Recording button on the Stop Recording toolbar. Use the taskbar to move back to the **WD1301-Inheritance** document. Press [Alt]+P.

The file is saved and printed.

Choose <u>T</u>ools, M<u>a</u>cro, <u>M</u>acros from the menu.

The Macros dialog box is displayed. Your two new macros (along with any other on your machine) are displayed.

New macros

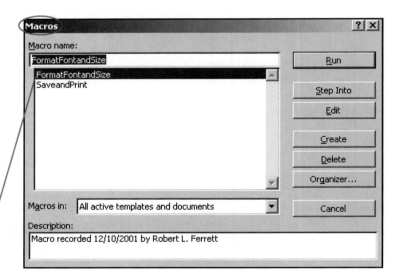

9 Click the Cancel button in the Macros dialog box. Close the open documents, but leave Word open for the next lesson.

CAUTION

One of the potential problems with using macros is the possibility of using a reserved name that will change the operation of Word. For example, if you had named the first macro in this lesson FormatFont, it would have taken the place of the Format, Font menu option. Instead of getting a dialog box when you use the menu option, the macro would be run instead. To help avoid this problem, do not use a series of menu options as a macro name. For example, do not call a macro FilePrint. Instead, call it PrintTheFile.

IN DEPTH

When you are planning your macros, it might be a good idea to have a list of keyboard shortcuts that are already used. Even if you are not writing macros, this list can come in very handy if you keep it close to your computer. To get a list of shortcuts, choose Tools, Macro, Macros from the menu. In the Macros dialog box, choose Word commands from the **Macros in** list box. In the **Macro name** box, choose ListCommands and click the <u>R</u>un button. Choose the **Current menu and keyboard settings** option and click OK. A list of all the shortcuts is placed in a table in a new Word document.

Task 2
CREATING A BUTTON-ACTIVATED MACRO

Why would I do this?

In the first task, you created two macros and attached them to keystroke combinations. A second option is to place a macro button on a toolbar. This option doesn't require that you memorize special keystroke combinations. It is especially useful if someone else is going to be using the macro. The procedure is similar to the one you used in the first task.

The document you use in this task is a long story. It has end-of-paragraph marks at the end of each line of text and has an empty paragraph between the text paragraphs. This type of formatting often occurs when you copy text from a Web page or convert text from some non-Microsoft formats. There are about 250 paragraph marks at the end of lines of text, although there are really far fewer actual paragraphs. You want to remove the end-of-paragraph marks from the end of each line, except the one at the end of the paragraph. A simple Find-and-Replace operation to delete all the paragraph marks doesn't work in this situation.

The process you need takes three steps. First, you find all the pairs of paragraph marks that characterize the end of a paragraph and replace them with an unusual character that you can find and replace later. Second, you replace all the remaining paragraph marks with a space. Third, you replace the unusual characters with pairs of paragraph marks. This process is a bit tricky and takes time to perform. If you record it as a macro, you can use it quickly and accurately to fix any document you receive that has this formatting problem.

In this task, you create and test a button-activated macro.

Dots indicate spaces

① Click the **Open** button. Change **Files of type** to **All Files**, if necessary. Find and open **WD1303**. Choose **File**, **Save As** from the menu. Change **Save as type** to Word Document and save it as **WD1303-Tiger**. Click the **Print Layout View** button, if necessary.

The short story is displayed. You now want to see how the document is formatted.

Type your name at the top of the document where indicated. Click the **Show/Hide** button.

Notice the paragraph marks at the end of each line. Also notice that you will need to insert a space when the extra paragraph marks are removed. Existing spaces are indicated with dots.

Extra paragraph mark indicates end of paragraph

Paragraph marks at the end of each line

```
THE·LADY,··OR·THE·TIGER?¶
¶
by·Frank·R.·Stockton¶
¶
formatted·by·<your·name>¶
¶
In·the·very·olden·time·there·lived·a·semi-barbaric·king,·whose¶
ideas,··though·somewhat·polished·and·sharpened·by·the¶
progressiveness·of·distant·Latin·neighbors,·were·still·large,¶
florid,·and·untrammeled,·as·became·the·half·of·him·which·was¶
barbaric.·He·was·a·man·of·exuberant·fancy,·and,·withal,·of·an¶
authority·so·irresistible·that,·at·his·will,·he·turned·his·varied¶
fancies·into·facts.·He·was·greatly·given·to·self-communing,·and,¶
when·he·and·himself·agreed·upon·anything,·the·thing·was·done.¶
When·every·member·of·his·domestic·and·political·systems·moved¶
smoothly·in·its·appointed·course,·his·nature·was·bland·and·genial;¶
but,·whenever·there·was·a·little·hitch,·and·some·of·his·orbs·got¶
out·of·their·orbits,·he·was·blander·and·more·genial·still,·for¶
nothing·pleased·him·so·much·as·to·make·the·crooked·straight·and¶
crush·down·uneven·places.¶
¶
Among·the·borrowed·notions·by·which·his·barbarism·had·become¶
semified·was·that·of·the·public·arena,·in·which,·by·exhibitions·of¶
manly·and·beastly·valor,·the·minds·of·his·subjects·were·refined¶
and·cultured.¶
¶
But·even·here·the·exuberant·and·barbaric·fancy·asserted·itself¶
The·arena·of·the·king·was·built,·not·to·give·the·people·an¶
opportunity·of·hearing·the·rhapsodies·of·dying·gladiators,·nor·to¶
enable·them·to·view·the·inevitable·conclusion·of·a·conflict¶
between·religious·opinions·and·hungry·jaws,·but·for·purposes·far¶
better·adapted·to·widen·and·develop·the·mental·energies·of·the¶
people.·This·vast·amphitheater,·with·its·encircling·galleries,·its¶
```

2 Choose **T**ools, **M**acro, **R**ecord New Macro from the menu.

The Record Macro dialog box is displayed

Type **StripParagraphMarks** in the **Macro name** box.

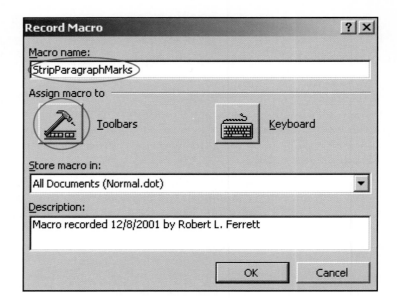

3 Click the **T**oolbars button. Click the **C**ommands tab, if necessary

*The Command for the macro is shown in the Comman**d**s box. You will drag this up to a toolbar.*

Click and drag the Normal.NewMacros. StripParagraphMarks command to the right end of the Standard toolbar. Place the I-bar to the right of the Zoom box.

The I-bar shows the future location of the macro.

Zoom button

The macro will be placed at the I-bar location

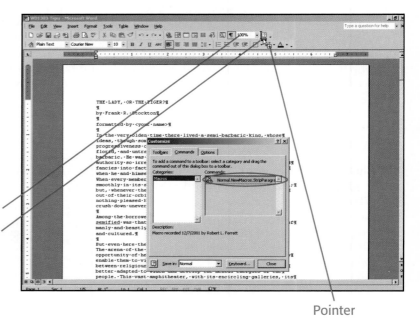

Pointer

4 Release the mouse button.

The macro is placed in the toolbar. If you are using a low screen resolution, the button may wrap.

Click the **Close** button.

The Stop Recording toolbar indicates that you are now ready to record a new macro.

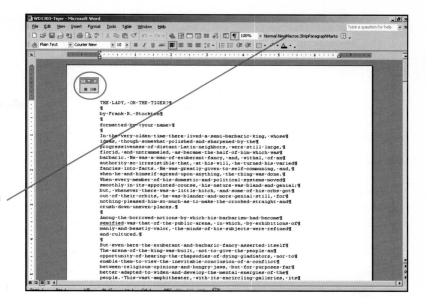

New macro button

5 Select **Edit**, **Replace** from the menu.

The Find and Replace dialog box is displayed.

Click the **More** button.

More options are displayed. You now need to use the Special button to place the paragraph mark symbol in the Find and Replace boxes. The first thing you want to do is mark the ends of actual paragraphs. You do that by finding two successive paragraph marks and replacing them with an unused character. You will then remove the rest of the paragraph marks, and finally put the actual paragraph marks back in.

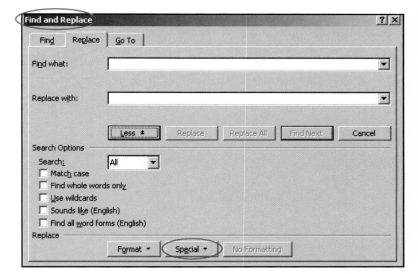

6 Place the insertion point in the **Find what** box, delete anything in the box, and click the **Special** button. Choose **Paragraph Mark** from the list.

The paragraph mark code, ^p, is placed in the box.

Repeat the procedure to place a second paragraph mark code in the **Find what** box.

The end of the paragraph is characterized by two successive paragraph marks whereas the end of each line has only one paragraph mark. The program will now look for two successive paragraph marks. You need to identify the character you want to replace them with.

QUICK TIP

If you know the code for the special character you want to insert, you can simply type the code into either box. The two most commonly used codes are for paragraph marks (**^p**) and tab characters (**^t**).

7 Place the insertion point in the **Replace with** box. Click the **Special** button and choose **Em Dash** from the list.

The em dash character, ^+, is placed in the box. An em dash is a long dash used in printing, and is as long as the letter M. It is a character that is not supported in a text file, so you can be certain that none exist in this document.

Click the **Replace All** button. Click **OK** to accept the 26 replacements.

All the double paragraph marks are replaced by em dashes.

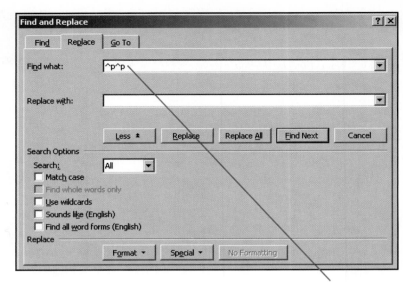

Paragraph mark codes

Replace All button

The em dash represents the end of a paragraph

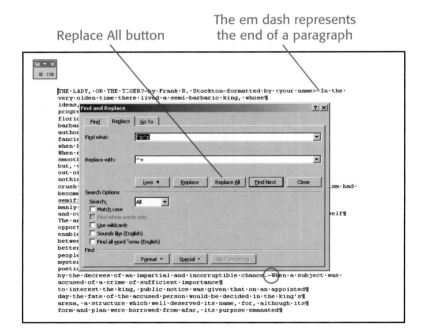

8 Move back to the **Find what** box and remove one of the paragraph mark codes.

The box should contain only a single paragraph mark code (^p).

Select and delete the contents of the **Replace with** box and then press Spacebar.

This will replace each remaining paragraph mark with a space.

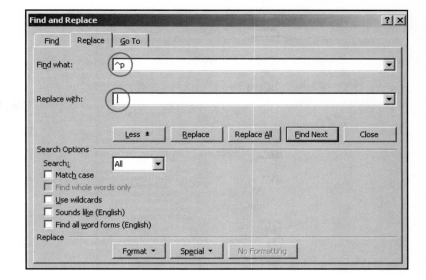

9 Click the **Replace All** button. Click **OK** to accept the 225 replacements.

All the paragraph marks are replaced by single spaces.

Place the insertion point in the **Find what** box and backspace over the existing characters to delete them. Click the **Special** button and choose **Em Dash** from the list. Move to the **Replace with** box, remove the space character, click the **Special** button, and then choose **Paragraph Mark** from the list. Repeat this procedure to add a second paragraph mark

This will replace each em dash with two paragraph marks, leaving a blank line between the paragraphs.

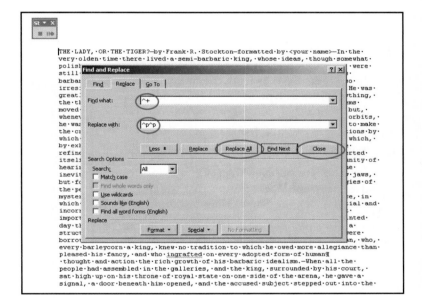

10 Click the **Replace All** button. Click **OK** to accept the 26 replacements.

All the em dashes are replaced by two paragraph marks.

Click the **Close** button, and then click the **Show/Hide** button.

The extraneous paragraph marks are gone from the document, which now looks like a word processing document rather than a text document.

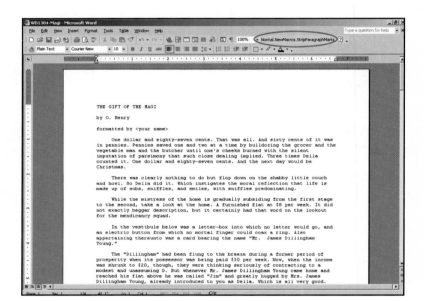

11 Click the **Stop Recording** button. Click the **Open** button. Find and open **WD1304**. Choose **File, Save As** from the menu. Change **Save as type** to Word Document and save it as **WD1304-Magi**.

This document has the same format as the WD1303-Tiger document did before you recorded the macro.

Click the **Normal.NewMacros. StripParagraphMarks** button that you just created. Click the **Show/Hide** button.

The extraneous paragraph marks are gone from the document, and the text of the paragraphs wraps within the page margins properly. You can now manipulate the text as paragraphs rather than as a series of individual lines of text.

12 Type your name at the top of the document where indicated. Press [Alt]+P.

This activates the macro you recorded in Task 1 and prints the first page of the document.

Close the document. Save the **WD1303-Tiger** document. Leave this document open for the next task.

Task 3
EDITING MACROS USING THE VISUAL BASIC EDITOR

Why would I do this?

When you have spent a lot of time recording a macro, and you find one or two things that need to be changed, you have two choices. You can delete the macro and record a replacement, or you can edit it using the Visual Basic Editor. This means opening a Visual Basic window, making changes to the programming language, and then saving your changes.

The obvious drawback to the second method of editing a macro is that you need to work with a programming language. You do not, however, need to learn Visual Basic to make simple changes. Many of the changes will be obvious when you look at the code. To learn more about Visual Basic for Applications, there are several reference manuals available at major bookstores and libraries. The purpose of this task is to show you the procedure for editing a macro, not to give you a tutorial on VBA—that would take an entire book by itself!

In this task, assume that your company has decided on a consistent look for all of its documents, and this differs from your FormatFontandSize macro. You edit that macro to match the company's new style requirements. Along the way, you will see how Word stores the macros you have created.

1 With the **WD1303-Tiger** document still open, choose **Tools**, **Macro**, **Macros** from the menu.

The Macros dialog box is displayed.

    Choose **All active templates and documents** from the **Macros in** list box, if necessary. Make sure the FormatFontandSize macro is selected.

All three of the macros you created in the first two tasks are displayed, along with other macros on your machine.

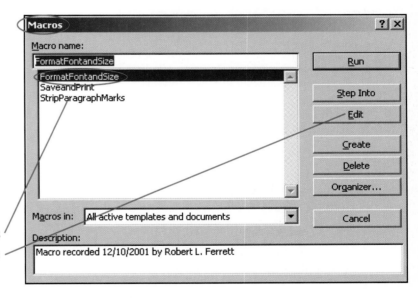

Three new macros

Edit button

> **QUICK TIP**
>
> You can use the Macros dialog box for several tasks. You can delete a macro here; you can also run a macro by selecting the macro name and clicking the Run button. This is particularly helpful when you forget the keyboard shortcut you assigned to the macro.

2 Click the **Edit** button.

The Microsoft Visual Basic Editor window opens. This window has a Project Explorer window on the left and the Code window on the right. There are several other VBE windows that might be open, but you do not need them for this task.

Your macros are stored here

Open documents

Project Window

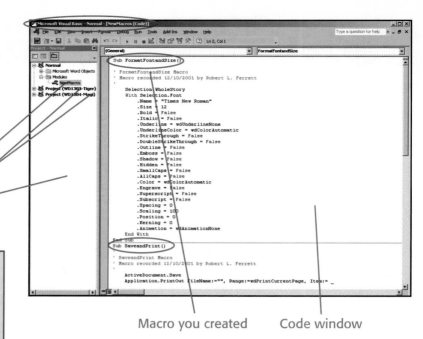

Macro you created   Code window

IN DEPTH

Notice the code for the FormatFontandSize macro. The macro you recorded only changed the font and font size, and yet there are many font attributes shown in the Code window. This is because you chose to make these changes in a dialog box. When you use a dialog box while recording a macro, the VBA code that is created must address every option in the dialog box. If you had used the buttons for font and font size, the code would have addressed only those two items. For example, the code for the two changes could have been:

```
Selection.WholeStory
With Selection.Font
    .Name = "Times New Roman"
    .Size = 12
End With
```

This makes the code easier to read and more efficient.

3 Change the font name from **Times New Roman** to **Arial**. Change the font size from **12** to **11** points.

These changes will be reflected only after you save them.

Click the **Save Normal** button on the Standard toolbar. Choose **File**, **Print** from the menu.

Your changes are saved, and the file is printed.

New font style   New font size

Save Normal button

4 Click the **Close** button in the VBE title bar.

The Visual Basic Editor window is closed.

Press Alt+C to run the macro. Click anywhere in the document to turn off the highlighting.

Notice that the document reflects the changes you made to the macro.

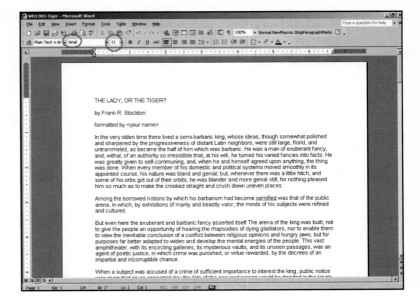

5 Click the **Show/Hide** button to turn it off, if necessary. Click the **Save** button to save your work. Leave the document open for the next task.

Task 4
CREATING A CUSTOM MENU

Why would I do this?

If you use a lot of macros, you end up with one of two problems—you either have to remember a lot of keystroke combinations, or you have a huge, unwieldy toolbar or group of toolbars cluttering the top of your screen. Fortunately, there is a really great solution to this problem. You can create your own menu option that contains all your macros (or other commands). The other strength of this technique is that you can rename the macros to something shorter and more descriptive than the long name in the toolbar.

In this task, you create a menu option that contains the three macros that you created in this lesson. You then give them more manageable names.

1 With the **WD1303-Tiger** document still open, choose **T**ools, **C**ustomize from the menu.

The Customize dialog box opens. There are three tabs at the top of the dialog box.

Click the **Commands** tab, if necessary. Scroll down in the **Categories** box and click the **New Menu** option.

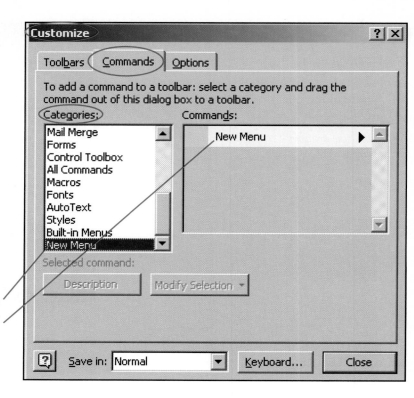

New Menu option
Menu choice to be added to a toolbar

2 Click the **New Menu** command in the **Commands** box and drag it up until the I-bar is to the left of the **H**elp menu option.

This is where you will place the new menu option. (Note: If you are using a computer in a lab, you need to remove the new menu option when you complete this task.)

I-bar indicates the location
of the new menu option

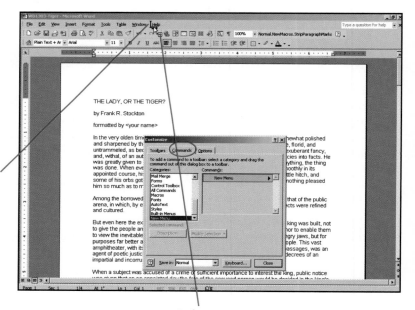

Pointer

3 Release the mouse button.

The menu option now appears in the menu bar.

Right-click the New Menu menu option on the menu bar and type **Macros** over the **New Menu** name.

This will give you a descriptive title for the menu option.

New title for the menu option

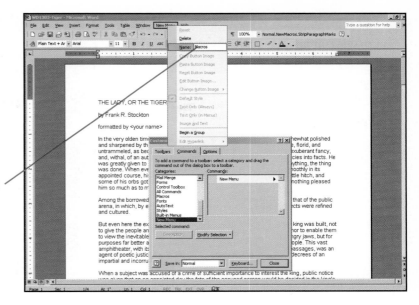

4 Press ⏎Enter.

The name is now changed on the menu bar.

Scroll up in the **Categories** box and click the **Macros** option.

The macros you created earlier in this lesson are displayed, along with any other macros that might be attached to the document.

Macros recorded in this lesson

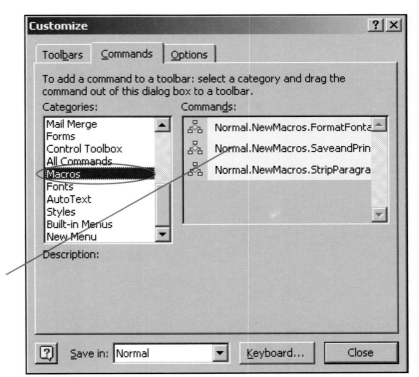

5 Drag the **Normal.NewMacros. FormatFontandSize** macro to the **Macros** menu option.

A box appears below the menu option. This is the list box that will display your macros.

Move the I-bar down into the box.

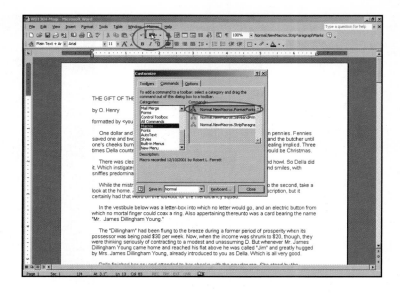

6 Release the mouse button.

The macro is placed in the list box.

Right-click the new menu option and change the name to **New Font**.

The new name will appear in the menu, but it will still be connected to the original macro.

New menu option

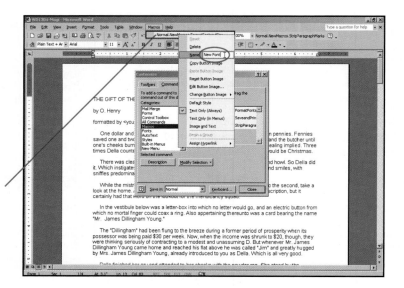

7 Press Enter to accept the name change. Drag the **SaveAndPrint** macro to the **Macros** menu option. Place the horizontal I-bar under the **New Font** menu option.

The horizontal I-bar shows where the new menu choice will be placed.

Horizontal I-bar

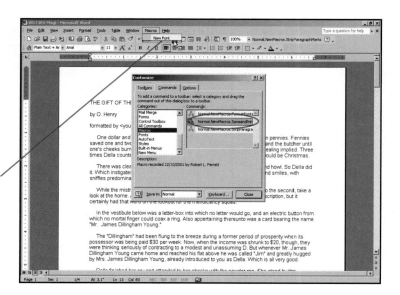

8 Right-click the new menu option and change the name to **Save and Print** and press ⏎Enter.

Your second macro is now renamed.

Use the same procedure you used in Steps 5-7 to move the StripParagraphMarks macro to the bottom of the new menu option. Rename it **Strip Paragraph Marks**.

Your new menu should look like the figure.

QUICK TIP

You do not have to use the same words in the menu names that you gave the macros. However, if you used descriptive names for the macros, they will probably end up with similar names.

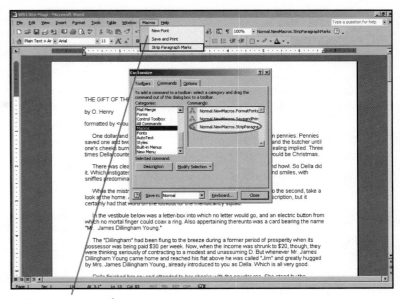

New menu options

9 Grab the **Normal.NewMacros. StripParagraphMarks** button from the Standard toolbar and drag it below the toolbars.

This removes a button that is no longer necessary. The Customize dialog box needs to be open to remove a button.

Close the Customize dialog box. Open **WD1305** and save it as **WD1305-Weather**. Type your name at the top of the document where indicated.

This is another document that has been scanned and contains text file formatting.

10 Choose **Macros, Strip Paragraph Marks** from the menu. Click the **Show/Hide** button to turn off formatting marks, if necessary. Choose **Macros, New Font** from the menu. Choose **Macros, Save and Print** from the menu.

You now have an easy way to run the macros you created. You can also add new macros to this menu as you create them.

Close the **WD1305-Weather** document. Leave the **WD1303-Tiger** document open for the next task.

A Forfeited Right

by Ambrose Bierce

formatted by <your name>

THE Chief of the Weather Bureau having predicted a fine day, a Thrifty Person hastened to lay in a large stock of umbrellas, which he exposed for sale on the sidewalk; but the weather remained clear, and nobody would buy. Thereupon the Thrifty Person brought an action against the Chief of the Weather Bureau for the cost of the umbrellas.

"Your Honour," said the defendant's attorney, when the case was called, "I move that this astonishing action be dismissed. Not only is my client in no way responsible for the loss, but he distinctly foreshadowed the very thing that caused it."

"That is just it, your Honour," replied the counsel for the plaintiff; "the defendant by making a correct forecast fooled my client in the only way that he could do so. He has lied so much and so notoriously that he has neither the legal nor moral right to tell the truth."

Judgment for the plaintiff.

Task 5
ADDING BUTTONS TO A TOOLBAR

Why would I do this?

There are probably buttons on your Standard and Formatting toolbars that you have never used. There are also buttons that are available, and could be very useful, but are not on the toolbars. Word gives you a way to remove unwanted buttons, and add potentially useful buttons to any toolbar. You can even create your own toolbar of often-used buttons!

In this task, you add buttons to Word toolbars.

1 With the **WD1303-Tiger** document still open, choose **Tools**, **Customize** from the menu.

The Customize dialog box opens. There are three tabs at the top of the dialog box.

Click the **Commands** tab, if necessary. With **File** selected in the **Categories** box, scroll down in the **Commands** box and click the Page Setup option.

If you need to use the options in the Page Setup dialog box on a regular basis, to change margins, orientation, printers, or paper source, this can be a real time-saver.

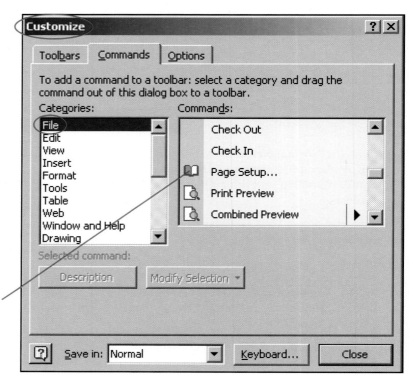

Page Setup option

2 Drag the button up to the left of the **Print** button on the Standard toolbar.

The button will be dropped in the I-bar location. It must be in a toolbar, not in an open area to the right of the toolbar.

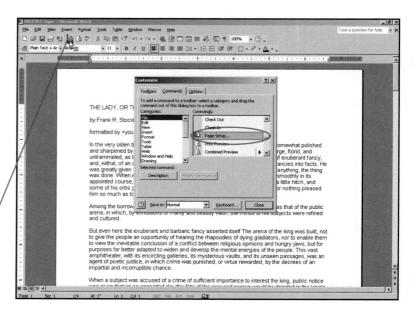

I-bar indicates new button location

3 Release the mouse button.

The new Page Setup button is placed at the I-bar location.

Click the **Format** option in the **Categories** box. Scroll down and select the **Grow Font 1 Pt** option.

This button, along with the one below it, enables you to quickly resize text in 1-point intervals until you have it exactly the right size. These are very important buttons when you are doing flyers, brochures, or newsletters.

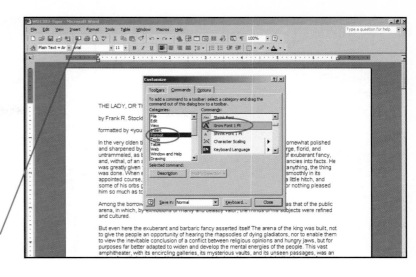

Page Setup button has been added

QUICK TIP

There are other ways to customize toolbars. To remove a button, you can hold down Alt and drag a button below the toolbar. To add a button, you can click the arrow at the end of a toolbar, choose Add or Remove Buttons, choose the name of the toolbar, and then select and deselect available buttons for that toolbar.

4 Drag the **Grow Font 1 Pt** command and drop it to the right of the **Font Size** button. Drag the **Shrink Font 1 Pt** command and drop it to the right of the new **Grow Font 1 Pt** button.

The buttons are now on the Formatting toolbar.

Click the **Close** button to close the Customize dialog box.

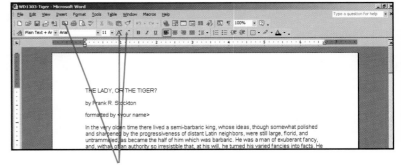

New buttons

5 Select the story title. Click the **Bold** button and the **Center** button on the Formatting toolbar.

The Title is now centered and bold, but could stand to be a little larger.

Click the **Grow Font 1 Pt** button four times.

Notice that the font increases by one point each time you click the button.

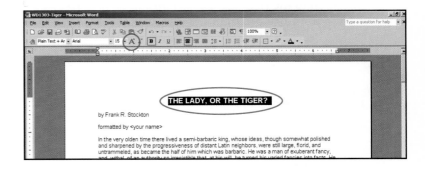

6 Click the new **Page Setup** button.

The Page Setup dialog box is displayed.

Change the left and right margins to **1.25** inches.

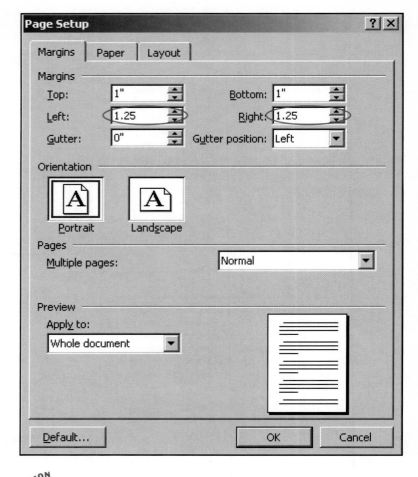

7 Click **OK** to close the dialog box. Choose **Macros**, **Save and Print** from the menu.

You just used a button you added to the toolbar, and a menu option you created to run a macro you recorded.

If you are working in a lab setting, check with the instructor to see if you need to remove the new menu option, buttons, and macros you created in this lesson. If so, see the Caution to the right for instructions. If not, close the Word program.

CAUTION

Some labs are set up so that Office applications change back to their original settings every time the computer is turned off, or at the end of each day. Some computers, however, do not have these features installed, so you will need to remove your customizations yourself.

To remove the new menu option, choose Tools, Customize from the menu. Click the Toolbars tab, highlight the Menu Bar option, click the Reset button, and click OK.

To remove the buttons you added, click the buttons, drag them below the ruler, and drop them.

To remove the macros, choose **Tools**, **Macro**, **Macros** from the menu. Select a macro you created and click Delete. Repeat this procedure for each macro you created.

IN DEPTH

The changes you make to your toolbars do not move with the document that is open at the time; rather, they stay with the computer on which they were created. You can, however, attach the changes you make to the current document, so that they will not appear in the toolbars when other programs are open. To do that, select the document name from the **Save in** box at the bottom of the Customize dialog box. You can also reset any toolbar to its original state, if necessary.

Task 6
MOVING WORD CUSTOMIZATIONS TO ANOTHER COMPUTER

Why would I do this?

Have you ever gotten a new computer and found that you had to re-create all the custom settings you had used on your old computer? Now that you are familiar with many of the ways to customize Word, you will probably make many more changes that will make your life easier. These customization options are also available in most of the other Office applications, so you could eventually end up with hundreds of customizations that you would need to repeat when you move to a new computer or begin using a portable computer on the road.

Office XP has added a feature that will save you an enormous amount of time setting up other computers. One of the new Microsoft Office Tools, called the Save My Settings Wizard, enables you to quickly transfer your templates, dictionaries, AutoCorrect, and AutoText entries, toolbars, menus, defaults, and other customizations to a file. You can then use the same wizard to install the customizations stored in the file onto the new computer.

In this task, you create a file containing all of your Microsoft Office customizations.

1 Close all Microsoft Office applications.

This feature will not work if any of the Office applications are open.

Click the **Start** button. Choose **All Programs, Microsoft Office Tools, Save My Settings Wizard** from the Start menu.

The first Microsoft Office Save My Settings Wizard is displayed.

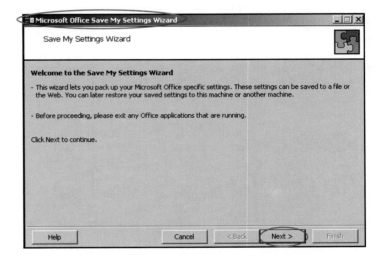

2 Click the **Next** button.

The second Microsoft Office Save My Settings Wizard is displayed. This is where you tell the program whether you want to create a file containing your Office settings, or update the current computer from an existing file.

Make sure the **Save the setting from this machine** option is selected.

> **CAUTION**
>
> You may get a warning message that the program cannot continue because Outlook is open. Close Outlook. If you get the same message, it may mean that you have a CE-based PDA that is running Microsoft ActiveSync. Remove your PDA from the cradle or disconnect the cable, and then close ActiveSync.

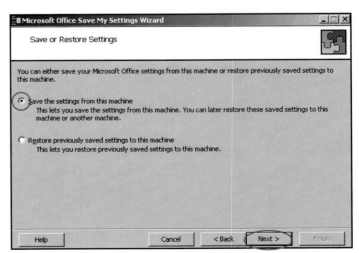

3 Click the **Next** button.

You can save your settings to a secure Web server, or to a file on a hard disk, Zip disk, or even a floppy disk, although if you have a lot of customizations, the file may be too large for a floppy disk.

Click the **Save the settings to a File** option.

The document, which has a .OPS extension, is placed in a default folder unless you change it.

Default file name
and location

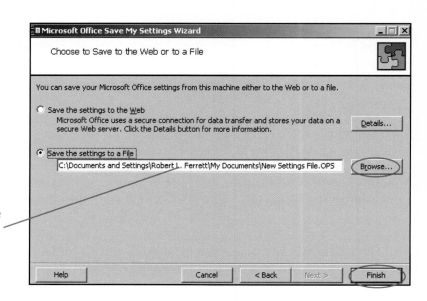

4 Click the **Browse** button. Find a folder in which you can store this file.

This could be a floppy disk, hard disk, shared network drive, or any other device to which you have access.

Type a descriptive name for your file.

You can add your first name to the existing name if you want.

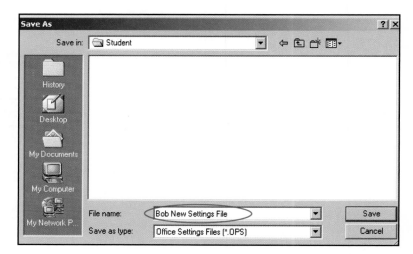

5 Click the **Save** button. Click the **Finish** button on the final Microsoft Office Save My Settings Wizard dialog box.

A confirmation dialog box tells you where the file was saved.

File location

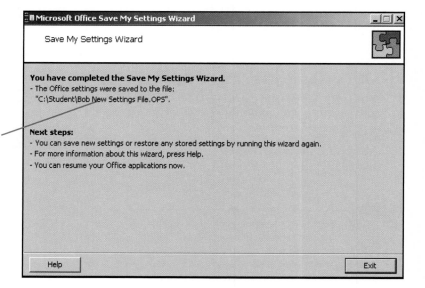

6 Click the **Exit** button.

You could now update another computer to match the settings on your current computer, if appropriate.

You may be required to print a screen showing your file. To do so, go to Windows Explorer and find the file, press [Alt]+[PrtSc] to place a copy of the screen in the clipboard, open a new Word document, and paste the image. Send the document to the printer. (Note: You may need to turn on the file extensions.)

The exercises that follow are designed for you to review and use what you have learned in this lesson. You also have the opportunity to practice your skills and then expand on them by applying them to new situations.

Explain It

Do It

Use It

COMPREHENSION

Comprehension exercises are designed to check your memory and understanding of the basic concepts in this lesson. You distinguish between true and false statements, identify new screen elements, and match terms with related statements. If you are uncertain of the correct answer, refer to the task number following each item (for example, T4 refers to Task 4) and review that task until you are confident that you can provide a correct response.

TRUE-FALSE

Circle either T or F.

T   F   **1.** You cannot use spaces in a macro name. **(T1)**

T   F   **2.** When you create a macro with the <u>T</u>oolbars option, the button is automatically added to the Standard toolbar. **(T2)**

T   F   **3.** You can delete a macro in the Macros dialog box. **(T3)**

T   F   **4.** If you use a dialog box while recording a macro, each of the options in that dialog box is addressed in the VBA code for that macro. **(T3)**

T   F   **5.** When you create a menu option from a macro, you must name the menu option the same name as the macro. **(T4)**

T   F   **6.** You can connect toolbar changes to a specific document only. **(T5)**

MATCHING QUESTIONS

A. VBA   **D.** OPS

B. VBE   **E.** Customize

C. Macro   **F.** Recorder

Match the following statements to the word or phrase that is the best match from the list. Write the letter of the matching word or phrase in the space provided next to the number.

1. _____ Dialog box from which you can drag buttons to be added to a toolbar **(T5)**

2. _____ Programming language for macros **(T4)**

3. _____ Program that runs several steps at one time **(Intro)**

4. _____ Editor used to edit macros **(T4)**

5. _____ One way to quickly create a macro **(T1)**

6. _____ File extension for Office settings file **(T6)**

IDENTIFYING PARTS OF THE WORD SCREEN

Refer to the figure and identify the numbered parts of the screen. Write the letter of the correct label in the space next to the number.

1. _____

2. _____

3. _____

4. _____

5. _____

6. _____

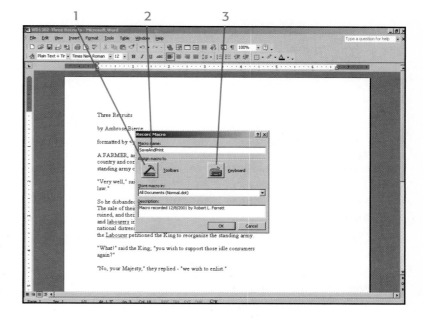

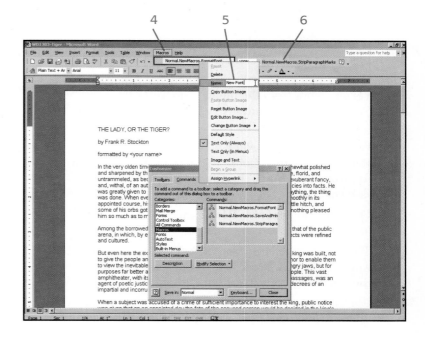

A. Assigns a macro to a keystroke combination (T1)

B. New menu choice (T4)

C. Macro button (T2)

D. Renames a menu list option (T4)

E. Assigns a macro to a button (T2)

F. New macro name (T1)

Reinforcement exercises are designed to reinforce the skills you have learned by applying them to a new situation. Detailed instructions are provided along with a figure, where appropriate, to illustrate the result. Complete the reinforcement exercises sequentially. Leave the workbook open at the end of each exercise for use in the next exercise until you are specifically directed to close it.

In these exercises, you work with an analysis of Alcona County through the end of the 19th century. This is a paper handed out at a historical society meeting. Different people are doing different parts of the presentation, such as population, literacy, and occupations. Because one person (you!) does the final formatting, the various writers have been asked not to do any formatting at all on the text or tables.

As in the tasks for this lesson, if you are working in a lab environment, you may need to remove any customizations you add in these exercises. See the Caution at the end of Task 5 for instructions.

R1—Creating a Keyboard Macro

1. Start Word, if necessary. Open the document **WD1306** and save it as **WD1306-Alcona Literacy**. Turn off the Task Pane and click the **Print Layout View** button, if necessary. Type your name at the top of the document where indicated.

2. Choose **Tools**, **Macro**, **Record New Macro** from the menu.

3. Type **FormatTheDocument** in the **Macro name** box. Click the **Keyboard** button.

4. Hold down Alt and press **D** and click the **Assign** button. (Note: If this combination is already in use, try another.) Click the **Close** button.

5. Choose **File**, **Page Setup** from the menu. Change the left and right margins to **1.25** inches and the bottom margin to **0.8** inches. Click **OK**.

6. Choose **Edit**, **Select All** from the menu. Choose **Format**, **Font** from the menu. Choose **11** from the **Size** box, choose **Times New Roman** from the **Font** box, and then click **OK**.

7. Click the **Stop Recording** button on the Stop Recording toolbar. Click anywhere in the document to turn off the highlight. Click the **Save** button to save your work.

8. Open the document **WD1307** and save it as **WD1307-Alcona Occupations**.

9. Type your name at the top of the new document where indicated. Press Alt+D. Click anywhere in the document to turn off the highlight.

10. Click the **Save** button to save your work. Leave the document open for the next exercise.

R2—Creating a Macro Attached to a Button

1. With the **WD1307-Alcona Occupations** document still open, place the insertion point anywhere in the first table.

2. Choose **Tools**, **Macro**, **Record New Macro** from the menu. Type **NewTableFormat** in the **Macro name** box.

3. Click the **Toolbars** button.

4. Click and drag the Normal.NewMacros. NewTableFormat command to the right of the Zoom box. Release the mouse button.

5. Click the **Close** button. Choose **Table**, **Select**, **Table** from the menu.

6. Choose **Table**, **Table AutoFormat** from the menu. Choose **Table List 3** from the **Table Styles** box and click the **Apply** button.

7. Choose **Table**, **AutoFit**, **AutoFit to Contents** from the menu.

8. Choose **Table**, **Table Properties** from the menu. Click the **Center** option and click **OK**.

9. Click the **Stop Recording** button. Scroll down and place the insertion point in the second table. Click the **Normal.NewMacros.NewTableFormat** button that you just created.

Occupations

Researcher: <your name>

During the period from 1860-1900, the occupations of Alcona County residents changed drastically. For the men, the biggest occupation by far in 1860 was fishing, with more than 60% of the men engaged in some aspect of that trade. Farming was being practiced, on a very small scale, by only six men. By 1900, nearly 60% (920) were involved in farming, while only two of 1,626 were involved in fishing. In between, there was a lumber boom; many of the men listed as general laborers in 1880 were working the lumber camps. The following table shows the major occupations by category:

	1860	1870	1880	1900
Farming	6	69	325	920
General labor	18		174	262
Lumbering	4	102	60	172
Retail		11	85	89
Skilled trades	2	19	45	44
Railroads			26	39
Other transportation			42	31
Teacher			2	29
Professional		3	23	22
Government		6	10	16
Fishing	47	44	1	2
Total	77	254	793	1,626

Female occupations remained similar throughout. In each of the census years, there were more servants than any other category of work outside the home. The occupation of keeping house was recorded in 1870 and 1880, but not in 1860 or 1900, and has thus been left off the table. Many of the women listed as farmers were widows who had inherited the family farm, and were listed as head of household. The only other category recorded in significant numbers was that of teacher, although by 1900, there were more male teachers than female teachers. The following table shows the major occupations by category:

	1860	1870	1880	1900
Servant	3	14	42	59
Farming				38
Teacher		1	9	23
Dress maker/milliner		2	2	5
Retail				4
Music teacher				3
Stenographer				3
Keeps hotel/boarding house			5	2
Cook			3	1
Laborer				1

10. Notice that the numbers are still left-aligned. Select the numbers in the second table and click the **Align Right** button on the Formatting toolbar. Repeat the procedure for the first table.

11. Click the **Save** button to save your work. Leave the document open for the next exercise. (Note: You may see light gridlines in your tables. These will not print.)

R3—Using the Visual Basic Editor to Modify a Macro

1. With the **WD1307-Alcona Occupations** document still open, choose **Tools**, **Macro**, **Macros** from the menu.

2. Select the **FormatTheDocument** macro and click the **Edit** button.

3. Scroll down until you can see the end of the macro. There will be a line between this macro and the next one.

4. Place the insertion point at the end of the last **End With** statement and press (↵Enter).

5. Type **ActiveDocument.Save** in the blank line. This is the command to save the current document.

6. Click the **Save Normal** button in the VBA Standard toolbar. Choose **File**, **Print** from the menu. Close the VBA window.

7. Change the title (first line) of the document to **Alcona County** Occupations. Press (Alt)+**D** (or whatever keystroke combination you assigned) to run the macro you just edited. Close the document and then reopen it to make sure the Save command you added has worked.

8. Leave the document open for the next exercise.

R4—Creating a Custom Menu

1. With the **WD1307-Alcona Occupations** document still open, choose **Tools**, **Customize** from the menu.

2. Scroll down in the **Categories** box and click the **New Menu** option.

3. Click the **New Menu** command in the **Commands** box and drag it up and drop it to the left of the **Help** menu option. This is to the right of the Macro menu option if it is still on your computer.

4. Right-click the New Menu menu option and type **Alcona** over the **New Menu** name. Press (↵Enter).

5. Scroll up in the **Categories** box and click the **Macros** option.

6. Drag the **Normal.NewMacros.FormatTheDocument** macro to the **Alcona** menu option and drop it in the list box.

7. Right-click the new menu option, change the name to **Format Document**, and press (↵Enter).

8. Use the same procedure to drag the **Normal.NewMacros.NewTableFormat** macro to the **Alcona** menu option list box. Change the name to **Format Table** and press (↵Enter).

9. Grab the **Normal.NewMacros.NewTableFormat** button from the Standard toolbar, drag it below the toolbars, and release the mouse button.

10. Close the Customize dialog box. Click the **Save** button. Leave the document open for the next exercise.

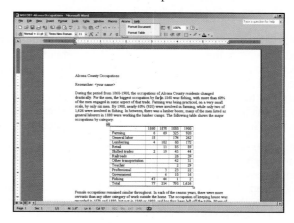

R5—Adding and Removing Toolbar Buttons

1. With the **WD1307-Alcona Occupations** document still open, choose **Tools**, **Customize** from the menu. Click the **Commands** tab, if necessary.

2. Choose the **View** option in the **Categories** box. Grab the **Ruler** button and drop it to the left of the **Print Preview** button.

3. If the **Page Setup** button is still on the Standard toolbar to the left of the **Print** button, drag it below the ruler and let go to remove it.

4. Click the Toolbars tab in the Customize dialog box. Click on the Formatting toolbar (not the check box) to select it.

5. Click the **Reset** button to remove the extra buttons you added in Task 5. Click **OK** to reset the changes for **Normal**.

6. Click the **Close** button in the Customize dialog box.

7. Print your document and exit Word.

Challenge exercises are designed to test your ability to apply your skills to new situations with less detailed instruction. These exercises also challenge you to expand your repertoire of skills by using commands that are similar to those you have already learned. The desired outcome is clearly defined, but you have more freedom to choose the steps needed to achieve the required result.

The following exercises use different files to illustrate procedures that you should find helpful. Because of the nature of customization features, some of these exercises may not be available to you if you are using a computer in a lab setting. If you are preparing for a certification test, read through the steps for the network exercises and do as many of the steps as possible to get a feel for the dialog boxes that you will need to work with.

As in the tasks for this lesson, if you are working in a lab environment, you may need to remove any customizations you add in these exercises. See the Caution at the end of Task 5 for instructions.

C1—Protecting Documents from Macro Viruses

In this lesson, you attached macros to the Normal.dot template. When you move the document to a different computer, the macros do not go with it, although they are available to all Word documents on the first machine. The other option is to attach the macros to the document, not to the Normal.dot template. This will ensure that the macros move with the document from machine to machine. This, however, causes a different set of problems.

One of the serious problems with macros in Office applications, particularly Word and Excel, is the opportunity for people to use them to transfer viruses. Because of this, security has been added to Office applications. You can set macro security to three levels—high, medium, and low. If high security is set, when you load a document with macros, there will be no indication that macros exist. If you try to run the macros from the menu, you will be told that macros are disabled. If medium security is set, you will be asked whether you want to activate them when you open the document. If low security is set, all macros will work. This setting is not recommended.

Goal: To test the different security levels.

1. Locate and open the **WD1308** document. This document has two macros attached to it. If a warning message appears, go ahead and enable the macros. The file has been carefully checked for viruses. If the file loads immediately, your security level is set either high or low.

2. Save the file as **WD1308-Alaska**. Type your name in the first paragraph where indicated. Choose **Tools**, **Options** from the menu. Click the Security tab.

3. Click the **Macro Security** button. Change the security to **High**, if necessary and click **OK** twice.

4. Choose **Tools**, **Macro**, **Macros** from the menu. Click the **SavePrint** macro (not the SaveandPrint macro). Click the **Run** button. Notice what happens.

5. Use the same procedure to change the security to **Medium**. Try running the macro. What happens?

6. Close and save the document and open it again, enabling the macro. Open the macro dialog box and run the macro. What was different this time?

7. Type a short document explaining what happened under the different security levels. Add your name, save, and print it. Close the document.

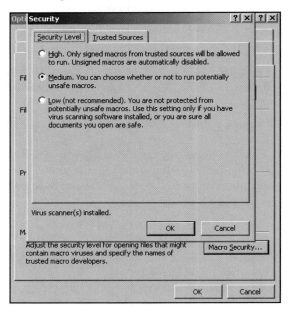

C2—Adding a Digital Signature to a Macro

You can certify a document by attaching a digital signature, which is an assurance to the receiver that the document came from you and has not been changed along the way. You can also attach a digital signature to a macro.

Digital signatures are your "signature" verified by a digital certificate—an electronic identification that verifies the source and also verifies that the document has not been changed since the signature was added. The digital certificate contains personal information about the person who signed the document.

You can obtain a digital certificate in one of three ways. The most secure, and the one with the widest acceptance, is to purchase a certificate from one of the commercial verification companies, such as VeriSign or E-Lock. You can also obtain a certificate that works company-wide from your company's network administrator. Finally, you can create a local certificate using Selfcert.exe, a program that is included with Microsoft Office XP, but which is not automatically installed when you install Office.

In this exercise, you create a digital certificate for yourself, attach that signature to a macro, and then describe the process you used to set up your certificate. If you created a certificate in Lesson 11, you can skip those steps in this exercise. (Note: If you are working in a lab, you may find that Selfcert.exe has already been installed, or that you cannot create certificates because of security. You will need to get the information to complete the exercise from the Help.)

Goal: To add a digital signature to a macro.

1. Locate and open the **WD1309** document. Enable macros, if necessary. Save the document as **WD1309-Signature**. This is the same document you used in the previous exercise, but the macro has been removed.

2. Use the Help menu to find out how to use Selfcert.exe. If it is not installed on your computer, you will need the original Office CD.

3. Run **Selfcert.exe** and create a certificate for yourself.

4. Create a macro that changes the font of the entire document to Broadway and attach it to the current document. Call the macro **BroadwayFont** and use Alt+**B** as the keyboard shortcut.

5. Open the Visual Basic Editor. Choose **Tools**, **Digital Signature** from the toolbar. Click the **Choose** button in the **Sign as** area. Select your certificate and click **OK**.

6. Set the macro security to the medium setting.

7. Save, close, and reopen the document. When asked about macros, click the **Details** button. Notice that you now have a certificate attached to the macro. If you do not have a trusted certificate, as is true with the figure below, a red **X** appears. If you want to make your digital signature trusted, use help to find out how to do it.

8. You may be required to print this screen. To do so, press Alt+PrtSc to place a copy of the open window in the clipboard. Open a new Word document and paste the image, and then send it to the printer.

9. Finish opening the document, and then close it without saving changes.

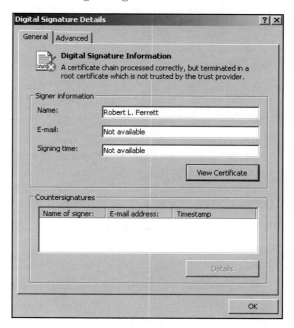

C3—Creating a Custom Toolbar

When you use Word extensively, you will find that you regularly use commands for which there are no buttons. Often the buttons to perform these tasks do exist, but are simply not considered important enough to put on the default toolbars. You will soon find that you differ from Microsoft in what you consider to be important buttons. Many advanced Word users create special toolbars that contain those special buttons that they use frequently.

In this exercise, you create a custom toolbar and add special formatting buttons to it.

Goal: To create a custom toolbar.

1. Locate and open the **WD1310** document and save it as **WD1310-Nuclear Energy**.

2. Choose **Tools**, **Customize** from the menu, select the **Toolbars** tab, and click the **New** button.

3. Call the toolbar **Formatting 2** and attach it to this document only.

4. Click the **Commands** tab. Choose **Format** from the **Categories** box. Scroll down and find the **Superscript** and **Subscript** buttons. Drag the **Subscript** button into the new toolbar. Drag the **Superscript** button and place it to the right of the **Subscript** button.

5. Use the same technique to add the **Small Caps, Strikethrough, Double Underline, Single Spacing, 1.5 Spacing,** and **Double Spacing** buttons to the new toolbar.

6. Close the Customize dialog box. Double-click the title bar of your new toolbar to dock it.

7. Scroll down to step five and select **92** in the first line. Click the **Subscript** button. Select **235** and click the **Superscript** button.

8. You may be required to print this screen. To do so, press PrtSc to place a copy of the screen in the clipboard. Open a new Word document and paste the image. Add your name, and then send it to the printer.

9. Save and close the document.

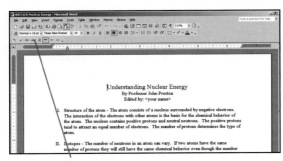

New toolbar

C4—Customizing the Keyboard

You have learned how to customize a toolbar and a menu. There are other customization features that can be used to great advantage by people with special requirements. Many people type documents in languages other than English that have marks on the letters. These are called diacritic characters, and they are not on standard keyboards. The same is true of other special characters, such as the copyright, trademark, or even paragraph symbols.

If you need special characters on a regular basis, there is a great way to make them easily available. Once again, it uses the Customize dialog box. Most special characters already have keyboard shortcuts, but they tend to have three parts and are difficult to remember. If you use these symbols regularly, you want shortcuts that are easy to remember. In this exercise, you create new shortcuts for several special characters. You use the same file that was used in the previous exercise.

Goal: To create new shortcuts for special characters.

1. Locate and open the **WD1310** document. Save the file as **WD1310-Shortcuts**.

2. Open the **Customize** dialog box. Click the **K**eyboard option and scroll down to the **Common Symbols** category.

3. In the **C**ommon **Symbols** box, scroll down and select the **Copyright** symbol.

4. Click in the **Press new shortcut key** box. Press Alt+**C**. This shortcut may still be assigned to a macro you created earlier in this lesson. Click the **Assign** button to reassign this shortcut.

5. Scroll to the top and select the **Em Dash**. Change the shortcut to Alt+**E** and assign it.

6. Move back to the document. Place the insertion point at the end of the title. Press Alt+**C** to add a copyright symbol.

7. Move to the first full paragraph. Select the dash after **Structure of the atom**. Make sure you select the spaces on either side of it. Press Alt+**E** to change a dash to an em dash.

8. Type your name at the top of the document where indicated. Save and print the document. Close Word.

> **Understanding Nuclear Energy©**
> By Professor John Preston
> Edited by: <your name>
>
> I. Structure of the atom—The atom consists of a nucleus surrounded by negative electrons. The interaction of the electrons with other atoms is the basis for the chemical behavior of the atom. The nucleus contains positive protons and neutral neutrons. The positive protons tend to attract an equal number of electrons. The number of protons determines the type of atom.
>
> II. Isotopes - The number of neutrons in an atom can vary. If two atoms have the same number of protons they will still have the same chemical behavior even though the number of neutrons may differ. They are the same type of atom. We call them **isotopes**, meaning "same type". The usual way of showing the difference between isotopes is to show the

ON YOUR OWN

In the first Challenge exercise, you set security levels for macros. In the second exercise, you added a digital signature. Both steps help in the fight against macro viruses, a particularly insidious type of virus that attacks computers by using some of the features of macros to create problems.

In this exercise, you research macro viruses and put together a report that gives brief descriptions of how they work, and what harm they can do. Go to the Internet and find Web sites that discuss macro viruses. Include hyperlinks to at least three sites that back up your research (one of them should be the Microsoft site). Make sure the report includes your name. Turn in the report as directed.

Lesson 9

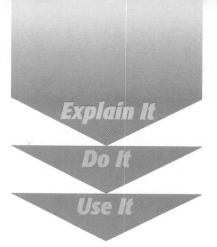

Explain It
Do It
Use It

Importing and Exporting Tables and Creating a Workspace

Task 1   Copying a Worksheet from Another Workbook
Task 2   Importing Data from a Web Page
Task 3   Importing Data from an Access Table
Task 4   Copying a Table from a Word Document
Task 5   Creating a Summary Sheet
Task 6   Saving a Sheet in CSV Format
Task 7   Publishing Interactive Web Pages
Task 8   Saving Related Files in a Workspace

INTRODUCTION

Excel is a good place to analyze and summarize data obtained from several different sources. Its charting and statistical capabilities make it ideal for this purpose. To make use of Excel as a summary tool, you import data into a workbook from several different sources.

Once you summarize the data and chart it, you may export the data to other programs using common data formats or you can create an interactive Web page that you can transfer to a Web server.

If you are working with a group of related workbooks, you can create a *workspace* which is a single name for a group of workbooks. Opening a workspace automatically opens all the workbooks.

In this lesson, you gather data about the budget of the United States from another workbook, a Web page, an Access Table, and a Word table. You create a summary sheet to compare the data from these sources and chart it for analysis. Once you have the summary sheet, you export it in a common format that many other programs can read and save it as an interactive Web page. Finally, you create a workspace that makes it convenient to open all the workbooks at once.

VISUAL SUMMARY

When you complete this entire lesson, you will have worksheets that look like these:

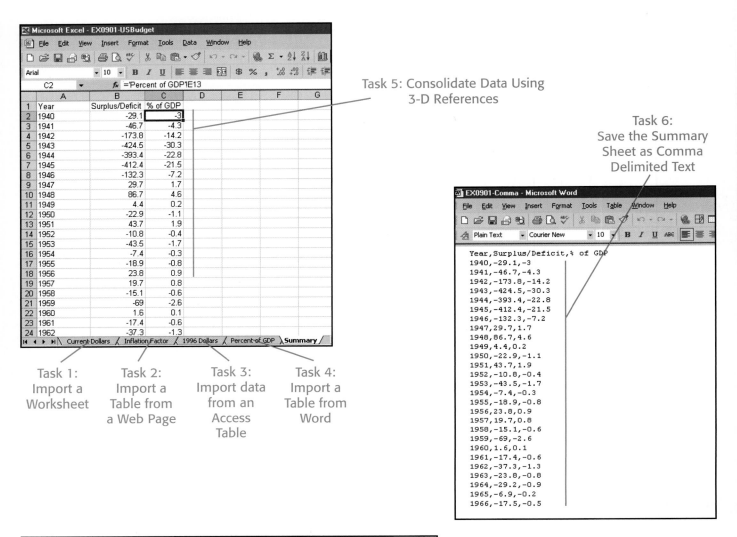

Task 5: Consolidate Data Using
3-D References

Task 6:
Save the Summary
Sheet as Comma
Delimited Text

Task 1:
Import a
Worksheet

Task 2:
Import a
Table from
a Web Page

Task 3:
Import data
from an
Access
Table

Task 4:
Import a
Table from
Word

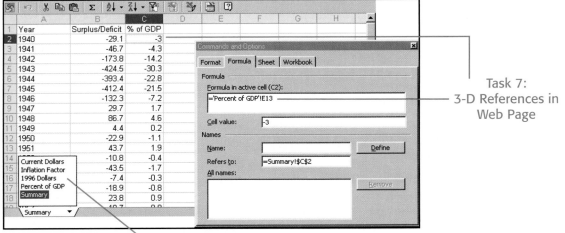

Task 7:
3-D References in
Web Page

Task 7: Save the Summary Sheet as an
Interactive Web Page

Task 1

COPYING A WORKSHEET FROM ANOTHER WORKBOOK

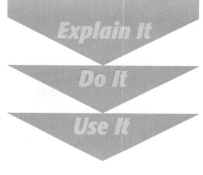

Why would I do this?

You can copy and paste worksheets within a workbook or between open workbooks. If you have a worksheet that is already set up the way you like it, it is faster to copy it and paste it into your current workbook than it is to create it again.

In this task, you learn how to copy a worksheet that shows information about the income and expenses of the United States government. This sheet displays the receipts, outlays, and the surplus or deficit for each year from 1901 to estimated values for 2001 through 2006.

1 Start Excel. Confirm that an empty workbook is displayed and choose <u>F</u>ile, Save <u>A</u>s. Select the folder on your disk in which you are saving your files in the **Save <u>in</u>** box.

The workbook will be saved on your disk.

Change the name in the **File <u>n</u>ame** box to **EX0901-USBudget**. Click the <u>S</u>ave button.

The empty workbook is saved on your disk with a new file name that appears in the title bar.

2 Open the Task Pane, if necessary, by choosing <u>V</u>iew, Ta<u>s</u>k Pane. Click **More workbooks** from the **Open a workbook** area of the task pane. Change the **Look <u>in</u>** box to display the student files for this lesson. Select **EX0901** and click the <u>O</u>pen button.

The workbook opens and displays a table that lists the receipts, outlays, and the surplus or deficit for each year from 1901 to estimated values through 2006.

> **IN DEPTH**
>
> The values in the Year column have small green triangles in the upper left corner to indicate that the Error Checking feature is turned on and there is something unusual about these cells. The cells in this column are formatted as text rather than number to accommodate the values at the end of the column which contains both dates and text.

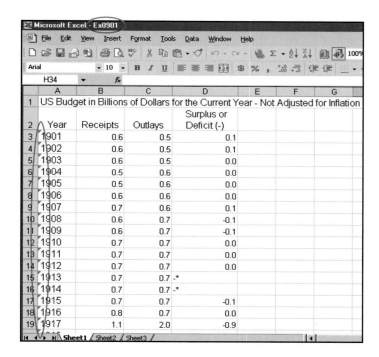

3 Choose **E**dit, **M**ove or Copy Sheet.

The Move or Copy dialog box opens.

> Click the arrow at the right side of the **T**o book box and select **EX0901-USBudget**. Click the **Create a copy** check box.

A copy of the current sheet will be placed before Sheet1 in the EX0901-Budget workbook.

4 Click the **OK** button.

A copy of the sheet is placed before Sheet1 in the EX0901-USBudget workbook and the display automatically switches to the EX0901-USBudget workbook.

> Double-click the sheet tab to select it and type **Current Dollars**. Press ↵Enter.

The sheet tab is renamed.

> Print this sheet if your instructor requires it.

5 Switch back to **EX0901** and close it.

Task 2

IMPORTING DATA FROM A WEB PAGE

Why would I do this?

Many Web pages contain useful tables that you can import into Excel. Web pages change often on the Internet so we have saved a simple table as a Web page as part of the student files to be used for this task. See the challenge or supplementary exercises to practice importing tables from Web pages on the Internet.

In this task, you learn how to import a table from a Web page.

1 Launch Internet Explorer. Choose <u>F</u>ile, <u>O</u>pen. Click the B<u>r</u>owse button.

You can locate Web pages stored on your disk or network using this method.

Locate the folder that contains the student files for this lesson and select **EX0902**. Click the <u>O</u>pen button. Click OK.

The table on this Web page is displayed.

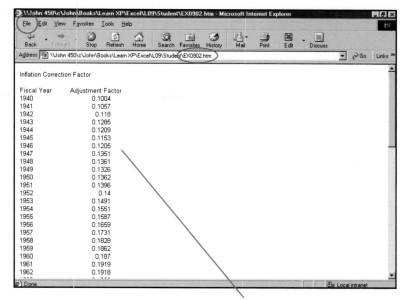

IN DEPTH

When you start the wizard that imports the table from a Web page, it has an address box into which you may type the Web address. Unfortunately, this dialog box does not have a browse option so you must have the address before you begin the process. To do this, you can use a Web browser like Internet Explorer to locate the desired page and copy its address to the clipboard for use in the Excel dialog box.

Table of data on the Web page

2 Select the address in the **A<u>d</u>dress** box. Choose <u>E</u>dit, <u>C</u>opy.

The address is copied to the Office Clipboard. Your address will differ from the one shown in the figure since your student files are stored in your folder.

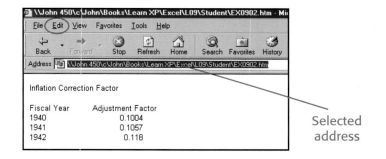

Selected address

3 Click the Close button on the title bar of the Internet Explorer window. Double-click the **Sheet1** tab to select it and type **Inflation Factor**. Press ⏎Enter.

The sheet tab is renamed. This sheet will display the factor used to convert current dollars into constant 1996 dollars so budgets from different years may be compared using the same dollar value.

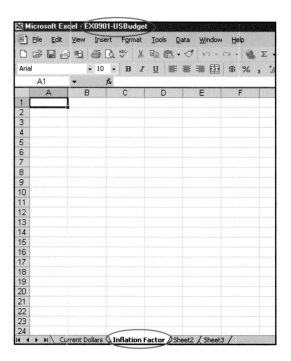

4 Choose **D**ata, Import External **D**ata, New **W**eb Query.

The New Web Query dialog box opens and displays the default Web page.

Confirm that the address is selected. Hold the Ctrl key and press **V.**

The address of the Web page is pasted into the box.

Click the **G**o button.

Tables in the Web page are identified with a small black arrow on a yellow background.

Address pasted from Office Clipboard

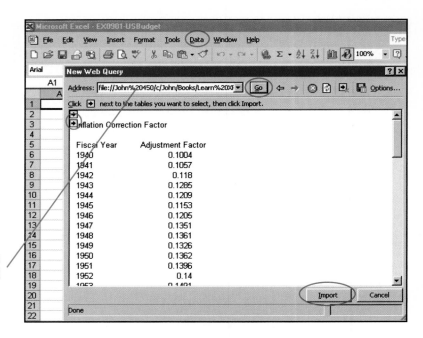

5 Click the arrow next to the title, **Inflation Correction Factor**.

The arrow changes to a check mark and the background changes to blue.

Click the **I**mport button.

The Import Data dialog box opens.

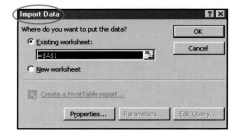

6 Type **=$A$2.**

The upper left corner of the table will be placed in the cell you choose and the rest of the table will be placed in the cells to the right and below the chosen cell.

Click **OK.** Close the Data toolbar if it appears.

The data is imported into the worksheet.

Print this sheet if your instructor requires it.

First cell of the imported table placed in cell A2

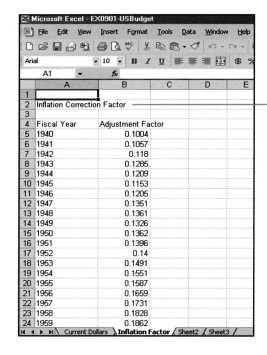

Task 3

IMPORTING DATA FROM AN ACCESS TABLE

Why would I do this?

Access is database management software that can store large tables of data. You import data from an Access table and filter the records to import only those records you need.

In this task, you learn how to import annual budget records from a table in Access that has been adjusted for inflation based on constant 1996 dollars. One of the records in the table is for an interim report and the value in the year field is TQ. You will import all the records except that one.

1 Double-click the **Sheet2** tab and type **1996 Dollars**. Press ⏎Enter.

The sheet tab is renamed.

Choose **Data, Import External Data, New Database Query**.

The Choose Data Source dialog box opens.

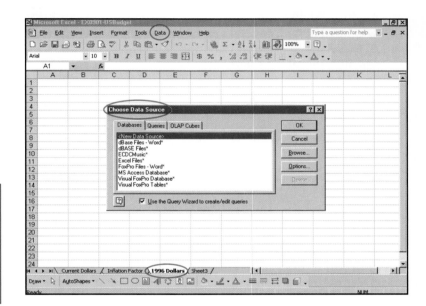

> **CAUTION**
>
> If this feature is not installed on your computer, you may be prompted to provide the installation disc. If you are working in a lab where this is not convenient and you know how to open a file in Access, you may start Access, open EX0903, copy the table, switch back to Excel and paste it into the sheet. Delete the last row that has TQ in place of the year.

2 Click the **Databases** tab, if necessary and click **MS Access Database***.

You can import data from a variety of database files.

Confirm that the checkbox next to **Use the Query Wizard to create/edit queries** displays a check mark.

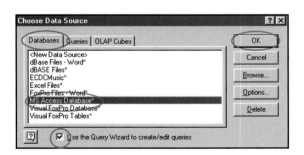

3 Click the **OK** button.

The Select Database dialog box opens.

Select the drive where the student files are located in the **Drives** box. Select the folder where the student files are located in the **Directories** box. Select **EX0903** in the **Database Name** box.

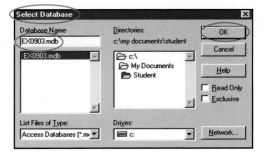

4 Click **OK**.

The Query Wizard starts.

Confirm that **Budget in Billions of 1996 Dollars** is selected and click the add button to add all of the table's columns to the query.

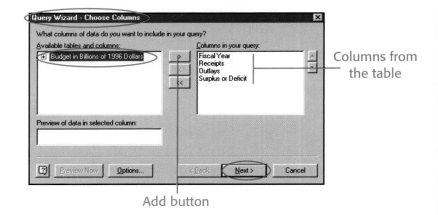

Columns from the table

Add button

IN DEPTH

You do not have to import all the columns. You may click the plus sign next to the name of the table then select and add the columns individually. If you are familiar with Access, these columns are the fields in the table.

---

5 Click the **Next** button to move to the **Filter Data** dialog box of the wizard. Click **Fiscal Year**.

This column contains the name of the year. One of the rows in this table has TQ in this column to indicate a special case which you do not want to import.

Click the arrow on the first box in the **Only include rows where** area and choose **does not equal**.

You want all the rows that do not have TQ in this column.

Type **TQ** in the second box.

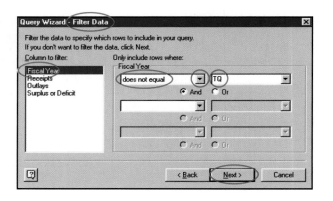

6 Click the **Next** button.

The Sort Order page of the wizard is displayed. The rows are already sorted by year, so no change is needed on this page.

Click the **Next** button.

The Finish dialog box of the wizard is displayed and provides three options for dealing with this data.

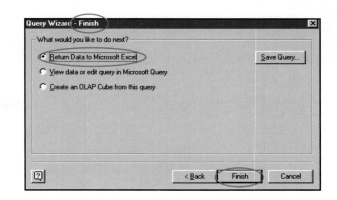

7 Confirm that **Return Data to Microsoft Excel** is selected. Click **Finish**.

The Import Data dialog box is displayed.

Confirm that **Existing worksheet** is selected and type **=$A$2**.

The upper left corner of the table will be placed in cell A2 to provide room for adding a label in the first row.

8 Click the **OK** button.

The table is imported to the worksheet without the row with TQ in the year cell.

Print this sheet if your instructor requires it.

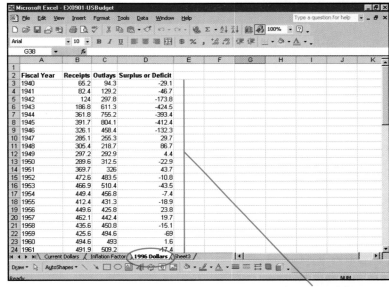

Data imported from
Access table

IN DEPTH

If you import data from an external source, you may want to update it if you think the data in the external source has changed. You can view the External Data toolbar by choosing View, Toolbars, External Data. You may use the Refresh Data button to refresh the selected range or the Refresh All button to refresh all references.

Task 4
COPYING A TABLE FROM A WORD DOCUMENT

Why would I do this?

Some people make tables of names and addresses in Microsoft Word that they use to create merged documents and mailing labels. Tables of data may also exist in research documents that are written in Word. You can import tables like these from Word into Excel without retyping them.

In this task, you learn how to select a table in a Word document, copy it, and paste it into a worksheet.

1 Double click the **Sheet3** tab and type **Percent of GDP**. Press ↵Enter.

The name of the sheet is changed.

IN DEPTH

GDP stands for Gross Domestic Product and is used in the field of economics to measure the economic productivity of a country. Comparing the surplus or deficit in the budget to the GDP provides some insight into how significant the deficit or surplus may be. For example, if a person with an annual income of $100,000 overspends his budget by $2,000 it isn't as significant as a person who overspends by the same amount but who only makes $20,000 per year.

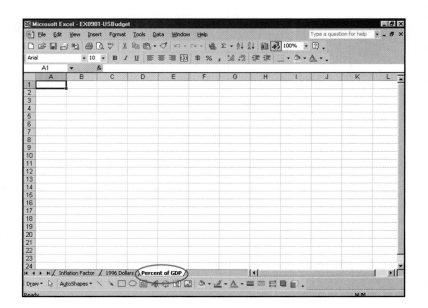

2 Start Word and click the **Open** button on the toolbar. Locate the folder where the student files for this lesson are stored. Select **EX0904** and click the **Open** button.

The Word file EX0904 opens and displays a table of data.

U.S. Budget as Percent of Gross Domestic Product

Year	GDP	Receipts	Outlays	Surplus or Deficit (-)
1930	97.4	4.2	3.4	0.8
1931	83.7	3.7	4.3	(0.6)
1932	67.5	2.9	6.9	(4.1)
1933	57.4	3.5	8.0	(4.5)
1934	61.2	4.8	10.7	(5.9)
1935	69.7	5.2	9.2	(4.0)
1936	78.5	5.0	10.5	(5.5)
1937	87.8	6.1	8.6	(2.5)
1938	89.0	7.6	7.7	(0.1)
1939	89.0	7.1	10.3	(3.2)
1940	96.7	6.8	9.8	(3.0)
1941	114.0	7.6	12.0	(4.3)
1942	144.2	10.1	24.4	(14.2)
1943	180.1	13.3	43.6	(30.3)
1944	209.0	20.9	43.7	(22.8)
1945	221.3	20.4	41.9	(21.5)
1946	222.7	17.6	24.8	(7.2)
1947	234.6	16.4	14.7	1.7

3 Click anywhere in the table to place the insertion point in one of its cells. Choose **Ta**ble, **Selec**t, **Ta**ble.

The table is selected but not the row of text above it.

Click the **C**opy button.

The table is copied to the Office Clipboard.

Selected table copied to the Office Clipboard

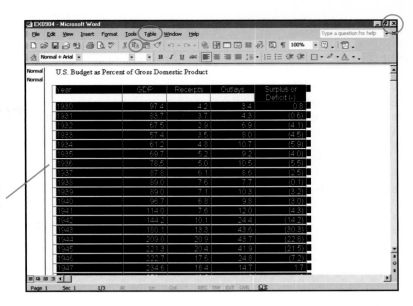

4 Close Word. Do not save any changes.

The table is still in the Office Clipboard.

Click cell **A2** in the **Percent of GDP** sheet to select it. Click the **P**aste button.

The table is imported with some of its formatting.

Table imported with borders around cells

5 Confirm that the table is still selected. Choose **E**dit, **C**lear, **F**ormats.

The formatting is removed from the table.

Print this sheet if your instructor requires it.

Save the workbook. Overwrite the original copy of the workbook, if necessary.

Leave the workbook open for use in the next task.

Task 5
CREATING A SUMMARY SHEET

Why would I do this?

It is easy to get overwhelmed by too much data spread across several worksheets. If you want to extract meaningful information from the data, it is a good idea to bring the important data together on a single worksheet and then chart it.

In this task, you learn how to create a summary sheet and use formulas to transfer data into it. The custom chart type allows you to chart two different sets of related data on the same chart using two different value axes.

1 Choose Insert, Worksheet.

A new worksheet is inserted.

> Double-click the tab on the new sheet and type **Summary**. Press ↵Enter.

The sheet is renamed.

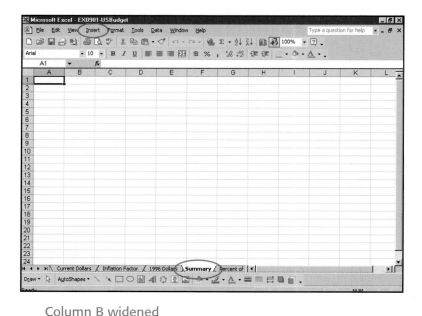

Column B widened

2 Move the mouse pointer onto the **Summary** sheet tab. Drag the sheet tab to the right of the **Percent of GDP** sheet tab and release the mouse.

The Summary sheet is moved to the last position in the list of sheets.

> Select cell **A1** and type **Year**. Select cell **B1**. Type **Surplus/Deficit**. Select cell **C1**. Type **% of GDP**. Press ↵Enter. Widen column **B** to display the full title.

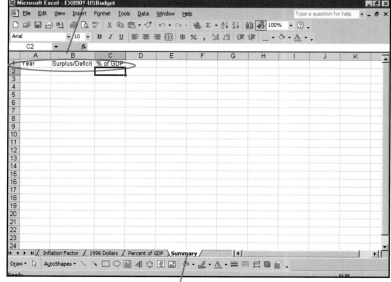

Sheet tab moved to the end

3 Click cell **A2**. Type = to start an equation.

Equations can refer to other worksheets. This type of reference is called a **three-dimensional reference**. *If you consider the sheets to be stacked on top of each other, the third dimension is the depth of the stack of worksheets.*

Click the **1996 Dollars** tab. Click cell **A3** on the 1996 Dollars sheet which contains the year **1940**. Press ↵Enter.

The formula on the Summary sheet refers to the first cell in the list of years on the 1996 Dollars sheet.

Select **A2** on the **Summary** sheet.

Notice the 3-D reference on the formula toolbar.

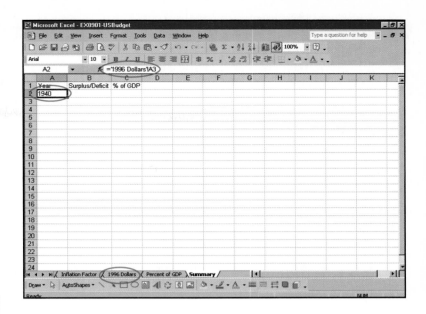

IN DEPTH

You can type a formula with a 3-D reference if you use the correct syntax. Like all formulas in Excel, it starts with an equal sign. The sheet name is enclosed in single quotation marks and followed by an exclamation mark. The cell name follows the sheet name. This combination of sheet name and cell name can be used with other cell names and mathematical functions.

Column widened

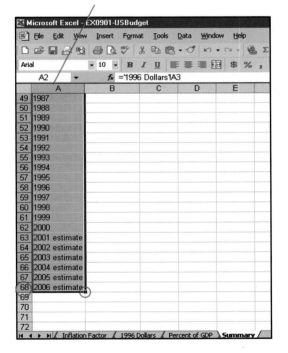

4 Click the fill handle on cell **A2** and drag it to cell **A68**. Release the fill handle.

The Summary sheet displays the values from the corresponding cells in the 1996 Dollars sheet. If actual values are used to replace the estimates in the last six cells in the 1996 Dollars sheet, the changes will be reflected in the Summary sheet.

Widen column **A** to accommodate the last six values.

5 Select cell **B2**. Type **=**, click the **1996 Dollars** sheet tab, click cell **D3**, and press ⏎Enter.

The Summary sheet displays the budget deficit for 1940.

Select cell **B2**. Drag the fill handle down to cell **B68**.

The formula in B2 is filled into the cells below it through cell B68.

QUICK TIP

If you are filling in columns of a table where the length of the column is the same length as the column next to it, you can double-click the fill handle instead of dragging it. The cells below the selected cell will fill automatically and stop when the length of the column matches the column next to it.

6 Select cell **C2**. Type **=**, click the **Percent of GDP** sheet tab, click cell **E13**, and press ⏎Enter.

The Summary sheet displays the budget deficit as a percent of GDP for 1940 .

Select cell **C2**. Drag the fill handle down to cell **C68**.

The summary sheet has the surplus or deficit value in 1996 dollars and the percent of GDP for each year. You can now compare and evaluate this data.

Print this sheet if your instructor requires it.

Save the workbook and leave it open for use in the next task.

CAUTION

Be sure to save your workbook. If you do not, you may lose some of your work when you save the file again in the next task.

IN DEPTH

Summary sheets like this allow you to make comparisons. Notice that the United States ran a deficit during the Gulf War (1990–1992) almost as large as during World War II (1941–1946) but the deficit was a much smaller percentage of gross domestic product.

Task 6
SAVING A SHEET IN CSV FORMAT

Why would I do this?

Programs that handle data use proprietary formats to display the data. Codes that control the format are saved as part of the data and can confuse a program made by a different vendor.

Data can be transferred between different programs if the proprietary formatting codes are removed. The result is a series of text or numbers separated by a character such as a comma, tab, or semicolon that is used to separate the values that were formerly in different columns in the sheet. If commas are used, the file format is called *CSV*, which stands for *Comma Separated Values*. When a character such as a comma is used to separate values, the characters are called *delimiters*. This type of file is also called a comma delimited file. A CSV file can be imported into almost any other program that manages data.

In this task, you learn how to save a worksheet as a CSV file and open it in a word processor to view the file structure.

1 Confirm that the **Summary** sheet is selected. Choose <u>F</u>ile, Save <u>A</u>s. Click the arrow next to the **Save as type** box and select **CSV (Comma delimited)**.

The worksheet will be saved with a file extension of .csv.

Select the file name and type **EX0901-Comma**.

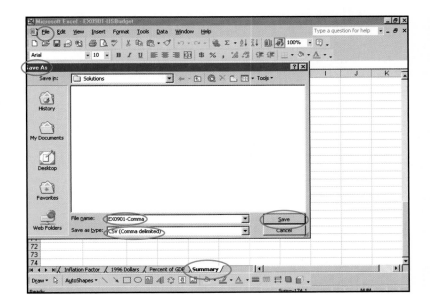

You can display the file extension as part of the file name or you can hide the file extensions for known file types. If you want to see the file extensions for the known file types, start Windows Explorer and choose <u>T</u>ools, Folder <u>O</u>ptions. Click the View tab and deselect the option, Hide file extensions for known file types.

2 Confirm that the folder in which you store your solutions is selected in the **Save in** box. Click **Save**.

A dialog box opens and explains that this format does not work with multiple worksheets and that only the currently selected sheet will be saved.

      Click **OK**.

Another dialog box opens to warn you that your worksheet contains features that will be lost. This worksheet uses formulas. Only the values will be saved, not the formulas

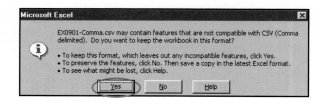

3 Click **Yes**.

The Summary worksheet is saved as a comma separated values file named EX0901-Comma. The name on the sheet tab is changed to the new name. If you close this file and open it again, the other sheets will not be there.

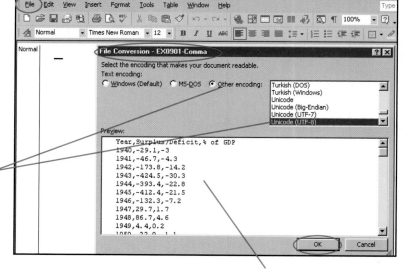

4 Close Excel and the workbook. When asked if you want to save your changes, click **No**.

      Start Microsoft Word. Choose **File, Open**. Locate the folder in which you store your files. Change the **Files of type** box to **All Files**. Select **EX0901-Comma** and click **Open**.

The File Conversion dialog box opens. The default settings will work to open this file.

Default settings

Preview of data before it is imported

CAUTION

In some cases, you may not see this dialog box and the program proceeds to the final step.

5 Click **OK**.

The file opens and displays the data from the summary sheet separated by commas.

Print this sheet if your instructor requires it.

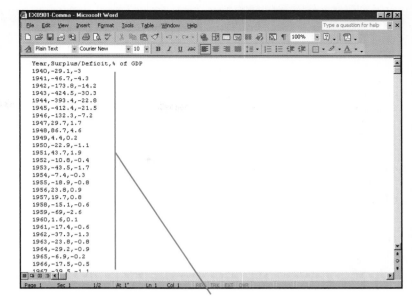

Comma Separated Values

6 Close the file and close Word.

Task 7

PUBLISHING INTERACTIVE WEB PAGES

Why would I do this?

Interactive Web pages allow you to interact with the worksheet using a Web browser. You can provide the data to the entire company or a small workgroup where people can sort, filter, and calculate values for themselves. The people who view the Web page cannot alter the data permanently so you do not have to worry about them corrupting the data. They can download a working copy of the worksheet if they want to use it off-line as a normal Excel worksheet.

In this task, you learn how to save the budget pages as a Web page that you can view with a browser.

1 Start Excel. Open **EX0901-USBudget** from the folder where you store your work.

CAUTION

This workbook should have all the worksheets. If you did not save the workbook at the end of Task 5, you may have lost most of your work when you saved the file as CSV in Task 6. If the workbook only has one worksheet, you need to start this lesson over. Be sure to save the work as directed in Task 5.

QUICK TIP

Excel keeps a short list of recently opened workbooks that you can use to open a workbook again without taking the time to look for it. One of these lists is part of the File menu and the other is found in the task pane under Open a workbook. You can use either one to open the recently used workbook.

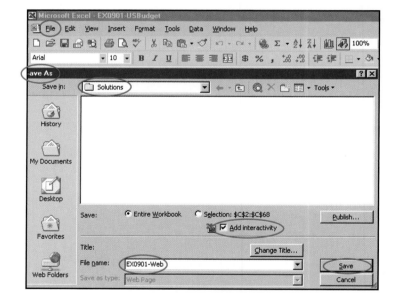

2 Choose File, Save as Web Page.

The Save As dialog box opens.

Click the **Add interactivity** box. Select the current name in the **File name** box and type **EX0901-Web**. Confirm that the folder in the **Save in** box is the one where you save your work.

When you choose the Add interactivity option, the page is saved using the XML language which provides more interactivity with Web pages. XML stands for eXtensible Mark-up Language.

3 Click the <u>S</u>ave button. Close Excel. Do not save any changes if asked.

The workbook is saved as a Web page.

Start Internet Explorer. Choose <u>F</u>ile, <u>O</u>pen, and click the B<u>r</u>owse button. Locate the folder where you saved the Web page, select **EX0901-Web**, and then click the **Open** button.

The Open dialog box displays the location of the file in your folder.

Click **OK**.

The browser opens the Web page.

4 Click the **Summary** tab.

A list of the other worksheets in the workbook is displayed.

Click **Percent of GDP** on the list.

The Percent of GDP sheet is displayed and its name is displayed on the sheet tab.

5 Click the **Percent of GDP** sheet tab and choose **Summary** from the list. Click cell **C2** to select it.

This cell had a formula with a 3-D reference in it in the Excel workbook.

Click the **Commands and Options** button on the toolbar.

The Commands and Options dialog box opens.

Click the **Formula** tab.

The formula is still there.

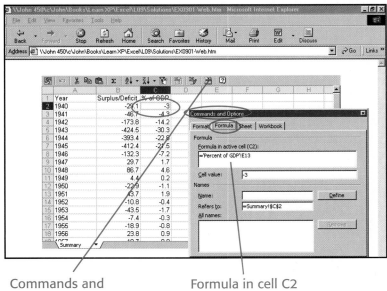

Commands and Options button

Formula in cell C2

6 Print this page if your instructor requires it.
Close the browser.

Task 8
SAVING RELATED FILES IN A WORKSPACE

Why would I do this?

When you regularly work with several related Excel files, it is convenient to create a workspace. This is a file that automatically opens several workbooks at once.

In this task, you learn how to create a workspace that opens the budget files you have been using.

1 Start Excel. Choose **File**, **Open**. Locate the folder you use to store your work in the **Look in** box. Click the arrow at the right of the **Files of type** box and select **All Files.**

All the files in this folder are displayed. You may have more files than those shown in the figure. Confirm that there are three different files that begin with EX0901.

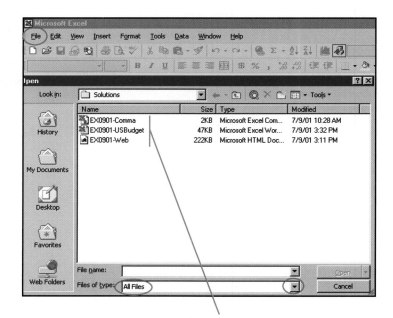

Three files to be placed in a workspace

2 Select **EX0901-USBudget** and click the **Open** button. Repeat this process to open **EX0901-Comma** and **EX0901-Web**.

You have a workbook, a CSV file, and a Web page open at the same time.

Choose <u>W</u>indow.

A list of the open files is displayed at the bottom of this menu.

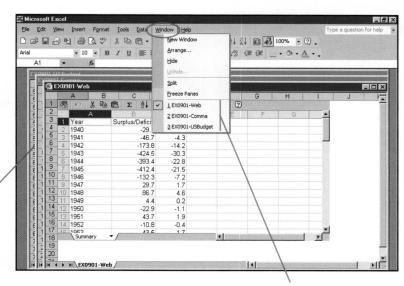

Three open files

List of open Excel files

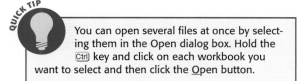

The three windows are arranged using the Cascade option. If your windows do not display this way by default, choose <u>W</u>indow, Arrange, <u>C</u>ascade, and click OK.

You can open several files at once by selecting them in the Open dialog box. Hold the [Ctrl] key and click on each workbook you want to select and then click the <u>O</u>pen button.

3 Choose <u>F</u>ile, Save <u>W</u>orkspace.

The Save Workspace dialog box opens.

Confirm that the folder where you store your work is selected in the **Save <u>i</u>n** box. Select the default name in the **File name** box and type **EX0901-Workspace**.

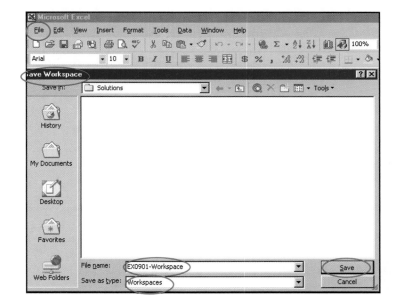

4 Click <u>S</u>ave. Choose <u>N</u>o if you are asked if you want to save changes.

The workspace is created.

    Close all three files. Do not save any changes.

This time, you can open all three files at once by opening the workspace file. It will open the other files for you automatically.

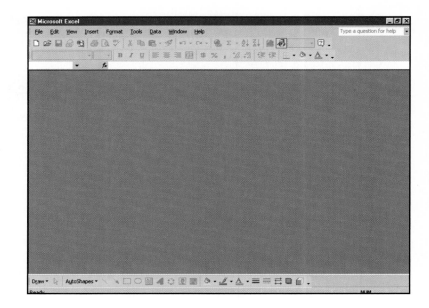

5 Choose <u>F</u>ile, <u>O</u>pen. Select your folder in the **Look in** box. Change the **Files of type** box to **All Files**, if necessary.

The file names are listed.

    Click the arrow on the **Views** button and choose **Details** if this view is not already in use.

This view displays the file size. Notice that the workspace file is very small. It only contains instructions on how to open the other files.

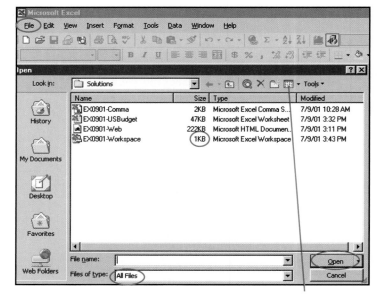

View button

6 Select **EX0901-Workspace** and click **Open**.

The three files in the workspace open automatically.

Choose **Window** to display the list of open files.

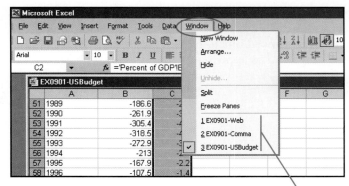

List of files opened automatically

7 Close Excel. Do not save any changes.

The exercises that follow are designed for you to review and use what you have learned in this lesson. You also have the opportunity to practice your skills and then expand on them by applying them to new situations.

Explain It

Do It

Use It

COMPREHENSION

Comprehension exercises are designed to check your memory and understanding of the basic concepts in this lesson. You distinguish between true and false statements, identify new screen elements, and match terms with related statements. If you are uncertain of the correct answer, refer to the task number following each item (for example, T4 refers to Task 4) and review that task until you are confident that you can provide a correct response.

TRUE-FALSE

Circle either T or F.

T   F   **1.** To import a table from Access, you must first convert it to a CSV file. **(T3)**

T   F   **2.** When you copy a table from a Word document and paste it in an Excel worksheet, the existing formatting is automatically removed. **(T4)**

T   F   **3.** A 3-D reference can include cells from other worksheets. **(T5)**

T   F   **4.** When you save an Excel worksheet as a CSV file, formulas will be saved. **(T6)**

T   F   **5.** Only one worksheet can be selected at a time when viewing your Excel workbook as a Web page in a Web browser. **(T7)**

T   F   **6.** A workspace is a file that automatically opens several workbooks at once. **(T8)**

MATCHING QUESTIONS

A. CSV   **D.** Add Interactivity box

B. Workspace   **E.** Import External <u>D</u>ata

C. 3-D reference   **F.** Move or Copy dialog box

Match the following statements to the word or phrase that is the best match from the list. Write the letter of the matching word or phrase in the space provided next to the number.

1. _____ An option when saving the file as a Web page to use the XML language to provide more interaction with Web pages **(T7)**

2. _____ A file format that uses commas to separates values **(T6)**

3. _____ A menu item that allows you to create a new Web or database query **(T2 & T3)**

4. _____ An equation that can use references to other worksheets **(T5)**

5. _____ A place where you indicate where you want to copy a worksheet **(T1)**

6. _____ A file that automatically opens several workbooks at once **(T8)**

IDENTIFYING PARTS OF THE EXCEL SCREEN

Refer to the figure and identify the numbered parts of the screen. Write the letter of the correct label in the space next to the number.

1. _____

2. _____

3. _____

4. _____

5. _____

6. _____

7. _____

8. _____

9. _____

10. _____

A. Database query dialog box (T3)

B. 3-D reference (T5)

C. Name of Access database table (T3)

D. Button to add database columns to your query (T3)

E. Web query dialog box (T2)

F. Address of Web page that contains table to import (T2)

G. Identified Web table to import (T2)

H. Formatting marks to indicate number (T6)

I. Formatting marks to indicate separation of data (T6)

J. CSV file (T6)

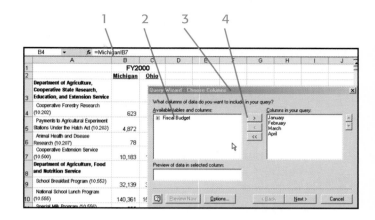

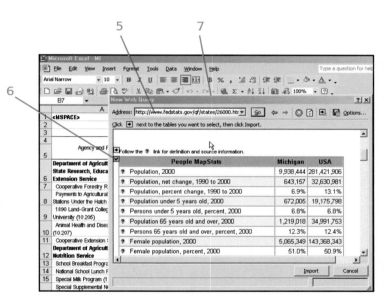

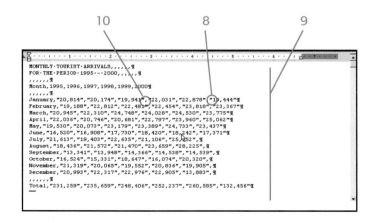

Reinforcement exercises are designed to reinforce the skills you have learned by applying them to a new situation. Detailed instructions are provided along with a figure, where appropriate, to illustrate the result. Complete the reinforcement exercises sequentially. Leave the workbook open at the end of each exercise for use in the next exercise until you are specifically directed to close it.

R1—Copying a Worksheet from another Workbook

In this exercise, you create a new workbook and then copy information from another workbook into it. The information you will be copying is a list of how many employees the executive branch of the U.S. government employed between 1962 and 2000.

1. Start Excel. Confirm that an empty workbook is displayed and save it in your folder as **EX0905-USEmployees**.

2. Open the Task Pane, if necessary, by choosing <u>V</u>iew, Tas<u>k</u> Pane. Click **More workbooks** from the **Open a workbook** area. Change the **Look <u>in</u>** box to display the student files for this lesson. Select **EX0905** and click the <u>O</u>pen button.

3. Choose <u>E</u>dit, <u>M</u>ove or Copy Sheet.

4. Click the down arrow at the right side of the **To book** box and select **EX0905-USEmployees**.

5. Click the **<u>C</u>reate a copy** check box, and then click the **OK** button.

6. Double-click the sheet tab to select it and type **Executive**. Press ↵Enter.

7. Switch back to EX0905 and close it.

8. Save the workbook, and leave it open for the next exercise.

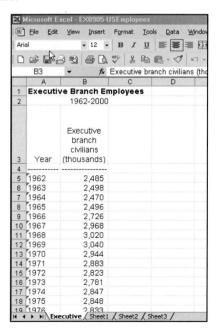

R2—Importing Data from a Web Page

The information that lists how many employees the legislative and judicial branches employ is located on a Web page. You will import this information into your workbook using a New Web Query.

1. Launch Internet Explorer. Choose <u>F</u>ile, <u>O</u>pen. Click the **B<u>r</u>owse** button.

2. Locate the folder that contains the student files for this lesson and select **EX0906**. Click the <u>O</u>pen button. Click **OK**.

3. Select the address in the **Address** box. Choose <u>E</u>dit, <u>C</u>opy.

4. Click the **Close** button on the title bar of the Internet Explorer window. Double-click the **Sheet1** tab and type **Legislative & Judicial**. Press ↵Enter.

5. Choose <u>D</u>ata, Import External <u>D</u>ata, New <u>W</u>eb Query.

6. Confirm that the address is selected. Hold the Ctrl key and press **V**, then click the <u>G</u>o button.

7. Click the **<u>I</u>mport** button; then click the **OK** button. Widen column **B** to accommodate the heading.

8. Save the workbook, and leave it open for the next exercise.

	A	B
1	Year	Legislative and judicial branch personnel (thousands)
2	-	-
3	1962	30
4	1963	30
5	1964	31
6	1965	32
7	1966	33
8	1967	34
9	1968	35
10	1969	36
11	1970	38
12	1971	40
13	1972	42
14	1973	44
15	1974	46
16	1975	49
17	1976	50
18	1977	53
19	1978	55
20	1979	53
21	1980	55
22	1981	54
23	1982	55
24	1983	56

◄ ◄ ► ►◄ Executive \ **Legislative & Judicial** / Sheet2 / Sheet3 /

R3—Importing Data from an Access Table

Information on how many people the U.S. military employs is located in an Access database. You will use a new database query to import this information into your workbook.

1. Double click the **Sheet2** tab and type **Military**. Press ⏎Enter.

2. Choose **Data**, **Import External Data**, **New Database Query**.

3. Click the **Databases** tab, if necessary, and click **MS Access Database***. Confirm that the checkbox next to **Use the Query Wizard to create/edit queries** displays a check mark.

4. Click the **OK** button. Select the drive where the student files are located in the **Drives** box. Select the folder where the student files are located in the **Directories** box. Select **EX0907** in the **Database Name** box.

5. Click **OK**. Confirm that **Military Table** is selected and click the add button to add all of the table's columns to the query.

6. Click the **Next** button twice to move to the **Sort Order** box. Click the down arrow to the right of the **Sort by** box, and select **Year**.

7. Click **Next**. Confirm that **Return Data to Microsoft Excel** is selected. Click **Finish**.

8. Confirm that **Existing worksheet** is selected and click **OK**.

9. Save the workbook, and leave it open for the next task.

	A	B	C	D	E	F
1	**Year**	**Military**				
2	1962	2840				
3	1963	2732				
4	1964	2719				
5	1965	2687				
6	1966	3129				
7	1967	3413				
8	1968	3584				
9	1969	3499				
10	1970	3104				
11	1971	2752				
12	1972	2360				
13	1973	2289				
14	1974	2198				
15	1975	2164				
16	1976	2119				
17	1977	2112				
18	1978	2099				
19	1979	2063				
20	1980	2090				
21	1981	2122				
22	1982	2147				
23	1983	2163				
24	1984	2178				

Executive / Legislative & Judicial / **Military** / Sheet3 /

R4—Getting a Table from a Word Document

In this exercise, you retrieve state and local employment numbers from a Word document and paste them in your workbook.

1. Double click the **Sheet3** tab and type **State & Local**. Press ⏎Enter.

2. Start Word and click the **Open** button on the toolbar. Locate the folder where the student files for this lesson are stored. Select **EX0908** and click the **Open** button.

3. Click anywhere in the table to place the insertion point in one of its cells. Choose **Table**, **Select**, **Table**. Click the **Copy** button. Close Word.

4. Click cell **A1** in the **State & Local** sheet to select it. Click the **Paste** button.

5. Choose **Edit**, **Clear**, **Formats**. Widen column **B** to accommodate heading.

6. Save the workbook, and leave it open for the next task.

	A	B	C
1	Year	State and local governments (thousands)	
2	1962	6549	
3	1963	6868	
4	1964	7248	
5	1965	7696	
6	1966	8221	
7	1967	8673	
8	1968	9102	
9	1969	9437	
10	1970	9822	
11	1971	10184	
12	1972	10649	
13	1973	11069	
14	1974	11446	
15	1975	11937	
16	1976	12138	
17	1977	12400	
18	1978	12920	
19	1979	13174	
20	1980	13375	
21	1981	13259	
22	1982	13098	
23	1983	13096	
24	1984	13216	

Executive / Legislative & Judicial / Military / **State & Local**

R5—Creating a Summary Sheet

In this exercise, you create a summary worksheet that uses formulas with 3-D references to the Executive and State & Local worksheets.

1. Choose **Insert**, **Worksheet**. Double click the tab on the new sheet and type **Summary**. Press ⏎Enter.

2. Move the mouse pointer onto the **Summary** sheet tab. Click and drag the sheet tab to the right of the **State & Local** sheet tab and release the mouse.

3. Select cell **A1** and type **Year**. Press Tab⇥ to move the selection to cell **B1**. Type **Executive**. Press Tab⇥. Type **State & Local**. Press ⏎Enter. Widen column **C** to display the full title.

4. Click cell **A2**. Type = to start an equation. Click the **Executive** sheet tab. Click cell **A5**, and then press ⏎Enter. Select **A2** on the **Summary** sheet. Click the fill handle on cell **A2** and drag it to cell **A40**. Release the fill handle.

5. Select cell **B2**. Type =, click the **Executive** sheet tab, click cell **B5**, and then press ⏎Enter. Select cell **B2**. Click and drag the fill handle down to cell **B40**.

6. Select cell **C2**. Type =, click the **State & Local** sheet tab, click cell **B2**, and then press ⏎Enter. Select cell **C2**. Click and drag the fill handle down to cell **C40**.

7. Select column **C**. Click the **Comma Style** button to format the numbers. Click the **Decrease Decimal** button twice to remove zeros.

8. Print each sheet of the workbook if your instructor requires it.

9. Save the workbook, and leave it open for the next task.

	A	B	C	D	E	F
1	Year	Executive	State & Local			
2	1962	2,485	6,549			
3	1963	2,498	6,868			
4	1964	2,470	7,248			
5	1965	2,496	7,696			
6	1966	2,726	8,221			
7	1967	2,968	8,673			
8	1968	3,020	9,102			
9	1969	3,040	9,437			
10	1970	2,944	9,822			
11	1971	2,883	10,184			
12	1972	2,823	10,649			
13	1973	2,781	11,069			
14	1974	2,847	11,446			
15	1975	2,848	11,937			
16	1976	2,833	12,138			
17	1977	2,840	12,400			
18	1978	2,875	12,920			
19	1979	2,823	13,174			
20	1980	2,821	13,375			
21	1981	2,806	13,259			
22	1982	2,770	13,098			
23	1983	2,820	13,096			
24	1984	2,854	13,216			

⁴ ◄ ► ▶◄ Executive / Legislative & Judicial / Military / State & Local \ Summar

R6—Saving a Sheet in CSV Format

1. Confirm that the **Summary** sheet is selected. Choose **File, Save As**. Click the down arrow next to the **Save as type** box and select **CSV (Comma delimited)**. Select the file name and type **EX0905-Comma**.

2. Confirm that the folder in which you store your solutions is selected in the **Save in** box. Click **Save**. Click **OK**.

3. Click **Yes**. Close Excel and the workbook. When asked if you want to save your changes, click **No**.

4. Start Microsoft Word. Choose **File, Open**. Locate the folder in which you store your files. Change the **Files of type** box to **All Files**. Select **EX0905-Comma** and click **Open**. Click **OK**.

5. Print this sheet if your instructor requires it. Close the file and close Word.

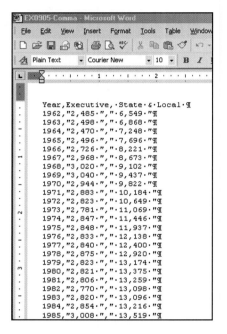

R7—Publishing Interactive Web Pages

1. Start Excel. Open **EX0905-USEmployees** from the folder where you store your work.

2. Choose **File, Save as Web Page**. Click the **Add interactivity** box. Select the current name in the **File name** box and type **EX0905-Web**. Confirm that the folder in the **Save in** box is the one where you save your work.

3. Click the **Save** button. Close Excel. Do not save any changes if asked.

4. Start Internet Explorer. Choose **File, Open**, and click the **Browse** button. Locate the folder where you saved the Web page, select **EX0905-Web**, and then click the **Open** button. Click **OK**.

5. Click the arrow on the sheet tab and choose **Military**.

6. Click the arrow on the sheet tab and choose **Summary**. Click cell **C2** to select it.

7. Print this page if your instructor requires it. Close the browser.

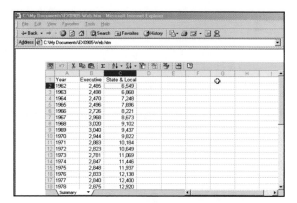

R8—Saving Related Files in a Workspace

1. Start Excel. Choose **File**, **Open**. Locate the folder you use to store your work in the **Look in** box. Click the arrow at the right of the **Files of type** box and select **All Files.** Confirm that there are three different files that begin with EX0905. Select **EX0905-USEmployees** and click the **Open** button. Repeat this process to open **EX0905-Comma** and **EX0905-Web**.

2. Choose **File**, **Save Workspace**. Confirm that the folder where you store your work is selected in the **Save in** box. Select the default name in the **File name** box and type EX0905-Workspace.

3. Click **Save**. Choose **No** if you are asked if you want to save changes. Close all three files. Do not save any changes.

4. Choose **File**, **Open**. Select your folder in the **Look in** box. Change the **Files of type** box to **All Files**, if necessary. Click the arrow on the **Views** button and choose **Details** if this view is not already in use.

5. Select **EX0905-Workspace** and click **Open**. All three Excel files in the workspace open.

6. Close Excel. Do not save any changes.

	A	B	C	D	E	F	G
1	Year	Executive	State & Local				
2	1962	2,485	6,549				
3	1963	2,498	6,868				
4	1964	2,470	7,248				
5	1965	2,496	7,696				
6	1966	2,726	8,221				
7	1967	2,968	8,673				
8	1968	3,020	9,102				
9	1969	3,040	9,437				
10	1970	2,944	9,822				
11	1971	2,883	10,184				
12	1972	2,823	10,649				
13	1973	2,781	11,069				
14	1974	2,847	11,446				
15	1975	2,848	11,937				
16	1976	2,833	12,138				
17	1977	2,840	12,400				
18	1978	2,875	12,920				
19	1979	2,823	13,174				
20	1980	2,821	13,375				
21	1981	2,806	13,259				
22	1982	2,770	13,098				
23	1983	2,820	13,096				
24	1984	2,854	13,216				

Challenge exercises are designed to test your ability to apply your skills to new situations with less detailed instruction. These exercises also challenge you to expand your repertoire of skills by using commands that are similar to those you have already learned. The desired outcome is clearly defined, but you have more freedom to choose the steps needed to achieve the required result.

The following exercises use separate sheets in the same workbook. The exercises are not sequential and do not depend on each other.

C1—Copying and Importing Information into the Same Worksheet

When you copy or import information into an Excel workbook from another file, you do not need to place it in its own worksheet. You can place it in your active worksheet beside existing information and then reformat it if necessary.

In this exercise, you obtain information from three different weather service agencies that are responsible for tracking temperature data. All three services use a different software application, and you will create a single worksheet from the separate files. You will also deal with some of the formatting issues that arise when you create a single worksheet from several different files.

Goal: Retrieve information from other files and place in an existing worksheet.

1. Open **EX0909** and save it in your folder as **EX0909-Challenge1**.

2. Start Word and open **EX0910.** Place your mouse pointer at the top of the second column (above **May**) so it becomes a down button. Click and drag to the right to highlight all columns containing names of months. Click the **Copy** button, and close Word.

3. Select cell F4 in the Temperatures worksheet and click the **Paste** button. Clear the formats.

4. Select cell J4. Choose **Data**, **Import External Data**, **New Database Query**. On **Databases** tab, click **MS Access Database***, and click **OK**. Locate the student files, select **EX0911** and click **OK**.

5. Click the add button. In the **Columns in your query** box, select **Year**. Click the remove button that has a single arrow to remove Year from your query.

6. Click **Next** three times to advance to the **Finish** dialog box. Confirm that **Return Data to Microsoft Excel** is selected, and click **Finish**.

7. In the **Import Data** dialog box, click **OK**. Place your name in **A3**.

8. Remove bold formatting from the month headings. Adjust the column widths and size of the font to fit the data on one printed sheet. (Hint: Use the **Fit to** option in Page Setup.) Change the titles in rows 1 and 2 to merge across all the columns of data.

9. Save the changes, print the **Temperatures** worksheet, and then close the file.

C2—Consolidating Data in a Summary Sheet

When you create a summary worksheet, is it useful to obtain numbers from different worksheets and have them automatically totaled when placed in the summary sheet. Excel allows you to do this with the Consolidate feature. You create references to the desired cells in various worksheets, and Excel then adds them together.

The U.S. Census Bureau tracks total monthly income by region and income bracket. In this exercise you use a workbook that contains two worksheets: one for households whose total monthly income is $0–$24,999 and one for households whose total monthly income is $25,000–$49,999. The summary sheet you create will take the totals in each worksheet and automatically sum them.

Goal: Use the Consolidate feature in a summary worksheet.

1. Open **EX0912** and save it in your folder as **EX0912-Challenge2**.

2. Double-click **Sheet3** and rename it **Summary**.

3. Select the **Under25k** worksheet. Select cells **A6** through **A19**. Click the **Copy** button. Select cell **A2** in the Summary worksheet, and click the **Paste** button. Widen column **A** to accommodate the information.

4. Select cell B2 and type **Total**.

5. Select cell **B3**. Choose **D**ata, **Co**nsolidate. Confirm that **SUM** is selected in the **Function** box and the insertion point is in the **Reference** box.

6. Click the **Under25k** worksheet, and select cells L7 to L19. You may need to move the open dialog box to view the worksheet. Click **A**dd in the **Consolidate** dialog box.

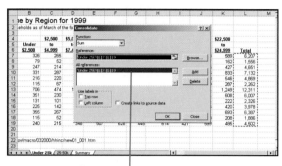

Stores the formulas to be used again

7. Click the **25-50k** tab, and select cells **L7** to **L19**. Click **A**dd.

8. Click **OK**. The numbers added to your worksheet are summed by region.

9. Type your name in **A1**. Save the changes, print the **Summary** worksheet and close the workbook.

C3—Saving Excel Workbook in Different File Formats

Goal: Save an Excel workbook in different file formats and compare them in Word.

1. Open **EX0913**. Choose **F**ile, **S**ave **A**s. Click the arrow next to the **Save as type** box and select **CSV (Comma delimited)**. Select the file name and type **EX0913-CSV**.

2. Click **OK**. Click **Y**es when prompted about certain features not being compatible with CSV format. Notice that you were not prompted about the selected file not being compatible with multiple worksheets (as you were in Task 6) since the file only contains a single worksheet.

3. Close **EX0913-CSV**, and do not save changes.

4. Reopen **EX0913**. Choose **F**ile, **S**ave **A**s. Click the arrow next to the **Save as type** box and select **Text (Tab delimited)**. Select the file name and type **EX0913-Text**.

5. Click **S**ave. Click **Y**es when prompted, and do not save changes. Close Excel.

6. Start Word. Click **F**ile, **O**pen. Confirm that **All Files** is selected in the **Files of type** box. Open **EX0913-CSV**. Click **OK** when prompted. Click the **Show/Hide** button if formatting is not displayed.

7. Click **F**ile, **O**pen. Confirm that **All Files** is selected in the **Files of type** box. Open **EX0913-Text**. Click **OK** when prompted. Click the **Show/Hide** button if formatting is not displayed.

8. Create a new Word document and save it as **EX0913-Questions**. Enter your name and section number then type and answer the following questions regarding **EX0913-CSV** and **EX0913-Text**. Keep the two files open for reference and toggle between them using the **W**indows menu or clicking on them in the Task bar.

   1) **What font do the files use and why do you think the fonts are different from the original worksheet?**

   2) **How are the files similar?**

   3) **What differences do you notice between the files?**

   4) **The CSV file uses commas to separate the numbers. How does the file treat the column headings that contain commas versus the column heading that contains no commas? What could be done so that all headings are treated equally?**

9. Save **EX0913-Questions** and print the file. Close all files.

C4—Using Multiple Worksheets in 3-D References

You previously learned how to create a 3-D reference that used a cell located on another worksheet. A 3-D reference can also contain functions using cells from multiple worksheets, providing that the desired information is located in the same cell on each worksheet.

This exercise uses an Excel workbook that contains multiple worksheets. Each worksheet contains information on a single department of the U.S. Executive branch. In the Summary worksheet you create a 3-D reference that uses cells in each worksheet.

Goal: Using Microsoft Help to create a 3-D reference that refers to the same cell on multiple worksheets.

1. Open **EX0914** and save it on your disk as **EX0914-Challenge4**.

2. View the various worksheets to become familiar with them.

3. Select the **Summary** worksheet, which is the first worksheet in the workbook.

4. Select **H**elp, **Microsoft Excel H**elp. Search for information on 3-D reference and locate the item that explains how to refer to the same cell on multiple sheets. Print the help screen titled **Refer to the same cell or range on multiple sheets**. Close the Help window.

5. Create a 3-D reference in cell **D7** of the **Summary** worksheet to sum all the values that occur in cell **B4** in each of the other worksheets. The function you will use in the 3-D reference is **SUM**.

6. Click the fill handle of cell D7 and drag it down to cell D26. Format the numbers to include a decimal and no zeros and the comma separator. Place your name in **A1** or in a location your instructor prefers.

7. Print the Summary worksheet.

8. Save the changes and close the workbook.

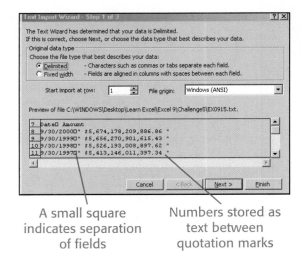

A small square indicates separation of fields

Numbers stored as text between quotation marks

C5—Importing Data from a Text File

In addition to importing data from the Internet and Access, Excel contains a wizard to import data from other file types. In this exercise, you import a text file.

Goal: Use Paste Special to copy formula values to another worksheet.

1. Start Excel, and save the blank workbook on your floppy disk as **EX0915-Challenge5**.

2. Choose **D**ata, **Import External D**ata, **Import Data**.

3. Confirm that **All Data Sources** is displayed in the **Files of type** box. In the **Look in box**, select **EX0915**. Click **O**pen.

4. In **Step 1** of the **Text Import Wizard** box, click the arrow of the scroll bar to view the data that will be imported.

5. Click **N**ext. **Step 2** previews how the data will look when imported into your worksheet. Notice that Excel has removed the quotation marks from the numbers and correctly guessed that tabs were used as delimiters.

6. Click **N**ext. **Step 3** allows you to set the data format. In the **Data preview** box, **General** appears above each column and the first column is highlighted. This dialog box allows you to format each column separately. The General format recognizes the date and currency formats automatically so you do not need to specify them in this box.

7. Click **F**inish. Confirm that **Existing worksheet** is selected, and click **OK**.

8. Save the file, print the worksheet, and close the workbook.

C6—Copying Values Produced by Formulas

Creating and using formulas in Excel is an easy and accurate way to manipulate numbers. Once you create them, these formulas can even be copied to adjacent cells using the click and drag method. However, if you want to use the resulting values in another worksheet or application, using copy/paste will not work since it is the formula that gets copied and not the number. This results in a reference error message. Excel provides an option called Paste Special to copy values produced by formulas. Paste Special also allows you to copy formulas, formats, and comments.

In this exercise you use a workbook that contains two worksheets. One worksheet contains Michigan travel information that is broken down by regional areas. The SUM function is used in cells to total each region. The second worksheet contains headings but no numbers. You will copy information from the first worksheet and paste it into the second worksheet using Paste Special.

Goal: Use Paste Special to copy formula values to another worksheet.

1. Start Excel and open **EX0916** from the folder of student files. Save the new workbook on your floppy disk as **EX0916-Challenge6**.

2. Select the **Regional Breakdown** worksheet, and click cell **D9**. Notice that the cell contains a SUM function. In fact, all cells located beneath **Total** headings contain SUM functions.

3. Select the **Region Totals** worksheet. Notice that the headings in the first column match the **Regional Breakdown** worksheet. The other four columns contain only region names.

4. Select the **Regional Breakdown** worksheet. Highlight cells **D9** through **D51**. Click the **Copy** button.

5. Select the **Region Totals** worksheet. Click cell **B5**.

6. Choose **Edit, Paste Special**. Under **Paste**, click **Values**. Click **OK**.

7. Repeat steps 4 through 6 to finish filling in the Region Totals worksheet. The following cell ranges need to be selected for each region: Midwest, **G9** through **G51**; South, **K9** through **K51**; and West, **N9** through **N51**.

8. Select cells **E5** through **E47** and add a right border.

9. Add your name to **A2** or a location your instructor prefers. Make any formatting changes your instructor requires. Save the file, and print the **Region Totals** worksheet.

10. Close the file and close Excel.

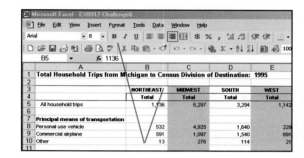

Value pasted, not the formula

ON YOUR OWN

Pick a topic that draws information from at least two different types of tables which are stored as text: a database table, or a table on a web page. Tables should come from at least two different types of files, not including Excel worksheets.

Criteria for grading will be:

1. Demonstrate the ability to import the tables into separate sheets in the same workbook.

2. In a separate sheet in the same workbook, create a summary sheet using 3-D references or the Consolidate option.

To complete the project:

• Submit the source files and/or the Web address for the tables you imported.

• Save your file on your own disk. Name it **EX0918-Importing**.

• Check with your instructor to determine if you should submit the project in electronic or printed form. If necessary, print out a copy of the worksheet to hand in.

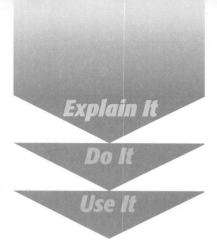

Lesson 10

Templates and Macros

Task 1   Creating and Running Macros

Task 2   Editing Macros Using VBA Editor

Task 3   Creating a Custom Toolbar

Task 4   Adding and Removing Buttons from Toolbars

Task 5   Assigning a Macro to a Toolbar Button

Task 6   Customizing Menus

Task 7   Creating Templates

Task 8   Applying Templates

INTRODUCTION

If you use Excel in the workplace, you may find yourself doing the same task repeatedly. It could be formatting the title of a worksheet to conform to company standards or performing a series of moves and operations on a range of cells. If you or your employees are spending time doing the same tasks over and over, you can automate these steps to make the operation faster and to assure that it is done the same way each time. One way to accomplish this objective is to record the steps in a *macro*. A macro in Excel is a program that is created automatically by recording a sequence of commands. It can be assigned to menus, buttons, or keys on the keyboard. You can edit the macro using the *Visual Basic Editor*, which is a text editor that allows you to see and edit the programming code that was created automatically when you recorded the macro.

If your work uses a collection of toolbar commands that are not usually available or are found on several different toolbars, you can create your own toolbar to make it easier to use these commands. You can *customize* the new toolbar by adding existing buttons to it. You can also create your own buttons and assign macros to them. Your toolbar can even have menus with a selection of options just like the standard menu toolbar.

Once you create a worksheet with its own macros and customized toolbars, you can use it as a *template*. Templates are workbooks that are already formatted with formulas in place. They only lack the specific information the user provides in certain cells.

In this lesson, you record a macro to format a title with a given font, color, alignment, and background. You edit the macro using the Visual Basic Editor to change the selected font. You also create a new toolbar to which you add a button that runs your macro. Then you add other buttons and a menu to the new toolbar. Finally, you save this worksheet as a template and apply it to a new worksheet.

VISUAL SUMMARY

When you complete this entire lesson, you will have a worksheet that looks like this:

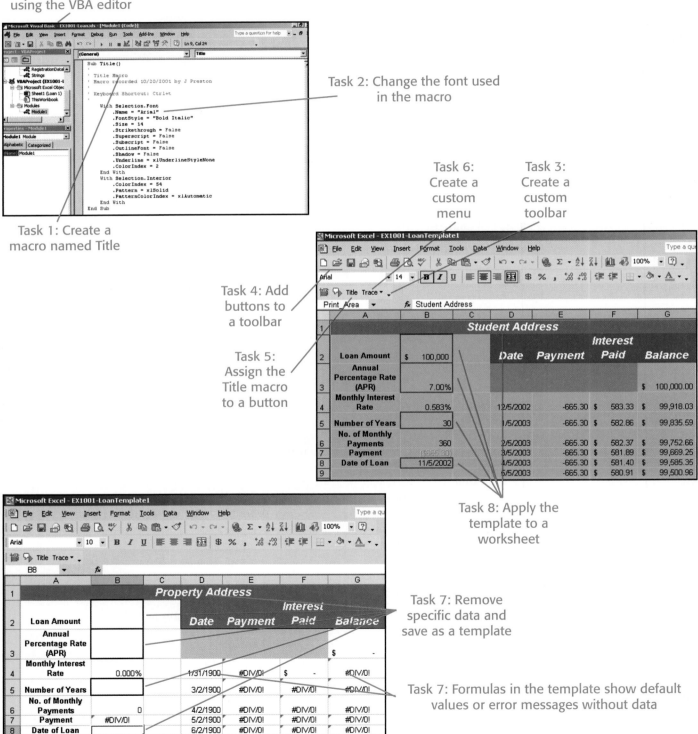

Task 2: Edit the macro using the VBA editor

Task 2: Change the font used in the macro

Task 1: Create a macro named Title

Task 6: Create a custom menu

Task 3: Create a custom toolbar

Task 4: Add buttons to a toolbar

Task 5: Assign the Title macro to a button

Task 8: Apply the template to a worksheet

Task 7: Remove specific data and save as a template

Task 7: Formulas in the template show default values or error messages without data

Task 1

CREATING AND RUNNING MACROS

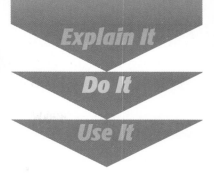

Why would I do this?

Companies spend a lot of advertising money on creating a company name that customers recognize. The company name is represented by the same font and colors wherever it appears to take advantage of this investment. If you have to go through numerous steps to format the company name every time you type it into a worksheet, you can automate this process by using a macro.

If you know Visual Basic programming code, you can write sophisticated macros. Fortunately, Excel has a feature that writes this code for you. If you know how to do what you want in Excel, the program can create a macro for you by recording your actions. It is a good idea to practice the process you want to record so you can do it without errors while you are recording the macro.

In this task, you set the security level to allow the creation of macros and then record a macro to format the company name.

1 Launch Excel and click the **Open** button. Find **EX1001** in the **Student** folder and open it.

This worksheet calculates the repayment schedule for an amortized loan.

Save the new file as **EX1001-Loan** on your disk.

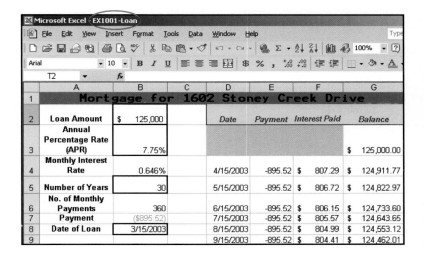

2 Choose <u>T</u>ools, <u>M</u>acro, <u>S</u>ecurity from the menu.

The Security dialog box displays security options for the workbook.

Click the **Security Level** tab, if necessary. Click the **Medium** option to select it.

This allows you to create a macro and run it without allowing unknown macros to run without your approval.

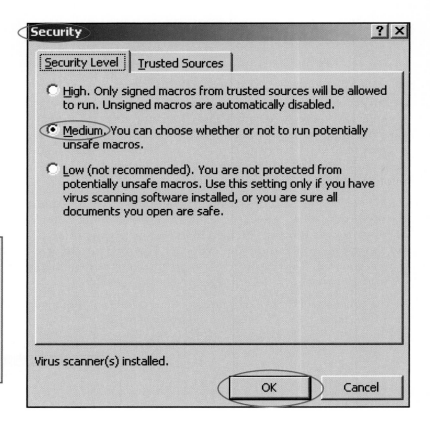

> ⚠ **CAUTION**
>
> Macros are designed to help you with repetitive tasks, but be aware that malicious people can use macros to destroy your work. Macros that are written for these purposes are called *macro viruses*. If you receive a worksheet or other file from someone else and it has a macro in it, do not run the macro unless you know what it is supposed to do and you trust the creator of the file. If you are in doubt, scan the file with a security program to check for known macro viruses.

3 Click **OK**.

The Security dialog box closes.

Click in **A1** to select cells **A1** through **G1**, type **Property Address**, and press ↵Enter.

The marketing department wants document and worksheet titles to appear as white letters on a plum colored background using bold, italic, Bookman Old Style font.

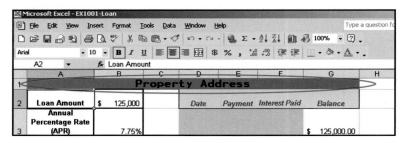

4 Select the title in cells **A1** through **G1**. Choose <u>T</u>ools, <u>M</u>acro, <u>R</u>ecord New Macro from the menu.

The Record Macro dialog box opens.

Confirm that the default name is selected in the **Macro name** box and type **Title**. Confirm that **This Workbook** is selected in the **Store macro in** box. Select the **Shortcut key** box and type **t**.

The macro is stored in the workbook with the name you typed. You can run it using the Ctrl *key plus the letter t.*

Confirm that your name is used in the **Description** box or replace the default name with your name, if necessary.

Your name

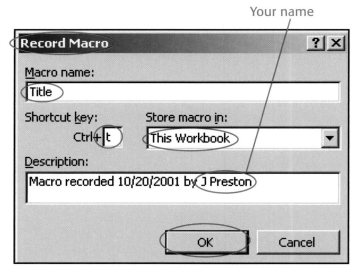

5 Click **OK**.

The Record Macro toolbar is displayed. The program is ready to record each step you take and write a program to reproduce them.

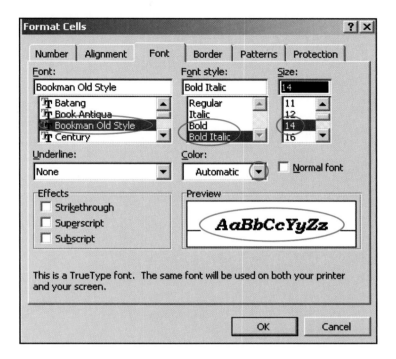

6 Choose **Format**, **Cells** and click the **Font** tab.

You can make all the formatting changes from this dialog box.

> Change the **Font** to **Bookman Old Style**. Change the **Font style** to **Bold Italic**. Change the **Size** to **14**.

An example is displayed in the Preview box.

7 Click the **Color** arrow to display the options for font colors. Click the White box.

The font will be white. While the background is still white, the font cannot be seen in the preview box.

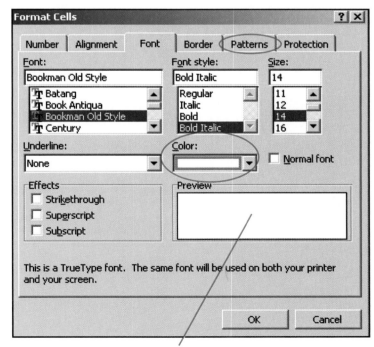

White text on white background

8 Click the **Patterns** tab. Click the plum color in the fourth row.

This color contrasts with the white font.

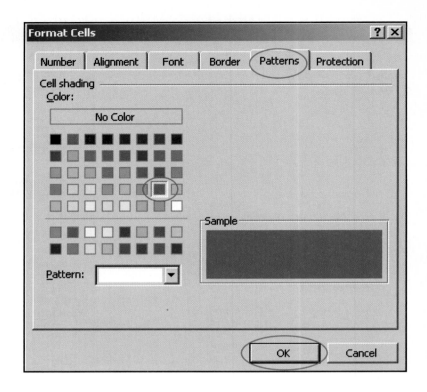

9 Click **OK**.

The title is formatted and the Record Macro toolbar is displayed to indicate that you are recording these steps.

Click the **Stop Recording** button on the Record Macro toolbar.

The macro is recorded and named Title.

Formatted title

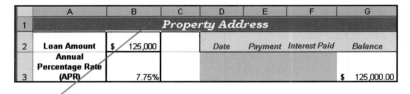

CAUTION
If you do not see the Stop Recording button on the Record Macro toolbar, the toolbar may be hidden behind another window. You can stop recording by selecting Tools, Macro, Stop Recording option.

10 Scroll down and select cell **A365**. Type your name and press ↵Enter. Select the cell again.

You can duplicate all the formatting steps required to format a title by running the macro.

Confirm that your name is selected. Hold the Ctrl and press the letter **t**. If your name is wider than a single cell, select cell **A365** and as many cells to the right as necessary and click the **Merge and Center** button.

Your name is formatted just like the title.

QUICK TIP

If want to move to a particular cell in a large worksheet, you can enter the cell address in the Name box. If you want to go to the end of a long column, use Ctrl + End.

	A	B	C	D	E	F	G
348				12/15/2031	-895.52	$ 87.61	$ 12,757.40
349				1/15/2032	-895.52	$ 82.39	$ 11,944.27
350				2/15/2032	-895.52	$ 77.14	$ 11,125.89
351				3/15/2032	-895.52	$ 71.85	$ 10,302.22
352				4/15/2032	-895.52	$ 66.54	$ 9,473.24
353				5/15/2032	-895.52	$ 61.18	$ 8,638.90
354				6/15/2032	-895.52	$ 55.79	$ 7,799.17
355				7/15/2032	-895.52	$ 50.37	$ 6,954.02
356				8/15/2032	-895.52	$ 44.91	$ 6,103.41
357				9/15/2032	-895.52	$ 39.42	$ 5,247.31
358				10/15/2032	-895.52	$ 33.89	$ 4,385.68
359				11/15/2032	-895.52	$ 28.32	$ 3,518.48
360				12/15/2032	-895.52	$ 22.72	$ 2,645.68
361				1/15/2033	-895.52	$ 17.09	$ 1,767.25
362				2/15/2033	-895.52	$ 11.41	$ 883.14
363				3/15/2033	-895.52	$ 5.70	$ (6.68)
364	**Prepared by:**						
365	*<Student Name>*						
366							

Formatted using the macro

11 Click the **Save** button to save your work.

The macro is saved as part of the workbook and is available for use any time the workbook is open.

Task 2

EDITING MACROS USING VBA EDITOR

Why would I do this?
The macro you created in the previous task is a program written in *VBA* that you can edit. *Visual Basic for Applications* or VBA is a programming language and the VBA Editor is a program that allows you to edit the programs.

Learning how to write programs in Visual Basic could be a separate course and is beyond the scope of this text. You can use the VBA editor to make some simple changes to an existing program without knowing how to write the program yourself. Using the VBA editor also provides insight as to how macros work.

In this task, you learn how to open the Title macro in the VBA editor and change the font used for the title.

❶ Choose **Tools**, **Macro**, **Macros**. Select the **Title** macro and click the **Edit** button.

The Microsoft Visual Basic editor starts and the EX1001-Loan.xls-Module1(code) window opens.

> Maximize the **EX1001-Loan.xls-[Module1(code)]** window.

This is the VBA program that runs when you run the Title macro. Notice the name of the font.

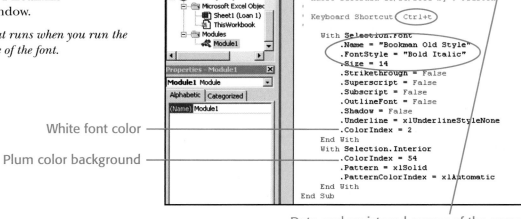

White font color ⎯⎯⎯⎯⎯

Plum color background ⎯⎯⎯⎯⎯

Date and registered owner of the computer

❷ Drag to select **"Bookman Old Style"**. Type **"Arial"**.

Arial is the name of one of the fonts available in Excel.

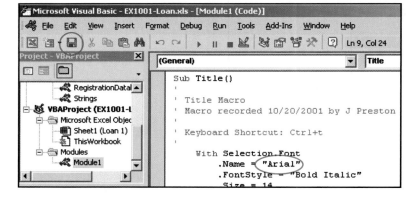

❸ Click the **Save** button. Close the VBA editor program.

You can use the macro to apply the new formatting to selected cells.

> Select the title in cells **A1** through **G1**. Hold the Ctrl key and press **t**.

The same colors and font size are used but the font is now Arial. This does not affect the formatting of your name, which is still in Bookman Old Style.

> Save the workbook.

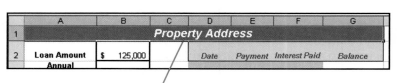

Font changed to Arial

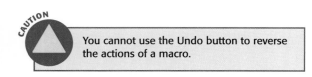

CAUTION

> You cannot use the Undo button to reverse the actions of a macro.

Task 3
CREATING A CUSTOM TOOLBAR

Why would I do this?

There are many buttons available for use on toolbars that are not normally displayed on the Standard or Formatting toolbar. You can add or remove buttons from existing toolbars or create your own toolbar and add buttons to it. You can add buttons that run macros and you can also add menus.

In this task, you create a new toolbar that can display buttons that do not normally appear on the other toolbars.

1 Choose <u>V</u>iew, <u>T</u>oolbars, <u>C</u>ustomize.

The Customize dialog box is displayed.

Click the **Tool<u>b</u>ars** tab.

A list of toolbars is displayed. Checkmarks indicate toolbars that are currently displayed on the worksheet.

Displayed toolbars

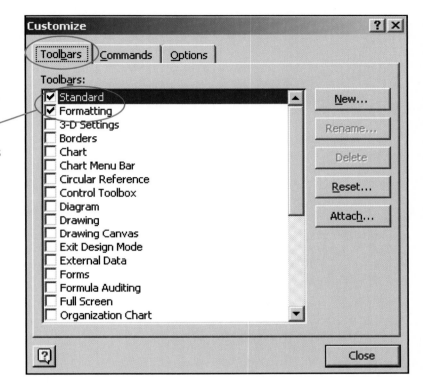

 CAUTION

Your screen may show other toolbars that are open. For example, it is common for the Drawing toolbar to be open in Excel.

2 Click the <u>N</u>ew button.

The New Toolbar dialog box is displayed.

> Select the default name in the **Toolbar name** box and type your last name.

The toolbar will be referred to by your last name.

Your last name

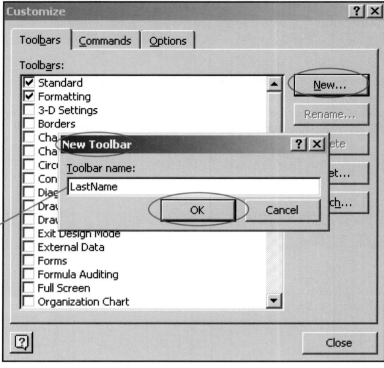

3 Click the **OK** button.

A short toolbar with no buttons is displayed on the worksheet and the toolbar name is added to the list. A check indicates the toolbar is displayed. The toolbar appears on the worksheet. This is called a floating toolbar.

> Leave this dialog box open for use in the next task.

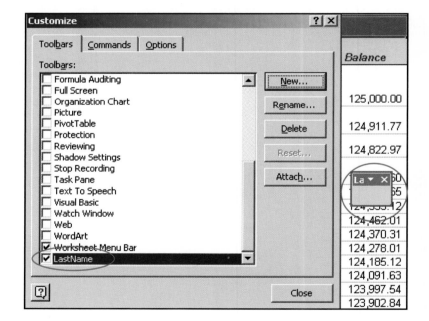

Task 4

ADDING AND REMOVING BUTTONS FROM TOOLBARS

Why would I do this?

You can add many special buttons to your toolbar. If there is a function that you use often but have to go through several layers of menus to get to it, you can probably find a button for it to add to your toolbar.

In this task, you add the Set Print Area button and the Speak Cells button to your toolbar.

1 Click the **Commands** tab in the **Customize** dialog box.

The Categories pane on the left of the dialog box displays the categories of buttons. Buttons within the category are displayed on the right in the Commands pane.

Choose the **File** category on the left and scroll down the commands to the button labeled **Set Print Area**.

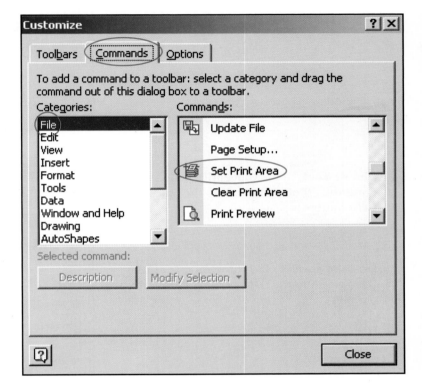

Your screen may show the Standard and Formatting toolbars on one row. You can move the formatting toolbar to a position under the standard toolbar by dragging the move handle of the formatting toolbar below the standard toolbar.

2 Drag the **Set Print Area** button from the Commands pane to your toolbar.

A vertical line on the toolbar indicates where the button will be placed.

Release the mouse button and a copy of the Set Print Area button is added to the toolbar.

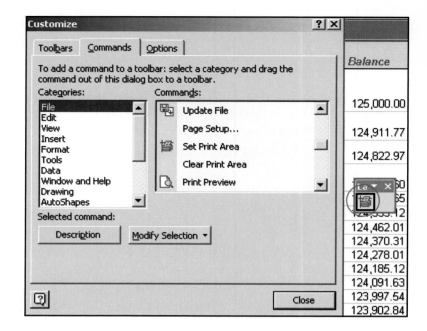

3 Choose **Tools** in the **Categories** pane. Scroll down the list of commands to the **Speak Cells** button.

If your computer has speakers and they are turned on, Office XP will speak the contents of selected cells.

Drag the **Speak Cells** button onto your toolbar. Place it to the right of the **Set Print Area** button.

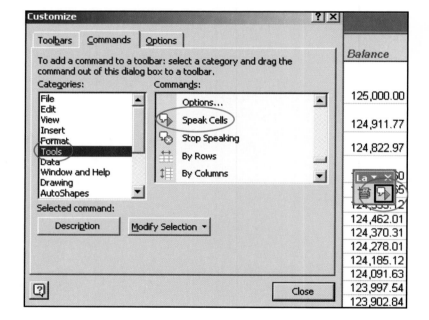

The new toolbar is small and may be in a different location on your screen.

4 Drag the **Stop Speaking** button onto your toolbar.

The stop speaking command cancels the Speak Cells command. The stop speaking command can be used if you select a large range of cells and do not wish to wait until they are all spoken. Pressing the Esc *key accomplishes the same thing. This button is not as useful as the Speak Cells button, so it would be a good one to remove.*

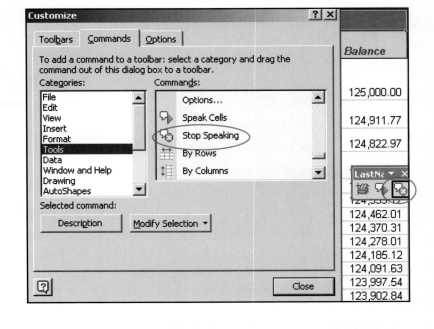

5 Move the mouse pointer onto the **Stop Speaking** button. Drag the button off of the toolbar onto any other part of the screen except another toolbar. Release the mouse button.

The Stop Speaking button is removed from the toolbar. You can use this method to add or remove command buttons from existing toolbars as well as toolbars you create.

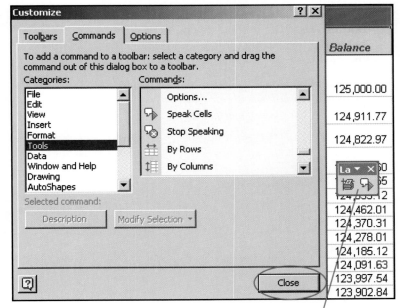

Stop Speaking button removed

6 Click the **Close** button on the Customize dialog box.

The new toolbar is active.

Select cells **A2** through **B8**. Click the **Set Print Area** button.

A dotted line is displayed around the selected area.

Click the **Print Preview** button.

The range of cells you selected is now the print area.

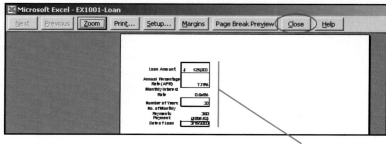

Selected print area

Speak Cells button

7 Click the **Close** button on the toolbar. Confirm that cells **A2** through **B8** are still selected and click the **Speak Cells** button.

If you have speakers attached to your computer and they are turned on, you hear a computer-generated voice speak the content of the cells.

Move the mouse pointer onto the title bar of the new toolbar but not onto one of the buttons. Drag the toolbar to a point just below the formatting toolbar and release the mouse.

*The toolbar becomes a **docked toolbar** below the formatting toolbar. Docked toolbars are located at the top, bottom, or either side of the window.*

Docked toolbar

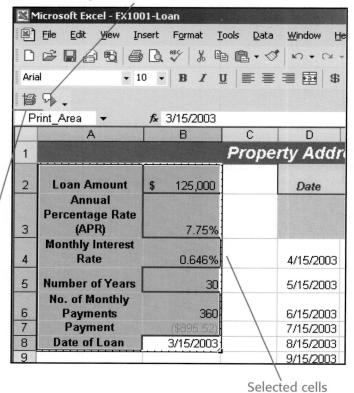

Selected cells

CAUTION

The Speak Cells feature will try to pronounce abbreviations like APR and No. as if they were words. This could be confusing if someone was relying on this feature to determine the content of cells.

Task 5

Why would I do this?

A toolbar button can run a macro. This is faster than using the menus and doesn't require that you remember a keyboard shortcut.

In this task, you learn how to add a custom button to the toolbar and use it to run the Title macro.

1 Choose **View**, **Toolbars**, **Customize**. Click the **Commands** tab if necessary. Scroll down the list of **Categories** and select **Macros**.

Two commands are listed in the Commands pane.

Drag the **Custom Button** from the **Commands** pane to a position just to the right of the **Speak Cells** button on your new toolbar. Release the mouse button.

The Custom button is placed on your toolbar and it is still selected.

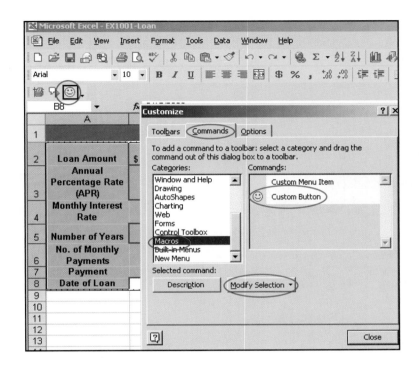

2 Click the **Modify Selection** button.

A menu of options is displayed.

Select the default name in the **Name** box and type Title.

The new name of the button is Title.

> **IN DEPTH**
>
> A *hotkey* is a letter in a menu or button name that can be used in place of clicking on the menu or button item. To turn one of the letters in your button name into a hotkey, place an ampersand, &, to the left of the letter when you type the name of the button in the Name box. Check the other menus displayed on the screen to be sure that the letter you want to use is not a hotkey in another menu. To use a hotkey, hold the Alt key and press the hotkey letter on the keyboard.

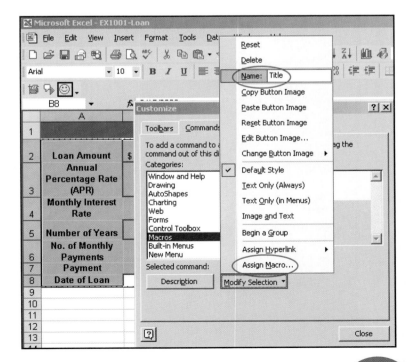

3 Choose **Assign Macro**.

The Assign Macro dialog box is displayed and existing macros are listed on the Macro Name pane.

Click **Title** to select it.

The Title macro is assigned to the custom button.

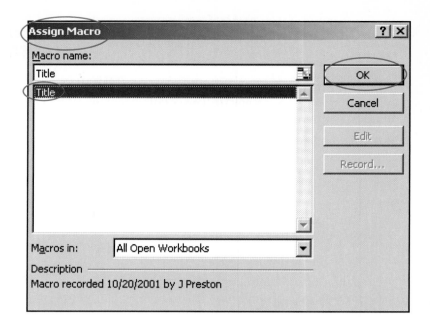

4 Click **OK**.

The Assign Macro dialog box closes.

Click the **Modify Selection** button.

The menu of modifications is displayed.

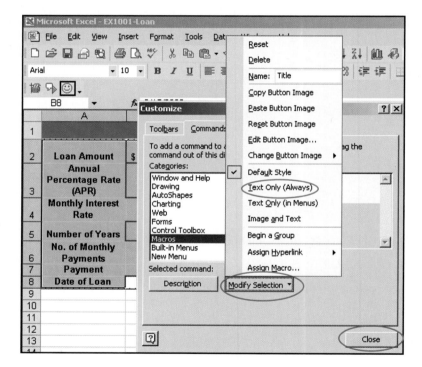

5 Click **Text Only (Always)**.

The button displays the name instead of the icon.

Click the Close button on the Customize dialog box.

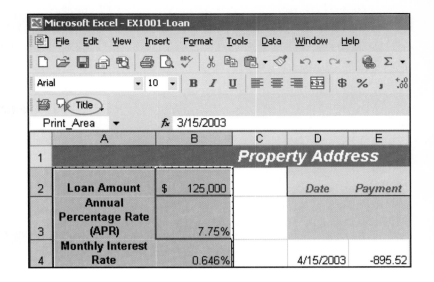

6 Select cells **D2** through **G2** and click the new Title button on your toolbar.

The column headings are reformatted to match the title.

Adjust the width of column **E** to display the larger heading. Save the workbook and leave it open for the next task.

Column widened

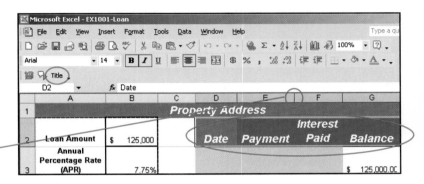

Task 6
CUSTOMIZING MENUS

Why would I do this?

You can add your own menus to toolbars or customize existing menus. First you add the menu item to the toolbar and then you populate it with command buttons. Generally, you use menus when you have a group of related commands. Just like adding buttons, you may want to customize a menu for frequently used tasks that do not otherwise appear on buttons.

In this task, you add a menu to your toolbar that has command buttons designed to help you troubleshoot formulas.

1 Choose <u>V</u>iew, <u>T</u>oolbars, Customize. Click the **<u>C</u>ommands** tab, if necessary.

The Customize dialog box opens.

Scroll down the list in the **Categories** pane and select **New Menu**.

The New Menu command is displayed in the Comman<u>d</u>s pane.

QUICK TIP

To view the Customize dialog box in fewer steps, right-click on one of the toolbars and choose Customize from the shortcut menu.

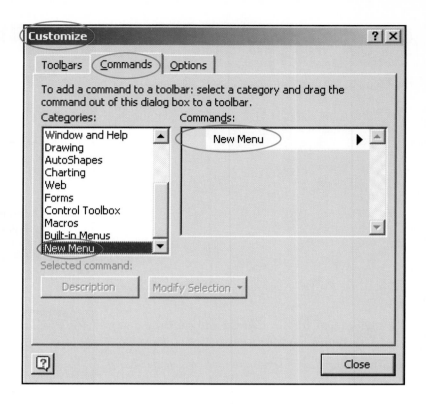

2 Drag the **New Menu** command from the **Comman<u>d</u>s** pane onto your toolbar. Place it at the right end of the toolbar.

The New Menu is part of the toolbar.

Click the arrow on the **New Menu** button on your toolbar.

A blank menu item is displayed below the New Menu button. The first command button will be placed in this area.

First menu item

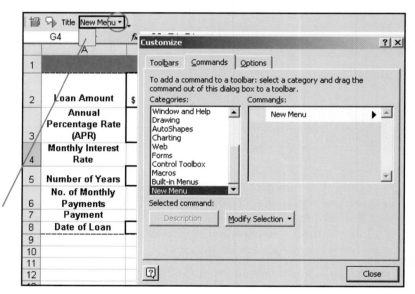

3 Select **Tools** in the **Categories** pane. Scroll down the list of commands in the **Commands** pane and locate **Trace Precedents**.

You can add a menu item by dragging a command button onto the blank area.

Drag the **Trace Precedents** command to the blank area below the **New Menu** button.

The first menu item is Trace Precedents. You can add more command buttons by dragging them from the Commands pane to the menu.

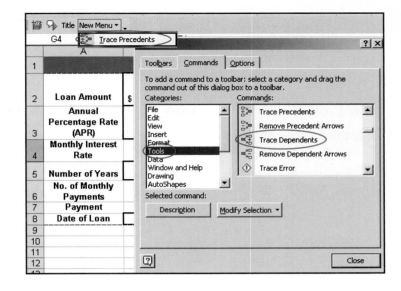

4 Drag **Remove Precedent Arrows** from the command list to the new menu. Position the pointer to drop the **Remove Precedent Arrows** below the **Trace Precedents** menu item.

A horizontal line indicates where the new menu item will appear in the list.

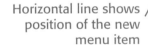

Horizontal line shows position of the new menu item

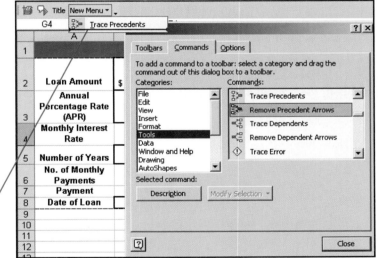

5 Release the mouse button. The **Remove Precedent Arrows** command is the second menu option.

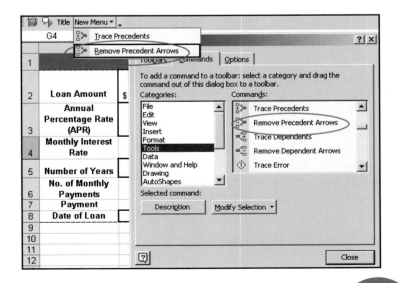

6 Drag the **Trace Dependents** command to a position between the other two menu items so that it is second on the list. Release the mouse button.

You can place new commands anywhere in the list of menu items.

Drag the **Remove All Arrows** command to the bottom of the list of menu options.

In this example, you do not need the Remove Precedent Arrows option. You will remove it in the next step.

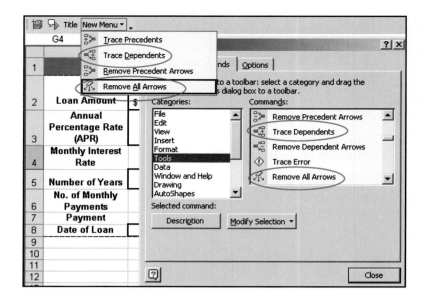

7 Move the pointer onto the **Remove Precedent Arrows** item in the new menu. Drag the menu item off the menu.

You can remove an item from the menu by dragging it off the menu. It does not matter where you drag it as long as it is off the menu and not on another toolbar.

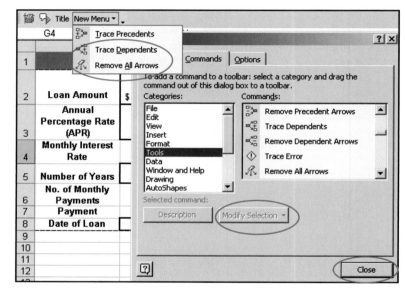

8 Click the New Menu button on your toolbar to select it. Click the Modify Selection button.

A shortcut menu appears.

Select the default name for the menu in the **Name** box and type **Trace**. Press ⏎Enter. Click the Close button on the Customize dialog box.

The new name appears on the menu bar. Keep the menu names short to conserve space on the menu bar. You will learn to use these commands to audit formulas in Lesson 11.

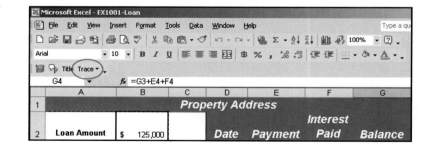

Save the workbook and leave it open for use in the next task.

Task 7
CREATING TEMPLATES

Why would I do this?

If you invest a lot of time designing a workbook and creating toolbars and macros to do a particular task, you can use it again and share it with others who do similar work. You can remove the data but leave the formulas and formatting. You can also attach custom toolbars. The resulting workbook can be used as a template. Templates are workbooks that contain formulas, formatting, and other special features that allow you to simply enter specific data to achieve a sophisticated result.

There are two common ways to use a workbook as a template. The first is to save the workbook normally. Whenever you want to use it, you locate the file, open it, add the data, and save it with a different name. The problem with this method is that you may accidentally save the file without changing the name and overwrite the original file with new data. The second method is to save the file as a template file type in a special folder that the Windows operating system uses for templates. Your file will display with the other template files and is not easily overwritten when you save the file.

In this task, you learn how to attach a toolbar and save a workbook as an Excel template. You also learn how to save the file as a normal workbook that you can use as a template.

1 Delete the values in cells **B2**, **B3**, **B5**, and **B8**.

The values that determine the specifics of a particular loan are removed. The formulas that depend upon these values show errors, zeros, or dates that start at the beginning of the century.

Division by zero errors

Loan values deleted

Default date when no input to formula

	A	B	C	D	E	F	G
1				Property Address			
2	Loan Amount				Date	Payment	Interest Paid	Balance
3	Annual Percentage Rate (APR)						$ -
4	Monthly Interest Rate	0.000%		1/31/1900	#DIV/0!	$ -	#DIV/0!
5	Number of Years			3/2/1900	#DIV/0!	#DIV/0!	#DIV/0!
6	No. of Monthly Payments	0		4/2/1900	#DIV/0!	#DIV/0!	#DIV/0!
7	Payment	#DIV/0!		5/2/1900	#DIV/0!	#DIV/0!	#DIV/0!
8	Date of Loan			6/2/1900	#DIV/0!	#DIV/0!	#DIV/0!
9				7/2/1900	#DIV/0!	#DIV/0!	#DIV/0!

CAUTION

If you are working in a laboratory that restores the computers to original settings on a regular basis, the security setting may have been changed since you set it to Medium in Task 1. If you cannot run your macro because the security setting is High, return to Task 1 and follow the directions to set it to Medium for this task.

2 Choose <u>V</u>iew, **Toolbars**, <u>C</u>ustomize. Click the **Tool<u>b</u>ars** tab, if necessary. Scroll down and select your new toolbar.

You can attach a toolbar to a workbook so that it will be available to someone else.

IN DEPTH

Toolbars are normally saved on a computer rather than in a workbook. If you send the workbook to another person who will use it on a different computer, you must attach the toolbar to the workbook to make it available to them. The same is true of templates that are shared by people who work on other computers.

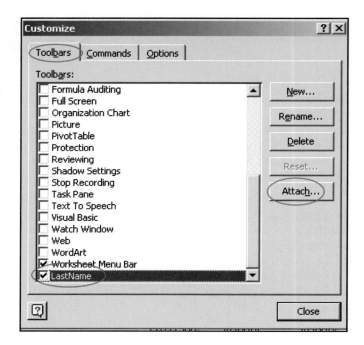

3 Click the Attac<u>h</u> button.

A list of custom toolbars is displayed on the left.

Select your toolbar and click the <u>C</u>opy button.

Your toolbar will be attached to the workbook.

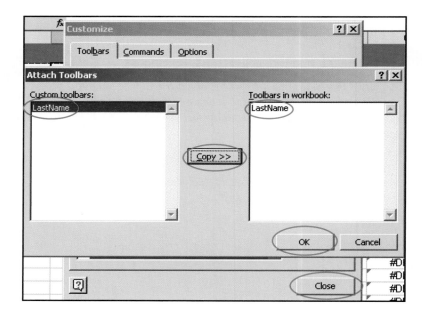

4 Click OK.

Your toolbar is attached.

Click the Close button.

You can save this workbook as a template that you can use whenever you need to calculate a loan repayment schedule.

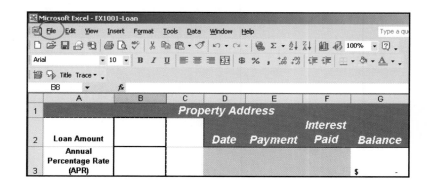

5 Choose <u>F</u>ile, Save <u>A</u>s. Click the arrow next to the **Save as <u>t</u>ype** box and choose **Template**. Change the name of the file to EX1001-LoanTemplate.

The Templates folder is automatically displayed in the Save in box.

Click the drop-down arrow next to the **Save <u>i</u>n** box.

The location of the Templates folder for your computer is displayed. The location of this folder depends on the operating system so your screen may not match the figure. Leave this folder selected.

This folder may be in a different location on your computer

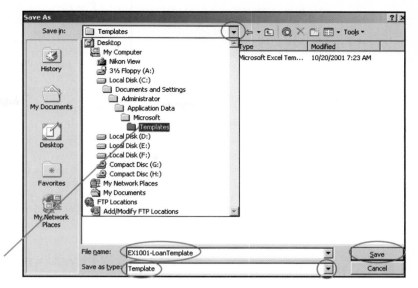

Templates are stored in a special folder. When you choose <u>F</u>ile, <u>N</u>ew, a list of the templates in this folder is available from the task pane under General Templates. The Templates folder is usually located in an administrative area of the disk. It may be protected from change if you are using a computer in a school lab or at work. The exact location of the Templates folders depends on the version of Windows you are using and may not match the figure.

6 Click the <u>S</u>ave button.

The workbook is saved as a template. If you do not have permission to save files to this folder, you may get an error message. Proceed to the next step.

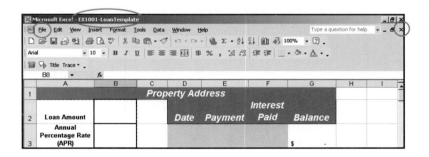

7 Choose <u>F</u>ile, Save <u>A</u>s. Choose the folder where you keep the other solution files for this book. Change the file type to **Microsoft Excel Workbook** and click the <u>S</u>ave button.

Your workbook is stored with your other files as a normal workbook. If you are not allowed to save files in the template folder, you can open this file from your folder as you would a normal file.

Close the workbook but leave Excel open.

Task 8
APPLYING TEMPLATES

Why would I do this?

Templates are designed to be used repeatedly without accidentally overwriting them. When you create a new workbook using a template, the Save command does not save the new workbook over the template but opens the Save As dialog box and automatically chooses the workbook file type. If you were not able to save your template to the Templates folder on a shared computer, you may use a normal workbook as a template but you must remember to save it with a different name to avoid overwriting the original file.

In this task, you learn how to apply a template and save the resulting workbook without changing the template.

1 Start Excel. Choose <u>F</u>ile, <u>N</u>ew.

The New Workbook task pane opens.

> **CAUTION**
>
> If you were able to save your template to the Templates folder on your computer, the EX1001-LoanTemplate file will be available from General Templates. The EX1001-LoanTemplate file may be listed by name under the New from template heading in the task pane. However, it may not be listed if you have changed computers since you did Task 7. If you cannot find the EX1001-LoanTemplate file in General Templates, open the file from your folder and go to step 3.

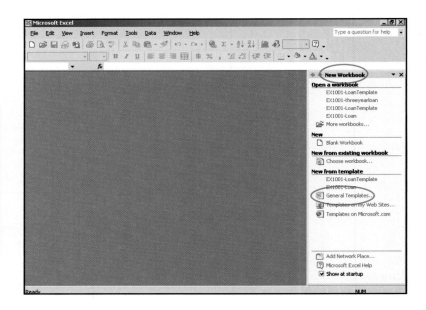

2 Click **General Templates**. Click the **General** tab, if necessary.

If you were able to save your template to the Templates folder on your computer, it will be listed in this window.

Click the icon that represents **EX1001-LoanTemplate**.

The selected template is applied to a new workbook.

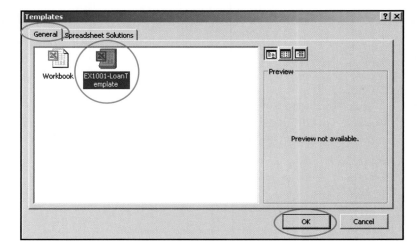

3 Click **OK**.

If your security setting is still Medium, a dialog box opens that allows you to enable macros.

Click the **Enable Macros** button.

A new workbook opens with the formatting and formulas from the template.

If your custom toolbar is not displayed, choose **View**, **Toolbars**. Select your toolbar from the list.

4 Select **B2** and type **100000**. Select **B3** and type **7**. Select **B5** and type **30**. Select **B8** and enter today's date.

The formulas calculate the loan.

Select the title in cells **A1** through **G1** and enter your personal home address.

A loan repayment schedule is ready to print.

Loan values

5 Select **A1** through **G39**.

The loan information and three years of payments are selected.

Click the **Set Print Area** button on your custom toolbar.

The print area is set.

Click the **Print** button.

A copy of the first three years of the loan repayment schedule is printed.

Selected print area

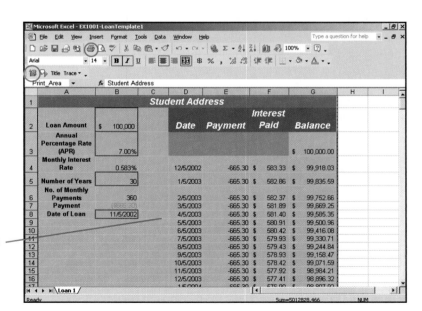

6 Choose File, Save As.

The Save As dialog box opens and the Save as type box is automatically set to Microsoft Excel Workbook.

Select the folder where you save your files in the **Save in** box. Change the name of the file in the **File name** box to EX1001-threeyearloan. Confirm that the type of file is **Microsoft Excel Workbook**.

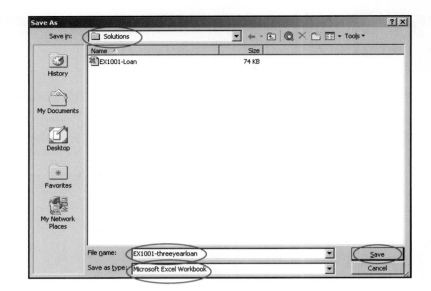

If you applied the template to the workbook from the General Templates option, it will open the Save As dialog box if you choose the Save or the Save As options.

7 Click the Save button. Close the workbook. Leave Excel open.

The exercises that follow are designed for you to review and use what you have learned in this lesson. You also have the opportunity to practice your skills and then expand on them by applying them to new situations.

COMPREHENSION

Comprehension exercises are designed to check your memory and understanding of the basic concepts in this lesson. You distinguish between true and false statements, identify new screen elements, and match terms with related statements. If you are uncertain of the correct answer, refer to the task number following each item (for example, T4 refers to Task 4) and review that task until you are confident that you can provide a correct response.

TRUE-FALSE

Circle either T or F.

T F **1.** The Security level must be set to High when you create a macro. **(T1)**

T F **2.** You can assign macros to a key on the keyboard and run them by holding the Ctrl key and pressing the assigned key. **(T1)**

T F **3.** To edit a macro, you use the Visual Basic editor. **(T2)**

T F **4.** You can create custom toolbars, but you have to choose a name for the toolbar from a list of names provided in the Customize dialog box. **(T3)**

T F **5.** To remove a button from a toolbar while the Customize dialog box is open, you double-click on the button. **(T4)**

T F **6.** You can assign a macro to a button on a toolbar. **(T5)**

T F **7.** You can add menu buttons to a toolbar that display a list of commands that you can customize. **(T6)**

T F **8.** Templates are stored in a special folder named Templates by default where the Excel program can find them automatically. **(T7)**

MATCHING QUESTIONS

A. VBA editor   **D.** Template

B. New Menu   **E.** Tools

C. Attach   **F.** Macro

Match the following statements to the word or phrase that is the best match from the list. Write the letter of the matching word or phrase in the space provided next to the number.

1. _____ The command used to link a custom menu to a workbook **(T7)**

2. _____ The type of program you create by recording a series of actions in Excel **(T1)**

3. _____ A workbook that has all the formulas and formatting but no specific data **(T7)**

4. _____ Allows you to edit a macro **(T2)**

5. _____ Name of the category of customized commands used to add a menu to a toolbar **(T3)**

6. _____ Name of the category of customized commands used to add the Speak Cells command to a toolbar **(T3)**

IDENTIFYING PARTS OF THE EXCEL SCREEN

Refer to the figure and identify the numbered parts of the screen. Write the letter of the correct label in the space next to the number.

1. _____

2. _____

3. _____

4. _____

5. _____

6. _____

7. _____

8. _____

9. _____

10. _____

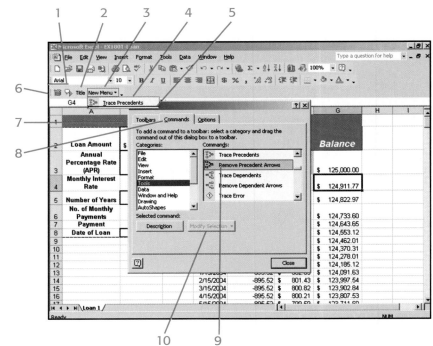

A. Command that can be added to a toolbar (T4)

B. Indicates where a new menu item will be placed (T6)

C. Buttons on a custom toolbar (T2)

D. Custom toolbar (T3)

E. Used to change names of buttons (T6)

F. Button used to run a macro (T5)

G. Custom menu (T6)

H. Command in a custom menu (T6)

I. Used to create a new custom toolbar (T3)

J. Displays available commands (T4)

REINFORCEMENT

Reinforcement exercises are designed to reinforce the skills you have learned by applying them to a new situation. Detailed instructions are provided along with a figure, where appropriate, to illustrate the result. Complete the reinforcement exercises sequentially. Leave the workbook open at the end of each exercise for use in the next exercise until you are specifically directed to close it.

Excel is commonly used to report quarterly sales of products. You can create a template to help with this task that provides consistent input. In the following exercises, you record macros to print each of the quarterly statements and the summary sheet. You assign these macros to buttons that you place on a custom menu in a custom tool-bar. You attach the toolbar to the workbook, remove the data but not the formatting or formulas, and save it to use as a template.

R1—Create Macros to Print Each Sheet of a Workbook

When you create the macros in this exercise, be sure to select the worksheet or menu option, even if they are already selected. The current default choice may not be the same the next time you run the macro.

1. Open **EX1002** and save it as **EX1002-Reinforcement** on your disk for use in the following exercises.

2. Choose **Tools**, **Macros**, **Record New Macro**. Type **PrintQ1** in the **Macro name** box (do not use a space between Print and Q1). Confirm that your name is displayed in the **Description** box and click **OK**.

3. Click the **First Quarter** sheet tab. Choose **File**, **Print**, **Active sheet(s)**, **OK**.

4. Choose **Tools**, **Macros**, **Stop Recording**.

5. Choose **Tools**, **Macros**, **Record New Macro**. Type **PrintQ2** in the **Macro name** box (do not use a space between Print and Q2) and click **OK**.

6. Click the **Second Quarter** sheet tab. Choose **File**, **Print**, **Active sheet(s)**, **OK**.

7. Choose **Tools**, **Macros**, **Stop Recording**.

8. Repeat this process for the third- and fourth-quarter sheets.

9. Choose **Tools**, **Macros**, **Record New Macro**. Type **PrintSum** in the **Macro name** box (do not use a space between Print and Sum) and click **OK**.

10. Click the **Year-End Summary** sheet tab. Choose **File**, **Print**, **Active sheet(s)**, **OK**.

11. Choose **Tools**, **Macros**, **Stop Recording**.

12. Choose **Tools**, **Macro**, **Macros**. A list of the five macros is displayed.

13. Capture a screen shot of the Macro Dialogue box by pressing and holding Alt and then pressing the PrtSc key. Launch Word and type your name and section number at the top of a blank page. Paste your screen shot. Save the file as **EX1002-R1** and print it if required by your instructor.

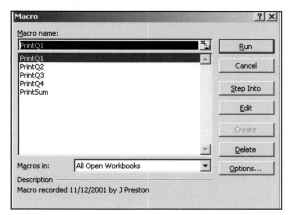

R2—Change the Name of the Macro in VBA Editor

The name for the macro that prints the summary may be misleading. Edit the macro to change the name.

1. Select **PrintSum** and click **Edit**.

2. Change **PrintSum** to **PrintSummary** in the first two lines of the macro.

3. Capture a screen shot of the VBA Editor window by pressing and holding Alt and then pressing the PrtSc key. Launch Word and type your name and section number at the top of a blank page. Paste your screen shot. Save the file as **EX1002-R2** and print it if required by your instructor. Close Word.

4. Save the changes and close the VBA editor.

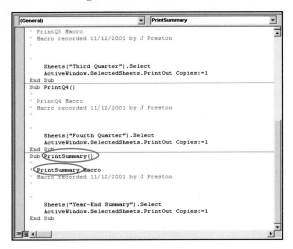

R3–Create a Custom Toolbar with a Custom Menu

You can add these print options to a custom toolbar. Create a custom toolbar and attach it to this workbook.

1. Choose **View**, **Toolbars**, **Customize**. Click the **Toolbars** tab and click the **New** button.

2. Type your initials in the **Toolbar name** box and click **OK**.

3. Double-click the title bar of the new toolbar to dock it.

4. Click the **Commands** tab. Scroll down the list of categories and click **New Menu**.

5. Drag the **New Menu** command to the custom toolbar.

6. Click **Modify Selection**. Select the default value in the **Name** box and type **Print Sheets**.

7. Click **Macros** in the Categories pane. Drag the **Custom Menu Item** onto the new menu on your toolbar, just below the name of the menu.

8. Click the **Modify Selection** button and choose **Assign Macro**. Select **PrintQ1** from the list of macros and click **OK**.

9. Click the **Custom Menu Item** that you just placed on your custom toolbar. Click the **Modify Selection** button and change the name of the button to **Q1**.

10. Repeat Steps 4-6 to create a total of five menu items on your toolbar to print the four quarterly sheets and the summary sheet.

11. Select the name of your toolbar in the **Toolbars** box and click the **Attach** button.

12. Select the custom toolbar named with your initials and click the **Copy** button. Click **OK**.

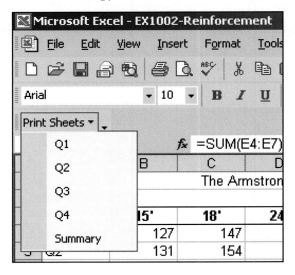

R4–Remove data and save as a template

You can use this workbook as a template without saving it to the Templates folder. Remove the data from the first four sheets but do not disturb the formulas in the Year-End Summary sheet.

1. Choose the **First Quarter** sheet. Select **B4** through **H11** and delete the data.

2. Repeat this process for the other three quarters.

3. Choose the **Year-End Summary** sheet. Do not delete the formulas.

4. Click the **Save** button to save your work, and then close the workbook.

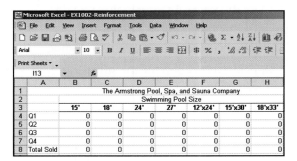

R5—Apply the template

You can use this workbook as a template if you open it, save it with a new name, and fill in the data.

1. Open **EX1002-Reinforcement**.

2. Choose the **First Quarter** sheet. Enter the following numbers in row 4 for sales at the Indianapolis store: **11, 16, 18, 17, 3, 10, 4**.

3. Choose the **Year-End Summary** sheet and confirm that the numbers you entered were added to the fourth row to show first-quarter sales.

4. Save the workbook as **EX1002-Applied Template**. Close the workbook.

	15'	18'	24'	27'	12'x24'	15'x30'	18'x33'
The Armstrong Pool, Spa, and Sauna Company							
Swimming Pool Size							
Q1	11	16	18	17	3	10	4
Q2	0	0	0	0	0	0	0
Q3	0	0	0	0	0	0	0
Q4	0	0	0	0	0	0	0
Total Sold	11	16	18	17	3	10	4

Challenge exercises are designed to test your ability to apply your skills to new situations with less detailed instruction. These exercises also challenge you to expand your repertoire of skills by using commands that are similar to those you have already learned. The desired outcome is clearly defined, but you have more freedom to choose the steps needed to achieve the required result.

C1—Use Templates Installed with Microsoft Office XP

A few templates are provided with Microsoft Office. Most of them use protection features to hide the formulas and prevent the user from making changes. You will learn how to add these features to your templates in a later lesson. The templates provided with Excel have little flexibility but are very fast and useful for specific needs.

Partial installations of Microsoft Office XP may not include these templates. If you have none listed when you do Step two of this exercise, you need to install them from the Microsoft Office XP CD-ROM. If you do not have that privilege on the computer you are using, contact the administrator or make arrangements with your instructor to do a different assignment.

Goal: Use the Loan Amortization template to determine two loans and comment on the benefits and limitations of the template.

1. Choose **File, New**. Select **General Templates** from the task pane under **New from template**.

2. Click the **Spreadsheet Solutions** tab to see the templates installed with Office.

3. Select **Loan Amortization** and click **OK**.

4. Select the cell to the right of **Loan Amount**, type **100000**, and press ↵Enter.

5. Enter the following values in the next three cells: **7.25%**, **30**, **12**. Enter today's date for the start date of the loan. Leave the **Optional Extra Payments** cell empty and enter your name as the lender.

6. Notice that the total interest you would pay on this loan is $145,583.46. Scroll to the bottom of the sheet and confirm that there are 360 payments on this 30-year loan.

7. Click the **Save** button. Notice that the **Save As** dialog box opens. This is a characteristic of templates that prevents you from saving your changes over the original template. Name the file **EX1003-CH1a**.

8. Select the cell to the right of **Optional Extra Payments** and enter **50**. Notice the actual number of combined payments is reduced to 290 if an extra $50 is added to each payment.

9. Start Word and open the file, **EX1003**. Save the file as **EX1003-CH1b**. Print this sheet and fill it out if required by your instructor. If your instructor prefers the file in electronic form, switch back and forth between this document and the worksheet and answer the questions in this document. Save it and close it when you are finished.

10. Close the workbook and do not save it again. Leave Excel open if you plan to continue with the Challenge exercises.

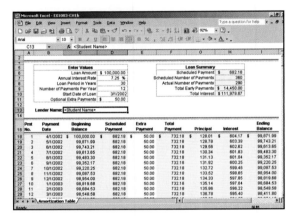

C2—Use a Finance and Accounting Template from the Microsoft Web Site

Microsoft maintains a library of templates that you can use if you have Internet access. The templates are organized by category and within each category are templates in Word, Excel, PowerPoint, and Access. Excel is primarily a financial tool and the greatest number of templates is in the Finance and Accounting section.

Goal: Use a finance or accounting template from the library of templates on Microsoft's Web site.

1. Choose **File, New**. Click **Templates on Microsoft.com** under **New from Template** in the task pane.

2. Choose the **Finance and Accounting** topic. Browse through the options and choose an Excel template that you may find useful in your major area of study or an area of personal interest. Do not choose the loan amortization with optional payments template if you did the first challenge exercise in this lesson.

3. Fill out the template with some sample data and save it as **EX1004-CH2**.

C3—Use Templates of Your Choice from the Microsoft Web Site

Explore Microsoft's library of templates. The templates are organized by category and within each category are templates in Word, Excel, PowerPoint, and Access. Excel is primarily a financial tool but it can be used for other purposes

Goal: Use a template of your choice that is not from the Finance and Accounting area of the library of templates on Microsoft's Web site.

1. Choose **File, New.** Click **Templates on Microsoft.com** under **New from Template** in the task pane.

2. Browse through the Template Gallery and choose an Excel template that you may find useful in your major area of study or an area of personal interest.

3. Fill out the template with some sample data and save it as **EX1004-CH3**.

C4—Manage Toolbar Attachments

A toolbar is stored in a special folder on the computer you are using and continues to reside there after the workbook is closed. You can attach it to another workbook. If you delete it from your list of toolbars, it will be restored when you open the workbook.

If you are working in a laboratory environment, the toolbars stored on your computer in the special folder may be erased periodically and replaced with the default toolbars. This is another good reason to attach them to specific workbooks.

Goal: Attach an existing toolbar to a new workbook.

1. Click the **New** button on the toolbar to automatically open a new workbook without opening the task pane.

2. Choose **View, Toolbars, Customize.** Click the **Toolbars** tab, if necessary. Click the **Attach** button.

3. Click the custom toolbar with your last name and click the **Copy** button. (This step assumes you have done the tasks in this lesson.) Click **OK**.

4. Type your name in cell **A1**. Save the workbook as **EX1004-CH4** and close the workbook.

5. Choose **View, Toolbars, Customize.** Click the **Toolbars** tab, if necessary. Scroll to find the custom toolbar named with your last name and click it to select it.

6. Click the **Delete** button. Click **OK** to confirm the deletion. Click the **Close** button to close the dialog box.

7. Confirm that the toolbar is no longer on your list of toolbars. Open **EX1004-CH4** and confirm that the toolbar is available.

8. If your instructor requires a printout for grading purposes, capture a screen shot that displays the toolbar by pressing and holding (Alt) and then pressing the (PrtSc) key. Launch Word and type your name and section number at the top of a blank page. Paste your screen shot. Print the page to hand in. Close Word and do not save the file (you have EX1004-CH4 to confirm you have done the work).

9. Close the workbook. If you are working on a computer that others share, delete the toolbar from the list of available toolbars on the computer.

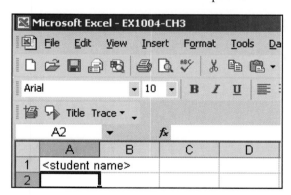

ON YOUR OWN

Create your own macro to do something you find repetitive and place it on a custom toolbar that is attached to a workbook.

Grading criteria will be:

1. Demonstrate the ability to record a macro.

2. Demonstrate the ability to create a custom toolbar.

3. Demonstrate the ability to attach a macro to a button on a toolbar.

4. Demonstrate the ability to attach a toolbar to a workbook.

Some examples of features that students have learned to use in previous classes to enhance their multipage printouts are listed below:

- Two or more ranges of cells on a single worksheet have buttons on a toolbar that are set to print each range.

- Several different text formats are attached to buttons that can be used for appropriate sections of the worksheet.

- Several different number formats, including specific number of decimal places displayed, are attached to buttons on a toolbar.

To complete the project, perform the following:

- Place your name in the header.

- Save your file on your own disk. Name it **EX1005-Macros**.

- Check with your instructor to determine if the project should be submitted in electronic or printed form. If necessary, capture an image of the screen using the (PrtSc) button on your keyboard and paste the image into a Word document that you can print to display your toolbar in a workbook.

Lesson 11

Managing Formulas

Task 1 Naming a Range

Task 2 Validating Data Input

Task 3 Using VLOOKUP and IF Functions

Task 4 Using Conditional Formats

Task 5 Using Custom Date and Number Formats

Task 6 Auditing Formulas and Resolving Errors

INTRODUCTION

The strength of Excel is its ability to perform sophisticated calculations and display the results in useful ways. As your workbooks grow in size and complexity, you need to learn how to simplify formulas, make them easy to change, and analyze them for errors.

In this lesson, you use a template to produce invoices for a small company that sells customized shirts. The company buys shirts in several styles and prints designs or logos on them in one, two, or three colors. The price of the shirt depends on the style, quantity, and number of colors used. The owner of the company would like to simply enter the code for the shirt, the number ordered, and the number of colors used to produce an invoice. The owner would also like to prevent errors that may occur while entering the data.

In this lesson, you learn how to use *named ranges* to validate input and look up prices from lists on other worksheets. A named range is a cell or range of cells that has a name of your choice. You use *conditional functions* to determine the price range based on quantity ordered and *conditional formatting* to draw attention to important issues. Conditional functions evaluate a conditional statement and then perform one of two other functions depending on whether the statement is true or false. Conditional formatting evaluates a statement and applies a format of your choice if the statement is true. You also trace the *precedents* and *dependents* of formulas to analyze them and resolve an error that results from modifying the original template. Precedents are cells that are used by a formula in the selected cell and dependents are cells that use the contents of the current cell to calculate their own values.

VISUAL SUMMARY

By the time you complete this lesson, you will have created an invoice worksheet that looks like this:

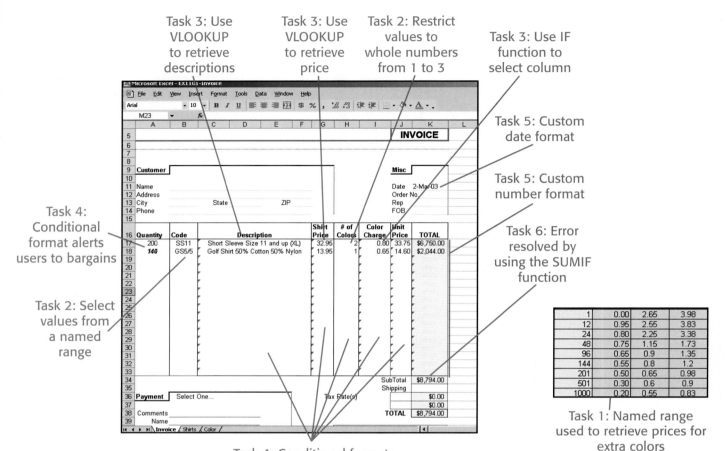

Task 3: Use VLOOKUP to retrieve descriptions

Task 3: Use VLOOKUP to retrieve price

Task 2: Restrict values to whole numbers from 1 to 3

Task 3: Use IF function to select column

Task 5: Custom date format

Task 5: Custom number format

Task 6: Error resolved by using the SUMIF function

Task 4: Conditional format alerts users to bargains

Task 2: Select values from a named range

Task 1: Named range used to retrieve prices for extra colors

Task 4: Conditional formats hide error messages

Task 3: Use VLOOKUP to retrieve descriptions

Task 1: Named range used to select codes

Task 2: Named range used to retrieve descriptions and prices

Task 6: Precedent cells

Task 6: Precedent named range

Task 6: Series of precedent cells

Task 6: Dependent cells

Task 6: Smart Tag

Task 6: Trace Precedents arrow

Task 6: Indicates cells identified by the background error-checking option

Task 6: Trace Dependents arrow

Task 1

Why would I do this?

Some formulas refer to a range of cells. If the range of cells is a table of data, you must rewrite the formula whenever you modify the table or change the number of rows or columns. If you name the range of cells in the table and use that name in the formulas, you only have to rename the range if you change the size of the table. It is also easier to understand the formulas when the ranges have names.

Excel 2002 has a new feature that places a small colored triangle in the corner of cells that may have problems or could be improved. You turn this feature off in this task and turn it back on when you are finished revising the worksheet to check for errors.

In this task, you name ranges in two tables of data.

1 Open **EX1101** from the **Student** folder. Save it as **EX1101-Invoice** on your disk.

The new title appears in the title bar. The cells in the Unit Price column have small markers in the corners. These markers warn the user that the cells are not protected from accidental change. This issue is dealt with in a later lesson.

> Choose **Tools, Options**. Click the **Error Checking** tab. Deselect **Enable background error checking**. Click **OK**.

Many cells are marked with indicators while you are revising the worksheet. Removing these marks reduces the clutter on the screen. You will turn them back on in the last task.

Error checking markers removed

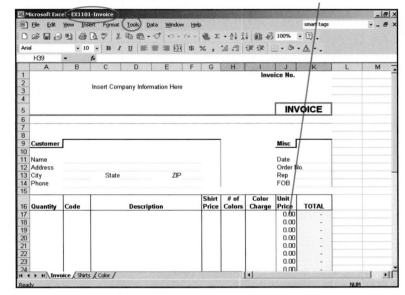

2 Click the **Shirts** worksheet tab.

This table of shirt products contains style codes, descriptions, and prices for quantities of less than, or more than, one case. In this example, a case holds 144 shirts.

> Select cells **A3** through **A12**.

This range of cells contains the shirt codes.

Data selected without column headings

3 Choose **Insert, Name, Define**.

The Define Names dialog box opens.

> Type **Codes**. Click the **Add** button.

The range of cells from A2 through A12 is named Codes. It will be used to validate the code entries.

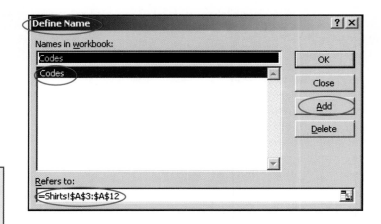

IN DEPTH

These tables are used in lookup functions in a later task. These functions do not use the column headings so they are not included in the selected range.

QUICK TIP

A faster way to name a range is to select the range of cells, click the Name box, and type the name of the range.

4 Click **OK**. Select cells **A3** through **D12**.

The table of shirt codes, descriptions, prices is selected.

> Choose **Insert, Name, Define**. Type **Shirts** and click the **Add** button.

The table of shirt information is named.

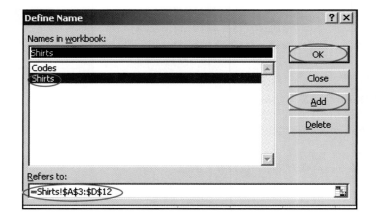

5 Click **OK**. Click the **Color** sheet tab and select cells **A3** through **D11**.

The table of prices for printing with color is selected.

> Choose **Insert, Name, Define**. Type **Colors** and click the **Add** button.

The table of prices for printing in color is named.

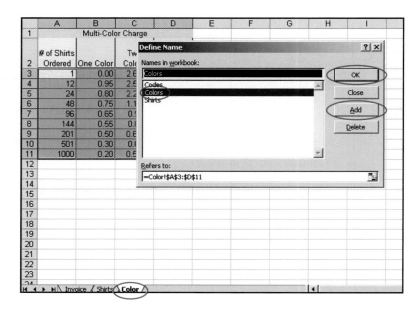

6 Click **OK**. Click the **Invoice** sheet tab. Click the arrow on the **Name** box.

Three ranges are named that you can use in formulas on this invoice.

Named ranges

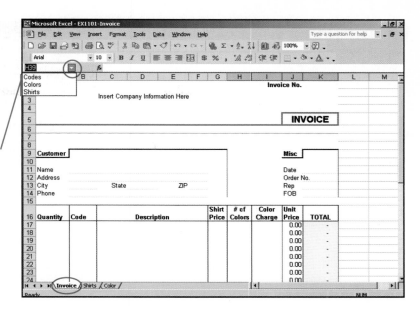

Task 2
VALIDATING DATA INPUT

Why would I do this?
You can use the validation option to restrict the input to a list of values or range of numbers. You can provide guidance to the user with a pop-up message that appears before the data is entered. You can also provide an error message that provides information on how the user can revise an incorrect entry. This makes data entry faster and more accurate.

In this task, you restrict the values entered in the Code column to those that exist in the table of shirts. You also restrict the values entered in the # of Colors column to integers from one to three.

1 Select cells **B17** through **B33**. Choose **Data**, **Validation**.

The Data Validation dialog box opens.

Click the **Settings** tab, if necessary. Click the **Allow** arrow and choose **List**. In the **Source** box, type **=Codes**.

Only values that exist in the named range are allowed.

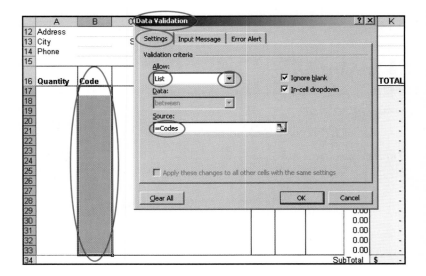

2 Click the **Input Message** tab. Select the **Title** box and type **Code Validation**.

The message is given a name for future reference.

Select the **Input Message** box and type **Enter a shirt code from the list**.

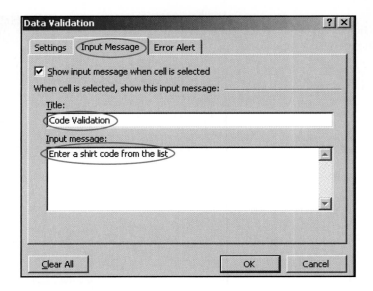

3 Click the **Error Alert** tab. Click in the **Title** box and type **Code validation error**.

Click the **Error message** box and type **Refer to the list of codes on the Shirts worksheet**.

The validation rule for this cell has been defined. It only allows values from the list and displays the messages you have entered.

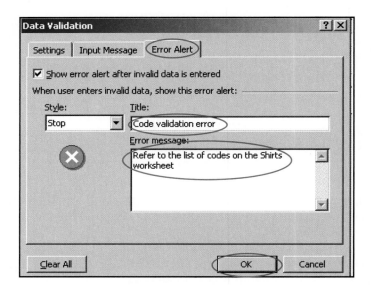

4 Click **OK**.

The input message is displayed next to the cell and an arrow is also displayed.

Select **B17**, type **SS1**, and press ⏎Enter.

The error message is displayed.

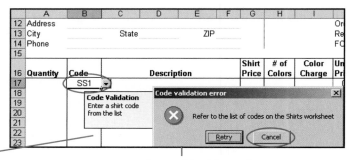

Input message

Error box with title and message

5 Click **Cancel**. Click the arrow next to the box and select **SS11** from the list.

This is a valid entry and no error message is displayed.

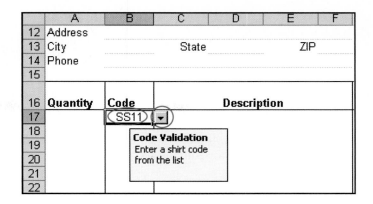

6 Select cells **H17** through **H33**. Choose **Data**, **Validation**.

The Data Validation dialog box opens.

Click the **Settings** tab. Click the **Allow** arrow and choose **Whole Number**. Click the **Data** arrow and choose **between**, if necessary. Select the **Minimum** box and type **1**. Select the **Maximum** box and type **3**.

The entry in this cell will be restricted to whole numbers from 1 to 3.

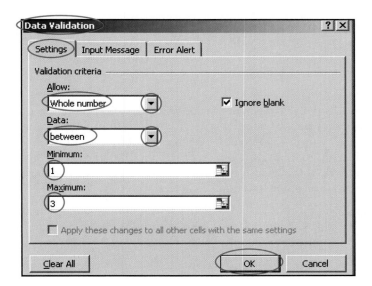

7 Click **OK**. Select cell **H17**.

No input message has been defined.

Type **4** and press ⏎Enter.

If you do not define an error message, a default error message is displayed.

Error warning with default title and message.

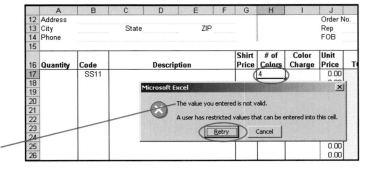

8 Click **Retry**, type **2**, and then press ⏎Enter.

The entry is successful. The number entered in this cell is restricted to whole numbers from 1 to 3.

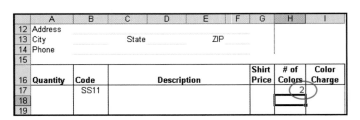

Task 3

USING VLOOKUP AND IF FUNCTIONS

Why would I do this?

If you need to retrieve data from tables for use in your formulas, lookup functions are powerful tools. The *VLOOKUP* function looks up values that are displayed vertically in a column. It is used most often because nearly all tables are arranged with a unique identifier in the first column. You use the *HLOOKUP* function to look up a value in a table by searching horizontally across a row of data. You will use the VLOOKUP function in this task.

The lookup functions can look up numbers or text. If you are searching for numbers, it is important to sort the column or row in ascending order.

If you name the table, you can use the name of the table in the lookup function. This has a major advantage. If you decide to add or remove rows or columns from the table, you simply redefine the table name to include the rows and columns of the revised table. You do not have to revise all the lookup formulas that refer to the table.

The *IF* function evaluates a statement and performs one of two options, depending on whether the statement is true or false. An IF function can be used to determine which column to look up by nesting it within the VLOOKUP function. The IF function has three arguments—a criterion, what to do if the criterion is true, and what to do if the criterion is false. The true and false results may be single values, blanks, or other functions.

In this task you use the VLOOKUP and IF functions to complete the body of the invoice. In steps 1 through 3, you use the VLOOKUP function to look up the description in the Shirts table.

In Steps 4 and 5, you fill this function into the other cells in the Description column and test it.

In Steps 6 through 8, you use the IF function to determine whether to use column 3 or 4 in the Shirts table to find the price. Column 3 has prices for quantities less than a case of 144 shirts and column 4 has prices for quantities of more than 144.

In Steps 9 and 10, you nest the IF function within a VLOOKUP function. This combination of functions lets you find the price per shirt based on the code and the quantity.

In Steps 11 and 12, you use a VLOOKUP function to find the additional charge for using colors by looking it up in the Color table.

1 Select the **Invoice** sheet, if necessary. Select cell **C17**. Choose **Insert**, **Function**. If the Office Assistant opens, click **No, don't provide help now**, to close it.

The Insert Function dialog box opens.

Click the arrow on the **Or select a category** box and choose **Lookup & Reference**. Scroll to the bottom of the list in the **Select a function** box and click **VLOOKUP**.

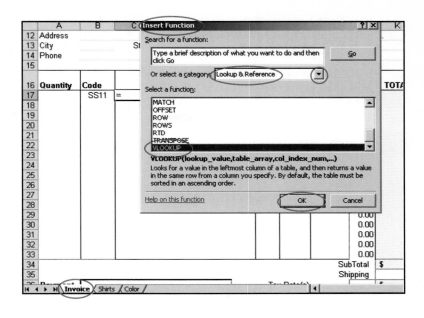

IN DEPTH

You may click the **Help on this function** link in the lower left corner of the Insert Function dialog box to learn more about this function.

CAUTION

The cells in the Description column are merged. If you try to click in D17, E17, or F17, you will still select C17. This isn't really a problem since you want to place the formula in cell C17 anyway.

2 Click **OK**.

The Function Arguments dialog box opens.

Click the **Lookup_value** box then type **B17**.

This is the code that will be looked up in the Shirts table.

Click the **Table_array** box and type **Shirts**. Click the **Col_index_num** box and type **2**.

You use the name of the range, defined in Task 1, in the Table_array box rather than the cell range for convenience. The column of the table that contains the descriptions is the second column in the table, which is why you entered the number 2 in the Col_index_num box.

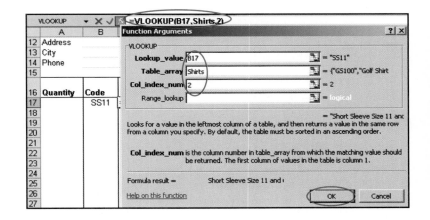

3 Click **OK**.

The description from the Shirts table is displayed for code SS11.

	A	B	C	D	E	F	G
12	Address						
13	City		State		ZIP		
14	Phone						
15							
16	Quantity	Code	Description			Shirt Price	
17		SS11	Short Sleeve Size 11 and up (XL)				
18							
19							

C17 fx =VLOOKUP(B17,Shirts,2)

4 Select cell **C17**. Drag the fill handle down to cell **F33** and release it.

The VLOOKUP function is filled into the cells below. When there is no value in the cell to the left, #N/A is displayed to indicate that the function is not applicable yet. You learn how to hide this in a later task.

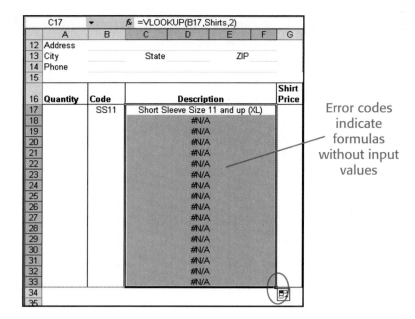

Error codes indicate formulas without input values

5 Select cell **B18**. Click the arrow and select **GSH5/5**.

The description is filled into cell C18.

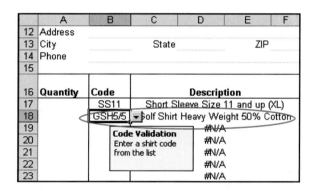

6 Select cell **A17** and type **200**. Select cell **A18**, type **140**, and press ⏎Enter.

The price of the shirt depends on how many are purchased. To determine the price per shirt, you need to determine if the quantity purchased is less than a case. A case of shirts holds 144 shirts (a gross). The prices for quantities of less than a case are found in column 3 of the Shirts table and prices for a case or more are found in column 4. You will use an IF function to determine the column number.

> Select **G17**. Choose **Insert**, **Function**. Click the arrow on the **Or select a category** box and choose **Logical**. Select **IF** in the **Select a function** box.

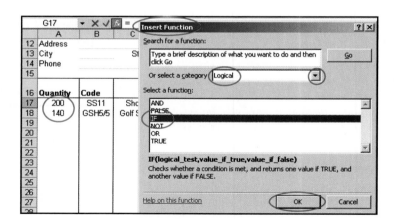

7 Click **OK**. In the **Logical_test** box, type
A17<144. In the **Value_if_true** box, type **3**.
In the **Value_if_false** box, type **4**.

*If the quantity in cell A17 is less than 144, the result of
the IF function will be 3, if the value is 144 or more,
the result will be 4.*

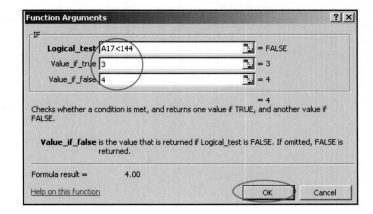

8 Click **OK**.

*The correct value is column 4. The Shirt Price column
is formatted with two decimal places to display the price.
Do not be concerned about the display at this time.
Next, this function will be nested within the VLOOKUP
function to find the correct column number.*

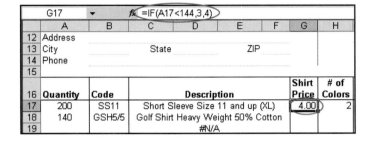

9 Select **G17** and press ⌫ Del.

*The IF function is deleted. You will start over and enter
this function as the third argument of the VLOOKUP
function to determine which column of the Shirts table
to use when determining the price.*

> Choose **Insert**, **Function**. Click the **Or select
> a category** arrow and choose **Lookup &
> Reference**. Scroll to the bottom of the list in
> the **Select a function** box and click
> **VLOOKUP**. Click **OK**.

The Function Arguments dialog box opens.

> In the **Lookup_value** box, type **B17**. In the
> **Table_array** box, type **Shirts**. In the
> **Col_index_num** box, type **IF(A17<144,3,4)**.

*The function looks up the code from cell B17 in the
Shirts range and uses the column determined by the IF
function to return the correct price. The formula results
are displayed in the dialog box.*

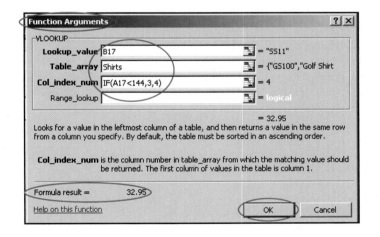

10 Click **OK**.

*The formula looks up the price for this type of shirt in
the fourth column of the Shirts table, which displays the
lower cost for purchases that exceed 144 shirts.*

11 Select **I17**. Choose **Insert**, **Function**. Click the **Or select a category** arrow and choose **Lookup & Reference**. Scroll to the bottom of the list in the **Select a function** box and click **VLOOKUP**. Click **OK**.

The Function Arguments dialog box opens. You will use the VLOOKUP function to find the price for extra colors in the color table. The color table has nine rows for different quantities ordered and three different columns for one, two, and three colors. The VLOOKUP function uses the value in the Quantity column and the value in the # of Colors column to find the additional price for extra colors. In this case the prices for one color are in column two of the table, the prices for two colors are in column three, and prices for three colors are in column four. The correct column number in this case is the number of colors plus one.

In the **Lookup_value** box, type **A17**. In the **Table_array** box, type **Colors**. In the **Col_index_num** box, type **H17+1**.

The function looks up the number of shirts from cell A17 in the Colors range and uses the column determined by the value entered in H17 plus one. The formula result shows 0.80 as the cost per shirt for the number of colors used.

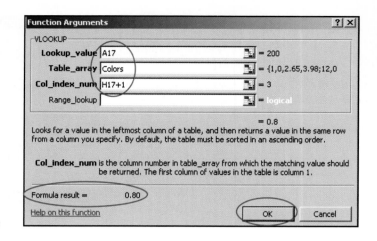

CAUTION

The first column of the table contains numbers to identify the minimum quantity for the prices in that row. The prices for one color start in column 2. In this example, you add 1 to the value the user enters in H17 to find the correct column in the table. This is specific to this particular example. You do not always add 1 to the cell used for the Col_index_num argument.

12 Click **OK**. Select **G17** and copy it. Select cells **G18** to **G33**. Choose **Edit**, **Paste Special**. Click **Formulas** then click **OK**. Repeat this process to copy the formula in **I17** to **I18** through **I33**.

Both functions display #N/A in the rows that lack values in column A or H.

Select **H18** and type **1** and then press ⏎Enter.

The charge for one color is displayed in I18.

Print the worksheet if your instructor requires it. Save your workbook and leave it open for the next task.

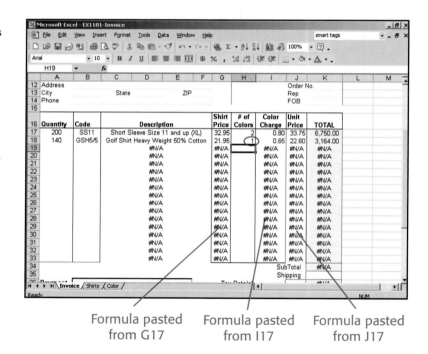

Formula pasted from G17   Formula pasted from I17   Formula pasted from J17

Task 4
USING CONDITIONAL FORMATS

Why would I do this?

You can change the format of a cell based on the value in the cell. This is called conditional formatting. Conditional formatting is often used to warn the person who is entering data that they may have made a mistake. It can also be used to hide error messages that are displayed because cells referenced in formulas are empty. In this circumstance, you can hide the error messages, and when valid entries are supplied, the formulas calculate the results.

In this example, there is a significant price reduction if the order exceeds 144 shirts. If an order is just under 144, the buyer could increase the quantity ordered and actually pay less. It would be useful to flag this situation so the person taking the order can suggest to the buyer that it would be in their best interest to increase the quantity ordered to take advantage of the decreased price.

There are also numerous error codes in the rows that do not have values yet. The error code, #N/A, indicates that no value is available. It would improve the appearance of the invoice to hide these codes. A single function, *ISNA,* can be used to identify when a cell contains this error. You can hide error codes by using a conditional format to format the error code font to be the same color as the background, thereby hiding them from view.

In this task, you use conditional formatting to draw attention to quantities that are slightly less than 144 and to hide the error codes by making their font color the same as the background.

1 Select A17 through A33. Choose **Format, Conditional Formatting.**

The Conditional Formatting dialog box opens.

Confirm that the first box displays **Cell Value is**. Click the arrow on the next box and choose **between**. In the third box, type **135**. In the fourth box, type **143**.

This condition will identify values from 135 to 143 in the quantity cells.

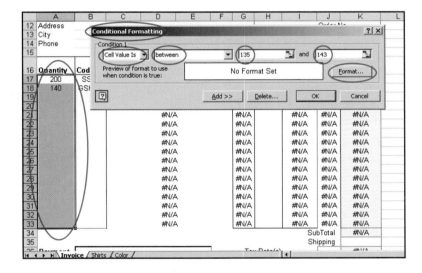

2 Click the **Format** button.

The Format Cells dialog box opens.

> Click **Bold Italic** in the **Font Style** box.

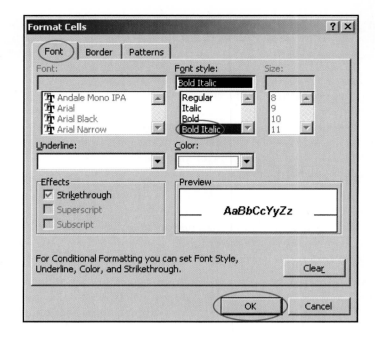

3 Click **OK**.

The Format Cells dialog box closes, and the selected format is displayed in the Conditional Formatting dialog box.

> Click **OK**.

The value in cell A18 is displayed in bold italic font because it is between 135 and 143. The value in cell A17 does not change.

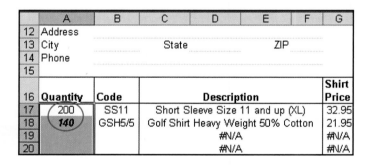

4 Select cells **C18** through **F33**. Choose **Format, Conditional Formatting**.

The Conditional Formatting dialog box opens. C17 is not selected because you would never have a blank invoice.

> Click the arrow on the first box and choose **Formula is**. Click the second box and type **=ISNA(C18)**.

The argument for the ISNA function is the cell address that contains the error code.

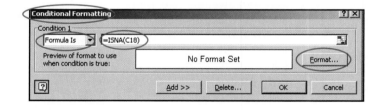

5 Click the **Format** button. Click the **Color** arrow and choose **white**.

To hide the code, format the font color to match the background in the cell, which in this case is white.

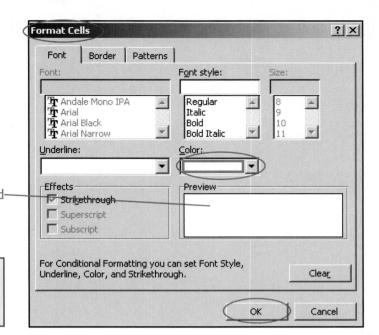

White font on white background ——

CAUTION

You must select the color white from the color palette, even though the color box appears to be white. The color box is actu-ally empty—no color is selected.

6 Click **OK**.

Cells that contain an error message are formatted with a white font that does not appear against a white background.

White font shows when the cell is selected ——

16	Quantity	Code	Description	Shirt Price	# of Colors
17	200	SS11	Short Sleeve Size 11 and up (XL)	32.95	2
18	*140*	GSH5/5	Golf Shirt Heavy Weight 50% Cotton	21.95	1
19				#N/A	#N/A
20				#N/A	#N/A
21				#N/A	#N/A
22				#N/A	#N/A
23				#N/A	#N/A
24				#N/A	#N/A
25				#N/A	#N/A
26				#N/A	#N/A
27				#N/A	#N/A
28				#N/A	#N/A
29				#N/A	#N/A
30				#N/A	#N/A
31				#N/A	#N/A
32				#N/A	#N/A
33				#N/A	#N/A

7 Select cells **G18** through **G33**. Choose **Format, Conditional Formatting**.

The Conditional Formatting dialog box opens.

Click the arrow on the first box and choose **Formula is**. Click the second box and type **=ISNA(G18)**. Set the format of the font color to white.

Repeat this process to hide the error mes-sages in the **Color Charge** and **Unit Price** columns.

The error messages are hidden in the columns with white backgrounds.

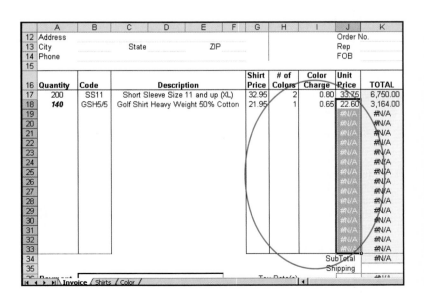

8 Select **K18** through **K38**. Use a conditional format to set the font color to light yellow when an error message is present.

To hide the error messages in this column, the font must match the light yellow color of the background. If you are unsure which color is light yellow, point at the color and wait for a screen tip to appear with the name of the color.

Click elsewhere on the worksheet to deselect the cells.

The error messages are hidden.

Save the workbook.

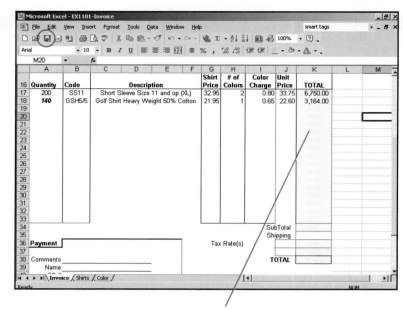

Yellow error code on
yellow background

Task 5

USING CUSTOM DATE AND NUMBER FORMATS

Why would I do this?

Excel has many options for displaying numbers and dates. You can control the placement of commas in large numbers, as well as control how negative numbers are displayed. You can choose the type of currency settings used, including the symbols for different international currencies.

In this task, you learn how use a custom format for the date cell that displays the date in an unambiguous format, and to set the currency format for the Total column.

1 Select **K11**. Type **3/2/03** and press ↵Enter. Select **K11** again.

The date is displayed using a four-digit format for the year.

CAUTION

You can choose from a variety of displays for dates. If you work in an environment where people of different nationalities are using your worksheets, you need to be careful how you display dates. Most Europeans use a day-month-year format while most Americans use month-day-year. A date such as 3/2/03 is interpreted as February 3rd by Europeans and March 2nd by most Americans. The system your computer uses was determined when the Windows operating system was installed. The instructions in this task assume your operating system was set to United States English when it was installed. If your computer's operating system is set to a different date system, ask your instructor for options on how to do this task.

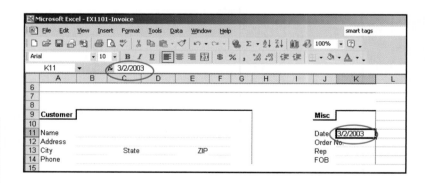

IN DEPTH

Notice the program converted 03 to 2003. To learn more about the assumptions Excel uses to convert two-digit years to four-digit years, use Help and search for: About Dates and Date Systems.

2 Choose F<u>o</u>rmat, C<u>e</u>lls.

The Format Cells dialog box opens.

Click the **Number** tab, if necessary. Select **Date** in the **<u>C</u>ategory** pane. Select **14-Mar-01** in the **<u>T</u>ype** pane. Confirm that the **Locale** is set to **English (United States)**.

The month will be displayed using a three-character format.

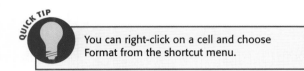

You can right-click on a cell and choose Format from the shortcut menu.

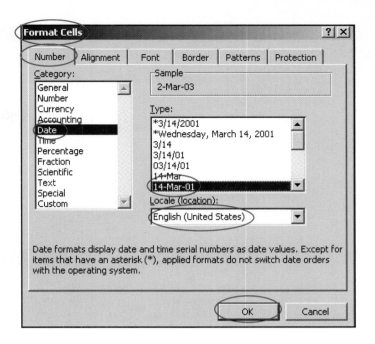

3 Click **OK**. Select **K17** through **K38**. Choose F<u>o</u>rmat, C<u>e</u>lls.

The Format Cells dialog box opens.

Select **Currency** in the **<u>C</u>ategory** pane. Click the arrow on the **Symbol** box.

A list of different currency styles is displayed.

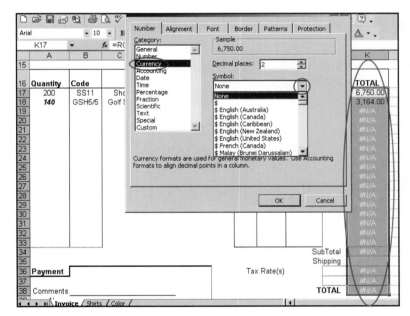

4 Select **$ English (United States)**. Select **($1,234.10)** in the **Negative numbers** pane— the third option listed.

Negative numbers, if they occur, are enclosed in parentheses.

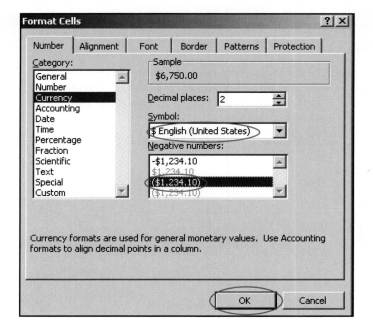

5 Click **OK**.

The numbers are formatted as currency in U.S. dollars. Negative numbers, if they occur, are enclosed in parentheses. The conditional format of the colors is not changed.

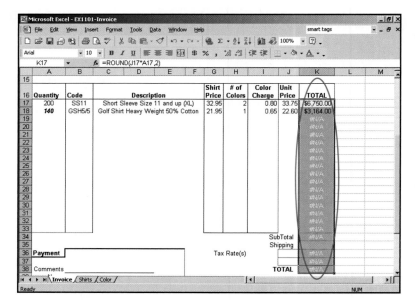

Task 6
AUDITING FORMULAS AND RESOLVING ERRORS

Why would I do this?

The formulas used in this lesson are more complex than most and are more difficult to troubleshoot when there is an error. You may use a feature in Excel called *Formula Auditing,* which helps you identify the cells that affect or are affected by the current cell. The program draws arrows on the worksheet to show the cells used to calculate the formulas in the current cell when you use the *Trace Precedents* option. Arrows show which cells use the value in the current cell when you use the *Trace Dependents* option. The Undo button does not remove the arrows. You must use the *Remove All Arrows* option.

If a formula uses a range of cells and one of those cells contains an error message, such as #N/A, the formula also displays an error message. You turn the background error checking feature on to help identify the problem and then resolve this problem by using the *SUMIF* function that only sums cells in one range that meet certain criteria in another range.

In this task, you trace the precedents for a formula in the Color Charge column and you trace the dependents for a cell in the Quantity column. You resolve the problem in the SubTotal and Total cells by tracing the dependents and using the SUMIF function.

1 Select **I17**. Choose **T**ools, Formula A**u**diting, **T**race Precedents.

The blue arrow indicates the precedent cells with a small circle in each precedent cell. The Shirts table is indicated with a small table and a dotted line to show that it is in another worksheet.

Indicates precedents | Range name in the formula | Cells in the formula | Precedent sheet

Precedent cells

2 Select **A18**. Choose **T**ools, Formula Auditing, Trace **D**ependents.

A blue line indicates the dependent cells by placing an arrowhead at each dependent cell.

Trace dependent line

Dependent cells

QUICK TIP

The Undo button does not remove the arrows. You can remove the arrows by using the Remove All Arrows option that is also found on the Formula Auditing toolbar.

3 Select **K34**. Choose **T**ools, Formula **A**uditing, **T**race Precedents.

The solid color line indicates that all the cells through which it passes are precedents of the selected cell.

K34 depends on all the cells from K17 through K33

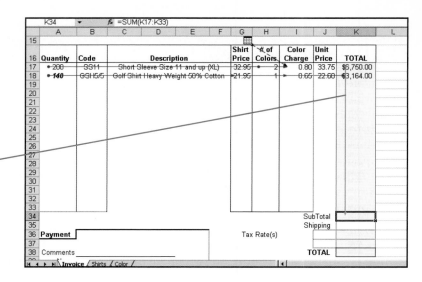

4 Choose **T**ools, **O**ptions. Click the **Error Checking** tab. Click **Enable background error checking**. Click **OK**.

Small green markers indicate the cells with error codes.

Select **K38**. Move the pointer onto the *smart tag.*

Smart tags detect situations in which you might need help. When you click on this one, it displays a message that tells you a value may not be available to this formula. The solid red trace precedent arrow tells you this formula uses values from the four cells above it and you can see that three of them have an error marker.

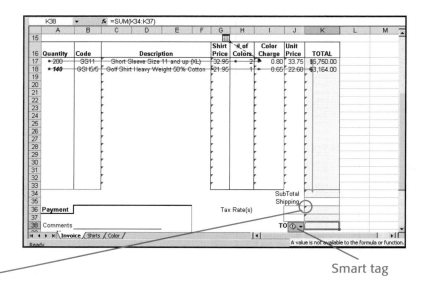

Error indicator

Smart tag

5 Select **K34**.

This cell has a formula that sums the cells above it, many of which have the #N/A error message. You will replace this formula with the SUMIF function.

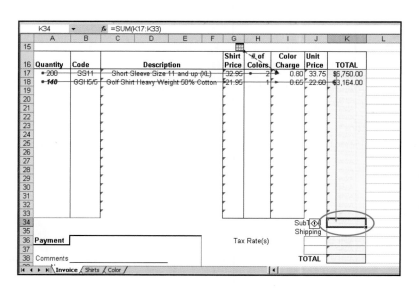

6 Press Del. Choose **Insert**, **Function**. Click **Or select a category** arrow and choose **Math & Trig**. Scroll down and select **SUMIF**.

This function examines one range of cells and sums the cells in a second range of cells if a criterion is met.

Click **OK**. In the **Range** box, type **A17:A33**. In the **Criteria** box, type **>0**. In the **Sum_range** box, type **K17:K33**.

The cells in the Total column that have a corresponding value greater than zero in the Quantity column will be summed. The cells with the #N/A error are not included and the SUMIF formula adds the cells that have values. The criteria is automatically enclosed in quotation marks that you do not have to type.

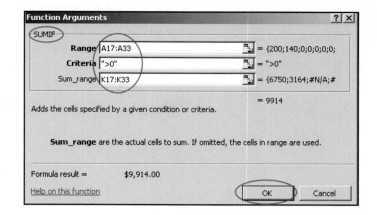

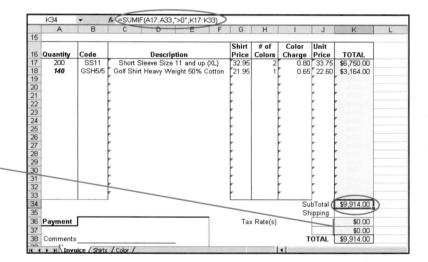

The two ranges in a SUMIF function must be the same size and consist of two columns that share the same rows. The criterion is applied to the cells in the range column one at a time. If the criterion is met, the corresponding cell in the sum_range is included in the summation.

7 Click **OK**.

The formula correctly sums the cells that have corresponding values in the Quantity column. This also removes the error markers in the three cells that are precedents of the Total formula in cell K38. The formula auditing lines are also removed.

Cells no longer depend on a cell with an error

8 Print the worksheet if your instructor requires it. Click **Save**. Close the workbook.

The exercises that follow are designed for you to review and use what you have learned in this lesson. You also have the opportunity to practice your skills and then expand on them by applying them to new situations.

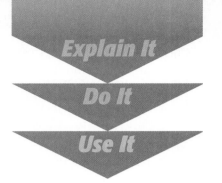

COMPREHENSION

Comprehension exercises are designed to check your memory and understanding of the basic concepts in this lesson. You distinguish between true and false statements, identify new screen elements, and match terms with related statements. If you are uncertain of the correct answer, refer to the task number following each item (for example, T4 refers to Task 4) and review that task until you are confident that you can provide a correct response.

TRUE-FALSE

Circle either T or F.

T F 1. If you use a named range in a formula, it must always be enclosed in double quotation marks. **(T1)**

T F 2. You can validate the input of a cell by requiring that the value entered matches one of the values in a range of cells. **(T2)**

T F 3. The VLOOKUP function finds a value in the first column of a range of data to determine the desired row. **(T3)**

T F 4. You can use conditional formatting to hide errors by utilizing the ERROR function as the criterion. **(T4)**

T F 5. The date, 3/2/2002, may be interpreted differently in the United States and Europe. You can use a custom date format to display the name of the month to reduce the likelihood of a misunderstanding. **(T5)**

T F 6. To display the cells that depend on the currently selected cell graphically, you use the Trace Precedents tool. **(T6)**

MATCHING QUESTIONS

A. Settings, Input message, Error Alert

B. Criteria, true, false

C. 2/3/2002

D. Define

E. Smart tags

F. Font color same as background color

Match the following statements to the word or phrase that is the best match from the list. Write the letter of the matching word or phrase in the space provided next to the number.

1. _____ Menu option used when naming a range for the first time **(T1)**

2. _____ Parts of defining validation **(T2)**

3. _____ Arguments of an IF statement **(T3)**

4. _____ Formatting method used to hide a message **(T4)**

5. _____ The way many Europeans would write March 2, 2002 **(T5)**

6. _____ Icons that display next to cells that may need attention **(T6)**

IDENTIFYING PARTS OF THE EXCEL SCREEN

Refer to the figure and identify the numbered parts of the screen. Write the letter of the correct label in the space next to the number.

1. _____

2. _____

3. _____

4. _____

5. _____

6. _____

7. _____

8. _____

9. _____

10. _____

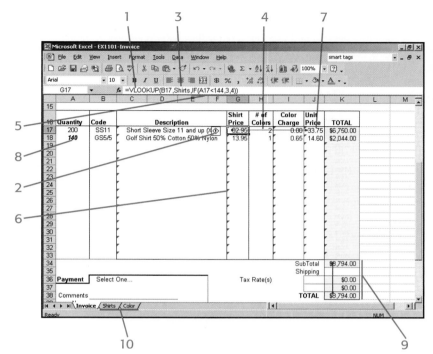

A. Precedents for K38 (T6)

B. Smart tag (T6)

C. Conditional format (T4)

D. A lookup function (T3)

E. IF function (T3)

F. Trace dependents line (T6)

G. Error marker (T6)

H. Dependent cell (T6)

I. Named range (T1)

J. Workheets where tables with named ranges are stored (T1)

REINFORCEMENT

Reinforcement exercises are designed to reinforce the skills you have learned by applying them to a new situation. Detailed instructions are provided along with a figure, where appropriate, to illustrate the result. Complete the reinforcement exercises sequentially. Leave the workbook open at the end of each exercise for use in the next exercise until you are specifically directed to close it.

The workbook employed in the following reinforcement exercises is used to prepare an invoice for Armstrong Pool, Spa, and Sauna. It utilizes three tables that contain information about products, customers, and installation contractors.

R1—Naming Ranges

You need two ranges for each of the four tables of data. One range will be used to validate the selection and the other will be used to look up specific information.

1. Open **EX1102** and save it as **EX1102-Armstrong** on your disk. Select the **Stores** worksheet. Select **A2** through **A9**. Define this range of cells as a named range with the name **StoreNumber**. Select **A2** through **G9** and name this range **StoreInfo**.

2. Select the **Products** worksheet. Select **A2** through **A20**. Define this range of cells as a named range with the name **ProductDescription**. Select **A2** through **D20** and name this range **ProductInfo**.

3. Select the **Customers** worksheet. Select **A2** through **A49**. Define this range of cells as a named range with the name **CustomerName**. Select **A2** through **I49** and name this range **CustomerInfo**.

4. Select the **Contractors** worksheet. Select **A2** through **A17**. Define this range of cells as a named range with the name **ContractorName**. Select **A2** through **I17** and name this range **ContractorInfo**.

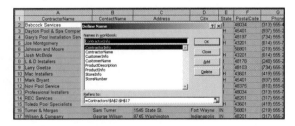

R2—Validating Store, Customer, Contractor, and Product Information

To be sure that your invoice has the correct and current information, you validate the data from the other tables.

1. Select the **Invoice** sheet. Select cell **B1**. Validate the data in this cell by using a list. Use **=StoreNumber** as the source. Use the list to select **MI-100** for cell **B1**.

2. Select cells **B7** and **C7** (they are merged). Validate the data in this cell by using a list. Use **=CustomerName** as the source. Use the list to select **Shepard, Lucinda**.

3. Select cells **B13** through **D13** (they are merged). Validate the data in these cells by using a list. Use **=ContractorName** as the source. Use the list to select **Professional Installers**.

4. Select cells **B20** through **D20** (they are merged). Validate the data in these cells by using a list. Use **=ProductDescription** as the source. Use the list to select **Pool Oval 15'x24'**.

	A	B	C	D	E	F	G
1	Store	MI-100					
2	Manager						
3	Address						
4	City		State		ZIP		
5	Phone						
6							
7	Customer	Shepherd, Lucinda					
8	First Name		Last Name				
9	Address						
10	City		State		ZIP		
11	Phone						
12							
13	Contractor	Professional Installers					
14	Contact						
15	Address						
16	City		State		ZIP		
17	Phone						
18							
19	Quantity		Description		Manufacturer	Unit Price	
20			Pool Oval 15'x24'				

R3—Using VLOOKUP functions to fill in the form

Once you have chosen the store, customer, contractor, and product, you can look up the related address and contact information.

1. Select the **Invoice** sheet, if necessary. The store manager's name is in column 2 of the StoreInfo range. Select the merged cells **B2** through **F2**. Type **=VLOOKUP(B1,StoreInfo,2)** and Press ↵Enter. Use a VLOOKUP function in each of the following cells, **B3:F3**, **B4**, **D4**, **F4**, and **B5:C5**, to look up the value in cell B1 in the StoreInfo range. The address, city, state, postal code, and phone numbers are in columns 3 through 7. For example, in cells **B2:F3** you type **=VLOOKUP(B1,StoreInfo,3)**. In cell **B4**, you type **=VLOOKUP(B1,StoreInfo,4)** and so on.

2. The customer name is in column **1** of the CustomerInfo range. The names in this column are a combination of the last name, a comma, and the first name. This is done to provide a column of unique names that can be used with a VLOOKUP function. Select the merged cells **B8** through **C8** where the first name should go. Type **=VLOOKUP(B7,CustomerInfo,3)**. Use a VLOOKUP function in each of the following cells, **E8:F8**, **B9:F9**, **B10**, **D10**, **F10**, and **B11:C11**, to look up the value in cell **B7** in the CustomerInfo range. The last name, address, city, state, postal code, and phone numbers are in columns **4** through **9** of the CustomerInfo range. For example, in cells **E8:F8** you type **=VLOOKUP(B7,CustomerInfo,4)**. In cells **B9:F9**, you type **=VLOOKUP(B7,CustomerInfo,5)** and so on.

3. The contractor name is in column **1** of the ContractorInfo range. Select the merged cells **B14** through **C14** where the contact name should go. Type **=VLOOKUP(B13,ContractorInfo,2)**. Use a VLOOKUP function in each of the following cells, **B15:F15**, **B16**, **D16**, **F16**, and **B16:C16**, to look up the value in cell **B13** in the ContractorInfo range. The address, city, state, postal code, and phone numbers are in columns **3** through **7** of the ContractorInfo range.

4. Place a VLOOKUP function in cell **E20** that can look up the description in **B20** in the **ProductInfo** range and return the manufacturer's name from column **2**.

5. Place a VLOOKUP function in cell **G20** that can look up the description in **B20** in the **ProductInfo** range and return the unit price from column **3**.

6. Place a VLOOKUP function in cell **H20** that can look up the description in **B20** in the **ProductInfo** range and return the installation cost from column **4**.

7. Select **A20** and type **1**. The unit price, installation cost, and total are filled in.

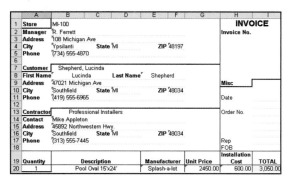

R4—Using Conditional Formatting to Hide Error Messages

When you copy the validation and the formulas into the other cells in the table, #REF error messages display due to the empty reference cells. You can hide them by formatting the font of the error messages to match the background color.

1. Select the description in cells **B20** through **D20** and click the **Copy** button. Select **B21** through **D36**. Choose **Edit**, **Paste Special**. Choose **Validation** and click **OK**.

2. Select the three formulas in cells **E20** through **H20** and click the **Copy** button. Select **E21** through **H36**. Choose **Edit**, **Paste Special**. Choose **Formulas** and click **OK**.

3. Select **E21** through **H36**. Choose **Format**, **Conditional Formatting**. Change the condition to **Formula is** and type **=ISNA(E21)**. Click the **Format** button and set the font to white, then click **OK** twice to close the dialog boxes.

4. Select **I21** through **I41**. Choose **Format**, **Conditional Formatting**. Change the condition to **Formula is** and type **=ISNA(I21)**. Click the **Format** button and set the font to light yellow, then click **OK** twice to close the dialog boxes.

5. Format the numbers in columns **G**, **H**, and **I** to **Currency** with two decimal places. Select cells **I20** through **I41**. Click the **Borders** arrow and select **Right Border**.

	A	B	C	D	E	F	G	H	I
19	Quantity	Description			Manufacturer		Unit Price	Installation Cost	TOTAL
20	1	Pool Oval 15'x24'			Splash-a-lot		2450.00	600.00	3,050.00
21									#N/A
22									#N/A
23									#N/A
24									#N/A
25									#N/A
26									#N/A
27									#N/A
28									#N/A
29									#N/A
30									#N/A
31									#N/A
32									#N/A
33									#N/A
34									#N/A
35									#N/A
36									#N/A
37								SubTotal	#N/A
38								Shipping	
39	Payment						Tax Rate(s)		#N/A
40									#N/A
41	Comments							TOTAL	#N/A

R5—Using Formula Auditing to Resolve Errors

The subtotals and total figures do not display at the bottom of TOTAL column.

1. Delete the formula in cell **I37**. Choose **Insert**, **Function**. Click the **Or select a category** arrow and choose **Math & Trig**. Scroll down and select **SUMIF**. Click **OK**. In the **Range** box, type **A20:A36**. In the **Criteria** box, type **>0**. In the **Sum_range** box, type **I20:I36**. Click **OK**.

2. Select **I37** and choose **T**ools, Formula A**u**diting, **T**race Precedents.

3. Print the **Invoice** sheet. Save the workbook and close it. The auditing arrows are not saved as part of the workbook.

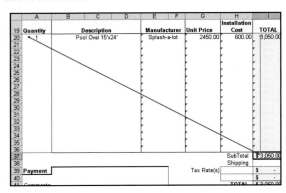

Challenge exercises are designed to test your ability to apply your skills to new situations with less detailed instruction. These exercises also challenge you to expand your repertoire of skills by using commands that are similar to those you have already learned. The desired outcome is clearly defined, but you have more freedom to choose the steps needed to achieve the required result.

C1–Using the INDEX function

If you know the row and column numbers of the cell you wish to look up from a table, you can use the INDEX function. The table used in this exercise is similar to the Colors table in EX1101-Invoice but it has been modified so that the number of shirts in the first column is in dozens and the number of colors ranges from 1 to 4 where 1 stands for black.

Goal: Use the INDEX function to find the cost of adding color to a printing job.

Use the following guidelines:

1. Locate **EX1103** in the student files and save it as **EX1103-C1-INDEX**.

2. Select **A22** and enter your name. Select **A12** and enter **Dozens of Shirts:**. Select **A13** and enter **Number of Colors:**. Select **A14** and enter **Cost per Shirt:**.

3. Enter a number between 1 and 8 in **B12** and a number between 1 and 4 in **B13**.

4. Select the data in cells **B3** through **E10**. Notice the row and column numbers are not included. Define a name for this range as **Colors**.

5. Select **B14**. Type **=INDEX(Colors,5,3)** and press **⏎Enter**. The answer should be **1.2,** which is the cost for five dozen shirts in three colors.

6. Select **B14** and type **=INDEX(Colors,B12,B13)**. Now the formula uses the values you selected in cells **B12** and **B13**.

7. Print the **Colors** sheet if your instructor requires it. Save the file. Close the workbook.

	B14	▼	*fx* =INDEX(Colors,B12,B13)		
	A	B	C	D	E
1	Dozens of Shirts		Number of Colors		
2		1	2	3	4
3	1	0.95	2.55	3.83	5.11
4	2	0.80	2.25	3.38	4.51
5	3	0.75	1.15	1.73	2.31
6	4	0.65	0.90	1.35	1.80
7	5	0.55	0.80	1.20	1.60
8	6	0.50	0.65	0.98	1.31
9	7	0.30	0.60	0.90	1.20
10	8	0.20	0.55	0.83	1.11
11					
12	Dozens of Shirts:	4.00			
13	Number of Colors	2.00			
14	Cost per Shirt:	0.9			
15					

C2–Selecting Ranges using Column Headers or Whole Worksheets

If you want to add values to a table, you have to revise the named ranges if they are based on a specific range of cells. You can get around this limitation by naming the entire worksheet or a particular column as the range. The worksheet must be modified to remove column headings and other labels as well as any merged cells. You also use a combination of the Ctrl and ◿ keys to display the formulas in each cell. The *accent grave* character, ◿, is similar to a single quotation mark and is usually found at the left end of the row of numbers on your keyboard.

Goal: Revise the Colors sheet and create ranges that you can expand without revising the range names.

Use the following guidelines:

1. Locate **EX1103** in the student files and save it as **EX1103-C2-Range**.

2. Select row **1** and row **2**. Choose **Edit, Delete**.

3. Click the small box in upper-left corner of the sheet. It is above the first row header and to the left of the column **A** header. The entire sheet is selected. Name this range **Colors**.

4. Click the header for column **A** to select the entire column. Name this range **Dozens**.

5. Click the **Sheet1** tab. Enter your name in **A1**.

6. Select **A3** and type **Dozens:**. Select **B3** and type **5**.

7. Select **A4** and type **Colors:**. Select **B4** and type **3**.

8. Select **A5** and type **Cost:**. Select **B5** and type **=VLOOKUP(B3,Colors,B4+1)** and press **⏎Enter**. In this example, the number of the column is one more than the number of the colors because the first column is used for the number of dozens.

9. Click the **Colors** sheet tab. Add another row to the table. The new values in row **9** are: **9, 0.18, 0.50, 0.78,** and **1.02**.

10. Click the **Sheet1** tab. Change the number of dozens to **9**. The correct cost per shirt for nine dozen with three colors should display.

11. Format **B5** to **Currency**.

12. Press Ctrl + ◿ to display the formulas and print the Sheet1.

13. Save the workbook and close it.

	A	B	C	D	E
1	1	0.95	2.55	3.83	5.11
2	2	0.80	2.25	3.38	4.51
3	3	0.75	1.15	1.73	2.31
4	4	0.65	0.90	1.35	1.80
5	5	0.55	0.80	1.20	1.60
6	6	0.50	0.65	0.98	1.31
7	7	0.30	0.60	0.90	1.20
8	8	0.20	0.55	0.83	1.11
9	9	0.18	0.50	0.78	1.02

Selects whole worksheet

Selects column

C3—Using the True/False Option in a VLOOKUP Function

If you use a VLOOKUP function to look up a number, you need to know what will happen if the number for which you are searching does not match any of the values in the first column. You also need to know what happens if the value is outside the range of numbers in the first column. You can use a fourth argument, called *range_lookup*, in the function to force exact matches or allow approximate matches.

Goal: Create a small table that shows what happens with you exceed the range or use nonmatching numbers in a VLOOKUP function with and without the range_lookup option.

1. Locate **EX1103** in the student files and save it as **EX1103-C3-TRUE**.

2. Select **A3:E10** and name the range **Colors**.

3. Select **A13** and type **Dozens:**. Select **B13** and type **5**.

4. Select **A14** and type **Colors:**. Select **B14** and type **3**.

5. Select **A15** and type **Cost:**. Select **B15** and type **=VLOOKUP(B13,Colors,B14+1,TRUE)** and then press ↵Enter. In this example, you use B14+1 as the third argument because the number of the column is one more than the number of the colors. This happens because the first column is used for the number of dozens. The fourth argument is used to determine if the match is approximate or exact.

6. Select **B12** through **D12**, click the **Merge and Center** button, and then type **TRUE**. Select **E12** through **G12**, click the **Merge and Center** button, and then type **FALSE**.

7. Select **B13** through **B15**. Drag the fill handle to column **G**.

8. Edit the three formulas in **E15** through **G15** and change the range_lookup options from TRUE to **FALSE**.

9. Replace the values in **B13:G13** to show three different options for both TRUE and FALSE: **0.50, 2.75, 9.00, 0.50, 2.75, 9.00**.

10. Select **A17** through **G23** and click the **Merge and Center** button. Choose F**o**rmat, C**e**lls, Alignment. Select **Left(Indent)** in the **Horizontal** box, **TOP**, in the **Vertical** box, and select **Wrap text**. Click **OK**.

11. Use this range of cells to write a short explanation of this function. Refer to the table of results in **A12** through **G15**. Describe how the range_error option deals with reference values that are less than the lowest value in the first column of the table (.5), how they each deal with a number that is between two values in the first column (2.75), and how they deal with numbers that are larger than the largest value in the first column (9).

12. Print the worksheet. Save your changes and close the workbook.

	A	B	C	D	E	F	G
3	1	0.95	2.55	3.83	5.11		
4	2	0.80	2.25	3.38	4.51		
5	3	0.75	1.15	1.73	2.31		
6	4	0.65	0.90	1.35	1.80		
7	5	0.55	0.80	1.20	1.60		
8	6	0.50	0.65	0.98	1.31		
9	7	0.30	0.60	0.90	1.20		
10	8	0.20	0.55	0.83	1.11		
11							
12			TRUE			FALSE	
13	Dozens:	0.50	2.75	9.00	0.50	2.75	9.00
14	Colors:	3.00	3.00	3.00	3.00	3.00	3.00
15	Cost:	#N/A	3.38	0.83	#N/A	#N/A	#N/A
16							
17	Analyze the behaviour of the range_error option in the table above and write your						
18	essay here.						
19							
20							
21							
22							
23							

C4—Using the HLOOKUP Function and Transpose

You can orient a table of data horizontally rather than vertically. If the value you want to look up is arranged in a row across the top of the table, you can use the HLOOKUP function instead of the VLOOKUP function.

In some cases, you may wish to change the orientation of a table. To accomplish this, you copy the table and then paste it in another location using the *Transpose* option.

Goal: Transpose the Colors table and use the HLOOKUP function to find the price for color printing.

1. Locate **EX1103** in the student files and save it as **EX1103-C4-Horizontal**.

2. Select **A2** through **E10** and click the **Copy** button.

3. Click **A12**. Choose **E**dit, Paste **S**pecial. Click the **Transpose** option and click **OK**. The number of colors is now listed in column **A**, and the number of dozens is in row **12**.

4. Select **B12** through **I16** and name the range **Colors**. You do not include the row headings in the HLOOKUP argument in the same manner that you did not include the column headings in a VLOOKUP argument.

5. Select **A18** and type **Dozens:**. Select **B18** and type **5**.

6. Select **A19** and type **Colors:**. Select **B19** and type **3**.

7. Select **A20** and type **Cost:**. Select **B20** and type **=HLOOKUP(B18,Colors,B19+1)** and press ⏎Enter. In this example, you use B19+1 as the third argument because the number of the rows is one more than the number of the colors. This happens because the first row is used for the number of dozens.

8. Select **A22** and enter your name. Print the sheet. Save the workbook and close it.

	A	B	C	D	E	F	G	H	I
1	Dozens of Shirts		Number of Colors						
2		1	2	3	4				
3	1	0.95	2.55	3.83	5.11				
4	2	0.80	2.25	3.38	4.51				
5	3	0.75	1.15	1.73	2.31				
6	4	0.65	0.90	1.35	1.80				
7	5	0.55	0.80	1.20	1.60				
8	6	0.50	0.65	0.98	1.31				
9	7	0.30	0.60	0.90	1.20				
10	8	0.20	0.55	0.83	1.11				
11									
12		1	2	3	4	5	6	7	8
13	1	0.95	0.80	0.75	0.65	0.55	0.50	0.30	0.20
14	2	2.55	2.25	1.15	0.90	0.80	0.65	0.60	0.55
15	3	3.83	3.38	1.73	1.35	1.20	0.98	0.90	0.83
16	4	5.11	4.51	2.31	1.80	1.60	1.31	1.20	1.11
17									
18	Dozens:	5.00							
19	Colors:	3.00							
20	Cost:	1.2							
21									
22	<student name>								

💲 ## C5—Using Custom Number Formats

Most formatting needs can be met using one of the pre-defined formatting options. If you want to control the number of digits displayed, how zero values are handled, or if you want to add different text labels to positive and negative numbers you can create your own rules for handling these options.

In this exercise, you learn about the options for formatting numbers and create your own formatting options to handle positive, negative, and zero values.

Goal: Create and describe your own custom number format.

1. Save a new, blank workbook as EX1104-C5.

2. Enter your name and section in A1.

3. Select the Ask a Question box in the upper right corner of the window and enter Create a custom number format. Choose the option Create or delete a custom number format. Read the instructions in this topic.

4. Select B3 and create a custom format that will display positive numbers as currency. Negative numbers display in blue followed by your last name.

5. Test your format by typing in positive and negative numbers. Print a copy to hand in if your instructor requires it. Save the workbook and close it.

B3	▼	ƒx -1
	A	B	C
1	<student name and section>		
2			
3		($1.00 lastname)	
4			
5			

Create a workbook that consists of at least two worksheets. The first sheet prepares a statement of some kind that uses values from the second sheet.

Criteria for grading will be:

1. Demonstration of the use of reference formulas such as VLOOKUP, HLOOKUP, and IF formulas that refer to a named range of cells on the second worksheet.

2. Demonstration of the ability to use conditional formatting.

3. Demonstration of the ability to check for errors and hide #N/A error messages with conditional formatting.

Some examples of projects that students have created that meet these criteria are:

- A workbook that creates a Material Safety Data Sheet (MSDS) for substances that contain several chemicals. A list of chemicals and the required warnings resided in a table on the second worksheet while VLOOKUP functions retrieved the various attributes of the chemicals.

- A workbook that determines the safety and cost of flying freight to various destinations. This project had tables of airport information and airplane characteristics. The student used VLOOKUP and IF statements to determine if the runways were long enough at a given airport to accommodate a selected aircraft. Conditional formatting was used to warn of a safety problem. The student also looked up the longitude and latitude of the airports and calculated the distance between them. Another lookup formula determined the fuel consumption of the selected aircraft and calculated the fuel needed to fly between the two airports. The final product allowed the user to select an aircraft and enter the airports on its route. The distance, fuel consumption, and flight time were calculated and the user was warned if the airport did not have long enough runways for the aircraft selected.

1. Identify yourself and the year. Place your name in a cell that is clearly visible on the first worksheet.

2. To complete the project:

- Save the workbook on your own disk. Name the workbook **EX1104-OnYourOwn**.

- Check with your instructor to determine if you should submit the project in electronic or printed form. If necessary, print out a copy of the workbook.

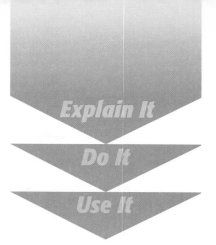

Lesson 12

Analyzing Data

Task 1   Filtering Data

Task 2   Sorting, Grouping, and Subtotaling Data

Task 3   Creating a PivotTable

Task 4   Charting a Trend

Task 5   Estimating Values

Task 6   Saving Scenarios

Task 7   Using Goal Seek and Using PivotTable to Compare Scenarios

INTRODUCTION

Many people who are not familiar with database management software, such as Microsoft Access, use Excel as a simple database manager to store records of invoices or other transactions. You can manage data in Excel if the data is stored in a simple table format where each row is a record of one transaction and the columns are types of data. The column headings should not be merged across columns and each column heading should be short and unique. If the data is stored in this form, you can sort, filter, group, and subtotal the columns of data. These features are especially useful for preparing reports that allow someone to focus on particular sections of the data. You can summarize the data by groups and categories by creating a *PivotTable* on another worksheet. You select the row and column headings and how the cells in the table will be calculated.

Excel can help you chart your data and find a line that is the best fit through your data points. This type of line is called a *trendline*. Excel can also provide the formula for that line and a statistical measurement called an *R-squared value* that gives you an idea of how well the trend line fits the data. You can use the formula to estimate other data points on the trend line.

If your calculations depend on several assumptions, you can calculate the best option for each variable using *Goal Seek* and save the result of each calculation as a separate *scenario*. Goal Seek is a tool that automatically tries different values to achieve a goal, and a scenario saves the values of the variable for use at a later time.

In this lesson, you learn how to sort the data by each of the columns and how to filter the data by selecting values within certain columns. You group the data and add subtotals. You create a PivotTable to compare sales by branch and product. Finally, you save different scenarios that result from changing the size limit and point values for large and small sales.

307

VISUAL SUMMARY

By the time you complete this lesson; you will have sorted, grouped, subtotaled, and filtered the data. You will have charted the data and added a trend line. You will also have calculated and compared four different scenarios. The worksheets will look like these:

Task 2:
Group data

Task 2:
Sort rows by column
used for grouping

Task 1: Filter
the rows

Task 2:
Add subtotals

Task 3: One column
for each product

Task 3: One row
for each branch

Task 3: Amount
for each branch
and product

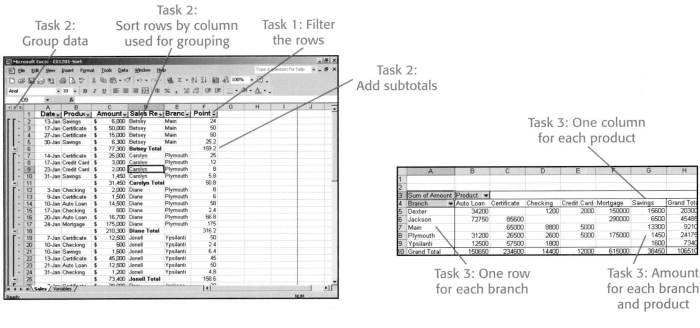

Task 4: Formula of
the straight line

Task 4: Best-fit
straight line

Task 4: Measure
of how well the
line fits the data

Task 4:
Data points
approximate a
straight line

Task 4: Equally spaced values
on the category axis

Task 7: PivotTable
summarizing scenarios

Task 6:
Four scenarios

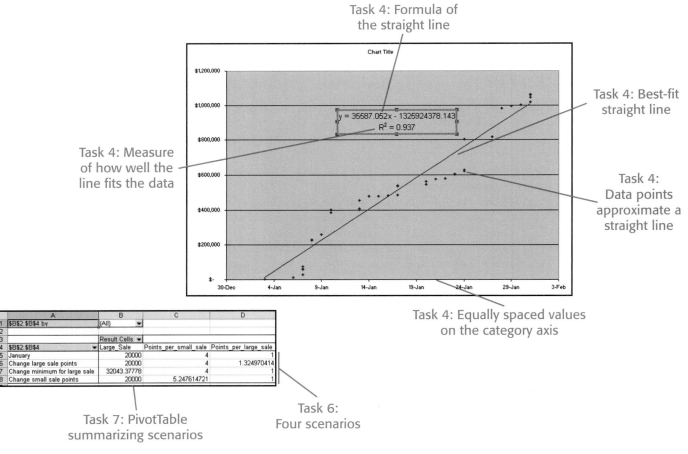

Task 1
FILTERING DATA

Explain It

Do It

Use It

Why would I do this?

If you have a lot of data that is mixed together, you can focus on one portion of the data by selecting the characteristics you want and only displaying the rows in the worksheet that meet those criteria.

In the example used in this lesson, you analyze the data from a sales contest at a bank. There are several branch banks and each branch has several employees. There are several different banking services they sell to bank customers for which they are awarded points. The points awarded depend on whether the sale is considered to be above or below a certain size.

In this task, you filter the data by matching names, using *comparison operators* and date ranges.

1 Open **EX1201** from the **Student** folder. Save it as **EX1201-Sort** on your disk.

The new title appears in the title bar.

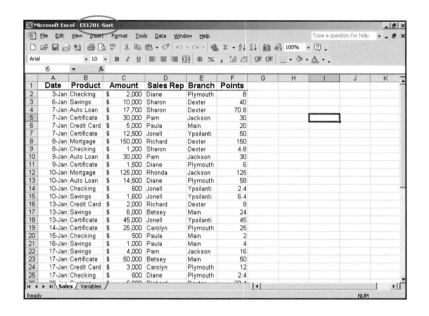

2 Select any cell in the table of data then choose **D**ata, **F**ilter, Auto**F**ilter.

Arrows are added in the column headings. The arrows display lists of options for filtering the rows based on the contents of the column.

IN DEPTH

The program assumes that the first row contains column headings. Do not merge column headings across columns. Keep the headings short and different for each column. Use only one row for column headings. Do not use empty rows or columns for visual spacing. If you ever decide to move an Excel worksheet into an Access database, it will be easier if you use simple rows and columns with simple column headings.

3 Click the arrow on the **Branch** heading and select **Jackson** from the list.

The rows for the Jackson branch are displayed. The row numbers change color to draw attention to the fact that all the rows are not displayed, and the small arrow in the heading changes color to show that a filter is active in that column. The cumulative total formulas in the last column still display the totals from all the rows even if they are not displayed.

	A	B	C	D	E	F
1	Date ▾	Produc ▾	Amount ▾	Sales Re ▾	Branc ▾	Point ▾
5	7-Jan	Certificate	$ 30,000	Pam	Jackson	30
10	9-Jan	Auto Loan	$ 30,000	Pam	Jackson	30
12	10-Jan	Mortgage	$ 125,000	Rhonda	Jackson	125
22	17-Jan	Savings	$ 4,000	Pam	Jackson	16
30	22-Jan	Savings	$ 2,500	Pam	Jackson	10
31	23-Jan	Certificate	$ 25,000	Pam	Jackson	25
33	24-Jan	Auto Loan	$ 17,750	Rhonda	Jackson	71
37	28-Jan	Mortgage	$ 165,000	Pam	Jackson	165
38	29-Jan	Certificate	$ 15,000	Rhonda	Jackson	60
41	31-Jan	Auto Loan	$ 25,000	Pam	Jackson	25
42	31-Jan	Certificate	$ 15,600	Pam	Jackson	62.4
46						

4 Click the arrow on the **Branch** heading and select **(All)** from the list.

All the rows are displayed.

All the rows are displayed again

	A	B	C	D	E	F
1	Date ▾	Produc ▾	Amount ▾	Sales Re ▾	Branc ▾	Point ▾
2	3-Jan	Checking	$ 2,000	Diane	Plymouth	8
3	6-Jan	Savings	$ 10,000	Sharon	Dexter	40
4	7-Jan	Auto Loan	$ 17,700	Sharon	Dexter	70.8
5	7-Jan	Certificate	$ 30,000	Pam	Jackson	30
6	7-Jan	Credit Card	$ 5,000	Paula	Main	20
7	7-Jan	Certificate	$ 12,500	Jonell	Ypsilanti	50
8	8-Jan	Mortgage	$ 150,000	Richard	Dexter	150
9	8-Jan	Checking	$ 1,200	Sharon	Dexter	4.8
10	9-Jan	Auto Loan	$ 30,000	Pam	Jackson	30
11	9-Jan	Certificate	$ 1,500	Diane	Plymouth	6
12	10-Jan	Mortgage	$ 125,000	Rhonda	Jackson	125
13	10-Jan	Auto Loan	$ 14,500	Diane	Plymouth	58
14	10-Jan	Checking	$ 600	Jonell	Ypsilanti	2.4
15	10-Jan	Savings	$ 1,600	Jonell	Ypsilanti	6.4

5 Click the arrow on the **Amount** heading and choose **Custom**.

The Custom AutoFilter dialog box opens.

Click the arrow on the first **Amount** box and choose **is greater than or equal to**. Click in the box to the right and type **50000**.

The filter limits the rows displayed to those with an amount greater than or equal to $50,000. This is an example of a comparison operator.

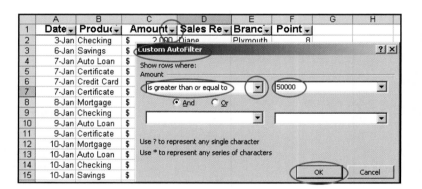

6 Click **OK**.

You can add filters to more than one column at the same time. Here, you want to see amounts of $50,000 or more that were sold between January 15, 2002, and January 31, 2002.

Click the arrow on the **Date** heading and choose (**Custom…**) from the list.

The Custom AutoFilter dialog box opens.

Click the arrow on the first box and choose **is greater than or equal to**. Click in the second box and type **January 15, 2002**. Click the arrow on the third box and choose **is less than or equal to**. Click in the fourth box and type **January 31, 2002**.

The **A**nd *option should be checked to require that both conditions are met.*

7 Click **OK**.

Three rows meet the combined criteria set in the date and amount columns.

Three rows match both criteria

8 Select **A50** and enter your name. Include your section number if your instructor requires it. Click the **Print Preview** button.

The three rows that meet the criteria can be printed with your name.

Click **Zoom** if necessary to display the top part of the page.

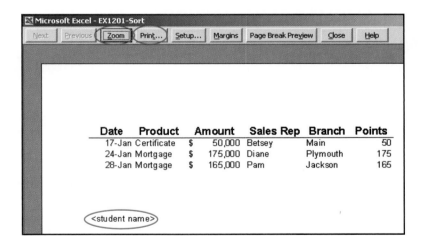

Date filter active   Amount filter active

9 Click **Print**. Select your printer and click **OK**.

The sheet is printed to display your work.

Click the **Save** button.

The filter settings are saved.

Click the arrow on the **Date** heading and choose **(All)**. Do the same on the **Amount** heading.

All the rows are displayed.

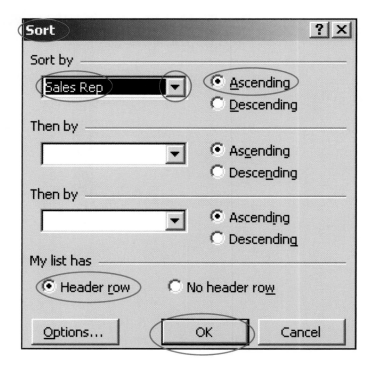

Task 2
SORTING, GROUPING, AND SUBTOTALING DATA

Why would I do this?

The table of data can be sorted, grouped, and subtotaled to provide summaries. You can use such summaries to prepare monthly reports about expenses or other activities. To prepare such reports, it is useful to sort the data by one or more of the columns and then create groups based on that column that can be collapsed to hide the individual records. You can customize reports for different levels of management showing only the data of interest to them. If some of the columns contain numeric values, you can add subtotals at each change in the group. You can also count the number of items in the group and display them in a subtotal.

In this task, you sort the rows by sales representative then group the records by sales representative. You add a subtotal to the Amount and Points columns. This display is useful when you want to see how individual people are doing in the contest.

1 Select any cell in the data. Choose **Data**, **Sort**.

The entire table of data is selected and the Sort dialog box opens.

Select **Header row**, if necessary. Click the arrow on the **Sort by** box and choose **Sales Rep**. Confirm that **Ascending** is chosen.

The rows will be sorted alphabetically by the sales representative's name.

2 Click **OK**.

The rows are sorted on the Sales Rep field.

Select **D2:D5**.

The cells with Betsey are selected.

Choose **D**ata, **G**roup and Outline, **G**roup.

The Group dialog box opens.

Sorted on Sales Rep
Selected for a group

	A	B	C	D	E	F
1	Date ▾	Produc ▾	Amount ▾	Sales Re ▾	Branc ▾	Point ▾
2	13-Jan	Savings	$ 6,000	Betsey	Main	24
3	17-Jan	Certificate	$ 50,000	Betsey	Main	50
4	27-Jan	Certificate	$ 15,000	Betsey	Main	60
5	30-Jan	Savings	$ 6,300	Betsey	Main	25.2
6	14-Jan	Certificate	$ 25,000	Carolyn	Plymouth	25
7	17-Jan	Credit Card	$ 3,000	Carolyn	Plymouth	12
8	23-Jan	Credit Card	$ 2,000	Carolyn	Plymouth	8
9	31-Jan	Savings	$ 1,450	Carolyn	Plymouth	5.8
10	3-Jan	Checking	$ 2,000	Diane	Plymouth	8
11	9-Jan	Certificate	$ 1,500	Diane		
12	10-Jan	Auto Loan	$ 14,500	Diane		
13	17-Jan	Checking	$ 600	Diane		
14	20-Jan	Auto Loan	$ 16,700	Diane		
15	24-Jan	Mortgage	$ 175,000	Diane		
16	7-Jan	Certificate	$ 12,500	Jonell		
17	10-Jan	Checking	$ 600	Jonell		

Group ? ☒
Group
• **R**ows
○ **C**olumns
OK   Cancel

3 Confirm that **R**ows is selected and click **OK**.

An outline pane opens on the left of the screen that displays the group. It is limited to the rows that contain the selected cells.

Outline pane

		A	B	C	D	E	F
1 2							
	1	Date ▾	Produc ▾	Amount ▾	Sales Re ▾	Branc ▾	Point ▾
	2	13-Jan	Savings	$ 6,000	Betsey	Main	24
	3	17-Jan	Certificate	$ 50,000	Betsey	Main	50
	4	27-Jan	Certificate	$ 15,000	Betsey	Main	60
	5	30-Jan	Savings	$ 6,300	Betsey	Main	25.2
	6	14-Jan	Certificate	$ 25,000	Carolyn	Plymouth	25
	7	17-Jan	Credit Card	$ 3,000	Carolyn	Plymouth	12
	8	23-Jan	Credit Card	$ 2,000	Carolyn	Plymouth	8

4 Click the minus sign on the outline box.

The rows in this group are hidden and the sign on the outline box changes to a plus.

Rows 2 through 5
are hidden

		A	B	C	D	E	F
1 2							
	1	Date ▾	Produc ▾	Amount ▾	Sales Re ▾	Branc ▾	Point ▾
⊕	6	14-Jan	Certificate	$ 25,000	Carolyn	Plymouth	25
	7	17-Jan	Credit Card	$ 3,000	Carolyn	Plymouth	12
	8	23-Jan	Credit Card	$ 2,000	Carolyn	Plymouth	8
	9	31-Jan	Savings	$ 1,450	Carolyn	Plymouth	5.8
	10	3-Jan	Checking	$ 2,000	Diane	Plymouth	8
	11	9-Jan	Certificate	$ 1,500	Diane	Plymouth	6

QUICK TIP

You can expand or collapse all the groups at once by using the small numbered buttons at the top of the outline pane.

5 Click the plus sign on the outline box.
Choose **D**ata, **G**roup and Outline, **U**ngroup.

The Ungroup dialog box opens.

Confirm that **R**ows is selected and click **OK**.

The group is removed. You will use grouping again when you create subtotals.

Outline pane
removed

Rows displayed

	A	B	C	D	E	F
1	Date ▾	Produc ▾	Amount ▾	Sales Re ▾	Branc ▾	Point ▾
2	13-Jan	Savings	$ 6,000	Betsey	Main	24
3	17-Jan	Certificate	$ 50,000	Betsey	Main	50
4	27-Jan	Certificate	$ 15,000	Betsey	Main	60
5	30-Jan	Savings	$ 6,300	Betsey	Main	25.2
6	14-Jan	Certificate	$ 25,000	Carolyn	Plymouth	25

6 Select a single cell in the table. Choose **D**ata, Su**b**totals.

The Subtotal dialog box opens, and the entire table is automatically selected.

> Click the **At each change in** arrow and choose **Sales Rep**. Confirm that the **Sum** function is selected in the **U**se function box. Select **Amount** and **Points** in the **A**dd **subtotal to** box.
>
> Confirm that **Replace current subtotals** and **Summary below data** are both selected.

The Amount and Points columns will be subtotaled for each sales representative.

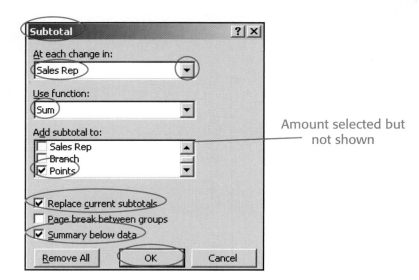

Amount selected but not shown

CAUTION

You can subtotal these data by Sales Rep because you have sorted by that column. You must sort the data before subtotaling. Prior to subtotaling, check the last row of data to see if there are any column totals. Remove any existing totals at the bottom of the columns, as they will be added automatically.

---

7 Click **OK**.

Subtotals for the Amount and Point values are displayed for each Sales Rep. The rows are also grouped automatically, and the outline for the entire group of data appears on the left.

Outline levels controlled here

Outline pane

Subtotal below change in Sales Rep

IN DEPTH

Outline level 1 only displays the grand total. Outline level 2 displays the subtotals and the grand total. Outline level 3 shows all the rows.

1 2 3		A	B	C	D	E	F
	1	Date	Produc	Amount	Sales Re	Branc	Point
	2	13-Jan	Savings	$ 6,000	Betsey	Main	24
	3	17-Jan	Certificate	$ 50,000	Betsey	Main	50
	4	27-Jan	Certificate	$ 15,000	Betsey	Main	60
	5	30-Jan	Savings	$ 6,300	Betsey	Main	25.2
	6			$ 77,300	**Betsey Total**		159.2
	7	14-Jan	Certificate	$ 25,000	Carolyn	Plymouth	25
	8	17-Jan	Credit Card	$ 3,000	Carolyn	Plymouth	12
	9	23-Jan	Credit Card	$ 2,000	Carolyn	Plymouth	8
	10	31-Jan	Savings	$ 1,450	Carolyn	Plymouth	5.8
	11			$ 31,450	**Carolyn Total**		50.8
	12	3-Jan	Checking	$ 2,000	Diane	Plymouth	8
	13	9-Jan	Certificate	$ 1,500	Diane	Plymouth	6
	14	10-Jan	Auto Loan	$ 14,500	Diane	Plymouth	58
	15	17-Jan	Checking	$ 600	Diane	Plymouth	2.4
	16	20-Jan	Auto Loan	$ 16,700	Diane	Plymouth	66.8
	17	24-Jan	Mortgage	$ 175,000	Diane	Plymouth	175
	18			$ 210,300	**Diane Total**		316.2

Level 3 detail collapsed

---

8 Click outline level **2**.

The outline collapses the details in level 3 and displays just the subtotals for each sales representative and the grand total.

Level 2 shows subtotals and grand totals

1 2 3		A	B	C	D	E	F
	1	Date	Produc	Amount	Sales Re	Branc	Point
	6			$ 77,300	**Betsey Total**		159.2
	11			$ 31,450	**Carolyn Total**		50.8
	18			$ 210,300	**Diane Total**		316.2
	25			$ 73,400	**Jonell Total**		158.6
	34			$ 297,100	**Pam Total**		363.4
	41			$ 14,800	**Paula Total**		59.2
	45			$ 157,750	**Rhonda Total**		256
	50			$ 174,100	**Richard Total**		246.4
	54			$ 28,900	**Sharon Total**		115.6
	55			$ 1,065,100	**Grand Total**		1725.4

9 Print this sheet if your instructor requires it. Save and close the workbook.

Task 3
CREATING A PIVOTTABLE

Why would I do this?

A PivotTable is a summary table produced by a wizard that allows you to try different columns from the selected data as column and row headings. If you don't like the arrangement of columns and rows, it is easy to switch them or exchange them for other columns from the table.

For example, if you are managing the sales contest at the bank, you may want to know the amount of sales for each product at every branch. You can create a PivotTable with branch names as row headings and product names as column headings. The sales amount is placed in the cells of the table. The PivotTable wizard calculates the total amount for each branch and product and displays it in each cell of the PivotTable.

Many of the data management features of Excel are similar to features found in Microsoft Access, and some of the terms used to describe the data are those used to describe database tables. In a database table, the types of data found in columns are called *fields*. The PivotTable wizard refers to the columns of the table as fields because they are similar to the fields in a database table.

In a PivotTable, you can use fields as row headings, column headings, cell contents, and page headings.

PivotTables produce output similar to sorting and subtotaling. However, you do not need to presort the data to summarize it using a PivotTable.

In this task, you create a PivotTable that summarizes the amount of sales by branch and by product.

1 Open **EX1202** from the **Student** folder. Save it as **EX1202-Pivot** on your disk.

The new title appears in the title bar.

Select any cell in the table. Choose **Data, PivotTable and PivotChart Report**.

The PivotTable and PivotChart Wizard opens. If the Office Assistant opens, close it.

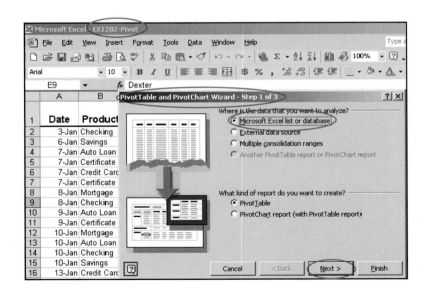

2 Confirm **Microsoft Excel list or database** and **PivotTable** are selected.

The table that contains the previously selected cell will be used to create a PivotTable.

Click **Next**.

A marquee displays around the table of data, including column headings in the first row, to indicate the selected area.

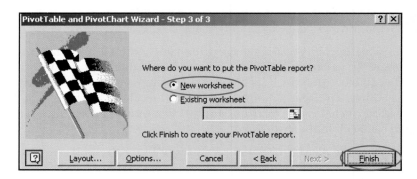

Selected area

3 Click **Next**.

The New worksheet option is selected by default.

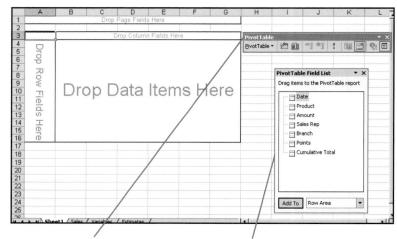

4 Click **Finish**.

A new sheet is added to the workbook. The wizard displays a list of fields. The PivotTable toolbar also appears on your screen.

If necessary, drag the **PivotTable Field List** box to the right so it is not on top of the PivotTable data area. Do the same for the PivotTable toolbar.

PivotTable toolbar   List of available fields

5 Drag **Branch** from the list of field names to the section of the PivotTable labeled **Drop Row Fields Here**.

Drag **Product** from the list to the section labeled **Drop Column Fields Here**. Drag **Amount** to the section labeled **Drop Data Items Here**.

The sales amounts are summarized by branch and by product. The branch and product headings have filter options that allow you to restrict the display to selected products and branches.

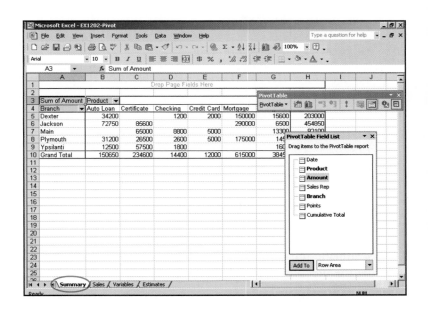

Branch fields   Product fields

CAUTION

If you drag a field to the wrong box, simply drag it back to the PivotTable Field List and try again. Your choices may result in very wide or very long tables that extend across more than one page or screen. If the table is much wider than it is long, switch the fields used for columns and rows to see if you can make the table one page wide and several pages long. This will make it easier to view and print.

6 Double-click the **Sheet1** tab and type **Summary**. Press ↵Enter. Save the workbook and leave it open for the next lesson.

Task 4

CHARTING A TREND

Why would I do this?

If you believe that one set of values in your data depends upon another set of values, you can chart them to visualize the relationship between the two. To view this type of relationship correctly, it is important that the labels on the category, or X axis, are equally spaced. To assure that the labels on the X axis are spaced evenly, use an XY Scatter chart, which adjusts the interval between category labels automatically. If the second set of numbers is a simple multiple of the numbers chosen as labels on the category (X) axis, a line drawn between the data points on the chart will be a straight line. Straight lines can be represented by formulas that can be used to estimate new dependent values.

Real data seldom conforms exactly to a simple mathematical formula. If the data points on an XY Scatter chart look like they approximate a straight line, Excel can calculate the line that minimizes the distance between all of the points and the line. This line is called a trend line. The technique for calculating this best-fit line is called *linear regression* and is done automatically. One measure of quality of the fit of the trend line to the data is represented by the R-squared number. A perfect fit has an R-squared value of 1. Data points that do not make an exact straight line produce R-squared values less than 1, such as .94.

For example, as the manager of the sales contest at the bank, you want to predict future sales totals. You chart the cumulative total of the sales against the date of the sales. As the date increases, so does the total sales. You have data for the month of January but you want to predict what that total will be if sales continue at their present rate for another month. A cumulative total column has been added to the worksheet for this purpose.

In this task, you chart the date and the cumulative total, add a trend line, and determine the formula for the trend line that you can use to estimate future total sales.

1 Click the **Sales** sheet tab. Click the header for column **A**. Hold the Ctrl key and click the header for column **G**.

Columns A and G are selected.

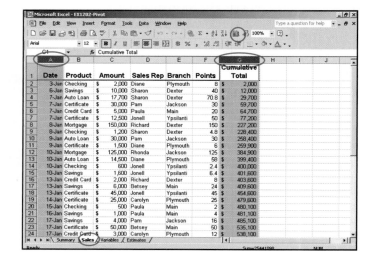

2 Click the Chart Wizard button. Click **XY (Scatter)** in the <u>C</u>hart type box. Confirm that the first option in the **Chart sub-type** is selected.

The data points will be charted without a connecting line. You will add the trend line in a subsequent step.

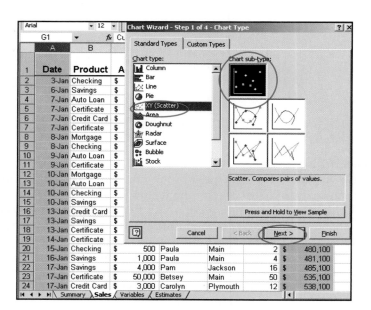

3 Click <u>N</u>ext.

An example of the chart is displayed. The program correctly identified the data as columns.

Chart shows total sales related to the passage of time

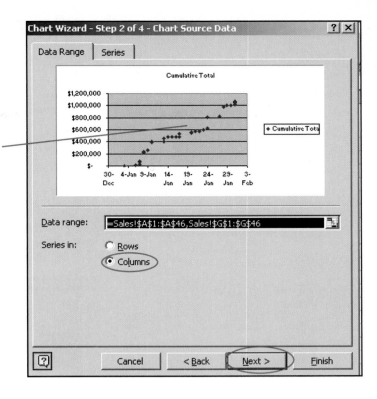

4 Click <u>N</u>ext. Click the **Legend** tab and deselect the **<u>S</u>how legend** option.

Notice that the data points do not make a perfectly straight line, but that there is a definite trend upwards to the data points.

Legend removed

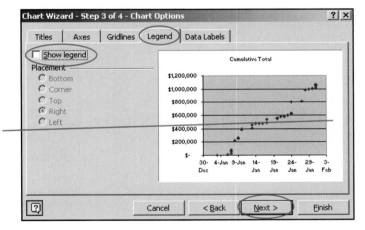

5 Click <u>N</u>ext. Click the **As new <u>s</u>heet** option. Select the default sheet name and type **Trend**.

The chart will be placed on its own sheet labeled Trend.

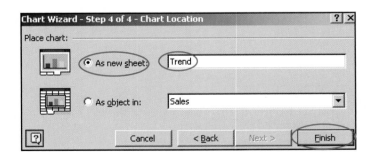

6 Click **Finish.**

The chart is displayed on its own sheet. Notice that the interval between dates is uniform on the chart even though the data provided did not have equal intervals.

Click one of the data points to select them.

All the data points are selected but all of them are not highlighted. This is normal.

All data points selected but only some are highlighted

Equal intervals of time

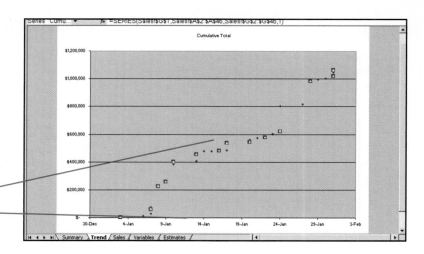

7 Choose **Chart, Add trendline.** Confirm that **Linear** is selected.

The data points in this example appear to fit a straight line better than one of the other curves with the possible exception of the polynomial.

> **IN DEPTH**
>
> A fourth order polynomial is a slightly better fit than a straight line, but its formula is more complex. The straight line is a reasonable choice in this example if you want to project approximate totals several weeks in advance. Be careful when making predictions about the future by extending a relationship from the past. If the basis for the relationship changes, your predictions might be grossly inaccurate.

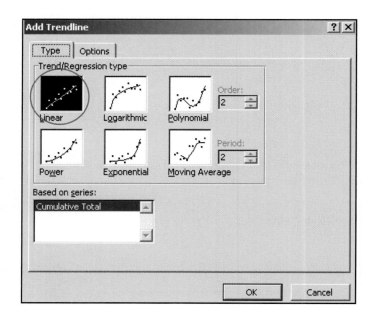

8 Click the **Options** tab. Select **Display equation on chart** and **Display R-squared value on chart.**

The straight trend line will be added along with its formula and the R-squared value.

> **IN DEPTH**
>
> The algebraic formula for a straight line is $y = mx + b$ where m is the slope of the line and b is a constant.

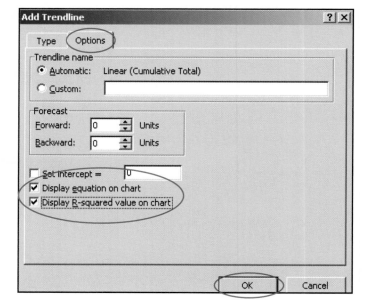

9 Click **OK**.

The trend line, its formula, and the R-squared value are added to the chart. The font is too small to read easily, and the numbers in the formula are rounded off too much for accurate use.

Click the formula.

A box outlines the formula and the R-squared value.

Choose **Format, Selected Data Labels**. Click the **Font** tab and change the font size to **14**.

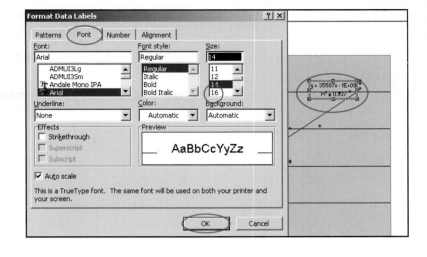

10 Click the **Number** tab. Change the **Category** to **Number** and the **Decimal places** to **3**.

The formula and R-squared value will be displayed in a larger font and the numbers will be displayed with sufficient accuracy.

IN DEPTH

The General format displays the formula constant in scientific notation because it is a large number. You may want to use these numbers to calculate values, in which case they must be displayed with more significant digits.

CAUTION

You may select to use commas in the numbers in this formula. This makes the formula easier to read. However, you have to remove the commas if you want to copy this formula and use it in a cell, which is what you do in the next task.

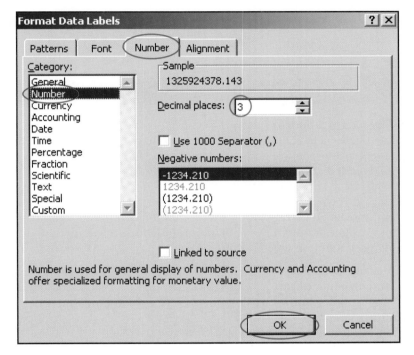

11 Click **OK**. Drag the box to the left between the grid lines where it is easier to read.

You can use the formula to predict other sales totals if you pick a date. An R-squared value greater than .9 indicates that the points are fairly close to the trend line.

Save the workbook and leave it open.

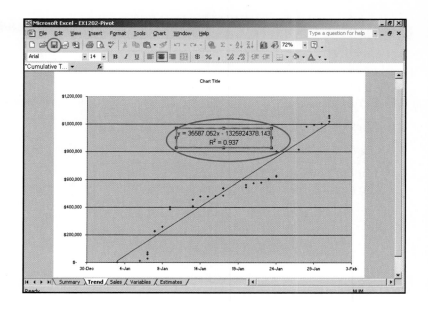

Task 5
ESTIMATING VALUES

Why would I do this?

If you have a chart of data that appears to have a linear relationship, you can estimate values between known data points with confidence. This type of estimation is called *interpolation*. If you try to estimate values beyond either end of the known data, you do so with much less confidence and you need to make assumptions. This type of estimate is called *extrapolation*. The most common assumption used when extrapolating data is that the conditions that produced the data do not change. Although extrapolation is much less accurate than interpolation, it is the most common type of estimate.

You can extrapolate a trend line by using the formula to calculate new dependant values from new category (X) values. This method works for all the trend line types. Another option is to use the *FORECAST* function, which estimates a value in one step.

In this task, you learn how to estimate future total sales using the formula from the trend line. You also learn how to use the FORECAST function.

1 Select the box containing the formula on the **Trend** sheet. Drag the formula to select it and click the **Copy** button.

The formula is copied to the Office Clipboard.

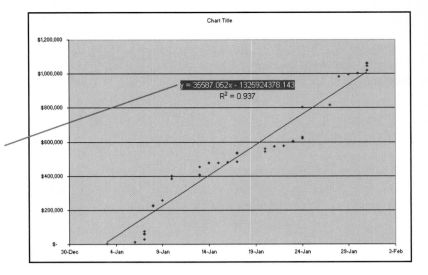

Selected formula

2 Click the **Estimates** sheet tab and select **B6**. Click the **Paste** button.

The formula is pasted into the cell. This formula is displayed using standard algebraic conventions. You need to convert it to the conventions used with formulas in a worksheet.

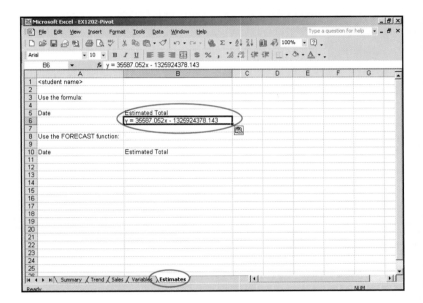

3 Select **A6**, type **2/28/02**, and then press ↵Enter.

	A	B
1	<student name>	
2		
3	Use the formula:	
4		
5	Date	Estimated Total
6	2/28/02	y = 35587.052x - 1325924378.143

4 Double-click **B6** to edit the formula. Delete the **y** and the space.

The equal sign should be the first character in the formula.

Replace **x** with ***A6**. Press <u>⏎Enter</u>. Select **B6** again.

The formula takes the date, multiplies by 35587.052, which is the slope of the line, then subtracts 1325924378.143, which is the constant that adjusts the height of the line above the category axis. These numbers were calculated when you added the trend line.

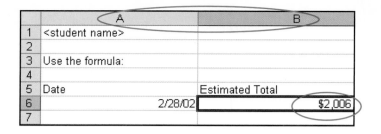

	A	B
1	<student name>	
2		
3	Use the formula:	
4		
5	Date	Estimated Total
6	2/28/02	$2,006
7		

5 Select cell **A11**, type **2/28/02**, and then press <u>⏎Enter</u>.

You will use the same date with the FORECAST function to estimate the value.

Select **B11**. Choose **Insert**, **Function**. Choose the **Statistical** category, scroll down the list, and select **FORECAST**.

The FORECAST function does all the work of finding the formula for the best-fit straight line and calculating the dependent value.

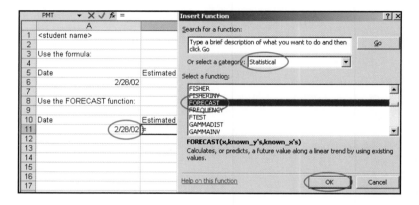

6 Click **OK**.

The Function Arguments dialog box opens.

Type **A11** to select it as the new value of **X**.

This is cell A11, not the word All. The FORECAST function estimates the total sales for the date in cell A11, which is February 28, 2002.

This is the cell in column A, row 11.

Collapse button

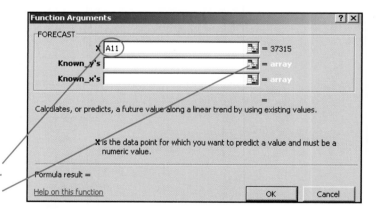

7 Click the **Known_y's** box. Click the **Collapse** button at the end of the box. Click the **Sales** tab and drag cells **G2** through **G45**

The range of dependent cells is selected. You are assuming that the total amount of sales depends on how long the contest goes on.

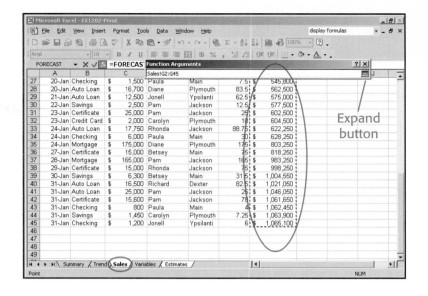

Expand button

8 Click the **Expand** button. Click the **Known_x's** box and click the **Collapse** button. Click the **Sales** tab and drag cells **A2** through **A45**.

The dates are selected and serve as the values along the category (X) axis.

Click the **Expand** button.

The date in A11 is used as the category. The FORE-CAST function will estimate the total amount of sales by that date using the linear regression method.

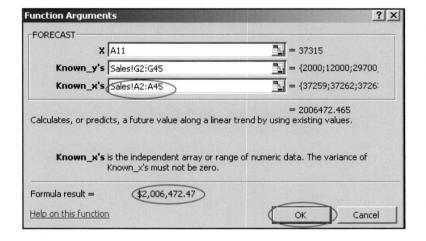

9 Click **OK**.

The value calculated by the FORECAST function is slightly different that the one calculated by the formula. The format of the formula did not display the data as accurately as possible. However, they are substantially the same.

Save the workbook.

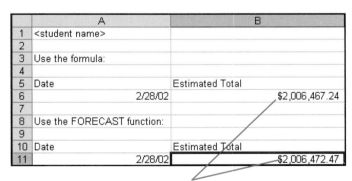

Slightly different answers
due to rounding of the
numbers in the formula

Task 6
SAVING SCENARIOS

Why would I do this?

When the electronic spreadsheet was first invented, users were thrilled by its ability to recalculate complex spreadsheets quickly so they could evaluate different scenarios. The average person is often confronted with making financial decisions that have several variables, such as buying a house or automobile. It is difficult to compare purchases that have different interest rates, closing costs, and monthly payments. You can try different combinations of key variables and save the results of each one as a separate scenario. The scenarios are part of the workbook and can be recalled to make comparisons. You can create a PivotTable that displays the results of the different scenarios.

In the bank sales contest, you decide that in addition to the prizes for first and second place, you want to give each employee a bonus for the points they get in the second month of the contest. You have evaluated the trend and have concluded that the amount and distribution of sales in the second month is likely to match the first month. You have a budget of $2,000 and would like to give a dollar per point to keep it simple. Points are awarded per thousand dollars of product sold, depending on whether the amount of the sale is above or below a certain figure. Sales of mortgages and certificates of deposit involve large sums, while the other products involve smaller amounts but take as much work to sell. Also, some employees are not allowed to sell the larger loans. To make the contest competitive among employees who sell different products, there are fewer points per thousand for the large sales. There are three variables that were used to determine the points given in the first month of the contest. Sales over $20,000 were awarded one point per thousand and sales under $20,000 were awarded four points per thousand. You plan to change one or more of these variables to get the total points to come out to 2,000, so you can give $1 per point and stay within your budget.

In this task, you save the variables used to calculate the points for January as a scenario.

---

1 Click the **Sales** sheet tab and select **F2**.

The formula uses named ranges to calculate the points. These named ranges are found on the Variables sheet.

2 Click the **Variables** sheet tab. Select **B2**.

The cells in B2, B3, and B4 have defined names that correspond to the labels in column A. The values in these cells are used to calculate the points on the Sales sheet.

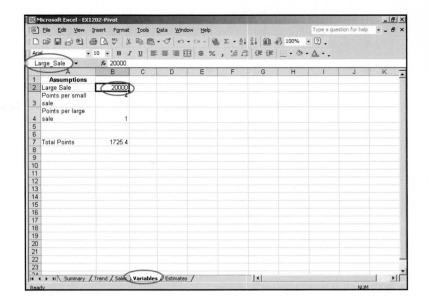

3 Select **B7**.

Notice the formula in the formula bar. The Points range includes the cells in the Sales sheet that display the points. Cell B7 displays the total points from the Sales sheet.

Select **B4**. Type **2** and press ⏎Enter.

All the formulas in the Sales sheet that depend on B4 are recalculated and the value in B7 is updated. Your goal is to change one of the three variables in B2, B3, or B4 to make the total in B7 come out to 2,000.

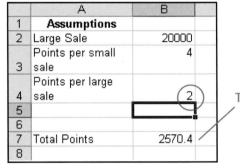

	A	B
1	**Assumptions**	
2	Large Sale	20000
3	Points per small sale	4
4	Points per large sale	2
5		
6		
7	Total Points	2570.4
8		

Total points from the Sales sheet

4 Select **B4**, change it back to **1**, and then press ⏎Enter.

This is the set of variables used to calculate the points for January.

Choose **Tools, Scenarios**.

The Scenario Manager dialog box opens.

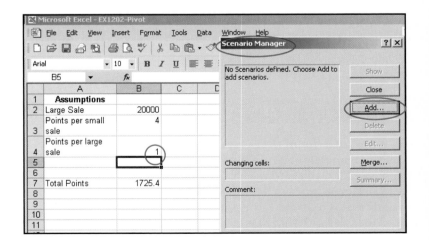

⑤ Click the **A**dd button. In the **Scenario name** box, type **January**.

These are the values used to calculate January's points.

Select the default value in the **Changing cells** box. Drag cells **B2** through **B4**. Add your name and section number to the **Comments** box, if your instructor requires it.

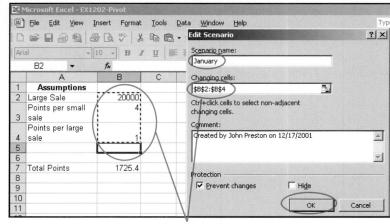

Cells to change

⑥ Click **OK**.

The Scenario Values dialog box opens. It displays the range name and the values.

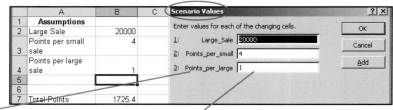

Range names created based on cells to the left of each range

Values in each range

The range names for cells B2, B3, and B4 were automatically generated using the Insert, Names, Create, Left commands.

⑦ Click **OK**. Click **Close**.

The original values of the variables are saved as a scenario named January. You use scenarios in the next task to compare several options.

Task 7

USING GOAL SEEK AND USING A PIVOTTABLE TO COMPARE SCENARIOS

Why would I do this?

You can manually enter different values for the points awarded for a small sale or a large sale, and you can try changing the minimum value considered to be a large sale. However, this is a time consuming process. Excel has a tool called Goal Seek that does this trial-and-error process. With Goal Seek, you specify the cell that contains the goal and what that goal should be. You then pick a cell to change and let the Goal Seek tool try different values in that cell until it gets as close as possible to your goal.

You can use Goal Seek to find the best value for each of the three variables and save each one as a scenario. You can then create a PivotTable to compare the scenarios.

In this task, you use Goal Seek to find the values of each of the three variables that would result in a total of 2,000 points. You save each one as a scenario, then you create a PivotTable to compare the results.

1 Confirm that the **Variables** sheet is selected. Choose <u>T</u>ools, <u>G</u>oal Seek. Select the default value in the **S<u>e</u>t cell** box and type **B7**.

This cell contains the value that is your goal. You want this number to be 2000.

Click the **To <u>v</u>alue** box and type **2000**. Click the **By <u>c</u>hanging cell** box and type **B3**.

In this scenario, you change the points awarded per thousand dollars for each small sale.

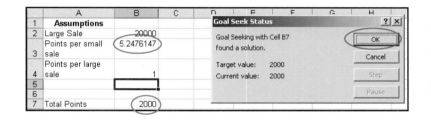

2 Click **OK**.

The program quickly tries many values of points for small sales to find the one necessary to produce a total of 2,000 points.

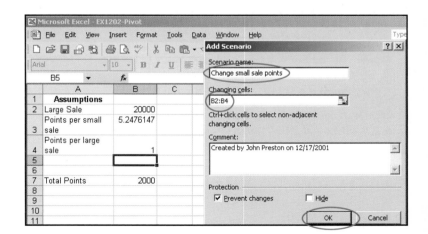

3 Click **OK**. Choose <u>T</u>ools, <u>S</u>cenarios. Click the <u>A</u>dd button. Click the **Scenario <u>n</u>ame** box and type **Change small sale points**.

Notice the range of cells, B2 through B4, is still selected from the earlier scenario.

4 Click **OK**.

The Scenario Values dialog box opens and displays the values that will be stored for this scenario.

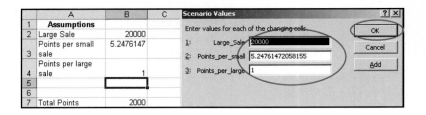

5 Click **OK**.

The Scenario Manager dialog box opens and displays the name of the new scenario.

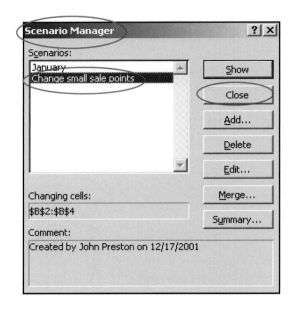

6 Click **Close**. Select **B3**, type **4**, and then press (↵Enter).

The value is changed back to the original amount. Next, you try different values of points for large sales.

Choose **Tools, Goal Seek**. Select the default value in the **Set cell** box and type **B7**. Click the **To value** box and type **2000**. Click the **By changing cell** box and type **B4**. Click **OK**.

A value is calculated and displayed in B4 that will produce a point total of 2,000 in B7.

7 Click **OK**. Choose **T**ools, Sc**e**narios. Click the **Add** button. Click the **Scenario name** box and type **Change large sale points**. Click **OK**. Click **OK**. Click **Close**.

The scenario for changing the points awarded per thousand points of large sales is saved.

Notice that the Undo button is gray. This operation cannot be undone.

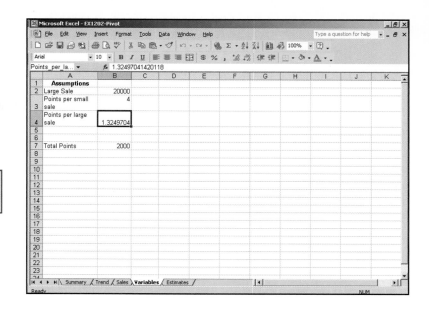

8 Select **B4**, type **1**, and then press **⏎Enter**.

Next, you try different minimum values that are used to define a large sale.

Choose **T**ools, **G**oal Seek. Select the default value in the **Set cell** box and type **B7**. Click the **To value** box and type **2000**. Click the **By changing cell** box and type **B2**. Click **OK**.

The program tries many options but cannot get any closer than 2130.4. Given the sales that occurred and the point values for large and small sales, this is the best the Goal Seek tool can do.

IN DEPTH

The number of tries that Goal Seek uses until it gives up is set under Tools, Options, Calculation, Iteration. An *iteration* is a repetition. The default setting is 100. Increasing the number of repetitions in this case will not make a difference due to the constraints of the other variables and the values of sales in the sales table.

9 Click **OK**. Choose **T**ools, Sc**e**narios. Click the **Add** button. Click the **Scenario name** box and type **Change minimum for large sale**. Click **OK**. Click **OK**. Click **Close**.

The scenario in which you try different values for the minimum large sale is saved.

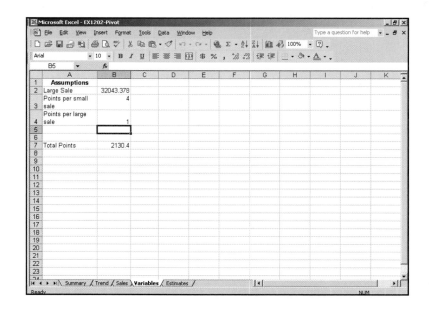

10 Click **Tools**, **Scenario**, and then click the **Summary** button.

The Scenario Summary dialog box opens.

Select **Scenario PivotTable report**. Select the **Result cells** box and enter **B2:B4**.

The four scenarios will be summarized in a PivotTable.

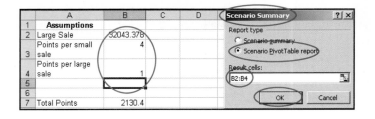

11 Click **OK**.

The Scenario PivotTable sheet is created where you can compare the four scenarios. Upon consideration, you decide that it is simplest to increase the points awarded for a small sale from four to five.

Changing points for a small sale to 5.25 would still yield 2,000 total points so changing it to 5 would stay within the budget and be a simple change.

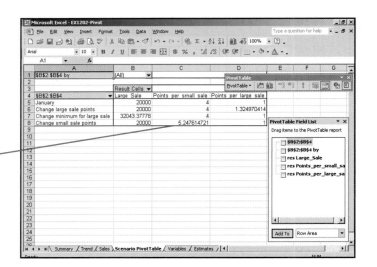

CAUTION

The PivotTable does not update automatically if you change one of the scenarios on which it is based.

12 Click the **Variables** sheet tab. Select **B3** and enter **5**.

The total points will be close to 2,000 but slightly under, which will meet the budget consideration.

Format **B2** to **Currency** style and format **B7** to **Comma** style.

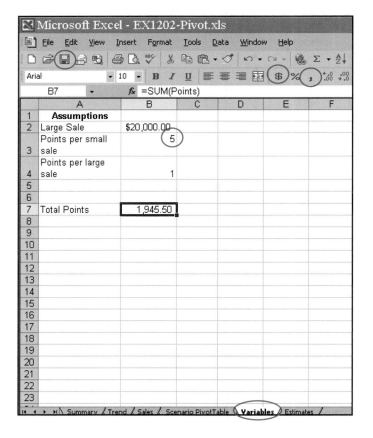

13 Save and close the workbook.

The exercises that follow are designed for you to review and use what you have learned in this lesson. You also have the opportunity to practice your skills and then expand on them by applying them to new situations.

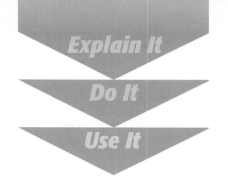

COMPREHENSION

Comprehension exercises are designed to check your memory and understanding of the basic concepts in this lesson. You distinguish between true and false statements, identify new screen elements, and match terms with related statements. If you are uncertain of the correct answer, refer to the task number following each item (for example, T4 refers to Task 4) and review that task until you are confident that you can provide a correct response.

TRUE-FALSE

Circle either T or F.

T   F   1. Before you add subtotals, it is a good idea to sort the table if it is not already sorted. **(T2)**

T   F   2. Grouping data places each group on a separate worksheet within the workbook and automatically creates a summary sheet. **(T2)**

T   F   3. The method used to determine the best-fit straight line for a set of data is called linear progression. **(T5)**

T   F   4. Scenarios save sets of values that you can use to recalculate the workbook to show different outcomes. **(T6)**

T   F   5. The filter feature works on one column at a time. If you want to filter on a combination of columns, you must use a database program like Access. **(T1)**

T   F   6. A PivotTable allows you to try different columns as row or column headings. **(T3)**

T   F   7. The Goal Seek function tries different numbers in a cell to get as close as possible to the desired result in another cell. **(T7)**

MATCHING QUESTIONS

A. Pivot   **E.** Scenario

B. Goal Seek   **F.** Subtotal

C. Filtering   **G.** Forecast

D. Linear Regression

Match the following statements to the word or phrase that is the best match from the list. Write the letter of the matching word or phrase in the space provided next to the number.

1. _____ Feature that displays rows of the table that match conditions **(T1)**

2. _____ Type of table that summarizes data from another table and allows the designer to choose which columns will be represented as row or column headings **(T3)**

3. _____ Allows you to save sets of critical values upon which the rest of the table depends **(T6)**

4. _____ Automatically tries different values into a selected cell to produce a desired result in another cell **(T7)**

5. _____ Method to find a best-fit straight line for two sets of data, where one set is dependent on the other **(T4)**

6. _____ Inserts a row at each change in a selected column **(T2)**

7. _____ Function used to predict a value from a trend **(T5)**

IDENTIFYING PARTS OF THE EXCEL SCREEN

Refer to the figure and identify the numbered parts of the screen. Write the letter of the correct label in the space next to the number.

1. _____

2. _____

3. _____

4. _____

5. _____

A. Collapse button (T2)

B. Filter button (T2)

C. Subtotal (T2)

D. Grouping levels (T2)

E. Sorted column (T2)

1. _____

2. _____

3. _____

A. Row fields (T3)

B. Column fields (T3)

C. Data items (T3)

1. _____

2. _____

3. _____

4. _____

A. Trend line (T4)

B. Data points (T4)

C. Formula of line (T4)

D. Measure of the "fit" (T4)

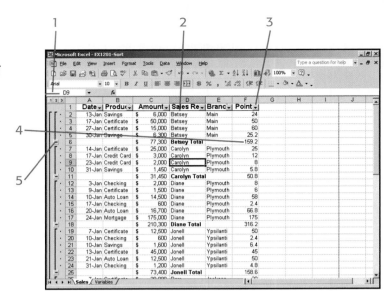

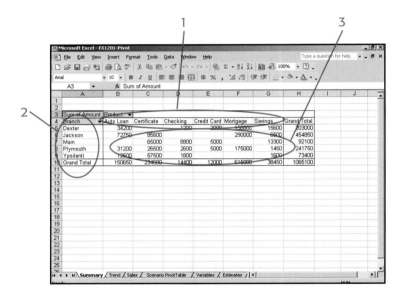

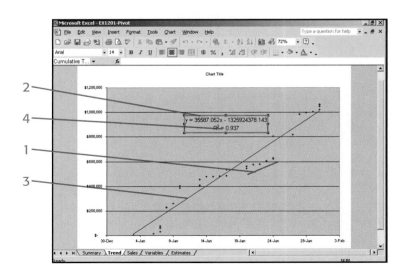

Reinforcement exercises are designed to reinforce the skills you have learned by applying them to a new situation. Detailed instructions are provided along with a figure, where appropriate, to illustrate the result.

As sales manager of Armstrong Pool, Spa, and Sauna Company, you are reviewing the method by which your salespeople are compensated. Currently they are paid a salary every two weeks without commission on sales. You are considering changing to a system that pays a lower percentage of their current salary plus a commission on sales. In the following reinforcement exercises, you use the analysis tools you have learned in this lesson to evaluate your options.

R1—Filtering, Sorting, and Subtotaling Sales Data

You have compiled the sales data from all the stores in the company for a two-week period. In this exercise, you sort the data by salesperson and subtotal their sales. You also filter it to look at sales by product description. This exercise gives you a look at the difference in sales by salesperson.

1. Open **EX1203** and save it as **EX1203-Reinforcement** in your folder. Select the **Two-Week Sales** tab, if necessary. Sort the table in ascending order by the **SalesRep** column.

2. Choose **Data, Subtotals**. In the **Subtotal** dialog box, add a subtotal at each change in **SalesRep**, use the **Sum** function, and then add a subtotal to the **Amount** column but not the **City** column.

3. Choose **Data, Filter, AutoFilter**. Click the arrow on the **City** column and select **Southfield**.

4. Enter your name and section number in cell **A95**.

1 2 3		A	B	C	D	E	F	
	1	OrderDate	SalesRi	FirstNam	LastNam	Description	Amount	
•	9	May 14, 2002	3	Margaret	Peacock	8 person spa	$4,200.00	So
•	10	May 18, 2002	3	Margaret	Peacock	4 person spa	$2,300.00	So
•	11	May 18, 2002	3	Margaret	Peacock	12'x24' oval pool	$1,695.00	So
•	12	May 18, 2002	3	Margaret	Peacock	4'x6' cedar sauna	$3,000.00	So
•	13	May 19, 2002	3	Margaret	Peacock	6'x10' cedar sauna	$4,750.00	So
•	14	May 19, 2002	3	Margaret	Peacock	8 person spa	$4,200.00	So
•	83	May 14, 2002	24	Matt	Brinkley	15'x24' oval pool	$2,450.00	So
•	84	May 16, 2002	24	Matt	Brinkley	8 person spa	$4,200.00	So
•	85	May 17, 2002	24	Matt	Brinkley	15'x24' oval pool	$2,450.00	So
•	86	May 17, 2002	24	Matt	Brinkley	4'x6' cedar sauna	$3,000.00	So
•	87	May 17, 2002	24	Matt	Brinkley	12'x24' oval pool	$1,695.00	So
•	88	May 19, 2002	24	Matt	Brinkley	15'x24' oval pool	$2,450.00	So

5. Print the worksheet if your instructor requires it.

6. Click the arrow on the **City** column and choose **All**. Leave the AutoFilter feature turned on.

7. Choose **Data, Subtotals**. Click the **Remove All** button.

8. Leave the workbook open for the next exercise.

R2—Creating a PivotTable to Analyze Sales by Person and by Store

Filtering and subtotals provide one method to review sales by individual or by store. You can get a better idea of how they compare by creating a PivotTable.

1. Select a cell in the table on the **Two-Week Sales** sheet. Choose **Data, PivotTable and PivotChart Report**.

2. Click **Finish**. A new sheet is added.

3. Drag **LastName** to the **Drop Row Fields Here** area. Drag **City** to the **Drop Column Fields Here** area. Drag **Amount** to the **Drop Data Items Here** area.

4. Right-click one of the cells in the **Items** area. Choose **Field Settings**. Change the **Summarize by** box to **Sum,** if necessary. Click **OK**.

5. Enter your name and section number in **A2**. Change the sheet name to **Sales by Person** and press ↵Enter.

6. Select all the cells in the data items area and in the column and row used for grand totals. Format these numbers to **Currency** with zero decimals.

7. Choose **File, Page Setup**, and then click the **Page** tab. Choose **Landscape** and choose **Fit to**. Choose **1** page wide. Click the **Sheet** tab and turn on the **Gridlines** option.

8. Click the **Print** button and print a copy of the sheet.

9. Leave the workbook open for the next exercise.

	A	B	C	D	E	F	G	H	I	J
1										
2	<name>									
3	Sum of Amount	City								
4	LastName	Columbus	Dayton	Fort Wayne	Indianapolis	Novi	Southfield	Toledo	Ypsilanti	Grand Tot
5	Armey							7295		72
6	Brinkley						16245			162
7	Buchanan			23345						233
8	Carman					13890				138
9	Creal					4900				49
10	Davolio				13040					130
11	Faulkner								3995	39
12	Ferrett								9700	97
13	Grayson		8195							81
14	Griffith					8395				83
15	Johnson								13500	135
16	McGuire				10540					105
17	Peacock						20145			201
18	Peters		11395							113
19	Smith	18945								189
20	Teacher	15045								150
21	Williams								7445	74
22	Grand Total	33990	19590	33885	21435	18790	36390	11290	30645	2060

Sales by Person / Two-Week Sales / Commission /

R3—Charting Money Paid to Salespeople versus Sales

You want to know if the amount the salespeople sell depends on how much they are paid. You can chart the sales versus the amount their current salary during the two-week period using an XY (Scatter) chart and add a trend line. The R-squared value will tell you how closely the sales relate to the salary. A value close to 1 is a very close relationship and a value close to 0 means the sales do not depend on the salary. Note that the Sales column uses the SUMIF function to add up all the sales by the person with the Rep # found in column D.

1. Click the **Commission** sheet tab. Select **E2** through **E18**. Hold the Ctrl key and select **G2** through **G18**.

2. Click the **Chart Wizard** button. Select the **XY (Scatter)** chart type. Click **Next** for Steps 1 through 3 of the chart wizard.

3. On Step 4 of the chart wizard, click **As new sheet**. Enter **Sales versus Salary**. Click **Finish**.

4. Right-click one of the data points and choose **Add Trendline**. Click the **Options** tab and select **Display R-squared value on the chart**. Click **OK**.

5. Drag the R-squared text to a place above the trendline and between the gridlines where it is easier to read. Change the font size to **18**. This R-squared value is almost 0, which means there is almost no relationship between the amount they sold during this two-week period and the salary they were paid. You could use this chart in a meeting to show that a change in compensation methods is necessary.

6. Leave the workbook open for the next exercise.

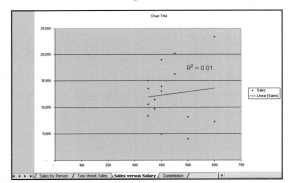

R4—Comparing Scenarios of Salary and Commission Options

You decide that you need to revamp the method by which the salespeople are compensated, but you don't want to discard completely the difference between their present salaries. A table has been set up to assist with this decision. The sales representative's number is in the first column. The columns to the right contain the current salary, the reduced salary, the sum of sales for that sales representative, the commission, the new total of salary plus commission, and the difference between the old salary and the new combination of reduced salary plus commission. The Sales column uses the SUMIF function and the Salary plus commission column uses a conditional format to display increases.

You use this table to examine different combinations of salary reductions and added commissions.

1. Select the **Commission** sheet. Select **D3**. It has the ID number of one of the sales representatives. Press → to move across the columns and see how formulas have been used to calculate the values in each column. Select **B3**. Press ↓ to move down the column to see how formulas have been used to calculate each of the values in this column.

2. Select **B4**, type **50%**, and then press ↵Enter. Observe the effect (you can use formula auditing arrows if you like).

3. Select **B3**, type **5%**, and then press ↵Enter. Observe the effect. Notice that all the values in column I turned blue. This conditional format shows which people would earn more than their current salary. Notice the total in cell B8 is much larger than the present salary total in cell B5. You want to find a commission rate that exactly offsets the decrease in salary. When that is the case, the total value in cell B8 will match the current salary total of $6,850.

4. Choose **Tools**, **Goal Seek**. In the **Set cell** box, type **B8**. In the **To value** box, type **6850**. In the **By changing cell** box, type **B3**. Click **OK**. Click **OK** to accept the change.

5. Choose **Tools**, **Scenarios**. Click the **Add** button. In the **Scenario name** box, type **50 percent**. In the **Changing cells** box, type **B3:B4**. Click **OK**. Click **OK**. Click **Close**.

6. Select **B4** and type **75**. Use Goal Seek to set cell **B8** to **6850** by changing cell **B3**. Save this scenario as **75 percent**.

7. Choose Tools, Scenarios. Click the Summary button. Click the **Scenario PivotTable report** option. Select the default option in the **Result cells** box and type **B3:B9**. Click OK.

8. A PivotTable is created that compares the options. You can observe that replacing 50% of the salary with commission can be accomplished with a commission rate of 1.72%, and a commission rate of 2.59% can be used to replace 75% of the current salary. Both methods result in the same total compensation for all employees, but 10 of the 16 salespeople will see increases.

9. Format the cells as shown in the figure. Add your name and section number to **A2**. Print the worksheet if your instructor requires it.

	A	B	C	D	E	F	G
	$B$3:$B$4 by	(All)					
	<name>						
		Result Cells					
	$B$3:$B$4	Commission_Rate	Salary_Reduction	Present_Salary	New_Salary	Commission	Total
	50 percent	1.72%	50%	6,850	3,425	3,425	6,850
	75 percent	2.59%	75%	6,850	1,713	5,138	6,850

R5—Forecasting What a New Salesperson Would Make

Under the current salary system, the amount the salespeople make is unrelated to the amount they sell. If a prospective employee asked you how much they would make if they sold as much as most of the other salespeople in a recent period, you couldn't answer that question. With the new method that replaces a large percentage of the salary with a commission, the employee's income should be more predictable.

You can generate another XY (Scatter) chart with a trendline to determine how predictable the total salary plus commission rate will be, and then you can use the FORECAST function to predict an income from an average amount of sales.

1. Select the **Commission** sheet. Select cells **H2:H18**. Hold the Ctrl key and select **I2** through **I18**.

2. Click the **Chart Wizard** button. Select the **XY (Scatter)** chart type. Click Next for Steps 1 through 3 of the chart wizard.

3. On Step 4 of the chart wizard, click **As new sheet**. Enter **Salary plus Commission Chart**. Click Finish.

4. Right-click one of the data points and choose **Add Trendline**. Click the **Options** tab and select **Display R-squared value on the chart**. Click OK.

5. Drag the R-squared text to a place above the trendline and between the gridlines where it is easier to read. Change the font size to **18**. This R-squared value is closer to 1 than the Sales versus Salary chart, which means the salary paid to the salespeople is more dependent on the amount they sold during this two-week period. This tells you that the FORECAST function will produce a forecast that won't be too far off.

6. Scroll to the **Commission** tab and click it. Select **B14**. Choose Insert, Function. Choose the **Statistical** category, scroll down the list, and then select **FORECAST**. Click OK. Type **B13** in the **X** box, **I3:I18** in the **Known_y's** box, and **G3:G18** in the **Known_x's** box. Click OK. The FORECAST function predicts a biweekly salary that the new person is likely to get if they make an average amount of sales.

7. Enter your name and section in cell **A1**. Format the cells with dollar values to **Currency** with no decimal places. Print this sheet and the **Salary plus Commission Chart** sheet if your instructor requires it.

	A	B	C	D	E	F	G	H	I	J
1	<name>									
2				Rep #	Current Bi-weekly Salary	New Salary	Sales	Commission	Salary plus Commission	Difference
3	Commission Rate	1.72%		1	400	200	13,040	225	425	25
4	Salary Reduction	50%		3	450	225	20,145	347	572	122
5	Present Salary	6,850		4	600	300	23,345	403	703	103
6	New Salary	3,425		5	375	188	9,700	167	355	(20)
7	Commission	3,425		10	350	175	8,395	145	320	(30)
8	Total	6,850		12	400	200	4,900	85	285	(115)
9	Increases	10		16	500	250	3,995	69	319	(181)
10				17	350	175	15,045	260	435	85
11				18	375	188	11,395	197	384	9
12				19	350	175	13,500	233	408	58
13	Average Sale	12410.63		20	400	200	18,945	327	527	127
14	Forecast	428.125		21	500	250	8,195	141	391	(109)
15				22	350	175	10,540	182	357	7
16				23	400	200	13,890	240	440	40
17				24	450	225	16,245	280	505	55
18				25	600	300	7,295	126	426	(174)

Scenario PivotTable / Salary plus Commission Chart \ Commission /

8. Save and close the workbook.

Challenge exercises are designed to test your ability to apply your skills to new situations with less detailed instruction. These exercises also challenge you to expand your repertoire of skills by using commands that are similar to those you have already learned. The desired outcome is clearly defined, but you have more freedom to choose the steps needed to achieve the required result.

C1—Using Pivot Charts

Charts are an excellent tool for making comparisons. You can combine the power of a PivotTable with a chart to analyze patterns and trends.

The file used in this exercise is much larger than most other files you have used. It has almost 38,000 rows and is 2.2 Megabytes in size. The solution file with its pivot table is 5.2 Megabytes. These files are too large to fit on a floppy disk.

Goal: Identify how tornadoes in individual states affect the overall pattern of fatalities by year.

Use the following guidelines:

1. Open **EX1204** and save it on your disk as **EX1204-Tornadoes**.

2. Choose **D**ata, **P**ivotTable and PivotChart Report. Choose the **PivotChart report (with PivotTable report)** option. Click the **Finish** button.

3. Drag the **Year** field to the **Drop Category Fields Here** area at the bottom of the chart. Drag the **Fatalities** field to the **Drop Data Items Here** area. Drag the **State Name** field to the **Drop Page Fields Here** area. Notice the button at the top left of the chart indicates that this is a count of the records, not a sum of the fatalities.

4. Click the **Sheet2** tab (it may have a different number). Select **B5** through **B50**. Right-click anywhere within the range of selected cells and choose **Field Settings**. Change the **Summarize by** option to **Sum**. Click **OK**.

5. Click the **Chart1** sheet tab. Notice that a few years have far higher numbers of fatalities than most of the others. Click the **Tornadoes** tab. Turn on the **AutoFilter** option. Filter the **Year** column for **74** and sort the table by the **Fatalities** column in descending order.

6. Notice which state has most of the deaths from tornadoes that year. Click the **Chart1** tab. Click the arrow on the **StateName** tab and choose the state with the most deaths from tornado in **74**.

7. Select the title. Change the font size to **18**. Replace **Total** with your name and section number. Right-click the legend and select **Clear**.

8. Print the chart if your instructor requires it.

9. Save and close the workbook.

C2—Using the Watch Window

Worksheets easily become too large to view all the cells on the screen at once. A cell that is off-screen may contain a formula that is dependent on a cell you are editing. If you want to see the effect of your changes on the dependent formula, you may find yourself scrolling back and forth. You can avoid this problem by using a Watch Window that displays the value of the dependent cell in a small window.

When you arrange a loan for a home, the size of the payments may be based on a long payout, but you are expected to pay off the entire loan after a shorter period. For example, the loan payments may be chosen to pay off the loan in 30 years but you have to pay off the outstanding balance after five years. This is called a *balloon payment*. You can change the terms of the loan at the top of the sheet and use a *Watch Window* to view what effect your changes will have on the balance after five years of payments.

Goal: Use the Watch Window to observe changes in an important cell that is off the screen.

Use the following guidelines:

1. Open **EX1205** and save it as **EX1205-Mortgage**.

2. Select **G63**. Choose **I**nsert, **N**ame, **D**efine. Type **Five_Year**. Click **OK**.

3. Choose **V**iew, **T**oolbars, **Watch Window**. Click the **Add Watch** button on the toolbar. Click **A**dd.

4. Scroll back to the top of the sheet. Move the toolbar to the right side of the screen.

5. You decide that you want to reduce the balance of the loan to approximately $100,000 at the end of five years. Try different values in cell **B6** to get the balance that shows in the Watch Window down to a value that is closest to $100,000. Restrict your choices to whole numbers of years.

6. Enter your name and section number in **A13**. Print the first page of the worksheet.

7. Close the workbook. Close the Watch Window toolbar.

C3—Using Solver

The Goal Seek function tries different values in one cell to get a target cell to match a given value. *Solver* is similar to Goal Seek except you can vary several cells and you can set the function to match a given value, find a maximum, or find a minimum and display it in the target cell. You can place constraints on the cells as well. The Solver function is an *Add-In* function, which means it is not usually installed on the Tools menu until you specifically choose to do so. It is a very powerful tool for finding optimum solutions to complex problems.

In this exercise, you have a loan amortization statement for a $125,000 loan. The payment is calculated to pay off the loan completely after a given number of years, but you expect to pay the remaining balance on the loan after five years. You want the balance of the loan to be $100,000 after five years. You plan to negotiate the terms of the loan to achieve this. You can vary the number of years on which the payment is calculated, but partial year values are not allowed. You can also vary the interest rate on the loan between 5% and 8%.

Goal: Find a combination of integer loan years and an interest rate between 5% and 8% that produces a loan balance of $100,000 after five years.

1. Open **EX1205** and save it as **EX1205-Solver**. Enter your name and section number in **A13**.

2. Choose **T**ools. Expand the menu to determine if the **Solver** option has been installed. If not, click **Add-I**ns. Select **Solver Add-in** and click **OK**.

3. Choose **T**ools, Sol**v**er. In the **Set Target Cell,** type **G63**.

4. Click the **V**alue of option. Select the box to the right of this option and type **100000**.

5. In the **By Changing Cells** box, type **B4, B6**.

6. Click the **A**dd button. In the **Cell R**eference box, type **B4**. Click the arrow on the middle box and select >=. In the **C**onstraint box, type **5%**.

7. Click the **A**dd button. In the **Cell R**eference box, type **B4**. Click the arrow on the middle box and select <=. In the **C**onstraint box, type **8%**.

8. Click the **A**dd button. In the **Cell R**eference box, type **B6**. Click the arrow on the middle box and select **int**. Click **OK**. The Solver Parameters dialog box displays the target cell, the value to which you want it set, the cells to be changed, and the three constraints.

9. Click S**o**lve. The value is calculated. Click **OK**. Scroll down to **G63** and confirm that it is $100,000. Scroll to the top of the screen. Confirm that the number of years is an integer and the annual percentage rate is between 5% and 8%.

10. Print the first sheet of the loan if your instructor requires it. Save and close the workbook.

C4—Using Other Types of Trend Lines for Scientific Experiments

Sometimes one set of data is dependent on another, but the relationship is not a simple multiple that produces a straight line on a chart. Excel has several other choices of trendlines that you can use to match the data. You can use the R-squared values and a visual examination of the chart to determine which type of line is

the best approximation to the data. There are sophisticated statistical analysis software programs available for detailed, professional analysis, but you can use Excel as a first step.

Radioactive materials lose their activity as time passes, but the relationship is not a simple multiple. For example, if a sample loses half of its activity in 10 years, it isn't gone after another 10 years.

In this exercise, the data represents the radioactivity measured in counts per minute. The first measurement is taken at zero time and then the measurement is taken each hour after that for 30 hours.

Goal: Chart the relationship between time and radioactivity of a sample and determine which trendline is the best fit.

1. Open **EX1206** and save it in your folder as **EX1206-Trendlines**. Place your name in **D2**.

2. Select columns **A** and **B**. Click the **Chart Wizard** button. Choose the **XY (Scatter)** chart type. Click **N**ext until you get to Step **4** of the chart wizard.

3. Choose **As new s**heet and type **Chart**. Click **F**inish. The relationship between activity and time is clearly not a straight line but some type of curve.

4. Right-click one of the data points and choose **Add Trendline**. Choose **P**olynomial and set the **O**rder box to **2**.

5. Click the **Options** tab and select **Display e**quation on chart and **Display R**-squared value on chart. Click **OK**.

6. Drag the box with the equation and R-squared value to the left corner of the chart and change the font size to **14**.

7. Right-click one of the data points and choose **Add Trendline**. Choose **Exponential**.

8. Click the **Options** tab and select **Display e**quation on chart and **Display R**-squared value on chart. Click **OK**.

9. Drag the box with the equation and R-squared value upward and change the font size to **14**. The exponential trendline has a higher R-squared value and is a better fit to the data points.

10. Select the chart title and type your name. Change the font size of the title to **14**.

11. Print the chart if your instructor requires it.

12. Save and close the workbook.

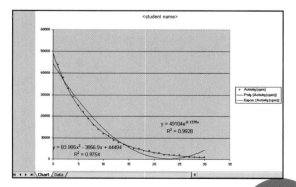

ON YOUR OWN

Find a situation where there is data that needs analysis. State your desired outcome. Demonstrate your ability to apply a variety of Excel tools to achieve that outcome.

Criteria for grading will be:

1. Demonstration of the ability to sort, subtotal, and group data.

2. Demonstration of the ability to chart data and estimate values using trendlines and the FORECAST function.

3. Demonstration of the ability to use Goal Seek or Solver to find solutions and to save possible solutions as scenarios.

4. Demonstration of the ability to use PivotTables or pivot charts.

Some examples of features that students have learned to use in previous classes to analyze their data are as follows:

- Use custom filters that define ranges of dates.

- Create two or more PivotTables on the same set of data that show different aspects of the data.

- Combine the use of charts and PivotTables to discover a fact or trend.

- Save several scenarios and create a summary PivotTable to compare them.

1. Identify yourself on at least one of the sheets you print out and place that sheet at the top of the group of papers.

2. To complete the project:

- Save the workbook on your own disk. Name the workbook **EX1207-Own**.

- Check with your instructor to determine if you should submit the project in electronic or printed form. If necessary, print out a copy of the workbook to hand in.

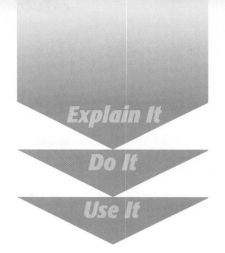

Explain It

Do It

Use It

Lesson 13

Working with Others

Task 1   Editing and Protecting a Template

Task 2   Sharing a Workbook and Tracking Changes

Task 3   Making Changes to a Shared Workbook

Task 4   Accepting Changes and Merging Revisions

Task 5   Querying Data from Other Sources and Saving as a Web Page

Task 6   Retrieving Data from Web Pages

INTRODUCTION

When you work with others you may find yourself in several different situations. You might have a worksheet you want others to use but with restricted options. For example, you might have a template you want people to use by entering data in a few cells, but you are concerned that they may overwrite the formulas in other cells. In this situation, you need to protect the worksheet from changes with the exception of certain cells.

If you are collaborating on a workbook, your partners may need to have more freedom to make changes but you want to retain control of the final product. For example, you have to prepare an annual report that requires input from other managers. You need to be able to track the changes they make and merge them into a single workbook.

If others have the data you want, you can import it from Web pages or from other data sources such as Access databases.

In this lesson, you learn how protect a template, share a workbook, and retrieve data from Web pages and an Access database using queries.

VISUAL SUMMARY

By the time you complete this lesson, you will have created a template that is protected from accidental changes, a shared workbook, and an invoice workbook that can be updated from a company Web site:

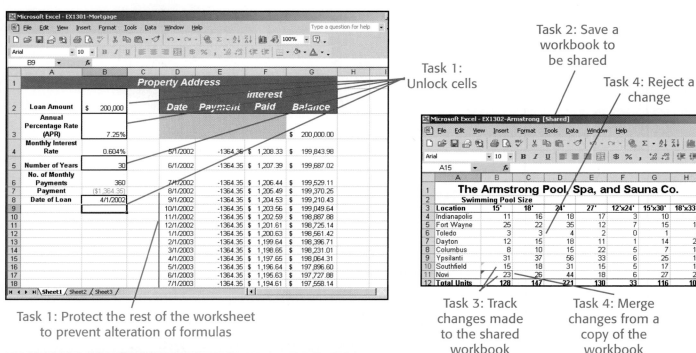

Task 1:
Unlock cells

Task 2: Save a workbook to be shared

Task 4: Reject a change

Task 1: Protect the rest of the worksheet to prevent alteration of formulas

Task 3: Track changes made to the shared workbook

Task 4: Merge changes from a copy of the workbook

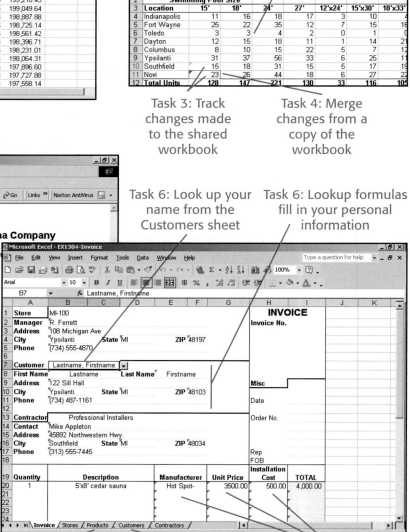

Task 6: Look up your name from the Customers sheet

Task 6: Lookup formulas fill in your personal information

Task 5: Extract data from an Access database and save it as a Web page

Task 6: Data imported to Products sheet from Web page

Task 6: Add your name to the list of customers and sort

Task 6: Lookup formulas use updated product information

Task 1
EDITING AND PROTECTING A TEMPLATE

Explain It

Do It

Use It

Why would I do this?

You have a template that works well but the formulas can be overwritten easily and users who are not familiar with Excel may become confused. You can prevent the user from changing any of the cells in the worksheet except those you choose to make available. This feature is called *protection*. Protecting cells in Excel is a two-step process. First, you choose the cells you want to make available, even when the rest of the cells are protected from change, and *unlock* them. The second step is to protect the entire sheet and give it a password. Users can change the unlocked cells while the rest of the cells in the sheet are protected. A user must know the password to unprotect the sheet and make changes to the *locked* cells. The terms, locked and unlocked, refer to the state of the cell when the sheet is protected and do not apply when the sheet is unprotected.

In this task, you learn how to edit the template. You unlock cells used to input the loan and address information, and protect the rest of the cells in the sheet from change.

1 Open **EX1301** and save it in your folder as **EX1301-Mortgage**.

You will protect all the cells in this worksheet except those designed to be altered by the user.

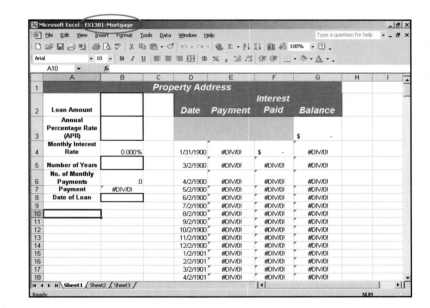

2 Select the title in **A1** through **G1**. Choose **Format**, **Cells**, and click the **Protection** tab in the **Format Cells** dialog box.

The selected cells are locked if the sheet is protected.

Click the **Locked** option to deselect it.

The user can change this title if the rest of the sheet is protected from change.

QUICK TIP

You can right-click on the cell and choose Format Cells from the shortcut menu.

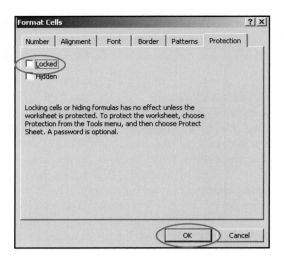

3 Click **OK**.

The dialog box closes.

Select cell **B2**. Hold down the Ctrl key and select cells **B3**, **B5**, and **B8**. Choose **Format**, **Cells**, **Protection**. Click the **Locked** option to deselect it. Click **OK**

The cells used to describe the loan are unlocked. A user can change the cells after the sheet is protected.

Unlocked cells

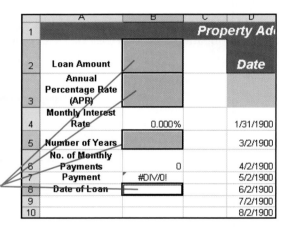

4 Choose **Tools**, **Protection**, **Protect Sheet**.

The Protect Sheet dialog box opens.

Select the **Password to unprotect sheet** box and type **Learn**.

The user must know the password to unprotect the sheet and make changes.

CAUTION

Passwords are case-sensitive. This means that **Learn** is a different password than **learn**.

Asterisks displayed to protect password

IN DEPTH

The first two options in the **Allow all users of this worksheet to** box are selected by default. They allow the user to select any of the cells in the worksheet regardless of their locked or unlocked condition. This allows the user to see the formulas in the locked cells, as well as to select and change the unlocked cells.

5 Click **OK**.

The Confirm Password dialog box opens.

Type **Learn** in the **Reenter password to proceed** box. Click **OK**.

The sheet is protected from changes to all the cells that are still locked, but the unlocked cells can be changed.

Unlocked cells can be changed

Formulas protected from change

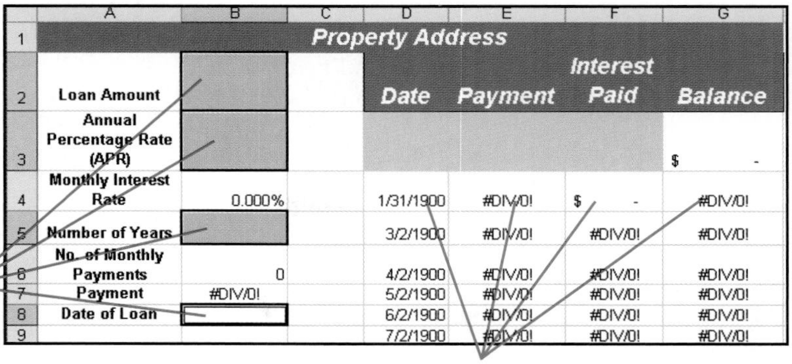

IN DEPTH

To make changes to the worksheet, you need to remove the sheet protection. Choose <u>T</u>ools, <u>P</u>rotection, Unprotect Sheet, and provide the password. This action does not change the locked/unlocked status of the cells but allows you to make changes to locked cells.

6 Select **B2** and enter **200000**.

Changes are allowed to the unlocked cells.

Select **G3** and try to type something.

A warning is displayed that informs you that you cannot change the contents of this cell without removing the protection from the sheet.

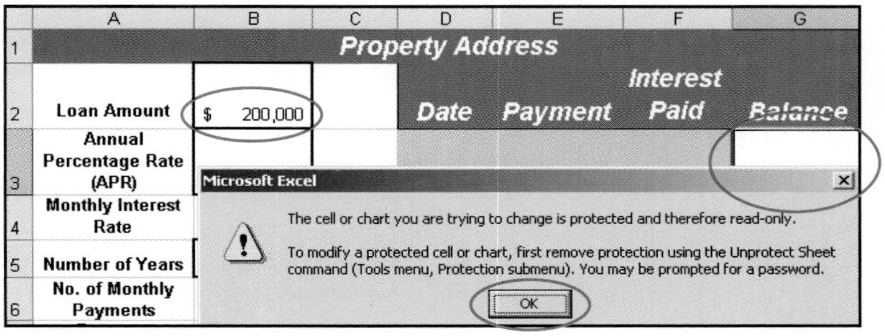

7 Click **OK**. Select **B3,** type **7.25**, and then press Enter.

The formula in B4 is updated automatically.

Select **B5**, type **30,** and then press Enter. Select **B8** and enter today's date.

The worksheet is updated.

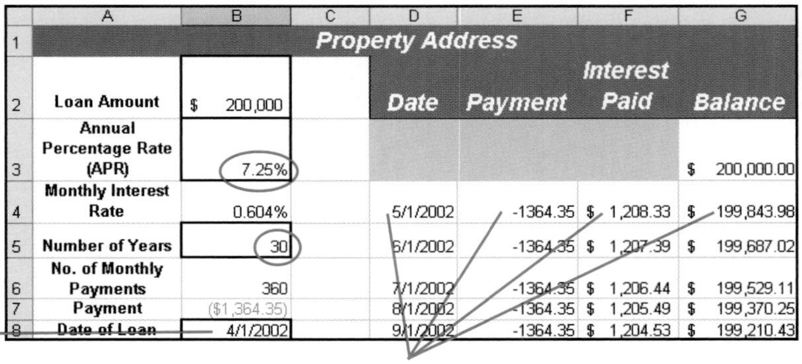

Use current date instead of the example

Updated formulas

QUICK TIP

If the cell is already formatted to display percentages, you do not need to type the percent sign. You have a choice of typing 7.25 or .0725. Excel interprets them both as 7.25%. When you start to type 7.25, Excel automatically adds a percent sign after you type the first number to indicate that it will interpret this number as a percent.

8 Select the title in **A1** through **G1** and enter your name and section number. Print the first sheet of the worksheet if your instructor requires it.

Save and close the workbook.

Task 2
SHARING A WORKBOOK AND TRACKING CHANGES

Why would I do this?

You have prepared a summary of sales from each of the stores in the Armstrong Pool, Spa, and Sauna Company and you want to have your store managers check it before you submit it to your supervisor. You can save the workbook in a folder to which most of the store managers have access and allow them to make changes, or you can send individual copies of the workbook and merge the changes into the final version when they return the edited copies. You can also do a combination of sharing and merging.

You play the role of three other store managers who make revisions to the original workbook and then you combine all the revisions into a final version. Two of the store managers are on the company network and can make the changes directly to the worksheet. The manager of the Novi store is not on the company network but has access to the Internet so you send a copy of the worksheet as an e-mail attachment and merge it into the original when it is returned.

To simulate changes made by three different users, you change the user name each time you make a change. If you were the actual store manager, you would not need to make this change. Be sure to return the user name to the original name when you are finished. This name is attached to all documents created by Microsoft Office applications on the computer you are using.

In this task, you open an existing copy of the workbook and save a version of it that can be reviewed. You also make a copy to be sent to the manager of the Novi store.

1 Open **EX1302** and save it in your folder as **EX1302-Armstrong**.

This file will be modified. If you get confused and wish to start over, the EX1302 file remains unchanged.

IN DEPTH

If this were a real situation, you would save the file in a folder that is shared with the other people who are supposed to make the changes. This folder could exist on a network server. In this exercise, you play the roles of the individual store managers, as well as the owner of the workbook. You store all the files on your own disk.

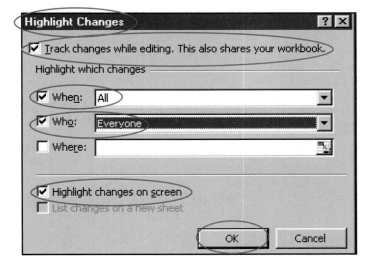

CAUTION

If you are working in a laboratory that does not allow you to change the user name, save the file to a floppy disk. Move to different computers in the lab and make the changes required by the other store managers. You will not be able to use the names as they are shown in the steps but the different names assigned to each computer will be displayed.

2 Choose **Tools**, **Track Changes**, **Highlight Changes**.

The Highlight Changes dialog box opens.

Click **Track changes while editing. This also shares the workbook**. Confirm that **When** and **All** are selected in the **When** box. Click the **Who** box to select it and confirm that **Everyone** is selected, the **Where** box is empty, and **Highlight changes on screen** is selected.

Other users can open this file if it is located in a folder shared with other users. If they make changes to it, you can see what the changes are and who made them.

IN DEPTH

If you do not choose **Highlight changes on screen,** the changes are tracked but not displayed. They can be displayed later by selecting this feature. You can also share the workbook without using the Track Changes option by choosing Tools, Share Workbook.

3 Click **OK**.

A notice is displayed informing you that the workbook will be saved again.

Click **OK**.

The workbook is saved and can be shared by others. Notice the change in the title bar. The actual name of the file does not include the [Shared] notation.

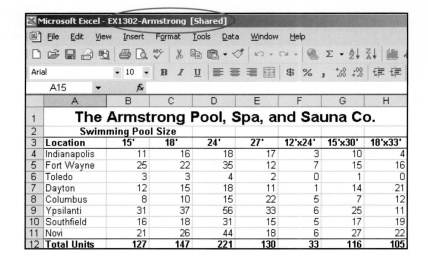

4 Close the workbook.

The workbook is available for other users who have access to the folder where the workbook is saved.

5 Choose **File, Open,** and locate the folder where you saved your file. Right-click on **EX1302-Armstrong** and choose **Copy** from the shortcut menu

The file is ready to be duplicated.

Right-click in an empty space below the list of files in your folder and choose **Paste** from the shortcut menu.

A copy of the file is created. You can send this file to other store managers.

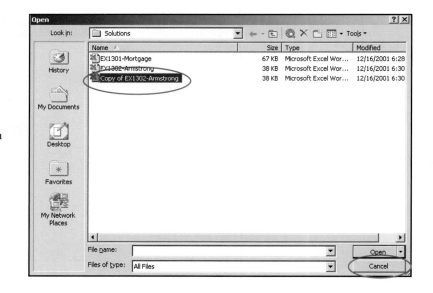

6 Click **Cancel**.

The Open dialog box closes. In the next task, you make changes to the workbook as if you are a store manager.

Task 3
MAKING CHANGES TO A SHARED WORKBOOK

Why would I do this?

You may be the one who is asked to review a workbook and make changes. You can make changes to the workbook as you would normally, but the program tracks your changes so the owner of the workbook can see who made the change. In order for you to simulate the changes made by another user, you must learn how to change the user name.

In this task, you learn how to make changes to a shared workbook as if you had access to the workbook in a shared folder, and as if you received a copy of the workbook as an e-mail attachment. You also learn how to change the user name that identifies who made the changes.

1 Open **EX1302-Armstrong**. Choose <u>T</u>ools, <u>O</u>ptions, and click the **General** tab.

The User name section displays the name that is shown when a comment is added to the presentation.

> Make note of the name so that you can replace it when you are finished with this task. Type your first name followed by **-Toledo** in the User <u>n</u>ame box.

CAUTION

Be sure to return the user name to the original name when you finish this task. Write down the original user name if you are sharing this computer or using a computer in the laboratory.

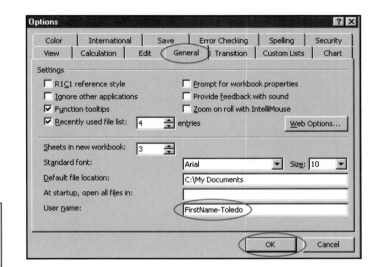

2 Click **OK**.

You will make changes to this review version as if you were the manager of the Toledo store.

> Choose the **First Quarter** sheet, select **B6**, type **5**, and then press ↵Enter.

3 Choose <u>T</u>ools, <u>T</u>rack Changes, <u>H</u>ighlight Changes.

The Highlight Changes dialog box opens.

Choose **All** in the **When** box. Click **Who** and select **Everyone**.

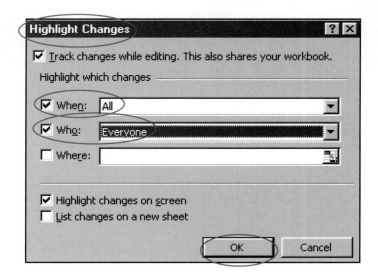

4 Click **OK**.

The dialog box closes and leaves a small colored triangle in the corner of the cell.

Move your mouse pointer onto **B6**.

The user name and information about the change is displayed.

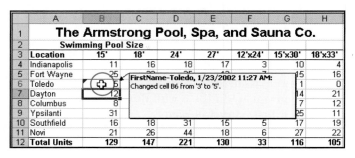

5 Click the **Close** button on the menu bar to close the workbook. Click <u>Y</u>es to save the changes.

The changes are saved, and the workbook closes. You have simulated a change made by the manager of the Toledo store. The user name is still set to your first name followed by the store name.

Choose <u>F</u>ile, <u>O</u>pen. Select **EX1302-Armstrong** from the folder where you saved it and click <u>O</u>pen.

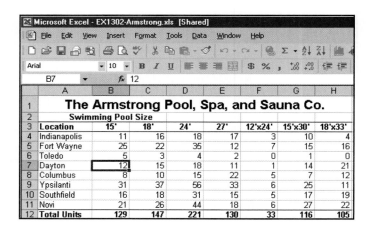

6 Choose <u>T</u>ools, <u>O</u>ptions, and then click the **General** tab.

You will make changes to this review version as if you were the manager of the Southfield store.

Select the **User <u>n</u>ame** box and enter your last name plus **-Southfield**.

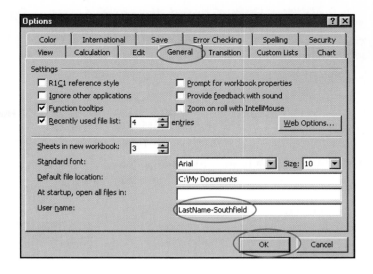

7 Click **OK**. Select **B10**. Change the value to **15**.

Track changes records the change but it will not automatically be displayed.

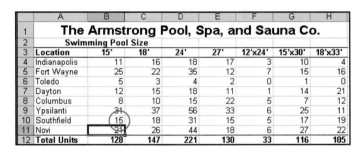

	A	B	C	D	E	F	G	H
1	**The Armstrong Pool, Spa, and Sauna Co.**							
2		**Swimming Pool Size**						
3	**Location**	**15'**	**18'**	**24'**	**27'**	**12'x24'**	**15'x30'**	**18'x33'**
4	Indianapolis	11	16	18	17	3	10	4
5	Fort Wayne	25	22	35	12	7	15	16
6	Toledo	5	3	4	2	0	1	0
7	Dayton	12	15	18	11	1	14	21
8	Columbus	8	10	15	22	5	7	12
9	Ypsilanti	31	37	56	33	6	25	11
10	Southfield	15	18	31	15	5	17	19
11	Novi	21	26	44	18	6	27	22
12	**Total Units**	**128**	**147**	**221**	**130**	**33**	**116**	**105**

8 Click the **Close** button on the menu bar to close the workbook. Click <u>Y</u>es to save the changes.

The changes are saved in the shared workbook.

Open **Copy of EX1302-Armstrong**. Choose <u>T</u>ools, <u>O</u>ptions, and then click the **General** tab. Change the **User <u>n</u>ame** to **John-Novi**.

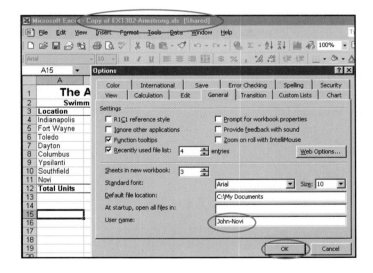

9 Click **OK**. Change the value of **B11** to **23**. Save the workbook.

You have made a change as if you were the manager of the Novi store.

Choose <u>T</u>ools, <u>O</u>ptions, and click the **General** tab. Change the **User <u>n</u>ame** back to the original name. Click **OK**. Close the workbook.

Task 4
ACCEPTING CHANGES AND MERGING REVISIONS

Why would I do this?

You have made two changes to the workbook posing as two different store managers who have access to the shared file in a shared folder on a network. You have also made a change to a copy of the file as if it had been sent to you as an e-mail attachment while identifying yourself as a manager of the Novi store.

In this task, you act as the home office manager and learn how to accept or reject changes and merge a copy of the file with the original file.

1 Open **EX1302-Armstrong**. Choose **Tools**, **Track Changes**, **Highlight Changes**.

The Highlight Changes dialog box opens.

Choose **All** in the **When** box. Click **Who** and select **Everyone**.

All the changes will be displayed.

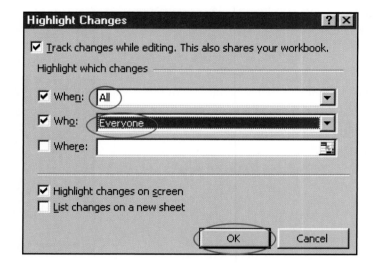

2 Click **OK**. Move the pointer to **B10**.

The change made using your last name as store manager is displayed.

Pointer activates pop-up message

CAUTION

Different users who make changes are represented by different colors, some of which are light colors and not easy to see. The colors used to identify different users are not easily changed in Excel.

③ Choose <u>T</u>ools, **Compare and Merge <u>W</u>orkbooks**.

The Select Files to Merge Into Current Workbook dialog box opens.

Locate the **Copy of EX1302-Armstrong** file in the folder where you saved it. Select the file and click **OK**.

The changes made in the copy are merged into the original.

Move the mouse pointer onto **B11**.

The change you made as the manager of the Novi store is displayed.

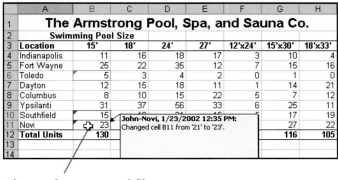

Change from merged file

④ Choose <u>T</u>ools, <u>T</u>rack Changes, <u>A</u>ccept or Reject Changes.

The Select Changes to Accept or Reject dialog box opens.

Confirm that **Not yet reviewed** is selected in the **When** box and **Everyone** is selected in the **Who** box.

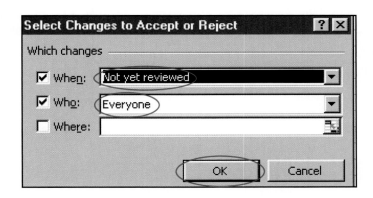

⑤ Click **OK**.

The Accept or Reject Changes dialog box opens and the first change is selected in B6.

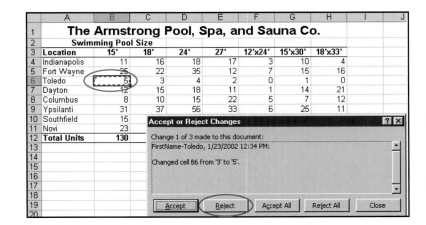

6 Click <u>R</u>eject.

The change is removed and the selection jumps to the next change in B10.

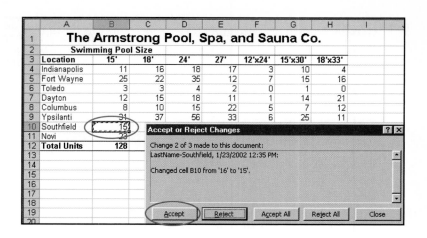

	A	B	C	D	E	F	G	H	I
1	The Armstrong Pool, Spa, and Sauna Co.								
2		Swimming Pool Size							
3	Location	15'	18'	24'	27'	12'x24'	15'x30'	18'x33'	
4	Indianapolis	11	16	18	17	3	10	4	
5	Fort Wayne	25	22	35	12	7	15	16	
6	Toledo	3	3	4	2	0	1	0	
7	Dayton	12	15	18	11	1	14	21	
8	Columbus	8	10	15	22	5	7	12	
9	Ypsilanti	31	37	56	33	6	25	11	
10	Southfield	15							
11	Novi	23							
12	Total Units	128							

Accept or Reject Changes

Change 2 of 3 made to this document:
LastName-Southfield, 1/23/2002 12:35 PM:

Changed cell B10 from '16' to '15'.

[Accept] [Reject] [Accept All] [Reject All] [Close]

7 Click <u>A</u>ccept.

The change in B10 is accepted and the next change in B11 is selected.

Click <u>A</u>ccept.

The changes for Southfield and Novi were accepted but the change made in B6 was not made.

	A	B	C	D	E	F	G	H
1	The Armstrong Pool, Spa, and Sauna Co.							
2		Swimming Pool Size						
3	Location	15'	18'	24'	27'	12'x24'	15'x30'	18'x33'
4	Indianapolis	11	16	18	17	3	10	4
5	Fort Wayne	25	22	35	12	7	15	16
6	Toledo	3	3	4	2	0	1	0
7	Dayton	12	15	18	11	1	14	21
8	Columbus	8	10	15	22	5	7	12
9	Ypsilanti	31	37	56	33	6	25	11
10	Southfield	15	18	31	15	5	17	19
11	Novi	23	26	44	18	6	27	22
12	Total Units	128	147	221	130	33	116	105

Change rejected   Changes accepted

CAUTION

If you made any errors while you worked through Tasks 3 or 4 and corrected them, an additional dialog box opens. It asks that you specify which version of the changes should be accepted or rejected. Should this happen, select the correct version by clicking on it and click OK.

8 Close the file and save the changes. Leave Excel open for the next task.

Task 5

QUERYING DATA FROM OTHER SOURCES AND SAVING AS A WEB PAGE

Why would I do this?

If your organization keeps detailed records of transactions, prices, customers, vendors, or other facts, they are probably stored in a database such as Microsoft Access. If you are not familiar with Access but want to extract data from a table stored in an Access database, you can do so using a ***database query***. A database query allows you to set conditions used to retrieve columns and rows of a table. Once the data is in a worksheet, you can save it as usual or you can save it as a Web page that store managers or salespeople can use.

In this task, you learn to extract a price list from an Access table and save it as a Web page.

1 Click the New button.

An empty worksheet is displayed.

> Choose **Data, Import External Data, New Database Query.**

The Choose Data Source dialog box opens.

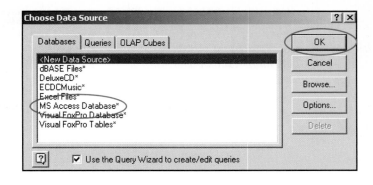

2 Select **MS Access Database*** and click **OK.**

*The Select Database dialog box opens, and a **Connecting to data source** icon is displayed.*

> Find the folder where the student files are kept in the **Directories** box. Select **EX1303.mdb** in the **Database Name** box.

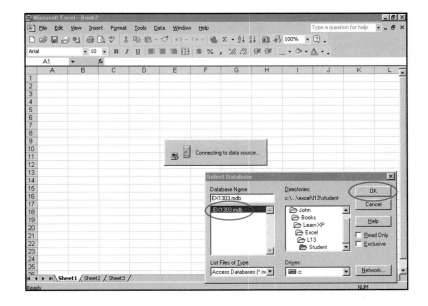

3 Click **OK.**

*The **Query Wizard-Choose Columns** dialog box opens. This database has several tables.*

> Click the plus sign next to **tblProducts.**

The column names within the tblProducts table are displayed. You can transfer the columns to the Columns in your query box one at a time or as a group.

> Click **Description.** Click the **Add** button. Repeat this process to add **Manufacturer, Amount,** and **InstallationCost.**

Four column names are moved into the Columns in your query box.

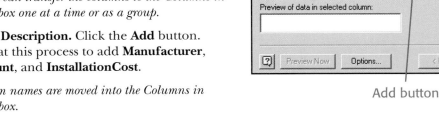

Add button

Unless you are familiar with the Access Table relationships, only select columns from a single Access table.

4 Click **Next**.

The Filter Data window of the wizard is displayed. You can use this window to limit the data by matching column contents to conditions specified in the boxes to the right. In this case, you want all the product prices so no restrictions are needed.

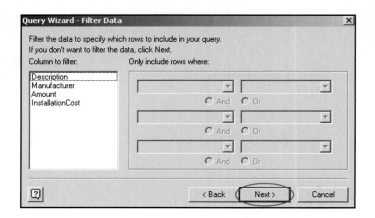

5 Click **Next**. Click the arrow on the **Sort by** box and choose **Description**.

The default sorting method is Ascending.

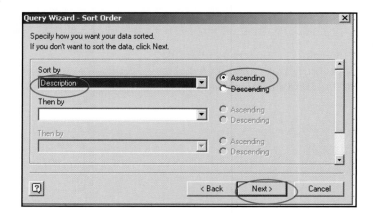

6 Click **Next**.

The last dialog box in the wizard displays.

Confirm that **Return Data to Microsoft Excel** is selected.

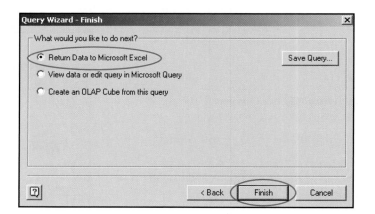

7 Click **Finish**.

The Import Data dialog box opens.

Confirm that **Existing worksheet** is selected and **=$A$1** is the selected cell.

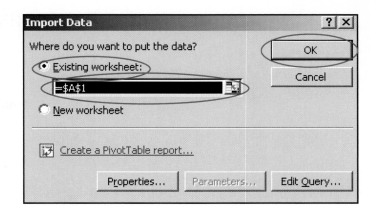

8 Click **OK**.

The data from the Access database is placed in the worksheet. You want to place this information on the Internet so all your store managers can receive it.

Tool bar used for refreshing data from the database

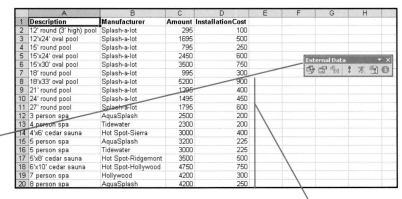

Data imported from the database with the latest product information

9 Choose **File**, **Save as Web Page**.

The Save As dialog box displays.

Choose **Selection: Sheet**. Select the default name in the **File name** box and type **EX1303-Web**.

The worksheet will be saved as a Web page.

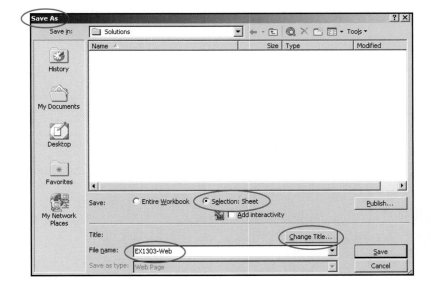

10 Click the **Change Title** button.

The Set Title box displays.

Type **Current Prices for Armstrong Pool, Spa, and Sauna Company**.

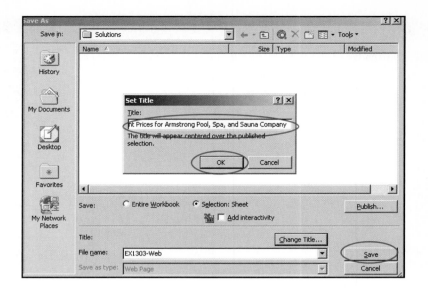

11 Click **OK**.

The Set Title box closes.

Click the **Save** button.

The worksheet is saved as a Web page but the Web page is not opened.

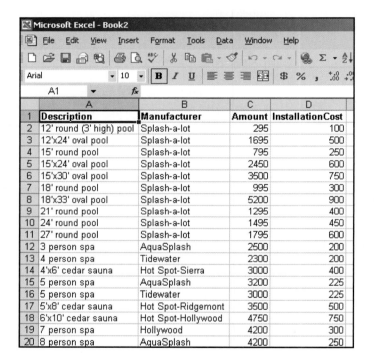

12 Close the worksheet. Do not save it.

This worksheet was created as an interim step and is no longer needed.

Task 6

RETRIEVING DATA FROM WEB PAGES

Why would I do this?

Maintaining current price lists that all the stores use can be a problem when they change rapidly. Instead of sending out updates for price catalogs, you can post the current list of prices as a Web page and then import this page into your workbooks. If the central office makes changes to the price list, you only need to click a button and the price list in your workbooks are updated with the latest values.

In this task, you locate the Web page you created in the previous task and open it in a browser. You copy the address of the file and close the browser, then you import this Web page into a worksheet.

1 Start Internet Explorer. Choose **File, Open.**

The Open dialog box opens.

> Click **Browse.** Locate **EX1303-Web** in your folder, select it, and then click **Open.**

The Open box displays the path to the EX1303-Web file on your computer.

> Click **OK.**

The Web page opens in Internet Explorer.

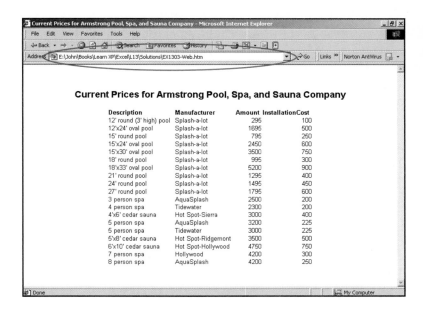

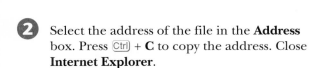

⚠ **CAUTION**

If Netscape is installed as the default Web browser on the computer you are using, it will start instead of Internet Explorer. This will not affect this step.

2 Select the address of the file in the **Address** box. Press Ctrl + **C** to copy the address. Close **Internet Explorer.**

The address is stored in the Office Clipboard and can be used to locate this Web page.

> Confirm that Excel is open and open **EX1304** from the folder of student files. Save this file as **EX1304-Invoice.**

An invoice workbook opens that is similar to the one you may have created in the reinforcement exercises in a previous lesson. The formulas in this invoice draw data from the products sheet where the current products and prices are stored.

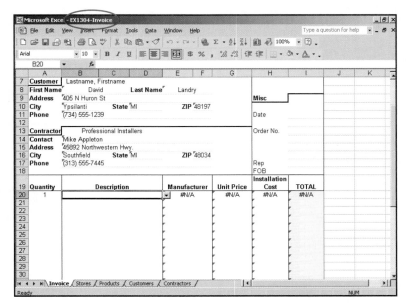

3 Click the **Products** sheet tab.

The sheet is empty. Columns A through D have already been defined as a named range called ProductInfo. The lookup formulas in the Invoice sheet will use whatever data you import into this sheet.

Choose **Data**, **Import External Data**, **New Web Query**.

The New Web Query window opens and displays the default Web page for your browser. The address line is selected.

Use Ctrl + **V** to paste the address of your Web page in the **Address** box.

The path to EX1303-Web on your machine differs from the example shown. The Web page displayed in the window is the default home page used by your browser and differs from the example shown.

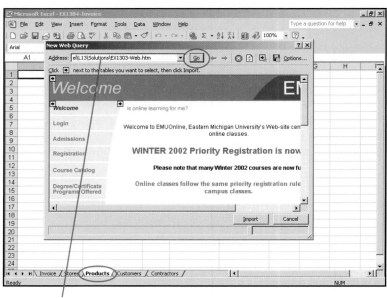

Path to EX1303-Web.htm on
your computer

4 Click the **Go** button.

The Web page, EX1303-Web, opens in the New Web Query window. Each table in the Web page is identified by a button with a small black arrow on it.

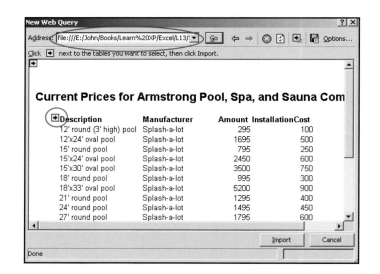

5 Click the button next to **Description**.

The button changes to a check box and the table is highlighted to indicate that it is selected.

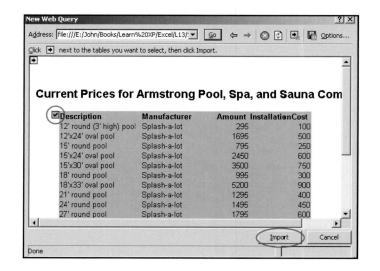

6 Click **I**mport.

The Import Data dialog box opens.

Confirm that **Existing worksheet** is selected and that **=$A$1** is chosen as the first cell in the table.

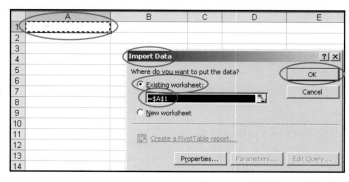

7 Click **OK**.

The data is imported into the worksheet and the External Data toolbar is displayed.

Note the price and installation cost for a 5'x8' cedar sauna. You will add this data to the invoice using lookup functions.

This data will be used in the Invoice sheet

Data imported from Web page

Refresh button used to refresh data from Web page

QUICK TIP

To update this sheet with any changes on the company Web page, you can simply click the Refresh Data button on the External Data toolbar.

8 Click the **Invoice** sheet tab.

The lookup formulas may use the new data.

Select cells **B20** through **D20**. Click the arrow next to the box and select **5'x8' cedar sauna** from the list.

The values used in the Manufacturer, Unit Price, and Installation Cost columns are located on the Products sheet and displayed in the appropriate cells on the Invoice.

Confirm that the lookup functions in **E20**, **G20**, and **H20** retrieved the correct values from the Products sheet.

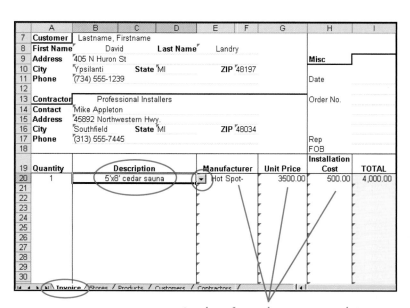

Lookup formulas use new data from the Products sheet

9 Click the **Customers** sheet tab. Scroll to row **50** and fill in your name and related information. Use **Y-787** as the CustomerNo in column **B**.

You will create an invoice with your name and address.

Click any of the names in column **A** and click the **Sort Ascending** button.

The customer data will be sorted and your name placed in proper alphabetical order. You must sort the list of names so that the lookup functions in the Invoice sheet work properly.

Enter your name
using this format

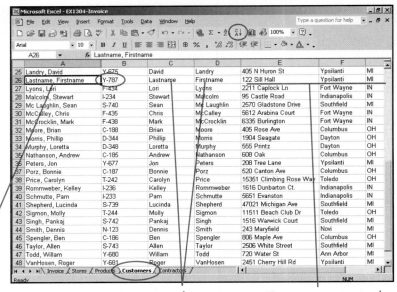

Enter your last name
and first name

Enter your personal
information

10 Click the **Invoice** sheet tab. Select **B7** through **B8**. Click the arrow next to the selected cells and choose your name from the list.

Your information is filled into the Customer information.

Print this page if your instructor requires it.

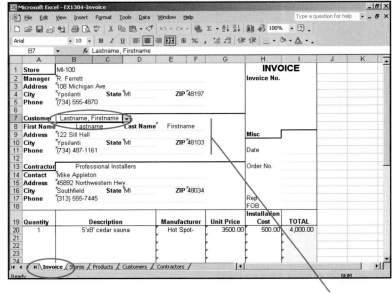

Your information

11 Save and close the workbook.

The exercises that follow are designed for you to review and use what you have learned in this lesson. You also have the opportunity to practice your skills and then expand on them by applying them to new situations.

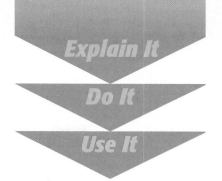

COMPREHENSION

Comprehension exercises are designed to check your memory and understanding of the basic concepts in this lesson. You distinguish between true and false statements, identify new screen elements, and match terms with related statements. If you are uncertain of the correct answer, refer to the task number following each item (for example, T4 refers to Task 4) and review that task until you are confident that you can provide a correct response.

TRUE-FALSE

Circle either T or F.

T F **1.** To protect worksheet cells from unintended changes, you can select them and choose **Format, Cells, Protection, Enable. (T1)**

T F **2.** When you type a password, the text is replaced by asterisks for added security. **(T1)**

T F **3.** When you enable the **Track Changes** feature and choose **Highlight Changes,** and the **Highlight changes on screen** option, you can tell what changes have been made to a worksheet. **(T3)**

T F **4.** You can accept or reject changes to a whole worksheet but not to individual cells. **(T4)**

T F **5.** Excel can import data from Access tables using the **New Database Query** command. **(T5)**

T F **6.** Once you import data from a table on a Web page, you can refresh the data by clicking on the **Refresh Data** button on the **External Data** toolbar. **(T6)**

T F **7.** When you choose the **Track changes while editing** option, you automatically share the workbook. **(T2)**

MATCHING QUESTIONS

A. [Shared]   **D.** Protect

B. Merge   **E.** Track changes

C. New Database Query   **F.** New Web Query

Match the following statements to the word or phrase that is the best match from the list. Write the letter of the matching word or phrase in the space provided next to the number.

1. _____ Prevent changes to cells **(T1)**

2. _____ Displayed next to the file name in the title bar when a workbook is made available to other users **(T2)**

3. _____ Combine copies of a shared workbook **(T4)**

4. _____ Import data from a Web page **(T6)**

5. _____ Import data from a database **(T5)**

6. _____ Display changes made to a workbook **(T4)**

IDENTIFYING PARTS OF THE EXCEL SCREEN

Refer to the figure and identify the numbered parts of the screen. Write the letter of the correct label in the space next to the number.

1. _____

2. _____

3. _____

4. _____

5. _____

6. _____

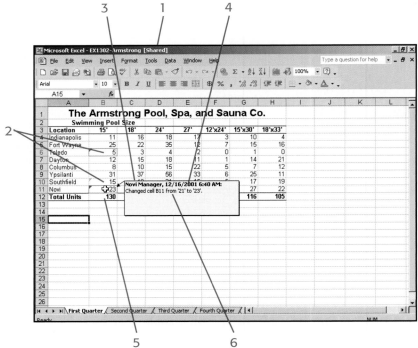

A. Mouse pointer (T4)

B. Changes made by two different users (T3)

C. Indicates the workbook is available to multiple users (T2)

D. Details of a change (T3)

E. Name of user who made the change (T4)

F. Date and time of the change (T4)

REINFORCEMENT

Reinforcement exercises are designed to reinforce the skills you have learned by applying them to a new situation. Detailed instructions are provided along with a figure, where appropriate, to illustrate the result. Complete the reinforcement exercises sequentially. Leave the workbook open at the end of each exercise for use in the next exercise until you are specifically directed to close it.

Open **EX1304** and save it as **EX1304-Reinforcement** on your disk for use in the following exercises.

R1—Importing Data from an Access Database

In this exercise, you import data directly from an Access database into the Contractors sheet of a workbook used to create invoices.

1. Click the **Contractors** sheet tab. Select **A1**.

2. Choose **Data, Import External Data, New Database Query**. Choose **MS Access Database** and click **OK**.

3. Locate and select **EX1303** in the student files and click **OK**. Click the plus sign next to **tblContractors**. Add all the columns in this table except the first one, ContractorID.

4. Click **Next** twice. Sort the data in ascending order by the **ContractorName** field. Click **Next** and **Finish**.

5. When the **Import Data** dialog box opens, click **Properties**. Select **Overwrite existing cells with new data, clear unused cells**. Click **OK**.

6. Confirm that the data will be placed in the existing worksheet and the cell reference is **=$A$1**. Click **OK**.

7. Add your name and information as a contractor to the bottom of the list in row **18**. Make up a company name but use your name as the contact person. Sort the table in ascending order on the ContractorName column.

R2—Protecting a Worksheet

Most of the data on this invoice is looked up from the other sheets. If a user tries to enter data directly in a cell with a formula, the formula could be lost. In this exercise, you unlock the cells intended for user input and protect the sheet with a password. The password in this example is a simple word that is easy to remember. Its purpose is to prevent accidental changes rather than intentional tampering. More secure passwords are collections of letters that cannot be found in the dictionary. The author prefers to take the first letter of each word in a phrase or saying. It is easy to remember but the collection of letters makes no sense by itself.

1. Click the **Invoice** sheet tab. Select **I2**. Choose **Format, Cells**, and then click the **Protection** tab. Remove the check mark next to **Locked**. Click **OK**. Repeat this process to unlock **B1**, **B7** through **C7**, **B13** through **D13**, **I11** through **I18**, **A20** through **D36**, and **B41** through **D44**.

2. Choose **Tools, Protection, Protect Sheet**.

3. Select the **Password to unprotect sheet** box and type **Invoice**. Click **OK**. Enter the password again and click **OK**.

4. Click the arrow next to **D13** and select your company as the contractor. Changes are allowed to this range of cells and your name is retrieved from the Contractors sheet.

5. Try to change your zip code in **F16**. The change is not allowed. Save the workbook.

R3—Share the Invoice Workbook and Track Changes

You want to make this invoice workbook available to several people in your store and give some of them the option of adding new customers. If anyone makes changes, you want to know who did it and when.

1. Choose **Tools, Track Changes, Highlight Changes**. Select the option to track changes and share the workbook. Choose **All** and **Everyone**. Click **OK** twice.

2. Click the **Customers** sheet tab. Locate **Daniel Cook.** He moved and changed addresses but kept the same phone number. Change his address to **1316 Glen Leven**.

3. Click the **Invoice** sheet tab. Change the customer to **Daniel Cook**.

4. Print the **Invoice** sheet.

5. Save and close the workbook.

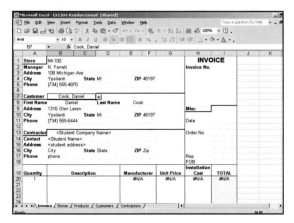

Challenge exercises are designed to test your ability to apply your skills to new situations with less detailed instruction. These exercises also challenge you to expand your repertoire of skills by using commands that are similar to those you have already learned. The desired outcome is clearly defined, but you have more freedom to choose the steps needed to achieve the required result.

C1—Use a Gantt Chart and Protect the Sheet

Many RFPs (Request for Proposals) require a chart to show the anticipated schedule for completion of the project. One of the most commonly used charts for this purpose is a Gantt chart. A Gantt chart is a method of depicting tasks in a project with horizontal bars that mark the duration of each task and the relationship between them. Diamonds denote milestones. Excel does not have a Gantt chart as one of its charting options but you can create one using the drawing tools. You can use track changes and a Gantt chart in a shared workbook to coordinate a project.

Goal: Create a Gantt chart and share the workbook with track changes turned on. Change user names and make changes to the project.

Use the following guidelines:

1. Open a blank worksheet and save it as EX1305-Gantt. Select cell **A1** and type **Term Project for** <your name and section>. Select cell **B3** and enter next Monday's date. Select cell **C3** and enter the date for the following Monday. Select both cells **B3** and **C3**. Use the fill handle to fill in a series of dates to the right. Stop at cell **J3**. You will have a series of dates one week apart.

2. Format row headings and increase row height. Select the row indicators for rows **4** through **9**. Choose **Format**, **Row**, **Height**. Set the row height to **24**. Select cells **A4** through **A10** and choose **Format**, **Cells**. Choose the Alignment tab and check the **Wrap text** option. Choose **Center** for **Horizontal** and **Vertical** text alignment then click **OK**.

3. In cells **A4** through **A10**, type the following row labels: **Develop Idea**, **Get Approval**, **First Draft**, **First Review**, **Make Changes**, and **Due Date**. Center the labels in their respective cells.

4. Draw rectangles, add your name, and use a fill color. Turn on the Drawing toolbar, if necessary. Click the Rectangle drawing tool and drag a long rectangle in row 4 that starts in the middle of cell **B4** and ends in the middle of cell **D4**. Type your name then click the **Center** button on the Formatting toolbar. Click outside the rectangle then click its edge to select it. Click the down-arrow next to the Fill Color button on the Formatting toolbar and choose **yellow**.

5. Draw a diamond to represent a milestone. Click **AutoShapes** on the drawing toolbar, then click **Basic Shapes** and click the diamond at the end of the first row of shapes. Move the pointer to the line between cells **D5** and **E5**. Click and drag to draw a small diamond that is about half the row's height. Fill the diamond with black.

6. Copy and paste the bar and rectangle to finish the chart. Copy the long rectangle and place it in row 6. Adjust its length and position to start in column **D** and end in column **H**. Copy the black diamond and paste it in row **7** between columns **H** and **I**. Repeat this process to show another task in row **8** and a milestone in row **9**. See the illustration.

7. Choose **Tools**, **Protection**, **Protect Sheet**. Use **Gantt** as the password. Scroll to the bottom of the list of items and select **Edit Objects**. Click **OK**. Reenter **Gantt** and click **OK**.

8. Move the diamond in row **5** to the line between columns **D** and **E**. Adjust the lengths of the bars above and below the diamond so the one above ends at the line between columns **D** and **E** and the one below starts at that line.

9. Try to change one of the cells to confirm that they are protected from change.

10. Print the worksheet. Save and close the workbook.

C2—List Changes on a Separate Sheet

If you need a log of the changes made to a workbook, you can use an option that will list the changes made on a separate sheet and print it.

This exercise uses the file you created doing the tasks in this lesson.

Goal: Open EX1302-Armstrong and print a log of the changes made to this file.

Use the following guidelines:

1. Open **EX1302-Armstrong.** Choose **T**ools, **T**rack Changes, **H**ighlight Changes.

2. Choose **All** in the **Whe**n box and **Everyone** in the **Wh**o box.

3. Choose **L**ist changes on a new sheet. Click **OK**. The History sheet appears with a log of all the changes made to the sheet.

4. Print the History sheet.

5. If your instructor requires it, press ⎡PrtSc⎤ on your keyboard to capture a copy of the screen. Open a blank Word document, type your name, and paste the screen image into the document. Save it as **EX1306-History** and close it.

6. Close the workbook. Do not save the changes.

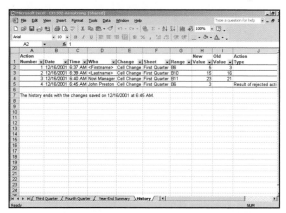

C3—Import Data from a Government Web Page

Government Web sites are useful for finding information about your own state or county. You can import tables of data from such Web sites.

Open a new workbook in Excel, and save it as **EX1307-Stats**. Choose **Data, Import External Data, New Web Query**. Go to **www.fedstats.gov**. Under **MapStats**, select your state and click the **Submit** button. Choose a table from this site and import it into your workbook. Add your name to cell **A1** on the sheet, and save the file. Print the worksheet or e-mail it to your instructor as directed.

Goal: Import data about your state and county.

1. Open a blank workbook and name it **EX1307-Stats**. Rename the **Sheet1** tab **State** and rename the **Sheet2** tab **County**. Select **A1** in the **State** sheet.

2. (Note: If this Web site has changed since publication of this book, check with your instructor. You may need to search for another table of data on a government Web site and use it instead.)

3. Scroll down to the top of the table of data, click the selection button, and import it to the **State** sheet.

4. Select **A1** in the **County** sheet. Choose **D**ata, **Import External D**ata, **New W**eb Query. Go to **www.fedstats.gov**. Under the **MapStats** heading, select your state and click the **Submit** button.

5. Select your county from the available list of counties for your state and click **Go**. Scroll down and select the table of county data and import it.

6. Insert your name in **A1** on the **State** and **County** sheets. Format both sheets in **Landscape** orientation and fit the text of each sheet to one page wide.

7. Print both sheets if your instructor requires it. Save and close the workbook.

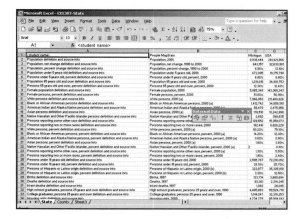

C4—Collaborating with People Who Have Special Needs

Office XP comes with a full speech recognition program. In Excel 2002, you can use the speech program to have the computer speak the content of the cells to you. This can be helpful if you need to compare data that has been entered with a paper record or if a person is visually impaired. The program can proceed across rows or down columns, and tell you with speech what has been entered in each cell. To do this exercise you must have speakers or headphones connected to your computer and they need to be turned on. Check the volume setting on your speakers before proceeding. The speech software must also be installed.

Goal: Use the Speak Cells feature to check accuracy of your entries.

1. Open a blank workbook and save it as **EX1308-Speech**.

2. Choose **T**ools, **Spee**ch, Show **T**ext To Speech Toolbar.

3. Click the **Speak On Enter** button on the right end of the Text To Speech Toolbar.

4. Select **A1**. Type your name and press ⎡↵Enter⎤.

5. Select **A2**. Type **20000000** and press ⏎Enter. If you typed the correct number of zeros, the program says **twenty million**.

6. Select cell **A4** and enter the following data in cells across this row: **19, 20-May-02, Y-681, 15x30 pool, $4,100.00, IN-4, 01-Jun-02.**

7. Select cells **A6:H20**. Choose Format, Cells, and then choose the **Alignment** tab. Set **Horizontal** to **General**, **Vertical** to **Top**. Select **Wrap text** and **Merge cells**. Click **OK**.

8. Write a brief essay describing your reaction to this feature. Answer such questions as:

   a) Did you find the Speak On Enter feature helpful?

   b) Did you have any problems getting it to work?

   c) In what circumstances do you think this might be useful?

   d) Do you think this would increase or decrease the speed of entering data?

9. Print this sheet and save it.

10. Click the **Speak On Enter** button on the right end of the Text To Speech Toolbar to turn off this feature. Close the toolbar. Close the workbook.

ON YOUR OWN

Create a set of worksheets that use data imported from a Web page to make calculations.

Criteria for grading will be:

1. Demonstration of the use of imported data to keep calculations up to date.

2. Formatting of one of the pages intended for public distribution.

3. Data must be easily updated from the Web page by clicking the refresh button on the Get External Data toolbar.

Some examples of applications that students have used in previous classes to make use of the import data feature are as follows:

- Set up a personal Web page on an Internet portal such as Yahoo.com and display a set of stock prices. The stock prices are imported into a worksheet and then used to calculate the current value of the shares of stock held. The sheet that displays the current status of the user's stock holdings is formatted for printing or may be saved as a Web page.

- Import current population or demographic data from a government site and use that data to make calculations.

- Locate a table of currency exchange rates that is updated daily. Given a mix of currencies that might be in the user's possession, calculate the current total value in U.S. dollars.

1. Place your name in a cell that is clearly visible on the summary worksheet and print it.

2. To complete the project:

   - Save the workbook on your own disk. Name the workbook **EX1309-Import**.

   - Check with your instructor to determine if you should submit the project in electronic or printed form. If necessary, print out a copy of the workbook to hand in.

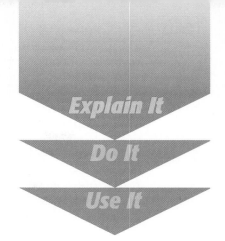
Explain It
Do It
Use It

Lesson 9

Modifying Table Properties and Joining Tables

Task 1   Setting Data Validation Properties
Task 2   Creating and Modifying Lookup Field Properties
Task 3   Adding Custom Input Masks
Task 4   Using the Linked Table Manager
Task 5   Creating Relationships Between Tables

INTRODUCTION

A database is useful only if the data that it contains is accurate. Table properties are used to help ensure consistency of format and accuracy of the data entered. This process starts when you select the data type for each field, which controls the type of data that can be entered. You can use a number of formatting properties to ensure that the data has a uniform appearance. You can also use table properties to restrict or control the data entered.

If the data being entered should always use parentheses, dashes, or a combination of numbers and letters in a consistent manner, you can reduce errors by using a custom *input mask* to control the input and format. If the data must meet certain criteria, or is limited to a range of dates or numbers, you can use a *validation rule* to assure that it does. If you need to enter a name or other text that must match existing data exactly, it is better to pick the value from a list rather than type it in with the chance of capitalization, spacing, and spelling errors. A *lookup field* allows you to select an existing value from another table or from a specific list. In this lesson, you learn how to use each of the properties to help ensure the accuracy of the data in your tables.

In some cases, the data that you need is located in another database, often stored on a mainframe or file server. In these situations you link to the data and then create the required queries, forms, or reports. If the database containing the data tables is moved, you can use the *Linked Table Manager* to help restore the links to all the tables. This lesson shows you how to link to a table in another database, and then reestablish that link using the Linked Table Manager.

305

The main advantage of using a *relational database*, such as Access, is that you avoid having redundant information in several places. With a relational database, you create relationships between tables to extract the information you need. Most databases contain many tables of data that can be related through a common field. In Access, you use the *primary key* field to create a *join* between tables. The most common type of relationship is a *one-to-many relationship*, where a single record in one table is related to many records in a second table. It is also common to have many records in one table that need to be related to many records in another table. You cannot do this directly between two tables in Access, but rather you create a third table called a *junction table*. A junction table includes the primary keys from each of the other tables. In the junction table, the primary key fields function as foreign keys. You can also include other fields in a junction table such as a transaction date or number.

In the databases that you use in this book, there are one or more *many-to-many relationships*. In the Armstrong database, used throughout the lessons, there are many stores with many sales representatives who sell many products to many customers. The company needs to produce reports that show how much was sold at each store and how much was sold by each sales rep. Table design and table relationships are critical to answering questions about the information contained in the database. With a properly designed database you can show the sales results by store, by employee, or by product.

In this lesson, you change some table properties, use the Linked Table Manager, and create table relationships for the Armstrong Pool, Spa, and Sauna database.

VISUAL SUMMARY

When you complete this lesson, you will have changed table properties, used the Linked Table Manager, and created relationships as displayed in the following figures:

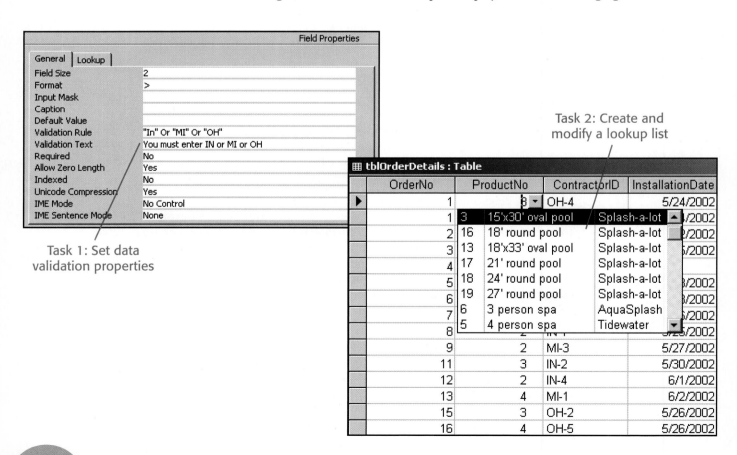

Task 1: Set data validation properties

Task 2: Create and modify a lookup list

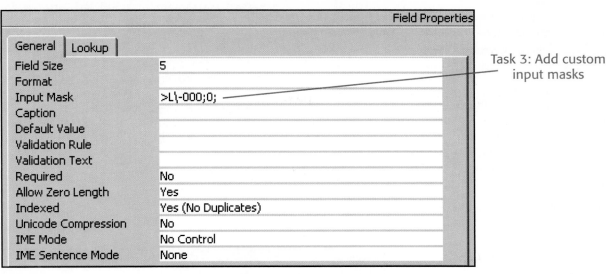

Task 3: Add custom input masks

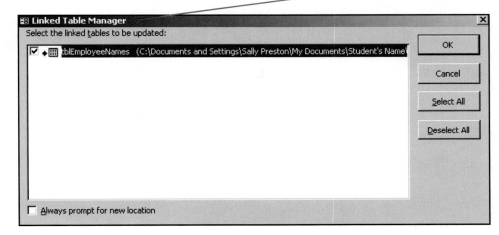

Task 4: Use the Linked Table Manager

Task 5: Create multiple relationships

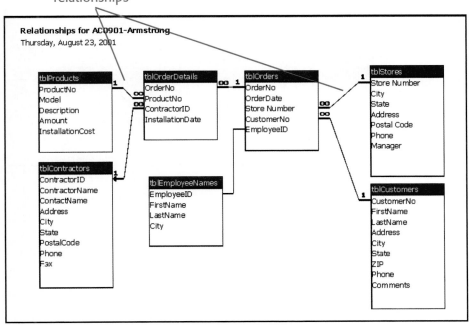

Task 1

SETTING DATA VALIDATION PROPERTIES

Why would I do this?
Validation rules are set to help ensure that only appropriate information is entered into a particular field. You use this property when the possible entries are limited to a few alternatives, or when the data is within a range of numbers or dates. Whenever you set a validation rule for a particular field, you should also set the *validation text* property so the message box provides a clear message to users if they enter invalid data.

In this task, you learn how to set the validation properties for a field in a table.

1 Start Microsoft Access. Click **More files** under the **Open a file** category. Locate **AC0901** in the **Student** folder for this lesson.

Transfer the files to the location where you are saving your files. Use either the **Send To**, **3 1/2" Floppy (A)** option, or **Copy** and **Paste** it to a folder on the hard drive. Remove the read-only property, if necessary, and rename the file **AC0901-Armstrong**. Open the file.

There are six tables in this database. In this task you work with tblContractors.

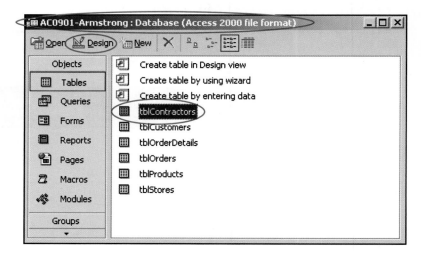

2 Click **tblContractors** to select it, and then click the **Design** button.

The table opens in Design view.

Click anywhere in the **State** field to make it the active field.

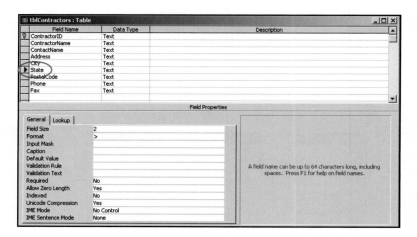

3 Click on the **Validation Rule** property box and type: **"IN"or "MI"or "OH"**.

This rule limits the data entered for the state field to one of these three state abbreviations.

IN DEPTH

Access interprets the characters within the quote marks as a valid string that is acceptable for a field. You usually do not need to include quote marks around the valid data; Access adds them automatically. In this example, however, the quote marks are included because the abbreviation IN for Indiana is also a programming term used in Access. The quote marks tell Access that this is a string of data rather than a programming term.

4 Click the **Validation Text** line and type: **You must enter IN or MI or OH**.

This is the message the user sees if an incorrect abbreviation is entered.

Click the Save button to save your changes.

A message box is displayed, warning you that data integrity rules have changed and some data may not meet the new rules.

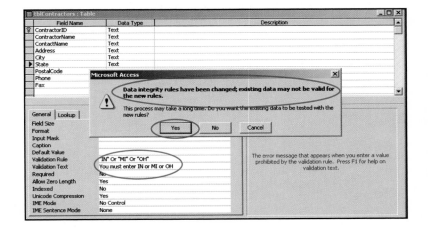

CAUTION

If the data does not match the validation rule, you see a second warning box advising you that existing data violates the validation rule. You then have to decide if you want to continue having the data tested, or revert to the old setting. The program does not identify which records violate the new rule. If this happens, you can create a query that searches for records that do not match the validation rule requirements. It may be that you overlooked another valid option, or that the data is incorrect.

5 Click **Yes**.

The data is tested and the message box closes.

Click the **View** button. Select the entry in the **State** field for the first record, type **IL**, and then press Tab↹.

A message box displays the warning you entered in the Validation Text property box. When you use a validation rule you should always test it to make sure it works as expected.

View button

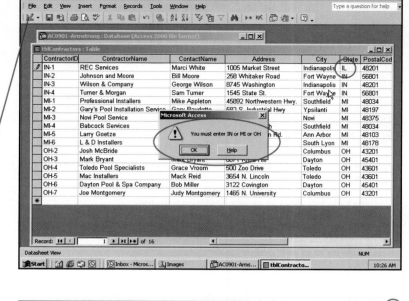

6 Click **OK**. Change the **State** field back to **IN** for the first record.

7 Click the **Close** button to close the table.

IN DEPTH

To enter a range of numbers or dates as a validation rule, you can use the Between . . . And operator, or use the comparison operators: greater than (>), less than (<), greater than or equal to (>=), less than or equal to (<=), or not equal (<>). For example, a validation rule for a range of dates might be Between 01/01/02 And 12/31/02. A validation rule for a range of numbers could be expressed (>1000 And <10000).

Task 2

CREATING AND MODIFYING LOOKUP FIELD PROPERTIES

Why would I do this?

The *Lookup* property is a powerful tool that helps maintain data integrity and makes it easier to enter new records into your database. Because Access is a relational database, pieces of information that need to be brought together are maintained in separate tables. A retail business might have a table containing customer information, a table containing product information, and a table containing information on each sale. When a customer buys a product, you want to be able to look up the product description so the information about the sale is entered correctly. For example, in the orders table, the product ID number is stored, but the description for the product is in the products table. To help you locate the correct product, you can use a lookup field property in the orders table. Then when you enter a sale in the orders table or form, you can look up the information about the product using the lookup list box.

This ensures that accurate product descriptions are used in all sales, rather than relying on the memory of your sales staff. There are several places in the Armstrong database where a lookup field property would be useful.

In this task, you learn how to add and modify a lookup field property.

① Select **tblOrdersDetails** and click the **Design** button.

You are going to add a lookup list for the ProductNo that also shows the product description.

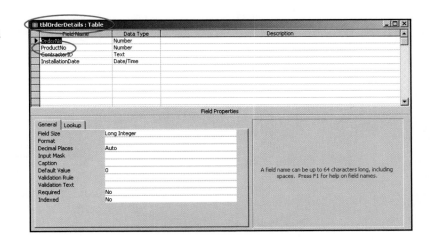

② Click in the **ProductNo** Data Type column, and click the arrow to display the list box.

You are going to use the Lookup Wizard to add a lookup property to this field.

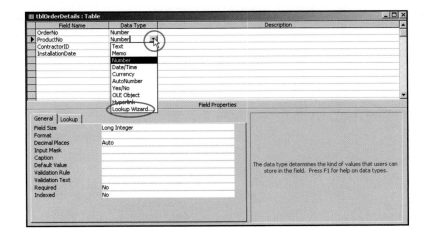

3 Click **Lookup Wizard** from the list.

The first Lookup Wizard dialog box is displayed. You have two options—to look up the values in a table or a query, or to type the values you want into a list. You want to look up the values from the product table.

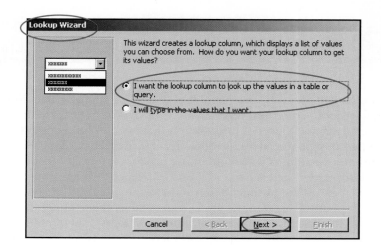

4 Make sure the first option button is selected, and then click <u>Next</u>.

In the second Lookup Wizard dialog box, you select the table or query that you want to use for looking up the necessary information.

> Click **Table: tblProducts.**

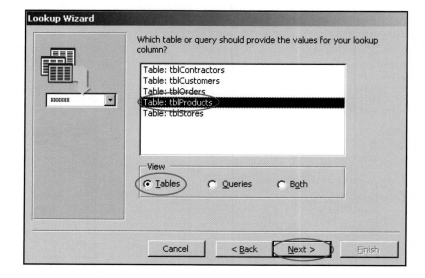

5 Click <u>Next</u>.

In the third Lookup Wizard dialog box you select the fields you want to include in your lookup list.

> Double-click **ProductNo**, **Model**, and **Description** to add these three fields to the Selected Fields box.

Add button

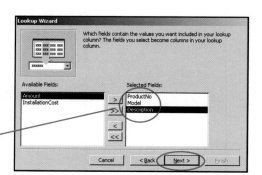

6 Click **Next**.

In the fourth Lookup Wizard dialog box you can adjust the field widths and choose to hide or display the primary key data.

Deselect the checkbox next to **Hide key column**. Double-click on the line separating each column heading to adjust each column to the width needed to display the information.

Column widths adjusted

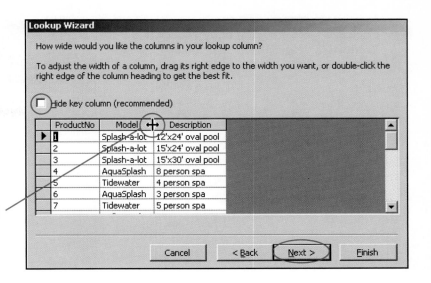

7 Click **Next**.

In the fifth Lookup Wizard dialog box you identify the value that is unique for this set of data. This is the same as the primary key field—in this case the ProductNo.

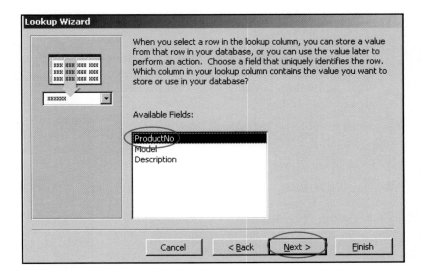

8 Make sure **ProductNo** is selected and click **Next**.

In the last page of the Lookup Wizard you choose a label for your lookup column. ProductNo displays by default, which you accept as the label when you click Finish.

Click **Finish**.

A message box is displayed, warning you that the table must be saved so relationships can be created.

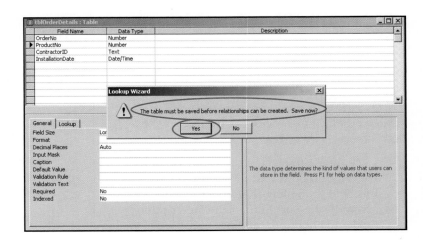

9 Click **Yes**. Click the **View** button. Click in the **ProductNo** field, and then click the arrow to display the lookup list you just created.

The description column is not fully displayed. You can adjust this. It would also be useful if the items were displayed in alphabetical order by description.

Lookup list

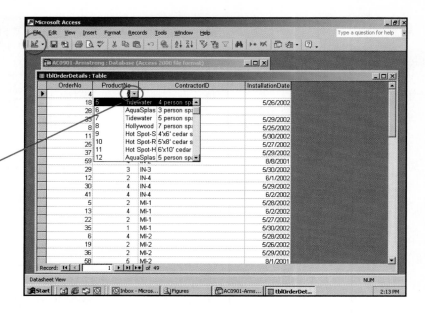

10 Click the **View** button. Click anywhere in the **ProductNo** field to make it active, and then click the **Lookup** tab in the Field Properties area of the window.

You can see the properties that were set when you created the lookup list.

Click in the **Row Source** property box.

A build button is displayed. You use this button to view the structure of the query that was created when you used the Lookup Query Wizard.

Build button

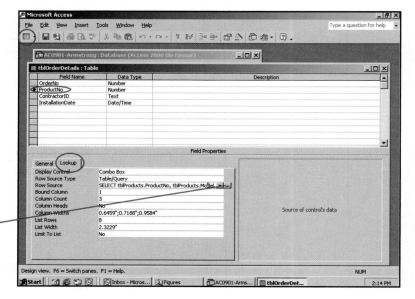

11 Click the **Build** button.

The Query Builder window displays the three fields that you selected for the lookup list. You use this window to make changes to the lookup list.

Click the field selector bar at the top of the **Description** field, and then click and drag this field to the left of **Model**. Click the arrow on the **Sort** line for the **Description** field and choose **Ascending**.

This causes the description field to sort in ascending order so it will be easier to find the products.

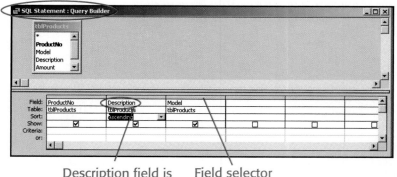

Description field is moved and sorted

Field selector bar

12 Click the **Close** button to close the Query Builder window. Choose **Yes** to save your changes.

The changes are saved and the Query Builder window closes.

In the **Column Widths** property, select the values, type **0.3;1.25;1,** and press ⏎Enter. Select the number in the **List Width** property, type **2.55,** and press ⏎Enter.

The program adds inch marks. The semicolons separate each column width. You need to change the list width property to accommodate the increase in total width of all the columns.

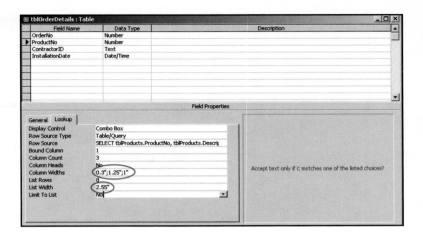

13 Click the **View** button and save your changes. Click anywhere in the **ProductNo** column and click the arrow to see your changes.

Now you can see the description and model information. Be careful not to inadvertently change the product number for the record you are viewing.

14 Click the arrow to close the list. Close the table.

Task 3

ADDING CUSTOM INPUT MASKS

Why would I do this?

You use an input mask to ensure that data entered follows the same format. For example, phone numbers use a (XXX) XXX-XXXX format, where the area code is placed in parentheses and the number is divided into a format of three numbers, a dash, and four numbers. You can create a custom input mask to format fields that follow a specific pattern. The Help system explains the various combinations of letters, spaces, and other characters you can use to create a customized input mask.

In this task, you create two customized input masks, one for the CustomerNo and another for the ContractorID field.

1 Select **tblContractors** and click the *Design* button. Make sure the **ContractorID** field is the active field, and then click the **Input Mask** property.

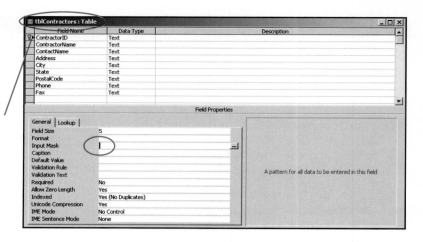

Active Field

2 Press the ꞥF1ꞩ function key. Maximize the window.

The related help screen opens and provides information about how to create an input mask.

Scroll through this Help topic. In particular, read the information about the three sections of an input mask, and the characters you use to define an input mask.

Characters used to define an input mask

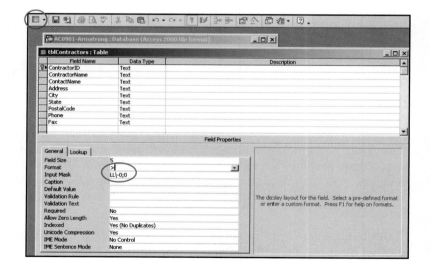

3 Close the Help window. On the **Input Mask** property line type **LL\-0;0**. On the **Format** line type **>**.

This creates an input mask that requires the first two characters to be letters, followed by a dash and a number. The zero in the second section indicates that all literal characters will be stored with the input mask. Nothing is required in the third section of this input mask, which is used to specify the placeholder that displays in the field. An underscore is used as a placeholder by default. The greater than symbol on the format line means that any new contractor ID will be formatted to capital letters.

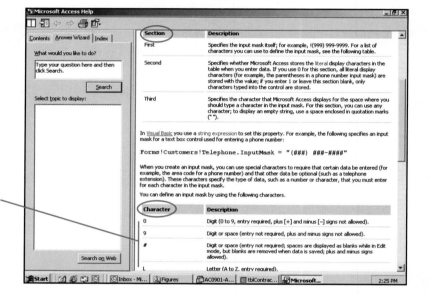

4 Click the **View** button and save the changes when prompted.

Click the **New Record** button. Type **22**.

The input mask prevents the numbers from being accepted and your computer may beep.

Type **mmm**.

This time the first two mm's are recorded, but not the third one, because the input mask requires that the third character be a number.

New Record button

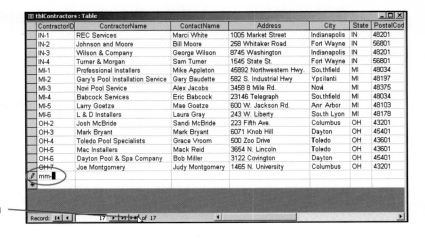

5 Press Esc, and close the table.

The new record is not entered and the Database window is displayed.

Select **tblCustomers** and click the **Design** button.

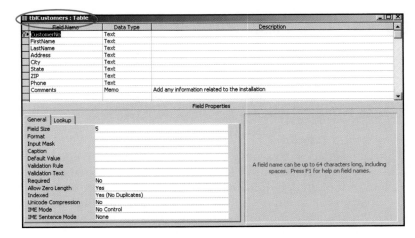

6 Make sure the **CustomerNo** field is the active field and click the **Input Mask** property line. Type **>L\-000;0;**.

This input mask requires a letter, followed by a dash and three numbers. The format symbol for capitalization (>) is included as part of the input mask.

Active Field

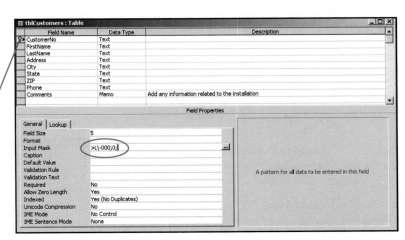

7 Click the **View** button and save the changes. Click the **New Record** button. Test the input mask by typing a number, then letters, to see if it is working correctly.

Whenever you create an input mask, you should test it to make sure it is working as expected.

CustomerNo	FirstName	LastName	Address	City	State	ZIP	P
S-739	Lucinda	Shepherd	47021 Michigan	Southfield	MI	48034	(419) 8
S-740	Sean	Mc Laughlin	2570 Gladstone	Southfield	MI	48034	(419) 8
S-741	James	Krammer	1736 Broadview	Southfield	MI	48034	(419) 8
S-742	Pankaj	Singh	1516 Warwick C	Southfield	MI	48034	(419) 8
S-743	Allen	Taylor	2506 White Stre	Southfield	MI	48034	(419) 8
S-744	Donald	Curtis	3600 Peach Lar	Southfield	MI	48034	(419) 8
S-745	Andrew	Jones	4362 Congress	Southfield	MI	48034	(419) 8
T-241	Willam	Bruno	1608 Hamilton	Toledo	OH	43601	(419) 8
T-242	Carolyn	Price	15351 Climbing	Toledo	OH	43601	(419) 8
T-243	Dan	Howard	6553 Berkridge	Toledo	OH	43601	(419) 8
T-244	Molly	Sigmon	11511 Beach Cl	Toledo	OH	43601	(419) 8
T-245	Barb	Cage	116 Sabre Drive	Toledo	OH	43601	(419) 8
Y-675	David	Landry	405 N Huron St	Ypsilanti	MI	48197	(734) 8
Y-676	Adrian	Zaner	520 Madison Av	Ann Arbor	MI	48103	(734) 8
Y-677	Jon	Peters	208 Tree Lane	Ypsilanti	MI	48197	(734) 8
Y-678	Allan	Bugbee	405 Elm Street	Ann Arbor	MI	48104	(734) 8
Y-679	Daniel	Cook	303 Tulip Street	Ypsilanti	MI	48197	(734) 8
Y-680	Willam	Todd	720 Water St	Ann Arbor	MI	48105	(734) 8
Y-681	Roger	VanHosen	2451 Cherry Hill	Ypsilanti	MI	48197	(734) 8
Y-							

Record: 49 of 49

8 Press Esc. Close the table.

Task 4
USING THE LINKED TABLE MANAGER

Why would I do this?
The data you need to use may be in another database. When that is the case, you can either import the data or link to the other database table. The decision to link or import is often determined by the size of the database and whether or not you have permission to import it. If another group or division controls the data, then linking to it may be your only alternative. This method also ensures that the data you are linked to is up-to-date with the main database files. If you link to a database table and the location of the table is moved on the mainframe, or host server, then you need to repair the link in order to reestablish access to the data. The *Linked Table Manager* is a tool in Access that you use to repair links when a database table has been moved.

In this task, you link to a sales rep table in the Personnel database, enter the sales rep number on several orders, and then learn how to use the Linked Table Manager.

1 Open Windows Explorer and click the **My Documents** folder. Choose **File**, **New**, **Folder** and type your name.

This creates a folder with your name on it in the My Documents folder on your computer's hard drive.

Locate file **AC0902** and copy it to your new folder.

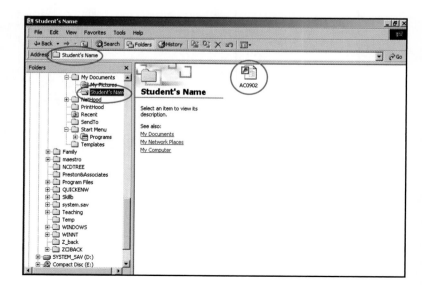

2 Click the **AC0901-Armstrong** button on the taskbar to reactivate Access. Choose **F**ile, **G**et External Data, **L**ink Tables.

The Link dialog box is displayed.

Change the Look-in box to your folder in the My Documents folder. Select file **AC0902**.

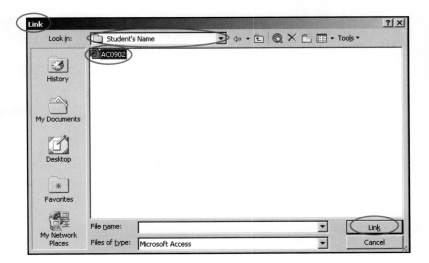

3 Click the **Link** button.

The Link Tables dialog box is displayed and three tables are listed.

Make sure **tblEmployeeNames** is selected.

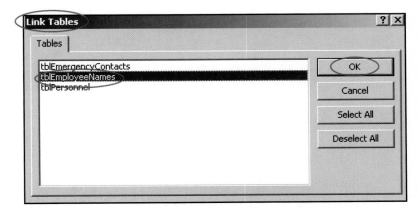

4 Click OK.

The tblEmployeeNames table is listed on the Tables list with an arrow next to it. The arrow indicates that this is a linked table.

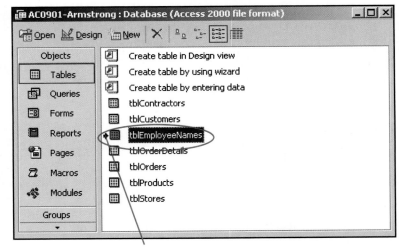

Linked table indicator

5 Select **tblOrders** and click the <u>Design</u> button.

You need to add the employee ID field to this table so you can record who takes each order.

In the next empty Field Name box type **EmployeeID**. Press Tab⇆ and type **N** to select Number as the data type, and then press Tab⇆ again.

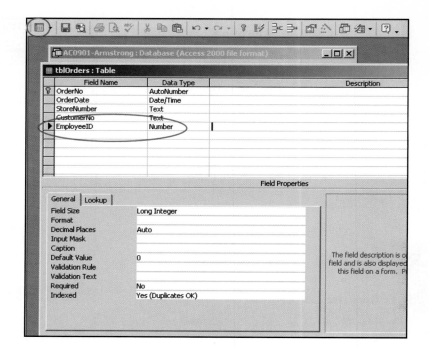

6 Click the View button and save the changes when prompted.

Next you add some employee numbers to the orders, to identify the person who made each sale.

With the tblOrders table open, click in the **EmployeeID** field for the first order and type **12**.

Press ↓ and type **20**. Continue to use the ↓ to move to each subsequent record and type the following EmployeeID numbers in the next eight records:

17, 19, 3, 24, 18, 1, 12, 23

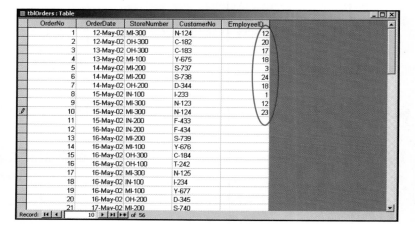

QUICK TIP

When the EmployeeID field is added to tblOrders you can also create a lookup list for the field so it is easier to identify the employees at each store location. This helps ensure that the correct employee ID is entered for each sale.

7 Close the table. Click the **Windows Explorer** button on the Task bar. Open the folder with your name. Move the **AC0902** file to the same location as the AC0901-Armstrong file.

Make sure you move the file and not copy it. Moving the file breaks the link you created, but now both files are in the same location on your computer.

Task bar ⟶

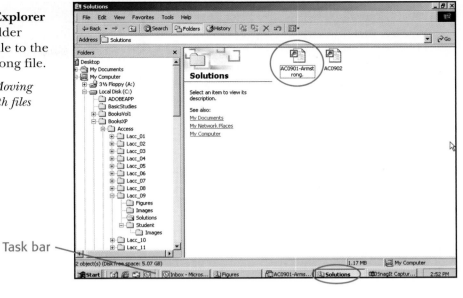

8 Click the **AC0901-Armstrong** button on the taskbar to reactivate the database. Double-click **tblEmployeesNames**.

A message is displayed, warning you that Access could not find the file where this table is located.

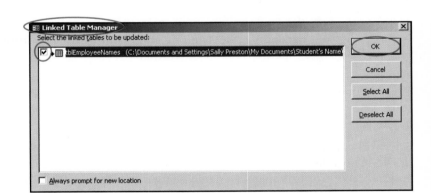

9 Click OK. Choose **Tools**, **Database Utilities**, **Linked Table Manager** from the menu.

The Linked Table Manager dialog box opens. This enables you to recreate the link to the database that has been moved.

Click the checkbox next to **tblEmployeeNames** listed in the dialog box.

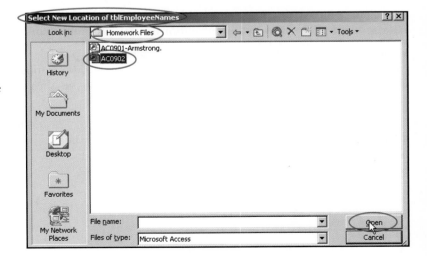

10 Click OK.

The Select New Location dialog box opens.

Change the **Look in** box to the location where you are saving your files and select file **AC0902**.

11 Click **Open**. Click **OK** to acknowledge the message that displays, advising you that the linked tables were refreshed. Close the Linked Table Manager dialog box.

Double-click **tblEmployeesNames** to verify that the link works again.

tblEmployeeNames : Table			
EmployeeID	FirstName	LastName	City
1	Nancy	Davolio	Indianapolis
3	Margaret	Peacock	Southfield
4	Steven	Buchanan	Fort Wayne
5	Bob	Ferrett	Ypsilanti
10	Marybeth	Griffith	Indianapolis
12	Dave	Creal	Novi
15	Patricia	Williams	Ypsilanti
16	Michael	Faulkner	Toledo
17	John	Teacher	Columbus
18	Thomas	Peters	Dayton
19	Frank (Butch)	Johnson	Ypsilanti
20	Larry	Smith	Columbus
21	Phil	Grayson	Dayton
22	Perry	McGuire	Fort Wayne
23	Bret	Carman	Novi
24	Matt	Brinkley	Southfield
25	George	Armey	Toledo
(AutoNumber)			

Record: 1 of 17

IN DEPTH

The Linked Table Manager is particularly efficient if you have linked to multiple tables in one database. The Linked Table Manager displays all the tables that are linked, and you can reestablish the links for all the tables in the same process. Obviously, to use the Linked Table Manager, you have to know the new location for the database to which you have linked.

12 Close the table.

Task 5
CREATING RELATIONSHIPS BETWEEN TABLES

Why would I do this?

In designing your database, understanding and planning the relationships between the tables is perhaps the most critical part.

The strength of a relational database is its ability to divide the data into several tables. When this is done correctly, it minimizes the amount of data you need to store. The relationships you create enable you to draw together information from all the tables.

The most common type of relationship is the ***one-to-many relationship***. In a one-to-many relationship, a record in one table may be related to many records in another table. For example, in a database used to record data about vendors and the products they supply, you enter contact information for your vendors in one table, and list the products they supply in a second table. The vendor is one side of the relationship, while the product table is the many side of the relationship. This allows for the probability that each vendor may supply more than one item.

You can also have a ***one-to-one relationship*** between two tables, where a record in one table relates to a single record in a second table. This is most often used when data is placed in a separate table because access to the information is restricted, such as sensitive employee information.

It is common to have two tables that are related in a ***many-to-many relationship***. You cannot create this type of relationship directly between two tables, but you can do so by introducing a third table and by using two one-to-many relationships. The third table is referred to as a junction table.

In the Armstrong database, the information about each order is divided into two tables, the order information and the order details. The tblOrders table assigns a number to each order, shows the order date, and then lists the store number, customer number, and employee ID, all three of which are primary keys in other tables. Using the primary keys enables you to determine who placed an order, the customer name and address, and the store where the order was taken. The customer, store, and employee information is all stored in separate tables. The relationship between those tables and the tblOrders table allows you to find the related information for each order.

The tblOrderDetails table shows what was ordered and which contractor is supposed to install each item ordered. This information is placed in a separate table so each order can be used for multiple products. Again, this table contains the order number, and uses the primary key fields from the tblProduct and tblContractor tables to identify the product and the contractor information related to each order. When you use a primary key in a second table, where it is not a primary key, it is referred to as the *foreign key*. A foreign key shows how the tables are related.

You formalize the relationship between tables using the Relationships window. This enables you to define the relationship and ensure that a proper relationship is established before you attempt to create forms or reports that use fields from more than one table. This is particularly important in complex databases that use many tables.

In this task, you use the Relationships window to create the relationships between the tables in the Armstrong database.

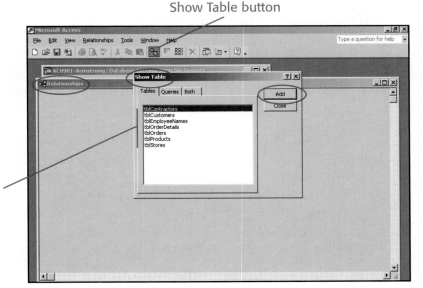

Show Table button

① Click the **Relationships** button. Click the **Show Table** button, if necessary, to display the Show Table dialog box.

The Relationships window opens and the Show Table dialog box displays a list of the tables in the database.

Tables in the database

2 Hold down ⬆Shift and click **tblStores**, the last table listed in the Show Table dialog box.

This selects all the tables so you can add them all at once to the Relationships window.

Click **A**dd.

The tables are displayed in the Relationships window.

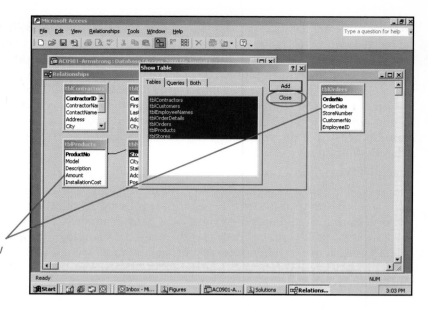

Tables added to
Relationships window

3 Click **C**lose to close the Show Table dialog box.

One relationship line is displayed between the tblProducts and tblOrderDetails tables due to the lookup list that you created in task 2.

Rearrange the field list boxes to match the figure by dragging on the title bar for each box. Expand the lower edge of each box as necessary to display all the fields.

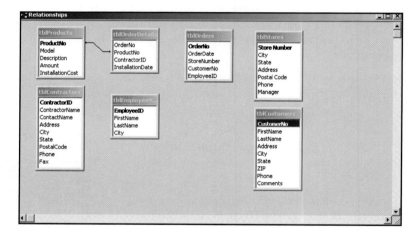

4 Right-click the diagonal portion of the join line between **tblProducts** and **tblOrderDetails** and choose **Edit Relationship** from the shortcut menu.

The Edit Relationships dialog box opens. Notice that this is identified as a One-To-Many relationship.

Click the **Enforce Referential Integrity** checkbox.

Join Line

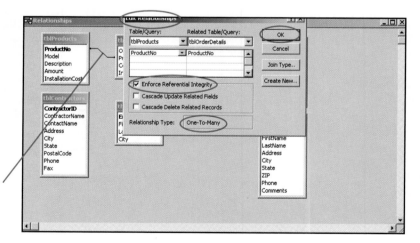

5 Click **OK**.

Referential integrity is enforced. This means that you cannot list a product number in an order if that product does not exist in tblProducts. The 1 indicates the one side of the relationship, and the infinity symbol represents the many side of the relationship.

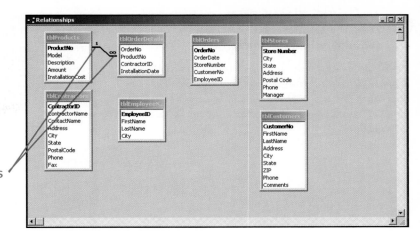

Referential integrity symbols

6 Drag the **OrderNo** field name from the **tblOrders** field list box and place it on top of **OrderNo** in **tblOrderDetails**.

When you release the mouse, the Edit Relationships dialog box is displayed.

Click the **Enforce Referential Integrity** checkbox.

Common field used to join tables

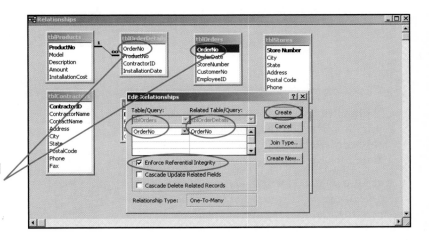

7 Click **Create**.

The second relationship is created.

Repeat this process (Steps 6 and 7) to create relationships between the following tables and fields:

Primary Table and Field	Foreign Table and Field
tblStores: StoreNumber	tblOrders: StoreNumber
tblCustomers: CustomerNo	tblOrders: CustomerNo
tblContractors: ContractorID	tblOrderDetails: ContractorID

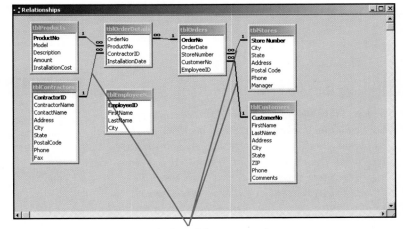

New relationships created

8 Drag the **EmployeeID** field from
tblEmployee to **tblOrders**.

*Notice in the Edit Relationships window that the
Enforce Referential Integrity box is not active. This
is because this is a relationship with a linked table
and you cannot enforce referential integrity in this
relationship.*

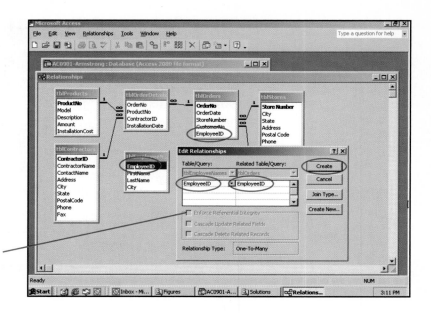

Referential integrity cannot be
enforced with a linked table

9 Click <u>C</u>reate.

Right-click the diagonal portion of the
join line between **tblContractors** and
tblOrdersDetails, and then choose **Edit
Relationship** from the shortcut menu.

*A customer who places an order does not have to use
one of the Armstrong contractors to have their pool, spa,
or sauna installed. This requires a special type of relationship to ensure that you can see all the orders, even
if a contractor is not assigned to the order.*

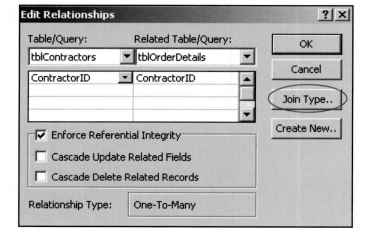

10 Click the <u>J</u>oin Type button.

*The Join Properties dialog box explains the three options
that are available when you create a relationship. The
first option, the default join type, known as an **inner
join**, displays only those records where there is a match
between both tables. In this situation, you want the
third option, which enables you to see all the orders,
even if a contractor has not been assigned to install the
order.*

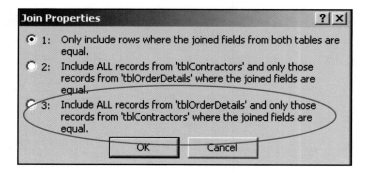

 QUICK TIP

This join type option could have been set at the time
the relationship was first created.

11 Click **3** to select the third option. Click **OK** twice to return to the Relationships window.

The join line displays an arrow pointing to the ContractorID field—the table contributing only the matching records. This type of join is known as an ***outer join***.

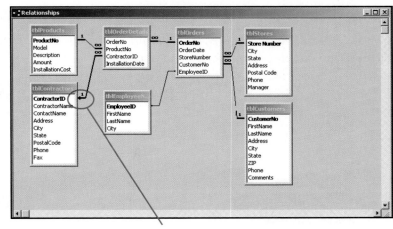

Arrow indicates an outer join

IN DEPTH

For more information about joins, type **join types** in the Ask a Question box. Select the Help topic About joining tables or queries in a query; then read the information under the topic Types of joins. This explains the difference between inner joins, outer joins, and other joins.

12 Choose **File**, **Print Relationships**, from the menu.

The relationships are displayed in a report format.

If necessary, return to the Relationships window and adjust the arrangement of the field list boxes to ensure that each list box is fully displayed.

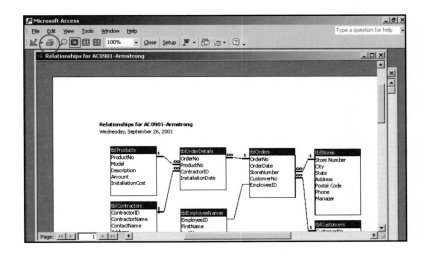

13 Click the **Print** button. Close the Relationships Report and save it when prompted. Accept the default report name.

The relationships report is saved. The Relationships window is again visible on the screen.

Close the Relationships window and save the changes when prompted. Compact the database, and then and close it.

QUICK TIP

You should always compact your database before you close it to reduce the size of the database. Choose Tools, Database Utilities, Compact and Repair Database to execute this command.

The exercises that follow are designed for you to review and use what you have learned in this lesson. You also have the opportunity to practice your skills and then expand on them by applying them to new situations.

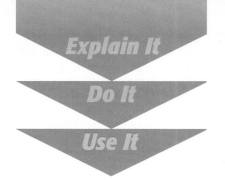

COMPREHENSION

Comprehension exercises are designed to check your memory and understanding of the basic concepts in this lesson. You distinguish between true and false statements, identify new screen elements, and match terms with related statements. If you are uncertain of the correct answer, refer to the task number following each item (for example, T4 refers to Task 4) and review that task until you are confident that you can provide a correct response.

TRUE-FALSE

Circle either T or F.

T F 1. A validation rule prevents incorrect data from being entered into a field. **(T1)**

T F 2. To use an input mask to format a field you must select from one of the predefined options provided by the Access Input Mask Wizard. **(T3)**

T F 3. When you add a lookup list property to a field you can have the program look up a value in a list or in another table. **(T2)**

T F 4. You use the Linked Table Manager to create relationships between tables in a database. **(T4)**

T F 5. In a custom input mask the first section defines the mask. **(T5)**

T F 6. You create many-to-many relationships by using a junction table. **(T5)**

MATCHING QUESTIONS

A. (>1000 And <10000)   **D.** Inner join

B. Outer join   **E.** Query Builder window

C. Semicolon   **F.** Linked Table Manager

Match the following statements to the word or phrase that is the best match from the list. Write the letter of the matching word or phrase in the space provided next to the number.

1. _____ The default join type **(T5)**

2. _____ Used to separate sections of an input mask **(T3)**

3. _____ Example of a validation rule **(T1)**

4. _____ Used to refresh the connection to tables in another database **(T4)**

5. _____ Used to modify a lookup list property **(T2)**

6. _____ Join used to ensure that all records from one of the tables are displayed **(T5)**

IDENTIFYING PARTS OF THE ACCESS SCREEN

Refer to the figure and identify the numbered parts of the screen. Write the letter of the correct label in the space next to the number.

1. _____

2. _____

3. _____

4. _____

5. _____

6. _____

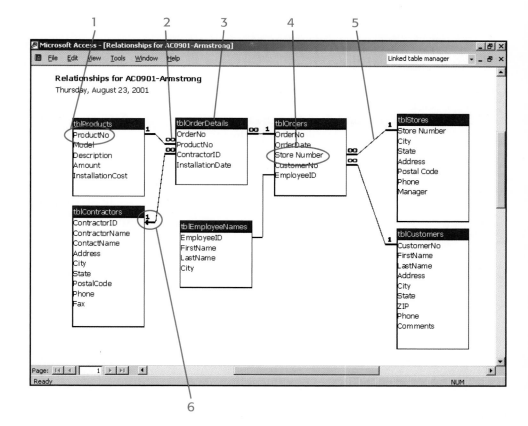

A. Primary key field (T5)

B. Foreign key field (T5)

C. Example of inner join (T5)

D. Example of outer join (T5)

E. Junction table (T5)

F. Many-side of a relationship (T5)

REINFORCEMENT

Reinforcement exercises are designed to reinforce the skills you have learned by applying them to new situations. Detailed instructions are provided along with a figure, where appropriate, to illustrate the result. Complete the reinforcement exercises sequentially. Leave the file open at the end of each exercise for use in the next exercise until you are specifically directed to close it.

In these exercises, you work with the Alumni Travel Club database.

R1—Setting Data Validation Properties

1. Open Access, and click **More files** under the **Open a file** category. Locate **AC0903** in the **Student** folder for this lesson. Transfer the file to the location where you are saving your files using either the **Send To, 3 1/2" Floppy (A)** option, or **Copy** and **Paste** it to a folder on the hard drive. Remove the read-only property, if necessary, and rename the file **AC0903-Travel**. Open the file.

2. Click the **Tables** object button, and open **tblMembers** in Design view.

3. Click in the **MembershipType** field to select it.

4. Click the **Validation Rule** box and type: **G or P or R.** In the **Validation Text** box type: **Must enter G for Golden, P for Premium, or R for Regular.**

5. Save the changes and click **Yes** to test the existing data with the new rules. Click the **View** button. Click **OK**.

6. Test the new validation rule by trying to change the MembershipType code for the first record to **F**. Acknowledge the warning box message and change the MembershipType back to **G**.

7. Close the table.

R2—Creating and Modifying Lookup Field Properties

1. Open **tblTransactions** in Design view.

2. Click the **Data Type** box of the **MemberID** field. Select **Lookup Wizard** from the Data Type list box.

3. Choose the first option button to look up values in a table or a query. Click **Next**.

4. Choose **tblMembers**, click **Next**, and then select **MemberID**, **FirstName,** and **LastName**.

5. In the next dialog box, deselect the **Hide Key Column** checkbox and adjust the column widths.

6. In the next dialog box, make sure **MemberID** is selected as the field that uniquely identifies the row.

7. Click the **Next** button and accept the suggested name for the lookup field. Finish the wizard and click **Yes** when prompted to save the table.

8. Change to Datasheet view and check the **MemberID** field to ensure that the MemberID and first and last names display in the list box.

9. Repeat this process to add a lookup list box to the **TripID** field. Include the **TripID** and **Description** fields from the **tblTrips** table. Test your results.

10. Close the table.

R3—Adding Custom Input Masks

1. Open **tblMembers** in Design view. Select the **MemberID** field.

2. Click the **Input Mask** box and type: **L\-000;;.**

3. Save the table and click the **View** button. Test the input mask by going to a new record and typing **R107**. If you entered the input mask correctly, this MemberID should be accepted. Now try typing a number in the first position and letters in the last three positions. You should not be able to make these entries. Press Esc to back out of the new record.

4. Close the table. Open **tblTrips** in Design view.

5. Create an input mask for the **TripID** field that requires letters in the first two positions, followed by dash (-) and then numbers in the last two positions. Press F1 if you need help with the proper code for this input mask.

6. Save the change and switch to Datasheet view. Test the new input mask to make sure it works as expected.

7. Close the table.

R4—Using the Linked Table Manager

1. Open **Windows Explorer** and click the **My Documents** folder. Choose <u>F</u>ile, <u>N</u>ew, <u>F</u>older and type your name, if necessary.

2. Locate file **AC0904** and copy it to your folder.

3. Return to the AC0903-Travel database. Choose <u>F</u>ile, <u>G</u>et External Data, <u>L</u>ink Tables. Select the **AC0904** file in your folder and click Lin<u>k</u>.

4. Select **tblContacts** and click **OK**.

5. Open **tblTrips** in Design view and add a new **TourGuide** field and select **Text** as the data type.

6. Change to Datasheet view. In the **TourGuide** field enter numbers **101** through **110** to each consecutive record.

7. Return to **Windows Explorer**. Move the **AC0904** database to the same folder location as the AC0903-Travel database.

8. Return to the **AC0903-Travel** database. Try to open **tblContacts**. Acknowledge the warning box that informs you the file cannot be located.

9. Choose <u>T</u>ools, <u>D</u>atabase Utilities, <u>L</u>inked Table <u>M</u>anager.

10. Select **tblContacts** from the Linked Table Manager dialog box and click **OK**. Locate **AC0904** in your folder and click <u>O</u>pen, and then click **OK** to acknowledge the update message. Close the Linked Table Manager dialog box.

11. Test the refreshed link by opening **tblContacts**. Close the table.

R5—Creating Relationships Between Tables

1. Click the **Relationships** button.

2. Click the Show Table button and add the four tables listed to the Relationships window. Close the Show Table dialog box.

3. Right-click the relationship line between **tblMembers** and **tblTransactions**. Choose **Edit Relationship** from the shortcut menu and enforce referential integrity. Save the change.

4. Enforce referential integrity between **tblTrips** and **tblTransactions**. Click the **Join Type** button and select the second option button so that all trips will display regardless of whether anyone has signed up for the trip. Save the change.

5. Click and drag the **GuideID** field in **tblContacts** to **TourGuide** in **tblTrips** to create a one-to-many relationship between these tables.

6. Resize the field list boxes and move them so the relationship lines do not cross other field list boxes.

7. Choose <u>F</u>ile, **Print** <u>R</u>elationships. Print the relationships report and save it with the default name.

8. Close the Relationships window. Close the database.

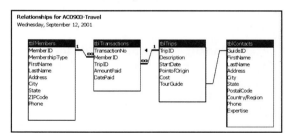

Challenge exercises are designed to test your ability to apply your skills to new situations with less-detailed instructions. These exercises also challenge you to expand your repertoire of skills by using commands that are similar to those you have already learned. The desired outcome is clearly defined, but you have more freedom to choose the steps needed to achieve the required result.

In the following Challenge exercise you work with the Armstrong database. Each exercise can be done independently.

C1—Creating and Modifying Lookup Fields

To gain a better understanding of how to create and modify lookup fields, in this exercise you create and modify several lookup fields for the tblOrderDetails and tblOrders table in the Armstrong database.

Goal: Add lookup fields to relevant fields in the Armstrong database.

1. Locate **AC0901** in the **Student** folder for this lesson. Transfer the file to the location where you are saving your files. Use either the **Send To, 3 1/2"** **Floppy (A)** option, or **Copy** and **Paste** it to a folder on the hard drive. Remove the read-only property, if necessary, and rename the file **AC0901-Challenge1**. Open the file.

2. Click the **Tables** object button. Open **tblOrdersDetails** in Design view.

3. Create a lookup list for the **ContractorID** that displays the **ContractorName**, and **City** fields from **tblContractors**. (Be sure to include the **ContractorID** field, but do not show it.) Accept the default label for this lookup column.

4. View the results to see how the list box displays the name and location. Return to the **Design** view and click the **Lookup** tab. Adjust the **List Width** and **Column Widths** so the contractor names are fully visible.

5. Click the **Build** button next to the **Row Source** box and sort the list alphabetically by **City**. Save your changes and view the results. Close the table.

6. Open **tblOrders** and create a lookup list for the **StoreNumber** field. Include the **StoreNumber** and

City fields from **tblStores**. Do not hide the key column. Accept the default label for this list column.

7. Click the **Lookup** tab and use the **Build** button to sort the list alphabetically by **City**. Test your results.

8. Add a lookup list to the **CustomerNo** field. Include **FirstName**, **LastName**, and **CustomerNo**, from **tblCustomers**. Do not hide the key column. Accept the default label for this list column.

9. Click the **Lookup** tab and use the **Build** button to sort the list alphabetically by **LastName**. Test your results. Close the table.

10. Compact and close the database.

C2—Using Cascade Update in a Relationship

When you set relationships you can choose to use the Cascade Update feature, which ensures that changes made to a primary key field are also made to records in related tables.

Goal: Use Cascade Update in a table.

1. Locate **AC0901** in the **Student** folder for this lesson. Transfer the file to the location where you are saving your files using either the **Send To, 3 1/2" Floppy (A)** option, or **Copy** and **Paste** it to a folder on the hard drive. Remove the read-only property, if necessary, and rename the file **AC0901-Challenge2**. Open the file.

2. Click the **Relationships** button. Click the **Show Table** button and add **tblStores** and **tblOrders** to the Relationship window.

3. Create a relationship based on the **Store Number** field and enforce referential integrity. Click the **Cascade Update Related Fields** checkbox. Click the **Create** button. Close the Relationship window and save your changes.

4. In the **Ask a Question** box type: **cascade update**. Select the topic: **About relationships in an Access database**. Scroll down the Help window and expand the topic: **Cascading updates and deletes**. Read this topic, and then close the Help window.

5. Open **tblOrders** and notice that the store number for orders 2 and 3 is OH-300. Close this table.

6. Open **tblStores**. Change the Store Number for the Columbus store from OH-300 to OH-303. Close this table.

7. Open **tblOrders** and verify that this table reflects the change in store number. Sort the table in descending order by store number. Print the datasheet for this table. Close the table and save the layout changes.

8. Compact and close the database.

	OrderNo	OrderDate	StoreNumber	CustomerNo
▶	49	19-Jul-01	OH-303	C-187
	48	19-Jul-01	OH-303	C-187
	46	19-May-02	OH-303	C-188
	39	19-May-02	OH-303	C-187
	32	18-May-02	OH-303	C-186
	23	17-May-02	OH-303	C-185
	15	16-May-02	OH-303	C-184
	3	13-May-02	OH-303	C-183
	2	12-May-02	OH-303	C-182
	45	19-May-02	OH-200	D-348
	38	19-May-02	OH-200	D-347
	34	18-May-02	OH-200	D-346
	20	16-May-02	OH-200	D-345
	7	14-May-02	OH-200	D-344
	42	19-May-02	OH-100	T-245
	31	18-May-02	OH-100	T-244
	24	17-May-02	OH-100	T-243
	16	16-May-02	OH-100	T-242
	44	19-May-02	MI-300	N-127
	26	17-May-02	MI-300	N-126
	17	16-May-02	MI-300	N-125
	10	15-May-02	MI-300	N-124
	9	15-May-02	MI-300	N-123
	1	12-May-02	MI-300	N-124
	47	19-May-02	MI-200	S-745
	40	19-May-02	MI-200	S-744

C3—Using Cascade Delete in a Relationship

The Cascade Delete feature is another option you can select when you set your relationships. This overrides the enforced referential integrity and enables you to remove a primary record and all related records in other tables. Use this feature very carefully so you do not unintentionally delete records in related tables. In the example used in this exercise, you delete records related to an employee who is no longer with the Armstrong Company. This is only done after the historical records for the employee are archived.

Goal: Use the Cascade Delete feature.

1. Locate **AC0902** in the **Student** folder for this lesson. Transfer the file to the location where you are saving your files. Use either the **Send To, 3 1/2" Floppy (A)** option, or **Copy** and **Paste** it to a folder on the hard drive. Remove the read-only property, if necessary, and rename the file **AC0902-Challenge3**. Open the file.

2. Click the **Relationships** button. Right-click the join line between tblPersonnel and tblEmergencyContacts and select **Edit Relationship** from the shortcut menu.

3. Enforce referential integrity and click the **Cascade Delete Related Records** checkbox. Click **OK**.

4. Right-click the join line between **tblPersonnel** and **tblEmployees** and select **Edit Relationship** from the shortcut menu. Click the **Cascade Delete Related Records** checkbox. Click **OK**. Close the Relationship window and save the changes.

5. Open **tblEmergencyContacts** and notice that there are two emergency records listed for **EmployeeID** 8. Click the list box in the **EmployeeID** field for this employee and note the employee's name. Close this table.

6. Open **tblPersonnel** and delete the record with **EmployeeID** 8. Read the warning box that is displayed before clicking **Yes** to delete the record.

7. Open the other two tables and verify that the related records for EmployeeID 8 have been deleted. Print the datasheet for the tblEmergencyContacts table. Close the table. Compact and close the database.

EmployeeID	Contact	Phone
1	Paul Davolio	(317) 555-0359
3	Michael Peacock	(313) 555-9873
3	Sara Darnell	(248) 555-4566
4	Mary Buchanan	(219) 555-6637
5	Mary Ferrett	(734) 555-1233
6	Anne Crammer	(937) 555-6599
7	Susan Preston	(734) 555-0239
9	Martha Spenser	(317) 555-3214
10	George Abrams	(317) 555-4111
11	Alice Markus	(810) 555-6588
12	Julianna Creal	(810) 555-2899
12	Jamie Creal	(810) 555-2899
13	Margaret Lacy	(313) 555-7211
14	Daniel McDonald	(734) 555-2365
15	Jim Williams	(734) 555-2145
16	Jenny Faulker	(419) 555-7744
17	Carrie Fisher	(614) 555-2444
18	Louise Peters	(937) 555-6558
19	Gretchen Johnson	(734) 555-3535
20	Henrietta Storey	(614) 555-2333
21	Sadie Collins	(937) 555-6745
22	Judy McGuire	(219) 555-5422
22	Jim Stevens	(810) 555-9874
23	Jean Carman	(810) 555-2644
24	Nancy Jordon-Brinkley	(313) 555-8465
25	Grace Armey	(419) 555-8721

C4—Using Linked Table Manager with More than One Table

The Linked Table Manager is especially useful when there is more than one table linked to a database. If the tables to which you have linked are in the same database, then you can reestablish the links to all of the tables at one time.

Goal: Reestablish links to multiple tables.

1. Open Windows Explorer and click the **My Documents** folder. Choose **File, New, Folder** and type your name. Locate file **AC0906** and copy it to the new folder that bears your name.

2. Locate **AC0905** in the **Student** folder for this lesson. Transfer the file to the location where you are saving your files. Use either the **Send To, 3 1/2" Floppy (A)** option, or **Copy** and **Paste** it to a folder on the hard drive. Remove the read-only property, if necessary, and rename the file **AC0905-Challenge4**. Open the file.

3. Link to the two tables in the **AC0906** database that you copied to the folder bearing your name.

4. Create a relationship between the three tables using their respective common fields.

5. Return to **Windows Explorer** and move the **AC0906** file to the same location where you are saving the rest of your files.

6. Return to **Access** and try to open either of the linked tables to verify that the link has been broken.

7. Open the **Linked Table Manager** and select both tables. Locate file **AC0906** and reestablish the link to both tables.

8. Test your results, then compact and close the database.

C5—Creating a Validation Rule for a Range of Values

You can use validation rules to ensure that data entered is within a range of numbers or dates.

Goal: Write a validation rule that allows a range of values.

1. Locate **AC0901** in the **Student** folder for this lesson. Transfer the file to the location where you are saving your files. Use either the **Send To, 3 1/2" Floppy (A)** option, or **Copy** and **Paste** it to a folder on the hard drive. Remove the read-only property, if necessary, and rename the file **AC0901-Challenge5**. Open the file.

2. Open **tblProducts** in **Design** view.

3. Click the **InstallationCost** field. In the **Validation Rule** box enter a validation rule that will ensure amounts less than 100 or greater than 1000 are not entered in this field. Enter an appropriate message in the **Validation Text** box.

4. Save the changes and test the results to ensure that you cannot enter more than $1,000 or less than $100.

5. Save the changes. Compact the database, and then close it.

ON YOUR OWN

This lesson focused on table design elements that help to ensure the accuracy of the data input. It also focused on relationships between tables, which are a key element to good database design. Here are some additional suggestions to help you learn more about controlling database input and table relationships.

- Look on the Internet for information about database design. Specifically look for information about table normalization rules. Write a brief report that explains how the normalization rules apply to database table design in Access. List all sources.

- Review the information in the Access Help program and create an input mask for an inventory number that is a combination of seven to nine letters, numbers, or other characters, and which is preceded by PROD. There must be at least seven characters and can be up to nine characters in the inventory number. You want the data that is entered to be filled from the left. Create a database table and enter data that meets these requirements.

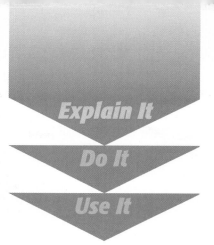

Explain It
Do It
Use It

Lesson 10

Working with Complex Query Designs

Task 1   Creating and Applying Advanced Filters
Task 2   Creating Queries with Multiple Criteria
Task 3   Designing Parameter Queries
Task 4   Creating an Update Query to Change Data
Task 5   Using Summary Queries

INTRODUCTION

A major goal of any database is to retrieve data in a manner that creates useful information. You can do this quickly using filters. Filters enable you to look at records containing data that matches one or more conditions. You can use the Advanced Filter/Sort command to create filters using a Filter Design window that is similar to the Query Design window. When you use filters you can only filter for information based on one table.

Queries provide greater flexibility for retrieving data. Extracting meaningful information depends on good table design and properly identified relationships. You can use multiple tables, and multiple *criteria* for restricting the results of your query. A special type of query, the *parameter query*, allows you to control the data that is being requested each time you run the query. With an *update query* you can change part of the data in a string of information, or change an entire field for specific records. *Summary queries* enable you to summarize information from several tables.

In this lesson, you use each of these techniques to retrieve specific information from the Armstrong Pool, Spa, and Sauna database.

VISUAL SUMMARY

When you complete this lesson, you will have used filters and queries to display the following information:

tblOrderDetails : Table

OrderNo	ProductNo	ContractorID	InstallationDate
13	4	MI-1	6/2/2002
35	1	MI-1	5/30/2002
5	2	MI-1	5/28/2002
22	2	MI-1	5/27/2002
58	10	MI-2	6/3/2002
58	5	MI-2	5/30/2002
36	2	MI-2	5/29/2002
6	4	MI-2	5/28/2002
19	2	MI-2	5/26/2002
17	1	MI-3	5/29/2002
26	2	MI-3	5/29/2002
9	2	MI-3	5/27/2002
40	2	MI-4	5/29/2002
47	4	MI-4	5/29/2002
21	1	MI-4	5/27/2002
43	2	MI-5	5/29/2002
27	4	MI-5	5/27/2002
44	4	MI-6	6/2/2002
*	0		

Task 1: Create a filter to display sales in Michigan

FirstName	LastName	Address	tblCustomers.C	State	ZIP	Description	tblSto
Philip	Morris	1904 Seagate	Dayton	OH	43401	12'x24' oval pool	Dayton
Carole	Yates	15115 Harbour	Columbus	OH	43201	15'x30' oval pool	Colum
Andrew	Nathanson	608 Oak	Columbus	OH	43201	15'x24' oval pool	Colum
Bonnie	Porz	520 Canton Ave	Columbus	OH	43201	15'x30' oval pool	Colum
Loretta	Murphy	555 Printz	Dayton	OH	45401	12'x24' oval pool	Dayton
Brian	Moore	405 Rose Ave	Columbus	OH	43201	15'x24' oval pool	Colum
Mary	Freeman	611 Sun Valley	Columbus	OH	43201	12'x24' oval pool	Colum
*							

Task 2: Create a query using four tables to display pools sold in Columbus and Dayton, Ohio.

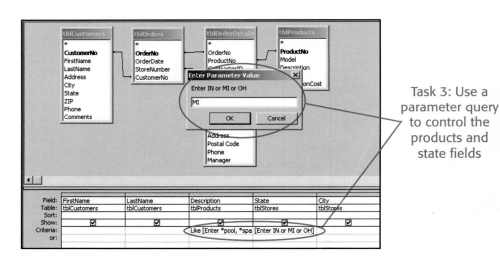

Task 3: Use a parameter query to control the products and state fields

Task 4: Update the area code for customers in Southfield

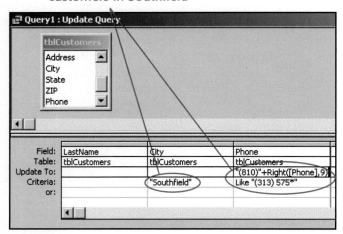

Task 5: Summarize products sold by store

Query1 : Select Query

City	CountOfDescrip	SumOfAmount	AvgOfInstallatio
Columbus	2	$6,500.00	$225.00
Dayton	3	$10,700.00	$233.33
Fort Wayne	3	$12,600.00	$250.00
Indianapolis	1	$2,300.00	$200.00
Novi	2	$8,400.00	$250.00
Southfield	4	$14,900.00	$237.50
Toledo	3	$8,800.00	$216.67
Ypsilanti	3	$8,800.00	$216.67

Task 1

CREATING AND APPLYING ADVANCED FILTERS

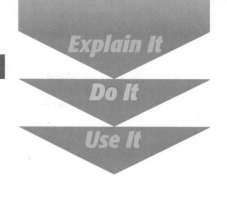

Why would I do this?

When you use advanced filters, you can sort one field in descending order and another field in ascending order. You can also apply limiting criteria to the table. In general, filters are a quick way to answer questions or locate data in a table. If you want to reuse a filter, you can save it as a query.

In this task, you learn how to use advanced filters.

1 Start Microsoft Access. Click **More files** under the **Open a file** category. Locate **AC1001** for this lesson.

Transfer the file to the location where you are saving your files. Remove the read-only property, if necessary, and rename the file **AC1001-Armstrong**. Open the file.

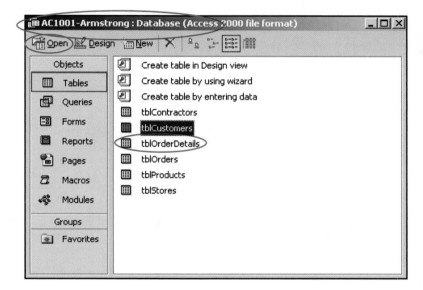

2 Click **tblOrderDetails** to select it and click the **Open** button.

The table Datasheet view is displayed. Notice there are 49 records in this table.

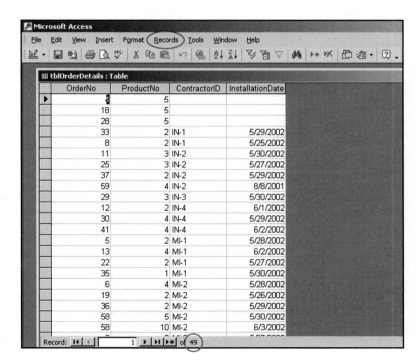

3 Choose <u>R</u>ecords, <u>F</u>ilter, <u>A</u>dvanced
Filter/Sort from the menu.

*A Filter window is displayed for the open table. This
window looks like the Query Design window.*

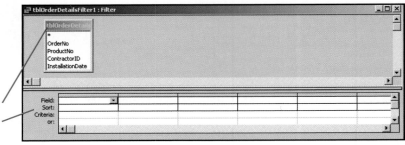

Field List box
Filter grid

4 In the field list box, double-click
ContractorID and **InstallationDate** to
add these fields to the filter grid.

Click in the Sort box under ContractorID,
click the arrow and choose **Ascending**
from the list. Click the Sort box under
InstallationDate, click the arrow and choose
Descending. On the Criteria line under
ContractorID, type **MI***.

*This filters the data to display all installations in
Michigan, and to sort in ascending order by contractor
and descending order by installation date.*

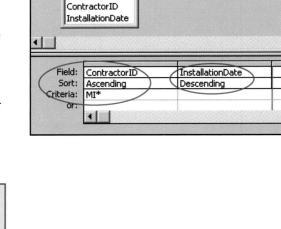

The asterisk is used as a *wildcard* in
Access when you want to match a pattern. It
is a placeholder for unspecified characters.
Where you place the wildcard determines the
unknown characters that you want to include. For
example, *son in a name field would find Thompson,
Danielson, or Peterson; whereas Mc* would find
McDonald, McDaniel, or McPherson. To replace
specific characters you can use a question mark in
a string of characters, such as m?n, or m??d. For
help with using wildcards, type wildcard in the Ask
a Question box.

5 Choose **Filter, Apply Filter/Sort** from the menu.

The table is filtered and displays 18 records for installations in Michigan. The records are sorted by contractor and date. Notice that all the fields still display, even though you only used two of the fields in the filter grid.

Only MI contractors are displayed

OrderNo	ProductNo	ContractorID	InstallationDate
▶ 13	4	MI-1	6/2/2002
35	1	MI-1	5/30/2002
5	2	MI-1	5/28/2002
22	2	MI-1	5/27/2002
58	10	MI-2	6/3/2002
58	5	MI-2	5/30/2002
36	2	MI-2	5/29/2002
6	4	MI-2	5/28/2002
19	2	MI-2	5/26/2002
17	1	MI-3	5/29/2002
26	2	MI-3	5/29/2002
9	2	MI-3	5/27/2002
40	2	MI-4	5/29/2002
47	4	MI-4	5/29/2002
21	1	MI-4	5/27/2002
43	2	MI-5	5/29/2002
27	4	MI-5	5/27/2002
44	4	MI-6	6/2/2002
✳ 0			

▦ tblOrderDetails : Table

Record: I◀ ◀ 1 ▶ ▶I ▶✳ of 18 (Filtered)

6 Choose **Records, Filter, Advanced Filter/Sort**.

The Filter Design window reopens. If you want to save the filter to use again, you can save it when you are in this view.

Choose **File, Save As Query** from the menu.

The Save As Query dialog box opens.

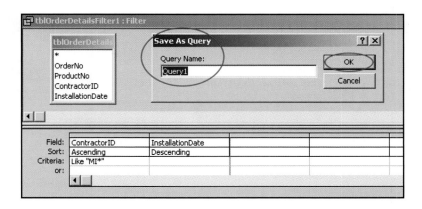

7 Type **qryMIinstalls** as the query name and click **OK**.

Notice that the name of the filter does not change.

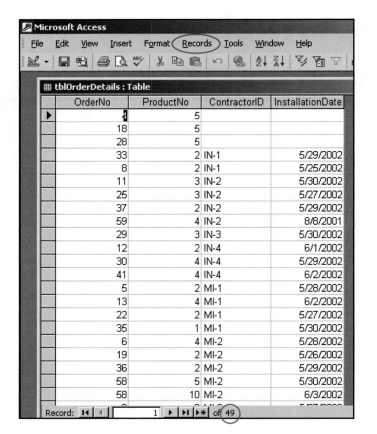

OrderNo	ProductNo	ContractorID	InstallationDate
13	4	MI-1	6/2/2002
35	1	MI-1	5/30/2002
5	2	MI-1	5/28/2002
22	2	MI-1	5/27/2002
58	10	MI-2	6/3/2002
58	5	MI-2	5/30/2002
36	2	MI-2	5/29/2002
6	4	MI-2	5/28/2002
19	2	MI-2	5/26/2002
17	1	MI-3	5/29/2002
26	2	MI-3	5/29/2002
9	2	MI-3	5/27/2002
40	2	MI-4	5/29/2002
47	4	MI-4	5/29/2002
21	1	MI-4	5/27/2002
43	2	MI-5	5/29/2002
27	4	MI-5	5/27/2002
44	4	MI-6	6/2/2002
0			

Record: 1 of 18 (Filtered)

8 Close the Filter Design window. Choose **Records**, **Remove Filter/Sort** from the menu.

The filter is removed and all the records are displayed.

OrderNo	ProductNo	ContractorID	InstallationDate
1	5		
18	5		
28	5		
33	2	IN-1	5/29/2002
8	2	IN-1	5/25/2002
11	3	IN-2	5/30/2002
25	3	IN-2	5/27/2002
37	2	IN-2	5/29/2002
59	4	IN-2	8/8/2001
29	3	IN-3	5/30/2002
12	2	IN-4	6/1/2002
30	4	IN-4	5/29/2002
41	4	IN-4	6/2/2002
5	2	MI-1	5/28/2002
13	4	MI-1	6/2/2002
22	2	MI-1	5/27/2002
35	1	MI-1	5/30/2002
6	4	MI-2	5/28/2002
19	2	MI-2	5/26/2002
36	2	MI-2	5/29/2002
58	5	MI-2	5/30/2002
58	10	MI-2	6/3/2002

Record: 1 of 49

9 Close the table and do not save the changes.

This ensures that the filter you created is not saved as part of the table.

Leave the database open for the next task.

Task 2

CREATING QUERIES WITH MULTIPLE CRITERIA

Why would I do this?

Queries are the main object used for retrieving information from Access tables. Queries are based on one or more tables, and are designed to include only the fields you need. You can sort on more than one field, and restrict the data displayed by using multiple criteria. Because queries are so vital in extracting useful information from a database, it is important that you understand and master techniques for developing useful queries. You have been asked to find the customers who bought pools from the Columbus store because the store manager wants to send them a promotional flyer for pool chemicals.

In this task, you learn how use multiple criteria with several tables.

1 Click the **Queries** object button and double-click the **Create query in Design view** command.

The query design window opens along with the Show Table dialog box.

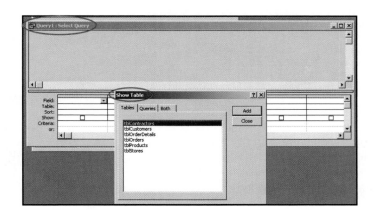

2 Add all the tables to the Query Design window except tblContractors, and then close the Show Table dialog box.

Field list boxes for the selected tables are added to the top of the query window. Join lines between each table display the relationships between the common fields.

IN DEPTH

If you have not created relationships between your tables, Access will create a join between tables in a query provided both fields are the same data type and have the same field name. One of the fields must be designated as a primary key for this join to automatically display. The "one" and "many" symbols do not display because referential integrity has not been enforced.

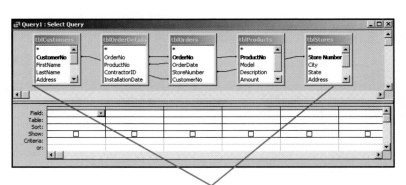

Tables added to the Query Design window

3 Maximize the window. Resize the window panes as shown in the figure. Move the field list boxes so the join lines do not cross, and resize the field list boxes as needed so you can see all the field names.

When working with multiple tables you want to clearly see the relationships between the tables and the field names.

Drag the lower edge of the field list box to see all the fields

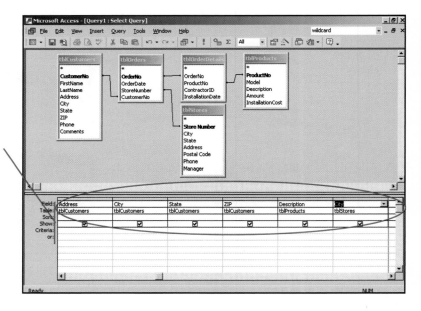

Use dividing bar to change the size of the window panes

Move field list boxes to clearly display relationships

IN DEPTH

In this example, you add the tblOrders and tblOrderDetail tables even though you are not going to use fields from either of them. The join to the customer table from the store and products tables is dependent on the two order tables. Without the order tables the query would result in what is known as a *cross product* or *Cartesian product* join. This is not a good thing! Without a valid join, Access does not know how to join the tables, so it displays every combination of records between the existing tables in the query.

4 Add the name and address information (including the **City**, **State,** and **Zip** fields) from tblCustomers to the query grid. Then add **Description** from tblProducts, and **City** from tblStores. Scroll to the right to verify that the fields are added.

Query grid

QUICK TIP

To add multiple contiguous fields at one time, select the first field name in a list, press and hold ◆Shift, and then click the last field name in the list. Then drag the selected list to the next field box in the query grid. If the fields you want to select are noncontiguous, press Ctrl while you click on the fields you want.

5 On the criteria line under the **Description** field, type ***Pool**. Under the **City** field for the tblStores table, type **Columbus** and press Enter.

The asterisk (*) wildcard is used to look for any product that ends in the word "pool." Notice that the program automatically adds the Like operator to the criteria statement. The second criterion, Columbus, is on the same criteria line as the first, which results in an And criterion. Both conditions have to be met for a record to be included in the results.

CAUTION

Because there are two city fields included in this query, one from the customer table and the other from the store table, it is important that you add the criteria to the correct field to get the desired results.

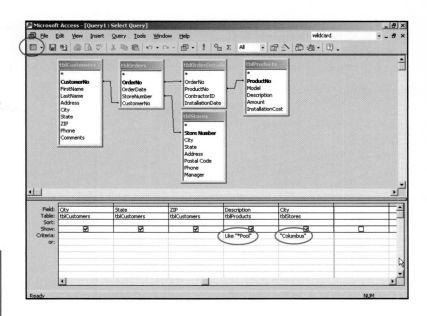

6 Click the View button to see the results.

There are five customers who bought pools from the Columbus store.

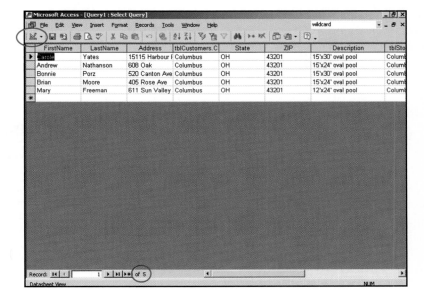

7 Click the **View** button to return to the Design view. On the **or** line under Columbus, type **Dayton** and press ↵Enter.

A second criterion is added to the City field.

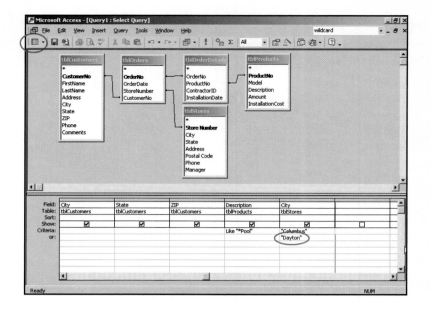

8 Click the **View** button.

This time the results include spas that were sold in Dayton, as well as the pools. To limit the results to just pools, you need to add the first criterion (*pool) to the same row as Dayton.

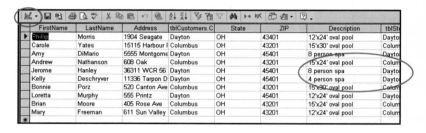

9 Click the **View** button. On the **or** line under the **Description** field box type ***pool** and press ↵Enter.

The Like operator is again added to the wildcard criterion. In this situation, Access is not case sensitive, so it will find records whether you use upper- or lowercase letters in your search criteria.

Click the **View** button again.

This time you see only the pools that were sold by the Dayton and Columbus stores.

Only pools sold in Columbus and Dayton are shown

10 Click the **Save** button. Type **qryColumbusandDaytonPools** as the query name.

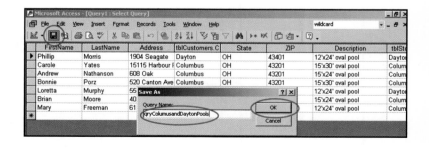

11 Click **OK**. Close the query. Leave the database open.

Task 3
DESIGNING PARAMETER QUERIES

Why would I do this?

A parameter query is designed to give you control over the information that is displayed each time you run the query. This can be based on one or more tables and can use multiple criteria on multiple fields. You can use wildcards in the query design for greater flexibility in the query outcome. In this case, you want to be able to tell what products have been sold by state.

In this task, you modify the query you created in Task 2 and add a parameter to one of the fields.

1 Open the **qryColumbusandDaytonPools** in Design view. Select and delete the criteria on the **Criteria** and **or** lines under the Description and City fields.

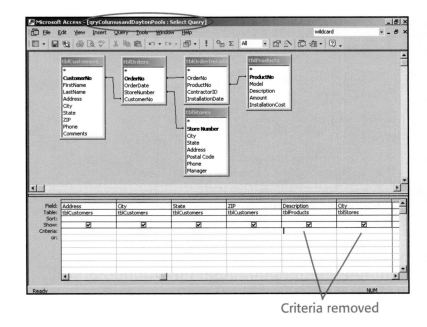

Criteria removed

2 Point to the field selection bar at the top of Address and drag to the right until you have selected all of the customer address fields.

You are not going to use these fields in this query, so you want to remove them from the query grid.

Field selection bar

Downward pointing selection arrow

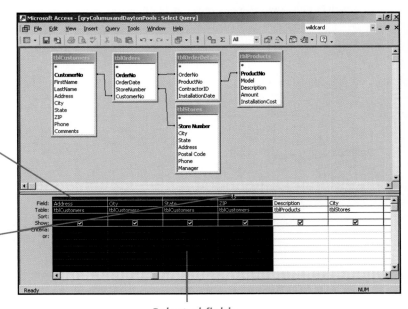

Selected fields

3 Press Del to remove the selected fields from the query grid. Drag the **State** field from tblStores and place it on top of the **City** field.

The fields for the customer's address are removed, and the State field is inserted between the Description and City fields.

State field inserted ————

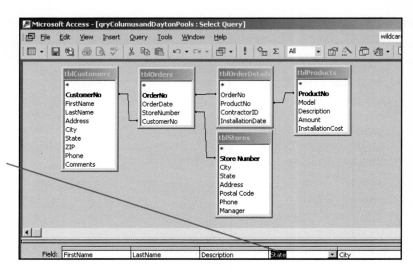

4 On the Criteria line under State type **[Enter IN or MI or OH]**.

This creates a parameter value box that allows you to control the state that displays when you run the query.

On the Criteria line under Description type **Like [Enter *pool, *spa, or *sauna]**. Use the Zoom box if it helps you enter the parameter message.

This creates a parameter value box that allows you to enter a specific type of product, or enter a wildcard to display all products. (Note: The Description column has been widened so you can see the entire parameter.)

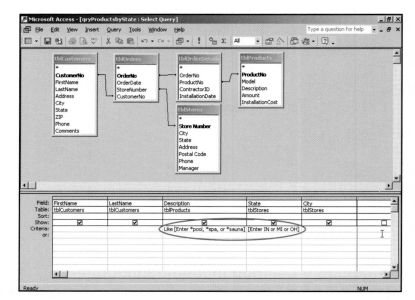

CAUTION

It is important that you use square brackets when you write a parameter criterion, not parentheses or curly braces.

QUICK TIP

You can open the Zoom box to see what you are typing in a query by right-clicking on the field or criteria line that is being used and choosing **Zoom** from the shortcut menu. You can also press ◆Shift + F2 to activate the Zoom box.

IN DEPTH

In this case, the wildcard (*) is also necessary because the words pool, spa, or sauna are the last part of the description field.

5 Click the View button. In the first parameter value box, type ***spa**.

Notice that even though you wrote the Description field parameter second, it displays first. The query fields are read left to right, which results in the Description field parameter displaying first.

Parameter Value box

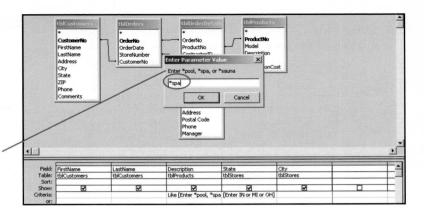

6 Click **OK**. In the second parameter value box type **MI**.

This limits the query results to only those spas sold in Michigan.

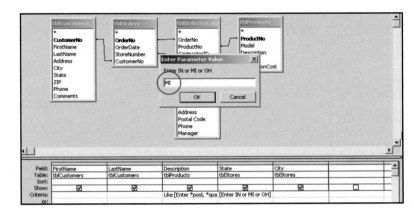

7 Click **OK**.

The query results are displayed.

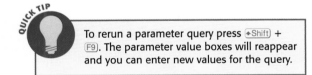

To rerun a parameter query press ⊛Shift + F9. The parameter value boxes will reappear and you can enter new values for the query.

FirstName	LastName	Description	State	City
David	Landry	4 person spa	MI	Ypsilanti
Nancy	Holmes	8 person spa	MI	Southfield
Lucinda	Shepherd	8 person spa	MI	Southfield
Allan	Bugbee	8 person spa	MI	Ypsilanti
Pankaj	Singh	4 person spa	MI	Southfield
Carl	Clark	8 person spa	MI	Novi
Andrew	Jones	8 person spa	MI	Southfield
Michael	Crock	8 person spa	MI	Novi
Adrian	Zaner	4 person spa	MI	Ypsilanti

8 Choose File, Save As, and save the new query with the name **qryProductsbyState**.

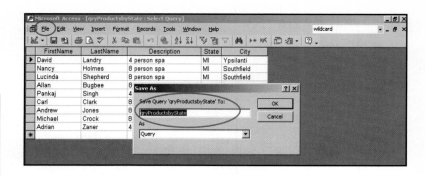

9 Close the query. Leave the database open.

Task 4

CREATING AN UPDATE QUERY TO CHANGE DATA

Why would I do this?
Action queries enable you to create an archive of old records that need to be preserved, but are no longer active. The *update query* is one of the action queries, and it can also be used to update a group of records in a database. If data such as street name, area code, or city name changes, you can use an update query to locate and change that data for any of the records in your database. If you are only changing part of a field, such as the area code in a telephone number, then you need to write the query so it changes only that specific data, while leaving the rest of the data unchanged.

In this task, you change the area code from 313 to 810 for customers in the 575 exchange in Southfield.

1 Make sure the **Queries** object button is selected, and then double-click the **Create query in Design view** command. Add **tblCustomers** to the Query Design window and close the Show Table dialog box.

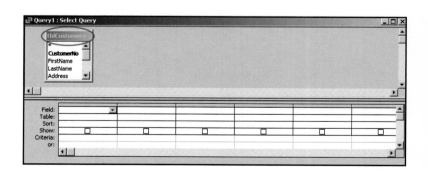

2 Add the **LastName**, **City**, and **Phone** fields to the query grid. Type **Southfield** on the Criteria line under the City field. On the Criteria line under the Phone field, type **"(313) 575*"**.

First you will select the fields and run a select query to determine how many records the change will affect. Because you are using parentheses in the criterion for the phone field, you need to type the quote marks around the string of data that you want to retrieve.

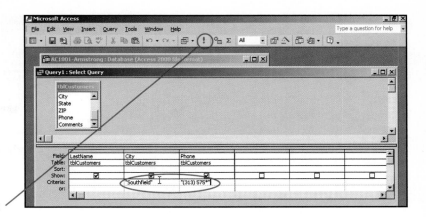

Run button

IN DEPTH

The expression to search for the phone number could have been written as Left([Phone],9) = "(313) 575". This would search for nine matching characters in the Phone field starting from the left.

3 Click the **Run** button.

Four records are displayed. When you run an update query, you do not see the results, or **dynaset***, like you do with a select query; therefore, it is a good idea to make a copy of the records that are to be changed.*

Print the results of this query showing the records that will be affected.

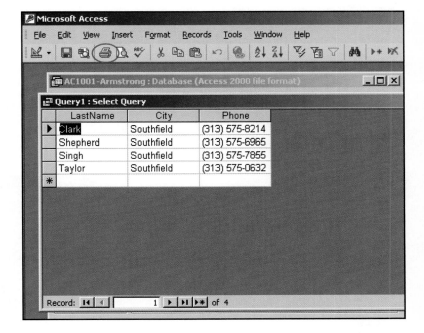

4 Click the **View** button to return to the Design view. Click the list arrow to the right of the **Query Type** button and select **Update Query**.

The query grid changes to include an Update To row. On this row you indicate the change you want to make to the data. The icon on the Query Type button changes to the Update Query icon.

Under the **Phone** field on the **Update To** row type **"(810)"+Right([Phone],9)**.

This expression creates a new phone number that begins with the new area code and then attaches the nine characters from the right end of the phone number. (Note: The Phone field column was widened, so you can see the full expression.)

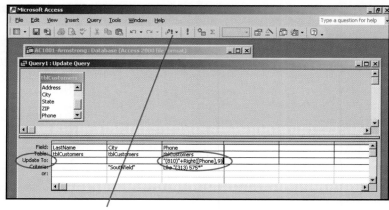

Query Type button

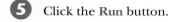

The Left and Right expression use character counts based on the actual characters stored in the table. If the table was designed to use an input mask, the character count may be different. In the example in this lesson, the input mask was set to store the mask as characters with the data; therefore the character count includes the parentheses, a space, and a dash for a total of 14 characters. If the input mask did not store the mask as characters, then the count would be the actual number of characters that were typed.

5 Click the **Run** button.

A message box informs you that you are about to update four rows. This agrees with the number of records that were identified when you ran the select query. If the number did not match, you would click No, and then determine why there is a discrepancy.

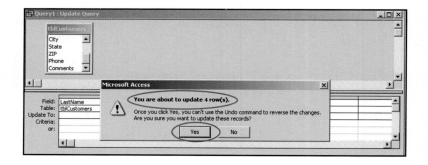

An update query is not actually done until you click the Run button. If you click the View button, the results of the criteria match would be displayed, but the records would not be changed. When you click the Run button, the records are changed, but you do not see the results in a dynaset, like you do with a select query.

6 Click **Yes**.

You do not see a dynaset to show that the change was effective. If you click the View button, you will not find any matching records because there are no longer any phone numbers that match the criteria in this query.

Click the **Save** button and name this query **qryUpdateAreaCode**. Close the query.

The query is displayed on the Queries Object page with the Update icon.

Update query icon —

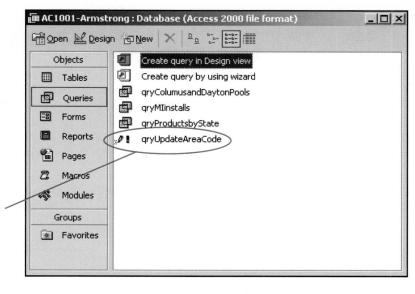

7 Click the **Tables** object button and open **tblCustomers**. Sort the table in descending order by phone. Verify that the four records identified in Step 3 have been changed.

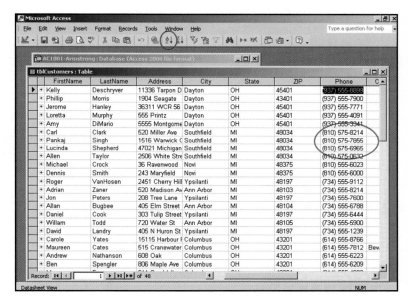

8 Close the table, but do not save the changes. Leave the database open.

IN DEPTH

A third expression is similar to the Right and Left. The Mid expression selects characters from the inside string of characters. To select the exchange number 575 from a phone number in this lesson you would use the expression Mid([Phone],7,3). It would start at the seventh character and select the next three characters.

Task 5
USING SUMMARY QUERIES

Why would I do this?

Queries also enable you to summarize data. The summary functions in Access are similar to the summary functions used in Microsoft Excel. You can summarize fields from different tables to create useful information. The summary functions include the standard sum, average, minimum, maximum, standard deviation, and variance functions. You can also create "*where*" statements to specify a condition that must be met.

In this task, you create a summary query that uses fields from several tables to determine the average installation costs by product type and location.

1 Make sure you have the **Queries** object button selected and then double-click **Create query in Design View**. Add **tblStores** **tblOrders**, **tblOrderDetails**, and **tblProducts**, to the query design window.

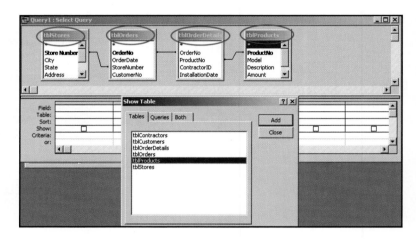

2 Close the **Show Table** dialog box. Rearrange the field list boxes, if necessary, so the join lines do not cross.

Add the following fields to the query grid: **City** from tblStores, **Description**, **Amount**, and **InstallationCost** from tblProducts.

This is another example where you have to include the two order tables in the query even though you are not using fields from these tables. Without them there would not be a join line connecting the stores and products tables.

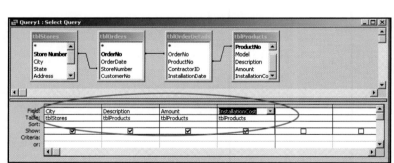

3 Click the **Totals** button.

The Total row is displayed on the query grid and the default option of Group By shows for each field.

Totals button
Total row

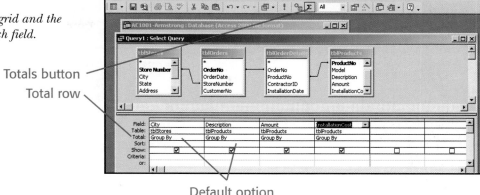

Default option

4 Click the list arrow on the Total row under **Description** and select **Count**.

You want to count the number of each product sold.

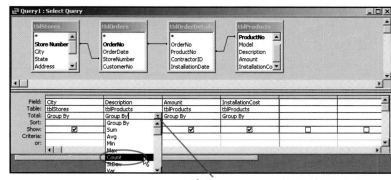

List arrow

5 Click the list arrow on the Total row under **Amount** and select **Sum**. On the Total row for the **InstallationCost** field select **Avg**.

You have identified how each field is going to be summarized in this query.

Sort in **ascending** order on the **Description** field.

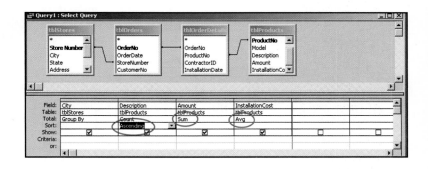

IN DEPTH

When you create a summary query it is important that you determine how you will use each field in the query. In particular, you want to avoid having extraneous fields that result in groups of one. If the field does not create a meaningful group, is not going to be summarized (average, sum, minimum, etc.), or is not used as a where condition, it should not be included in the query.

6 Click the **Run** button.

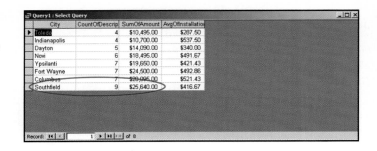

The dynaset shows that the Southfield store has the most installations.

7 Click the **View** button to return to Design view. Add the **Description** field from **tblProducts** to the query.

You can use fields in a summary query more than once. This time you will limit the results by product description.

Click the list arrow on the Total row under the second **Description** and select **Where**. Type ***spa** as the criterion. Press ⏎Enter.

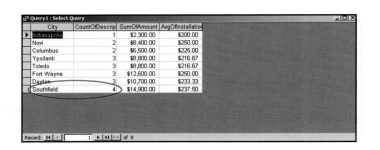

The results will be limited to only the spas that have been sold by each location. Notice that the Like operator and quote marks are added to the criterion.

8 Click the **Run** button.

The Southfield store sold four spas for an average installation cost of $237.50

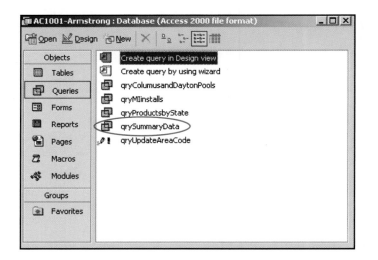

9 Save the query with the name **qrySummaryData**. Close the query.

10 Compact and close the database.

The exercises that follow are designed for you to review and use what you have learned in this lesson. You also have the opportunity to practice your skills and then expand on them by applying them to new situations.

COMPREHENSION

Comprehension exercises are designed to check your memory and understanding of the basic concepts in this lesson. You distinguish between true and false statements, identify new screen elements, and match terms with related statements. If you are uncertain of the correct answer, refer to the task number following each item (for example, T4 refers to Task 4) and review that task until you are confident that you can provide a correct response.

TRUE-FALSE

Circle either T or F.

T   F   1. Using advanced filter procedures, you can filter data based on more than one table. **(T1)**

T   F   2. The expression **"(810)"+Right([Phone],9)** creates a new phone number that begins with (810) and then attaches the nine characters from the right end of the Phone field. **(T4)**

T   F   3. Using a summary query, you can determine the standard deviation for a field. **(T5)**

T   F   4. The order in which multiple Parameter Value boxes display cannot be controlled except by changing the order of the fields in the query. **(T3)**

T   F   5. When you design a query you only include tables that contain the fields you need for your query. **(T2)**

T   F   6. If you want to save a filter, it can be saved as a query. **(T1)**

MATCHING QUESTIONS

A. Square brackets   **D.** Run button

B. Mid([Phone],7,3)   **E.** Where

C. Totals button   **F.** Asterisk

Match the following statements to the word or phrase that is the best match from the list. Write the letter of the matching word or phrase in the space provided next to the number.

1. ____ Expression to select three characters within a string of characters **(T4)**

2. ____ Used to summarize data **(T5)**

3. ____ Used to create a parameter value statement **(T3)**

4. ____ Used to locate unspecified data **(T2)**

5. ____ Used to activate an update query **(T4)**

6. ____ Used to restrict data in a summary query **(T5)**

IDENTIFYING PARTS OF THE ACCESS SCREEN

Refer to the figure and identify the numbered parts of the screen. Write the letter of the correct label in the space next to the number.

1. _____

2. _____

3. _____

4. _____

5. _____

6. _____

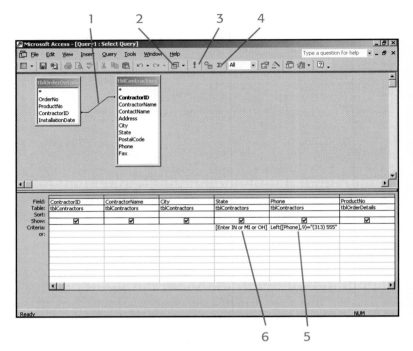

A. Totals button (T5)

B. Join (T1)

C. Run button (T2)

D. Parameter criteria (T3)

E. Query Type button (T4)

F. Expression used to isolate part of a field (T5)

Reinforcement exercises are designed to reinforce the skills you have learned by applying them to new situations. Detailed instructions are provided along with a figure, where appropriate, to illustrate the result. Complete the reinforcement exercises sequentially. Leave the file open at the end of each exercise for use in the next exercise until you are specifically directed to close it.

In these exercises, you work with a database that is designed to track funds raised for a charitable organization. The database consists of three tables: one that contains member data, another for pledges, and a third that tracks payments.

R1—Creating and Applying Advanced Filters

1. Open Access and click **More files** under the **Open a file** category. Locate **AC1002** in the **Student** folder for this lesson. Transfer the file to the location where you are saving your files. Remove the read-only property, if necessary, and rename the file **AC1002-Charity**. Open the file.

2. Open **tblMembers**. Add your name and information as a new member. Use **115-6** for the MemberID. Close the table.

3. Open **tblPledges**. This table uses the AutoNumber data type for the PledgeNum field. Click the **New Record** button and enter a pledge of **$1,000** for member **1156** dated **6/06/01**. Open **tblPayments** and record a payment of **$100** dated **06/07/01** for your pledge number.

4. Return to **tblPledges**. Choose **Records**, **Filter**, **Advanced Filter/Sort** from the menu.

5. Add **PledgeAmount** and **PledgeDate** to the filter grid. Sort in descending order by **PledgeAmount** and ascending order by **PledgeDate**.

6. On the **Criteria** row, under **PledgeDate,** type **<=06/30/01** to view only those pledges made before July 1, 2001.

7. Choose **Filter**, **Apply Filter/Sort** from the menu. Print the results.

8. Choose **Records**, **Filter**, **Advanced Filter/Sort** to return to the Filter Design window and choose **File**, **Save As Query**. Name the query for this filter **qryFilter6/30/01**.

9. Close the Filter Design window. Close the table and do not save the changes.

qryFilter6/30/01 : Select Query			
PledgeNum	MemberID	PledgeAmount	PledgeDate
2 1012		$5,000.00	01-Apr-01
4 1034		$2,500.00	30-Apr-01
10 1101		$2,250.00	08-Jun-01
3 1023		$2,000.00	13-Apr-01
9 1045		$2,000.00	31-May-01
7 1056		$1,700.00	01-Jun-01
8 1067		$1,200.00	03-Jun-01
1 1003		$1,000.00	10-May-01
15 1156		$1,000.00	06-Jun-01
(AutoNumber)		$0.00	

R2—Creating Queries with Multiple Criteria

1. Click the **Queries** object button and double-click **Create query in Design view.**

2. Add all three tables to the Query Design window.

3. Add the member's first and last name fields to the query grid, then add **PaymentDate** and **PaymentAmount**.

4. Sort in ascending order by **PaymentDate**.

5. On the Criteria row under **PaymentDate** type **Between 3/30/01 and 6/30/01**. On the Criteria row under **PaymentAmount** type **>=100**.

6. Run the query and print the results.

7. Save the query as **qry2ndQtrPayments**. Close the query.

qry2ndQtrPayments : Select Query			
FirstName	LastName	PaymentDate	PaymentAmour
Samantha	Miller	15-Apr-01	$100.00
Samantha	Miller	18-May-01	$100.00
Angela	Peters	04-Jun-01	$500.00
David	Kirch	05-Jun-01	$500.00
Martha	Waters	06-Jun-01	$200.00
Preston	Sally	07-Jun-01	$100.00
Peter	Smith	14-Jun-01	$100.00
Cheryl	McMasters	17-Jun-01	$100.00

R3—Designing Parameter Queries

1. Create a new query in Design view. Add all three tables to the Query Design window.

2. Add **Salutation**, **FirstName**, **LastName**, **PledgeAmount**, **PaymentAmount**, and **PaymentDate** to the query grid.

3. On the Criteria row under **LastName** type [Enter member's last name]. On the criteria row under **PaymentDate** type Between [Enter beginning search date] And [Enter ending search date].

4. Run the query. Type Miller in the first Parameter Value box, 01/01/01 in the second box, and 06/30/01 in the last box. Print the results.

5. Save the query as **qryFindMemberPayments**. Close the query.

Salutation	FirstName	LastName	PledgeAmount	PaymentAmour	PaymentDat
Dr.	Samantha	Miller	$2,000.00	$100.00	18-May-
Dr.	Samantha	Miller	$2,000.00	$50.00	04-Apr-
Dr.	Samantha	Miller	$2,000.00	$100.00	15-Apr-
Dr.	Samantha	Miller	$2,000.00	$75.00	30-Apr-
Dr.	Samantha	Miller	$2,000.00	$50.00	15-May-

R4—Creating an Update Query to Change Data

1. Create a new query in Design view based on **tblMembers**.

2. Add the **LastName**, **City,** and **Telephone** fields.

3. Type **Ypsilanti** on the Criteria line under **City**. Type "734556*" on the Criteria line under **Telephone**. The input mask characters are not stored as part of the phone number for this field.

4. Run the query and note the two customer names whose phone numbers will be affected by the change.

5. Return to the Design view and change the query type to Update Query. On the **Update To** line under the Telephone field, type "733"+ Right ([Telephone], 7).

6. Run the query. Confirm that two records will be updated. Save the query as **qryPhoneUpdate**. Close the query. (Note: If you view the design of the update query after it has been saved, you will see that the LastName field has been dropped because it is not used, and the field that is changed displays in the first field box. This is a change the Access program made.)

7. Open **tblMembers** and confirm that the two records have been updated. Print the results, and then close the table.

R5—Using Summary Queries

1. Create a new query in Design view. Include all three tables.

2. Add the member's **first and last name**, the **PledgeAmount**, and the **PaymentAmount** fields.

3. Click the Totals button. On the Total row select **Sum** for the **PaymentAmount** field.

4. Run the query. Notice that two members' names appear more than once, because they have made more than one pledge. Save the query as **qrySummaryPledge&Payments**.

5. Print the results. Close the query.

6. Compact and close the database.

FirstName	LastName	PledgeAmount	SumOfPayment
Angela	Peters	$1,700.00	$600.00
Cheryl	McMasters	$2,000.00	$100.00
David	Kirch	$1,000.00	$500.00
David	Kirch	$5,000.00	$635.00
James	Stewart	$1,000.00	$50.00
Martha	Waters	$2,500.00	$200.00
Peter	Smith	$2,250.00	$100.00
Phyllis	Gracia	$3,000.00	$500.00
Roberta	Schmanski	$1,000.00	$0.00
Roberta	Schmanski	$1,500.00	$250.00
Sally	Preston	$1,000.00	$100.00
Samantha	Miller	$2,000.00	$375.00

More than one pledge made by these members

CHALLENGE

Challenge exercises are designed to test your ability to apply your skills to new situations with less-detailed instructions. These exercises also challenge you to expand your repertoire of skills by using commands that are similar to those you have already learned. The desired outcome is clearly defined, but you have more freedom to choose the steps needed to achieve the required result.

The following exercises use different files to illustrate procedures you should find helpful.

C1—Creating a Summary Query that Uses the Sums in a Calculated Field

When you use the summary function in Access, the dynaset produces a new field heading for the data that has been summarized. You can use this new field name in a calculation in a summary query. You might want to do this to calculate the percentage one number is of another. This exercise uses the charity database used in the reinforcement exercises.

Goal: Create a summary query that calculates what percent of the pledge amount contributors have paid.

1. Locate **AC1002** in the **Student** folder for this lesson. Transfer the file to the location where you are saving your files. Remove the read-only property, if necessary, and rename the file **AC1002-Challenge1**. Open the file.

2. Create a new query that includes all three tables. Add the **FirstName, LastName**, **PledgeAmount,** and **PaymentAmount** fields.

3. Add the **Total** row to the query and sum the **PaymentAmount** field. Run the query to see the dynaset.

4. Click in the next empty field box and enter the following calculation: **Percentage Paid: 1-([PledgeAmount]-[SumofPaymentAmount])/ [PledgeAmount]**. Press ↵Enter. (You may want to use the Zoom box to help you see what you are typing.) Change the **Total** row for the calculated field to **Expression**.

5. Right-click on the new calculated field and choose **P**roperties from the shortcut menu. Set the **Format** property to **Percent.**

6. View the dynaset. Save the query as **qryPercentofPledgePaid**. Print the results.

7. Close the query. Close the database.

FirstName	LastName	PledgeAmount	SumOfPayment	Percentage Pai
Angela	Peters	$1,700.00	$600.00	35.29%
Cheryl	McMasters	$2,000.00	$100.00	5.00%
David	Kirch	$1,000.00	$500.00	50.00%
David	Kirch	$5,000.00	$635.00	12.70%
James	Stewart	$1,000.00	$50.00	5.00%
Martha	Waters	$2,500.00	$200.00	8.00%
Peter	Smith	$2,250.00	$100.00	4.44%
Phyllis	Gracia	$3,000.00	$500.00	16.67%
Roberta	Schmanski	$1,000.00	$0.00	0.00%
Roberta	Schmanski	$1,500.00	$250.00	16.67%
Samantha	Miller	$2,000.00	$375.00	18.75%

qryPercentofPledgePaid : Select Query

C2—Using Expressions in Update Queries

In this lesson you learned to use the Right expression in an update query. The Mid and Left expressions are also useful when you need to replace part of a field using an update query. This exercise uses the charity database used in the reinforcement exercises.

Goal: Use the Mid expression in an update query to change data.

1. Locate **AC1002** in the **Student** folder for this lesson. Transfer the file to the location where you are saving your files. Remove the read-only property, if necessary, and rename the file **AC1002-Challenge2**. Open the file.

2. Create a new query based on **tblMembers**. Add **LastName** and **Telephone** to the query grid.

3. Write a criterion to search for the 556 exchange in the middle of the telephone number: **Mid([Telephone],4,3)="556"**. This expression starts at the fourth character and looks for the next three characters to match 556.

4. Run the query to locate the records that match this criterion.

5. Change the query type to an **U**pdate Query. On the Update To line write a Right expression to change the exchange to 665. (Hint: The area code for both numbers is the same.)

6. Save the query as **qryUpdate665**. Run the query. View the table to see the results. Print the table.

7. Close the database.

	MemberID	Salutation	LastName	FirstName	Address	City	State	Zip	Telephone
▶ +	100-3	Ms.	Schmanski	Roberta	349 Huron River Drive	Dexter	MI	48130-	(734) 555-1247
+	101-2	Mr.	Kirch	David	1221 Memorial	Plymouth	MI	48170-	(734) 555-2189
+	102-3	Dr.	Miller	Samantha	2131 E. Jefferson	Ypsilanti	MI	48197-	(734) 555-2302
+	103-4	Ms.	Waters	Martha	1367 Lakeshore Blvd.	Pinckney	MI	48169-	(734) 555-3514
+	104-5	Ms.	McMasters	Cheryl	2324 River St.	Milan	MI	48160-	(734) 555-2652
+	105-6	Ms.	Peters	Angela	526 Pear St	Ann Arbor	MI	48108-	(734) 555-9672
+	106-7	Mr.	Brown	Michael	735 N. 7th St	Chelsea	MI	48118-	(734) 555-2365
+	107-8	Mr.	Austin	Jack	2346 E. Maple	Saline	MI	48176-	(734) 555-4125
+	108-9	Dr.	Markley	Susan	1234 Easy Street	Dexter	MI	48130-	(734) 555-6112
+	109-0	Mr.	Lyors	Mark	874 Jackson	Ypsilanti	MI	48197-	(734) 665-2456
+	110-1	Mr.	Smith	Peter	424 Mark Hannah	Pinckney	MI	48176-	(734) 555-2587
+	111-2	Mr.	Stewart	James	457 E. Liberty St.	Dexter	MI	48178-	(734) 555-1235
+	112-3	Ms.	Allen	Grace	56 Park Lane	South Lyon	MI	48176-	(248) 555-2431
+	113-4	Mr.	Mathews	Darrell	3581 Torrance Plance	Ypsilanti	MI	48197-	(734) 665-2431
+	114-5	Ms.	Gracia	Phyllis	321 N. Madison	Manchester	MI	48169-	(734) 555-1229
*							MI		

C3—Using an Update Query to Increase Price

Update queries are useful when you want to calculate a new value. This might result in a price increase, or a penalty for late payments based on the original value of an order. When you use this type of query it is important not to run it multiple times. Every time you run the query, or open the query, the records will be updated and the price, or other value will be altered. This exercise uses the Armstrong database.

Goal: Use a calculation in an update query.

1. Locate **AC1001** in the **Student** folder for this lesson. Transfer the file to the location where you are saving your files. Remove the read-only property, if necessary, and rename the file **AC1001-Challenge3**. Open the file.

2. Create a new query that includes the Products table. Add the **Model**, **Description,** and **Amount** fields. There has been a 20% price increase for the Splash-a-lot oval pools. You are going to pass this cost on to the consumer and need to change your Product table to reflect the price increase.

3. Write the appropriate criteria to locate Splash-a-lot model oval pools. Note the number of records affected by the price increase.

4. In a new field box write an expression to calculate the new price that is 20% higher than the previous price. Change the **Format** property for the new field to **Currency**.

5. Run the query and verify that the new values make sense. Modify the calculation, if necessary, until you have determined a new price that is 20% higher than the current price.

6. Change the query type to an **Update Query**. Write the calculation on the **Update To** line. Run the query. Save the query as **qryUpdatePrice**. (Do not run the query multiple times or you will increase the price by 20% every time you run it.)

7. Open the **Products** table and verify that the price has increased by 20% for the Splash-a-lot oval pools. Print the table. Close the database.

	ProductNo	Model	Description	Amount	InstallationCost
▶ +	1	Splash-a-lot	12'x24' oval pool	$2,034.00	$500.00
+	2	Splash-a-lot	15'x24' oval pool	$2,940.00	$600.00
+	3	Splash-a-lot	15'x30' oval pool	$4,200.00	$750.00
+	4	AquaSplash	8 person spa	$4,200.00	$250.00
+	5	Tidewater	4 person spa	$2,300.00	$200.00
+	6	AquaSplash	3 person spa	$2,500.00	$200.00
+	7	Tidewater	5 person spa	$3,000.00	$225.00
+	8	Hollywood	7 person spa	$4,200.00	$300.00
+	9	Hot Spot-Sierra	4'x6' cedar sauna	$3,000.00	$400.00
+	10	Hot Spot-Ridgemont	5'x8' cedar sauna	$3,500.00	$500.00
+	11	Hot Spot-Hollywood	6'x10' cedar sauna	$4,750.00	$750.00
+	12	AquaSplash	5 person spa	$3,200.00	$225.00
+	13	Splash-a-lot	18'x33' oval pool	$6,240.00	$900.00
+	14	Splash-a-lot	12' round (3' high) pool	$295.00	$100.00
+	15	Splash-a-lot	15' round pool	$795.00	$250.00
+	16	Splash-a-lot	18' round pool	$995.00	$300.00
+	17	Splash-a-lot	21' round pool	$1,295.00	$400.00
+	18	Splash-a-lot	24' round pool	$1,495.00	$450.00
+	19	Splash-a-lot	27' round pool	$1,795.00	$600.00
*	(AutoNumber)			$0.00	$0.00

C4—Creating a Parameter Query to Match Any Part of a Field

The power of parameter queries increases when you use the Like operator to search for incomplete data. This helps to locate data when you do not know the specific information, or when the data you want is part of a field. This exercise uses a different version of the Armstrong database.

Goal: Create a parameter query that you can use to search for data contained anywhere in a field.

1. Locate **AC1003** in the **Student** folder for this lesson. Transfer the file to the location where you are saving your files. Remove the read-only property, if necessary, and rename the file **AC1003-Challenge4**. Open the file.

2. Create a new query that includes all the tables except tblContractors.

3. Include the customer name fields, the store location (City from tblStores), the product model, description, and amount.

4. On the Criteria line under the **Description** field type **Like"*"+[Enter round or oval for pool type]+"*"**. This creates a parameter value box that will look for round or oval in the description field.

5. Run the query and type **oval** in the Parameter Value box. Press ⬆Shift + F9 and type **round** in the Parameter Value box. Print the results for the round pools.

6. Save the query as **qryPoolType**. Close the database.

	FirstName	LastName	City	Model	Description	Amount
▶	Charles	Bloom	Southfield	Splash-a-lot	27' round pool	$1,795.0
	Jon	Peters	Ypsilanti	Splash-a-lot	15' round pool	$795.0
	James	Krammer	Southfield	Splash-a-lot	24' round pool	$1,495.0
	Andrew	Nathanson	Columbus	Splash-a-lot	18' round pool	$995.0
	Kelley	Rommweber	Indianapolis	Splash-a-lot	15' round pool	$795.0
	Pam	Schmutte	Indianapolis	Splash-a-lot	21' round pool	$1,295.0
*						

ON YOUR OWN

In this lesson you learned how to use several different query techniques. Proficiency in using queries comes with practice, especially when you need to create more complex queries. In particular, update queries can help you maintain database records. For example, you can design a query to update records that is based on data in another table. The sample database provided for this exercise is a database of training records maintained by the Human Resources department for the Armstrong Pool, Spa, and Sauna Company.

- Locate and copy the **AC1004** file to your disk and rename it **AC1004-OnYourOwn**. In the Software table, one (1) is displayed if an employee has completed the course. A zero (0) indicates that the course has not been completed.

- Create a relationship between the common fields in the two tables in this database.

- Create queries to update the Microsoft Software Level table with the word "Completed" for those employees who have taken the courses in each of the software applications. (You will need more than one query.) Each query should be named so it can be rerun each month.

- Hint: After you have successfully tested one query, you can reuse the query and modify the fields selected by using the drop-down menu in the Field box.

- Create another query based on the Microsoft Software Level table that enters a checkmark (Yes) in the Office Expert field for those individuals who have completed courses for all six applications.

- Save your queries and print the results of the Microsoft Software Level table.

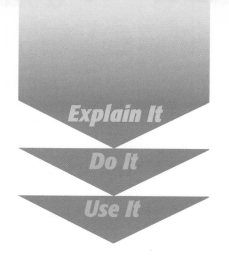

Lesson 11

Creating and Modifying Customer Forms and Reports

Task 1   Creating a Form in Design View
Task 2   Adding a Subform to a Form
Task 3   Creating a Report in Design View
Task 4   Modifying a Report in Design View
Task 5   Adding Subreport Controls to a Report
Task 6   Adding PivotTable Views
Task 7   Adding PivotChart Views

INTRODUCTION

Forms and reports are the input and output objects you use to enter and present data in an Access database. The wizards provided by the program are great tools that help you make choices when you are designing either of these objects. Sometimes, however, you will need to start from scratch to create a form or report that better suits your needs. You can include text fields and other *controls* to customize a form or report to your specifications. Controls are any objects selected from the Toolbox, such as text boxes, check boxes, or option boxes.

You can add a *subform* to a form to show related records in another table. You can do the same with a report by adding a *subreport* that displays related records in a report. When you create a form or report from scratch, there is a Toolbox control that can be used to add a subform or subreport to the primary object.

Two other types of analysis tools that are usually associated with forms are *PivotTables* and *PivotCharts*. PivotTables summarize and analyze data from a table or a query in an interactive format. You select fields to display in columns along the top and rows on the side. The field selected for the intersection of the rows and columns is summarized as a sum, count, average, or some other function. A PivotChart is an interactive graphical analysis of data. You can create a PivotTable or PivotChart as a view that is saved with a table or a query, or you can create either one as a separate form. To create these views or forms, you drag fields from the field list to the various parts of the PivotChart or PivotTable. You can move the fields from one part of the PivotTable or PivotChart simply by dragging them from one area to another. PivotCharts and PivotTables can also be displayed as a data access page. You will learn how to do this in Lesson 13.

In this lesson, you work with the Armstrong Pool, Spa, and Sauna Company database to learn how to create these objects and views.

VISUAL SUMMARY

When you complete this lesson, you will have used Design view to create a form and add a subform, and to create and modify a report. You will also have created a PivotTable view and a PivotChart view.

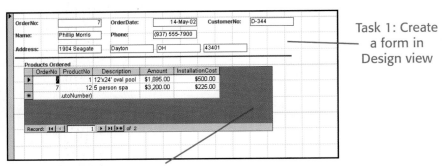

Task 1: Create a form in Design view

Task 2: Add a subform in Design view

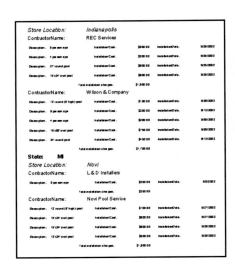

Task 3 and 4: Create and modify a report in Design view

Task 5: Add a subreport to a report

Task 6: Create a PivotTable view

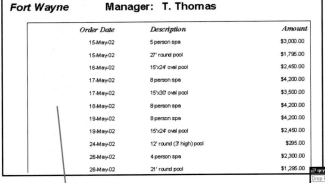

Task 7: Create a PivotChart view

Task 1
CREATING A FORM IN DESIGN VIEW

Explain It

Do It

Use It

Why would I do this?

When you create a form in Design view you have complete control over all elements of the form. For some purposes, this may be a more effective choice for creating a form. When you design a form from scratch, you learn more about the elements in a form and can better understand the form sections and how they are used. The *detail section* is the main area of the form where records are displayed. You can also add *form headers* (top of form) or *form footers* (bottom of form). Either area can be used to display titles, dates, page numbers, summary data, or other controls. Information in these three sections displays on your screen when you look at the form in Form view. You can also add *page headers* and *page footers*, which are not visible onscreen in Form view but will appear if you print the form. Other elements you can add to a form include drop-down lists, groups of option buttons, graphic objects, and much more.

In this task, you learn how to create a basic form in Design view.

1 Start Microsoft Access. Click **More files** under the **Open a file** category. Locate **AC1101** for this lesson.

Transfer the file to the location where you are saving your files. Remove the read-only property and rename the file **AC1101-Armstrong**. Open the file.

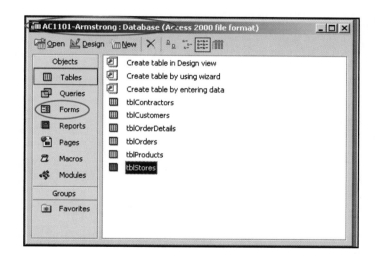

2 Click the Forms object button and click New.

The New Form dialog box opens. You select the method you want to use and the object upon which to base your form.

Make sure **Design View** is selected, and then click the arrow next to the **Choose the table or query** list box and select **qryCustomerOrders**.

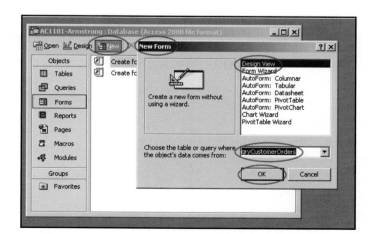

3 Click **OK**.

The Form Design view is displayed, along with a Field List box for the qryCustomerOrders query, and the Toolbox, which is used to add controls to a form.

Maximize the window, and drag the title bar to move the Field List box and Toolbox out of the way of the form grid.

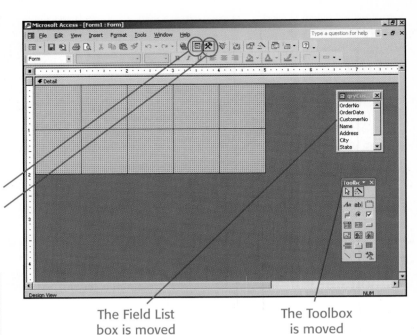

Field List button
Toolbox button

⚠️ **CAUTION**

If the Toolbox does not display on your screen, click the Toolbox button on the Form Design toolbar to open it. If the Field List box does not appear on the screen, click the Field List button to display it.

The Field List box is moved

The Toolbox is moved

4 Click **OrderNo** in the Field List box, scroll down the Field List, press ⬆Shift, and then click **Phone**.

This selects all the fields in the list so you can add them as a group to the design grid.

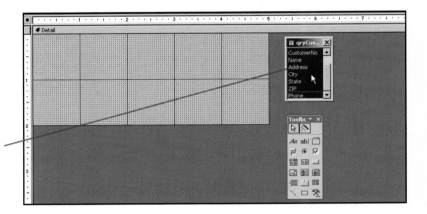

All fields are selected

AutoFormat button

Preview area

5 Drag the highlighted fields to the design grid and place them at the 1-inch mark on the horizontal ruler.

The field text boxes and labels are displayed in a column on the design grid.

Click the **AutoFormat** button on the Form Design toolbar.

The AutoFormat dialog box opens. You can click on different formats to see how they will look. The selected format is displayed in the preview window on the dialog box.

Click the **Blueprint** format.

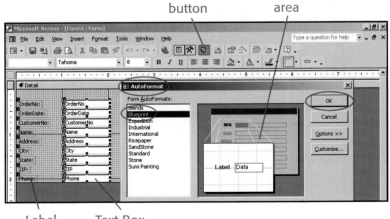

Label controls

Text Box controls

6 Click **OK**.

The format is applied and the dialog box closes.

Click in an open area to deselect the controls, and then drag the **OrderDate** to the right of OrderNo and place the left edge of the label control at the 2.25-inch mark on the horizontal ruler. Drag **CustomerNo** to the 4.5-inch mark as shown in the figure.

Both the label and the text boxes move together. The mouse pointer is shaped like an open hand when you are moving controls. When you move a control out of the grid area, the grid expands to accommodate the control when you release the mouse button.

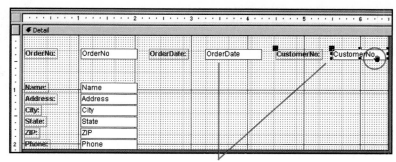

Fields moved

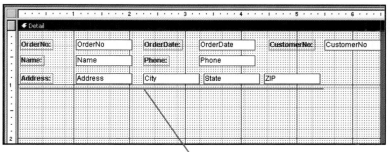

CAUTION

Make sure that you see the open hand mouse pointer before you drag the mouse to move controls in a form. If you point to one of the handles you will see a two-headed arrow that is used to resize the control. If you point to the large box in the upper-left corner of the control, you will see a pointing-finger pointer. Using this enables you to move the text box, or label, separately from the other.

7 Click the **City** label, press **Shift**, and click the **State** and **Zip** labels. Press **Del**.

If you do not need labels you can delete them.

Drag the rest of the fields to rearrange them on the design grid as shown in the figure.

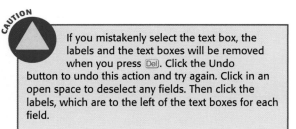

Text Box and Labels rearranged

CAUTION

If you mistakenly select the text box, the labels and the text boxes will be removed when you press **Del**. Click the Undo button to undo this action and try again. Click in an open space to deselect any fields. Then click the labels, which are to the left of the text boxes for each field.

8 Save the form with the name **frmCustomerOrders**. Click the **Line** button on the Toolbox, and move the mouse pointer to the left edge of the form under all the controls.

The mouse pointer becomes a plus sign (+) with a line attached. You will draw a line across the bottom of the data to create a visual break on the form. Later you will add a subform.

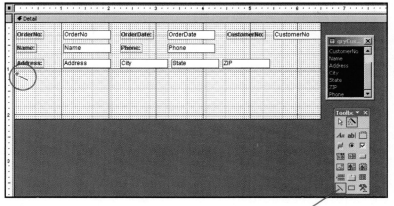

Line button

9 Press ⬆Shift while you drag the mouse to the right across the form to draw a line. Release the mouse and ⬆Shift when you reach the right edge of the form.

Holding down ⬆Shift while you drag creates a straight line. When you release the mouse the line is displayed and sizing handles are shown at each end and in the middle of the line.

With the line still selected, click the **Properties** button on the Form Design toolbar. Click the **Format** tab. Scroll down and click the arrow on the **Border Width** property. Change this property from Hairline to **2 pt**.

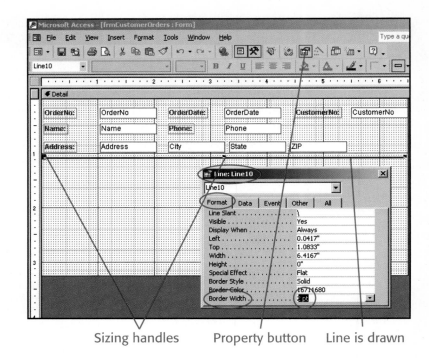

Sizing handles   Property button   Line is drawn

10 Close the Property sheet. Drag the line up if necessary so it is just under the address controls. Click the **View** button to see the results.

Click the **Save** button to save your changes and leave the form open.

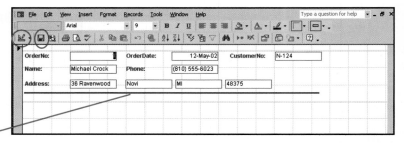

Line widened

Task 2
ADDING A SUBFORM TO A FORM

Why would I do this?

You can create a form with a subform by using the Form Wizard. You can also add a subform to an existing form by using the Subform/Subreport control. This gives you the option to change a form that has already been created. Of course, the value of a subform is that it shows the records that are related to the data displayed in the main part of the form. For example, in the Armstrong database, if the main part of a form shows a contractor, then the subform could display the installations assigned to that contractor.

In this task, you learn how to add a subform to the form you created in Task 1.

1 Click the **View** button to return to the frmCustomerOrders form Design view.

Click the **Subform/Subreport** button on the Toolbox and move the mouse pointer to the left edge of thedesign grid under the drawn line.

The mouse pointer changes to a plus sign (+) with the Subform/Subreport icon attached.

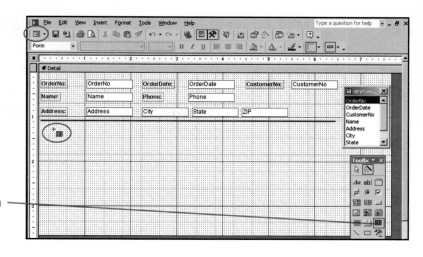

Subform/Subreport button

2 Drag an area that is approximately 1-inch tall by 4-inches wide.

*The Subform Wizard opens. In the first dialog box of the Subform Wizard you choose whether to use an existing table, query, or form as the basis for the subform. The first option—**Use existing Tables and Queries**— is the default choice.*

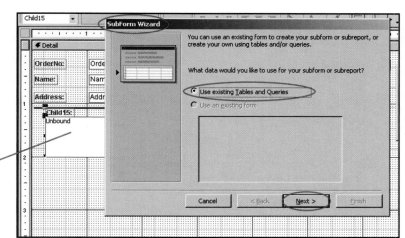

Area drawn for subform

> **QUICK TIP**
>
> It is not necessary to drag an area to launch the Subform Wizard. You can simply click on the form and the wizard will open. You adjust the size of the subform after it is created.

3 Click **Next**.

On the second Subform Wizard dialog box you choose the table or query you want to use and select the fields to include in your subform.

Select **Query:qryProductOrderDetails** from the Tables/Queries box and select all the fields to include in the subform.

> **IN DEPTH**
>
> The OrderNo field is specifically included in this query because it is needed to match the product sold to the customer. If you look at the design of this query you see that it is based on the tblOrderDetails and tblProduct tables. The query used for the main part of the form used the tblOrders and tblCustomers tables.

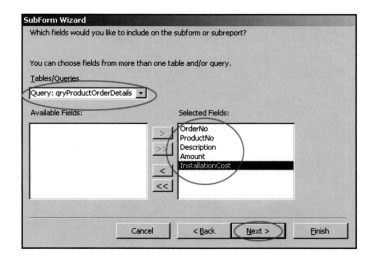

4 Click **Next**.

*On the third Subform Wizard dialog box, you define the field that links the two parts of the form. You can choose from the relationship identified in the box, or click the **Define my own** option button and create the link. In this case, the link displayed in the box is correct.*

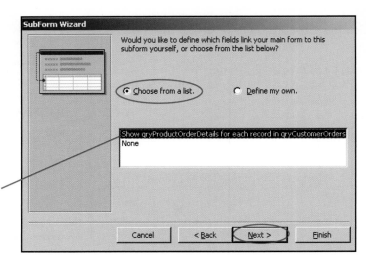

Link identified by Access

5 Click **Next**.

The last dialog box of the Subform Wizard is used to name the subform.

> Change the name to **frmProductsOrdered subform**, and then click **Finish**.

The subform is displayed on your form.

> Click the **Save** button to save the changes to the frmCustomerOrders form.

Subform added

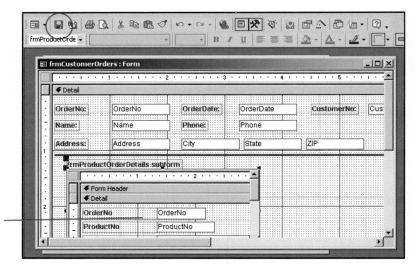

6 Click the **View** button to see the results. Maximize the window if necessary.

Only the first three fields included in the subform are displayed. The size and shape of the subform needs to be adjusted so you can see all the fields.

Title needs to be changed
Only three fields displayed

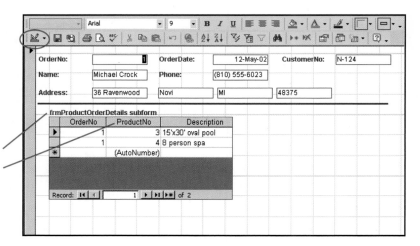

7 Click the **View** button to return to the Design view. Click the top edge of the subform to select it. Drag the right sizing handle to the 6-inch mark on the horizontal ruler.

Resizing the perimeter of the box enables you to see all the fields and to adjust the width of the columns in the Form view.

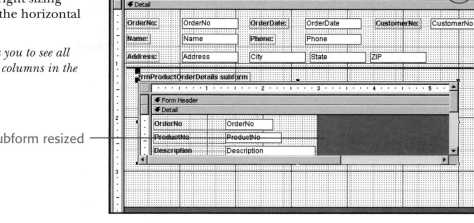

Subform resized

8 If necessary, move the subform down slightly so the title is not on top of the drawn line. Right-click the qryProductsOrdered subform title and choose **P**roperties from the short-cut menu. Click the **Format** tab. On the **Caption** property line, type **Products Ordered** and press ↵Enter.

The name shown for the subform is changed.

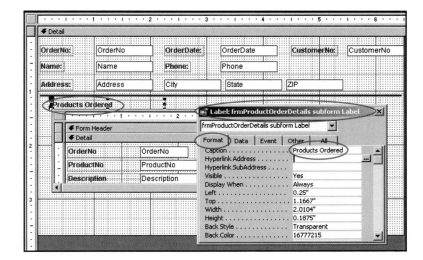

9 Close the property sheet. Click the **View** button to see the results.

You can now adjust the width of the columns in the subform by double-clicking on the line dividing each column heading. This is the same technique you use in tables or queries to adjust column widths.

Double-click the line between each column heading to automatically adjust each column to the width needed to display the data.

Click the **Next Record** button on the main form several times to make sure each field in the subform is fully displayed.

Next Record button

Double-click column divider to adjust column widths

10 Return to Design view. Choose <u>V</u>iew, **Form <u>H</u>eader/Footer.**

The Form Header and Form Footer sections are added to the form.

Click the **Label** button in the Toolbox and drag a rectangle in the **Form Footer** section that is approximately 0.25-inches tall by 1-inch wide. Type your name.

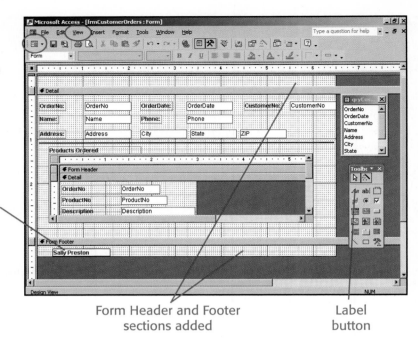

Label added
with your name

Form Header and Footer
sections added

Label
button

11 Click the **View** button. Click the **Save** button to save the changes. Choose <u>F</u>ile, <u>P</u>rint.

The Print Dialog box opens. To print just one form, you view the record you want to print, then go the Print dialog box and choose the Selected Record(s) option. You can also remember the record number of the main form and type that in to the Print Range box to print the selected record.

Click the **Selected Record(s)** options button.

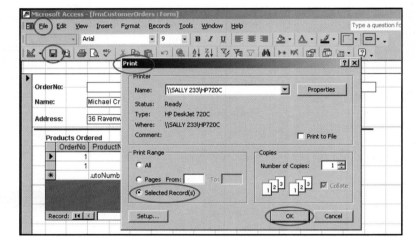

12 Click **OK.**

The form for the first record is printed.

Close the form.

Task 3
CREATING A REPORT IN DESIGN VIEW

Why would I do this?

Just like you would create a form, you can create a report using the Report Wizard, or you can create one from scratch using Report Design view. Building a report from scratch can help you better understand the components of a report and how data is controlled in each section of the report. The records in a report are displayed in the detail section. You can add page header or footer, or report header or footer sections. You can also group data, which can result in a *group header* or *group footer* section.

In this task, you create a report in Design view that is based on a query that contains fields from four tables.

1 Click the **Queries** object button and open the **qryInstallationsbyStore** query in Design view.

This query includes five tables, and fields from four of the tables. The State and City fields are taken from the store table because you want to create the report based on store location. The tblOrders table is included because it joins tblStores to the rest of the tables.

Right-click the join line between tblContractors and tblOrderDetails.

A shortcut menu displays.

Shortcut menu allows you to modify the join

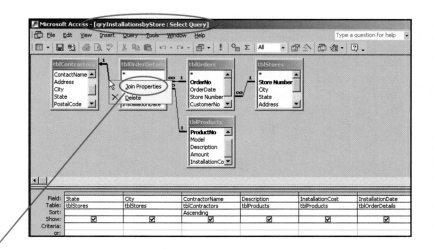

2 Choose **Join Properties** from the shortcut menu. Change the join type from 3 to 1.

This change is needed so the report will only show those installations that have been assigned to one of Armstrong's contractors—it excludes orders with an empty ContractorID field.

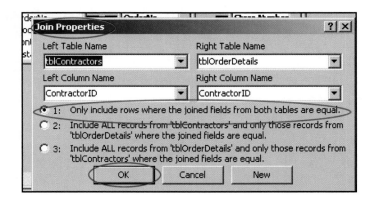

3 Click **OK**. Close the query and save the change. Click the **Reports** object button and click **New**.

The New Report dialog box opens and lists the methods you can use to create a report. In this dialog box you select the type of report you want to create and the object you want to use as the basis for the report. Design view is selected as the default choice.

Click the arrow next to the **Choose the table or query** box and point to **qryInstallationbyStore**.

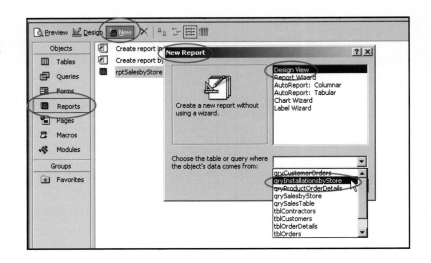

4 Select qryInstallationbyStore and click **OK**.

The Report Design view is displayed along with the Toolbox and a Field List box for the selected query. Notice that there is a Page Header and Page Footer area already open in the report design.

Field list box

Toolbox

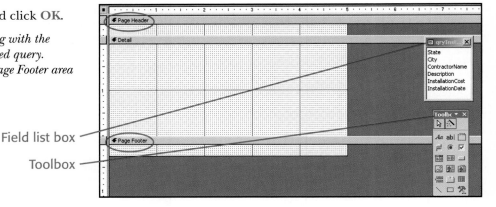

5 In the Field List box click **State**, then press ⬆Shift and click **InstallationDate**.

All the fields are selected.

Drag the selected fields to the report Detail section at about the 1-inch mark on the horizontal ruler. Click in an open area to deselect the fields.

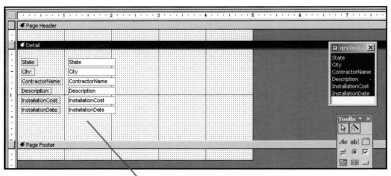

Fields added to the
Detail section

6 Maximize the window, if necessary. Drag the **InstallationCost** field to the right so it is next to the **Description** field. Move the **InstallationDate** field to the right of the **InstallationCost** field. Make sure you do not exceed the 6.5-inch mark on the horizontal ruler.

You move fields and other controls on a report using the same techniques you use with a form.

The edge of the report should not exceed 6.5-inches

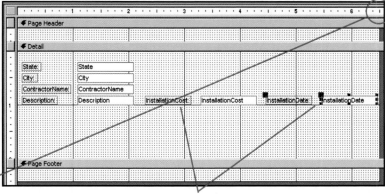

Fields moved

CAUTION

When objects are printed, Access uses 1-inch margins all around. If the design grid of a report with portrait orientation exceeds the 6.5-inch mark on the horizontal ruler, you will have blank pages between every page of data. You can change the width of the side margins by going to File, Page Setup, and selecting the Margins tab to change the margins. If the grid area accidentally extends beyond the allowable width—6.5 inches in this case—simply drag the edge to the left to reduce it to the appropriate dimension.

7 Choose <u>V</u>iew, Report <u>H</u>eader/Footer from the menu.

The Report Header and Report Footer sections are added to the report.

Move the mouse pointer to the top edge of the **Page Header** section bar. When the pointer changes to a two-headed arrow, drag down about a half-inch to expand the Report Header area.

Report Header area expanded

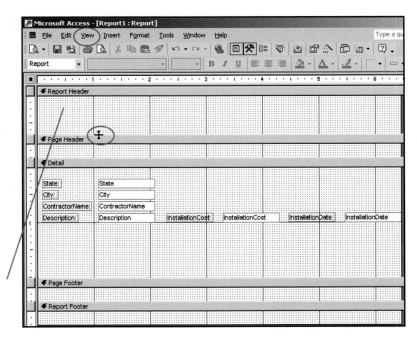

8 Click the **Label** button on the Toolbox. Move the mouse pointer to the Report Header section and drag a box that is approximately 0.5-inches high by 3.5-inches long.

*After you click the Label button, the mouse pointer changes to a plus sign (+) with an **A** attached.*

Area drawn for label
Label button

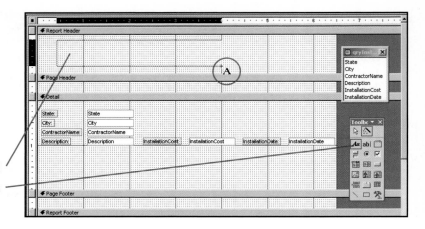

9 Type **Installations by Store** and press ↵Enter.

The title for the report is entered and the label box is selected so you can format the title.

Change the font size to **20**. Click the **Bold** button, and then click the **Center** button to center the title in the box.

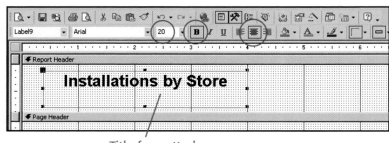

Title formatted

10 Click the **Save** button and name the report **rptInstallationsbyStore**.

Leave the report open for the next task.

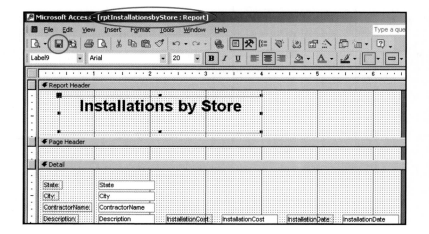

Task 4
MODIFYING A REPORT IN DESIGN VIEW

Why would I do this?

When you create a report, whether with a wizard or in Design view, you often need to modify the report in some manner. At the very least you may need to move and resize fields so all the data is displayed. The report that you created in Task 3 needs to be modified to group data by state, store location (City field), and contractor. In addition, you need to add labels to the Page Header and delete them from the Detail section of the report. You also need to add a calculation to one of the group footers so you can display the total amount owed to each contractor for the installations.

In this task, you make the changes described above to the report created in Task 3.

1 Click the **Sorting and Grouping** button on the Report Design toolbar.

The Sorting and Grouping dialog box is used to sort data and to group records based on common data.

Click the arrow in the first Field/Expression box and choose **State**. In the Group Properties area, change the **Group Header** to **Yes**.

The State field is sorted in ascending order and the State Header section is added to the report design.

Group header for
State field added

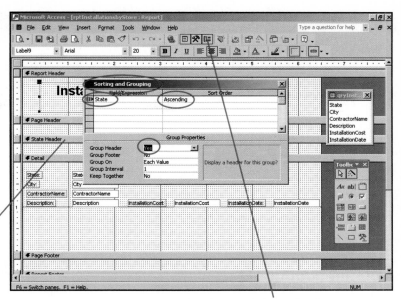

Sorting and Grouping button

2 Click in the next empty box in the Field/Expression column and select **City**. Change the **Group Header** to **Yes**.

The City field is sorted in ascending order and a City header section for City is added to the report design.

In the third box under the Field/Expression column select **ContractorName**. Change the **Group Header** and the **Group Footer** properties to **Yes**.

Both a header and a footer section are added to the report to group the data by the ContractorName field. (You may need to scroll the window down to see the footer.)

City Header added
ContractorName Header

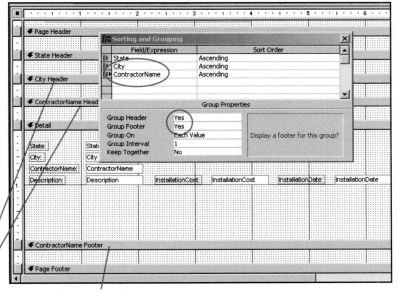

ContractorName
Footer added

IN DEPTH

Each section you add to a report for grouping takes on the selected field name. Generically, these sections are referred to as group header or footer sections, although the name on the section bar is for the specific field name upon which the data is being grouped.

3 Close the **Sorting and Grouping** dialog box. Drag the State field to the **State Header** section.

After you create a group header, you need to move the related field to that section.

Drag the **City** field to the **City Header** section, and the **ContractorName** field to the **ContractorName** Header.

The data for each field will now appear as a group.

Fields moved

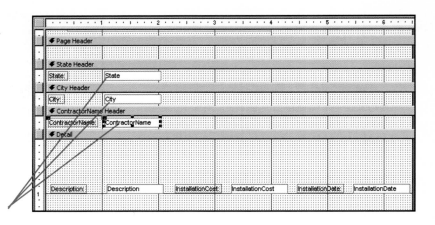

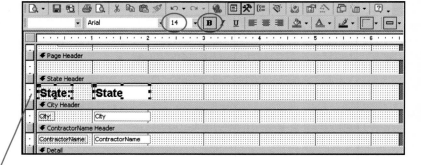

When you move a field control from one section to another, you must move both the text box and the label. You cannot move just one of the controls. Make sure you use the open hand pointer when you move these controls.

4 Click in the vertical ruler to the left of the **State** controls.

This selects both the label and the text box control so you can format them.

Change the font size to **14**, and click the **Bold** button. Double-click a sizing handle to automatically adjust the size of the controls to fit the larger font.

Clicking in the vertical ruler to select both controls

5 Click the **City** label, then click it a second time to change to an editing mode. Replace City: with **Store Location:**.

Click in the vertical ruler next to the City controls to select both controls. Change the font size to **14** and click the **Italic** button. Double-click on a sizing handle to resize the controls.

The City text box needs to be moved to the right so the Store Location label will be fully displayed.

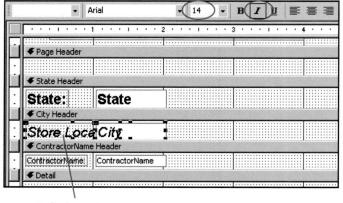

Label caption changed

6 Point to the large move box in the upper-left corner of the **City** text box.

The pointer changes to a pointing finger.

Use the pointing-finger pointer to drag the **City** text box to the right until the left edge aligns with the 2-inch mark on the horizontal ruler. Click in an open space to deselect the controls. Click the **City** text box and drag the right sizing handle to the 4-inch mark on the horizontal ruler.

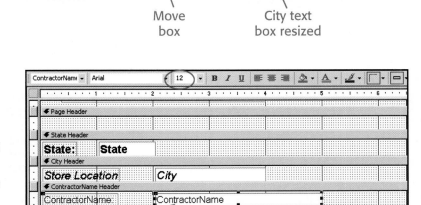

Move box

City text box resized

7 Select the **ContractorName** controls and change the font size to **12** points. Double-click a sizing handle to automatically adjust the sizing. Move the **ContractorName** text box to the 2-inch mark. Drag the right sizing handle to the 5-inch mark.

By changing the formatting of group labels you improve the readability of the report because the groups are more easily identified.

Contractor Name field modified

8 Click in the vertical ruler to the left of the controls in the **Detail** section.

The controls remaining in the detail section are selected. You can move these controls up and reduce the size of the detail section.

Move the controls up just under the Detail section bar. Scroll down the window and drag the top of the ContractorName Footer bar up to just under the controls in the Detail section.

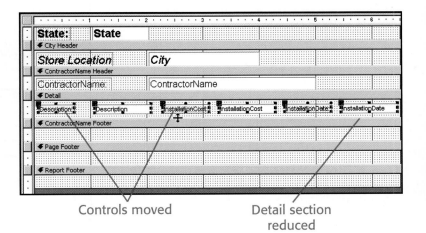

Controls moved

Detail section reduced

9 Click the **Text Box** button and click in the **ContractorName Footer** section under the **InstallationCost** text box.

An unbound text box opens with a label to the left.

Change the label to read **Total installation charges:**. Use the large move box to move the label left to the 1.75-inch mark on the horizontal ruler. Click outside the control to deselect it.

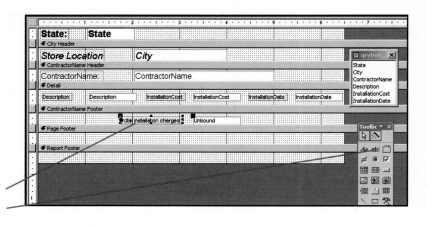

Label moved and caption added

Text Box button

10 Double-click the **Unbound** text box.

The property sheet for this text box opens. You can enter the calculation to sum the installation costs in the Control Source property box, or you can type it directly in the unbound text box control.

Click the **Data** tab if necessary. In the **Control Source** property box, type **=Sum([InstallationCost]).**

This calculation will total the installation costs. Because you added this control to the ContractorName group footer, a total is calculated by contractor.

11 Click the **Format** tab and change the **Format** property to **Currency**. Close the property sheet. Click the **View** button to see the results.

As you create a report it is a good idea to frequently look at the results so you can determine how the changes are affecting the overall look of the report.

Scroll through the report.

Notice that some of the product descriptions are not fully displayed. Also notice that some companies start on one page and end on the next page. (Your report will probably break in different places than shown in the figure.) You can control where a group breaks in a report. If the sum of the installation costs is not aligned under the Installation Cost column, you might want to adjust that alignment.

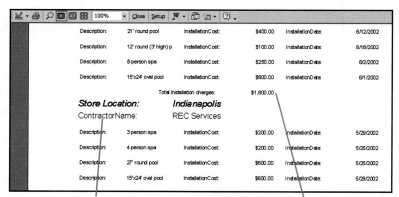

Contractor started on page 1

Calculated control added to ContractorName footer

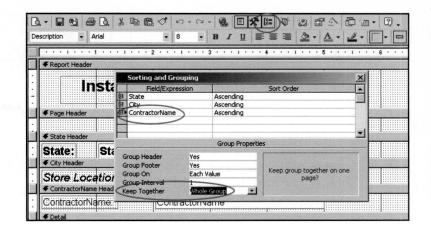

12 Click the View button to return to Design view. Click the **Description** text box and drag the left sizing handle to the left to increase the size of this field.

This enlarges the control used to display the product description data.

Click the **Sorting and Grouping** button. Click the **ContractorName** field and change the **Keep Together** property to **Whole Group**.

This ensures that the records for each contractor are displayed on the same page in the report.

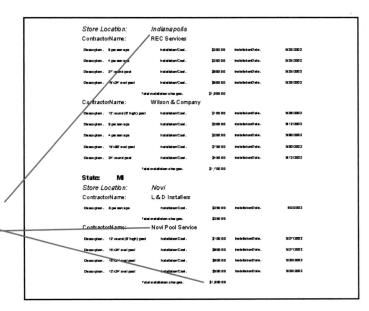

13 Click the **City** field in the Sorting and Grouping dialog box and change the **Keep Together** property to **With First Detail**.

This ensures that the store location is kept with the first contractor listed for that city.

Close the Sorting and Grouping dialog box. Click the View button to see the final results. Scroll through the report to see the effect of your changes.

City kept with first record

Contractor data kept together on one page

14 Return to Design view and add a label to the Report Footer and type your name. Print the report and save your changes. Close the report.

Task 5

ADDING SUBREPORT CONTROLS TO A REPORT

Why would I do this?

You can add a subreport to a report just like you added a subform to a form. With a report, however, you have to complete this procedure in Design view using the Subform/Subreport button. You cannot create a subreport by using one of the Report Wizards like you can with the Form Wizard. The subreport displays records related to the main part of the report but in a separate section. You can add a subreport to any section in a report. Which section you add it to controls how many times it is displayed when you print the report.

In this task, you add a subreport to the detail section of a report that displays the sales by store.

1 Make sure you have the **Reports** object button selected and then open the **rptSalesbyStore** report in **Design** view. Maximize the window.

The main part of this report has already been created. You will add a subreport to it.

Click the **Subform/Subreport** button on the Toolbox, and then click in the detail section of the report under the **City** field at the half-inch mark on the horizontal ruler.

The SubReport Wizard opens. You can select a table, query, form, or report as the basis for the subreport. The Use Existing Tables and Queries option button is selected by default.

Options available for subreport source data

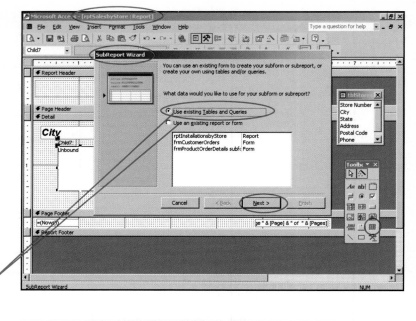

2 Make sure the first option button is selected and then click **Next**.

In the second SubReport Wizard dialog box, you select the table or query you want to use, and then you select the fields you want to include.

Select **qrySalesbyStore** from the **Tables/Queries** list box. Then add all the fields to the Selected Fields box.

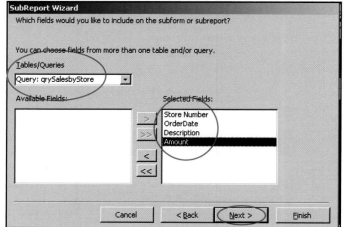

3 Click **Next**.

In the third SubReport Wizard dialog box, the link between the data in the main part of the report and the subreport is identified. In this case, the common field is Store Number.

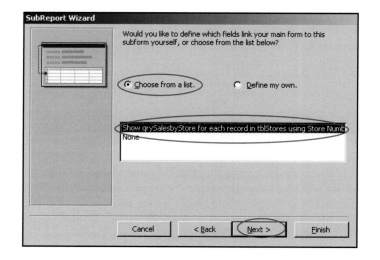

4 Click <u>N</u>ext.

In the last SubReport Wizard dialog box you name the subreport.

Change the name to **rptSalesbyStore subreport** and click the <u>F</u>inish button.

The subreport is added to the detail section of the report.

Maximize the window again, if necessary.

Subreport added

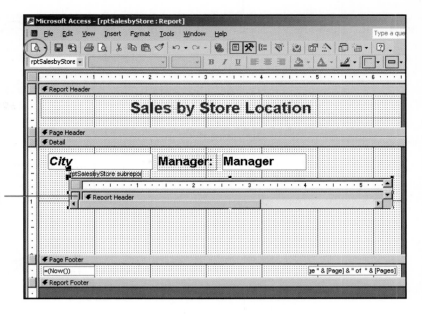

5 Click the View button.

A few minor adjustments are needed. You can delete the title for the subreport. It is redundant to display the Store Number for every record in the subreport, so you can hide this field in the subreport. And the spacing between the OrderDate and Description fields needs to be adjusted.

Remove title

Hide repetitive data

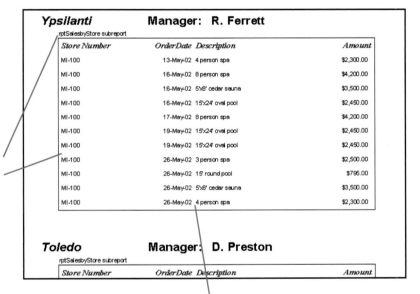

Adjust spacing

6 Click the **View** button. Click the **subreport title** and press Del.

The title is removed because it is not necessary.

Click the upper edge of the subreport to select it. Drag the bottom-middle sizing handle down until you can see the field text boxes in the Detail section of the subreport.

The Detail section of the main part of the report automatically expands while you increase the size of the subreport.

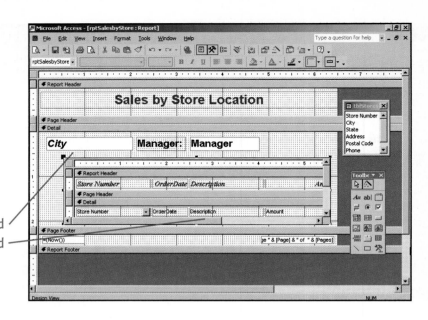

Subreport title removed

Subreport expanded

7 Click the **Store Number** label in the subreport Report Header section and press Del. Double-click the Store Number text box.

The Store Number label is removed from the report and the property sheet for the Store Number text box is displayed.

Click the **Format** tab and change the **Visible** property to **No**.

This keeps the store number data from displaying on the subreport.

Store Number label removed

8 Close the property sheet.

Now you need to resize the Store Number text box and move the other controls to adjust the spacing on the report.

Drag the right sizing handle to the left to reduce the size of the **Store Number** field to approximately one-quarter-inch wide. Edit the **OrderDate** label to **Order Date**. Move the Order Date label and text box to the 1-inch mark on the horizontal ruler.

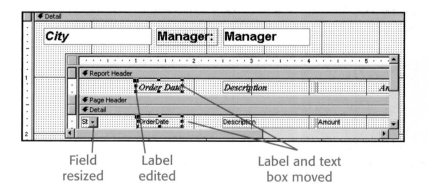

Field resized

Label edited

Label and text box moved

9 Click the **Save** button to save the changes. Click the **View** button to see the results.

Scroll through the report to see if it needs any final adjustments. Click the **Next Page** button to view each page in the report.

Next Page button

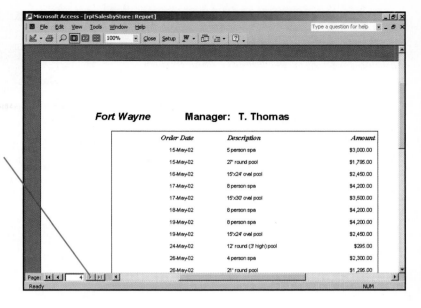

10 Click the **View** button. Add a label to the middle of the page footer section and type your name. Print the report. Save the changes again and then close the report.

Task 6
ADDING PIVOTTABLE VIEWS

Why would I do this?

PivotTables are another tool you can use to summarize data. You can create one by selecting PivotTable from the New Form dialog box. However, a PivotTable is not like other forms. You can view data with a PivotTable, but you cannot edit or enter data, and you do not view the information one record at a time. It is simply another method used to view data. A PivotTable is similar to a crosstab query because the data is grouped by rows and columns, and then summarized on a third value at the intersection of the rows and columns. Once you create a PivotTable view, you can move the fields between the rows and columns. With a PivotTable you can have two column headings, which is unlike a crosstab query where you can have more than one row heading, but only one column heading. You can also create a PivotTable view based on a datasheet or form, and then save the view as part of the original object.

In this task, you create a PivotTable that summarizes products sold by description and store.

1 Click the **Queries** object button and open the **qrySalesTable** query.

This query is based on the tblProducts and tblStores tables.

Click the arrow on the **View** button and point to **PivoTable View**.

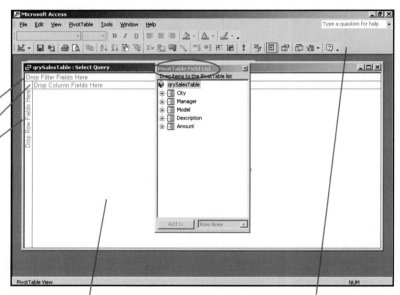

2 Click **PivoTable View** from this list box.

A blank PivoTable view window opens. You can drag fields onto the various parts of the window from the PivoTable Field List box.

Add filters here
Place fields for columns here
Place fields for rows here

IN DEPTH

You can also get to this window by clicking the New button on the Forms object page, and then selecting PivotTable Wizard and the table, query, or form that you want to use as the basis for the PivotTable.

Data to be summarized
is placed here

PivotTable toolbar

3 Drag **City** from the PivotTable Field List and drop it in the **Drop Column Fields Here** area.

The City field is added to the PivotTable as a column heading.

Drag **Manager** from the PivotTable Field list box and place it next to City.

You can add multiple column headings to a PivotTable. Notice that fields that have been added to the PivotTable are now bolded in the PivotTable Field List box.

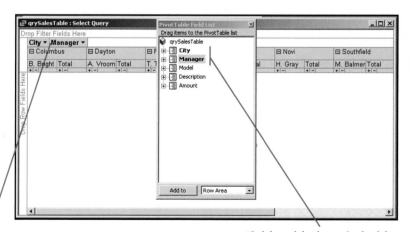

City and Manager added
to column heading

Fields added are in bold

4 Drag **Model** to the **Drop Row Fields Here** area.

You can also add multiple fields to the row area.

Select **Description**. Make sure **Row Area** is displayed in the list box at the bottom of the PivotTable Field List box, and click the **Add to** button.

You can add fields to the PivotTable view by dragging them to the appropriate area, or by selecting the field and using the Add to button.

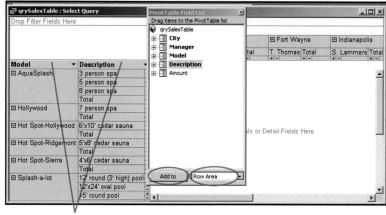

Model and Description fields added as row headings

5 Drag **Amount** to the **Drop Totals or Detail Fields Here** area. Close the PivotTable Field List box.

The details for the PivotTable are displayed.

Scroll through the PivotTable to see the results.

Notice that no totals are displayed. Each category has a Show/Hide detail button that you can use to hide or display the data.

Details displayed for AquaSplash

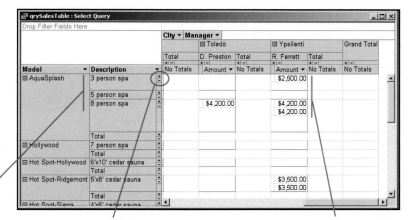

Show/Hide Detail buttons

Amounts by model, description, and store location are displayed

IN DEPTH

The highest level for the column and row headings automatically displays the details. In this example, the AquaSplash row heading displays all the related products sold for that company.

6 Click the **Amount** column heading under any one of the city/manager groups.

The amounts under each City/Manager group are selected.

Choose **PivotTable**, **AutoCalc** from the menu.

A list of calculation options is displayed.

List of calculation options

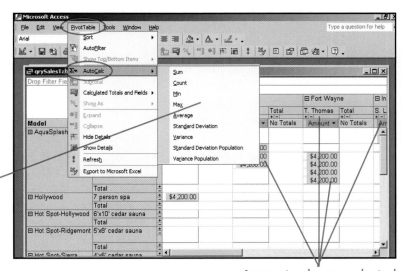

Amount columns selected

7 Click **Sum**. Maximize the window, if necessary.

A Sum of Amount column is added to the right of each of the columns under the City/Manager grouping.

Scroll to the bottom of the PivotTable.

The Grand Total has also been calculated by each City/Manager group.

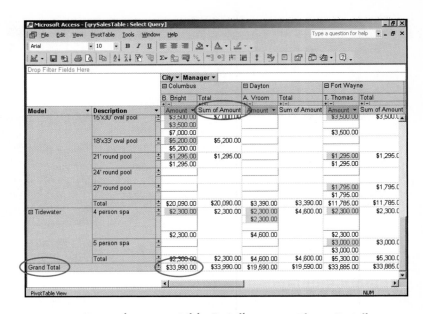

Expand button   Hide Details button   Show Details button

8 Scroll down and to the right to see the lower-right corner of the PivotTable view.

Sums have also been calculated by the description field and a grand total for all sales is displayed.

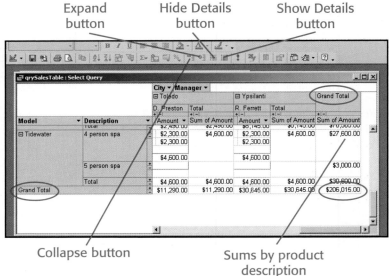

Collapse button   Sums by product description

QUICK TIP

You can show or hide the details by clicking the Hide Details button or Show Details button on the Formatting (PivotTable/PivotChart) toolbar. You can also use the Expand or Collapse buttons to control the subcategories that are displayed.

9 Click the **Save** button.

The PivotTable view is saved as part of the query.

Close the PivotTable.

IN DEPTH

The next time you open this query you can view the PivotTable you just created by choosing View, PivotTable View, from the menu or by using the View button.

Task 7
ADDING PIVOTCHART VIEWS

Why would I do this?

Charts provide a graphical representation of data. You can chart data using the PivotChart view, which is an interactive program similar to a PivotTable. Once you create a PivotChart view, it is saved as part of the table or query upon which it is based. Like a PivotTable, this object presents data, but cannot be used to enter or alter the underlying data. When you create a PivotTable view for a table or a query datasheet, a PivotChart view of the same data is automatically created. If you create a PivotChart based on the same object, it alters the contents of any PivotTable that has been created for that object. To preserve the PivotTable you created in the previous task, you use a separate query to create the PivotChart. Using a separate query also allows you to group the data differently.

In this task, you create a PivotChart view based on the qrySalesChart.

1 Make sure you have the **Queries** object button selected, and then open the **qrySalesChart**.

Click the arrow to the right of the **View** button and select **PivotChart View**.

An empty PivotChart view is displayed, along with a Chart Field list box that lists the fields displayed in the selected query. This query uses the same fields as qrySalesTable with the exception of the Manager field.

Place the field used for filtering data here
Place the summary field here

Place the series field here

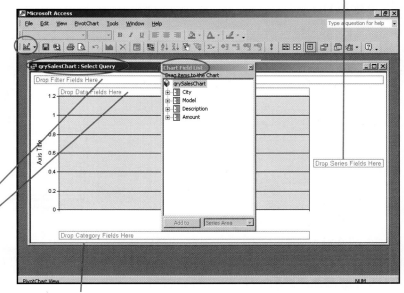

Place the category axis field here

> **IN DEPTH**
>
> You can also create a PivotChart as a form. On the Forms object page, click the New button and choose PivotChart from the list of design options, and then select the object you want to use as the basis for the chart. You select the fields you want to include and then follow the same steps to add the fields to the chart.

2 Drag the **City** field to the **Drop Category Fields Here** box.

The names of the store locations will be displayed across the bottom of the chart.

Drag the **Description** field to the **Drop Series Fields Here** box.

A description list box will show all the categories of products sold.

Drag the **Amount** Field to the **Drop Data Fields Here** box.

The chart is displayed as a column chart.

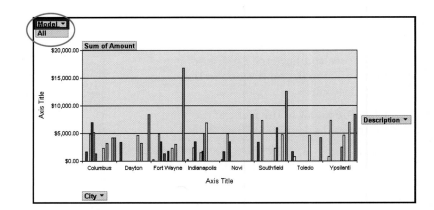

Fields used are in bold

3 Drag the **Model** field to the **Drop Filter Fields Here** box.

You can use Model as a filter to display only those products sold for a particular company. Initially, all products are shown.

Close the Chart Field List box.

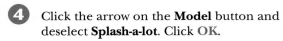

4 Click the arrow on the **Model** button and deselect **Splash-a-lot**. Click **OK**.

The chart is altered to display the products sold by all companies except Splash-a-lot.

Point to the tallest column on the chart.

A ScreenTip displays describing the product and dollar value represented by this bar for sales at Fort Wayne.

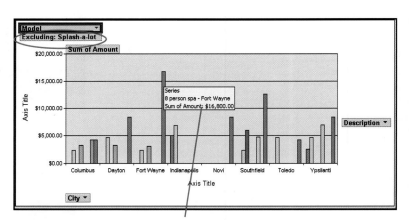

ScreenTip describes the data
represented by the column

5 Right-click **Axis Title** at the bottom of the chart and choose Properties from the shortcut menu.

The Properties dialog box opens for this control.

Click the **Format** tab and type **Store Location** and your last name in the **Caption** box. Change the font size to **12**.

The title at the bottom of the chart is changed.

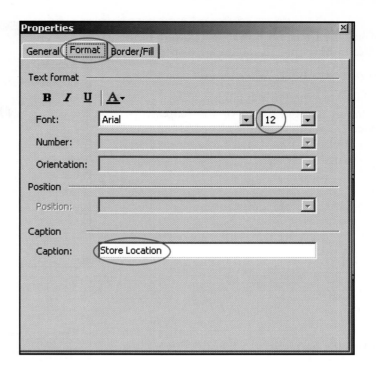

6 Click **Axis Title** at the left edge of the chart.

The property sheet is changed to the control you just selected.

Type **Sales by Product** in the **Caption** box and change the font size to **12**.

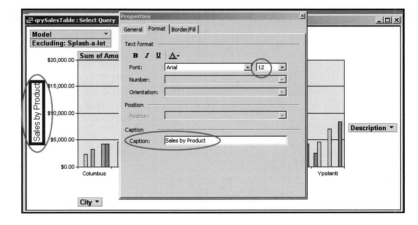

7 Click the **Value Axis** on the left of the chart.

The property sheet changes to this control. You can format the values to display as currency.

Make sure the **Format** tab is selected. Click the arrow next to the **Number** box and select **Currency**. Change the font size to **10**.

Amounts formatted as currency

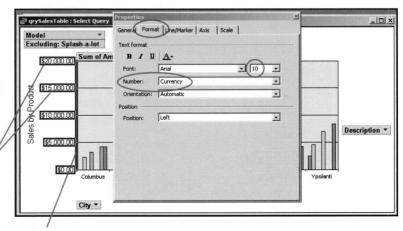

Value Axis

8 Click the **Category Axis** at the bottom of the chart where the city names are displayed.

The property sheet is now pointed to the Category Axis.

Make sure the **Format** tab is selected. Change the font size to **10**. Close the property sheet. Click the **Show Legend** button on the Formatting (PivotTable/PivotChart) toolbar.

Show Legend button

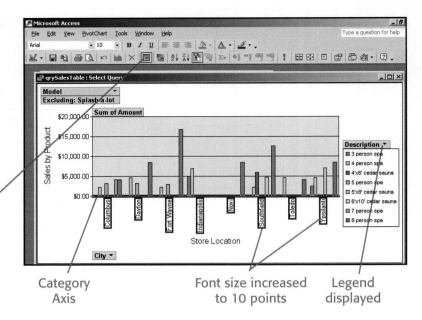

Category Axis

Font size increased to 10 points

Legend displayed

9 Click the **Save** button. Print the PivotChart, and then close it. Compact and close the database.

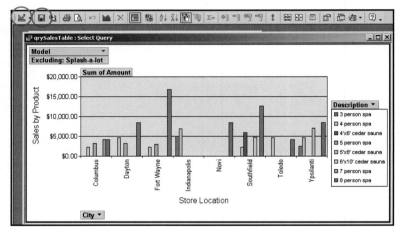

IN DEPTH

If you had created the PivotChart as a form, then when you saved it, it would have been saved as an object on the Forms page in the Database window.

The exercises that follow are designed for you to review and use what you have learned in this lesson. You also have the opportunity to practice your skills and then expand on them by applying them to new situations.

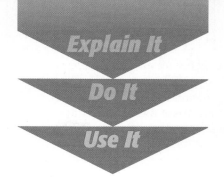

COMPREHENSION

Comprehension exercises are designed to check your memory and understanding of the basic concepts in this lesson. You distinguish between true and false statements, identify new screen elements, and match terms with related statements. If you are uncertain of the correct answer, refer to the task number following each item (for example, T4 refers to Task 4) and review that task until you are confident that you can provide a correct response.

TRUE-FALSE

Circle either T or F.

T F 1. When you delete a text box from a form, the related label box still remains on the form. **(T1)**

T F 2. To create a subform, you must use content that includes a field that can be joined to the main part of the form. **(T2)**

T F 3. To summarize data by groups, you can add a calculated field in a text box in the related group footer. **(T4)**

T F 4. You can alter the data in an underlying table by changing the figures that are displayed in a PivotTable View. **(T6)**

T F 5. To draw a straight line on a form, press ⇧Shift while you drag the line pointer across the form. **(T1)**

T F 6. You can include a subreport in a report when you use the Report Wizard. **(T5)**

MATCHING QUESTIONS

A. Detail section
B. Equal sign
C. PivotChart view
D. PivotTable view
E. Sorting and Grouping button
F. Design view

Match the following statements to the word or phrase that is the best match from the list. Write the letter of the matching word or phrase in the space provided next to the number.

1. _____ Similar to a crosstab query **(T6)**

2. _____ Used to add sections to a report to help organize data **(T4)**

3. _____ Used to display a graphical representation of data **(T7)**

4. _____ Used to create a report from scratch **(T3)**

5. _____ Area on a form or report that displays records **(T1)**

6. _____ Used to calculate a value in a text box **(T4)**

IDENTIFYING PARTS OF THE ACCESS SCREEN

Refer to the figure and identify the numbered parts of the screen. Write the letter of the correct label in the space next to the number.

1. _____

2. _____

3. _____

4. _____

5. _____

6. _____

A. Legend (T7)

B. Sorting and Grouping button (T4)

C. Value axis (T7)

D. Group header section (T4)

E. Category axis (T7)

F. Helps control where data breaks across pages (T4)

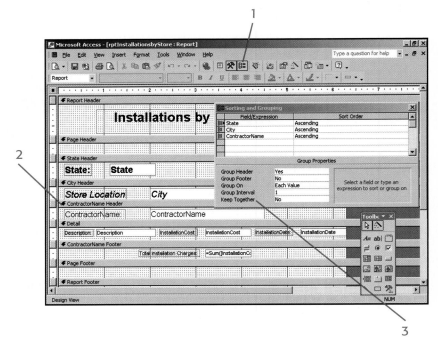

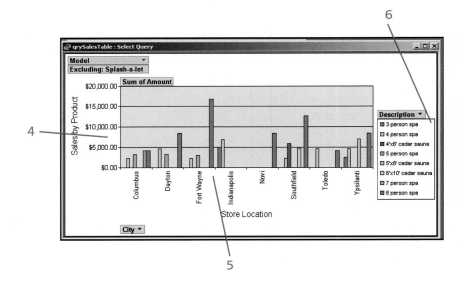

REINFORCEMENT

Reinforcement exercises are designed to reinforce the skills you have learned by applying them to new situations. Detailed instructions are provided along with a figure, where appropriate, to illustrate the result. Complete the reinforcement exercises sequentially. Leave the file open at the end of each exercise for use in the next exercise until you are specifically directed to close it.

In these exercises, you use the Alumni Travel Club database.

R1—Creating a Form in Design View and Adding a Subform

1. Open Access and click **More files** under the **Open a file** category. Locate **AC1102** in the **Student** folder for this lesson. Transfer the file to the location where you are saving your files. Remove the read-only property, and rename the file **AC1102-Travel**. Open the file.

2. Click the **Forms** object button and click **New**. Select **Design View** and then select **tblTrips**. Click **OK**.

3. Drag **TripID, Description**, **StartDate**, and **TourGuide** to the design grid.

4. Rearrange the fields on the design grid as shown in the figure. Use the large move handle and the pointing-finger pointer to move the labels and place them directly over the text box for each field.

5. Click the **Line** button on the Toolbox. Press ◆Shift and drag a line below the text boxes. Click the **Property** button and change the **Border Width** property to **2-pt**.

6. Choose **View, Form Header/Footer**. Add a label to the header and type **Members Signed up for Trips**. Change the font size to **20** and the font color to **blue**. Double-click a sizing handle to resize the label.

7. Click the **Subform/Subreport** button on the Toolbox. Click on the design grid under the drawn line. In the Tables/Queries box select **Query: qryMembersByTrip**. Include all the fields except Description. Link the main form and subform on the **TripID** field. Name the subform: **frmMembers Subform**.

8. Expand the size of the subform to the 6.25-inch mark on the horizontal ruler. Change to the **Form** view and adjust the widths of the columns in the subform so you can see all the data.

9. Change the caption for the subform label to **Registered Members**. Save the form as **frmTrips and Members**, and then close it.

10. Open **tblMembers** and change the name for MemberID **P-512** to your name. Close the table.

11. Reopen **frmTrips** and **Members**. Display the record for the **African Safari** trip. Choose **File, Print**, and choose **Selected Record(s)** to print this record. Close the form.

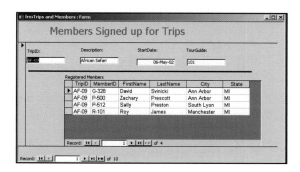

R2—Creating a Report in Design View and Adding a Group Header

1. Click the **Reports** object button and click **New**. Make sure **Design View** is selected, and then choose **qryMembersByTrips**.

2. Add all the fields except **City** and **State** to the detail section of the report design.

3. Click the **Sorting and Grouping** button and add a group header for **TripID**. Close the Sorting and Grouping dialog box. Move **TripID** and **Description** to the TripID Header section. Change the font of the controls in the group header to **12-point Bold**. Adjust the size of the controls as needed. Make sure all the trip descriptions are fully displayed.

4. Rearrange the field text boxes and labels as shown in the figure on the next page. Increase the font size to **10-point** for all the controls in the Detail section. Adjust the size of the controls as needed.

5. Add a label to the Page Header. Type **Registered Member's Report** and press ◄Enter.

6. Change the font of the label to **20**-point. Add **Bold** and **Italic** emphasis. Change the font color to **Green**. Adjust the size of the label control as needed.

7. Save the report with the name **rptRegisteredMembers**. Leave the report open for the next exercise.

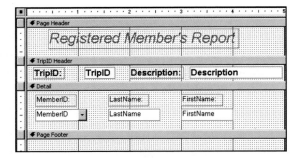

R3—Adding a Subreport to a Report

1. With the **rptRegisteredMembers** report open, click the **Subform/Subreport** button and click under the **MemberID** text box in the detail section of the report.

2. Select **tblTransactions**, and include the **MemberID**, **AmountPaid**, and **DatePaid** fields. Link the fields based on **MemberID**—the first choice highlighted in the third SubReport Wizard dialog box. Save the report as **rptMemberPayments subreport**.

3. Maximize the window and move the subreport down, if necessary, so it does not overlap the fields in the detail section.

4. Change the caption of the subreport label control to **Payments**. Change the font size of the subreport label control to **12**-point and add **Bold** emphasis. Adjust the size of the control so it is fully displayed.

5. Adjust the size of the detail section so it ends just below the subreport control.

6. View the report to ensure that all the data is visible. Examine how the data breaks across pages. Return to Design view.

7. Open the **Sorting and Grouping** dialog box and change the **Keep Together** property for the **TripID** group to **Whole Group**.

8. Save the report with the name **rptMemberPayments**. Print the first page of the report.

R4—Creating a PivotTable View

1. Open the **tblTrips** table. Click the arrow next to the **View** button and choose **PivotTable View**.

2. Drag the **Description** field to the **Drop Column Fields Here** area.

3. Drag the **StartDate by Month** field to the **Drop Row Fields Here** area.

4. Drag the **Cost** field to the **Drop Totals or Detail Fields Here** area. Close the PivotTable Field List box.

5. Click the **Expand** button next to 2002 in the row area. Quarters are displayed.

6. Click the **Expand** button next to the three quarters that are displayed.

7. Click the **Expand** button next to the months that are displayed.

8. Choose **File**, **Page Set Up**. Click the **Page** tab and choose **Landscape**. Print the PivotTable. (The Cost figures will not display on the printout.)

9. Save the PivotTable view as part of the tblTrips table.

R5–Creating a PivotChart View

1. Open the **qryMemberTripPayments** query. Click the arrow next to the View button and choose **PivotChart View.**

2. Drag the **StartDate** field to the **Drop Category Fields Here** area. Drag **Description** and place it to the right of **StartDate** in the **Drop Category Fields Here** area.

3. Drag the **MemberID** field to the **Drop Series Fields Here** area.

4. Drag the **AmountPaid** field to the **Drop Data Fields Here** area.

5. Right-click the **Category Axis Title** and select Properties. Change the caption to **Trips**.

6. Right-click the **Value Axis Title** and select Properties. Change the caption to **Amount Paid per Member**.

7. Choose File, Page Set Up. Click the **Page** tab and select **Landscape**. Print the PivotChart.

8. Save the PivotChart view as part of the query. Compact and close the database.

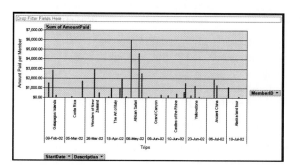

Challenge exercises are designed to test your ability to apply your skills to new situations with less-detailed instructions. These exercises also challenge you to expand your repertoire of skills by using commands that are similar to those you have already learned. The desired outcome is clearly defined, but you have more freedom to choose the steps needed to achieve the required result.

In the following Challenge exercise you work with the Armstrong Pool, Spa, and Sauna Company database. Each exercise can be done independently. For Challenge Exercise 4, you will need the file Armstrong Logo.jpg.

 ## C1—Creating a Form that Uses Option Buttons

There are many controls included in the toolbox that you can use when you design a form. One of the more interesting controls is the Option Group. You can add individual option buttons or check boxes to a form, but with the Option Group control, you restrict the choice to one of the options listed in the group box. Once you have created the control, you then activate it by attaching macros to each of the option buttons. You will learn how to attach macros to option buttons in a Challenge exercise in Lesson 12.

Goal: Create a form with an Option Group control.

1. Locate **AC1101** in the **Student** folder for this lesson. Transfer the file to the location where you are saving your files. Remove the read-only property, and rename the file **AC1101-Challenges**. Open the file.

2. Click the **Forms** object button and open the **Design** view window for a new form.

3. Add a 2-inch square label on the left side of the form and type **Customer Records**. Increase the font to **28**-point, **italic**. Change the font and font color to something you like.

4. Click the **Option Group** button on the toolbox and click on the right side of the form.

5. In the first Option Group Wizard dialog box, type **Add New Customer**, then press Tab↹. Type **Edit Customer Record**, press Tab↹, and type **Find Customer**.

6. In the second Option Group Wizard dialog box, select **Find Customer** as the default choice.

7. In the third Option Group Wizard dialog box, accept the values assigned to each option.

8. In the fourth Option Group Wizard dialog box, choose **Option buttons** and then select a style of your choice.

9. In the last Option Group Wizard dialog box, type the caption **Select Option.**

10. Change the font size of the Select Option control to **12**-point, and change the font size of the other option controls to **10**-point. Adjust the size of the controls and their alignment as needed.

11. Add your name in a label on the form. Add a background color of your choice to the form.

12. Save the form as **frmCustomerRecords**. Print the form.

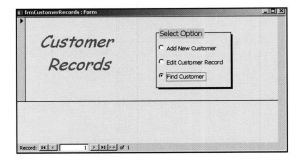

 ## C2—Creating a PivotTable as a Form

In this lesson, you learned to create a PivotTable view as part of a datasheet. You can also create a PivotTable or a PivotChart as a form. The PivotTable Wizard that opens in the Form window enables you to select the fields you want to use.

Goal: Create a PivotTable and save it as a form.

1. If you completed the previous exercise, continue to use that file. Otherwise, locate **AC1101** in the **Student** folder for this lesson. Transfer the file to the location where you are saving your files. Remove the read-only property, and rename the file **AC1101-Challenges**. Open the file.

2. On the **Forms** object page, click the **New** button and choose **PivotTable Wizard**. Select **tblOrderDetails** from the list box.

3. When you click **OK**, the PivotTable Wizard opens. Read this first dialog box to familiarize yourself with PivotTables.

4. In the second PivotTable Wizard dialog box, add **ProductNo**, **ContractorID**, and **InstallationDate** to the **Fields Chosen for Pivoting** box.

5. In the PivotTable window, add the **ContractorID** as the column heading, **ProductNo** as the row heading, and **InstallationDate** as the data for the center of the table.

6. Click the arrow next to the **ContractorID** heading and deselect the **Blank** contractor ID to hide it. Save the PivotTable as **frmInstallationsPivotTable**.

7. Show just the **Michigan** contractors. Change the **Page Setup** to print landscape and adjust the margins as needed to show the data for the Michigan contractors on one page. Print the PivotTable.

8. Save the changes and close the form.

ProductNo ▾	MI-1 InstallationDate ▾	MI-2 InstallationDate ▾	MI-3 InstallationDate ▾	MI-4 InstallationDate ▾	MI-5 InstallationDate ▾	MI-6 InstallationDate ▾	Grand Total No Totals
1	5/30/2002			5/29/2002			
2	5/29/2002	5/26/2002	5/27/2002	5/29/2002			
	5/27/2002	5/29/2002	5/29/2002				
4	6/2/2002	5/29/2002		5/29/2002	5/27/2002	6/2/2002	
		5/26/2002					
5		6/3/2002					
6					6/12/2002		
9	5/27/2002			6/3/2002			
10		5/28/2002					
		6/3/2002					
11				5/29/2002			
14			5/27/2002				
15					6/10/2002		
Grand Total							

C3—Creating a Report Based on Multiple Tables

The challenge in using any database is to understand its structure so you can extract the information you need. So far in this lesson, you have been given fairly detailed instructions about how to create objects and what fields to include. In the world of work, instructions are rarely that clear. Your boss may say, "I need a report that shows me sales by store." It is up to you to figure out what to include and how to create the report. In this exercise, you create a report with minimal instructions.

Goal: Create a report based on a general description of the desired outcome.

1. If you completed one of the previous exercises, continue to use that file. Otherwise, locate **AC1101** in the **Student** folder for this lesson. Transfer the file to the location where you are saving your files. Remove the read-only property, and rename the file **AC1101-Challenges**. Open the file.

2. Create a new report that shows the products sold by store. Also include the customers' names and the installation dates for each product sold.

3. Organize the report so you can print a separate page for each store manager that shows all the products sold and the customers and installation dates for that location.

4. Make sure that all the data is visible. Place your name in a label on the page footer.

5. Save the report as **rptProductsSoldbyStore**.

6. Print the report. (The figure is an example of how the report might look.)

Products Sold by Store

Store Location		Manager
Columbus	OH	B. Bright

Customer Name Andrew Nathanson

Installation Date	Description
5/29/2002	15'x24' oval pool

Customer Name Ben Spengler

Installation Date	Description
5/30/2002	4 person spa

Customer Name Bonnie Porz

Installation Date	Description
5/29/2002	15'x30' oval pool
6/5/2002	21' round pool

C4—Adding an Image to a Report

Some of the controls on the toolbox can be used to add images to a report or a form. There are three options: an Image control, a Bound Object control, or an Unbound Object control. In this exercise, you examine the Help explanation that describes these three options, and then add a logo to an Armstrong Report.

Goal: Understand the different types of image controls and add an image to a report.

1. If you completed one of the previous exercises, continue to use that file. Otherwise, locate **AC1101** in the **Student** folder for this lesson. Transfer the file to the location where you are saving your files. Remove the read-only property, and rename the file **AC1101-Challenges**. Open the file.

2. Open the report **rptSalesbyStore** in Design view. Using the **What's This?** Help command, click on each of the three image controls in the toolbox. Read the explanations to learn the differences between the **Image** button, the **Unbound Object** button, and the **Bound Object** button.

3. Open the **Page Header** section to approximately one-half inch. Move the **Sales by Store Location** label from the Report Header section to the Page Header section.

4. Click on the toolbox control that you think would be the best one to use to add a static image to a report. Click in the **Report Header** section.

5. Locate the **Armstrong Logo** file in the **Student** folder for this lesson. Reduce the size of the logo to approximately 1.25-inches tall. Make sure it does not extend beyond the 6.5-inch margin for a portrait printout.

6. Add your name to a label in the Page Header section and save the report. Print the first page of the report.

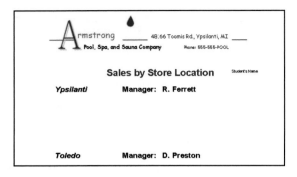

ON YOUR OWN

 In this lesson you learned more about creating reports and forms. To extend your practice and knowledge, you can create your own reports based on other database files or on paper records that you use. Any of the following ideas can be used as a basis for further practice.

- Work with a database of your own design and create forms and reports that serve the needs of your database and the users who may need information from the database.

- Look at paper reports that you may use and see if you can recreate them using an Access database.

- Try to design an invoice as a report or a form for billing customers for services provided.

- Take a bill that you regularly receive, such as a utility bill, and analyze the data necessary to generate the bill. Determine 1) how many tables would be required to gather the information, 2) what relationships would need to be created, 3) whether a query should be created to extract the necessary data, 4) how the report should be designed.

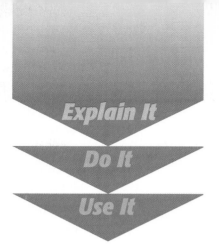

Lesson 12

Working with Macros and Modules

Task 1   Creating a Macro and Attaching It to a Command Button
Task 2   Creating a Command Button
Task 3   Adding a Command Button to a Form Using the Wizard
Task 4   Modifying a VBA Module
Task 5   Attaching a Module to a Command Button

INTRODUCTION

Once you have created your database structure, you can automate the database using a variety of tools. Adding automated features to your database makes it usable by someone who is not familiar with Access. You can make it easy for someone else to add new records, edit existing records, search for information, or print reports. There are three methods you can use to help automate your database

One way to automate functions in your database is to use *macros*. Macros are pre-defined commands that you can invoke and apply to objects in your database. By using macros you can automate a wide range of tasks, such as opening and closing forms or reports, printing information, or updating records. Macros are often attached to buttons. When you click on the button, it activates the macro to perform the specified action.

You can also add *command buttons* to a form to automate an action. You create command buttons by using a wizard or by setting the property values of the command button control. When you make a command button it creates an *event procedure*. An event procedure is a series of steps that must occur for a command to take effect. For example, if you create a command button to open a form, the event of clicking the button causes the open action to take place, and the specified form opens on your screen. Event procedures are written in a language called *Visual Basic for Applications (VBA)*. VBA is a common programming language used in many Microsoft products. It enables you to integrate data across applications. You can view and edit the event procedure module that is created when you add a command button.

The last procedure to automate your database is to write *modules*. Modules are programming routines written using Visual Basic code. The command button event procedures are an example of a module. Modules give you great flexibility and control over your database design, but you need to know and understand Visual Basic to use them effectively. This book does not teach you Visual Basic, but rather introduces the concept of modules and how they are used.

In this lesson, you work with the Armstrong Pool, Spa, and Sauna Company database to learn how to add macros and command buttons. You also edit a command button module and create a VBA module.

VISUAL SUMMARY

When you complete this lesson, you will have added command buttons, attached macros to buttons, and written a VBA module attached to a button.

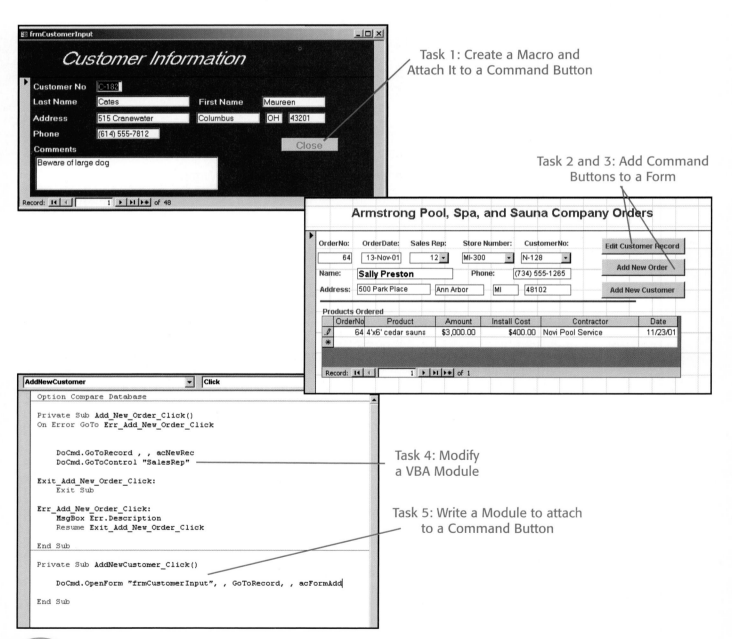

Task 1
CREATING A MACRO AND ATTACHING IT TO A COMMAND

Explain It

Do It

Use It

Why would I do this?

Someone may have responsibility for updating or entering records in a database, but not have any knowledge of Access or how to design a database. Macros are tools that can be used to help automate a database for use by someone else. Macros consist of *actions* and *arguments*. Actions are Access-defined functions that perform a task, while arguments are user-defined values that specify how and where a macro performs its function. You can create generic macros for use with several different objects, or an object-specific macro that causes an action to take place for one particular object.

In this task, you learn how to create a simple Close macro and attach it to the Customer Input form.

1 Start Microsoft Access. Click **More files** under the **Open a file** category. Locate **AC1201** and **AC1202** for this lesson. Transfer the files to the location where you are saving your files.

Remove the read-only property, if necessary, from both files. Rename the AC1201 file **AC1201-Armstrong** and open the file.

The Armstrong database you have been using contains the records of orders for the company. The company uses a second database for personnel, which contains a table of the sales representatives. From the Armstrong Orders database you are going to link to a table in the Armstrong Personnel database so you can display the sales representative for each order.

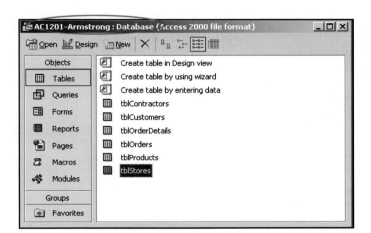

2 Choose File, Get External Data, Link Tables. Select **AC1202** in the **Link** dialog box. Click the **Link** button. Select **tblSalesReps** in the **Link Tables** dialog box and click **OK**.

The tblSalesReps table shows as a linked table in the Database window.

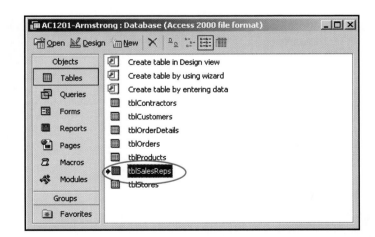

3 Click the **Macros** object button and click <u>N</u>ew.

The Macro window opens. You use the Action column to select the action you want to take. A macro consists of one or more actions. You use the Comment column to document the purpose for each action in a macro. In this macro, only one action is used.

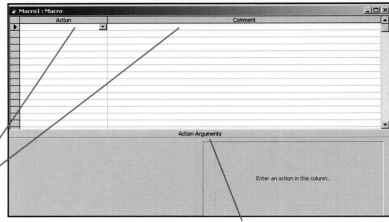

Actions listed in this column

Description of action documented here

Action Arguments display once an action has been selected

IN DEPTH

Two additional columns—the Macro Name column, and the Condition column—are sometimes used to define macros. Two buttons on the Macro toolbar are used to open and close these options. If either column appears on your screen, click the Macro Names or Conditions button, as appropriate, to remove the columns from your screen.

4 Click the arrow in the first **Action** box and select **Close** from the list of actions.

The Action Arguments area becomes active once you select an action. The arguments that display depend on the macro action you select. Normally, you specify an object to which the selected action should apply. In this case, you want the close action to be generic so it can be applied to several forms; therefore no action arguments are needed.

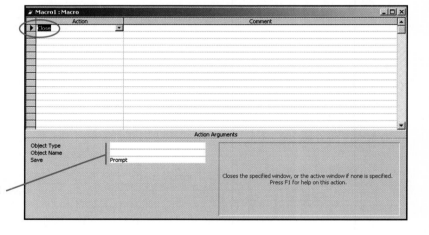

Action Arguments left blank

5 Save the macro and name it **mcrClose**. Close the Macro window.

The Close macro displays on the Macro page of the database window.

CAUTION

You can accidentally close the database using the button you created in this database. If you click the macro from the Macros window, the database will close. You will not lose any information if this happens—just reopen the database.

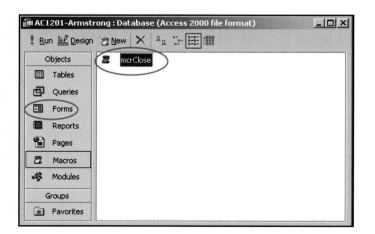

6 Click the **Forms** object button and open **frmCustomerInput** in **Design** View.

You will attach the Close macro you just created to a button on this form.

Click the **Control Wizards** button to turn off the wizards.

The Control Wizards is usually active by default. This is a toggle button used to turn on and off the wizards incorporated in the Toolbox controls. You deselect the Control Wizard because you do not use the Command Button Wizard in this task.

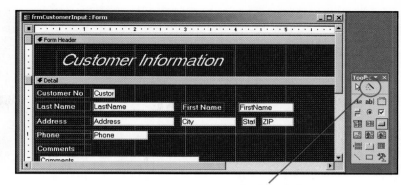

Control Wizards button

7 Click the **Command** button. Move the mouse pointer to the lower-right corner of the form and click.

A button is created. The Command number that appears on the button may vary.

Select the Command label, type **Close**, and press ↵Enter. Change the font size to **12**, the font color to **red**, and add **bold** emphasis.

Next, you attach the Close macro to this button.

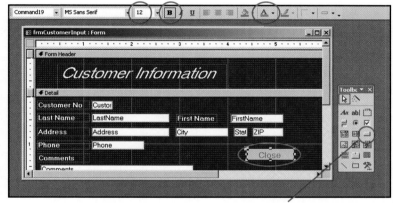

Command button

8 Right-click on the button and choose **Properties** from the shortcut menu. Click the **Event** tab and click in the **On Click** property box.

An arrow displays and a Build button appears to the right of the On Click property.

Click the arrow and select **mcrClose** from the list.

The items listed are the macros that have been created for this database.

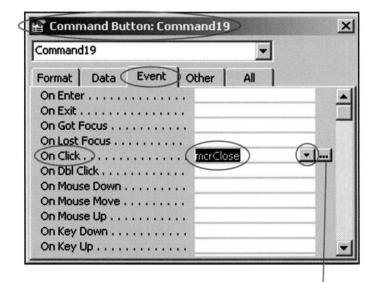

Build button

9 Close the property sheet. Click the **Save** button and then click the **View** button.

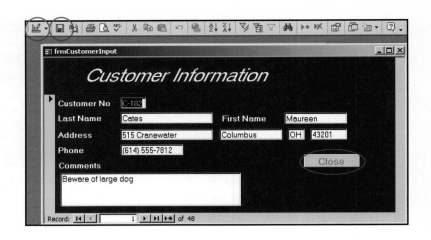

10 Click the **Close** button you just created to test it.

The form closes and the database window is displayed.

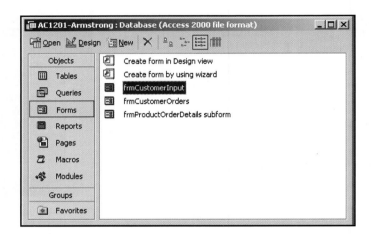

Task 2
CREATING A COMMAND BUTTON

Why would I do this?
The Windows environment uses a *Graphical User Interface (GUI)* that enables you to interact with the computer and the computer applications to accomplish tasks. A main component of this environment is the ability to click on buttons to execute commands. The toolbar at the top of your window is an example of buttons used to execute commands. In the previous task, you created a macro and then attached it to a command button. Clicking buttons is a familiar procedure when working in any application. The use of command buttons adds to the graphical interface environment, which enables you to work easily in your database.

In the previous task, you first created a macro and then attached it to a button. In this task, you create a command button first, and then learn how to use the Macro Builder to create the action you want the command button to execute.

1 Open the **frmCustomerOrders** form in **Design** View. Maximize the window. If necessary, close the field list box and open the toolbox.

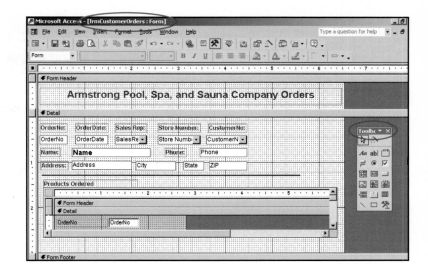

2 Click the Command button on the toolbox and then click on the form at the 5-inch mark, to the right of the CustomerNo label.

A command button is placed on the form. To make it functional, you will create a macro that is attached it. The number on your button may be different from the one shown in the figure.

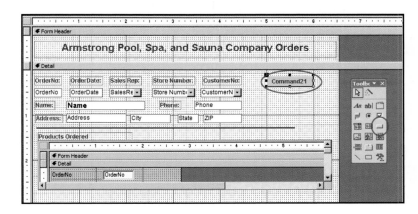

3 Open the property sheet for the command button. Click the **Event** Tab, and click the **On Click** property box.

You will use the Build button to open the Macro Builder where you can create a macro for this command button.

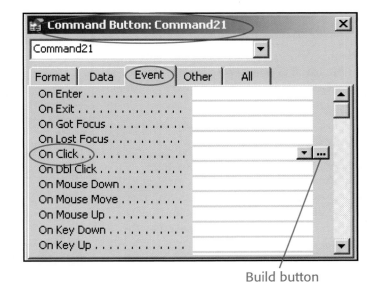

Build button

4 Click the **Build** button.

The Choose Builder dialog box opens and lists three options.

Click **Macro Builder** to select it.

The Macro Builder opens the Macro window so you can create a macro that is automatically attached to the selected command button.

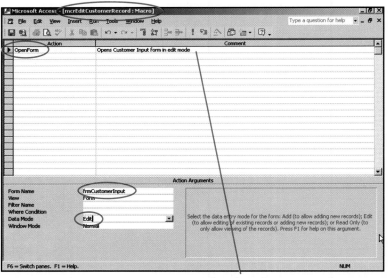

5 With Macro Builder selected, click **OK**.

The Macro window opens and a Save As dialog box is displayed. Before you can create the macro, you have to name and save it.

Replace the default name in the Save As dialog box with **mcrEditCustomerRecord**.

6 Click **OK**.

The macro is saved. Now you need to select the actions for this macro. The purpose of this macro is to open the Customer Input form so you can edit a record. You want the record that displays in the input form to match the record that is currently active in the Customer Orders form.

In the first Action box, select **OpenForm** from the list of actions. Press Tab⇄ and type **Opens Customer Input form in edit mode** in the **Comment** area.

This sets the first macro action and explains the purpose of the action.

In the Action Argument area, click the **Form Name** box. Click the arrow and select **frmCustomerInput** from the list of available objects. Click the **Data Mode** box and select **Edit** from the list of options displayed by the list arrow.

This specifies the form that opens when the button is clicked and sets the way you can work with the form.

Purpose of action documented

QUICK TIP

In the Action box you can simply type the first letter of the action you want to take. The list moves to the beginning of all actions that start with the letter you typed. This is a way to move quickly through the alphabetized list of actions to select the one you want. For example, if you type O, the first open action will display in the Action box, and then you can expand the list and select the open action you want.

7 Click in the second **Action** box and type **M**.

The Maximize action displays as the next action in the macro. This causes the window that is opened by the previous action to expand to a maximized window. No arguments are needed for this action.

Click in the third **Action** box and type **F**, then select **FindRecord** from the list of actions. Press ⎄Tab⎄ and type **Find current record**.

This action is used to locate the record in the Customer Input form that matches the one displayed in the Customer Orders form.

In the **Find What** argument type **=[CustomerNo]**.

This argument causes the Customer Input form to find the record that matches the CustomerNo field in the first form—in this case the Customer Orders form.

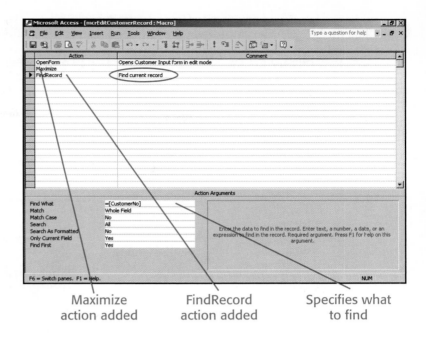

Maximize
action added

FindRecord
action added

Specifies what
to find

8 Click the **Close** button on the macro window, and click **Yes** to save the changes.

The Macro window closes, and the Design view of the frmCustomerOrders form is displayed. The property sheet for the command button displays the name of the macro you just created.

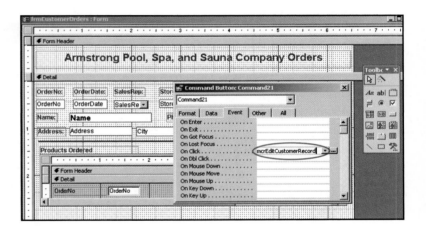

9 Close the property sheet. Change the caption on the button to read **Edit Customer Record**. Increase the size of the button as needed to see the entire caption. Click the **View** button to see the results.

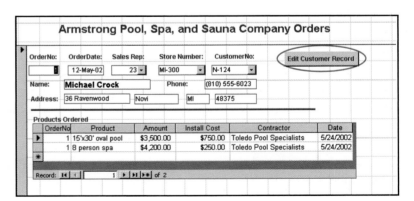

10 Click the **Next Record** button on the main part of the form four times until you see the record for **Charles Bloom**.

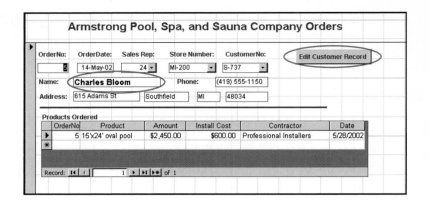

11 Click the **Edit Customer Record** button.

The record for Charles Bloom is displayed in the Customer Input form.

In the comments box type **Installer: Call customer on cell phone at (419) 555-2341 before going to house.**

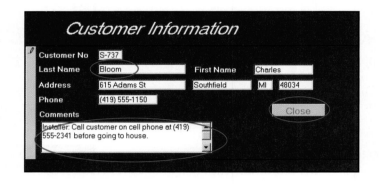

12 Click the **Close** command button.

The frmCustomerInput form closes and the frmCustomerOrders form is redisplayed on your screen.

Leave the **frmCustomerOrders** form open for the next task.

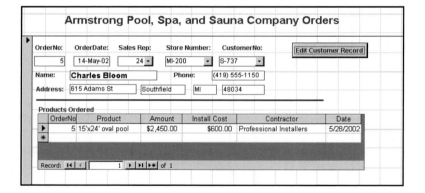

Task 3

ADDING A COMMAND BUTTON TO A FORM USING THE WIZARD

Why would I do this?

In the first two tasks you created command buttons attached to macros. You can also create command buttons using the Command Button Wizard. When you use this method, the Access program creates an event procedure module that executes the command. The wizard is simple and easy to follow, and you do not have to create a macro.

In this task, you use the wizard to create a command button to add a new order.

1 Click the View button to return to the Design view of the frmCustomerOrders form.

To use the Command Button Wizard you first need to reactivate the wizards.

Click the Control Wizards button to make it active. Click the Command button and then click on the form under the Edit Customer Record button.

The Command Button Wizard dialog box opens. The left column lists the available categories. The right column displays the actions available for the selected category.

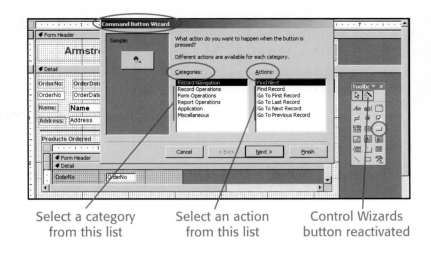

Select a category from this list   Select an action from this list   Control Wizards button reactivated

2 Select Record Operations from the **Categories** list. Select Add New Record from the **Actions** list.

This action will clear the fields on the form so you can add a new record to the frmCustomerOrders form.

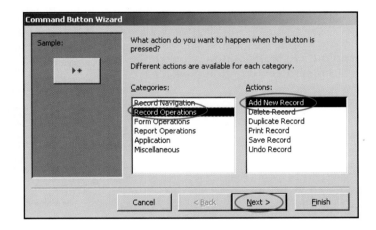

3 Click Next.

In the second Command Button Wizard dialog box you can choose to have the command button display text or an image.

Click the **Text** option button and type Add New Order.

The text displays in the sample button to the left. This is the caption property, which controls what displays on the button.

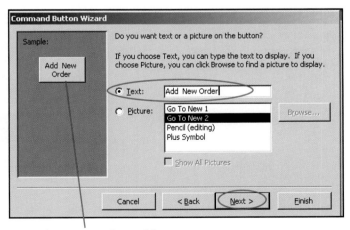

Sample text previewed here

4 Click <u>N</u>ext. Type **Add New Order** in the name box.

You want to use a meaningful name for the command button in case you need to refer to it later. What is typed here shows on the name property line for this button.

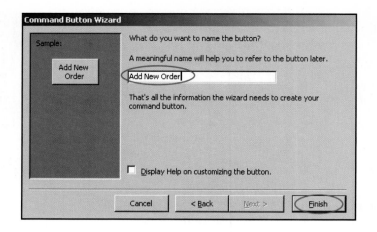

5 Click <u>F</u>inish.

The wizard closes and the command button displays the new name.

Expand the size of the button to match the Edit Customer Record button. Save the changes.

Button expanded

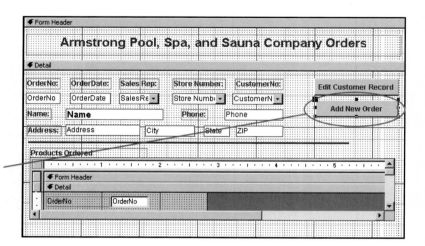

6 Click the <u>V</u>iew button. Click the **Add New Order** button.

The fields are emptied and you are now ready to add a new order. This has the same effect as clicking the New Record button on the toolbar or on the navigation bar.

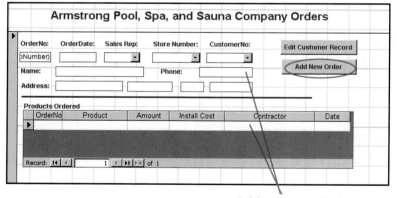

Fields are emptied

7 Click in the **OrderNo** field box and then press Tab↹ to move to the OrderDate field. Type the current date. Press Tab↹ and select sales rep **3 Margaret Peacock**. Press Tab↹ and select **MI-200 Southfield**. Press Tab↹ and select **S-743 Taylor** for the CustomerNo field.

The OrderNo field is an AutoNumber field, so the next order number is automatically filled in after you enter a date. Once you select the customer record number, the customer information is filled in.

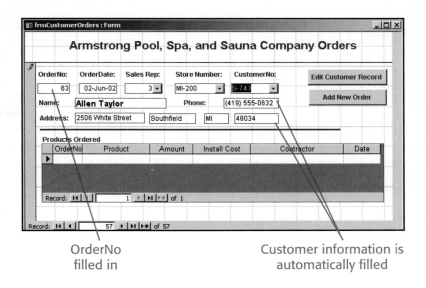

OrderNo
filled in

Customer information is
automatically filled

In order for the customer information to fill in automatically, the query that is used for this form was created using the foreign key field from the related table. If you look at the design of the qryCustomerOrders query, you will see that the CustomerNo field is taken from the tblOrders table. In this table, the CustomerNo field is a foreign key that is joined to the primary key field in the tblCustomers table. The use of the foreign key field causes the information for the other fields selected from the primary table to be filled automatically. If the CustomerNo field from the tblCustomer had been used, where it is the primary key, then the related data would not fill in automatically.

8 Click the **OrderNo** field in the subform and press Tab↹ to move to the **Product** field. Select **15' round pool** from the list.

The information for the product is automatically filled and the same order number is displayed in the subform.

Tab to the **Contractor** field and select **Babcock Services Southfield** from the list. Press Tab↹ and type a date that is 10 days after the current date you entered for the **OrderDate** field.

The order form is complete.

Leave the form open for the next task.

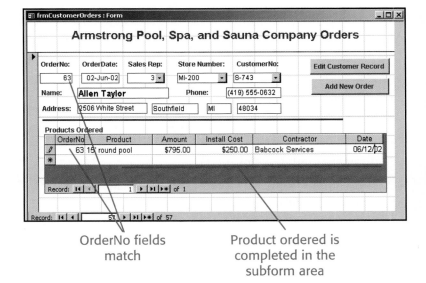

OrderNo fields
match

Product ordered is
completed in the
subform area

Task 4
MODIFYING A VBA MODULE

Why would I do this?

When you create a command button using the Command Button Wizard, an event procedure is created. You can view this event procedure as a VBA module. You may want to modify the module in some manner to make it more effective. For example, you can modify the module for the Add New Order button so the insertion point is placed automatically in the OrderDate field.

In this task, you modify the Add New Order module.

1 Click the <u>View</u> button to return to the Design view of the **frmCustomerOrders** form. Right-click the **Add New Order** button and choose **Build <u>E</u>vent** from the shortcut menu.

The Microsoft Visual Basic window opens and the module for the selected button is displayed. Each module in the VBA window begins with the phrase "Private Sub" followed by the name of the action or subroutine program that has been invoked. In this case, this includes the name of the button and the click event.

Maximize the Microsoft Visual Basic window and maximize the module.

Add New Order module

Click identified as the event

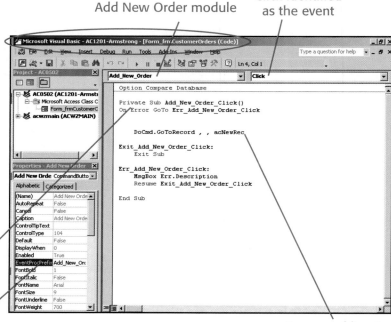

Beginning of Private Subroutine

Event Procedure is selected in the Properties Window

Command line to go to a new record

2 Press the ↓ key four times.

This moves the insertion point to just under the GoToRecord command.

Press Tab⇄ and type **DoCmd.GoToControl "SalesRep"** and press ↵Enter.

This enters a command to go to the field named SalesRep. Instructions are indented so it is easier to read the code.

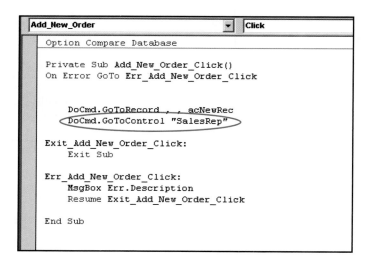

IN DEPTH

As you type you will see a list of suggested actions. You can select an action from the list and press Tab⇄ to accept the action. Then you type the rest of the instructions. DoCmd is a Visual Basic instruction that directs the program to execute the command or action that follows. The commas indicate arguments for the command. In this example you do not need to include any arguments.

3 Close the **Microsoft Visual Basic** window.

The frmCustomerOrders Design window is redisplayed.

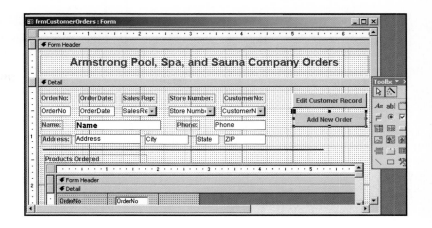

4 Click the View button. Click the Add New Order button to test the change you made to the module.

The fields are cleared and the insertion point moves to the Sales Rep field. To further enhance this form you can add a default value to the OrderDate field so the current date is automatically displayed when a new order is entered.

Insertion point displays here

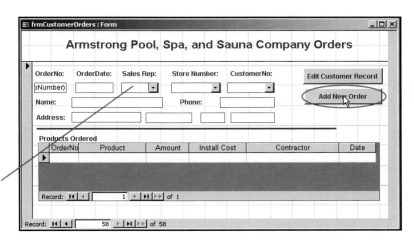

5 Return to Design view and open the property sheet for the **OrderDate** field.

The OrderDate property sheet opens.

Click the **Data** tab and type **Date()** in the **Default Value** property box.

This is the code to enter the current date in the selected field.

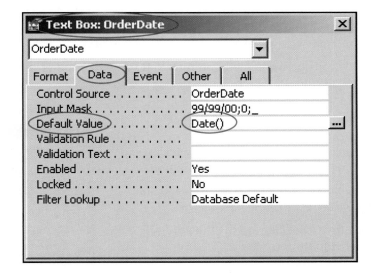

6 Close the property sheet and return to Form view.

Whenever you make a change to a form, you need to test it to make sure it works as intended.

Click the **Add New Order** button

The current date is entered in the OrderDate field and the insertion point moves to the SalesRep field.

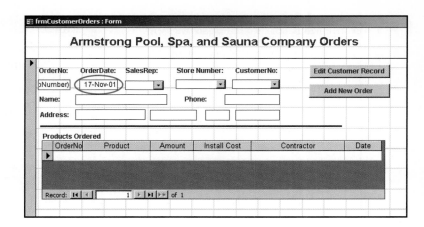

7 Click the **Save** button to save the changes to your form. Leave the form open for the next task.

Task 5

ATTACHING A MODULE TO A COMMAND BUTTON

Why would I do this?

So far, you have learned how to create a macro and attach it to a button, create a command button and then create the macro for that button, create a command button by using the Command Button Wizard, and modify the event procedure module that the wizard creates. You can also write a module for a command button. This procedure is similar to creating a button and then writing the macro to make the button work. In this case, however, you use the Visual Basic window to write code for the button. The end goal is the same for all of these techniques—to help automate your database for someone else to use.

In this task, you add a command button to add a new customer, and then create a module to execute the action.

1 Click the **View** button. Click the **Command** button on the toolbox and then click on the form under the Add New Order button.

The Command Button Wizard dialog box opens. You are not going to use the wizard.

Click the **Cancel** button to close the Command Button Wizard.

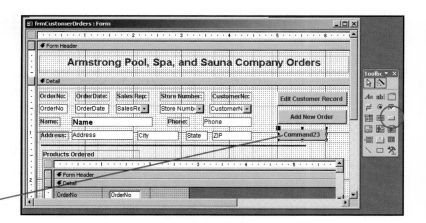

New Command button added to the form

2 Right-click the command button you just added to your form and choose **Properties** from the shortcut menu.

The properties sheet for command button control is displayed.

Click the **Format** tab and change the **Caption** property to **Add New Customer** and press ⏎Enter.

The new caption shows on the command button.

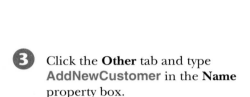

3 Click the **Other** tab and type **AddNewCustomer** in the **Name** property box.

The name of the button is used to identify it when you are working in a module. Naming conventions for Visual Basic modules do not allow spaces.

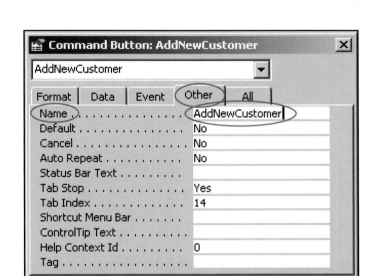

4 Click the **Event** tab and click the **On Click** Property.

A Build button displays next to the On Click property.

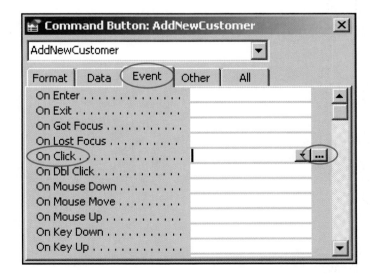

⑤ Click the **Build** button and choose **Code Builder** from the **Choose Builder** dialog box. Click **OK**.

The Microsoft Visual Basic window opens. A new Private Sub routine is started for the AddNewCustomer button. Notice that the name of the button appears in the list box at the top of the form. The "Click" event displays in the second list box. EventProcPrefix is highlighted in the Properties window on the left.

Declaration of a new subroutine

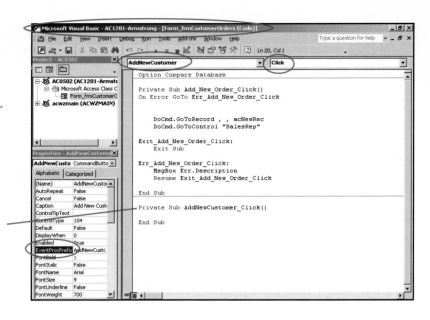

⑥ Move your insertion point to the empty line following the Private Sub declaration, if necessary.

The first statement in a module is a declaration of the classification and purpose of the code that follows.

Press ⏎Enter to add another empty line, then press Tab⇥ and type **DoCmd.OpenForm "frmCustomerInput", , GoToRecord, , acFormAdd**.

*This code executes the command to open a form and then identifies the form as **frmCustomerInput**. The next command is the go to record command. The last command clears the fields so a new record can be added.*

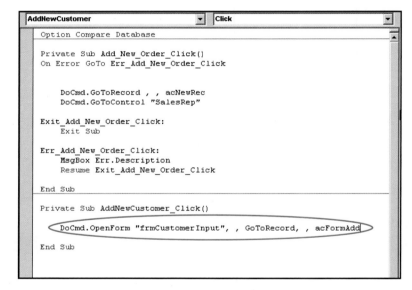

⑦ Close the **Microsoft Visual Basic** window.

The code is automatically saved when you close the window. The Form Design window is redisplayed on your screen. [Event Procedure] displays on the property sheet.

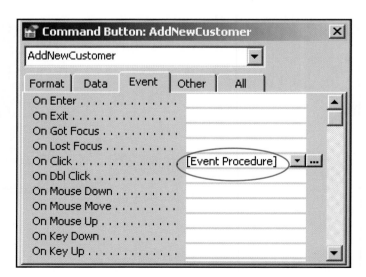

8 Close the property sheet and increase the size of the **Add New Customer** button to match the other command buttons. Click the **View** button, and then click the **Add New Customer** button.

The frmCustomerInput form opens and the fields are cleared so you can add a new record.

> **Type N-128 in the Customer No** field, and then fill in the rest of the information with your name, address, and phone number.

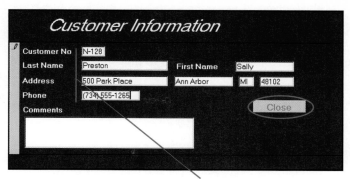

New record added

9 Click the **Close** button on the form.

The frmCustomerOrders form is redisplayed on your screen.

> Click the **Add New Order** button. Select **12 Dave Creal** as the sales rep and then select **MI-300 Novi** for the Store Number. Type **N-128** in the CustomerNo field box and press Tab.

Your name and address information is filled in automatically. The new customer record does not show in the list box until you refresh the form. You can refresh the form by closing it and opening it again. In this case, it is simply easier to type in the new customer number.

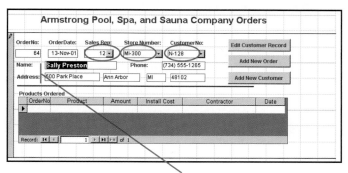

Your name and address information displays automatically

10 Complete the order by filling in a product of your choice. Select a Novi-based contractor to install it, and set the date for 10 days from the **OrderDate**.

A new record and a new order have been entered.

> Choose **File**, **Print**, **Selected Record(s)** to print the record showing your name. Save the form and close it.

Order completed

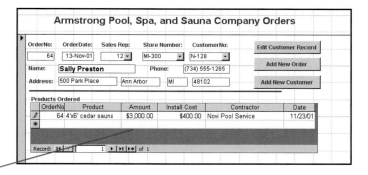

> **IN DEPTH**
>
> If your database contains modules, you may want to save it as an MDE file before you share it with other users. This protects the code and the design of your forms, reports, and modules so others cannot alter them. Saving the database as an MDE file compiles all modules, removes all editable code, and compacts the destination database. Before you can do this, however, there are a number of things you should know. First, the file must be an Access 2002 file. You should make a backup copy of the database so you can alter the objects if needed. The Design view of the forms and reports will not be accessible in the MDE file. If the database uses tables from other databases, the linked database must also be changed to an MDE file. If you are interested in learning more about this feature, be sure to do the Challenge 4 exercise at the end of this lesson.

11 Compact and close the database.

The exercises that follow are designed for you to review and use what you have learned in this lesson. You also have the opportunity to practice your skills and then expand on them by applying them to new situations.

COMPREHENSION

Comprehension exercises are designed to check your memory and understanding of the basic concepts in this lesson. You distinguish between true and false statements, identify new screen elements, and match terms with related statements. If you are uncertain of the correct answer, refer to the task number following each item (for example, T4 refers to Task 4) and review that task until you are confident that you can provide a correct response.

TRUE-FALSE

Circle either T or F.

T F 1. Once you have created a module, it cannot be modified. **(T4)**

T F 2. The ability to click on buttons to execute commands is a feature of a GUI. **(T2)**

T F 3. In order for information to fill in automatically on a form, the query that is used as the basis for the form must use the primary key field from the main table. **(T3)**

T F 4. When you use the Command Button Wizard, the Access program creates an event procedure module that executes the command. **(T3)**

T F 5. Macros are the only method used in Access to create a command button. **(T1)**

T F 6. DoCmd is used in a module to instruct the program to do the command that follows. **(T5)**

MATCHING QUESTIONS

A. Macros   D. VBA

B. Modules   E. Arguments

C. Event Procedure   F. Actions

Match the following statements to the word or phrase that is the best match from the list. Write the letter of the matching word or phrase in the space provided next to the number.

1. ____ A common programming language used in many Microsoft products **(Intro)**

2. ____ A series of steps that must occur for a command to take effect **(Intro)**

3. ____ Predefined commands that you can invoke and apply to objects in a database **(Intro)**

4. ____ Access-defined functions that perform a task **(T1)**

5. ____ Values that specify how and where a macro performs its function **(T1)**

6. ____ Programming routines that are written using Visual Basic code **(Intro)**

IDENTIFYING PARTS OF THE ACCESS SCREEN

Refer to the figure and identify the numbered parts of the screen. Write the letter of the correct label in the space next to the number.

1. _____

2. _____

3. _____

4. _____

5. _____

6. _____

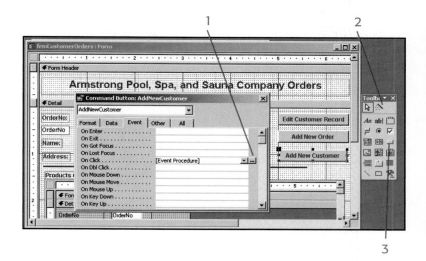

A. Command button **(T2)**

B. Argument for FindRecord action **(T2)**

C. Causes form that opens to fill the screen **(T2)**

D. Documents the purpose of the action **(T1)**

E. Build button **(T2)**

F. Control Wizards **(T4)**

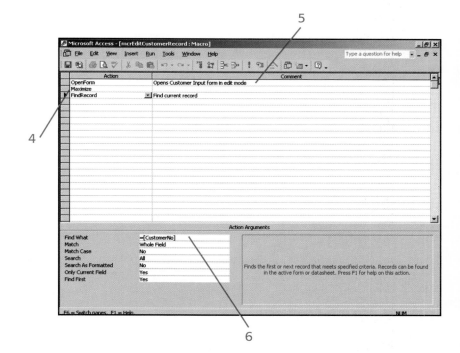

Reinforcement exercises are designed to reinforce the skills you have learned by applying them to new situations. Detailed instructions are provided along with a figure, where appropriate, to illustrate the result. Complete the reinforcement exercises sequentially. Leave the file open at the end of each exercise for use in the next exercise until you are specifically directed to close it.

In these exercises, you use a database designed to track fund-raising efforts for a nonprofit organization. The main function of the database is to track member pledges and their payments.

R1— Creating a Macro and Attaching It to a Command Button

1. Open Access and click **More files** under the **Open a file** category. Locate **AC1203** in the **Student** folder for this lesson. Transfer the file to the location where you are saving your files. Remove the read-only property, and rename the file **AC1203-FundRaising**. Open the file.

2. Click the **Macro** object button and click **New**. In the Macro window select **PrintOut** in the first action box. Press (Tab↹), and then type **Print current record** in the Comment column.

3. In the **Print Range** argument box, use the arrow to choose **Selection** from the list.

4. Close the macro and save it as **mcrPrintSelection**.

5. Click the **Forms** object button and open **frmMemberPledges** in Design view.

6. Click the **Command** button and then click in the Form Header area. Cancel the Command Button Wizard and open the property sheet for this new button.

7. Click the **On Click** property and select **mcrPrintSelection** from the list. Change the **Caption** property to **Print Record**.

8. Close the property sheet and click the **View** button.

9. Change the name of the first member (MemberID 100-3) to your name. Click the **Print Record** button to make sure it works.

10. Close the form and save your changes.

R2—Creating a Command Button

1. Open **frmMemberPledges** in Design view. Click the **Command** button and click to the right of FirstName on the form. Cancel the wizard.

2. Open the property sheet for this new button and click the **On Click** property. Click the **Build** button and choose **Macro Builder** in the **Choose Builder** dialog box. Click **OK**.

3. In the **Save As** dialog box type **mcrEditMemberRecord** as the macro name.

4. Click in the first **Action** box and select **OpenForm**. Press (Tab↹), and then type **Open frmMemberInformation in edit mode**. Click in the **Form Name** box in the Action Arguments area and select **frmMemberInformation**. Change the **Data Mode** to **Edit**.

5. Click the second **Action** box and type **M**. The **Maximize** action is selected.

6. Click the third **Action** box and select **FindRecord**. Press (Tab↹), and then type **Find current record**.

7. On the **Find What** argument type =[MemberID].

8. Close the macro and save the changes. Change the caption on the command button to **Edit Member Record**. Resize the button as needed.

9. Click the **View** button. Click the **Next Record** button until you see the record for **Martha Waters**. Click the **Edit Member Record** button and add the following comment: **Chair of the Board of Trustees**.

10. Print the form for Martha Waters. Close **frmMemberInformation**. Close **frmMemberPledges** and save the changes.

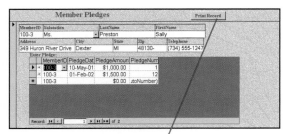

Print Record button added

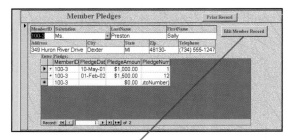

Edit Member Record button added

R3—Adding a Command Button to a Form Using the Wizard

1. Open **frmMemberPledges** in Design view.

2. Click the **Command** button and click on the form under the Edit Member Record button.

3. In the first Command Button Wizard dialog box, choose **Record Operations** under <u>C</u>ategories, and **Add New Record** as the <u>A</u>ction.

4. In the second Command Button Wizard dialog box, choose **<u>T</u>ext**.

5. In the third Command Button Wizard dialog box, type **Add Record** as the name for the button. Click **<u>F</u>inish**.

6. Click the **View** button and test it to make sure it works. Do not add a record at this time.

7. Close the form and save the changes.

R4—Modifying a VBA Module

1. Open the **frmMemberPledges** form in Design View.

2. Right-click the **Add Record** button and choose **Build <u>E</u>vent** from the shortcut menu.

3. In the Add Record module, press ↓ four times. With the insertion point on the line below the DoCmd line, press Tab⇄ and type **DoCmd.GoToControl "MemberID"**. Press ⏎Enter.

4. Close the **Module** window. Click the **View** button. Click the **Add Record** button to make sure the insertion point moves to the MemberID field box.

5. Save the changes and close the form.

R5—Attaching a Module to a Command Button

1. Open **frmMemberPledges** in Design view. Add another new command button on the form under the Add Record button. Cancel the Wizard.

2. Open the property sheet for the new button. Change the **Caption** property to **Add New Member**. Change the **Name** property to **AddNewMember**.

3. Click the **On Click** property. Click the **Build** button and choose **Code Builder** from the **Choose Builder** dialog box.

4. In the Module Window, make sure the insertion point is on the blank line under the AddNewMember subroutine declaration statement. Press ⏎Enter, then press Tab⇄ and type **DoCmd.OpenForm "frmMemberInformation", , GoToRecord, , acFormAdd**. Press ⏎Enter again to add an empty line.

5. Close the **Microsoft Visual Basic** window. Close the property sheet. Adjust the size of the three buttons you added to the same size.

6. Click the **View** button and click the new **Add New Member** button. Add your information in the new record. Use **114-5** as the MemberID and print the results.

7. Save and close the database.

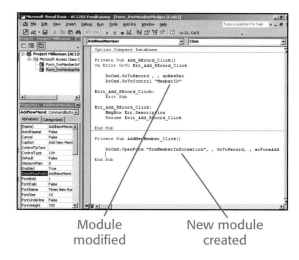

Module modified   New module created

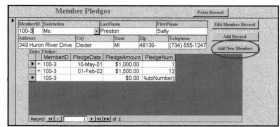

Challenge exercises are designed to test your ability to apply your skills to new situations with less-detailed instructions. These exercises also challenge you to expand your repertoire of skills by using commands that are similar to those you have already learned. The desired outcome is clearly defined, but you have more freedom to choose the steps needed to achieve the required result.

 ## C1—Create a Group Macro to Preview Reports

You can create a blank form that contains buttons used to print or preview reports. In this exercise, you add buttons to a blank form and create the macros needed to view or print reports. It is important the macros are precisely named to indicate what action they will perform. This exercise uses the fund-raising database.

Goal: Create a group macro to use for printing reports.

1. If you completed the Reinforcement exercise, you can use the **AC1203-FundRaising** file you created. Otherwise, locate **AC1203** in the **Student** folder for this lesson. Transfer the file to the location where you are saving your files. Remove the read-only property, and rename the file **AC1203-Ch1**. Open the file.

2. Click the **Macros** object button and click **New**. Click the **Macro Names** button to add that optional column to the window. You can create a group of macros to use with one object and save all the macros with one name. This is known as a group macro.

3. Type **PreviewMemberPayments** in the **Macro Name** column and press Tab. Choose **OpenReport** as the action and type **Preview Member Payments report** in the Comment column. Select **rptMemberPayments** as the Report Name argument and change View to **Print Preview**.

4. Skip a line, then type **PreviewMemberPledges** in the third **Macro Name** box, select **OpenReport** as the action, and then type **Preview Member Pledges report** in the Comment column. Select **rptMemberPledges** as the Report Name argument and change View to **Print Preview**.

5. Repeat this process to preview **rptMembers** and **rptPayments**. The macro window should look like the one in the figure. Close the macro and save it as **mcrPreviewReports**.

6. Create a new blank form in design view that is not based on a table or a query. Turn off the Control Wizards. Add four command buttons to the form. Using the **On Click** property, attach each of the buttons to one of the macros in the ReportOptions macro group. (You may need to widen the property sheet to see the macro names.) Select a different macro for each button and then name the button appropriately to match the action of the macro.

7. Add a label to the form that instructs the user what to do. Change the font size, and the font color to make the buttons easier to read. Resize the buttons so they are evenly sized. Change other formatting characteristics of the form to make it attractive. The figure that follows is an example of how you might design the form.

8. Add your name to the form and print a copy. Save it as **frmPreviewReports**.

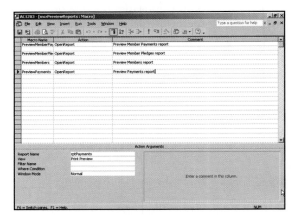

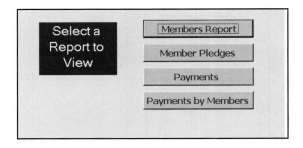

C2—Adding Conditional Macros to an Option Group Control

There are a lot of controls included in the toolbox that you can use when you design a form. One of the more interesting controls is the Option Group. You can add individual option buttons or check boxes to a form, but with the Option Group control you restrict the choice to one of the options listed in the group box. Once you have created the control, you then activate it by attaching macros to each of the option buttons. In the previous lesson you learned how to add a group option control to a form. In this lesson you add the macros to activate the Option group control.

Goal: Activate option buttons in an Option Group control.

1. Locate **AC1204** in the **Student** folder for this lesson. Transfer the file to the location where you are saving your files. Remove the read-only property, and rename the file **AC1204-Challenges**. Open the file.

2. Click the **Forms** object button and open **frmCustomerRecords** in the Design view. Maximize the form.

3. Click the **Control Wizards** button to turn off the wizards. Add a **Command** button to the right of the Select Options group control. Change the name on the button to **Continue** and change the font to **12-point bold**.

4. Add a second **Command** button under the first. Change the name to **Cancel** and change the font to **12-point bold**.

5. Click the option button for each of the three options and examine the **Option Value** property (found on the Data tab) for each button. Each button is given a different number to identify it in the group. Close the form and save the changes.

6. Open a new Macro window. Click the **Macro Name** and **Conditions** buttons to add these two optional columns to the macro window.

7. Type **RecordOptions** in the Macro Name column and press Tab⇆. Type **[SelectOption]=1** in the Condition column. SelectOption is the name of the option group box. In the Action column select **OpenForm**. In the Comment column, type **Open CustomerInput form in Add mode**. Select **frmCustomerInput** in the Form Name argument, and **Add** in the Data Mode argument.

8. In the second Condition box type **[SelectOption]=2**; the Action is **OpenForm**. Type **Open CustomerInput form in Edit mode**. Change the Form Name argument to **frmCustomerInput**, and the Data Mode to **Edit**.

9. In the third Condition box type **[SelectOption]=3**. Set the rest of this option to open **frmCustomerInput** in **Read Only** mode.

10. Leave an empty line and type **Cancel** as a new Macro Name. The Action is **Close**. Type **Close Record Options form** in the comment area. Save the macro and name it **mcrOptions**.

11. Choose <u>F</u>ile, <u>P</u>rint. Make sure all the check boxes are selected in the **Print Macro Definition** dialog box and then click **OK**. Close the macro.

12. Open **frmCustomerRecords** in Design View. Open the property sheet for the **Continue** command button. Select **mcrOptions.RecordOptions** for the **On Click** event. Click the **Cancel** button and select **mcrOptions.Cancel** for the On Click event.

13. Change to the Form view and test your buttons. Notice that when you click the **Find Customer** button, the form opens and displays the customer records, but you cannot add a new record or make any changes. Print the **frmCustomerRecords** form. Save your changes.

C3—Deleting a Command Button and Its Related Module

In this lesson you learned to create command buttons using a wizard, and you learned to edit the related VBA module for that button. Sometimes you may create a button and then decide you want to delete it. When you delete the button you should also delete the VBA module for that button.

Goal: Create and delete a command button.

1. If you completed the previous exercise, continue to use that file. Otherwise, locate **AC1204** in the **Student** folder for this lesson. Transfer the file to the location where you are saving your files. Remove the read-only property, and rename the file **AC1204-Challenges**. Open the file.

2. Open the **frmCustomerInput** in Design view. Maximize the window.

3. Make sure the **Control Wizards** button is active, and then add a **Command** button to the lower-left corner of the form. Choose **Record Operations** from

the **Categories** list and **Add New Record** from the **Actions** list.

4. Select **Text** in the next Command Button Wizard dialog box, and then name the button **Add Record**.

5. Add a second command button to the right of the Add Record button. Select **Delete Record** from the **Record Operations** category. Add a third button to print a record. Add a fourth button that uses the Go To Previous Record command. Name it **Previous Record**. Align the buttons on the form and save your changes.

6. Click the View button. Click the **Add Record** button. Use customer number **C-189** and enter your name and address information as a new record. Click the **Print Record** button.

7. Click the **Delete Record** button to remove your record. Click the **Previous Record** button.

8. Return to the Design view and select the **Previous Record** button and press Del. Add a new **Previous Record** button that uses a picture instead of text. Name it **Previous Record**. You should see an error message telling you that there is already an On Click event procedure by that name. Change the name to **PreviousRecord**.

9. Go to the Form view and test the new **Previous Record** button. Return to the Design view. Right-click the **PreviousRecord** button and choose **Build Event** from the shortcut menu.

10. Review the subroutines written for the command buttons. Select the text between the lines for the **Private Sub Previous_Record_Click()** down through **End Sub** and press Del to remove this code. This is the code for the button that you deleted.

11. Save the changes. Print the VBA module. Close the VBA module window and then test the button again. Print the form and save the changes.

C4—Saving a Database as an MDE File

If you add macros and modules to a database, it is usually to help automate the database so others can use it. Before you share the database with others, however, you should make a backup copy. Then you can save the database you want to share as an MDE file. This compacts and removes the code so someone else cannot alter it. This exercise uses the AC1201-Armstrong file you created in the lesson.

Goal: Save a database as an MDE file.

1. Open Access and open the file **AC1201-Armstrong** that was created when you completed the tasks in this lesson.

2. Choose **Tools, Database Utilities, Convert Database, To Access 2002 File Format**. In the **Convert Database Into** dialog box type **AC1201-Ch4** in the **File name** box and change the **Save in** box to the folder where you have your other files. Click **Save**. Click **OK** to acknowledge the warning message box. Close the file.

3. Choose **Tools, Database Utilities, Make MDE File**.

4. Select the **AC1201-Ch4** file in the **Database to Save as MDE** dialog box. Click the **Make MDE** button.

5. Click the **Save** button in the **Save MDE As** dialog box.

6. Open the **AC1201-Ch4.mde** file. If the file extensions are not showing on your computer, look for the Access icon with the lock on it. This is the MDE file.

7. Look at the **Forms** page of the Database window. The command buttons are not displayed and the **Design** and **New** buttons are gray. Open the **frmCustomerOrders** form and test the buttons.

8. Look at the other object pages in the Database window. What differences do you see from a regular mdb database window? Can you find any method to view the design of the forms? Open Word and respond to these two questions. Write a brief explanation of the differences you detected.

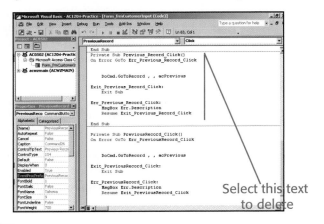

Select this text to delete

ON YOUR OWN

 In this lesson you learned about creating macros and modules. To extend your practice and knowledge, you can create your own macros or modules based on other database files. Use any of the following ideas as a basis for further practice.

1. Work with a database of your own design and create macros and modules that serve the needs of your database and the users who may need information from the database.

   - Demonstrate the ability to create a macro.

   - Demonstrate the ability to attach a macro to a button.

   - Demonstrate the ability to create a command button that runs from a macro or a module.

2. Explore the macro window and examine some of the other macro functions that are part of the Access program. Look at the different action arguments that accompany each action.

   - Create a macro for a database of your choice that uses an expression or a filter in the action argument area. This might be used to restrict the records that are displayed when a report is printed.

3. Save your file on your own disk. Name it **AC1205-Macros**.

4. Check with your instructor to determine if you should submit the file in electronic or printed form. If necessary, capture an image of the screen using the PrtScn button on your keyboard and paste the image into a Word document that you can print to display the macros or modules you have created.

5. For further information on using VBA in Access, go to your local bookstore and look for a book that teaches how to use VBA modules in Access. Not all books cover this topic, so examine the content of the book to determine if the information covered is detailed enough for your needs.

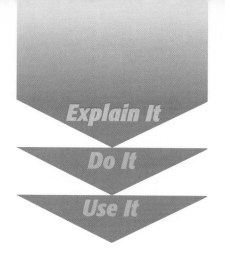

Lesson 13

Collaborating with Access

Task 1   Creating and Modifying a Data Access Page
Task 2   Saving PivotTable Views to a Data Access Page
Task 3   Saving PivotChart Views to a Data Access Page
Task 4   Exporting Access Data to XML Documents
Task 5   Importing XML Documents into Access

INTRODUCTION

Information in a database may need to be shared with vendors, customers, or branch locations. You can use a variety of methods to make this information available to others. This lesson introduces some of those options.

You can create a *data access page* to display information as a Web page. Access uses *Hypertext Markup Language* (HTML) to control how the information looks when it is viewed with a Web browser. This process creates a separate file and folder and places a shortcut on the *Pages* object page in the Database window. The data access page is connected to the database, and can be used interactively. This method enables a company to post database information to a Web site for the purpose of viewing or updating information in the database.

You can also save PivotTables and PivotCharts as data access pages. As you learned in Lesson 11, PivotTables are dynamic views that enable you to easily alter the layout of the view to show totals across different categories. PivotCharts present graphical representations of data that help you see trends, or visualize differences in categories across time.

Access 2002 adds *eXtensible Markup Language (XML)* support, which enables Access data to be transformed to and from other formats. XML is a standard language for describing and delivering data on the Web, while HTML controls how a Web page looks. The capability to import or export data using XML gives you the option of sharing your data with organizations that use other database formats. This increases the flexibility of your Access database to be used collaboratively with other organizations. With XML you can share information with vendors and tell them how the data should be structured.

In this lesson, you learn how to create a data access page in Design view, create PivotTables and PivotCharts as data access pages, and import and export data using XML.

431

VISUAL SUMMARY

When you complete this lesson, you will have created a data access page, created a PivotTable and a PivotChart as data access pages, and exported and imported data using XML:

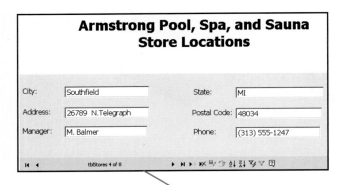

Task 1: Create and modify a data access page

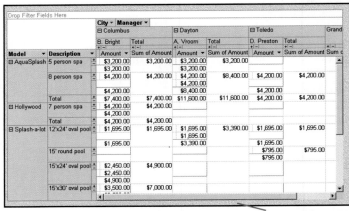

Task 2: Save a PivotTable as a data access page

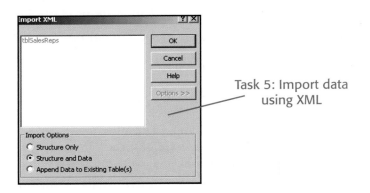

Task 5: Import data using XML

Task 4: Export data using XML

Task 3: Save a PivotChart as a data access page

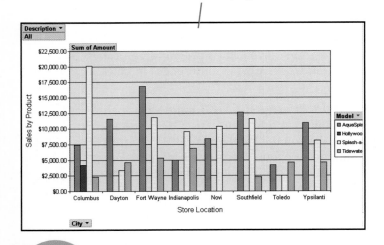

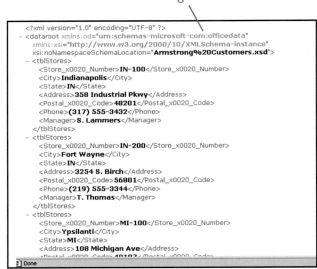

Task 1

CREATING AND MODIFYING A DATA ACCESS PAGE

Explain It

Do It

Use It

Why would I do this?

You can use data access pages to make information from your database available through a Web site. You might use this method to provide information to branch locations, customers, or suppliers for your business. To access this information using the Web, users have to have Internet Explorer 5.5 or later. If you want end users to be able to interact with the data and make changes to the underlying database, then the database has to be available to them on a Web server. Posting a data access page to a Web server is beyond the scope of most classroom environments and is not specifically addressed in this book.

There are several methods you can use to create a data access page. You can create one quickly in a columnar layout, similar to an AutoForm, which includes all the fields and records for a table or query. You can use the Page Wizard to select fields and other options. You can use an existing HTML document to create a data access page, or you can create one in Design view.

In this task, you learn how to create a data access page using Design view.

1 Start Microsoft Access. Click **More files** under the **Open a file** category. Locate **AC1301** for this lesson. Transfer the file to the location where you are saving your files.

Remove the read-only property, if necessary. Rename the file **AC1301-Armstrong** and open it.

The Armstrong database opens.

2 Click the **Pages** object button. Click **New**.

The New Data Access Page dialog box opens.

Make sure **Design View** is selected, and choose **tblStores** from the **Choose the table or query** list box.

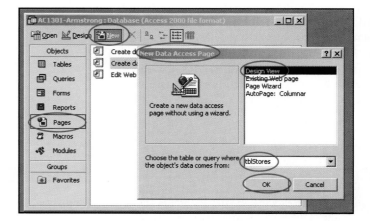

3 Click **OK**.

A message box displays (unless a previous user turned it off). The message warns you that data access pages created using Access XP cannot be opened in Design view with Access 2000. Also, you must install the Microsoft Office XP Web Components to be able to view the page in Page view when using Access 2000. This is a concern only if there are people in your office who use Access 2000 and will need to use this database object in an Access environment.

4 Click **OK** to acknowledge the message.

The data access page Design view opens. The Field list displays in a pane on the right side of the window.

> Maximize the **Page1:Data Access Page** window. If the Toolbox is not displayed, click the **Toolbox** button. Drag the title bar of the **Toolbox** to the right side of the screen to dock it.

To add fields to the page, you can simply drag them from the field list and drop them on the page. This works the same as designing a form. When you drag a field, a text box opens with a label to the left of it.

CAUTION

> To maximize the data access page, you may have to drag the title bar to the left so you can see the Maximize button in the upper-right corner of the window.

Instructions tell you how to add fields

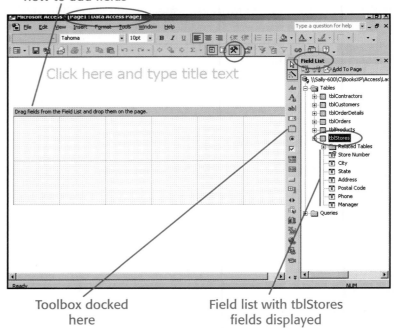

Toolbox docked here

Field list with tblStores fields displayed

5 Drag the **City** field to the second grid box as shown in the figure.

The City label displays to the left of the text box.

> Add the rest of the fields to the Page and place them as shown in the figure. (Do not include the Store Number.) If you need to adjust the placement of the fields, use the same methods and techniques that you use in the Form Design view.

QUICK TIP

> To add a field you can also select the field and then click the Add to Page button at the top of the Field List pane. Double-clicking a field is another quick way to add fields.

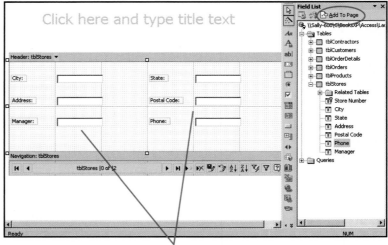

Fields added to the page

6 Click the title area and type **Armstrong Pool, Spa, and Sauna**. Press ⇧Shift+↵Enter and type **Store Locations** on the second line

A title is added to the page.

Select all the controls except the title. Change the font size to **12pt** and click the **Bold** button.

The font size is increased and bold emphasis is added. Now the controls need to be resized.

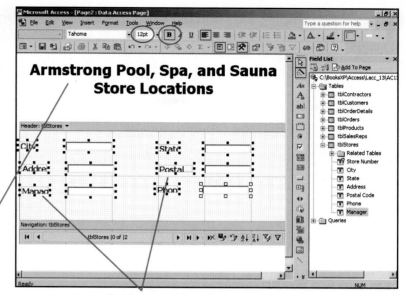

Title added

Font size increased and
bold emphasis added

> **QUICK TIP**
>
> To select a group of controls quickly, click below and to the right of the controls and drag up and to the left of the first control. A box indicates the area that will be selected. When you release the mouse button, every control enclosed in or touching the box will be selected. You use this same technique when selecting a group of controls in a form.

7 With the controls still selected, choose F**ormat**, **S**ize, To **F**it.

The text boxes and labels are resized. The text boxes need to be made even larger so all of the data will display.

Close the **Field List** pane. Deselect the controls, and then click the background of the grid area. Use the sizing handle on the right side to drag the grid so it is just over seven squares wide.

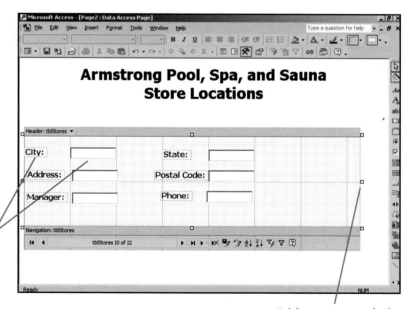

Labels and text
boxes expanded

Grid area expanded

8 Select the **State, Postal Code,** and **Phone** fields and drag them to the right so the left edge of the text box aligns with the left edge of the sixth grid line.

These fields are moved to the right so you can increase the size of the text boxes for all the fields.

Select the text boxes for each field and use the sizing handles to increase the size of the text boxes as shown. Each text box should stretch across two grid squares.

The size of the text boxes is increased.

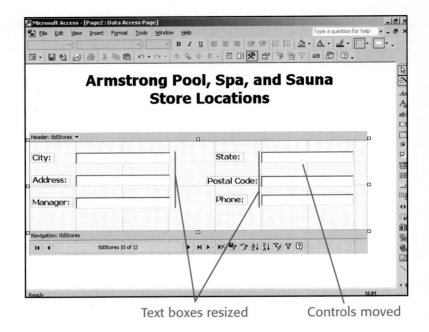

Text boxes resized   Controls moved

> ⚠ **CAUTION**
>
> In a data access page, you can move the labels separately from the text boxes, but you cannot move the text boxes without also moving the labels. This is slightly different from how you move controls in a form.

9 Click in an open area on the grid and click the arrow to the right of the **Back/Fill** button. Select the **pale blue** color, the fifth color in the last row.

A color is added to the grid background

Click the **View** button to see the results. Use the navigation buttons to move through the records to make sure that all the data displays.

You can use the toolbar to move through the records, and to sort or filter records. Also notice that there are buttons that enable you to add or delete records.

If necessary, return to Design view to adjust the size of the text boxes, and then return to the Page view.

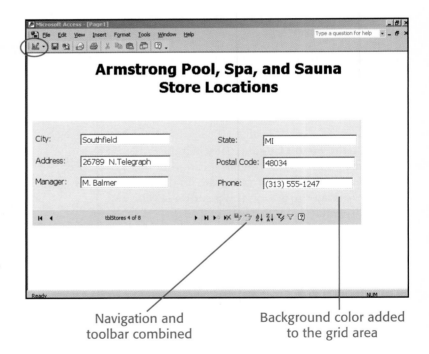

Navigation and
toolbar combined

Background color added
to the grid area

10 Click the **S**ave button.

The Save As Data Access Page opens so you can save this as a new file. It is important to save the file in the same location as the database.

Make sure the **Save in** box displays the location where the database file is stored, and then type **Store Locations Page** in the **File name** box.

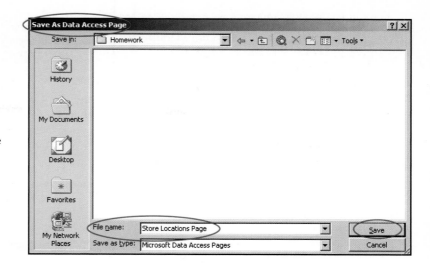

11 Click the **S**ave button.

A warning box displays advising you that the page specifies an absolute path. If you want to use this on a network, you need to edit the connection to specify a network path. Since you will not be posting this to a network, you do not need to be concerned about this warning. (This warning box does not display if a prior user turned it off.)

Click **OK**. Close the window.

A shortcut to the Store Locations Page displays on the Pages object page.

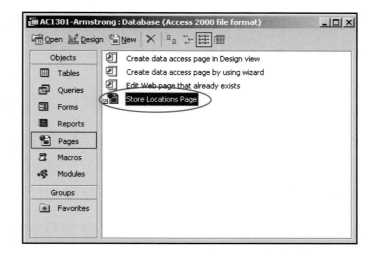

IN DEPTH

To view a data access page with a Web browser, launch Internet Explorer 5.5 or higher and choose File, Open on the Menu. Click Browse and locate the Store Locations Page.htm file. Open the file and view it with your browser. To view an Access XP data access page with a browser, you must have the Office XP Web Components installed on your computer. In addition, if you want users to edit the database they must have permissions to the database to which the page is connected.

Task 2
SAVING PIVOTTABLE VIEWS TO A DATA ACCESS PAGE

Why would I do this?

You can create a PivotTable as a view for a query or a table. You can also save it as form. If you save a PivotTable as a form, you can then convert it to a data access page. You can also create a PivotTable in the data access page Design view. As you learned in Lesson 11, PivotTables are a good tool for comparing and summarizing data.

In this task, you open a PivotTable form that is based on a query, and then save it as a data access page.

1 Click the **Forms** object button. Open the **frmSalesPivotTable** form.

This is the same PivotTable as the view you created for the sales table query in Lesson 11. Here it has been created as a separate form object.

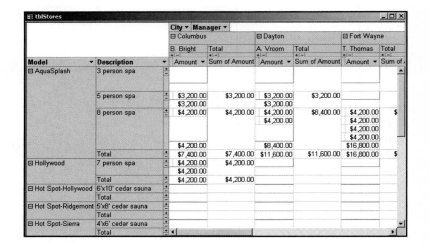

2 Choose **File, Save As** from the menu. Type **Sales PivotTable** in the Save To box and use the arrow to select **Data Access Page** in the As box.

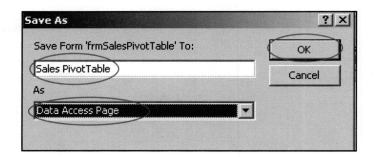

3 Click **OK.**

The New Data Access Page dialog box opens. Here you identify the location and name for the data access page file.

Make sure the **Save in** location is the same as the one you used for your database. Verify that **Sales PivotTable** displays as the file name.

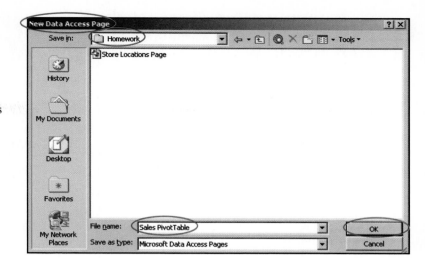

4 Click **OK.**

After a short delay, the data access page for the PivotTable opens on your screen. You can distinguish the PivotTable from the data access page by verifying the name that appears in the title bar of each window.

Close both the PivotTable and the data access page windows and click on the **Pages** object button.

The Sales PivotTable shortcut is listed on the Pages page of your Database window.

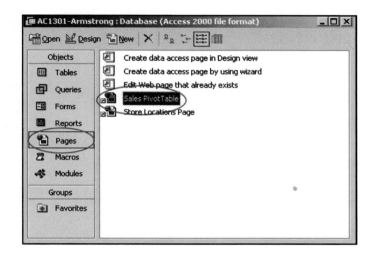

5 Double-click the **Sales PivotTable** shortcut to view it. Maximize the window.

The PivotTable displays with a background around it. You can use scroll bars to move around in the table.

Click the arrow next to the **City** box and deselect all the cities except **Columbus**, **Dayton**, and **Toledo**.

These are the store locations in Ohio.

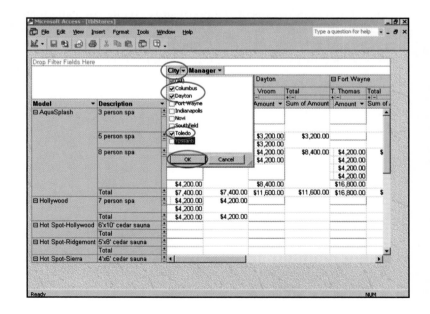

6 Click OK.

The PivotTable displays the records for just the sales in the Ohio stores. When you view a PivotTable as a data access page you can modify the results by selecting the data you want to see.

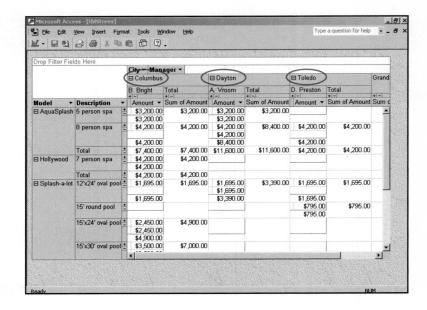

7 Close the data access page.

IN DEPTH

You can open the PivotTable data access page using Internet Explorer, just like you did for the data access page created in Task 1.

Task 3

SAVING PIVOTCHART VIEWS TO A DATA ACCESS PAGE

Why would I do this?

You can save PivotCharts as data access pages for easy access and viewing by others using a Web browser. PivotCharts are dynamic, graphical representations of data such as sales figures by region or store. While you can create a PivotTable in the data access page Design view, to create a PivotChart you must first create the PivotChart as a view for another object, or save it as a form. You open the PivotChart view or form and then save it as a data access page.

In this task, you view a PivotChart and then save it to a data access page.

1 Click the **Queries** object button and open **qrySalesChart**.

A PivotChart view has already been created for this query.

Click the arrow to the right of the **View** button and select **PivotChart View**.

The PivotChart for this query is displayed.

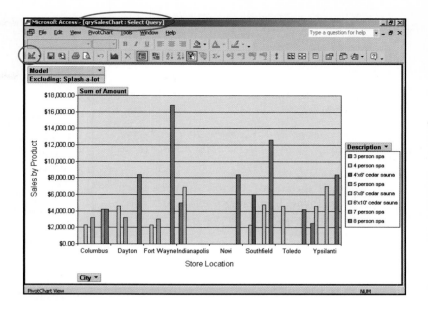

2 Choose **File**, **Save As** from the menu.

The Save As dialog box opens.

Type **Sales PivotChart** in the Save Query 'qrySalesChart' To box and select **Data Access Page** using the arrow on the right of the As box.

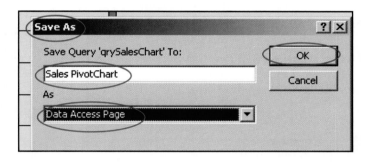

3 Click **OK**.

The New Data Access Page dialog box opens.

Verify that the Save in box is pointing to the same location as the database, and that the name is Sales PivotChart.

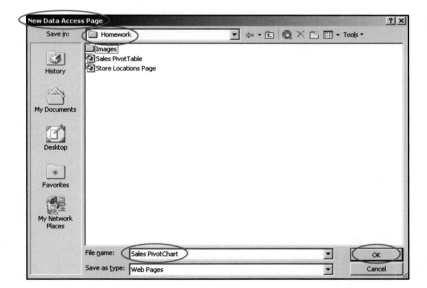

4 Click **OK**.

A second window opens that displays the chart as a data access page.

Close both the data access page and the PivotChart query view.

You can distinguish the query from the data access page by verifying the name that appears in the title bar of each window.

Click the **Pages** object button and then open the **Sales PivotChart** using the shortcut displayed on the page. Maximize the screen, if necessary.

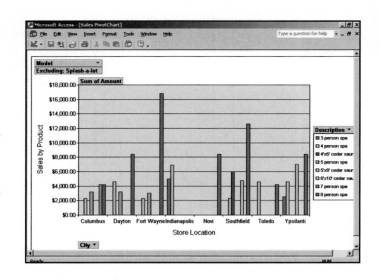

5 Reverse the Description and Model fields by dragging **Description** to the **Filter Fields** area, and then dragging **Model** to the **Series Fields** area.

You can work interactively with PivotCharts as data access pages the same as you would if you worked directly with the PivotChart form or view.

CAUTION

The city names along the bottom of the chart may change to display vertically instead of horizontally. If you go to the Design view of the data access page, you can expand the plot area which should enable the city names to be displayed horizontally again.

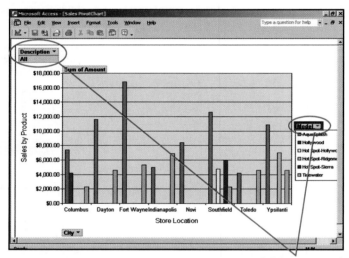

Fields reversed

6 Click the arrow on the **Model** field button and select **Splash-a-Lot**, and then deselect the three **Hot-Spot** models. Click **OK**.

The chart is redrawn to reflect your changes.

IN DEPTH

You can open the PivotChart data access page using Internet Explorer, just like you did for the data access page created in Task 1.

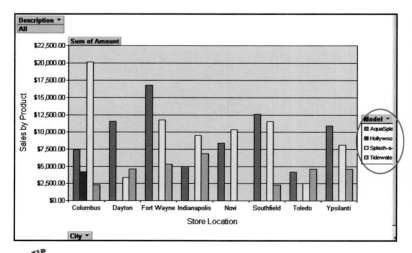

7 Close the PivotChart page.

QUICK TIP

When you open the chart again it will display in its original layout, based on the PivotChart View that was created as part of the qrySalesChart.

Task 4

EXPORTING ACCESS DATA TO XML DOCUMENTS

Why would I do this?

You may need to share your data with another company that uses a different database format. You might need to share inventory information with a just-in-time supplier so they can anticipate when to ship new parts. Or you may need to use an outside vendor to do a special mailing of information to customers. You can create an XML file for your Access data to facilitate collaboration with others. XML uses tags, similar to HTML, which define how the data should be structured. This structure is known as a *schema*.

In this task, you export an Access table as an XML file.

1 Click the **Tables** object button and select **tblCustomers**.

To export a file as an XML document you do not open the file, but merely select it to identify the object you want to export.

Choose **File**, **Export** from the menu.

The Export To dialog box opens.

In the **File name Insert box** type **Armstrong Customers**. Click the arrow at the end of the **Save as type** box and select **XML Documents**. Make sure the **Save in** box displays the location where you are saving your files.

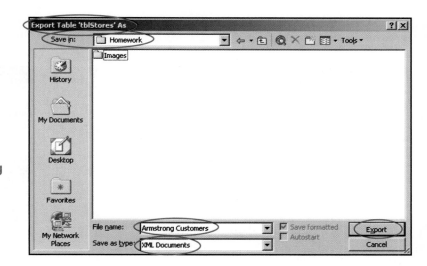

2 Click **Export**.

The XML Export dialog box opens. Here you choose whether the schema is exported with the data.

Make sure the **Data (XML)** and **Schema of the data** checkboxes are checked.

Selected Table

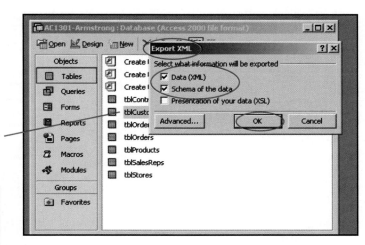

IN DEPTH

The Data (XML) option exports the data for table, query, form, and report objects. The Schema of the data option creates an XML schema document, which supports the XML Schema standard. This is saved as a separate file with an .xsd extension. The Presentation of your data (XLS) option can be used to select different schema formats.

3 Click **OK**.

The dialog box closes. To verify that the file was created you can look at it with your browser.

> Open your **Internet Explorer 5.5** (or higher) browser. Choose **File, Open** from the menu. Click the **Browse** button and locate the folder where you are saving your files. Change the **Files of type** box to **All Files**.

The Armstrong Customer XML document is listed.

> Select the **Armstrong Customers** file. Do not select the file with the .xsd extension.

This is the schema file that was created when you exported the schema.

4 Click the **Open** button.

The file path and name show in the Open dialog box.

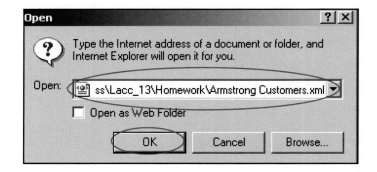

5 Click **OK**.

The data is displayed in the XML format.

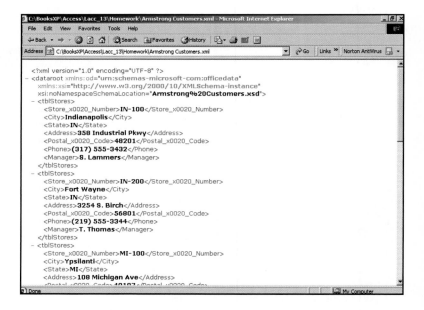

6 Close your browser.

The Database window returns to your screen.

Task 5
IMPORTING XML DOCUMENTS INTO ACCESS

Why would I do this?

Knowing how to export files as XML documents is helpful when you need to share information with someone who uses a different file format. Likewise, you may need to obtain information from another source to include in your database. If they can convert their file to an XML format, you can easily import the data into your Access database.

In this task, you import the sales rep data that has been saved as an XML document.

1 Choose, **File**, **Get External Data**, **Import** from the menu.

The Import dialog box opens.

Change the **Look in** box to the folder that contains the student files for this lesson. Change the **Files of type** box to **XML Documents**. Select the **SalesReps** file.

A SalesReps.xsd file is also displayed. This is the schema file that was created when the SalesReps file was created.

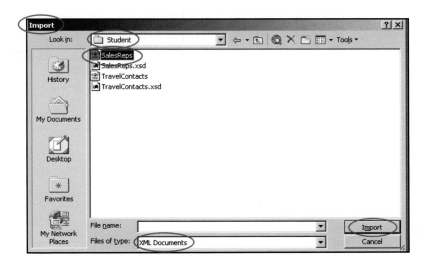

2 Click **Import**.

The Import XML dialog box opens.

Click the **Options** button to reveal the Import Options area. Make sure the **Structure and Data** option is selected.

IN DEPTH

In the Import XML dialog box, the Import Options enable you to import just the structure, the data and the structure, or to append the data to an existing table. Each of these choices has different consequences. Be aware that if you create a new table, it could overwrite an existing table that has the same name.

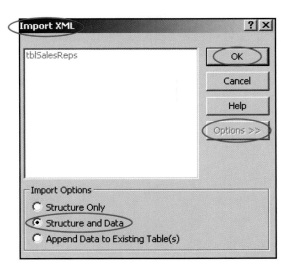

3 Click **OK**.

A message box advises you that the program has finished importing the data.

Click **OK** to acknowledge the message. Select **tblSalesReps** and open it.

The sales rep data is displayed.

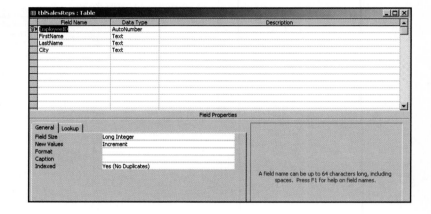

4 Click the **View** button to see the design of the data.

Since this data came from another Access database, the data types are correctly defined in the Table Design view. If the file came from another source, you might have had to make some adjustments to the data types to match Access protocols.

5 Close the table. Compact and close the database.

The exercises that follow are designed for you to review and use what you have learned in this lesson. You also have the opportunity to practice your skills and then expand on them by applying them to new situations.

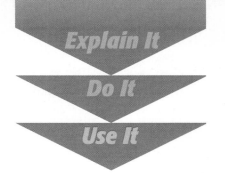

COMPREHENSION

Comprehension exercises are designed to check your memory and understanding of the basic concepts in this lesson. You distinguish between true and false statements, identify new screen elements, and match terms with related statements. If you are uncertain of the correct answer, refer to the task number following each item (for example, T4 refers to Task 4) and review that task until you are confident that you can provide a correct response.

TRUE-FALSE

Circle either T or F.

T   F   1. Using data access pages and XML helps you share data with others who may not use Access. **(Intro)**

T   F   2. To view a PivotTable on the Web you have to create it from scratch using the Pages Design view. **(T2)**

T   F   3. To view a PivotChart on the Web it has to first be created as a view or a form, and saved as part of the database. **(T3)**

T   F   4. Data exported in XML format can be viewed with Internet Explorer 5.5 or higher. **(T4)**

T   F   5. When you import XML data you can import just the structure, or the data and the structure. **(T5)**

T   F   6. To be able to access a data access page on the Web you can use Netscape Navigator 4.0 or higher. **(T1)**

MATCHING QUESTIONS

A. eXtensible Markup Language

B. Hypertext Markup Language

C. Schema

D. Data access page

E. Internet Explorer 5.5

F. Pages

Match the following statements to the word or phrase that is the best match from the list. Write the letter of the matching word or phrase in the space provided next to the number.

1. _____ You create this when you save an Access object so it can be viewed on the Web **(Intro)**

2. _____ Controls how the information looks when it is viewed with a Web browser **(Intro)**

3. _____ Displays shortcuts to data access pages **(Intro)**

4. _____ Defines how the data should be structured when it is exported as XML **(T5)**

5. _____ Enables Access data to be transformed to and from other formats **(Intro)**

6. _____ Used to view data access pages **(T1)**

IDENTIFYING PARTS OF THE ACCESS SCREEN

Refer to the figure and identify the numbered parts of the screen. Write the letter of the correct label in the space next to the number.

1. _____

2. _____

3. _____

4. _____

5. _____

6. _____

A. Navigation and toolbar (T1)

B. Toolbox (T1)

C. Toolbox button (T1)

D. Available fields (T1)

E. Title area (T1)

F. Task pane Field List (T1)

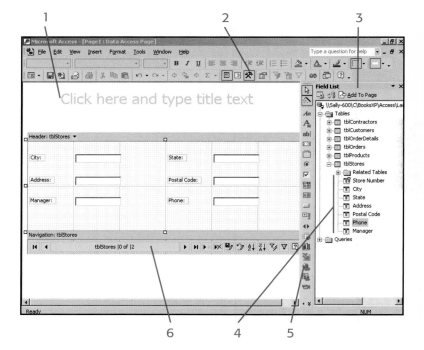

REINFORCEMENT

Reinforcement exercises are designed to reinforce the skills you have learned by applying them to new situations. Detailed instructions are provided along with a figure, where appropriate, to illustrate the result. Complete the reinforcement exercises sequentially. Leave the file open at the end of each exercise for use in the next exercise until you are specifically directed to close it.

In these exercises, you use the Alumni Travel Club database.

R1—Creating and Modifying a Data Access Page

1. Open Access and click **More files** under the **Open a file** category. Locate **AC1302** in the **Student** folder for this lesson. Transfer the file to the location where you are saving your files. Remove the read-only property, and rename the file **AC1302-Travel**. Open the file.

2. Click the **Pages** object button. Click <u>N</u>ew. Make sure **Design View** is selected, and choose **tblTrips** from the Choose the table or query list box.

3. Click **OK** twice. Drag the **Description** field to the second grid box as shown in the figure. Add **PointofOrigin**, **StateDate**, and **Cost** fields to the page and place them as shown in the figure. Close the Field List pane.

4. Click the title area and type **Alumni Travel Club Tours**.

5. Select all the controls and change the font size to **12**, Change the font to **Bookman Old Style**. Click in the labels and add a space between the words in the labels for **Point of Origin** and **Start Date**.

6. Adjust the size of the labels and field boxes as needed to ensure that the data and labels are fully displayed. Realign the controls as shown in the figure. Increase the size of the grid area so the title is centered over the fields.

7. Click in an open area of the design grid and click the arrow on the **Fill/Back Color** button. Select pale green as the background color.

8. Use the **Label** button on the Toolbox to add a label to the lower-right corner of the page, and then type your name.

9. Click the **View** button to see the results. Save the page as **Alumni Tours**. Print one data access page and then close it.

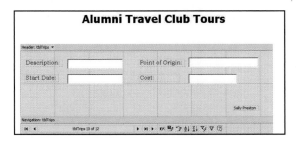

R2—Saving PivotTable Views to a Data Access Page

1. Click the **Tables** object button. Open the **tblTrips** table. Click the arrow on the **View** button and select **PivotTable View**.

2. Choose **File**, **Save As** from the menu. Type **Trips PivotTable** in the Save To box and use the arrow to select **Data Access Page** in the As box.

3. Click **OK**. In the New Data Access Page dialog box, make sure the file is being saved in the same folder as the rest of your files. The file name should display **Trips PivotTable**. Click **OK**.

4. After you create the PivotTable data access page, close both PivotTable windows and click on the **Pages** object button. Choose **Yes** if prompted to save the changes to tblTrips.

5. Double-click the **Trips PivotTable** shortcut to view it. Maximize the window.

6. Click the **View** button. (Note: In the Design view the page is empty. In the data area you will see a No Details notice stating that the query could not be processed. If you want to change the contents of the PivotTable, you have to do it in the original object. You can change the format of a PivotTable that has been created as a view of another object, but you cannot change the contents in the data access page design view.)

7. Click the **Toolbox** button to open the Toolbox. Click the **Label** button and draw a small label above the Drop Filter Fields Here area, outside the table area. Type your name in the label. Click the **View** button to see the results.

8. Click the arrow next to the **Description** box and deselect **Alaska land tour** and **Grand Canyon**. Click **OK**.

9. Change the layout to landscape and print the results. Save the changes, and then close the page. (Note: Only the first page will print.)

Sally Preston								
Drop Filter Fields Here								
				Description ▾				
				African Safari	Ancient China	Castles of the Rhine	Costa Rica
Years ▾	Quarters	Months	Days	Cost ▾	Cost ▾	Cost ▾	Cost ▾
⊟ 2002	⊟ Qtr1	⊟ Feb	⊟ 09-Feb				
			Total				
		⊟ Mar	⊟ 05-Mar				$3,000.00
			⊟ 26-Mar				
			Total				
		Total					
	⊟ Qtr2	⊟ Apr	⊟ 18-Apr				
			Total				
		⊟ May	⊟ 06-May	$6,800.00			
			Total				
		⊟ Jun	⊟ 10-Jun			$2,600.00	
			⊟ 23-Jun				
			Total				
		Total					
	⊟ Qtr3	⊟ Jul	⊟ 06-Jul		$4,500.00		
			Total				
		Total					
	Total						
Grand Total							

R3—Saving PivotChart Views to a Data Access Page

1. Click the Queries object button and open **qryMemberTripPayments.** Click the arrow on the **View** button and select **PivotChart View.** Maximize the window.

2. Choose **File, Save As** from the menu. Type **Member Payments** in the **Save Query To** box, and change the **As** box to **Data Access Page**.

3. Click **OK**. Verify that the file will be saved in the same location as the database, and that the file name is **Member Payments**. Click **OK**.

4. Close both windows that display the chart. Click the **Pages** object button and double-click the **Members Payment** shortcut to view the PivotChart as a data access page. The chart may be oversized for the window.

5. Click the **View** button to see the design of the chart. No data is displayed in the chart design. Close the Field List panel.

6. Scroll to the right and click on the chart to see the sizing handles. Use the sizing handles on the side and bottom of the chart to reduce the chart area, so the entire grid area is fully displayed in the window. When the entire chart area is contained within the window, the scroll bars will disappear.

7. If necessary, click the **Toolbox** button to open the Toolbox. Click the **Label** button and draw a small label outside the chart area. Type your name in the label. Click the **View** button to see the results.

8. Click the arrow on the **Description** field button and deselect **Alaska land tour**, and **Grand Canyon**.

9. Change the print layout to landscape and print the results. Save and close the page.

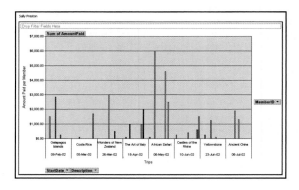

R4—Exporting Access Data to XML Documents

1. Click the **Tables** object button and select the **tblMembers** table.

2. Choose **File, Export** on the menu. Make sure the **Save in** box displays the location where you are saving your files. In the **File name** box type **Alumni Members**. Select **XML Documents** from the **Save as type** box. Click **Export**.

3. In the **Export XML** dialog box, make sure the **Data (XML)** and **Schema of the data** are selected, and then click **OK**.

4. Open **Internet Explorer 5.5** and choose **File, Open** from the menu. Click the **Browse** button. Change **Files of type** to **All Files**. Locate and open the **Alumni Members** XML Document file.

5. Print the result. Close the browser.

```xml
<?xml version="1.0" encoding="UTF-8" ?>
- <dataroot xmlns:od="urn:schemas-microsoft-com:officedata"
    xmlns:xsi="http://www.w3.org/2000/10/XMLSchema-instance"
    xsi:noNamespaceSchemaLocation="Alumni%20Members.xsd">
  - <tblMembers>
      <MemberID>G-328</MemberID>
      <MembershipType>G</MembershipType>
      <FirstName>David</FirstName>
      <LastName>Svinicki</LastName>
      <Address>3840 Packard St</Address>
      <City>Ann Arbor</City>
      <State>MI</State>
      <ZIPCode>48103</ZIPCode>
      <Phone>(734) 555-5400</Phone>
    </tblMembers>
  - <tblMembers>
      <MemberID>G-329</MemberID>
      <MembershipType>G</MembershipType>
      <FirstName>Josh</FirstName>
      <LastName>Melton</LastName>
      <Address>2610 W Liberty St</Address>
      <City>Dexter</City>
      <State>MI</State>
      <ZIPCode>48130</ZIPCode>
      <Phone>(734) 555-0991</Phone>
    </tblMembers>
  - <tblMembers>
```

R5–Importing XML Documents into Access

1. Choose **File**, **Get External Data**, **Import**. Change the **Files of type** box to **XML Documents.**

2. Locate the **Travel Contacts** XML document in the folder that contains the files for this lesson. Select the file and click the **Import** button.

3. In the Import XML dialog box, click the **Options** button and make sure the **Structure and Data** option is selected. Click **OK** twice.

4. Open **tblContacts**. For **GuideID 101**, change the name to your name.

5. Print and close the table.

6. Compact and close the database.

GuideID	FirstName	LastName	Address	City	State	PostalCode	Country/R	Phone	Expertise
101	Sally	Preston	604 Flamingo Drive	San Diego	CA	92101		619 555-8484	Curator of San Diego Zoo,
102	Frank	Mainzer	4597 Bay View Blvd. Apt 15C	Key West	FL	33041		305 555-7411	Certified scuba diver and
103	Joan	Navarre	711 Hilltop Drive	San Francisco	CA	94101		650 555-4574	Joan spent her youth in China
104	Antonio	Iglesias	72 Villa Grazioli	Rome			Italy	43/568421125	A citizen of Europe,
105	Johan	Graichen	Rathenower Strasse 96	Berlin		10559	Germany	49/368242497	Johan has been the
106	Miles	Davison	2647 Bahama Drive	Miami	FL	33102		786 555-9877	Ecologist and marine
107	Jon	Mathews	501 Washington	New York	NY	10011		917 555-3232	Biologist with a special
108	Mary	Robbins	2369 Bear Run	Anchorage	AK	99502		907 555-4513	Geologist with a particular
109	Scott	Michaels	584 N. Hibiscus Apt. 301	Tempe	AZ	85281		602 555-4321	Archaeologist with a focus on
110	Jerome	Baird	56 Deerpath Trail	Boise	ID	83701		208 555-3456	Naturalist, writer, and

CHALLENGE

Challenge exercises are designed to test your ability to apply your skills to new situations with less-detailed instructions. These exercises also challenge you to expand your repertoire of skills by using commands that are similar to those you have already learned. The desired outcome is clearly defined, but you have more freedom to choose the steps needed to achieve the required result.

In the following Challenge exercises you work with a fundraising database designed by a charity. Each exercise can be done independently.

C1—Create a Grouped Data Access Page

When you create a data access page, you group data by placing fields above or below the first section that displays on the design grid. In this exercise, you create a list of members and then add their pledge amounts under each member's name and address.

Goal: Create a grouped data access page.

1. Locate **AC1303** in the **Student** folder for this lesson. Transfer the file to the location where you are saving your files. Remove the read-only property, and rename the file **AC1303-Challenges**. Open the file.

2. Click the **Pages** object button and click **New**. In the New Data Access Page dialog box, choose **Design View**, and select **tblMembers** from the list box. Click **OK**. Acknowledge the warning if it displays.

3. Add the member name and address fields, including salutation, from **tblMembers**. Arrange the fields as shown in the figure. Remove the labels for all the fields except address. Use the **Label** button on the Toolbox to add a label for the first line. Type **Name** in the label.

4. Select all the controls and increase the font size to **12**. Resize each text box so it is just large enough to display the data for that field. Check the **Pages** view to see if all the data is displayed.

5. Click the plus sign (+) next to the **Related Tables** folder under tblMembers. Click the plus sign (+) next to **tblPledges** to reveal the available fields. Drag **PledgeDate** to the area below the member information. A blue frame appears and an area labeled **Create new section below tblMembers** displays. Drop the field on the left side of the Create new section below tblMembers box.

6. In the Layout Wizard dialog box that appears, select **Tabular** and click **OK**. Two new sections are added to the design—a caption area and a header area for tblPledges. The data displays in the Header: tblPledges area.

7. Drag the **PledgeAmount** field to the **Header: tblPledges** area. The label for this field automatically displays in the caption area.

8. Click in the title area and type **Members and Pledges**. Use the **Label** button on the Toolbox to add a label in the title area and type your name.

9. Use the sizing handle on the corner of the Header: tblMembers grid to reduce the size of the grid and eliminate the extra space below the member information.

10. Save the data access page in the folder where you have been saving your files using the same name as the title

11. View the results. Click the **Expand** button (+) next to the first record to display the pledge amounts. Print the results.

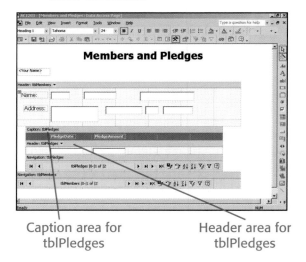

Caption area for tblPledges   Header area for tblPledges

Members and Pledges

<Your Name>

Name: | Ms. | Roberta | Schmanski

Address: | 349 Huron River Drive | Dexter | MI | 48130

PledgeDate	PledgeAmount
10-May-01	$1,000.00
01-Feb-02	$1,500.00

|◄ ◄ tblPledges 1-2 of 2 ► ►| ►* ▶X ⤴ ⤵ ↓₁ ↕₁ ⍍ ▽ ⑦

Name: | Mr. | David | Kirch

Address: | 1221 Memorial | Plymouth | MI | 48170

Name: | Dr. | Samantha | Miller

Expand button   Pledge amounts for the first record

C2—Using Data Access Page Controls

Most of the controls used in a data access page are the same as those used with a form or a report. Some of the controls included, however, are new and are particularly appropriate to an online environment. With a data access page, you can also apply a theme, similar to the layout design selections available for a form. In this exercise, you add a theme to a data access page and then add a scrolling text box.

Goal: Use design elements and toolbox controls in a data access page.

1. If you completed the previous exercise, continue to use that file. Otherwise, locate **AC1303** in the **Student** folder for this lesson. Transfer the file to the location where you are saving your files. Remove the read-only property, and rename the file **AC1303-Challenges**. Open the file.

2. Click the **Pages** object button to create a new data access page based on **tblMembers**.

3. Add the member name and address information to the data access page as shown in the figure.

4. Add **Charity Members** in the title area. Add a label in the title area and enter your name.

5. Choose **F**ormat, **T**heme from the menu. Look through the available themes and select one you like. Do not use one with a dark background if you need to print the page to turn in.

6. Click the **Scrolling Text** button on the Toolbox and drag a rectangle on the screen under the member fields. Type **Welcome to the Charity Web Site. Renew your pledge today.**

7. Save the page in the location with your other files. Name it **Members**.

8. View the results and print the page.

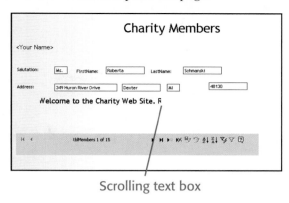

Scrolling text box

C3—Creating a PivotChart in a Data Access Page

In this lesson you learned to create a PivotTable in a data access page by using the Save As dialog box. You can also create a PivotTable from scratch in the data access page design window.

Goal: Create a PivotTable in the data access page design window.

1. If you completed the previous exercise, continue to use that file. Otherwise, locate **AC1303** in the **Student** folder for this lesson. Transfer the file to the location where you are saving your files. Remove the read-only property, and rename the file **AC1303-Challenges**. Open the file.

2. In the **Pages** page, double-click **Create data access page in Design view**. Click **OK** to acknowledge the warning message that displays. Click the **Field List** button and **Toolbox** button if necessary to open the Field List pane and the Toolbox. Click the **Expand** button next to queries. Click the **Expand** button next to **qryPayments&Pledge**. Maximize the data access page window.

3. Click the **Office PivotTable** button on the Toolbox. In the detail grid area drag a rectangle that is approximately 4-inches wide and 3-inches high.

4. Drag **MemberID** to the **Drop Column Fields Here** area. Drag **PledgeAmount** to the **Drop Row Fields Here** area. Drag **PaymentAmount** and then **PaymentDate** to the **Drop Totals or Detail Fields Here** area in the center. Add **PledgeDate** to **Filter** area at the top of the PivotTable

5. Use the sizing handles to increase the size of the grid to fill the window. Then resize the table to fill the grid area. Add a label and type your name.

6. Click the **View** button. Click the **PaymentAmount** heading for any member. Click the **AutoCalc** button and select **Sum** from the list. Click the **Hide Details** button on the toolbar to collapse the detail.

7. Click the **PledgeDate** filter button and deselect the last two dates in the list.

8. Save the page as **Pledges and Payments**. Your results should look like the figure below. Print your results.

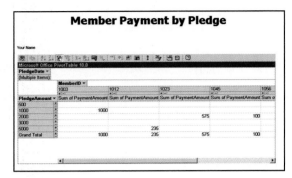

ON YOUR OWN

In this lesson you learned about creating data access pages and using XML to share data with others. To extend your practice and knowledge, you can create your own data access pages based on other database files. Use any of the following ideas as a basis for further practice.

1. Work with a database of your own design and create data access pages that serve the needs of your database and the users who may need information from the database.

- Demonstrate the ability create a data access page.

- Demonstrate the ability to export data in XML format.

- Demonstrate the ability to import data in XML format.

2. Investigate publishing a data access page to a Web site. Once you have created the data access page, you may want to find an Internet service provider that can host the page for you.

- Check with your school to see if they offer this option.

- Check with an ISP to find out what is involved and what it costs.

- Write a brief report detailing the results of your investigation.

3. There are many other tools you can use with a data access page. Create new pages using one of the files provided by your book and try adding some other elements to the page. Some options include:

- Change group property settings.

- Add background images to a page.

- Add a spreadsheet to a page.

- Add a hyperlink to a page.

4. Save your file on your own disk. Name it **AC1305-Collaboration**.

5. Check with your instructor to determine if you should submit the file in electronic or printed form.

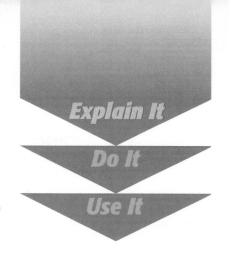

Explain It

Do It

Use It

Lesson 14

Protecting Your Database While Sharing It with Others

Task 1   Splitting a Database
Task 2   Setting Passwords for Databases
Task 3   Encrypting and Decrypting Databases
Task 4   Creating a Switchboard
Task 5   Setting Startup Options

INTRODUCTION

Databases are usually shared with people who need to access records, look up data, run reports, add, and change, or delete information. To help ensure the database integrity, there are a number of tools you can use to protect the database, while making it easy for others to use.

In an organization where many people need to access the same data, you can use the *database splitter* to place the tables into a separate database from the rest of the objects. Then every user can access the information and create their own forms and reports to use for their particular needs. When you do this, the forms, queries, and reports that each user creates are maintained on their individual workstations.

You can also protect a database by requiring a *password* to open it. This is a combination of letters and numbers that must be entered to open a database file. Use a password if you want to prevent someone else from gaining access to a database on your computer.

Another method you can use to secure data is to *encrypt* it. Encrypting a database changes the data into unreadable text. This prevents someone from being able to open a database with a word processing program, or other utility text program to decipher the data. You may want to follow this process if you need to send a database to someone at another location over the Internet.

Finally, to make a database easy for others to use, you can create a *switchboard,* which functions like a main menu. The switchboard menu contains command buttons that are used to navigate around the database. You can also set the startup options for Access to control the toolbars and other window elements that appear, and cause the switchboard menu to display when the database opens.

455

In this lesson, you work with the Armstrong Pool, Spa, and Sauna database to learn how to use various means to protect the database, and to make the database easier for others to use.

VISUAL SUMMARY

When you complete this lesson, you will have split a database, encrypted it, and added a password. You will have also created a switchboard menu and set the startup options.

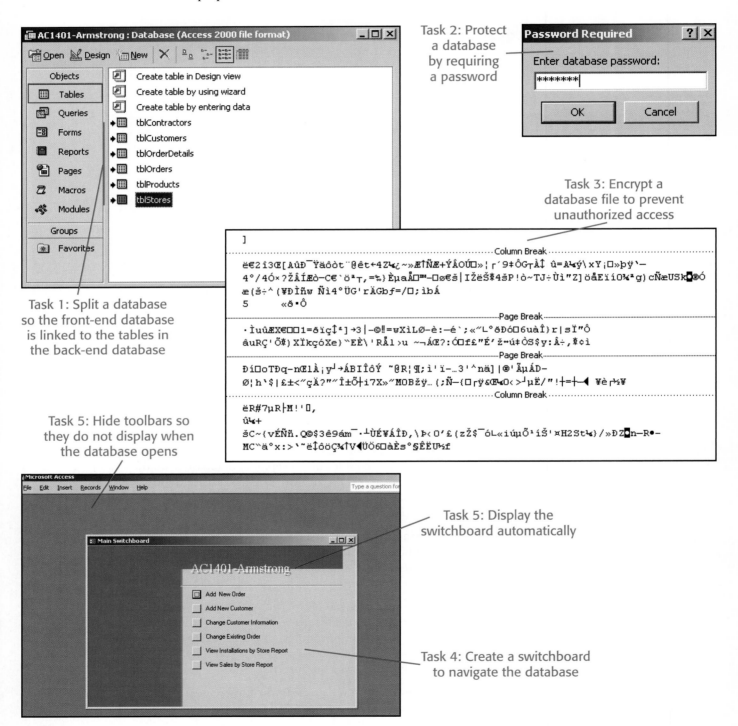

Task 2: Protect a database by requiring a password

Task 3: Encrypt a database file to prevent unauthorized access

Task 1: Split a database so the front-end database is linked to the tables in the back-end database

Task 5: Hide toolbars so they do not display when the database opens

Task 5: Display the switchboard automatically

Task 4: Create a switchboard to navigate the database

Task 1
SPLITTING A DATABASE

Explain It

Do It

Use It

Why would I do this?

When a database is used in a multiuser environment the easiest approach is to place the entire database on a server so many users can access the same set of objects. Use this method if you want everyone to use the same forms, queries, and reports, and you do not want people to customize the database to their own needs. This works best when everyone has similar responsibilities and uses the database for the same activities.

In some situations, however, it may be better to separate the data in the tables from the other objects in the database. This approach is best when the users of the database have different responsibilities and reasons to access the data. This allows the users to customize database objects to their particular needs. It also provides protection for their objects from change by other users.

To separate a database into two parts, you use the database splitter. The main database that houses the tables is known as the *back end*, and the one containing the other objects is called the *front end*. The back end is stored on a network server, while the front-end database is stored on each individual workstation. Access must be installed on the workstations as well as on the server.

In this task, you learn how to use the database splitter to split a database.

1 Start Microsoft Access. Click **More files** under the **Open a file** category. Locate **AC1401** for this lesson. Transfer the file to the location where you are saving your files.

Remove the read-only property, if necessary, and rename the file **AC1401-Armstrong**. Open the file.

Before you split a database, make sure you have a copy of it, because it is not easy to undo what the Database Splitter Wizard does. By copying the file, and opening the copy, you have the original file to use for the other tasks in this lesson.

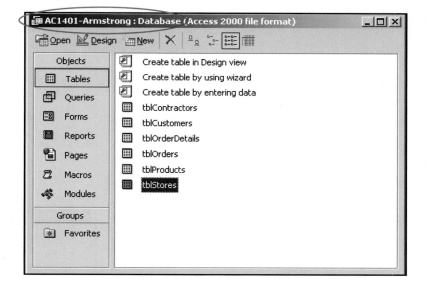

2 Choose **T**ools, **D**atabase Utilities, **D**atabase Splitter.

The first page of the Database Splitter opens.

Read the explanation on this page.

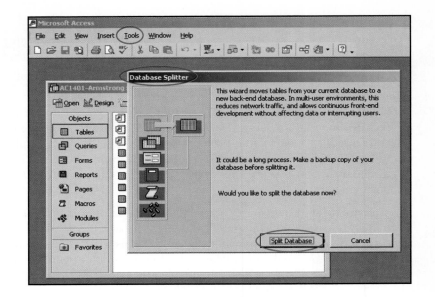

3 Click the **Split Database** button.

The Create Back-end Database dialog box opens.

If necessary, change the **Save in** box to the location where you are saving your files.

Notice that the default file name is the original file name with _be attached at the end of the name. Accept this as the file name for the back-end database.

> **CAUTION**
>
> If you are saving your files to a floppy disk, make sure you have enough room on the disk. When the database is split, there will be two files totaling approximately 760KB. If there is not sufficient space on your disk, the database-splitting process cannot be completed.

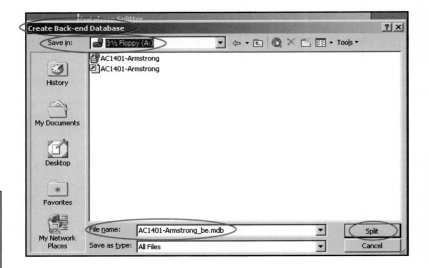

4 Click the **Split** button.

A message box displays advising you that the database has been split.

Click **OK** to acknowledge the message.

The front-end database displays on your screen showing that all the tables are now linked.

Arrows indicate linked tables

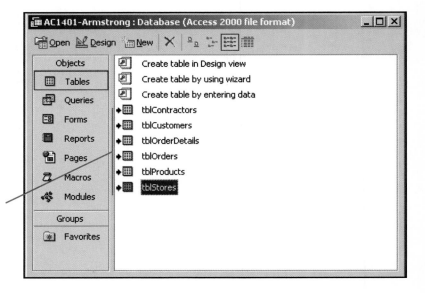

5 Open **tblCustomers** and locate the record for CustomerNo **N-128**. Replace the author's name with your name for this record.

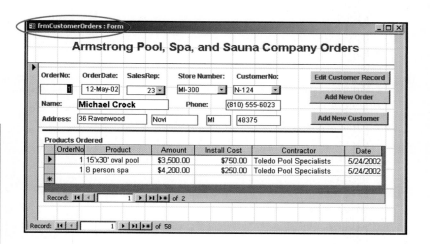

6 Close the table. Click the **Forms** object button and open **frmCustomerOrders**.

The objects from the original database are still functional.

> **IN DEPTH**
>
> When you split a database, the front-end database resides on each user's workstation, and the back-end database, which contains the tables, resides on the network. The objects in the front-end database cannot be changed by another user through the network unless they have permission to access the files on your hard drive. This process enables you to create the objects you need to do your work, and protect them from change by others. Later in this lesson you learn to add passwords. You can add a password to your copy of the front-end database file to ensure that no one else accesses the file.

7 Close the form and close the database. Click the **Open** button.

The Open dialog box is displayed.

Locate and select the **AC1401-Armstrong_be** file.

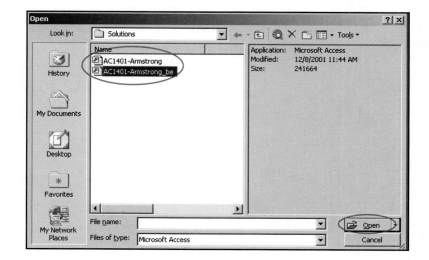

8 Click the **Open** button.

The back-end database opens. Notice that the tables listed are not linked—no arrows are displayed next to the tables.

Open tblCustomers and locate the record for CustomerNo N-128.

The record displays your name.

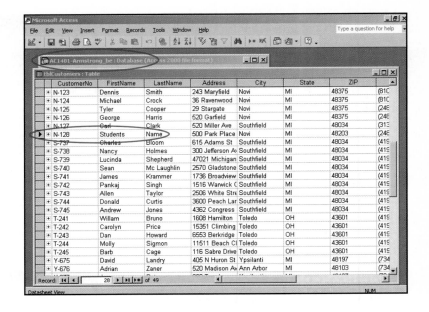

9 Close the table. Click on each of the other object buttons.

No other objects are included in this database.

Forms page is empty

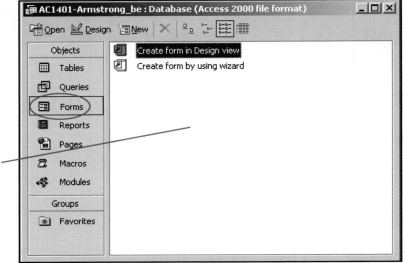

10 Close the database.

IN DEPTH

If you do not work in a networked environment, but more than one person needs to use the database, you can create a *replica* of the database. A replica is a copy of the original database that includes additional tables used to keep track of any changes made to the database. You then *synchronize* the two versions of the database so changes that have been made to either version are updated in both. You can also use this technique if your work takes you out of the office but you still need to work with the database. You learn more about *replicating* a database in the Challenge 2 exercise at the end of the lesson.

Task 2
SETTING PASSWORDS FOR DATABASES

Why would I do this?

Adding a password to your database is like putting a new lock on a door. It provides a measure of protection from some intruders. But putting a lock on a door also has several drawbacks:

- It slows you down every time you want to pass through the door.
- Other people who need to pass through the door must ask you for the key.
- If you give a duplicate key to someone, you do not know what he or she has done with it.
- There are people who have master keys to that type of lock.
- There are people who understand how the lock works and know how to pick it.
- If you lose the only key, it can be very inconvenient.

In spite of these disadvantages, most of us still use locks on our doors. Similarly, you may also want to add a measure of security to your database.

In this lesson, you learn how to require a password to open a database. Passwords are a mix of letters, numbers, and symbols used to identify an authorized user.

1 With Access open, click the **Open** button. Locate **AC1401** for this lesson. Transfer the file to the location where you are saving your files. Remove the read-only property, if necessary, and rename the file **AC1401-Armstrong2**. Do not open the file yet.

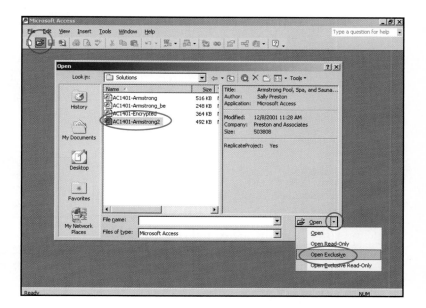

Before you can add a password to a database, you must open the file in Exclusive mode.

Select the **AC1401-Armstrong2** database and click the arrow next to the **Open** button in the Open dialog box.

Several options are displayed. You need to use the Open Exclusive mode. Exclusive mode prevents any other users from accessing the database while you are making this change. You must select this option to add a password even if you are not using Access in a network environment.

2 Click **Open Exclusive**.

The database window opens on your screen.

Choose **Tools, Security** from the menu, then select **Set Database Password**.

The Set Database Password dialog box opens.

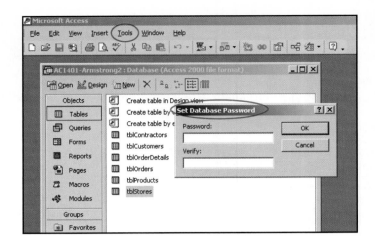

3 Type **ABCabc!** in the **Password** text box.

Asterisks are displayed in the Password box instead of the letters you typed. This prevents someone from looking over your shoulder and seeing your password.

If you are not sure what you typed, press 〔←Backspace〕 and try again carefully. Then press 〔Tab⇄〕 and type the same password in the **Verify** box.

Again, asterisks are displayed in the Verify box instead of the letters you typed.

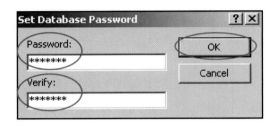

IN DEPTH

Passwords in Access can be very simple and short, or complex and up to 14 characters in length. To get the best security out of your password, do not use a date or a word that would be listed in a dictionary. Do not use passwords others might be able to guess, such as a family member's name, your social security number, or a commonly used phone number. Make the password at least six characters long and include a character that is not a letter. Use a combination of upper- and lowercase letters. If you do want to use an easily recalled word or date, insert an extra symbol. In this example, the password includes an exclamation mark for this purpose.

4 Click **OK**. Close the database.

To test if the password works, you need to close the database and open it again.

Choose **File** from the menu and click **AC1401-Armstrong2** from the list of recently used files displayed at the bottom of the **File** menu.

The Password Required dialog box is displayed.

Type **ABCabc!** in the **Enter database password** box.

The password is displayed as asterisks.

QUICK TIP

A list of recently used files is available at the bottom of the File menu. This is a list of files recently used on the individual computer. If the file you want was used recently, it is faster to select it from this list. You can change the number of files displayed in the list by choosing Tools, Options. Select the General tab and then change the number in the Recently used file list box.

5 Click **OK**.

The database opens. To remove the password you have to open the database in Exclusive mode, and you have to know the password.

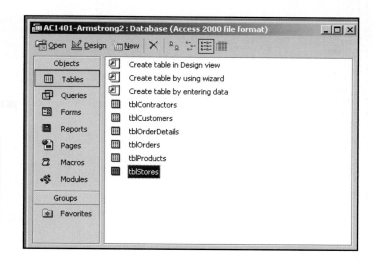

CAUTION

The database opens if you correctly matched the password. If you did not match the password exactly, including the proper upper- and lowercase characters, you see a warning box and then return to the Password Required dialog box to try again.

6 Close the database. This time click the **Open** button on the toolbar. Locate and select the **AC1401-Armstrong2** file in the Open dialog box.

To open the database in exclusive mode you have to select this option using the Open button.

Click the arrow next to the **Open** button and point to **Open Exclusive**.

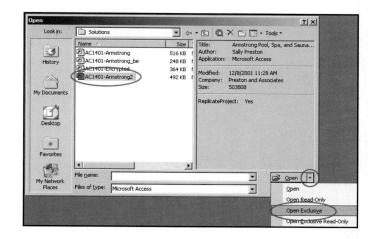

7 Click **Open Exclusive**. Type the password in the Password dialog box.

The database opens.

Choose **Tools, Security, Unset Database Password** from the menu.

The Unset Database Password dialog box opens.

Type **ABCabc!** in the **Password** box.

Again, the password is displayed as asterisks.

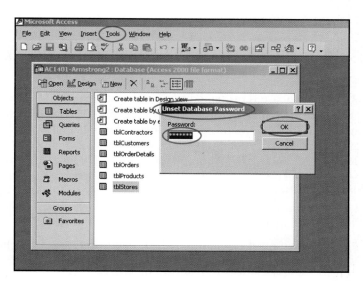

IN DEPTH

If you want to change the password, you need to open the file in Exclusive mode, remove the first password, and then set a new password. If you select a file from the list of recently opened files, it reopens the file in the same mode that was previously used for that file. For example, in Step 4, when you reopened the AC1401-Armstrong2 file by selecting it from the recently used file list, the file was actually opened in Exclusive mode and you could have removed and changed the password.

8 Click **OK**. Close the database.

The password is removed. To verify that the password has been removed, you need to close and reopen the database again.

> Choose **File** from the menu and select **AC1401-Armstrong2** from the list of recently opened files.

The database opens without requiring a password.

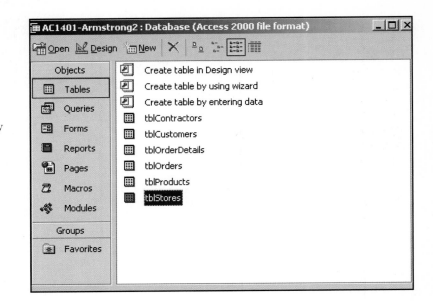

9 Close the database.

> Using a password provides protection for a single-user database that is maintained on one computer. Password protection does not allow you to control which objects can be used, or whether the user can change the design of the objects. If a person has the password, they have full access to the entire database. Access also provides a more sophisticated level of security called *user-level* security. User-level security provides control over who has permission to different objects and details what they can do to those objects. This type of security is particularly useful in a network environment. You learn more about user-level security in the challenge exercises at the end of this lesson.

Task 3
ENCRYPTING AND DECRYPTING DATABASES

Why would I do this?

Even though a database is protected by a password, it is still possible to view the data by opening the database with a word processing program. Most of what displays with a word processing program is unrecognizable characters, but you can still decipher some of the data in the tables. When you encrypt a database it compacts the database and makes it completely unreadable by a word processing or a utility program. Decrypting the database reverses the process and returns the file to its original condition. Before you encrypt a database, make sure you have enough storage space for both the original file and the encrypted file. You can use this procedure in addition to password protection.

In this task, you encrypt the personnel database for the Armstrong Pool, Spa, and Sauna Company.

1 With Access open, click the Open button. Locate **AC1402** for this lesson. Transfer the file to the location where you are saving your files. Remove the read-only property, if necessary. Do not rename or open the file.

You will rename the file when you encrypt it. To encrypt a database, the database must be closed.

File moved to your folder

2 Close the **Open** dialog box. Choose Tools, Security, Encrypt/Decrypt Database from the menu.

You select the database you want to encrypt in the Encrypt/Decrypt dialog box.

If necessary, change the **Look in** box to the location where you are saving your files. Select **AC1402**.

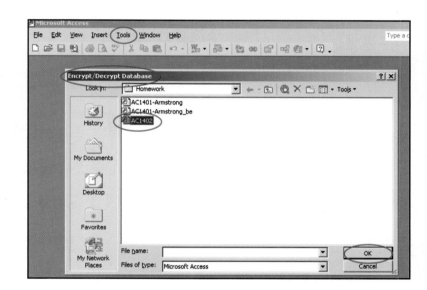

3 Click OK.

The Password Required dialog box opens.

Type **Learn** in the Password box and press ⏎Enter.

The Encrypt Database As dialog box is displayed. Here you name the database and identify the location where you want to save it.

Type **AC1402-Encrypted** in the **File name** box. Make sure the Look-in box displays the folder where you are saving your files.

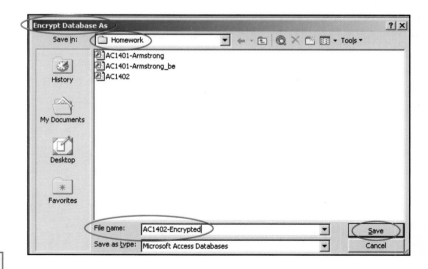

QUICK TIP

If you choose to save the encrypted file with the same name as the original file, Access will ask for confirmation before it overwrites the original file.

4 Click the <u>S</u>ave button. Type **Learn** in the **Password Required** dialog box and click **OK**.

The dialog box closes. The empty Access window remains on your screen.

Start **Microsoft Word**. Click the Open button. If necessary, change the **Files of type** box to **All Files**. Locate the **AC1402-Encrypted** file.

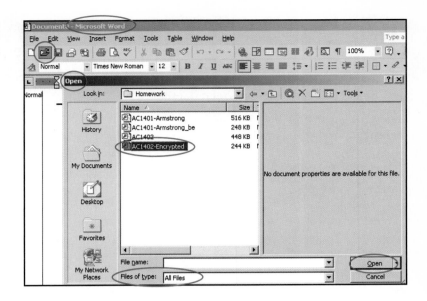

5 Select the **AC1402-Encrypted** file and click the <u>O</u>pen button.

The File Conversion dialog box opens. You have three choices for converting the text.

Make sure the **Windows (Default)** option button is selected.

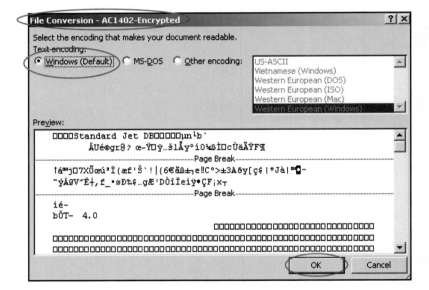

6 Click **OK**.

The file opens.

Scroll through the document. Notice that there are several hundred pages and the whole thing looks like gibberish.

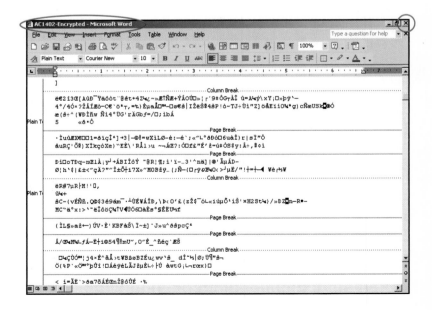

7 Close **Word**.

The Access window returns to your screen.

Click the **Open** button. Locate and open the **AC1402-Encrypted** file. Type the password when prompted. Open the **tblPrivate** table.

The data is still viewable in Access

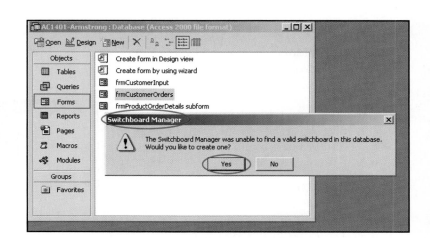

8 Close the table and close the database.

> **IN DEPTH**
>
> To decrypt the file, you simply reverse the process. Make sure the database is closed and not in use by anyone else. Select Tools, Security, Encrypt/Decrypt Database. Select the encrypted database and click OK. Enter the password, and then provide a name for the decrypted database.

Task 4
CREATING A SWITCHBOARD

Why would I do this?
Access databases are often used by people who do not know Access or anything about designing a database. You want to make the process of working with the data as easy as possible. One of the features you can add to make it easier to work with Access is a switchboard. This creates a menu system that enables users to navigate the database by clicking on buttons. The switchboard itself is a form. Each button on the switchboard performs a specific task, such as opening a form or printing a report. With this approach, you can open the database, search for records, change records, and add new records, or preview and print reports.

In this task you learn how to create a switchboard using the Switchboard Manager. You use the Armstrong database file.

1 Open the **AC1401-Armstrong** file that you copied to your folder in Task 1.

The database opens on your screen.

Choose **Tools**, **Database Utilities**, **Switchboard Manager** from the menu.

Because there is no switchboard to manage yet, a dialog box appears that asks if you would like to create one.

2 Click **Yes**.

The Switchboard Manager dialog box opens. The Main Switchboard is listed in the Switchboard Pages box. This switchboard is created by default by the Switchboard Manager.

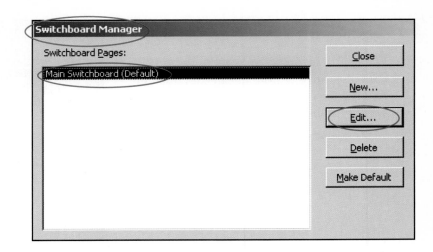

3 Click **Edit**.

The Edit Switchboard Page dialog box opens. The Main Switchboard is listed in the Switchboard Name box. This is the switchboard you are going to edit. Currently no items are listed on the Main Switchboard.

No items listed for the
Main Switchboard

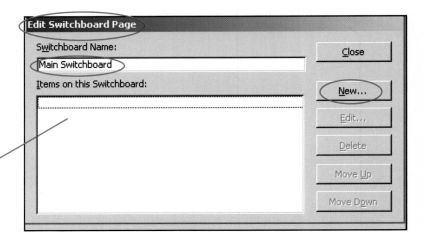

4 Click the **New** button.

The Edit Switchboard Item dialog box opens. This is used to add or edit items on the selected switchboard. When you add an item to a switchboard, it creates a button. You use the Text box to label each button on the switchboard. The Command box is used to select the type of action you want to occur, such as opening a form. The third box, currently labeled Switchboard, changes based on the selection made in the Command box. For example, if you select the command "Open Form in the Add Mode" the third box changes from Switchboard to Form, so you can select the form you want to open.

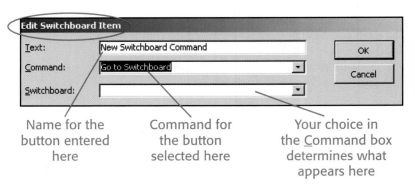

Name for the
button entered
here

Command for
the button
selected here

Your choice in
the Command box
determines what
appears here

5 In the **Text** box, select the text and type **Add New Order**. Use the arrow at the end of the **Command** box and select **Open Form in Add Mode**.

The third box changes to Form. The next step is to select the form you want to open.

Click the arrow at the end of the **Form** box and select **frmCustomerOrders**.

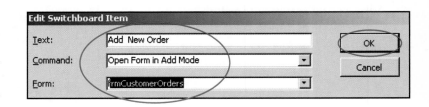

6 Click **OK**.

A new item is shown on the Edit Switchboard Page. To add other items to the main switchboard you repeat this process until all the items are listed.

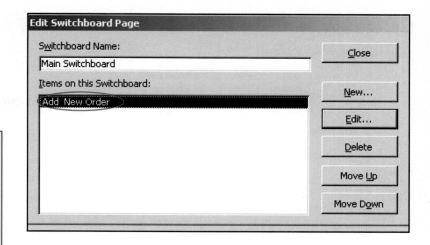

IN DEPTH

The same form can be opened three different ways and each can have its own button on the switchboard. The Add mode displays the form with all the fields empty so you can enter a new record. The Edit mode is used to view or change existing records, or to add new records. You can also open a form in Read Only mode, so records can be viewed but not added or changed. To use the Read Only option you first create a macro using the Macro object page and set the Data Mode Action Argument to Read Only. Then in the Edit Switchboard Item dialog box you select Run Macro as the command, and then select the macro you created from the Macro list box.

Items listed on the
Main Switchboard

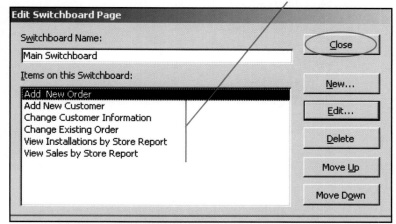

7 Click the **New** button. In the **Text** box type **Add New Customer**, change the **Command** box to **Open Form in Add Mode**, and select **frmCustomerInput** in the **Form** box. Click **OK**.

A second item is added to the Main Switchboard.

Repeat this process to add the following buttons:

Text Box	Command	Form or Report to open
Change Customer Information	Open Form in Edit Mode	frmCustomerInput
Change Existing Order	Open Form in Edit Mode	frmCustomerOrders
View Installations by Store Report	Open Report	rptInstallationsbyStore
View Sales by Store Report	Open Report	rptSalesbyStore

After you add all the items, there should be six items in the Items on this Switchboard box.

QUICK TIP

When you are building your own switchboard, it may be easier to add items by selecting the command first, then selecting the object you want to open or view in the third box. Last, you type an appropriate label in the Text box to match the object opened and the action or view used.

8 Click <u>C</u>lose.

The Edit Switchboard dialog box closes.

Click <u>C</u>lose again to close the **Switchboard Manager** dialog box. Click the **Forms** object button.

The Switchboard is listed as a form on this page.

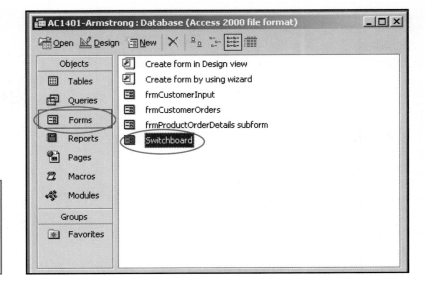

CAUTION

You may also notice there is a Switchboard table listed on the Tables object page. Do not do anything with the Switchboard table. It controls the organization of the form. If you make changes to it, it can cause the form to not function properly.

9 Double-click the **Switchboard** form to open it.

The Main Switchboard is displayed.

Switchboard buttons ——

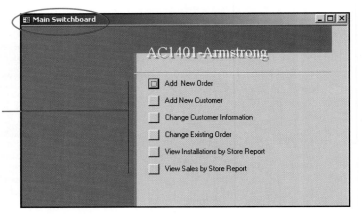

10 Test the buttons by clicking on each one to verify that they open the correct form or report in the correct view. Close the Switchboard after you have tested each button.

IN DEPTH

When you create a switchboard, you can use the Main Switchboard as a vehicle to list secondary switchboards. To do this, you create additional switchboards, and add them to the Main Switchboard. This creates a nested set of switchboards. For example, you might use one switchboard to list all the forms, and another one to list the reports. The buttons on the Main Switchboard open the secondary switchboards. The secondary switchboards list buttons that open specific forms, reports, or other objects.

If you want to add more items to your switchboard, you can return to Switchboard Manager the same way you opened it. Simply choose <u>T</u>ools, <u>D</u>atabase Utilities, <u>S</u>witchboard Manager. Select the Main Switchboard and click the <u>E</u>dit button. Follow the same procedures you used in this task to add new items. If you want to delete an item, select it in the Edit Switchboard Page dialog box and click the <u>D</u>elete button. You can delete all the items from your switchboard, but you cannot delete the Main Switchboard.

Task 5
SETTING STARTUP OPTIONS

Why would I do this?

Often databases are used by people who need to locate, edit, or add new records, or perhaps run reports. You can help simplify the interface so they see only what they need to do their work. You can control the way the database appears when it first opens by selecting which toolbars are available to the user. You can also set the switchboard form to open automatically. Using these tools helps ensure that the user is not overwhelmed by the full Access window. It also can provide a measure of protection by keeping the user from altering the design of objects.

In this task, you learn how to open the switchboard automatically whenever the database is opened. You also disable several features that are very useful while the database is being designed, but that are not necessary while someone else is using it.

1 With the **AC1401-Armstrong** file open, choose **T**ools, **Startup** from the menu.

The Startup dialog box opens.

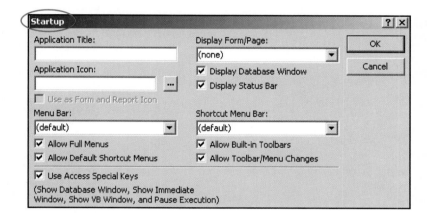

2 Click the arrow at the end of the **Display Form/Page** box and select **Switchboard** from the list.

This causes the Switchboard to open automatically when the database is opened.

Click the checkbox to deselect **Display Database Window**.

This prevents the Database window from opening, so the user cannot get into the design of the database.

Click **Allow Full Menus**, **Allow Default Shortcut Menus**, **Allow Built-in Toolbars**, and **Allow Toolbar/Menu Changes** to deselect these items.

Display Database Window is deselected

Menu and toolbar choices are deselected

3 Click **OK**. Close the database. Choose **File**, and select **AC1401-Armstrong** from the list of recently opened databases.

The Main Switchboard for the Armstrong database is displayed. The toolbar is not shown, and the items on the menu are limited.

The menu has fewer choices
The toolbar is not available

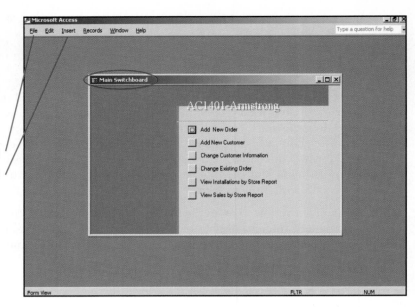

4 Close the switchboard.

The blank Access window is displayed. The database window is not available.

Click the **File** menu.

The normal list of commands is not available. You cannot open another database from within Access. To return Access to its normal state you have to close Access and reopen it.

Menu commands limited

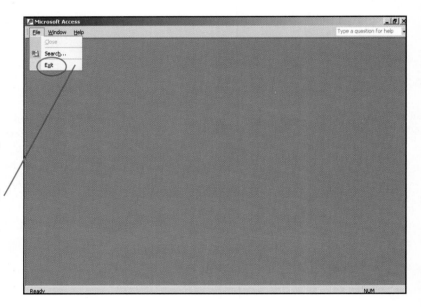

5 Click **Exit**, and then reopen Access to see the full menu toolbar options.

Access is restored to its normal state.

Menu and toolbar
are displayed

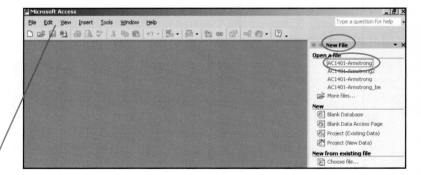

6 Hold down ⟨Shift⟩ while you double-click **AC1401-Armstrong** on the **New File** task pane.

The AC1401-Armstrong Database window opens with the toolbar and menu bar displayed. To override the startup parameters, hold down ⟨Shift⟩ as you open the file.

7 Close the file and close Access.

The exercises that follow are designed for you to review and use what you have learned in this lesson. You also have the opportunity to practice your skills and then expand on them by applying them to new situations.

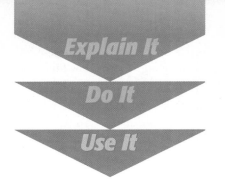

COMPREHENSION

Comprehension exercises are designed to check your memory and understanding of the basic concepts in this lesson. You distinguish between true and false statements, identify new screen elements, and match terms with related statements. If you are uncertain of the correct answer, refer to the task number following each item (for example, T4 refers to Task 4) and review that task until you are confident that you can provide a correct response.

TRUE-FALSE

Circle either T or F.

T   F   **1.** To split a database you must first open the database in Exclusive mode. **(T1)**

T   F   **2.** You can add a password to an open database by choosing **Tools, Database Utilities, Add Password. (T2)**

T   F   **3.** Replication is a process that is used to copy a database so it can be used in more than one location. **(T1)**

T   F   **4.** When you use the Switchboard Manager you can open a form in edit mode or in add mode. **(T4)**

T   F   **5.** You can use the Startup options to control how a database appears when it opens. **(T5)**

T   F   **6.** When a database is encrypted it prevents someone from viewing the data in Access. **(T3)**

MATCHING QUESTIONS

A. front end   **D.** back end

B. password   **E.** switchboard

C. encrypt   **F.** permission

Match the following statements to the word or phrase that is the best match from the list. Write the letter of the matching word or phrase in the space provided next to the number.

1. ____ Used to create a menu system to make it easier for people to use Access **(T4)**

2. ____ The process of giving users access to parts of a database based on job-related activities **(T2)**

3. ____ In a split database, the file that has the queries, forms, and reports **(T1)**

4. ____ Made unreadable by a word processing program **(T3)**

5. ____ Should include numbers and letters and other characters **(T2)**

6. ____ In a split database, the file where the data resides **(T1)**

IDENTIFYING PARTS OF THE ACCESS SCREEN

Refer to the figure and identify the numbered parts of the screen. Write the letter of the correct label in the space next to the number.

1. _____

2. _____

3. _____

4. _____

5. _____

6. _____

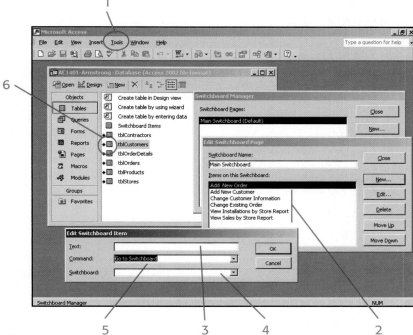

A. Enter name to appear on the switchboard button **(T4)**

B. Indicates linked tables **(T1)**

C. Select object to activate **(T4)**

D. Used to set security and startup options **(T2, T5)**

E. Select action to occur here **(T4)**

F. List of switchboard items **(T4)**

REINFORCEMENT

Reinforcement exercises are designed to reinforce the skills you have learned by applying them to new situations. Detailed instructions are provided along with a figure, where appropriate, to illustrate the result. Complete the reinforcement exercises sequentially. Leave the file open at the end of each exercise for use in the next exercise until you are specifically directed to close it.

In these exercises, you use the Alumni Travel Club database. A number of the concepts taught in this lesson can best be verified by opening the database file to see if the password and switchboard function as expected. Your instructor may direct you to submit the file on disk or by e-mail for evaluation, in addition to the printouts specified in the instructions.

R1—Splitting a Database

1. Open Access and click **More files** under the **Open a file** category. Locate **AC1403** in the **Student** folder for this lesson. Transfer the file to the location where you are saving your files. Remove the read-only property, and rename the file **AC1403-Travel**. Open the file.

2. Choose **Tools**, **Database Utilities**, **Database Splitter** from the menu. Click the **Split Database** button.

3. In the **Create Back-end Database** dialog box, change the **Save in** box to the location where you are saving your files. Click the **Split** button, and then click **OK** to acknowledge the message.

4. Click the **Forms** object button and open **frmMemberInformation.** Replace the name of the first member listed (Donor ID 1003) with your name. Choose **File**, **Print**, **Selected Record(s)**, and then click **OK** to print the form with your name. Close the form. Close the database.

5. Open the **AC1403-Travel_be** database. Open the **tblMembers** table. Scroll to the right and enter a comment in the Comment field for the record that displays your name.

6. Choose **File**, **Page Setup**. Click the **Page** tab on the **Page Setup** dialog box, choose **Landscape**, and then click **OK**. Click the **Print Preview** button to make sure the table will print on one page. Print the table. Close the database.

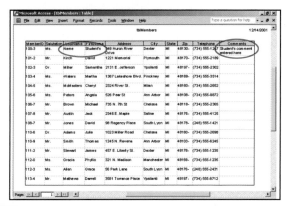

R2—Setting Passwords for Databases

1. With Access open, click the **Open** button. In the **Open** dialog box, locate the **AC1403-Travel** database. Select the file and click the arrow next to the **Open** button. Click **Open Exclusive**.

2. Choose **Tools**, **Security**, and **Set Database Password** from the menu.

3. Type **Learn!** in the **Password** text box. Press `Tab` and type the same password in the **Verify** box. Click **OK**. Close the database.

4. Choose **File** from the menu and select **AC1403-Travel** from the list of available files. Type the password in the **Enter database password** box and press `↵Enter`.

5. Close the database.

R3—Encrypting and Decrypting Databases

1. With Access open, choose **Tools**, **Security**, **Encrypt/Decrypt Database** from the menu.

2. In the **Encrypt/Decrypt Database** dialog box, change the **Look in** box to the location where you are saving your files. Select **AC1403-Travel** and click **OK**.

3. Type **Learn!** in the **Enter database password** box and press `↵Enter`.

4. Type **AC1403-Encrypted** in the **File name** box. Make sure the **Look-in** box displays the folder where you are saving your files.

5. Click the **Save** button. Type the password in the **Password Required** dialog box.

6. Start **Microsoft Word**. Click the **Open** button. If necessary, change the **Files of type** box to **All Files**. Locate and open the **AC1403-Encrypted** file.

7. In the **File Conversion** dialog box, make sure the **Windows (Default)** option button is selected. Click **OK**.

8. Make sure the insertion point is at the top of the document and type your name. Choose **File**, **Print**, from the menu and then select **Current page**. The first page of the encrypted file is printed. Close the Word document without saving the file.

R4—Creating a Switchboard

1. Open the **AC1403-Travel** file. Enter the password when prompted.

2. Choose **Tools**, **Database Utilities**, **Switchboard Manager** from the menu. Click **Yes** to create a new switchboard. Click **Edit** to edit the Main Switchboard.

3. Click the **New** button. In the **Text** box type **Add New Member**, change the **Command** box to **Open Form in Add Mode**, and select **frmMemberInformation** in the **Form** box. Click **OK**.

4. Repeat Step 3 to create the following menu items:

Text	Command/ Form or Report
Add New Pledge	Open Form in Add Mode/ frmMemberPledges
Member Payments	Open Form in Edit Mode/ frmRecordPayments
Pledges by Member	Open Report/ rptPledgesbyMembers
Member Payments Report	Open Report/ rptMemberPayments
Close Database	Exit Application

5. Click **Close** twice to exit the **Switchboard Manager** dialog boxes.

6. Click the **Forms** object button, and open the **Switchboard**. Click the **Print** button to print a copy of the **Main Switchboard** form.

7. Test the buttons by clicking on each one to verify that it opens the correct report or form in the correct mode.

R5—Setting Startup Options

1. Open AC1403-Travel again, and choose **Tools**, **Startup** from the menu.

2. Click the arrow at the end of the **Display Form/Page** box and select **Switchboard** from the list.

3. Click the checkbox to deselect **Display Database Window**.

4. Click **Allow Full Menus**, **Allow Default Shortcut Menus**, **Allow Built-in Toolbars**, and **Allow Toolbar/Menu Changes** to deselect these items

5. Click **OK**. Close the database. Choose **File**, and select **AC1403-Travel** from the list of recently opened databases to confirm that the startup parameters work as expected. Enter the password when prompted.

6. Locate the print screen key PrtSc to the right of the function keys on your keyboard. Press PrtSc. Open **Microsoft Word** and click the **Paste** button. A copy of the Access window is pasted into Word.

7. Type your name on the page and then click the **Print** button on the Word toolbar. Close Word. Close the database, and close Access.

8. If your instructor requests it, submit a copy of the file, by email or on disk, so the functionality of your database can be verified.

9. Close Access.

Paste button

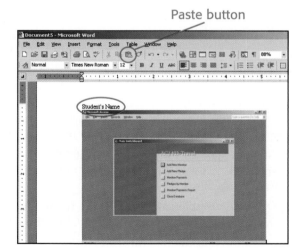

Challenge exercises are designed to test your ability to apply your skills to new situations with less-detailed instructions. These exercises also challenge you to expand your repertoire of skills by using commands that are similar to those you have already learned. The desired outcome is clearly defined, but you have more freedom to choose the steps needed to achieve the required result.

In the following Challenge exercise you work with the charity fund-raising database.

C1—Updating the Connection to a Back-End Database File

When you work with a split database file, you may need to use the Link Table Manager to update the link to the back-end database. This is necessary if you move your file, or the back-end file gets moved. In this exercise, you split a database, then move the back-end database and update the link.

Goal: Update a link to a back-end database using the Linked Table Manager.

1. Locate **AC1404** in the **Student** folder for this lesson. Transfer the file to the location where you are saving your files. Remove the read-only property, and rename the file **AC1404-Ch1**. Open the database.

2. Choose **Tools**, **Database Utilities**, **Database Splitter**. Split the database and save the back-end file in the same location as your other files.

3. Close the front-end database file. Open **Windows Explorer** or **My Computer**. Create a new folder and label it with your name. Move the **AC1404-Ch1_be** file to the new folder bearing your name.

4. Return to **Access** and open the **AC1404-Ch1** file. Try to open the **tblMembers** table. A message box displays warning you that the file AC1404-Ch1_be cannot be found. Click **OK**.

5. Choose **Tools**, **Database Utilities**, **Linked Table Manager**. Select all three tables displayed in the Linked Table Manager dialog box and click **OK**.

6. Find the new location of the **AC1404-Ch1_be** file. Select the file and click the **Open** button. Click **OK**, then click **Close**.

7. Open **tblMembers** and change the name for the first record (100-3) to your name. Close the table.

8. Open the **frmMemberInformation** and print the single form showing your name. Close the file.

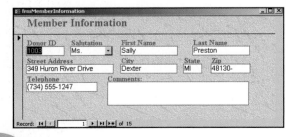

C2—Replicating a Database

If you travel and need access to a database file that is normally maintained on a network or on a workstation, you can replicate the file and take a copy with you. When you return to the office, you can synchronize the two files so records and changes in both database files are updated. While creating a replicate file is not difficult, there are many ramifications to using this process and it should not be done without first reading extensively about this topic. You can start by reading the Help files provided by Access. In this lesson you read the Help files related to replicating a file, and then you create a replicated file.

Goal: Replicate the Armstrong database file.

1. In the **Ask a question box**, type **create a replicated database** and press ↵Enter. Select the topic, **Create a replicated database**. Maximize the **Help** window and click the **Show All** arrow at the top-right corner of the window. Read and print this topic.

2. Use the **Ask a question box** to locate the topic, **Changes made to your database when you use replication**. Expand this topic, read it, and print the full contents. Close the Help window

3. Make a copy of the **AC1401** file. Rename the copy **AC1401-Ch2**. Follow the steps detailed in **Create a replica of your database by using the menu bar** found under the **Create a replicated database** Help topic. Use default values for anything not specified in the instructions. This will result in a file titled **AC1401-Ch2-Design Master**.

4. Choose **Tools**, **Options**, and click the **View** tab. Click the **Hidden objects** and **System objects** check boxes to turn on these options. Click **OK**. The additional objects that have been created as a result of the replication process are displayed. (You may need to use the scroll bar at the bottom of the database window to see the objects displayed in the figure.)

5. Make sure the Tables objects are displayed and click (PrtSc) on your keyboard. This places a copy of the database window in the Office Clipboard. Open **Microsoft Word** and click the **Paste** button.

6. Open **Windows Explorer** or **My Computer** and look at the files that have been created by the replication process. Change the **View** to **Details** to see the file size.

7. Add your name to the Word document. Then list the files that were created by this replication process and the size of each file.

8. Print the Word document and then close it without saving the changes.

9. Return to Access and choose <u>T</u>ools, <u>O</u>ptions, and click the **View** tab. Click the **Hidden objects** and **System objects** check boxes to deselect these options. Click **OK**. The additional objects that have been created as a result of the replication process are hidden again. Close the file.

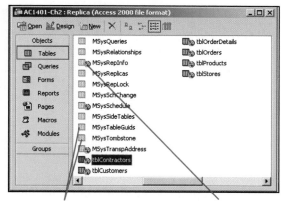

Files created by the replication process   Replication icon

 ### C3—Preventing Changes to Data in One Field

There are various levels of security. In many cases, you just want to prevent accidental changes made by a well-meaning person. In such cases, it is sufficient to change the property of a field in a form to prevent accidental entries.

In the following exercise, you protect the member ID number in a form to prevent accidental change.

Goal: Prevent changes to one field in a form.

1. Locate **AC1404** in the **Student** folder for this lesson. Transfer the file to the location where you are saving your files. Remove the read-only property, and rename the file **AC1404-Ch3**. Open the file.

2. Click the **Forms** button and open **frmMemberInformation** in **Design** view.

3. Right-click on the **MemberID** text box (not the label box) and select <u>P</u>roperties from the shortcut menu.

4. Click the **Data** tab. Change the **Locked** option from No to **Yes**.

5. Press PrtSc to capture the change made to the property sheet. Close the properties sheet.

6. Open **Word** and click the **Paste** button. Add your name to the Word document and print the file. Close Word without saving the changes.

7. Return to Access and save the changes to the Form. Switch to the Form view. Try to change the MemberID number under the label Donor ID. It is not changeable. Close the form.

8. Click the **Tables** object button and open the **tblMember** table. Attempt to edit one of the **MemberID** numbers. You can still edit the table—locking the field in the form simply prevents accidents. Press Esc to restore the MemberID number. Close the database.

C4—Learning about User-Level Security

Throughout this book you learned how to create and design database objects. Often, the person who designs a database is not the person who will be working with the data on a daily basis. Occasionally, you may be asked to modify the design of the objects, but the day-to-day maintenance of records, querying the data, and running reports is done by the end user. If the database is going to be used in a multiuser environment, you want to guarantee that the design is protected from alteration.

To protect your design, you need to work with the network administrator to create a user-level security system for your database. User-level security can ensure that each group of users has access to the information they need to do their jobs, while preventing unauthorized use or modification.

When you install Access, two groups are created by default, Admins and Users. The Admins group has full control over all the objects in the database. There is also a default user name, Admin. The user Admin is a member of both groups by default. Normally, this happens in the background and you are unaware of it. It makes Access easy to use and allows full *permissions* to administer and use a database when anyone opens it because everyone is automatically identified as the user, Admin, and is a member of the Admins group.

If you change the default settings, it is possible to control what rights other users have to the various objects in a database. It is also possible to lock yourself and others out of the database.

In the following exercise, you learn about the predefined accounts in Access and the security risk of using the default settings. We recommend that you limit your activity in this exercise to learning about the process so that you can assist your network administrator in setting up user-level security.

Goal: Learn about the predefined accounts in Access and the security risks of using the default settings.

1. Start Access. Type **User-level security** in the **Ask a question box** and press Enter. Choose **About user-level security** from the list of topics.

2. Read the topic, **About user-level security**.

3. Open the Word document AC1405 and save it as **AC1405-Security**. Write an answer to the first question in your own words.

4. Read the topic **About organizing security accounts**.

5. Write answers to questions 2 and 3 in your own words.

6. Print the Word document. Save and close the document.

This is a difficult subject to learn from these pages. Do not attempt to apply what you learn on these pages to a computer that is used on a network without consulting with the network administrator. You can easily make a mistake that would result in locking people out of databases and causing a great deal of trouble. Even if you are working on your own computer that is not attached to a network, you could end up reinstalling Access and permanently locking yourself out of some databases.

 ### C5—Determining User-Level Groups

It is recommended that you do Challenge exercise C4 if you are not familiar with user-level security.

You may be better qualified than the network administrator when it comes to determining what kinds of control and access different people should have to various objects in your database. It is possible to grant permissions to different people on an individual basis, but this is very cumbersome to administer if there are more than a few people involved. Generally, it is better to create groups with certain permissions, determine what job classifications need those

permissions, and then assign users who have those jobs to the groups. If you hire a new employee or someone changes jobs, the administrator can simply determine what job they have and assign them to the appropriate group or groups.

In this exercise, you examine the activities each type of job requires and determine what group or groups are appropriate for each job.

Goal: Determine what user groups should be established to enable each store in the Armstrong Pool, Spa, and Sauna Company to access the information they need, while protecting the database design.

1. Open Word and open the file **AC1406**. Save the form with the name **AC1406-Groups**. Add your name and section number at the top of the form.

2. Review the table on the first page that describes the list of permissions granted to each group.

3. Look at each job in the table on the second page. All the job activities are related to sales recorded in the Armstrong Orders database that you have been working with throughout this book.

4. Assign a group to each job that provides the minimum set of permissions necessary to do the job.

5. Add your name as the Network Administrator in the last cell of the table. Print the form. Save and close the document.

ON YOUR OWN

 In this lesson you learned about several methods of protecting a database so it can be shared with others. Use any of the following ideas as a basis for further practice.

1. Work with a copy of a database of your own design and use any of the techniques that have been taught to add security to your database.

- Split the database and place the back-end database on a network and the front-end database on one or more workstations. Add different objects to the front-end databases to create unique objects for different users.

- Add a password to your database.

- Encrypt your database.

- Document the protection you have applied to your database. Check with your instructor to determine if you should submit the file in electronic or printed form. If necessary, capture an image of screens using (PrtSc) and paste the image into a Word document as a means of documenting your work.

2. For further information on user-level security, go to your local bookstore and look for a book that teaches how to add user-level security in Access. Not all books cover this topic, so you need to examine the content of the book to determine if the information covered is detailed enough for your needs.

- Work with a network administrator at your workplace to learn more about creating groups and adding permissions to users.

- Work with your instructor or network administrator to add groups to a database at your school.

3. For further information on replicating a database, go to your local bookstore and look for a book that discusses how to replicate a database. After researching this topic, replicate a database, make changes to both copies of the file, and then follow the instructions you found to synchronize the files.

- Provide copies of the files before and after the synchronization to your instructor.

Glossary

#N/A error message displayed when a formula refers to cells that do not have values in them.

Actions in a macro, Access-defined functions that perform a task.

Add-In tools not usually installed.

Arguments user-defined values that specify how and where a macro performs its function.

Back end the term used to identify the main database that houses the tables in a split database setup.

Balloon payment a single payment that is made to pay off the balance of a loan.

Bookmark a marker that enables you to go directly to a section of the document or a particular document feature, such as a graphic or a table.

Cartesian product the results of a query when there is no valid join between the tables used in the query.

Cascade windows placed on top of each other slightly displaced so you can read the title bar.

Comma Separated Values (CSV) database values that are separated from each other by a comma.

Command buttons a control placed on a form that when clicked executes a specific action.

Comparison operators mathematical operators such as less than and greater than.

Conditional Formatting formatting of the selected cell is applied when a condition is met.

Controls any object on a form or report this is selected from a field list box or from the Toolbox, such as text boxes, check boxes, or option boxes

Criteria values entered to limit the records to those that match the criterion.

Cross product (see Cartesian product)

Customize make changes to suit an individual's preferences.

Data access page used to display Access objects as a Web page.

Database query extracts data from a database.

Database splitter an Access tool that is used to split a database into two parts, resulting in one database that holds the tables of data, and another database that holds all of the other database objects.

Decrypt reverses the process of encrypting a database file.

Delimiters characters used to separate values in a database.

Detail section the part of a form or report that displays the data from the underlying object.

Digital signature uses a digital certificate, obtained by using the SelfCert.exe program, or from a system administrator or commercial site, to confirm that the document originated from the signer, and also confirms that it has not been altered.

Document map an outline based on the Heading styles included with Word. To move around the document, you turn the document map on and click on the outline heading of the section you want to see.

Dynaset the results of a query.

Em dash a long dash used in printing to indicate a sudden break in thought or an important parenthetical expression. It is about four times as long as a hyphen.

Embed to copy a picture, chart, or other object from another application and place it in the document, where it takes on the characteristics of a picture.

Encrypt a method used to change data into unreadable text.

Endnote identifies a source of information, and is placed at the end of the document or document section.

Event procedure an event procedure is a series of steps that must occur for a command to take effect.

eXtensible Markup Language (XML) a standard language for describing and delivering data on the Web

Extrapolation estimating values beyond known data points.

Fields types of data in a database.

Floating toolbar a moveable toolbar that is not located in a specific position on the screen.

Font styles   a set of formatting characteristics that you can use to change the look of selected text. Some font styles are built into Word, but you can create your own styles.

Footnote   identifies a source of information, and is placed at the bottom of the page that contains the referenced information.

FORECAST   a function that estimates values from a given set of data.

Foreign key   the common field that is used to join with a primary key field in another table.

Form footers   the bottom section of a form, generally used to display dates, page numbers or summary data.

Form headers   the top section of a form, generally used to display titles, dates, page numbers or summary data.

Formula Auditing   a group of features that may be used to display the relationships between the selected cell and other cells using arrows.

Front end   In a split database, the database that houses all of the objects except the tables. This is the database used by the end-user.

Gantt chart   a chart that uses bars to represent duration and relationships between tasks.

GDP   Gross Domestic Product, a measure of a country's economic performance.

Goal Seek   a tool that determines the value required to produce a desired outcome in a selected cell.

Graphical User Interface (GUI)   term used to describe the Windows environment that enables you to interact with the computer by using a mouse to click on buttons and select commands from menus.

Group footer   a section in a report that displays summary data for the field upon which the report is grouped.

Group header   a section in a report that displays the name of the field upon which the report is grouped, and which controls the grouping of the data.

HLOOKUP   a function that looks up the reference value in the first row of the selected range and then displays the value in a given row. It may be used when the orientation of the table is horizontal.

Hotkey   a letter in a menu or button name that can be used in place of clicking on the menu or button item.

Hypertext Markup Language   programming language that is used to create Web pages.

IF   the IF function examines a criterium and then chooses one of two options to perform depending on whether the criterium evaluate as true or false.

Inner join   the default join type which displays only those records where there is a match between related tables.

Input mask   a field property designed to guide the user when entering data so that data containing dashes or parentheses is entered in a consistent way.

Interpolation   estimating a value between known data points.

ISNA   determines if the selected cell has the #N/A error message.

Iteration   a synonym for repetition.

Join   a relationship between common fields in two or more tables used to retrieve related information from multiple tables.

Junction table   a third table used to list the primary keys from two other tables in order to establish a many-to-many-relationship between the two tables. In the junction table, the primary key fields function as foreign keys.

Landscape   a page layout orientation where the document is printed or displayed with the width greater than the height.

Linear regression   a statistical method of determining the minimum difference between a line and a set of data points.

Link   to place an object, such as a chart or table, into a document and keep the relationship between the source and the destination file. If you make a change in the source document, it is automatically updated in the Word document.

Linked Table Manager   a feature that enables you to repair links to tables in a database that has been moved.

Locked   changes not allowed if the worksheet is protected.

Lookup field   a text box that includes a list box that enables the user to select an existing value from another table or from a specific list

Macro virus   an unauthorized program that utilizes the macro options in Microsoft Office.

Macro   pre-defined commands that can be applied to selected text, objects or files. They are often used to automate repetitive, multi-step procedures.

Many-to-many relationships   A type of relationship that is accomplished by introducing a third table and using two one-to-many relationships.

Master document   the controlling file that coordinates and compiles each individual section of a collaborative document. The individual parts of the document are known as subdocuments.

Microsoft Graph   a program built into Word that enables the user to place data in a datasheet and create a chart.

Modules   modules are programming routines written using Visual Basic code.

named range   one or more cells that have been assigned a name. The name may be used in formulas in place of the cell references.

Normal style   the default paragraph style in the Normal.dot template. The normal style produces the paragraph settings and font characteristics you start with when you begin a document.

Normal.dot   the default global template that contains built-in styles. It is the base template for all other templates. The style defaults in the Normal.dot template can be modified by the user.

One-to-many relationship   the most common type of relationship, where a record in one table may be related to many records in another table.

One-to-one relationship   a relationship between two tables, where a record in one table is related to a single record in a second table.

Orphan   the first line of a paragraph that is alone at the bottom of a page.

Outer join   a join type that enables the user to display all the records from one table, whether or not it matches another record in the related table.

Page footers   a section of a report that contains information that displays at the bottom of every page of the report, such as the date and/or page numbers. Forms can also have page footers.

Page headers   a section near the top of a form or report. In a report this area displays column headings.

Pages   the Access Database object that displays a short cut to a data access page.

Paragraph styles   a set of formatting characteristics that can be used to quickly change the characteristics of a paragraph or paragraphs. Paragraph styles control such things as margins, indents, line spacing, and even font characteristics.

Parameter query   a query that uses values to define the output as part of the query structure.

Password   a combination of letters and numbers that must be entered to open a database file.

PivotCharts   an interactive graphical analysis of data.

PivotTables   a reporting tool that summarizes and analyzes data from a table or a query in an interactive format.

Portrait   a page layout orientation where the document is printed or displayed with the height greater than the width. This is by far the most common document orientation.

Primary key   A field in a table that contains a unique value for each record.

Property   a field or object attribute that can be set to define one of the object's characteristics, such as size, color, border, or pattern.

Protection   prevents unauthorized changes.

Range_lookup   the VLOOKUP and HLOOKUP functions have an optional argument named range_lookup that may be used to force exact matches when looking for numbers.

Relational database   a database that contains tables of data that are related through common fields.

Remove All Arrows   arrows displayed by the Trace Dependents and Trace Precedents commands may be removed by using the Remove All Arrows command.

Replica   a copy of the original database that includes additional tables used to keep track of any changes made to the database.

Replicating   the process of creating a copy of the original database so multiple users can make changes to the database. This process is best used when network access is not available.

R-squared value   a statistical measurement that describes how well the trend line fits the data.

Scenario   a method of saving a set of values.

Schema   the XML tags that define how data should be structured in an XML file.

Section   a part of a Word document that is formatted differently than other parts of the document.

Smart Tag   a small icon with context-sensitive options and advice.

Solver   a tool that is similar to Goal Seek except the user can specify several different cells that affect the outcome and place constraints on the values used in the process.

Styles   a style is a set of formatting characteristics that the user can apply to text, tables, and lists in your document to quickly change their appearance.

Subdocument   an individual piece of a master document. Subdocuments can be worked on independently, and then combined in the master document, where indexes, footnotes, page numbers, and other document components can be updated.

Subform   a form within a form used to display a one-to many relationship between records in related tables.

Subreport   a report within a report used to display a one-to-many relationship between records in related tables.

SUMIF   a sum function is combined with criteria to allow the user to sum only those cells in the selected range that meet the criteria in a corresponding range.

Summary queries   a query feature that enables the user to summarize data, and use common statistical functions such as sum, average, minimum, maximum and count.

Switchboard   a main menu that is used to navigate in an Access database.

Synchronize   the process of integrating changes made to a database that has been replicated for use by multiple users.

Task Pane   a window, usually on the right side of the screen, that enables the user to quickly access and use common commands.

Template   a set of standard settings that may be used to reduce the time it takes to create a new worksheet.

Three-dimensional reference   references to cells in another worksheet.

Trace Dependents   cells that depend on the selected cell for calculations are identified with arrows.

Trace Precedents   cells on which the selected cell depends for calculations are identified with arrows.

Transpose   axes may be switched when pasting a table using the Transpose option in the Paste Special command.

Trend line   a line that displays the general trend of a set of data points.

Unlock   allows changes to be made to selected cells when the rest of the worksheet is protected.

Update query   an action query that is used to change the same data for many records.

User-level   a sophisticated level of security that provides control over who has access to different objects in a database.

Validation rule   a field property that is set to ensure only acceptable data is entered in the field.

Validation text   a field property used to create a message box that displays when a validation rule is violated.

Version   a revision that you save with the current document. If you save versions, you can open any previous revision along with the current version and cut-and-paste between documents.

Visual Basic Editor (VBE)   a text editor that enables the user to make changes to macros after they have been created. The editor can also be used write macros from scratch.

Visual Basic for Applications (VBA)   a common programming language used in many Microsoft products.

VLOOKUP   a function that looks up the reference value in the first column of the selected range and then displays the value in a given column.

Watch Window   a window that displays the values of selected cells.

Widow   the last line of a paragraph that appears by itself at the top of a page.

Wildcard   a symbol that is used to search for unspecified characters. An asterisk (*) can be used at the beginning or the end of an entry to search for any number of unspecified letters, numbers, or other characters.

Workspace   a group of workbooks.

XML (eXtensible Markup Language)   an abbreviation for Extensible Markup Language which is a standard for describing data in web pages. The older web page design language, HTML, defines how elements of a web page are displayed while XML defines what those elements contain.

Index

C

formatting documents

editing shared workbooks using

protecting whole worksheets
    adding passwords, EXC344-345, EXC365
    locking/unlocking cells, EXC344
    removing passwords, EXC345
saving
    as interactive Web page, EXC225-228, EXC236
    CSV format for, EXC223-225, EXC236
templates for, creating, EXC263-264
three-dimensional (3-D) references, EXC239-240
Watch Windows, EXC338
worksheets (Excel)
copying/pasting to Word documents, WRD253-254

linking to Word documents, WRD257-258, WRD275
    table formatting, WRD258
updating/modifying data, WRD259
workspaces
creating, EXC228-230, EXC237
defined. 209, EXC228
opening files, EXC230-231

X

XML (eXtensible Markup Language)
Access support for, ACC431
schemas, ACC443
XML Export dialog box (File, Export menu), ACC443

XML files
exporting data to, ACC433-444, ACC450
importing into Access, ACC445-446, ACC451
XY Scatter charts
adding trend lines, EXC320, EXC337
creating, EXC318-319, EXC336
defined, EXC317

Z

zoom box, ACC348